Lecture Notes in Computer Science 8414

Commenced Publication in 1973
Founding and Former Series Editors:
Gerhard Goos, Juris Hartmanis, and Jan van Leeuwen

Advanced Research in Computing and Software Science

Subline of Lectures Notes in Computer Science

Martín Abadi   Steve Kremer (Eds.)

Principles of Security and Trust

Third International Conference, POST 2014
Held as Part of the European Joint Conferences
on Theory and Practice of Software, ETAPS 2014
Grenoble, France, April 5-13, 2014
Proceedings

 Springer

Volume Editors

Martín Abadi
Microsoft Research
Mountain View, CA, USA
E-mail: abadi@microsoft.com

Steve Kremer
Inria Nancy - Grand'Est
Villers-lès-Nancy, France
E-mail: steve.kremer@inria.fr

ISSN 0302-9743   e-ISSN 1611-3349
ISBN 978-3-642-54791-1   e-ISBN 978-3-642-54792-8
DOI 10.1007/978-3-642-54792-8
Springer Heidelberg New York Dordrecht London

Library of Congress Control Number: 2014933674

LNCS Sublibrary: SL 4 – Security and Cryptology

Typesetting: Camera-ready by author, data conversion by Scientific Publishing Services, Chennai, India

Printed on acid-free paper

Springer is part of Springer Science+Business Media (www.springer.com)

Foreword

ETAPS 2014 was the 17th instance of the European Joint Conferences on Theory and Practice of Software. ETAPS is an annual federated conference that was established in 1998, and this year consisted of six constituting conferences (CC, ESOP, FASE, FoSSaCS, TACAS, and POST) including eight invited speakers and two tutorial speakers. Before and after the main conference, numerous satellite workshops took place and attracted many researchers from all over the globe.

ETAPS is a confederation of several conferences, each with its own Program Committee (PC) and its own Steering Committee (if any). The conferences cover various aspects of software systems, ranging from theoretical foundations to programming language developments, compiler advancements, analysis tools, formal approaches to software engineering, and security. Organizing these conferences in a coherent, highly synchronized conference program, enables the participation in an exciting event, having the possibility to meet many researchers working in different directions in the field, and to easily attend the talks of different conferences.

The six main conferences together received 606 submissions this year, 155 of which were accepted (including 12 tool demonstration papers), yielding an overall acceptance rate of 25.6%. I thank all authors for their interest in ETAPS, all reviewers for the peer reviewing process, the PC members for their involvement, and in particular the PC co-chairs for running this entire intensive process. Last but not least, my congratulations to all authors of the accepted papers!

ETAPS 2014 was greatly enriched by the invited talks of Geoffrey Smith (Florida International University, USA) and John Launchbury (Galois, USA), both unifying speakers, and the conference-specific invited speakers (CC) Benoît Dupont de Dinechin (Kalray, France), (ESOP) Maurice Herlihy (Brown University, USA), (FASE) Christel Baier (Technical University of Dresden, Germany), (FoSSaCS) Petr Jančar (Technical University of Ostrava, Czech Republic), (POST) David Mazières (Stanford University, USA), and finally (TACAS) Orna Kupferman (Hebrew University Jerusalem, Israel). Invited tutorials were provided by Bernd Finkbeiner (Saarland University, Germany) and Andy Gordon (Microsoft Research, Cambridge, UK). My sincere thanks to all these speakers for their great contributions.

For the first time in its history, ETAPS returned to a city where it had been organized before: Grenoble, France. ETAPS 2014 was organized by the Université Joseph Fourier in cooperation with the following associations and societies: ETAPS e.V., EATCS (European Association for Theoretical Computer Science), EAPLS (European Association for Programming Languages and Systems), and EASST (European Association of Software Science and Technology). It had support from the following sponsors: CNRS, Inria, Grenoble INP, PERSYVAL-Lab and Université Joseph Fourier, and Springer-Verlag.

The organization team comprised:

General Chair: Saddek Bensalem
Conferences Chair: Alain Girault and Yassine Lakhnech
Workshops Chair: Axel Legay
Publicity Chair: Yliès Falcone
Treasurer: Nicolas Halbwachs
Webmaster: Marius Bozga

The overall planning for ETAPS is the responsibility of the Steering Committee (SC). The ETAPS SC consists of an executive board (EB) and representatives of the individual ETAPS conferences, as well as representatives of EATCS, EAPLS, and EASST. The Executive Board comprises Gilles Barthe (satellite events, Madrid), Holger Hermanns (Saarbrücken), Joost-Pieter Katoen (chair, Aachen and Twente), Gerald Lüttgen (treasurer, Bamberg), and Tarmo Uustalu (publicity, Tallinn). Other current SC members are: Martín Abadi (Santa Cruz and Mountain View), Erika Ábrahám (Aachen), Roberto Amadio (Paris), Christel Baier (Dresden), Saddek Bensalem (Grenoble), Giuseppe Castagna (Paris), Albert Cohen (Paris), Alexander Egyed (Linz), Riccardo Focardi (Venice), Björn Franke (Edinburgh), Stefania Gnesi (Pisa), Klaus Havelund (Pasadena), Reiko Heckel (Leicester), Paul Klint (Amsterdam), Jens Knoop (Vienna), Steve Kremer (Nancy), Pasquale Malacaria (London), Tiziana Margaria (Potsdam), Fabio Martinelli (Pisa), Andrew Myers (Boston), Anca Muscholl (Bordeaux), Catuscia Palamidessi (Palaiseau), Andrew Pitts (Cambridge), Arend Rensink (Twente), Don Sanella (Edinburgh), Vladimiro Sassone (Southampton), Ina Schäfer (Braunschweig), Zhong Shao (New Haven), Gabriele Taentzer (Marburg), Cesare Tinelli (Iowa), Jan Vitek (West Lafayette), and Lenore Zuck (Chicago).

I sincerely thank all ETAPS SC members for all their hard work in making the 17th ETAPS a success. Moreover, thanks to all speakers, attendants, organizers of the satellite workshops, and Springer for their support. Finally, many thanks to Saddek Bensalem and his local organization team for all their efforts enabling ETAPS to return to the French Alps in Grenoble!

January 2014   Joost-Pieter Katoen

Preface

This volume contains the papers presented at POST 2014, the Third Conference on Principles of Security and Trust. The conference was held as part of ETAPS 2014, in Grenoble, France, during April 6–7, 2014.

POST 2014 attracted 55 submissions in response to the call for papers. The submissions included 54 research papers and one tool-demonstration paper. Each of them was assigned to at least three members of the Program Committee; in many cases, reviews were solicited from outside experts. The Program Committee discussed the submissions electronically, judging them on their originality, importance, appropriateness, and clarity.

As a result of these discussions, the Program Committee decided to accept 15 research papers and the tool-demonstration paper. The papers that appear in this volume may differ from the initial submissions; it is expected that some of them will be further revised and submitted for publication in refereed archival journals.

In addition to these papers, the volume contains contributions that correspond to two invited lectures: one given by David Mazières, as the POST invited speaker, and one given by Geoffrey Smith, as an ETAPS unifying speaker.

We would like to thank the members of the Program Committee, the external reviewers, the POST Steering Committee, and the ETAPS Steering Committee and local Organizing Committee, who all contributed to the success of POST 2014. Finally, we gratefully acknowledge the use of EasyChair for organizing the submission process, the Program Committee's work, and the preparation of this volume.

January 2014

Martín Abadi
Steve Kremer

Organization

Program Chairs

Martín Abadi   MSR and UCSC, USA
Steve Kremer   Inria Nancy, France

Program Committee

Bruno Blanchet	Inria Paris, France
Ran Canetti	Boston University, USA and Tel Aviv University Israel
Claude Castelluccia	Inria Grenoble, France
George Danezis	University College London, UK
Anupam Datta	CMU, USA
Stéphanie Delaune	CNRS, ENS Cachan, France
Riccardo Focardi	University of Venice, Italy
Somesh Jha	University of Wisconsin, USA
Ninghui Li	Purdue University, USA
Sergio Maffeis	Imperial College, UK
Andrew Myers	Cornell University, USA
Catuscia Palamidessi	Inria Saclay, École Polytechnique, France
Benjamin Pierce	University of Pennsylvania, USA
Frank Piessens	KU Leuven, Belgium
David Pointcheval	CNRS, ENS Paris, France
David Sands	Chalmers University of Technology, Sweden
Hovav Shacham	UCSD, USA
Nikhil Swamy	MSR, USA
Paul Syverson	NRL, USA
Ankur Taly	Google, USA
Bogdan Warinschi	Bristol University, UK

Additional Reviewers

Adão, Pedro
Austin, Thomas
Bielova, Nataliia
Broberg, Niklas
Bursuc, Sergiu
Cadé, David

Calzavara, Stefano
Cheval, Vincent
Chowdhury, Omar
Chrétien, Rémy
Davidson, Drew
De Carli, Lorenzo

De Groef, Willem
Delignat-Lavaud, Antoine
Deyoung, Henry
Ferrara, Anna Lisa
Filaretti, Daniele
Fredrikson, Matt
Garg, Deepak
Goessler, Gregor
Harris, Bill
Harris, William
Hirschi, Lucca
Hritcu, Catalin
Jaggard, Aaron D.
Joaquim, Rui
Johnson, Aaron
Kaynar, Dilsun
Kordy, Barbara
Köpf, Boris
Lauradoux, Cédric
Luchaup, Daniel

Martin, Dan
Meadows, Catherine
Milushev, Dimiter
Mohsen, Rabih
Muehlberg, Jan Tobias
Mödersheim, Sebastian
Pereira, Olivier
Pironti, Alfredo
Planul, Jérémy
Rafnsson, Willard
Scerri, Guillaume
Schwoon, Stefan
Sen, Shayak
Sharma, Divya
Sharma, Rahul
Smyth, Ben
Tiplea, Ferucio
van Delft, Bart
van der Meyden, Ron
Zhang, Danfeng

Security and the Average Programmer[*]
(Invited Contribution)

Daniel Giffin, Stefan Heule, Amit Levy, David Mazières,
John Mitchell, Alejandro Russo*, Amy Shen, Deian Stefan,
David Terei, and Edward Yang

Stanford and *Chalmers

Software security research spans a broad spectrum of approaches. At one end, experts attempt to build systems that are secure by construction. At the other end, people deploy faulty software and leave it to security practitioners to clean up the mess. But cleaning up the mess isn't working: experience shows that post-hoc fixes can't be deployed in time to prevent damage. Moreover, fixing faulty software is an arms race, and the security community shows no signs of winning it. Worse, the war is spreading to new fronts: even cars [5], televisions and refrigerators [2] are now vulnerable to network attack.

How can we make software secure from the start? For most software to be secure, the median programmer will have to produce secure code. Attempts to achieve this by building a culture of good security practices have met with limited success. For example, despite attempts to educate them, web programmers continue to misuse **postMessage** authentication [8]. Even Linux kernel developers have committed vulnerable code three times in a row for a single bug [9].

Rather than focus on the abstract notion of security culture, we argue it is more effective to change programmer behavior through APIs and programming languages. Designing APIs and programming languages with security in mind allows us to make common operations less error-prone, and, more importantly, to restrict the damage that leads from inevitable mistakes. This requires security mechanisms that, within the context of a single application, can protect programmers from themselves as well as from each other. What should such mechanisms look like?

To provide maximum benefit, any security mechanism must be objective: it should provide concrete, formally specifiable, and (in the event of a design error) falsifiable guarantees. Security mechanisms that evolve with systems tend not to have this property. For example, enforcement of the same-origin policy is split across multiple locations in Firefox—permission to load a resource is checked in a completely different place from iframe DOM access. Without a suitable security mechanism, the same-origin policy had to be expressed and enforced in a series

---

[*] This work was funded by the DARPA Clean-Slate Design of Resilient, Adaptive, Secure Hosts (CRASH) program, BAA-10-70, under under contract #N66001-10-2-4088 (*Bridging the Security Gap with Decentralized Information Flow Control*), as well as multiple gifts from Google.

of conditional statements. As software evolves with new features, extending such a regime in a consistent way becomes a subjective exercise.

An equally important property for a security mechanism is to capture real-world security concerns in a direct, declarative way. The issues people actually care about tend to be high-level questions—e.g., Who can see this photograph?—rather than low-level details—e.g., Does this image filter access the network? Ideally, the security mechanism can capture such policy concerns in a manner substantially divorced from the complex inner workings of an application.

One promising family of mechanisms is those based on decentralized information flow control, or DIFC [7]. DIFC allows one to specify policy in terms of who can read and write various data, and enforces these constraints throughout an application or system regardless of its structure or the sequence of operations performed. Specifying policy on data naturally captures high-level concerns in a direct and declarative way, fulfilling one of our criteria. (Indeed, the generality of DIFC is demonstrated by its ability to enforce policies uniformly across hardware [14,1], operating systems [3,12], programming languages [7], distributed systems [13,6], and browsers [11,10].) Moreover, DIFC guarantees can be formally specified (for example, as non-interference), fulfilling the other criterion.

Historically, two weak points of DIFC have been, first, the discrepancy between formal models and actual implementations (notably, where covert channels violate non-interference) and, second, limited adoption by non-experts. However, we have made progress on both fronts in recent years. This talk will report on our experience with Hails [4], a DIFC framework for building extensible web applications. Hails structures a web application as a collection of mutually distrustful "apps" and database policies. Hails has been used to build production web sites with minimal trusted code, making it one of the largest real-world examples of DIFC. Moreover, the system has been used by novices, giving us invaluable insight into the obstacles DIFC faces for adoption by average programmers.

References

1. de Amorim, A.A., Collins, N., DeHon, A., Demange, D., Hrițcu, C., Pichardie, D., Pierce, B.C., Pollack, R., Tolmach, A.: A verified information-flow architecture. In: Proceedings of the 41st Symposium on Principles of Programming Languages, POPL (January 2014)
2. Bort, J.: For the first time, hackers have used a refrigerator to attack businesses. Business Insider (January 2014), http://www.businessinsider.com/hackers-use-a-refridgerator-to-attack-businesses-2014-1
3. Efstathopoulos, P., Krohn, M., van DeBogart, S., Frey, C., Ziegler, D., Kohler, E., Mazières, D., Kaashoek, F., Morris, R.: Labels and event processes in the Asbestos operating system, pp. 17–30
4. Giffin, D.B., Levy, A., Stefan, D., Terei, D., Mazières, D., Mitchell, J., Russo, A.: Hails: Protecting data privacy in untrusted web applications. In: 10th Symposium on Operating Systems Design and Implementation (October 2012)
5. Koscher, K., Czeskis, A., Roesner, F., Patel, S., Kohno, T., Checkoway, S., Mccoy, D., Kantor, B., Anderson, D., Shacham, H., Savage, S.: Experimental security

analysis of a modern automobile. In: Proceedings of IEEE Symposium on Security and Privacy (2010)

6. Liu, J., George, M.D., Vikram, K., Qi, X., Waye, L., Myers, A.C.: Fabric: A platform for secure distributed computation and storage. In: Proceedings of the 22nd Symposium on Operating Systems Principles, pp. 321–334 (October 2009)

7. Myers, A.C., Liskov, B.: A decentralized model for information flow control. In: 16th ACM Symposium on Operating Systems Principles, pp. 129–142 (1997)

8. Son, S., Shmatikov, V.: The postman always rings twice: Attacking and defending postMessage in HTML5 websites. In: 20th Network and Distributed System Security Symposium (2013)

9. Wang, X., Chen, H., Jia, Z., Zeldovich, N., Frans Kaashoek, M.: Improving integer security for systems with KINT. In: 10th USENIX Symposium on Operating Systems Design and Implementation (October 2012)

10. Yang, E.Z., Stefan, D., Mitchell, J., Mazières, D., Marchenko, P., Karp, B.: Toward principled browser security. In: 14th Workshop on Hot Topics in Operating Systems (May 2013)

11. Yip, A., Narula, N., Krohn, M., Morris, R.: Privacy-preserving browser-side scripting with bflow. In: Proceedings of the 4th ACM European Conference on Computer Systems, pp. 233–246. ACM (2009)

12. Zeldovich, N., Boyd-Wickizer, S., Kohler, E., Mazières, D.: Making information flow explicit in HiStar. In: 7th Symposium on Operating Systems Design and Implementation, Seattle, WA, pp. 263–278 (November 2006)

13. Zeldovich, N., Boyd-Wickizer, S., Mazières, D.: Securing distributed systems with information flow control. In: 6th Symposium on Networked Systems Design and Implementation, San Francisco, CA, pp. 293–308 (April 2008)

14. Zeldovich, N., Kannan, H., Dalton, M., Kozyrakis, C.: Hardware enforcement of application security policies using tagged memory. In: Eighth Symposium on Operating Systems Design and Implementation, San Diego, CA, pp. 225–240 (December 2008)

Operational Significance and Robustness in Quantitative Information Flow
(Invited Contribution)

Geoffrey Smith

Florida International University
smithg@cis.fiu.edu

Protecting sensitive information from improper disclosure is a fundamental security goal, but one that is clearly not being achieved well in today's cyber infrastructure. The issue is complicated by the realization that some leakage of sensitive information is often unavoidable in practice, due either to system functionality (e.g. a statistical database must by design reveal information derived from the database entries, even if those entries should be confidential) or due to side channels (e.g. it is difficult to prevent running time or power consumption from depending on secrets). For this reason, the last decade has seen growing interest in *quantitative* theories of information flow, which let us talk about "how much" information is leaked and perhaps allow us to tolerate "small" leaks.

One major theme has been the development of leakage measures with strong *operational significance*, so that the amount of information leaked is associated with strong security guarantees. In this respect, notable measures include *min-entropy leakage* [1], which measures leakage based on the secret's *vulnerability* to be guessed correctly in one try by the adversary, and *g-leakage* [2], which generalizes vulnerability with a *gain function*, which can model diverse operational scenarios, including those where the adversary gains from guessing the secret approximately, partially, or within k tries, or where there is a penalty for incorrect guesses.

A second major theme aims at *robustness*, trying to minimize sensitivity to (perhaps questionable) assumptions about the adversary's prior knowledge and goals, as modeled by the secret's prior distribution and by the gain function. One important approach is to focus on *capacity*, the maximum leakage over *all* prior distributions. Of particular interest are capacity relationships between different leakage measures—for instance, the *Miracle Theorem* of [2] shows that *min-capacity* (the maximum min-entropy leakage over all priors) is an upper bound on g-leakage for every prior and every gain function. A second approach to robustness concerns *comparisons* between channels, aimed at showing that one channel never leaks more than another, regardless of the prior and gain function. The *Coriaceous Theorem* of [3] shows that this strong g-leakage ordering is equivalent to a structural ordering called *composition refinement*, which says that the first channel is equivalent to the second followed by some "post-processing". This means that it is safe to replace channel B with A (e.g. in a stepwise refinement methodology) if and only if A is composition refined by B.

This talk will survey these and other recent developments in quantitative information flow, and will also discuss directions for future research.

References

1. Smith, G.: On the foundations of quantitative information flow. In: de Alfaro, L. (ed.) FOSSACS 2009. LNCS, vol. 5504, pp. 288–302. Springer, Heidelberg (2009)
2. Alvim, M.S., Chatzikokolakis, K., Palamidessi, C., Smith, G.: Measuring information leakage using generalized gain functions. In: Proc. 25th IEEE Computer Security Foundations Symposium (CSF 2012), pp. 265–279 (June 2012)
3. McIver, A., Morgan, C., Smith, G., Espinoza, B., Meinicke, L.: Abstract channels and their robust information-leakage ordering. In: Abadi, M., Kremer, S. (eds.) POST 2014. LNCS, vol. 8414, pp. 86–105. Springer, Heidelberg (2014)

Table of Contents

Invited Contributions

Analysis of Cryptographic Protocols

Quantitative Aspects of Information Flow

Information Flow Control in Programming Languages

Cryptography in Implementations

Policies and Attacks

A Reduced Semantics for Deciding Trace Equivalence Using Constraint Systems[*]

David Baelde[1], Stéphanie Delaune[1], and Lucca Hirschi[1,2]

[1] LSV, ENS Cachan & CNRS & Inria Saclay Île-de-France
[2] ENS Lyon, France

Abstract. Many privacy-type properties of security protocols can be modelled using trace equivalence properties in suitable process algebras. It has been shown that such properties can be decided for interesting classes of finite processes (*i.e.,* without replication) by means of symbolic execution and constraint solving. However, this does not suffice to obtain practical tools. Current prototypes suffer from a classical combinatorial explosion problem caused by the exploration of many interleavings in the behaviour of processes. Mödersheim *et al.* [18] have tackled this problem for reachability properties using partial order reduction techniques. We revisit their work, generalize it and adapt it for equivalence checking. We obtain an optimization in the form of a reduced symbolic semantics that eliminates redundant interleavings on the fly.

1 Introduction

Security protocols are widely used today to secure transactions that rely on public channels like the Internet, where dishonest users may listen to communications and interfere with them. A secure communication has a different meaning depending on the underlying application. It ranges from the confidentiality of data (medical files, secret keys, etc.) to, *e.g.,* verifiability in electronic voting systems. Another example is the notion of privacy that appears in many contexts such as vote-privacy in electronic voting or untraceability in RFID technologies.

Formal methods have proved their usefulness for precisely analyzing the security of protocols. In particular, a wide variety of model-checking approaches have been developed to analyse protocols against an attacker who entirely controls the communication network, and several tools are now available to automatically verify cryptographic protocols [8,15,5]. A major challenge faced here is that one has to account for infinitely many behaviours of the attacker, who can generate arbitrary messages. In order to cope with this prolific attacker problem and obtain decision procedures, approaches based on symbolic semantics and constraint resolution have been proposed [17,20]. This has lead to tools for verifying reachability-based security properties such as confidentiality [17] or, more recently, equivalence-based properties such as privacy [22,12,10].

---

[*] This work has been partially supported by the project JCJC VIP ANR-11-JS02-006, and the Inria large scale initiative CAPPRIS.

M. Abadi and S. Kremer (Eds.): POST 2014, LNCS 8414, pp. 1–21, 2014.

In both cases, the practical impact of most of these tools is limited by a typical state explosion problem caused by the exploration of the large number of interleavings in the protocol's behaviour. In standard model-checking approaches for concurrent systems, the interleaving problem is handled using partial order reduction techniques [19]. For instance, the order of execution of two independent (parallel) actions is typically irrelevant for checking reachability. Things become more complex when working with a symbolic semantics: the states obtained from the interleaving of parallel actions will differ, but the sets of concrete states that they represent will have a significant overlap. Earlier work has shown how to limit this overlap [18] in the context of reachability properties for security protocols, leading to high efficiency gains in the OFMC tool of the AVISPA platform [5].

In this paper, we revisit the work of [18] to obtain a partial order reduction technique for the verification of equivalence properties. Specifically, we focus on trace equivalence, requiring that two processes have the same sets of observable traces and perform indistinguishable sequences of outputs. This notion is well-studied and several algorithms and tools support it [9,14,22,12,10]. Contrary to what happens for reachability-based properties, trace equivalence cannot be decided relying only on the reachable states. The sequence of actions that leads to this state plays a role. Hence, extra precautions have to be taken before discarding a particular interleaving: we have to ensure that this is done in both sides of the equivalence in a similar fashion. Our main contribution is an optimized form of equivalence that discards a lot of interleavings, and a proof that this reduced equivalence coincides with trace equivalence. Furthermore, our study brings an improvement of the original technique [18] that would apply equally well for reachability checking. Detailed proofs of our results can be found in [6].

Outline. In Section 2, we introduce our model for security processes. We consider the class of simple processes introduced in [13], with else branches and no replication. Then we present two successive optimizations in the form of refined semantics and associated trace equivalences. Section 3 presents a *compressed* semantics that limits interleavings by executing blocks of actions. Then, this is lifted to a symbolic semantics in Section 4. Finally, Section 5 presents the *reduced* semantics which makes use of dependency constraints to remove more interleavings. We conclude in Section 6, mentioning a preliminary implementation that shows efficiency gains in practice and some directions for future work.

2   Model for Security Protocols

In this section, we introduce the cryptographic process calculus that we will use to describe security protocols. This calculus is close to the applied pi calculus [1].

2.1   Messages

A protocol consists of some agents communicating on a network. Messages sent by agents are modeled using a term algebra. We assume two infinite and disjoint sets of variables, $\mathcal{X}$ and $\mathcal{W}$. Members of $\mathcal{X}$ are denoted x, y, z, whereas members of $\mathcal{W}$ are denoted w and used as *handles* for previously output terms. We also assume a set $\mathcal{N}$ of *names*, which are used for representing keys or nonces, and a signature Σ consisting of a finite set of function symbols. Terms are generated inductively from names, variables, and function symbols applied to other terms. For $S \subseteq \mathcal{X} \cup \mathcal{W} \cup \mathcal{N}$, the set of terms built from S by applying function symbols in Σ is denoted by $\mathcal{T}(S)$. Terms in $\mathcal{T}(\mathcal{N} \cup \mathcal{X})$ represent messages and are denoted by u, v, etc. while terms in $\mathcal{T}(\mathcal{W})$ represent *recipes* (describing how the attacker built a term from the available outputs) and are written M, N, R. We write $fv(t)$ for the set of variables (from $\mathcal{X}$ or $\mathcal{W}$) occurring in a term t. A term is *ground* if it does not contain any variable, *i.e.*, it belongs to $\mathcal{T}(\mathcal{N})$. We may rely on a sort system for terms, but its details are unimportant for this paper.

To model algebraic properties of cryptographic primitives, we consider an equational theory E. The theory will usually be generated for finite axioms and enjoy nice properties, but these aspects are irrelevant for the present work.

Example 1. In order to model asymmetric encryption and pairing, we consider:
$$\Sigma = \{\mathsf{aenc}(\cdot, \cdot), \ \mathsf{adec}(\cdot, \cdot), \ \mathsf{pk}(\cdot), \ \langle \cdot, \cdot \rangle, \ \pi_1(\cdot), \ \pi_2(\cdot)\}.$$

To take into account the properties of these operators, we consider the equational theory $\mathsf{E}_{\mathsf{aenc}}$ generated by the three following equations:
$$\mathsf{adec}(\mathsf{aenc}(x, \mathsf{pk}(y)), y) = x, \quad \pi_1(\langle x_1, x_2 \rangle) = x_1, \text{ and } \pi_2(\langle x_1, x_2 \rangle) = x_2.$$
For instance, we have $\pi_2(\mathsf{adec}(\mathsf{aenc}(\langle n, \mathsf{pk}(ska) \rangle, \mathsf{pk}(skb)), skb)) =_{\mathsf{E}_{\mathsf{aenc}}} \mathsf{pk}(ska)$.

2.2 Processes

We do not need the full applied pi calculus to represent security protocols. Here, we only consider public channels and we assume that each process communicates on a dedicated channel.

Formally, we assume a set $\mathcal{C}$ of *channels* and we consider the fragment of *simple processes* without replication built on *basic processes* as defined in [13]. A basic process represents a party in a protocol, which may sequentially perform actions such as waiting for a message, checking that a message has a certain form, or outputting a message. Then, a simple process is a parallel composition of such basic processes playing on distinct channels.

Definition 1 (basic/simple process). *The set of* basic processes *on $c \in \mathcal{C}$ is defined using the following grammar (below $u, v \in \mathcal{T}(\mathcal{N} \cup \mathcal{X})$ and $x \in \mathcal{X}$):*

$$
\begin{array}{lll}
P, Q := 0 & \quad & null \\
\quad | \ \text{if } u = v \text{ then } P \text{ else } Q & \quad & conditional \\
\quad | \ \text{in}(c, x).P & \quad & input \\
\quad | \ \text{out}(c, u).P & \quad & output
\end{array}
$$

A simple process $\mathcal{P} = \{P_1, \ldots, P_n\}$ is a multiset of basic processes P_i on pairwise distinct channels c_i. We assume that null processes are removed.

For conciseness, we often omit brackets, null processes, and even "else 0". Basic processes are denoted by the letters P and Q, whereas simple processes are denoted using $\mathcal{P}$ and $\mathcal{Q}$.

During an execution, the attacker learns the messages that have been sent on the different public channels. Those messages are organized into a *frame*.

Definition 2 (frame). *A frame Φ is a substitution whose domain is included in $\mathcal{W}$ and image is included in $\mathcal{T}(\mathcal{N} \cup \mathcal{X})$. It is written $\{w \triangleright u, \ldots\}$. A frame is closed when its image only contains ground terms.*

An *extended simple proces* (denoted A or B) is a pair made of a simple process and a frame. Similarly, we define *extended basic processes*. Note that we do not have an explicit set of restricted names. Actually, all names are restricted and public ones are explicitly given to the attacker through a frame.

Example 2. We consider the protocol given in [2] designed for transmitting a secret without revealing its identity to other participants. In this protocol, A is willing to engage in communication with B and wants to reveal its identity to B. However, A does not want to compromise its privacy by revealing its identity or the identity of B more broadly. The participants A and B proceed as follows:

$$A \to B \; : \; \{N_a, \mathsf{pub}_A\}_{\mathsf{pub}_B}$$
$$B \to A \; : \; \{N_a, N_b, \mathsf{pub}_B\}_{\mathsf{pub}_A}$$

Moreover, if the message received by B is not of the expected form then B sends out a "decoy" message: $\{N_b\}_{\mathsf{pub}_B}$. This message should basically look like B's other message from the point of view of an outsider.

Relying on the signature and equational theory introduced in Example 1, a session of role A played by agent a (with private key ska) with b (whose public key is pkb) can be modeled as follows:

$$P(ska, pkb) \stackrel{\mathsf{def}}{=} \mathsf{out}(c_A, \mathsf{aenc}(\langle n_a, \mathsf{pk}(ska) \rangle, pkb)).$$
$$\mathsf{in}(c_A, x).$$
$$\mathsf{if} \; \langle \pi_1(\mathsf{adec}(x, ska)), \pi_2(\pi_2(\mathsf{adec}(x, ska))) \rangle = \langle n_a, pkb \rangle \; \mathsf{then} \; 0$$

Here, we are only considering the authentication protocol. A more comprehensive model should include the access to an application in case of a success. Similarly, a session of role B played by agent b with a can be modeled by the following basic proces where $N = \mathsf{adec}(y, skb)$.

$$Q(skb, pka) \stackrel{\mathsf{def}}{=} \mathsf{in}(c_B, y).$$
$$\mathsf{if} \; \pi_2(N) = pka \; \mathsf{then} \; \mathsf{out}(c_B, \mathsf{aenc}(\langle \pi_1(N), \langle n_b, \mathsf{pk}(skb) \rangle \rangle, pka))$$
$$\mathsf{else} \; \mathsf{out}(c_B, \mathsf{aenc}(n_b, \mathsf{pk}(skb)))$$

To model a scenario with one session of each role (played by the agents a and b), we may consider the extended process $(\mathcal{P}; \Phi_0)$ where:

- $\mathcal{P} = \{P(ska, \mathsf{pk}(skb)), Q(skb, \mathsf{pk}(ska))\}$, and
- $\Phi_0 = \{w_0 \triangleright \mathsf{pk}(ska'), w_1 \triangleright \mathsf{pk}(ska), w_2 \triangleright \mathsf{pk}(skb)\}$.

The purpose of $\mathsf{pk}(ska')$ will be clear later on. It allows us to consider the existence of another agent a' whose public key $\mathsf{pk}(ska')$ is known by the attacker.

2.3 Semantics

We first define a standard concrete semantics. Thus, in this section, we work only with closed extended processes, *i.e.*, processes $(\mathcal{P}; \Phi)$ where $fv(\mathcal{P}) = \emptyset$.

THEN $(\{$if $u = v$ then Q_1 else $Q_2\} \uplus \mathcal{P}; \Phi) \xrightarrow{\tau} (\{Q_1\} \uplus \mathcal{P}; \Phi)$ if $u =_\mathsf{E} v$

ELSE $(\{$if $u = v$ then Q_1 else $Q_2\} \uplus \mathcal{P}; \Phi) \xrightarrow{\tau} (\{Q_2\} \uplus \mathcal{P}; \Phi)$ if $u \neq_\mathsf{E} v$

IN $(\{$in$(c,x).Q\} \uplus \mathcal{P}; \Phi) \xrightarrow{\text{in}(c,M)} (\{Q\{x \mapsto u\}\} \uplus \mathcal{P}; \Phi)$
$$\qquad\qquad\qquad\qquad \text{if } M \in \mathcal{T}(\text{dom}(\Phi)) \text{ and } M\Phi = u$$

OUT $(\{$out$(c,u).Q\} \uplus \mathcal{P}; \Phi) \xrightarrow{\text{out}(c,w)} (\{Q\} \uplus \mathcal{P}; \Phi \cup \{w \triangleright u\})$
$$\qquad\qquad\qquad\qquad\qquad\qquad \text{if } w \text{ is a fresh variable}$$

where $c \in \mathcal{C}, w \in \mathcal{W}$ and $x \in \mathcal{X}$.

A process may input any term that an attacker can build (rule IN): $\{x \mapsto u\}$ is a substitution that replaces any occurrence of x with u. In the OUT rule, we enrich the attacker's knowledge by adding the newly output term u, with a fresh handle w, to the frame. The two remaining rules are unobservable (τ action) from the point of view of the attacker.

The relation $A \xrightarrow{a_1 \dots a_k} B$ between extended simple processes, where $k \geq 0$ and each a_i is an observable or a τ action, is defined in the usual way. We also consider the relation $\xRightarrow{\text{tr}}$ defined as follows: $A \xRightarrow{\text{tr}} B$ if, and only if, there exists $a_1 \dots a_k$ such that $A \xrightarrow{a_1 \dots a_k} B$, and tr is obtained from $a_1 \dots a_k$ by erasing all occurrences of τ.

Example 3. Consider the process $(\mathcal{P}; \Phi_0)$ introduced in Example 2. We have:
$$(\mathcal{P}; \Phi_0) \xrightarrow{\text{out}(c_A, w_3) \cdot \text{in}(c_B, w_3) \cdot \tau \cdot \text{out}(c_B, w_4) \cdot \text{in}(c_A, w_4) \cdot \tau} (\emptyset; \Phi).$$

This trace corresponds to the normal execution of one instance of the protocol. The two silent actions have been triggered using the THEN rule. The resulting frame Φ is as follows:
$$\Phi_0 \uplus \{w_3 \triangleright \mathsf{aenc}(\langle n_a, \mathsf{pk}(ska)\rangle, \mathsf{pk}(skb)),\; w_4 \triangleright \mathsf{aenc}(\langle n_a, \langle n_b, \mathsf{pk}(skb)\rangle\rangle, \mathsf{pk}(ska))\}.$$

2.4 Trace Equivalence

Many interesting security properties, such as privacy-type properties studied *e.g.*, in [4], are formalized using the notion of *trace equivalence*. We first introduce the notion of *static equivalence* that compares sequences of messages.

Definition 3 (static equivalence). *Two frames Φ and Φ' are in* static equivalence, *$\Phi \sim \Phi'$, when we have that $\text{dom}(\Phi) = \text{dom}(\Phi')$, and:*
$$M\Phi =_\mathsf{E} N\Phi \;\;\Leftrightarrow\;\; M\Phi' =_\mathsf{E} N\Phi' \;\text{ for any terms } M, N \in \mathcal{T}(\text{dom}(\Phi)).$$

Intuitively, two frames are equivalent if an attacker cannot see the difference between the two situations they represent, *i.e.*, they satisfy the same equalities.

Example 4. Consider the frame Φ given in Example 3 and the frame Φ' below:

$$\Phi' \stackrel{\text{def}}{=} \Phi_0 \uplus \{w_3 \triangleright \mathsf{aenc}(\langle n_a, \mathsf{pk}(ska')\rangle, \mathsf{pk}(skb)), \ \ w_4 \triangleright \mathsf{aenc}(n_b, \mathsf{pk}(skb))\}.$$

Actually, we have that $\Phi \sim \Phi'$. Intuitively, the equivalence holds since the attacker is not able to decrypt any of the ciphertexts, and each ciphertext contains a nonce that prevents him to build it from its components. Now, if we decide to give access to n_a to the attacker, *i.e.*, considering $\Phi_+ = \Phi \uplus \{w_5 \triangleright n_a\}$ and $\Phi'_+ = \Phi' \uplus \{w_5 \triangleright n_a\}$, then the two frames Φ_+ and Φ'_+ are not in static equivalence anymore. Let $M = \mathsf{aenc}(\langle w_5, w_1\rangle, w_2)$ and $N = w_3$. We have that $M\Phi_+ =_{\mathsf{E}_{\mathsf{aenc}}} N\Phi_+$ whereas $M\Phi'_+ \neq_{\mathsf{E}_{\mathsf{aenc}}} N\Phi'_+$.

Definition 4 (trace equivalence). *Let A and B be two simple processes. We have that $A \sqsubseteq B$ if, for every sequence of actions tr such that $A \stackrel{\mathsf{tr}}{\Longrightarrow} (\mathcal{P}; \Phi)$, there exists $(\mathcal{P}'; \Phi')$ such that $B \stackrel{\mathsf{tr}}{\Longrightarrow} (\mathcal{P}'; \Phi')$ and $\Phi \sim \Phi'$. The processes A and B are trace equivalent, denoted by $A \approx B$, if $A \sqsubseteq B$ and $B \sqsubseteq A$.*

Example 5. Intuitively, the private authentication protocol presented in Example 2 preserves anonymity if an attacker cannot distinguish whether b is willing to talk to a (represented by the process $Q(skb, \mathsf{pk}(ska))$) or willing to talk to a' (represented by the process $Q(skb, \mathsf{pk}(ska'))$), provided a, a' and b are honest participants. This can be expressed relying on the following equivalence:

$$(Q(skb, \mathsf{pk}(ska)); \Phi_0) \stackrel{?}{\approx} (Q(skb, \mathsf{pk}(ska')); \Phi_0).$$

For illustration purposes, we also consider a variant of the process Q, denoted Q_0, where its else branch has been replaced by else 0. We will see that the "decoy" message plays a crucial role to ensure privacy. We have that:

$$(Q_0(skb, \mathsf{pk}(ska)); \Phi_0) \xrightarrow{\mathsf{in}(c_B, \mathsf{aenc}(\langle w_1, w_1\rangle, w_2)) \cdot \tau \cdot \mathsf{out}(c_B, w_3)} (\emptyset; \Phi)$$

where $\Phi = \Phi_0 \uplus \{w_3 \triangleright \mathsf{aenc}(\langle \mathsf{pk}(ska), \langle n_b, \mathsf{pk}(skb)\rangle\rangle, \mathsf{pk}(ska))\}$.

This trace has no counterpart in $(Q_0(skb, \mathsf{pk}(ska')); \Phi_0)$. Indeed, we have that:

$$(Q_0(skb, \mathsf{pk}(ska')); \Phi_0) \xrightarrow{\mathsf{in}(c_B, \mathsf{aenc}(\langle w_1, w_1\rangle, w_2)) \cdot \tau} (\emptyset; \Phi_0).$$

Hence, we have that $(Q_0(skb, \mathsf{pk}(ska)); \Phi_0) \not\approx (Q_0(skb, \mathsf{pk}(ska')); \Phi_0)$. Actually, it can been shown that $(Q(skb, \mathsf{pk}(ska)); \Phi_0) \approx (Q(skb, \mathsf{pk}(ska')); \Phi_0)$. This is a non trivial equivalence that can be checked using the tool APTE [11] within few seconds for a simple scenario as the one considered here, and that takes few minutes/days as soon as we want to consider 2/3 sessions of each role.

3 Reduction Based on Grouping Actions

A large number of possible interleavings results into multiple occurrences of identical states. The compression step lifts a common optimization that partly tackles this issue in the case of reachability properties to trace equivalence. The key idea is to force processes to perform all enabled output actions as soon as possible. In our setting, we can even safely force them to perform a complete *block* of input actions followed by ouput actions.

Example 6. Consider the process $(\mathcal{P}; \Phi)$ with $\mathcal{P} = \{\text{in}(c_1, x).P_1, \text{ out}(c_2, b).P_2\}$. In order to reach $(\{P_1\{x \mapsto u\}, P_2\}; \Phi \cup \{w \triangleright b\})$, we have to execute the action $\text{in}(c_1, x)$ (using a recipe M that allows one to deduce u) and the action $\text{out}(c_2, b)$ (giving us a label of the form $\text{out}(c_2, w)$). In case of reachability properties, the execution order of these actions only matters if M uses w. Thus we can safely perform the outputs in priority.

The situation is more complex when considering trace equivalence. In that case, we are concerned not only with reachable states, but also with *how* those states are reached. Quite simply, traces matter. Thus, if we want to discard the trace $\text{in}(c_1, M).\text{out}(c_2, w)$ when studying process $\mathcal{P}$ and consider only its permutation $\text{out}(c_2, w).\text{in}(c_1, M)$, we have to make sure that the same permutation is available on the other process. The key to ensure that identical permutations will be available on both sides of the equivalence is our restriction to the class of simple processes.

3.1 Compressed Semantics

We now introduce the compressed semantics. Compression is an optimization, since it removes some interleavings. But it also gives rise to convenient "macro-actions", called *blocks*, that combine a sequence of inputs followed by some outputs, potentially hiding silent actions. Manipulating those blocks rather than indiviual actions makes it easier to define our second optimization.

For sake of simplicity, we consider *initial* simple processes. A simple process $A = (\mathcal{P}; \Phi)$ is *initial* if for any $P \in \mathcal{P}$, we have that $P = \text{in}(c, x).P'$ for some channel c, *i.e.*, each basic process composing A starts with an input action.

Example 7. Continuing Example 2, $(\{P(ska, \text{pk}(skb)), Q(skb, \text{pk}(ska))\}; \Phi_0)$ is not initial. Instead, we may consider $(\{P_{\text{init}}, Q(skb, \text{pk}(ska))\}; \Phi_0)$ where:

$$P_{\text{init}} \stackrel{\text{def}}{=} \text{in}(c_A, z).\text{if } z = \text{start then } P(ska, \text{pk}(skb))$$

assuming that start is a (public) constant in our signature.

The main idea of the compressed semantics is to ensure that when a basic process starts executing some actions, it actually executes a maximal block of actions. In analogy with focusing in sequent calculus, we say that the basic process takes the focus, and can only release it under particular conditions. We define in Figure 1 how blocks can be executed by extended basic processes. In that semantics, the label ℓ denotes the stage of the execution, starting with i^+, then i^* after the first input and o^* after the first output.

Example 8. Going back to Example 5, we have that:

$$(Q_0(skb, \text{pk}(ska)); \Phi_0) \xrightarrow{\text{in}(c_B, \text{aenc}(\langle w_1, w_1 \rangle, w_2)) \cdot \text{out}(c_B, w_3)}_{i^+} (0; \Phi)$$

where Φ is as given in Example 5. As illustrated by the prooftree below, we have also $(Q_0(skb, \text{pk}(ska)); \Phi_0) \xrightarrow{\text{tr}}_{i^+} (\bot; \Phi_0)$ with $\text{tr} = \text{in}(c_B, \text{aenc}(\langle w_1, w_1 \rangle, w_2))$.

$$\text{IN} \quad \frac{(P;\varPhi) \xrightarrow{\text{in}(c,M)} (P';\varPhi') \quad (P';\varPhi') \xrightarrow{\text{tr}}\!\!\!\twoheadrightarrow_{i^*} (P'';\varPhi'')}{(P;\varPhi) \xrightarrow{\text{in}(c,M).\text{tr}}\!\!\!\twoheadrightarrow_\ell (P'';\varPhi'')} \quad \text{with } \ell \in \{i^*; i^+\}$$

$$\text{OUT} \quad \frac{(P;\varPhi) \xrightarrow{\text{out}(c,w)} (P';\varPhi') \quad (P';\varPhi') \xrightarrow{\text{tr}}\!\!\!\twoheadrightarrow_{o^*} (P'';\varPhi'')}{(P;\varPhi) \xrightarrow{\text{out}(c,w).\text{tr}}\!\!\!\twoheadrightarrow_\ell (P'';\varPhi'')} \quad \text{with } \ell \in \{i^*; o^*\}$$

$$\text{TAU} \quad \frac{(P;\varPhi) \xrightarrow{\tau} (P';\varPhi') \quad (P';\varPhi') \xrightarrow{\text{tr}}\!\!\!\twoheadrightarrow_\ell (P'';\varPhi'')}{(P;\varPhi) \xrightarrow{\text{tr}}\!\!\!\twoheadrightarrow_\ell (P'';\varPhi'')} \quad \text{with } \ell \in \{o^*; i^+; i^*\}$$

$$\text{PROPER} \quad \frac{}{(0;\varPhi) \xrightarrow{\epsilon}\!\!\!\twoheadrightarrow_{o^*} (0;\varPhi)} \quad \frac{}{(\text{in}(c,x).P;\varPhi) \xrightarrow{\epsilon}\!\!\!\twoheadrightarrow_{o^*} (\text{in}(c,x).P;\varPhi)}$$

$$\text{IMPROPER} \quad \frac{}{(0;\varPhi) \xrightarrow{\epsilon}\!\!\!\twoheadrightarrow_{i^*} (\bot;\varPhi)}$$

Fig. 1. Focused semantics on extended basic processes

$$\frac{(Q_0(skb,\text{pk}(ska));\varPhi_0) \xrightarrow{\text{tr}} (Q';\varPhi_0) \qquad \dfrac{(Q';\varPhi_0) \xrightarrow{\tau} (0;\varPhi_0) \quad \dfrac{}{(0;\varPhi_0) \xrightarrow{\epsilon}\!\!\!\twoheadrightarrow_{i^*} (\bot;\varPhi_0)}\text{IMPROPER}}{(Q';\varPhi_0) \xrightarrow{\epsilon}\!\!\!\twoheadrightarrow_{i^*} (\bot;\varPhi_0)}\text{TAU}}{(Q_0(skb,\text{pk}(ska));\varPhi_0) \xrightarrow{\text{tr}}\!\!\!\twoheadrightarrow_{i^+} (\bot;\varPhi_0)}\text{IN}$$

where $Q' \stackrel{\text{def}}{=} \text{if } \text{pk}(ska) = \text{pk}(ska) \text{ then } \text{out}(c_B,u)$ for some message u.

Then we define the compressed reduction $\to_c$ between extended simple processes as the least reflexive transitive relation satisfying the following rules:

$$\text{BLOCK} \quad \frac{(Q;\varPhi) \xrightarrow{\text{tr}}\!\!\!\twoheadrightarrow_{i^+} (Q';\varPhi') \quad Q' \neq \bot}{(\{Q\} \uplus \mathcal{P};\varPhi) \xrightarrow{\text{tr}}_c (\{Q'\} \uplus \mathcal{P};\varPhi')} \qquad \text{FAILURE} \quad \frac{(Q;\varPhi) \xrightarrow{\text{tr}}\!\!\!\twoheadrightarrow_{i^+} (Q';\varPhi') \quad Q' = \bot}{(\{Q\} \uplus \mathcal{P};\varPhi) \xrightarrow{\text{tr}}_c (\emptyset;\varPhi')}$$

A basic process is allowed to *properly* end a block execution when it has performed outputs and it cannot perform any more. Accordingly, we call *proper block* a non-empty sequence of inputs followed by a non-empty sequence of outputs, all on the same channel. For completeness, we also allow improper termination of a block, when the basic process that is currently executing is not able to perform any visible action (input or output) and it has not yet performed an output.

Example 9. Continuing Example 8, using the rule BLOCK, we can derive that:

$$(\{P_{\text{init}}, Q_0(skb,\text{pk}(ska))\};\varPhi_0) \xrightarrow{\text{in}(c_B,\text{aenc}(\langle w_1,w_1\rangle,w_2)).\text{out}(c_B,w_3)}_c (P_{\text{init}};\varPhi).$$

We can also derive $(\{P_{\text{init}}, Q_0(skb,\text{pk}(ska'))\};\varPhi_0) \xrightarrow{\text{in}(c_B,\text{aenc}(\langle w_1,w_1\rangle,w_2))}_c (\emptyset;\varPhi_0)$ (using the rule IMPROPER). Note that the resulting simple process is reduced to $\emptyset$ even though P_{init} has never been executed.

At first sight, killing the whole process when applying the rule IMPROPER may seem too strong. Actually, even if this kind of scenario is observable by the attacker, it does not bring him any new knowledge, hence it plays only a limited role: it is in fact sufficient to consider such improper blocks at the end of traces.

Example 10. Consider $\mathcal{P} = \{\texttt{in}(c, x).\texttt{in}(c, y),\ \texttt{in}(c', x')\}$. Its compressed traces are of the form $\texttt{in}(c, M).\texttt{in}(c, N)$ and $\texttt{in}(c', M')$. The concatenation of those two improper traces cannot be executed in the compressed semantics. Intuitively, we do not loose anything for trace equivalence, because if a process can exhibit those two improper blocks they must be in parallel and hence considering their combination is redundant.

We define the notion of *compressed trace equivalence* (resp. *inclusion*) accordingly relying on $\to_c$ instead of $\Rightarrow$, and we denote them $\approx_c$ (resp. $\sqsubseteq_c$).

3.2   Soundness and Completeness

The purpose of this section is to establish the soundness and completeness of the compressed semantics. More precisely, we show that the two relations $\approx$ and $\approx_c$ coincide on initial simple processes.

Intuitively, we can always permute output (resp. input) actions occurring on distinct channels, and we can also permute an output with an input if the outputted message is not used to build the inputted term. More formally, we define an *independence relation* $\mathcal{I}_a$ over *actions* as the least symmetric relation satisfying:

- $\texttt{out}(c_i, w_i)\ \mathcal{I}_a\ \texttt{out}(c_j, w_j)$ and $\texttt{in}(c_i, M_i)\ \mathcal{I}_a\ \texttt{in}(c_j, M_j)$ as soon as $c_i \neq c_j$,
- $\texttt{out}(c_i, w_i)\ \mathcal{I}_a\ \texttt{in}(c_j, M_j)$ when in addition $w_i \notin fv(M_j)$.

Then, we consider $=_{\mathcal{I}_a}$ to be the least congruence (w.r.t. concatenation) satisfying $\texttt{act} \cdot \texttt{act}' =_{\mathcal{I}_a} \texttt{act}' \cdot \texttt{act}$ for all $\texttt{act}$ and $\texttt{act}'$ with $\texttt{act}\ \mathcal{I}_a\ \texttt{act}'$, and we show that processes are equally able to execute equivalent (w.r.t. $=_{\mathcal{I}_a}$) traces.

Lemma 1. *Let A, A' be two simple extended processes and tr, tr' be such that $\mathsf{tr} =_{\mathcal{I}_a} \mathsf{tr}'$. We have that $A \overset{\mathsf{tr}}{\Longrightarrow} A'$ if, and only if, $A \overset{\mathsf{tr}'}{\Longrightarrow} A'$.*

Now, considering traces that are only made of proper blocks, a strong relationship can be established between the two semantics.

Proposition 1. *Let A, A' be two simple extended processes, and tr be a trace made of proper blocks such that $A \overset{\mathsf{tr}}{\longrightarrow}_c A'$. Then we have that $A \overset{\mathsf{tr}}{\Longrightarrow} A'$.*

Proposition 2. *Let A, A' be two initial simple processes, and tr be a trace made of proper blocks such that $A \overset{\mathsf{tr}}{\Longrightarrow} A'$. Then, we have that $A \overset{\mathsf{tr}}{\longrightarrow}_c A'$.*

Theorem 1. *Let A and B be two initial simple processes. We have that:*
$$A \approx B \iff A \approx_c B.$$

Proof. (Sketch) The main difficulty is that Proposition 2 only considers traces composed of proper blocks whereas we have to consider all traces. To prove the $\Rightarrow$ implication, we have to pay attention to the last block of the compressed trace that can be an improper one (composed of several inputs on a channel c). The $\Leftarrow$ implication is more difficult since we have to consider a trace tr of a process A that is an interleaving of some prefix of proper and improper blocks. We will first complete it to obtain an interleaving of complete blocks and improper blocks. We then reorganize the actions providing an equivalent trace tr' w.r.t. $=_{\mathcal{I}_a}$ such that $\mathrm{tr}' = \mathrm{tr_{io}} \cdot \mathrm{tr_{in}}$ where $\mathrm{tr_{io}}$ is made of proper blocks and $\mathrm{tr_{in}}$ is made of improper blocks. For each improper block b of $\mathrm{tr_{in}}$, we show by applying Lemma 1 and Proposition 2 that A is able to perform $\mathrm{tr_{io}} \cdot b$ in the compressed semantics and thus B as well. Finally, we show that the executions of all those (concurrent) blocks b can be put together, obtaining that B can perform tr'.   □

Note that, as illustrated by the following example, the two underlying notions of trace inclusion do *not* coincide.

Example 11. Let $P = \mathtt{in}(c, x)$ and $Q = \mathtt{in}(c, x).\mathtt{out}(c, n)$. Actually, we have that $(P; \emptyset) \sqsubseteq (Q; \emptyset)$ whereas $(P; \emptyset) \not\sqsubseteq_c (Q; \emptyset)$ since in the compressed semantics Q is not allowed to stop its execution after its first input.

4 Deciding Trace Equivalence via Constraint Solving

In this section, we propose a symbolic semantics for our compressed semantics following, *e.g.*, [17,7]. Such a semantics avoids potentially infinite branching of our reduction semantics due to inputs from the environment. Correctness is maintained by associating with each process a set of constraints on terms.

4.1 Constraint Systems

Following the notations of [7], we consider a new set $\mathcal{X}^2$ of *second-order variables*, denoted by X, Y, etc. We shall use those variables to abstract over recipes. We denote by $fv^2(o)$ the set of free second-order variables of an object o, typically a constraint system. To prevent ambiguities, we shall use fv^1 instead of fv for free first-order variables.

Definition 5 (constraint system). *A constraint system $\mathcal{C} = (\Phi; \mathcal{S})$ consists of a frame Φ, and a set of constraints $\mathcal{S}$. We consider three kinds of constraints:*

$$D \vdash^?_X x \qquad u =^? v \qquad u \neq^? v$$

where $D \subseteq \mathcal{W}$, $X \in \mathcal{X}^2$, $x \in \mathcal{X}$ and $u, v \in \mathcal{T}(\mathcal{N} \cup \mathcal{X})$.

The first kind of constraint expresses that a recipe X has to use only variables from a certain set D, and that the obtained term should be x. The handles in D represent terms that have been previously outputted by the process.

We are not interested in general constraint systems, but only consider constraint systems that are *well-formed*. Given $\mathcal{C}$, we define a dependency order on

$fv^1(\mathcal{C}) \cap \mathcal{X}$ by declaring that x depends on y if, and only if, $\mathcal{S}$ contains a deduction constraint $D \vdash^?_X x$ with $y \in fv^1(\Phi(D))$. For $\mathcal{C}$ to be a well-formed constraint system, we require that the dependency relationship is acyclic and that for every $x \in fv^1(\mathcal{C}) \cap \mathcal{X}$ (resp. $X \in fv^2(\mathcal{C})$) there is a unique constraint $D \vdash^?_X x$ in $\mathcal{S}$. For $X \in fv^2(\mathcal{C})$, we write $D_{\mathcal{C}}(X)$ for the domain $D \subseteq \mathcal{W}$ of the deduction constraint $D \vdash^?_X x$ associated to X in $\mathcal{C}$.

Example 12. Let $\Phi = \Phi_0 \uplus \{w_3 \triangleright \mathsf{aenc}(\langle \pi_2(N), \langle n_b, \mathsf{pk}(skb)\rangle\rangle, \mathsf{pk}(ska))\}$ with $N = \mathsf{adec}(y, skb)$, and $\mathcal{S}$ be a set containing two constraints:

$$\{w_0, w_1, w_2\} \vdash^?_Y y \text{ and } \pi_2(N) =^? \mathsf{pk}(ska).$$

We have that $\mathcal{C} = (\Phi; \mathcal{S})$ is a well-formed constraint system. There is only one first-order variable $y \in fv^1(\mathcal{C}) \cap \mathcal{X}$, and it does not occur in $fv^1(\Phi(\{w_0, w_1, w_2\}))$, which is empty. Moreover, there is indeed a unique constraint that introduces y.

Our notion of well-formed constraint systems is in line with what is used *e.g.*, in [17,7]. We use a simpler and (slightly) more permissive variant because we are not concerned with constraint solving procedures in this work.

Definition 6 (solution). *A solution of a constraint system $\mathcal{C} = (\Phi; \mathcal{S})$ is a substitution θ such that $\mathrm{dom}(\theta) = fv^2(\mathcal{C})$, and $X\theta \in \mathcal{T}(D_{\mathcal{C}}(X))$ for any $X \in \mathrm{dom}(\theta)$. Moreover, we require that there exists a ground substitution λ with $\mathrm{dom}(\lambda) = fv^1(\mathcal{C})$ such that:*

- *for every $D \vdash^?_X x$ in $\mathcal{S}$, we have that $(X\theta)(\Phi\lambda) =_\mathsf{E} x\lambda$;*
- *for every $u =^? v$ in $\mathcal{S}$, we have that $u\lambda =_\mathsf{E} v\lambda$; and*
- *for every $u \neq^? v$ in $\mathcal{S}$, we have that $u\lambda \neq_\mathsf{E} v\lambda$.*

The set of solutions of a constraint system $\mathcal{C}$ is denoted $\mathsf{Sol}(\mathcal{C})$. Since we consider constraint systems that are well-formed, the substitution λ is unique modulo E given $\theta \in \mathsf{Sol}(\mathcal{C})$. We denote it by λ_θ when $\mathcal{C}$ is clear from the context.

Example 13. Consider again the constraint system $\mathcal{C}$ given in Example 12. We have that $\theta = \{Y \mapsto \mathsf{aenc}(\langle w_1, w_1\rangle, w_2)\}$ is a solution of $\mathcal{C}$. Its associated first-order solution is $\lambda_\theta = \{y \mapsto \mathsf{aenc}(\langle \mathsf{pk}(ska), \mathsf{pk}(ska)\rangle, \mathsf{pk}(skb))\}$.

4.2 Symbolic Processes: Syntax and Semantics

From a simple process $(\mathcal{P}; \Phi)$, we compute the constraint systems capturing its possible executions, starting from the symbolic process $(\mathcal{P}; \Phi; \emptyset)$. Note that we are now manipulating processes that rely on free variables.

Definition 7 (symbolic process). *A symbolic process is a tuple $(\mathcal{P}; \Phi; \mathcal{S})$ where $(\Phi; \mathcal{S})$ is a constraint system and $fv^1(\mathcal{P}) \subseteq (fv^1(\mathcal{S}) \cap \mathcal{X})$.*

We give below a standard symbolic semantics for our symbolic processes.

IN $\quad (\text{in}(c,y).P; \Phi; \mathcal{S}) \xrightarrow{\text{in}(c,X)} (P\{y \mapsto x\}; \Phi; \mathcal{S} \cup \{\text{dom}(\Phi) \vdash^?_X x\})$

$\qquad$ where X (resp. x) is a fresh second-order (resp. first-order) variable

OUT $\quad (\text{out}(c,u).P; \Phi; \mathcal{S}) \xrightarrow{\text{out}(c,w)} (P; \Phi \cup \{w \triangleright u\}; \mathcal{S})$

$\qquad$ where w is a fresh first-order variable

THEN $\quad (\text{if } u = v \text{ then } P \text{ else } Q; \Phi; \mathcal{S}) \xrightarrow{\tau} (P; \Phi; \mathcal{S} \cup \{u =^? v\})$

ELSE $\quad (\text{if } u = v \text{ then } P \text{ else } Q; \Phi; \mathcal{S}) \xrightarrow{\tau} (Q; \Phi; \mathcal{S} \cup \{u \neq^? v\})$

From this semantics, we derive our compressed symbolic semantics $\xrightarrow{\text{tr}}_c$ following the same pattern as for the concrete semantics. We consider interleavings that execute maximal blocks of actions, and we allow improper termination of a block only at the end of a trace.

Example 14. We have that $(Q_0(b,a); \Phi_0; \emptyset) \xrightarrow{\text{tr}}_c (\emptyset; \Phi; \mathcal{S})$ where:

- $\text{tr} = \text{in}(c_B, Y) \cdot \text{out}(c_B, w_3)$, and
- $\mathcal{C} = (\Phi; \mathcal{S})$ is the constraint system defined in Example 12.

We are now able to define our notion of (symbolic) trace equivalence.

Definition 8 (trace equivalence w.r.t. $\xrightarrow{\text{tr}}_c$). *Let $A = (\mathcal{P}; \Phi)$ and $B = (\mathcal{Q}; \Psi)$ be two simple processes. We have that $A \sqsubseteq_s B$ when, for every sequence tr such that $(\mathcal{P}; \Phi; \emptyset) \xrightarrow{\text{tr}}_c (\mathcal{P}'; \Phi'; \mathcal{S}_A)$, for every $\theta \in \text{Sol}(\Phi'; \mathcal{S}_A)$, we have that:*

- *$(\mathcal{Q}; \Psi; \emptyset) \xrightarrow{\text{tr}}_c (\mathcal{Q}'; \Psi'; \mathcal{S}_B)$ with $\theta \in \text{Sol}(\Psi'; \mathcal{S}_B)$, and*
- *$\Phi \lambda^A_\theta \sim \Psi \lambda^B_\theta$ where λ^A_θ (resp. λ^B_θ) is the substitution associated to θ w.r.t. $(\Phi'; \mathcal{S}_A)$ (resp. $(\Psi'; \mathcal{S}_B)$).*

We have that A and B are in trace equivalence w.r.t. $\xrightarrow{\text{tr}}_c$ *if $A \sqsubseteq_s B$ and $B \sqsubseteq_s A$.*

Example 15. We have that $(Q_0(b,a); \Phi_0) \not\sqsubseteq_s (Q_0(b,a'); \Phi_0)$. Continuing Example 14, we have seen that $(Q_0(b,a); \Phi_0; \emptyset) \xrightarrow{\text{tr}}_c (\emptyset; \Phi; \mathcal{S})$, and $\theta \in \text{Sol}(\Phi; \mathcal{S})$ (see Example 12). The only symbolic process that is reachable from $(Q_0(b,a'); \Phi_0; \emptyset)$ using tr is $(\emptyset; \Phi'; \mathcal{S}')$ with:

- $\Phi' = \Phi_0 \uplus \{w_3 \triangleright \text{aenc}(\langle \pi_2(N), \langle n_b, \text{pk}(skb) \rangle \rangle, \text{pk}(ska'))\}$, and
- $\mathcal{S}' = \{\{w_0, w_1, w_2\} \vdash^?_Y y; \ \pi_2(N) =^? \text{pk}(ska')\}$.

We can check that θ is not a solution of $(\Phi'; \mathcal{S}')$.

For processes without replication, the symbolic transition system is finite. Thus, deciding (symbolic) trace equivalence between processes boils down to the problem of deciding a notion of equivalence between sets of constraint systems. This problem is well-studied and several procedures already exist [7,14,12].

4.3 Soundness and Completeness

Using the usual approach, such as the one developed in [7,13], we can show soundness and completeness of our symbolic compressed semantics w.r.t. our concrete compressed semantics. We have:

- *Soundness*: each transition in the compressed symbolic semantics represents a set of transitions that can be done in the concrete compressed semantics.
- *Completeness*: each transition in the compressed semantics can be matched by a transition in the compressed symbolic semantics.

Finally, relying on these two results, we can establish that symbolic trace equivalence ($\approx_s$) exactly captures compressed trace equivalence ($\approx_c$).

Theorem 2. *For any extended simple processes A and B, we have that:*
$$A \sqsubseteq_c B \iff A \sqsubseteq_s B.$$

5 Reduction Using Dependency Constraints

Unlike compression, which is based only on the input/output nature of actions, our second optimization takes into account the exchanged messages.

Let us first illustrate one simple instance of our optimization and how dependency constraints [18] may be used to incorporate it in symbolic semantics. Let $P_i = \mathsf{in}(c_i, x_i).\mathsf{out}(c_i, u_i).P_i'$ with $i \in \{1, 2\}$, and $\Phi_0 = \{w_0 \triangleright n\}$ be a closed frame. We consider the simple process $A = (\{P_1, P_2\}; \Phi_0)$, and the two symbolic interleavings depicted below.

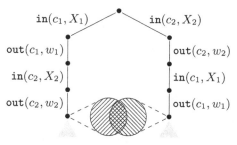

The two resulting symbolic processes are of the form $(\{P_1', P_2'\}; \Phi; \mathcal{S}_i)$ where:

- $\Phi = \Phi_0 \uplus \{w_1 \triangleright u_1, w_2 \triangleright u_2\}$,
- $\mathcal{S}_1 = \{w_0 \vdash^?_{X_1} x_1;\ w_0, w_1 \vdash^?_{X_2} x_2\}$,
- $\mathcal{S}_2 = \{w_0 \vdash^?_{X_2} x_2;\ w_0, w_2 \vdash^?_{X_1} x_1\}$.

The sets of concrete processes that these two symbolic processes represent are different, which means that we cannot discard any of those interleavings. However, these sets have a significant overlap corresponding to concrete instances of the interleaved blocks that are actually independent, *i.e.*, where the output of one block is not necessary to obtain the input of the next block. In order to avoid considering such concrete processes twice, we may add a *dependency constraint* $X_1 \bowtie w_2$ in $\mathcal{C}_2$, whose purpose is to discard all solutions θ such that the message $x_1\lambda_\theta$ can be derived without using $w_2 \triangleright u_2\lambda_\theta$. For instance, the concrete trace $\mathsf{in}(c_2, w_0) \cdot \mathsf{out}(c_2, w_2) \cdot \mathsf{in}(c_1, w_0) \cdot \mathsf{out}(c_1, w_1)$ would be discarded thanks to this new constraint.

The idea of [18] is to accumulate dependency constraints generated whenever such a pattern is detected in an execution, and use an adapted constraint resolution procedure to narrow and eventually discard the constrained symbolic states. We seek to exploit similar ideas for optimizing the verification of trace equivalence rather than reachability. This requires extra care, since pruning traces as described above may break completeness when considering trace equivalence. As before, the key to obtain a valid optimization will be to discard traces in a similar way on the two processes being compared. In addition to handling this necessary subtlety, we also propose a new proof technique for justifying dependency constraints. The generality of that technique allows us to add more dependency constraints, taking into account more patterns than the simple diamond shape from the previous example.

There are at least two natural semantics for dependency constraints. The simplest semantics focuses on the second-order notion of recipe. In the above example, it would require that recipe $X_1\theta$ contains the variable w_2. That is weaker than a first-order semantics requiring that *any* recipe deriving $x_1\lambda_\theta$ would involve w_2 since spurious dependencies may easily be introduced. Our ultimate goal in this section is to show that trace equivalence w.r.t. the first-order reduced semantics coincides with the regular symbolic semantics. However, we first establish this result for the second-order semantics, which is more easily analysed and provides a useful stepping stone.

5.1 Second-Order Reduced Semantics

We start by introducing *dependency constraints*, in a more general form than the one used above, and give them a second-order semantics.

Definition 9 (dependency constraint). *A dependency constraint is a constraint of the form* $\overrightarrow{X} \ltimes \overrightarrow{w}$ *where* $\overrightarrow{X}$ *is a vector of variables in* $\mathcal{X}^2$, *and* $\overrightarrow{w}$ *is a vector of handles, i.e. variables in* $\mathcal{W}$.

Given a substitution θ *with* $\text{dom}(\theta) \subseteq \mathcal{X}^2$, *and* $X\theta \in \mathcal{T}(\mathcal{W})$ *for any* $X \in \text{dom}(\theta)$. *We say that* θ *satisfies* $\overrightarrow{X} \ltimes \overrightarrow{w}$, *denoted* $\theta \models \overrightarrow{X} \ltimes \overrightarrow{w}$, *if either* $\overrightarrow{w} = \emptyset$ *or there exist* $X_i \in \overrightarrow{X}$ *and* $w_j \in \overrightarrow{w}$ *such that* $w_j \in fv^1(X_i\theta)$.

A constraint system with dependency constraints is called a *dependency constraint system*. We denote by $\mathcal{C}^\circ$ the regular constraint system obtained by removing all dependency constraints from $\mathcal{C}$. We only consider *well-formed* dependency constraint systems, that is those $\mathcal{C}$ such that $\mathcal{C}^\circ$ is well-formed. A solution of $\mathcal{C}$ is a substitution θ such that $\theta \in \text{Sol}(\mathcal{C}^\circ)$ and $\theta \models \overrightarrow{X} \ltimes \overrightarrow{w}$ for each dependency constraint $\overrightarrow{X} \ltimes \overrightarrow{w} \in \mathcal{C}$. We denote this set $\text{Sol}^2(\mathcal{C})$.

We shall now define how dependency constraints will be added to our constraint systems. For this, we fix an arbitrary total order $\prec$ on channels. Intuitively, this order expresses which executions should be favored, and which should be allowed only under dependency constraints. To simplify the presentation, we use the notation $\text{io}_c(\overrightarrow{X}, \overrightarrow{w})$ as a shortcut for $\text{in}(c, X_1) \cdot \ldots \cdot \text{in}(c, X_\ell).\text{out}(c, w_1) \cdot \ldots \cdot \text{out}(c, w_k)$ assuming that $\overrightarrow{X} = (X_1, \ldots, X_\ell)$ and $\overrightarrow{w} = (w_1, \ldots, w_k)$. Note that $\overrightarrow{X}$ and/or $\overrightarrow{w}$ may be empty.

Definition 10 (generation of dependency constraints). *Let c be a channel, and* $\text{tr} = \text{io}_{c_1}(\overrightarrow{X_1}, \overrightarrow{w_1}) \cdot \ldots \cdot \text{io}_{c_n}(\overrightarrow{X_n}, \overrightarrow{w_n})$ *be a trace. If there exists a rank $k \leq n$ such that $c_i \prec c \prec c_k$ for all $k < i \leq n$, then we define*

$$\text{dep}(\text{tr}, c) = \{ w \mid w \in \overrightarrow{w_i} \text{ with } k \leq i \leq n \}$$

Otherwise, we have that $\mathrm{dep}\,(\mathsf{tr}, c) = \emptyset$.

We obtain our reduced semantics by integrating those dependency constraints into the symbolic compressed semantics. We define $\mapsto_d$ as the least reflexive relation satisying the following rule:

$$\frac{(\mathcal{P};\Phi;\emptyset) \xmapsto{\mathsf{tr}}_d (\mathcal{P}';\Phi';\mathcal{S}') \quad (\mathcal{P}';\Phi';\mathcal{S}') \xmapsto{\mathrm{io}_c(\vec{X},\vec{w})}_c (\mathcal{P}'';\Phi'';\mathcal{S}'')}{(\mathcal{P};\Phi;\emptyset) \xmapsto{\mathsf{tr}\cdot\mathrm{io}_c(\vec{X},\vec{w})}_d (\mathcal{P}'';\Phi'';\mathcal{S}'' \cup \{\vec{X}\times\mathrm{dep}\,(\mathsf{tr}, c)\})}$$

Given a proper trace, we define $\mathrm{Deps}\,(\mathsf{tr})$ to be the accumulation of the generated constraints as defined above for all prefixes of tr (where each proper block is considered as an atomic action). We may observe that:

- if $A \xmapsto{\mathsf{tr}}_d (\mathcal{P};\Phi;\mathcal{S})$ then $\mathcal{S} = \mathcal{S}^\circ \cup \mathrm{Deps}\,(\mathsf{tr})$ and $A \xmapsto{\mathsf{tr}}_c (\mathcal{P};\Phi;\mathcal{S}^\circ)$;
- if $A \xmapsto{\mathsf{tr}}_c (\mathcal{P};\Phi;\mathcal{S})$ then $\mathcal{S} = \mathcal{S}'^\circ$ and $A \xmapsto{\mathsf{tr}}_d (\mathcal{P};\Phi;\mathcal{S}')$.

Example 16. Let a, b, and c be channels in $\mathcal{C}$ such that $a \prec b \prec c$. The dependency constraints generated during the symbolic execution of a simple process of the form $(\{\mathrm{in}(a, x_a).\mathrm{out}(a, u_a), \mathrm{in}(b, x_b).\mathrm{out}(b, u_b), \mathrm{in}(c, x_c).\mathrm{out}(c, u_c)\};\Phi)$ are depicted below.

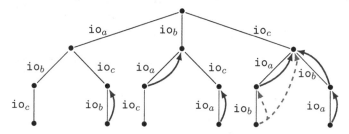

We use io_i as a shortcut for $\mathrm{in}(i, X_i)\cdot\mathrm{out}(i, w_i)$ and we represent dependency constraints using arrows. For instance, on the trace $\mathrm{io}_a \cdot \mathrm{io}_c \cdot \mathrm{io}_b$, a dependency constraint of the form $X_b\times w_c$ (represented by the left-most arrow) is generated. Now, on the trace $\mathrm{io}_c \cdot \mathrm{io}_a \cdot \mathrm{io}_b$ we add $X_a\times w_c$ after the second transition, and $X_b\times\{w_c, w_a\}$ (represented by the dashed 2-arrow) after the third transition. Intuitively, the latter constraint expresses that io_b is only allowed to come after io_c if it depends on it, possibly indirectly through io_a.

This reduced semantics gives rise to a notion of trace equivalence. It is defined as in Definition 8, relying on $\mapsto_d$ instead of $\mapsto_c$ and on Sol^2 instead of Sol. We denote it $\approx_d^2$, and the associated notion of inclusion is denoted $\sqsubseteq_d^2$

5.2   Soundness and Completeness

In order to establish that $\approx_s$ and $\approx_d^2$ coincide, we are going to study more carefully concrete traces made of (not necessarily proper) blocks. We denote by $\mathcal{B}$

the set of blocks $\mathtt{io}_c(\overrightarrow{M}, \overrightarrow{w})$ such that $c \in \mathcal{C}$, $M_i \in \mathcal{T}(\mathcal{W})$ for each $M_i \in \overrightarrow{M}$, and $w_j \in \mathcal{W}$ for each $w_j \in \overrightarrow{w}$. In this section, a concrete trace is necessarily made of blocks, *i.e.*, it belongs to $\mathcal{B}^*$. Note that all traces from executions in the compressed semantics are concrete traces in this sense. We show that we can view $\mathcal{B}^*$ as a partially commutative monoid in a meaningful way. This allows us to lift a classic result in which we ground our reduced semantics.

We lift the ordering on channels to blocks: $\mathtt{io}_c(\overrightarrow{M}, \overrightarrow{w}) \prec \mathtt{io}_{c'}(\overrightarrow{M'}, \overrightarrow{w'})$ if, and only if, $c \prec c'$. Finally, we define $\prec$ on concrete traces as the lexicographic extension of the order on blocks. We define similarly $\prec$ on symbolic traces.

Partially commutative monoid. We define an *independence relation* $\mathcal{I}_b$ over $\mathcal{B}$: we say that $\mathtt{io}_c(\overrightarrow{M}, \overrightarrow{w}) \, \mathcal{I}_b \, \mathtt{io}_{c'}(\overrightarrow{M'}, \overrightarrow{w'})$ when $c \neq c'$, none of the variables of $\overrightarrow{w'}$ occurs in $\overrightarrow{M}$, and none of the variables of $\overrightarrow{w}$ occurs in $\overrightarrow{M'}$. Then we define $=_{\mathcal{I}_b}$ as the least congruence satisfying

$$\mathtt{io}_c(\overrightarrow{M}, \overrightarrow{w}) \cdot \mathtt{io}_{c'}(\overrightarrow{M'}, \overrightarrow{w'}) =_{\mathcal{I}_b} \mathtt{io}_{c'}(\overrightarrow{M'}, \overrightarrow{w'}) \cdot \mathtt{io}_c(\overrightarrow{M}, \overrightarrow{w})$$

for all $\mathtt{io}_c(\overrightarrow{M}, \overrightarrow{w})$ and $\mathtt{io}_{c'}(\overrightarrow{M'}, \overrightarrow{w'})$ with $\mathtt{io}_c(\overrightarrow{M}, \overrightarrow{w}) \, \mathcal{I}_b \, \mathtt{io}_{c'}(\overrightarrow{M'}, \overrightarrow{w'})$. The set of concrete traces, quotiented by this equivalence relation, is the *partially commutative monoid* obtained from $\mathcal{I}_b$. Given a concrete trace tr, we denote by $\min(\mathsf{tr})$ the minimum for $\prec$ among all the traces that are equal to tr modulo $=_{\mathcal{I}_b}$.

First, we prove that the symbolic semantics is equally able to execute equivalent (w.r.t. $=_{\mathcal{I}_b}$) traces. Second we prove that the reduced semantics generates dependency constraints that are (only) satisfied by minimal traces.

Lemma 2. *Let* $(\mathcal{P}_0; \Phi_0; \emptyset) \xmapsto{\mathsf{tr}}_c (\mathcal{P}; \Phi; \mathcal{S})$ *with* tr *made of proper blocks, and* $\theta \in \mathsf{Sol}(\Phi; \mathcal{S})$. *For any concrete trace* $\mathsf{tr}_c =_{\mathcal{I}_b} \mathsf{tr}\theta$ *there exists a symbolic trace* $\mathsf{tr'}$ *such that* $\mathsf{tr}_c = \mathsf{tr'}\theta$, $(\mathcal{P}_0; \Phi_0; \emptyset) \xmapsto{\mathsf{tr'}}_c (\mathcal{P}; \Phi; \mathcal{S'})$ *and* $\theta \in \mathsf{Sol}(\Phi; \mathcal{S'})$.

Lemma 3. *Let* $A \xmapsto{\mathsf{tr}}_c (\mathcal{P}; \Phi; \mathcal{S})$ *and* $\theta \in \mathsf{Sol}(\Phi; \mathcal{S})$. *We have that* $\theta \models \mathsf{Deps}(\mathsf{tr})$ *if, and only if,* $\mathsf{tr}\theta = \min(\mathsf{tr}\theta)$.

Proof (Sketch). Let $A \xmapsto{\mathsf{tr}}_c (\mathcal{P}; \Phi; \mathcal{S})$ and $\theta \in \mathsf{Sol}(\Phi; \mathcal{S})$. We need a characterization of minimal traces. We exploit the following one, which is equivalent to the characterization of Anisimov and Knuth [3]:

> The trace t is minimal if, and only if, for all factors aub of t such that (1) $a, b \in \mathcal{B}$, $u \in \mathcal{B}^*$ and $d \prec b \prec a$ for all $d \in u$, we have (2) some $c \in au$ such that $c \, \mathcal{I}_b \, b$ does not hold.

We remark that condition (1) characterizes the factors of (symbolic) traces for which we generate a dependency constraint. Here, that constraint would be

$$\overrightarrow{X}_b \bowtie \cup_{d \in au} \overrightarrow{w}_d$$

where $\alpha \in \mathcal{B}$ is also written $\mathtt{io}_{c_\alpha}(\overrightarrow{X}_\alpha, \overrightarrow{w}_\alpha)$ to have an access to its components.

Then we note that (2) corresponds to the satisfaction of that dependency constraint in a concrete instance of the trace. $\qquad\square$

Finally, relying on these results, we can establish that trace equivalence ($\approx_d$) w.r.t. the reduced semantics exactly captures symbolic trace equivalence ($\approx_s$).

Theorem 3. *For any extended simple processes A and B, we have that:*
$$A \sqsubseteq_s B \iff A \sqsubseteq_d^2 B.$$

Proof (Sketch). Implication ($\Rightarrow$) is straightforward and only relies on the fact that dependency constraints generated by the reduced semantics only depend on the trace that is executed. The other direction ($\Leftarrow$) is more interesting. Here, we only outline the main idea, in the case of a trace made of proper blocks. We show that a concrete trace trθ which is not captured when considering $\mapsto_d$ (*i.e.*, a trace trθ that does not satisfy the generated dependency constraints) can be mapped to another trace, namely min(trθ), which manipulates the same recipes/messages but where blocks are executed in a different order. Lemma 2 is used to obtain an execution of the minimal trace, and Lemma 3 ensures that dependency constraints are satisfied in that execution. Thus the minimal trace can also be executed by the other process. We go back to trθ using Lemma 2. $\square$

5.3   First-Order Reduced Semantics

We finally introduce the stronger, first-order semantics for dependency constraints, and we prove soundness and completeness for the corresponding equivalence property by building on the previous theorem.

Definition 11. *Let $\mathcal{C} = (\varPhi; \mathcal{S})$ be a dependency constraint system. We define* $\mathsf{Sol}^1(\mathcal{C})$ *to be the set of substitutions $\theta \in \mathsf{Sol}(\mathcal{C}^\circ)$ such that, for each $\vec{X} \times \vec{w}$ in $\mathcal{C}$ with non-empty $\vec{w}$ there is some $X_i \in \vec{X}$ such that for all recipes $M \in \mathcal{T}(D_\mathcal{C}(X))$ satisfying $M(\varPhi\lambda_\theta) =_\mathsf{E} (X\theta)(\varPhi\lambda_\theta)$, we have $fv^1(M) \cap \vec{w} \neq \emptyset$.*

We define the notion of trace equivalence accordingly, as it has been done at the end of Section 5.1, relying on Sol^1 instead of Sol^2. We denote it $\approx_d^1$, and the associated notion of inclusion is denoted $\sqsubseteq_d^1$.

Theorem 4. *For any extended simple processes A and B, we have that:*
$$A \sqsubseteq_d^2 B \iff A \sqsubseteq_d^1 B.$$

Proof (Sketch). ($\Rightarrow$) This implication is relatively easy to establish. It actually relies on the fact that $\mathsf{Sol}^1(\mathcal{C}) \subseteq \mathsf{Sol}^2(\mathcal{C})$ for any dependency constraint system $\mathcal{C}$. This allows us to use our hypothesis $A \sqsubseteq_d^2 B$. Then, in order to come back to our more constrainted first-order reduced semantics, we may notice that as soon as θ is a solution of $\mathcal{C}$ and $\mathcal{C}'$ (w.r.t. Sol^2) with static equivalence of their associated frames, we have that: $\theta \in \mathsf{Sol}^1(\mathcal{C})$ if, and only if, $\theta \in \mathsf{Sol}^1(\mathcal{C}')$. ($\Leftarrow$) In order to exploit our hypothesis $A \sqsubseteq_d^1 B$, given a trace
$$A \overset{\mathsf{tr}}{\mapsto}_d (\mathcal{P}; \varPhi; \mathcal{S}) \text{ with } \theta \in \mathsf{Sol}^2(\varPhi; \mathcal{S}),$$
we build tr$'$ and θ' such that $A \overset{\mathsf{tr}'}{\mapsto}_d (\mathcal{P}; \varPhi; \mathcal{S}')$ with "tr $=_{\mathcal{I}_b}$ tr$'$", and $\theta' \in \mathsf{Sol}^1(\varPhi; \mathcal{S}')$. Actually, we do this without changing the underlying first-order

substitution, *i.e.*, $\lambda_\theta = \lambda_{\theta'}$. This is done by a sub-induction; iteratively modifying θ and tr. Whenever θ is not already a first-order solution, we slightly modify it. We obtain a new substitution θ' that is not a second-order solution anymore w.r.t. tr, and we use Lemmas 2 and 3 to obtain a new trace $\text{tr}' \prec \text{tr}$ for which θ' is a second-order solution. By induction hypothesis on tr' we obtain a first-order solution. We finally go back to the original trace tr, using an argument similar to the one in the first direction to handle static equivalence.   □

Example 17. We illustrate the construction of tr', which is at the core of the above proof. Consider $A = (\{P_1, P_2, P_3\}; \Phi)$ where $P_i = \text{in}(c_i, x_i).\text{out}(c_i, n_i)$, and $\Phi_0 = \{w_0 \triangleright n_0\}$, and $n_i \in \mathcal{N}$ for $0 \leq i \leq 3$. We assume that $c_1 \prec c_2 \prec c_3$, and we consider the situation where the nonces n_0 and n_2 (resp. n_1 and n_3) are the same.

Let $\text{tr} = \text{io}_{c_3}(X_3, w_3).\text{io}_{c_2}(X_2, w_2).\text{io}_{c_1}(X_1, w_1)$ and $(\Phi; \mathcal{S})$ the dependency constraint system such that $A \xrightarrow{\text{tr}}_d (\emptyset; \Phi; \mathcal{S})$. We consider the substitution $\theta = \{X_3 \mapsto \text{start}, X_2 \mapsto w_3, X_1 \mapsto w_2\}$. We note that $\theta \in \text{Sol}^2(\Phi; \mathcal{S})$ but we have that $\theta \notin \text{Sol}^1(\Phi; \mathcal{S})$ due to the presence of $X_1 \ltimes w_2$ in $\mathcal{S}$. We could try to fix this problem by building a "better" solution θ' that yields the same first-order solution: $\theta' = \{X_3 \mapsto \text{start}, X_2 \mapsto w_3, X_1 \mapsto w_0\}$ is such a candidate. Applying Lemmas 2 and 3, we obtain a smaller symbolic trace:

$$\text{tr}' = \text{io}_{c_1}(X_1, w_1) \cdot \text{io}_{c_3}(X_3, w_3) \cdot \text{io}_{c_2}(X_2, w_2).$$

Let $(\Phi; \mathcal{S}')$ be the constraint system obtained from the execution of tr'. We have that $\theta' \in \text{Sol}^2(\Phi; \mathcal{S}')$ but again $\theta' \notin \text{Sol}^1(\Phi; \mathcal{S}')$. This is due to the presence of $X_2 \ltimes w_3$ in $\mathcal{S}'$ — which was initially satisfied by θ in the first-order sense. With one more iteration of this transformation, we obtain a third candidate: $\theta'' = \{X_3 \mapsto \text{start}, X_2 \mapsto w_1, X_1 \mapsto w_0\}$ and

$$\text{tr}'' = \text{io}_{c_1}(X_1, w_1) \cdot \text{io}_{c_2}(X_2, w_2) \cdot \text{io}_{c_3}(X_3, w_3).$$

The associated constraint system does not contain any dependency constraint, and thus θ'' is trivially a first-order solution.

5.4   Applications

We first describe two situations showing that our reduced semantics can yield an exponential benefit. Then, we illustrate the effect of our reduced semantics on our running example, *i.e.*, the private authentication protocol.

Consider first the simple process $\mathcal{P} = \{P_1, P_2, \ldots, P_n\}$ where each P_i denotes the basic process $\text{in}(c_i, x).\text{if } x = \text{ok then } \text{out}(c_i, n_i)$ with $n_i \in \mathcal{N}$. There are $(2n)!/2^n$ different traces of size $2n$ (*i.e.*, containing $2n$ visible actions) in the concrete semantics. This number is actually the same in the standard symbolic semantics. In the compressed semantics (as well as the symbolic compressed semantics) this number goes down to $n!$. Finally, in the reduced semantics, there is only one trace such that the resulting constraint system admits a solution. Assuming that $c_1 \prec \ldots \prec c_n$, that trace is simply:

$$\text{tr} = \text{io}_{c_1}(\overrightarrow{X_1}, \overrightarrow{w_1}) \cdot \ldots \cdot \text{io}_{c_n}(\overrightarrow{X_n}, \overrightarrow{w_n}).$$

Next, we consider the simple process $\mathcal{P} = \{P_1^n, P_2^n\}$ where $P_i^0 = 0$, and P_i^{n+1} denotes the basic process $\mathsf{in}(c_i, x_j).\mathsf{if}\ x_j = \mathsf{ok}\ \mathsf{then}\ \mathsf{out}(c_i, n_j).P_i^n$. We consider traces of size $4n$. In the concrete semantics, there are $\binom{4n}{2n}$ different traces, whereas the number of such traces is reduced to $\binom{2n}{n}$ in the compressed semantics. Again, there is only one trace left in the reduced semantics.

Going back to our running example (see Examples 2 and 7), we represent some symbolic traces obtained using our reduced semantics. We consider:

$$(\{P_{\mathsf{init}}, Q_0(skb, \mathsf{pk}(ska))\}; \varPhi_0; \emptyset)$$

and we assume that $c_A \prec c_B$. We consider all symbolic traces obtained without considering the ELSE rule.

Those executions are represented in the diagram on the left, where

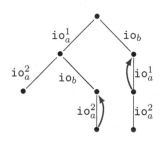

- $\mathtt{io}_a^1$ to denote $\mathtt{io}_{c_A}(X_a^1, w_a)$,
- $\mathtt{io}_a^2$ to denote $\mathtt{io}_{c_A}(X_a^2, \emptyset)$, and
- $\mathtt{io}_b$ to denote $\mathtt{io}_{c_B}(X_b, w_b)$.

The block $\mathtt{io}_a^2$ is an improper block since it only contains an input action. First, we may note that many interleavings are not taken into account thanks to compression. Now, consider the symbolic trace $\mathtt{io}_a^1 \cdot \mathtt{io}_b \cdot \mathtt{io}_a^2$. A dependency constraint of the form $X_a^2 \ltimes w_b$ is generated. Thus, a concrete trace that satisfies this dependency constraint must use the output of the role $Q_0(b, a)$ to build the second input of the role P_{init}.

Second, consider the rightmost branch. A dependency constraint of the form $X_a^1 \ltimes w_b$ is generated, and since X_a^1 has to be instantiated by a recipe that gives the public constant start (due of the constraint $x_a^1 =^? \mathsf{start}$ present in the system), the reduced semantics makes it possible to prune all executions starting with $\mathtt{io}_b \cdot \mathtt{io}_a^1$.

6   Conclusion

We have proposed two refinements of the symbolic semantics for simple processes. The first refinement groups actions in blocks, while the second one uses dependency constraints to restrict to minimal interleavings among a class of permutations. In both cases, the refined semantics has less traces, yet we show that the associated trace equivalence coincides with the standard one. In theory, this yields a potentially exponential algorithmic optimization.

In order to validate our approach, an experimental implementation has been developed[1]. This tool is based on SPEC [21] (which does not support else branches) and implements our modified semantics as well as an adapted constraint resolution procedure that takes (first-order) dependency constraints into account. The latter procedure is quite preliminary and far from optimal. Yet,

---

[1] Available at <http://perso.ens-lyon.fr/lucca.hirschi/spec_en.html>.

the modified checker already shows significant improvements over the original version on various benchmarks ([16], Figure 9).

We are considering several directions for future work. Constraint solving procedures should be studied in depth: we may optimize the one we already developed [16] and we are also interested in studying the problem in other frameworks, *e.g.*, [11]. We also believe that stronger reductions can be achieved: for instance, exploiting symmetries should be very useful for dealing with multiple sessions.

References

1. Abadi, M., Fournet, C.: Mobile values, new names, and secure communication. In: Proc. 28th Symposium on Principles of Programming Languages (POPL 2001), pp. 104–115. ACM Press (2001)
2. Abadi, M., Fournet, C.: Private authentication. Theoretical Computer Science 322(3), 427–476 (2004)
3. Anisimov, A., Knuth, D.: Inhomogeneous sorting. International Journal of Computer & Information Sciences 8(4), 255–260 (1979)
4. Arapinis, M., Chothia, T., Ritter, E., Ryan, M.: Analysing unlinkability and anonymity using the applied pi calculus. In: Proc. 23rd Computer Security Foundations Symposium (CSF 2010), pp. 107–121. IEEE Comp. Soc. Press (2010)
5. Armando, A., et al.: The AVISPA tool for the automated validation of internet security protocols and applications. In: Etessami, K., Rajamani, S.K. (eds.) CAV 2005. LNCS, vol. 3576, pp. 281–285. Springer, Heidelberg (2005)
6. Baelde, D., Delaune, S., Hirschi, L.: A reduced semantics for deciding trace equivalence using constraint systems. ArXiv e-prints (January 2014)
7. Baudet, M.: Deciding security of protocols against off-line guessing attacks. In: Proc. 12th Conference on Computer and Communications Security. ACM (2005)
8. Blanchet, B.: An Efficient Cryptographic Protocol Verifier Based on Prolog Rules. In: Proc. 14th Computer Security Foundations Workshop (CSFW 2001), pp. 82–96. IEEE Comp. Soc. Press (2001)
9. Blanchet, B., Abadi, M., Fournet, C.: Automated verification of selected equivalences for security protocols. Journal of Logic and Algebraic Programming (2008)
10. Chadha, R., Ciobâcă, Ş., Kremer, S.: Automated verification of equivalence properties of cryptographic protocols. In: Seidl, H. (ed.) ESOP 2012. LNCS, vol. 7211, pp. 108–127. Springer, Heidelberg (2012)
11. Cheval, V.: APTE (2011), http://projects.lsv.ens-cachan.fr/APTE/
12. Cheval, V., Comon-Lundh, H., Delaune, S.: Trace equivalence decision: Negative tests and non-determinism. In: Proc. 18th Conference on Computer and Communications Security (CCS 2011). ACM Press (2011)
13. Cheval, V., Cortier, V., Delaune, S.: Deciding equivalence-based properties using constraint solving. Theoretical Computer Science 492, 1–39 (2013)
14. Chevalier, Y., Rusinowitch, M.: Decidability of symbolic equivalence of derivations. Journal of Automated Reasoning 48(2) (2012)
15. Cremers, C.J.F.: The Scyther Tool: Verification, falsification, and fnalysis of security protocols. In: Gupta, A., Malik, S. (eds.) CAV 2008. LNCS, vol. 5123, pp. 414–418. Springer, Heidelberg (2008)
16. Hirschi, L.: Réduction d'entrelacements pour l'équivalence de traces. RR LSV-13-13, Laboratoire Spécification et Vérification, ENS Cachan, France (September 2013)

17. Millen, J., Shmatikov, V.: Constraint solving for bounded-process cryptographic protocol analysis. In: Proc. 8th ACM Conference on Computer and Communications Security (CCS 2001). ACM Press (2001)
18. Mödersheim, S., Viganò, L., Basin, D.A.: Constraint differentiation: Search-space reduction for the constraint-based analysis of security protocols. Journal of Computer Security 18(4), 575–618 (2010)
19. Peled, D.: Ten years of partial order reduction. In: Vardi, M.Y. (ed.) CAV 1998. LNCS, vol. 1427, pp. 7–28. Springer, Heidelberg (1998)
20. Rusinowitch, M., Turuani, M.: Protocol insecurity with finite number of sessions is NP-complete. In: Proc. 14th Computer Security Foundations Workshop (CSFW 2001), pp. 174–190. IEEE Comp. Soc. Press (2001)
21. Tiu, A.: Spec (2010), http://users.cecs.anu.edu.au/~tiu/spec/
22. Tiu, A., Dawson, J.E.: Automating open bisimulation checking for the spi calculus. In: Proc. 23rd IEEE Computer Security Foundations Symposium (CSF 2010), pp. 307–321. IEEE Computer Society Press (2010)

Stateful Applied Pi Calculus

Myrto Arapinis, Jia Liu, Eike Ritter, and Mark Ryan

School of Computer Science, University of Birmingham, UK

Abstract. We extend the applied pi calculus with state cells, which are used to reason about protocols that store persistent information. Examples are protocols involving databases or hardware modules with internal state. We distinguish between private state cells, which are not available to the attacker, and public state cells, which arise when a private state cell is compromised by the attacker. For processes involving only private state cells we define observational equivalence and labelled bisimilarity in the same way as in the original applied pi calculus, and show that they coincide. Our result implies Abadi-Fournet's theorem – the coincidence of observational equivalence and labelled bisimilarity – in a revised version of the applied pi calculus. For processes involving public state cells, we can essentially keep the definition of observational equivalence, but need to strengthen the definition of labelled bisimulation in order to show that observational equivalence and labelled bisimilarity coincide in this case as well.

Keywords: applied pi calculus, global state, bisimulation, security protocols.

1 Introduction

Security protocols are small distributed programs that use cryptography in order to achieve a security goal. The complexity that arises from their distributed nature motivates formal analysis in order to prove logical properties of their behaviour; fortunately, they are often small enough to make this kind of analysis feasible. Various logical methods have been used to model security protocols; process calculi have been particularly successful [3, 5, 31]. For example, the TLS protocol used by billions of users every day was analysed using ProVerif [11].

More recently, protocol analysis methods have been applied to stateful protocols – that is, protocols which involve persistent state information that can affect and be changed by protocol runs. Hardware devices that have some internal memory can be described by such protocols. For example, Yubikey is a USB device which generates one-time passwords based on encryptions of a secret ID, a running counter and some random values using a unique AES-128 key contained in the device. The trusted platform module (TPM) is another hardware chip that has a variety of registers which represent its state, and protocols for updating them. Radio-frequency identification (RFID) is a wireless technology for automatic identification and is currently deployed in electronic passports, tags for consumer goods, livestock and pets tracking, etc. An RFID-tag has a small area for storing secrets, which may be modified.

A process calculus can be made to work with such stateful protocols either by extension or by encoding. Extension means adding to the calculus explicit constructs for

M. Abadi and S. Kremer (Eds.): POST 2014, LNCS 8414, pp. 22–41, 2014.

working with the stateful aspects, while encoding means using combinations of the primitives that already exist. Encodings have the advantage that they keep the calculus simple and elegant, but (as argued in [3]) there may not be encodings for all the aspects we want, and in cases that encodings exist they may not be suitable for the analysis of security properties. StatVerif [7] demonstrates this: a natural way of encoding state using restricted channels prevents ProVerif from proving security. ProVerif also provides some built-in features, such as tables and phases, which provide only limited ways for modelling states. In particular, tables are defined as predicates which allow processes to store data by extending a predicate for the data. Hence there is no notion of the "current" state, and values cannot be deleted from tables. Phases are used to model the protocols with several stages. But there can be only finitely many phases, which can only be run in sequence, whereas a state may have infinitely many arbitrary values. Since our starting point is the applied pi calculus [3], we follow the philosophy adopted by its authors, which is to design a calculus that has the right primitives built in.

Our Contributions. We present an extension of the applied pi calculus by adding state cells, which are used to reason about protocols that store persistent information. We distinguish between private state cells, which are not available to the attacker, and public state cells, which arise when a private state cell is compromised by the attacker. In our stateful language, a private state cell is guarded by the scope restriction; its access is limited to some designated processes. When a private state cell gets compromised, the cell becomes public and this scenario is modelled by removing the scope restriction of that cell. We first define observational equivalence and labelled bisimilarity for processes having only private state cells, and we prove that two notions coincide as expected. By encoding the private state cells with restricted channels while keeping observational equivalence, our coincidence result can be seen to imply Abadi-Fournet's theorem [3, Theorem 1], in a revised version of applied pi calculus. As far as we can see, the only available proof for this theorem is [28] which is an unpublished manuscript. Despite having no published proof, this theorem has been widely used in many publications, for example [19, 8, 4, 18, 20].

We also discuss an extension of our language with public state cells. The obvious notion of labelled bisimilarity does not capture observational equivalence on public state cells. Designing a labelled bisimilarity on public state cells turns out to be unexpectedly difficult. Public state cells introduce many special language features which are significantly different from private state cells. Moreover, the addition of public state cells increases the capabilities of the attacker significantly. Hence we strengthen the definition of labelled bisimilarity to show that observational equivalence and labelled bisimulation coincide.

As an illustration, we analyse the OSK protocol [26] for RFID tags. We model its untraceability by private state cells and model its forward privacy by public state cells.

Related Work. StatVerif [7] is an extension of ProVerif process language [13] with private state cells. The main contribution there is to extend the ProVerif compiler to a compiler for StatVerif. The security property of interest there is secrecy which is modelled by reachability on the traces. This paper is a fundamental generalisation of the previous StatVerif work. The focus in this paper is to build a stateful language based on applied pi calculus, explore its language features and discuss indistinguishability, which is modelled by observational equivalence and analysed by labelled bisimilarity.

There are other languages that have been used to model protocols involving persistent state, but they are lower-level languages that are further away than our process language from the protocol design. Strand spaces have been generalised to work with the global state required by a trusted party charged with enforcing fair exchange [25]. The verifier Tamarin [33] uses multi-set rewriting (in which antecedents of applied rules are withdrawn from the knowledge set in order to represent state changes); it has been used to analyse hardware password tokens [27]. Multi-set rewriting is also used in [30], where state changes are important to represent revocation of cryptographic keys. Horn clauses rather than multiset rewriting are used in [22], in order to represent state changes made to registers of the TPM hardware module.

Reasoning about programming languages involving states has been extensively studied (e.g. [34, 23]). There are very strong interactions between programing language features and state, hence the reasoning principles are very specific to the precise combination of features. In this work we build on the work on reasoning principles for process calculi using bisimulation and show how to extend these principles to handle global state.

Outline. The next section defines syntax and semantics for the stateful applied pi calculus. Section 3 discusses the process equivalences and encoding for private state cells, and derives Abadi-Fournet's theorem. Section 4 extends our stateful language with public state cells. The paper concludes in Section 5.

2   Stateful Applied Pi Calculus

In this section, we extend the applied pi calculus [3] with constructs for states, and define its operational semantics. In fact, we do not directly build the stateful language on top of applied pi calculus, because we want to avoid working with the *structural equivalence* relation. More precisely, reasoning about the equivalent classes induced by structural equivalence turns out to be difficult and normally results in long tedious proofs [21, 18, 29, 17]. Our language inherits constructs for scope restriction, communication and active substitutions from applied pi calculus while having multisets of processes and active substitutions makes it possible to specify an operational semantics which does not involve any structural equivalence.

2.1   Syntax

We assume two disjoint, infinite sets $\mathcal{N}$ and $\mathcal{V}$ of *names* and *variables*, respectively. We rely on a sort system including a universal base sort, a cell sort and a channel sort. The sort system splits $\mathcal{N}$ into channel names $\mathcal{N}_{ch}$, base names $\mathcal{N}_b$ and cell names $\mathcal{N}_s$; similarly, $\mathcal{V}$ is split into channel variables $\mathcal{V}_{ch}$ and base variables $\mathcal{V}_b$. Unless otherwise stated, we use a, b, c as channel names, s, t as cell names, and x, y, z as variables. Meta variables u, v, w are used to range over both names and variables.

A signature Σ consists of a finite set of function symbols, each with an arity. A function symbol with arity 0 is a constant. Function symbols are required to take arguments and produce results of the base sort only. *Terms*, ranged over by M, N, are built up from variables and names by function application:

$M, N ::=$	terms
a, b, c, k, m, n, s	names
x, y, z	variables
$f(M_1, \dots, M_\ell)$	function application

We write $var(M)$ and $name(M)$ for the variables and names in M, respectively. Tuples such as $u_1 \cdots u_\ell$ and $M_1 \cdots M_\ell$ will be denoted by $\widetilde{u}$ and $\widetilde{M}$, respectively. Terms are equipped with an equational theory $=_\Sigma$ that is an equivalence relation closed under substitutions of terms for variables, one-to-one renamings and function applications.

The grammar for the *plain process* is given below. The operators for nil process 0, parallel composition $|$, replication $!$, scope restriction νn, conditional if - then - else , input $u(x)$ and output $\overline{u}\langle M \rangle$ are the same as the ones in applied pi calculus [3]. A state cell is a special process of the form $[s \mapsto M]$ where s is the cell name and M is the current value of s. The process lock $s.P$ locks the cell s for the subsequent process P. When the cell s is locked, another process that intends to access the cell has to wait until the cell is unlocked by a primitive unlock s. The process read s as $x.P$ reads the value in the cell and stores it in x in P. The process $s := M.P$ assigns the value M to the cell and continues as P.

$P, Q, R ::=$	plain process
0	nil process
$P \mid Q$	parallel composition
$! P$	replication
$\nu n.P$	name restriction
if $M = N$ then P else Q	conditional
$u(x).P$	input
$\overline{u}\langle M \rangle.P$	output
$[s \mapsto M]$	cell s, containing term M
$s := M.\,P$	writing a cell
read s as $x.P$	reading a cell
lock $s.P$	locking a cell
unlock $s.P$	unlocking a cell

subject to the following requirements:

- x, M, N are not of cell sort; $u \in \mathcal{N}_{ch} \cup \mathcal{V}_{ch}$ and $s \in \mathcal{N}_s$; additionally, M is of base sort in both $[s \mapsto M]$ and $s := M.\,P$;
- for every lock $s.\,P$, the part P of the process must not include parallel or replication unless it is after an unlock s.
- for a given cell name s, the replication operator $!$ must not occur between νs and $[s \mapsto M]$.

These side conditions rule out some nonsense processes, such as lock $s.!P$, lock $s.$ $(P \mid Q)$, $\nu s.![s \mapsto M]$ and $\nu s.([s \mapsto M] \mid [s \mapsto N])$, while keep some reasonable processes, such as lock $s.$unlock $s.!P$, lock $s.$unlock $s.\,(P \mid Q)$ and $!\nu s.[s \mapsto M]$.

An *extended process*, ranged over by A, B, C, is an expression of the form $\nu\tilde{n}.(\sigma, S, \mathcal{P})$ where

- $\nu\tilde{n}$ is a set of name restrictions;
- σ is a substitution $\{M_1/x_1, \ldots, M_n/x_n\}$ which replaces variables of base sort with terms of base sort; the domain $dom(\sigma)$ of σ is $\{x_1, \ldots, x_n\}$; the domain $dom(\nu\tilde{n}.(\sigma, S, \mathcal{P}))$ of the extended process $\nu\tilde{n}.(\sigma, S, \mathcal{P})$ is also $dom(\sigma)$; we require that $dom(\sigma) \cap fv(M_1, \ldots, M_n, \mathcal{P}, S) = \emptyset$;
- $S = \{s_1 \mapsto M_1, \ldots, s_m \mapsto M_m\}$ is a set of state cells such that $s_1, \ldots, s_m$ are pairwise-distinct cell names and terms $M_1, \ldots, M_m$ are of base sort; we write $dom(S)$ for $\{s_1, \ldots, s_m\}$ and $S(s_i)$ for M_i $(1 \leq i \leq m)$;
- $[s \mapsto M]$ can only occur at most once for a given cell name s, and if a cell name s is not restricted by any νs, a state cell $s \mapsto M$ can only occur in S;
- $\mathcal{P} = \{(P_1, L_1), \ldots, (P_k, L_k)\}$ is a multiset of pairs where P_i is a plain process and L_i is a set of cell names; $L_i \cap L_j = \emptyset$ for any $1 \leq i, j \leq k$ and $i \neq j$; for each $s \in L_i$, the part of the process P_i must not include parallel or replication unless it is after an `unlock` s; we write $locks(\mathcal{P})$ for the set $L_1 \cup \cdots \cup L_k$, namely the locked cells in $\mathcal{P}$.

In an extended process $\nu\tilde{n}.(\sigma, S, \mathcal{P})$, the substitution σ is similar to the active substitutions in applied pi calculus [3] which denote the static knowledge that the process exposes to the environment. A minor difference with [3] is that substitutions here are only defined on terms of base sort which will be explained later. State cells are mutable and the value of a cell may be changed during the running of processes. If a process P locks a cell s, then this status information will be kept as $(P, \{s\} \cup L)$ in $\mathcal{P}$. At any time, the cell s can be locked at most once in $\mathcal{P}$.

The variable x in "$u(x)$" and "`read s as x`" are bound, as well as the name n in νn. This leads to the usual notions of bound and free names and variables. We shall use $fn(A)$ for free names, use $fs(A)$ for free cell names, use $fv(A)$ for free variables, use $bn(A)$ for bound names, and use $bv(A)$ for bound variables of A. Let $fnv(A) = fn(A) \cup fv(A)$ and $bnv(A) = bn(A) \cup bv(A)$. Following the conventions in [32], we shall identify processes which are α-convertible. We write "$=$" for both syntactical equality and equivalence under α-conversion. Captures of bound names and bound variables are avoided by implicit α-conversion.

An extended process $\nu\tilde{n}.(\sigma, S, \mathcal{P})$ is called *closed* if each variable is either defined by σ or bound, each cell name s is defined by exactly one "$s \mapsto M$" (either in S or in $\mathcal{P}$), and $locks(\mathcal{P}) \subseteq dom(S)$. We may write $(\sigma, S, \mathcal{P})$ for $\nu\emptyset.(\sigma, S, \mathcal{P})$, and write $\nu\tilde{n}, \tilde{m}.(\sigma, S, \mathcal{P})$ for $\nu(\tilde{n} \cup \tilde{m}).(\sigma, S, \mathcal{P})$.

When we write $\sigma = \sigma_1 \cup \sigma_2$ for some substitution σ or $S = S_1 \cup S_2$ for some state cells S, we assume that $dom(\sigma_1) \cap dom(\sigma_2) = \emptyset$ as well as $dom(S_1) \cap dom(S_2) = \emptyset$. For variables $\tilde{x}$, we define $\sigma_{\backslash\tilde{x}}$ to be the substitution $\{z\sigma/z \mid z \in dom(\sigma) \text{ and } z \notin \tilde{x}\}$. If $A = \nu\tilde{n}.(\sigma, S, \mathcal{P})$, we write $A_{\backslash\tilde{x}}$ for $\nu\tilde{n}.(\sigma_{\backslash\tilde{x}}, S, \mathcal{P})$.

An *evaluation context* $\nu\tilde{n}.(\sigma\text{-}, S\text{-}, \mathcal{P}\text{-})$ is an extended process with holes "-" for substitution, state cells and plain processes. Let $\mathcal{C} = \nu\tilde{n}.(\sigma\text{-}, S\text{-}, \mathcal{P}\text{-})$ be an evaluation context and $A = \nu\tilde{m}.(\sigma_a, S_a, \mathcal{P}_a)$ be a closed extended process with $\tilde{m} \cap (\tilde{n} \cup fn(\sigma, S, \mathcal{P})) = dom(\sigma) \cap dom(\sigma_a) = dom(S) \cap dom(S_a) = \emptyset$. The result of applying

$$\nu\tilde{n}.\,(\sigma, S, \mathcal{P} \cup \{(!\,P, \emptyset)\}) \xrightarrow{\ \tau\ } \nu\tilde{n}.\,(\sigma, S, \mathcal{P} \cup \{(!\,P, \emptyset), (P, \emptyset)\})$$

$$\nu\tilde{n}.(\sigma, S, \mathcal{P} \cup \{(P \mid Q, \emptyset)\}) \xrightarrow{\ \tau\ } \nu\tilde{n}.(\sigma, S, \mathcal{P} \cup \{(P, \emptyset), (Q, \emptyset)\})$$

$$\nu\tilde{n}.(\sigma, S, \mathcal{P} \cup \{(\nu m.P, L)\}) \xrightarrow{\ \tau\ } \nu\tilde{n},\, m.(\sigma, S, \mathcal{P} \cup \{(P, L)\}) \text{ if } m \notin fn(\tilde{n}, \sigma, S, \mathcal{P}, L)$$

$$\nu\tilde{n}.(\sigma, S, \mathcal{P} \cup \{([s \mapsto M], \emptyset)\}) \xrightarrow{\ \tau\ } \nu\tilde{n}.(\sigma, S \cup \{s \mapsto M\}, \mathcal{P}) \text{ if } s \in \tilde{n} \text{ and } s \notin dom(S)$$

$$\nu\tilde{n}.(\sigma, S, \mathcal{P} \cup \{(a(x).P, L_1)\} \cup \{(\overline{a}(M).Q, L_2)\}) \xrightarrow{\ \tau\ } \nu\tilde{n}.(\sigma, S, \mathcal{P} \cup \{(P\{M/x\}, L_1), (Q, L_2)\}))$$

$$\nu\tilde{n}.(\sigma, S, \mathcal{P} \cup \{(\text{if } M = N \text{ then } P \text{ else } Q, L)\}) \xrightarrow{\ \tau\ } \nu\tilde{n}.(\sigma, S, \mathcal{P} \cup \{(P, L)\}) \text{ if } M =_\Sigma N$$

$$\nu\tilde{n}.(\sigma, S, \mathcal{P} \cup \{(\text{if } M = N \text{ then } P \text{ else } Q, L)\}) \xrightarrow{\ \tau\ } \nu\tilde{n}.(\sigma, S, \mathcal{P} \cup \{(Q, L)\}) \text{ if } M \neq_\Sigma N \text{ and } var(M, N) = \emptyset$$

$$\nu\tilde{n}.(\sigma, S \cup \{s \mapsto M\}, \mathcal{P} \cup \{(\text{read } s \text{ as } x.P, L)\}) \xrightarrow{\ \tau\ } \nu\tilde{n}.(\sigma, S \cup \{s \mapsto M\}, \mathcal{P} \cup \{(P\{M/x\}, L)\})$$
$$\text{if } s \in \tilde{n} \cup L \text{ and } s \notin locks(\mathcal{P})$$

$$\nu\tilde{n}.(\sigma, S \cup \{s \mapsto M\}, \mathcal{P} \cup \{(s := N.P, L)\}) \xrightarrow{\ \tau\ } \nu\tilde{n}.(\sigma, S \cup \{s \mapsto N\}, \mathcal{P} \cup \{(P, L)\})$$
$$\text{if } s \in \tilde{n} \cup L \text{ and } s \notin locks(\mathcal{P})$$

$$\nu\tilde{n}.(\sigma, S \cup \{s \mapsto M\}, \mathcal{P} \cup \{(\text{lock } s.P, L)\}) \xrightarrow{\ \tau\ } \nu\tilde{n}.(\sigma, S \cup \{s \mapsto M\}, \mathcal{P} \cup \{(P, L \cup \{s\})\})$$
$$\text{if } s \in \tilde{n} \text{ and } s \notin L \cup locks(\mathcal{P})$$

$$\nu\tilde{n}.(\sigma, S \cup \{s \mapsto M\}, \mathcal{P} \cup \{(\text{unlock } s.P, L)\}) \xrightarrow{\ \tau\ } \nu\tilde{n}.(\sigma, S \cup \{s \mapsto M\}, \mathcal{P} \cup \{(P, L \setminus \{s\})\}) \text{ if } s \in \tilde{n} \cap L$$

$$\nu\tilde{n}.(\sigma, S, \mathcal{P} \cup \{(a(x).P, L)\}) \xrightarrow{\ a(M)\ } \nu\tilde{n}.(\sigma, S, \mathcal{P} \cup \{(P\{M\sigma/x\}, L)\}) \text{ if } name(a, M) \cap \tilde{n} = \emptyset$$

$$\nu\tilde{n}.(\sigma, S, \mathcal{P} \cup \{(\overline{a}\langle c\rangle.P, L)\}) \xrightarrow{\ \overline{a}\langle c\rangle\ } \nu\tilde{n}.(\sigma, S, \mathcal{P} \cup \{(P, L)\}) \text{ if } a, c \notin \tilde{n}$$

$$\nu\tilde{n},\, c.(\sigma, S, \mathcal{P} \cup \{(\overline{a}\langle c\rangle.P, L)\}) \xrightarrow{\ \nu c.\overline{a}\langle c\rangle\ } \nu\tilde{n}.(\sigma, S, \mathcal{P} \cup \{(P, L)\}) \text{ if } a, c \notin \tilde{n} \text{ and } a \neq c$$

$$\nu\tilde{n}.(\sigma, S, \mathcal{P} \cup \{(\overline{a}\langle M\rangle.P, L)\}) \xrightarrow{\ \nu x.\overline{a}\langle x\rangle\ } \nu\tilde{n}.(\sigma \cup \{M/x\}, S, \mathcal{P} \cup \{(P, L)\})$$
$$\text{if } a \notin \tilde{n} \text{ and } M \text{ is of base sort and } x \text{ is fresh}$$

Fig. 1. Operational Semantics

$\mathcal{C}$ to A is an extended process defined by:

$$\mathcal{C}[A] = \nu\tilde{n}, \tilde{m}.(\sigma\sigma_a \cup \sigma_a, S\sigma_a \cup S_a, \mathcal{P}\sigma_a \cup \mathcal{P}_a)$$

An evaluation context $\mathcal{C}$ *closes* A when $\mathcal{C}[A]$ is a closed extended process.

2.2 Operational Semantics

The *transition* relation $A \xrightarrow{\alpha} A'$ is the smallest relation on extended processes defined by the rules in Figure 1. The action α is either an internal action τ, an input $a(x)$, an output of channel name $\overline{a}\langle c\rangle$, an output of bound channel name $\nu c.\overline{a}\langle c\rangle$, or an output of terms of base sort $\nu x.\overline{a}\langle x\rangle$. The transitions for conditional branch, communication, sending and receiving channel names and complex messages are typical and essentially the same as the ones in applied pi calculus. In particular, the output $\nu x.\overline{a}\langle x\rangle$ for term M generates an "alias" x for M which is kept in the substitution part of the extended process. As mentioned before, state cells are used to model the hardware or the database to which the access is usually mutually-exclusive. When a state cell is locked, the other process that intends to access the cell must wait until the cell is released.

3   Private State Cells

3.1   Equivalences for Private State Cells

We first discuss observational equivalence and labelled bisimilarity on the *extended processes with only private state cells*, that is, each cell name s occurring in the processes is within the scope of a restriction νs. We will discuss an extension of the language with public state cells in Section 4.

Observational equivalence [3] has been widely used to model properties of security protocols. It captures the intuition of indistinguishability from the attacker's point of view. Security properties such as anonymity [4], privacy [20, 6] and strong secrecy [12] are usually formalised by observational equivalence.

We write $\Longrightarrow$ for the reflexive and transitive closure of $\xrightarrow{\tau}$; we define $\overset{\alpha}{\Longrightarrow}$ to be $\Longrightarrow\xrightarrow{\alpha}\Longrightarrow$; we write $\overset{\widehat{\alpha}}{\Longrightarrow}$ for $\overset{\alpha}{\Longrightarrow}$ if α is not τ and $\Longrightarrow$ otherwise. We write $A \Downarrow_a$ when $A \Longrightarrow \nu\widetilde{n}.(\sigma, S, \mathcal{P} \cup \{(\overline{a}\langle M\rangle.P, L)\})$ with $a \notin \widetilde{n}$.

Definition 1. *Observational equivalence* ($\approx$) *is the largest symmetric relation $\mathcal{R}$ on pairs of closed extended processes with only private state cells, such that $A\ \mathcal{R}\ B$ implies*

(i) $dom(A) = dom(B)$;
(ii) if $A \Downarrow_a$ then $B \Downarrow_a$;
(iii) if $A \Longrightarrow A'$ then $B \Longrightarrow B'$ and $A'\ \mathcal{R}\ B'$ for some B';
(iv) for all closing evaluation contexts C with only private cells, $C[A]\ \mathcal{R}\ C[B]$.

Observational equivalence is a contextual equivalence where the contexts model the active attackers who can intercept and forge messages. In the following examples, we illustrate the use of observational equivalence in the stateful language by analysing the untraceability of the RFID tags.

Example 1. We start by analysing a naive protocol for RFID tag identification. The tag simply reads its id and sends it to the reader. We assume the attacker can eavesdrop on the radio frequency signals between the tag and the reader. In other words, all the communications between the tag and the reader are visible to the attacker. The operations on the tag can be modelled by: $P(s) = \texttt{read}\ s\ \texttt{as}\ x.\overline{a}\langle x\rangle$. One security concern for RFID tags is to avoid third-party attacker tracking. The attacker is not supposed to trace the tag according to its outputs. Using the definition in [6], the untraceability can be modelled by observational equivalence:

$$(\emptyset, \emptyset, \{(\,!\,\nu s, id.([s \mapsto id]\ |\ P(s)), \emptyset)\}) \approx (\emptyset, \emptyset, \{(\,!\,\nu s, id.([s \mapsto id]\ |\,!\,P(s)), \emptyset)\})$$

In the left process, each tag s can be used at most once. In the right process, each tag s can be used an unbounded number of times. The above equivalence does not hold, which means this protocol is traceable. By eavesdropping on channel a of the right process, the attacker can get a data sequence: "$id, id, id\cdots$", while a particular id can occur at most once in the first process.

Example 2. The OSK protocol [26] is a simple identification protocol for RFID tags which aims to satisfy third-party untraceability. The tag can perform two independent one-way functions g and h. An initial secret is stored in the tag and is known to the back-end database. On each run of the protocol, the tag computes the hash g of its current value and sends the result to the reader. The reader forwards the message to the back-end database for identification. The tag then updates its value with the hash h of its current value. The operations related to a tag s can be modelled by:

$$T(s) = \texttt{lock } s.\, \texttt{read } s \texttt{ as } x.\, \overline{a}\langle g(x)\rangle.\, s := h(x).\, \texttt{unlock } s$$

Let RD be process modelling the reader and back-end database. Similar to Example 1, the untraceability can be represented by

$$(\emptyset, \emptyset, \{(\,!\,\nu s, k.([s \mapsto k] \mid T(s) \mid RD), \emptyset)\})$$
$$\approx (\emptyset, \emptyset, \{(\,!\,\nu s, k.([s \mapsto k] \mid !\,T(s) \mid RD), \emptyset)\})$$

In the second process, for a particular tag s which contains value k, the data sequence observed by the attacker on channel a is "$g(k), g(h(k)), g(h(h(k))) \cdots$". Without knowing the secret k, these appear just random data to the attacker and so the attacker cannot link these data to the same tag. The observational equivalence between these two processes means the attacker cannot identify the multiple runnings of a particular tag. The "$\texttt{lock } s \cdots \texttt{unlock } s$" ensures exclusive access to the tag. After the reader reads the tag, the tag must be renewed before the next access to the tag; otherwise the tag would be traceable.

The universal quantifier over the contexts makes it difficult to prove observational equivalence. Hence labelled bisimilarity is introduced in [3] to capture observational equivalence. Labelled bisimilarity consists of static equivalence and behavioural equivalence.

Definition 2. *Two processes A and B are statically equivalent, written as $A \approx_s B$, if $dom(A) = dom(B)$, and for any terms M and N with $var(M, N) \subseteq dom(A)$, $M\sigma_1 =_\Sigma N\sigma_1$ iff $M\sigma_2 =_\Sigma N\sigma_2$ where $A = \nu\tilde{n}_1.(\sigma_1, S_1, \mathcal{P}_1)$ and $B = \nu\tilde{n}_2.(\sigma_2, S_2, \mathcal{P}_2)$ for some $\tilde{n}_1, \tilde{n}_2$ such that $(\tilde{n}_1 \cup \tilde{n}_2) \cap name(M, N) = \emptyset$.*

Our definition of static equivalence is essentially the same as the one in [3], as the definition in [3] is invariant under structural equivalence already. Although static equivalence is in general undecidable, there are well established ways, including tools, for verifying static equivalence [2, 15, 16, 9, 14]. Static equivalence defines the indistinguishability between the environmental knowledge exposed by two processes. The environmental knowledge is modelled by the substitutions in the extended processes. For example, let $A = \nu k, m.(\{k/x, m/y\}, \emptyset, \emptyset)$ and $B = \nu k.(\{k/x, h(k)/y\}, \emptyset, \emptyset)$. The test $h(x) = y$ fails under the application of A's substitution $\{k/x, m/y\}$, while succeeds under the application of B's substitution $\{k/x, h(k)/y\}$. Hence $A \not\approx_s B$.

Definition 3. *Labelled bisimilarity ($\approx_l$) is the largest symmetric relation $\mathcal{R}$ between pairs of closed extended processes with only private state cells such that $A \,\mathcal{R}\, B$ implies*

1. $A \approx_s B$;
2. if $A \xrightarrow{\alpha} A'$ and $fv(\alpha) \subseteq dom(A)$ and $bn(\alpha) \cap fn(B) = \emptyset$, then $B \xrightarrow{\hat{\alpha}} B'$ such that $A' \,\mathcal{R}\, B'$ for some B'.

$$\lfloor 0 \rfloor_S = 0 \qquad \lfloor P \mid Q \rfloor_S = \lfloor P \rfloor_S \mid \lfloor Q \rfloor_S \qquad \lfloor \nu n.P \rfloor_S = \nu n. \lfloor P \rfloor_S \ \text{if } n \notin \mathcal{N}_s$$

$$\lfloor !P \rfloor_S = ! \lfloor P \rfloor_S \qquad \lfloor u(x).P \rfloor_S = u(x). \lfloor P \rfloor_S \qquad \lfloor \overline{u}\langle M \rangle.P \rfloor_S = \overline{u}\langle M \rangle. \lfloor P \rfloor_S$$

$$\lfloor \text{if } M = N \text{ then } P \text{ else } Q \rfloor_S \ = \ \text{if } M = N \text{ then } \lfloor P \rfloor_S \text{ else } \lfloor Q \rfloor_S$$

$$\lfloor s \mapsto M \rfloor_S = \overline{c_s}\langle M \rangle \qquad\qquad \lfloor \nu s.P \rfloor_S = \nu c_s. \lfloor P \rfloor_S \ \text{if } s \in \mathcal{N}_s$$

$$\lfloor \text{lock } s.P \rfloor_S = \begin{cases} c_s(x). \lfloor P \rfloor_{S \cup \{s \mapsto x\}} & \text{if } s \notin dom(S) \text{ and } x \text{ is fresh} \\ 0 & \text{otherwise} \end{cases}$$

$$\lfloor \text{unlock } s.P \rfloor_S = \begin{cases} \overline{c_s}\langle M \rangle \mid \lfloor P \rfloor_T & \text{if } S = T \cup \{s \mapsto M\} \\ 0 & \text{otherwise} \end{cases}$$

$$\lfloor \text{read } s \text{ as } x.P \rfloor_S = \begin{cases} \lfloor P \{M/x\} \rfloor_S & \text{if } S = T \cup \{s \mapsto M\} \\ c_s(x).(\overline{c_s}\langle x \rangle \mid \lfloor P \rfloor_S) & \text{otherwise} \end{cases}$$

$$\lfloor s := M.P \rfloor_S = \begin{cases} \lfloor P \rfloor_{T \cup \{s \mapsto M\}} & \text{if } S = T \cup \{s \mapsto N\} \\ c_s(x).(\overline{c_s}\langle M \rangle \mid \lfloor P \rfloor_S) & \text{otherwise select fresh variable } x \end{cases}$$

Fig. 2. Encoding private state cells with restricted channels

Instead of using arbitrary contexts, labelled bisimilarity relies on the direct comparison of the transitions. The following theorem states that labelled bisimilarity can fully capture observational equivalence:

Theorem 1. *On closed extended processes with only private state cells, it holds that* $\approx = \approx_l$.

3.2 Encoding Private State Cells with Restricted Channels

Private state cells can be encoded by restricted channels. This is an important observation; moreover, we will use this to prove Abadi-Fournet's theorem in the following Section 3.3. However, when modelling security protocols, the drawback of representing private state cells by restricted channels is that it may introduce false attacks when using the automatic tool ProVerif as argued in [7]. The reason is that some features of restricted channels are abstracted away when ProVerif translates process calculus into Horn clauses [13]. To solve this problem, we introduce the primitives for lock, read, write and unlock which will help us design better translations for stateful protocols in ProVerif. This has been demonstrated by the verification of reachability [7], and will be useful in future for verifying observational equivalence.

We encode the extended processes with only private state cells into a subset of the extended processes which do not contain any cell name. Since the target language of the encoding does not have any cell name, we abbreviate extended processes $\nu \tilde{n}.$ $(\sigma, \emptyset, \{(P_i, \emptyset)\}_{i \in I})$ with no cell name to $\nu \tilde{n}.(\sigma, \{P_i\}_{i \in I})$.

First we define encoding $\lfloor P \rfloor_S$ in Figure 2 for the plain process P under a given set of state cells $S = \{s_1 \mapsto M_1, \ldots, s_n \mapsto M_n\}$. For each cell s, we select a fresh channel name c_s. The encoding in Figure 2 only affects the part related to cell names, leaving other parts like input and output unchanged. The state cell $s \mapsto M$ and unlock s are both encoded by an output $\overline{c_s}\langle M \rangle$ on the restricted channel c_s. The lock s is represented by an input $c_s(x)$ on the same channel c_s. To read the cell read s as x, we use the input $c_s(x)$ to get the value from the cell and then put the value back $\overline{c_s}\langle x \rangle$, which enables the other operations on cell s in future. To write a new value into the cell $s := N$, we need to first consume the existing $\overline{c_s}\langle M \rangle$ by an input $c_s(x)$ and then generate a new output $\overline{c_s}\langle N \rangle$. Our encoding ensures that there is only one output $\overline{c_s}\langle M \rangle$ available on a specified restricted channel c_s at each moment. When the cell is locked, namely $\overline{c_s}\langle M \rangle$ is consumed by some $c_s(x)$, the other processes that intend to access the cell have to wait until an output $\overline{c_s}\langle N \rangle$ is available.

Let $A = \nu \tilde{s}, \tilde{n}.\left(\sigma, \{s_i \mapsto M_i\}_{i \in I}, \{(P_j, L_j)\}_{j \in J} \right)$ be an extended process [1] where $\tilde{s} \subset \mathcal{N}_s$ and $\tilde{n} \cap \mathcal{N}_s = \emptyset$. We define the encoding $\lfloor A \rfloor$ as:

$$\lfloor A \rfloor = \nu \tilde{c_s}, \tilde{n}. \left(\sigma, \{\overline{c_{s_i}}\langle M_i \rangle\}_{i \in U} \cup \left\{ \lfloor P_j \rfloor_{S_j} \right\}_{j \in J} \right)$$

where $U = \{ i \mid s_i \notin \bigcup_{j \in J} L_j \text{ and } i \in I \}$ and $S_j = \{ s_i \mapsto M_i \mid s_i \in L_j \text{ and } i \in I \}$. Intuitively, U is the indices of the unlocked state cells in $\{s_i \mapsto M_i\}_{i \in I}$, and S_j is the set of state cells locked by L_j.

Example 3. Let $A = \nu s.(\emptyset, \{s \mapsto 0\}, \{(T(s), \emptyset)\})$ where $T(s)$ is defined in Example 2. Then $\lfloor A \rfloor = \nu c_s.(\emptyset, \{\overline{c_s}\langle 0 \rangle, \lfloor T(s) \rfloor_\emptyset\})$ with $\lfloor T(s) \rfloor_\emptyset = c_s(z).\overline{a}\langle g(z) \rangle.\overline{c_s}\langle h(z) \rangle$ obtained by:

$$
\begin{aligned}
\lfloor T(s) \rfloor_\emptyset &= \lfloor \texttt{lock } s.\texttt{read } s \texttt{ as } x.\overline{a}\langle g(x) \rangle.s := h(x).\texttt{unlock } s \rfloor_\emptyset \\
&= c_s(z). \lfloor \texttt{read } s \texttt{ as } x.\overline{a}\langle g(x) \rangle.s := h(x).\texttt{unlock } s \rfloor_{\{s \mapsto z\}} \\
&= c_s(z). \lfloor \overline{a}\langle g(z) \rangle.s := h(z).\texttt{unlock } s \rfloor_{\{s \mapsto z\}} \\
&= c_s(z).\overline{a}\langle g(z) \rangle. \lfloor s := h(z).\texttt{unlock } s \rfloor_{\{s \mapsto z\}} \\
&= c_s(z).\overline{a}\langle g(z) \rangle. \lfloor \texttt{unlock } s \rfloor_{\{s \mapsto h(z)\}} \\
&= c_s(z).\overline{a}\langle g(z) \rangle.\overline{c_s}\langle h(z) \rangle
\end{aligned}
$$

Theorem 2. *For two closed extended processes A, B with only private state cells, we have $A \approx B$ iff $\lfloor A \rfloor \approx^e \lfloor B \rfloor$ where $\approx^e$ is an equivalence defined exactly the same as Definition 1 except the context C does not contain any cell names.*

3.3 Overview of the Proof of Abadi-Fournet's Theorem

We shall use our Theorem 1 and Theorem 2 to derive Abadi-Fournet's theorem, namely Theorem 1 in [3]. We revise the original applied pi calculus [3] slightly: *active substitutions are only defined on terms of base sort*; otherwise Theorem 1 in [3] does not hold [10].[2] Since the active substitutions in applied pi calculus float everywhere in the extended processes, in order to prove Abadi-Fournet's theorem, we need to normalise

---

[1] We abbreviate the set $\{ s_i \mapsto M_i \mid i \in I \}$ as $\{s_i \mapsto M_i\}_{i \in I}$.

[2] Here is a counter example: let $A_r = \nu c.(\overline{c}.\overline{a} \mid \{c/x\})$ and $B_r = \nu c.(0 \mid \{c/x\})$. Obviously A_r and B_r are labelled bisimilar since their frames are the same and both have no transitions. However, they are not observationally equivalent. Consider the context $x(y)$, then $A_r \mid x(y) \Downarrow_a$ but $B_r \mid x(y) \not\Downarrow_a$.

the extended processes first. We can transform the extended processes in the applied pi calculus – denoted by A_r, B_r, C_r to avoid confusion – into the extended processes in stateful applied pi calculus by function $\mathcal{T}$ (assume bound names are pairwise-distinct and different from free names): [3]

$$\mathcal{T}(0) = (\emptyset, \emptyset) \qquad \mathcal{T}(\{M/x\}) = (\{M/x\}, \emptyset) \qquad \mathcal{T}(\nu n. A_r) = \nu n. \mathcal{T}(A_r)$$
$$\mathcal{T}(\nu x. A_r) = \nu \tilde{n}.(\sigma, P) \text{ if } \mathcal{T}(A_r) = \nu \tilde{n}.(\sigma \cup \{M/x\}, P)$$
$$\mathcal{T}(A_r^1 \mid A_r^2) = \nu \tilde{n}_1, \tilde{n}_2.((\sigma_1 \cup \sigma_2)^*, (P_1 \cup P_2)(\sigma_1 \cup \sigma_2)^*)$$
$$\text{if } \mathcal{T}(A_r^i) = \nu \tilde{n}_i.(\sigma_i, P_i) \text{ for } i = 1, 2$$
$$\mathcal{T}(A_r) = (\emptyset, \{A_r\}) \text{ in all other cases of } A_r$$

Intuitively, $\mathcal{T}$ pulls out name restrictions, applies active substitutions and separates them from the plain processes, and eliminates variable restrictions. For instance, $\mathcal{T}(\bar{a}\langle x \rangle.\nu n.\bar{a}\langle n \rangle \mid \nu k. \{k/x\}) = \nu k.(\{k/x\}, \{\bar{a}\langle k \rangle.\nu n.\bar{a}\langle n \rangle\})$. This normalisation $\mathcal{T}$ preserves both observational equivalence and labelled bisimilarity:

Theorem 3. *For two closed extended processes A_r and B_r in applied pi calculus,*

1. *A_r and B_r are labelled bisimilar in applied pi iff $\mathcal{T}(A_r) \approx_l \mathcal{T}(B_r)$;*
2. *A_r and B_r are observationally equivalent in applied pi iff $\mathcal{T}(A_r) \approx^e \mathcal{T}(B_r)$;*

With all the theorems ready, now we can prove Abadi-Fournet's theorem:

Corollary 1. *Observational equivalence coincides with labelled bisimilarity in applied pi calculus.*

4 Extending the Language with Public State Cells

4.1 Public State Cells

Hardware modules like TPMs and smart cards are intended to be secure, but an attacker might succeed in finding ways of compromising their tamper-resistant features. Similarly, attackers can potentially hack into databases [1]. We model these attacks by considering that the attacker compromises the private state cells, after which they are public. Protocols may provide some security properties that hold even under such compromises of the hardware or database. A typical example is forward privacy [24] which requires the past events remain secure even if the attacker compromises the device. This will be further discussed in the following Example 8 and Example 9. A cell s not in the scope of νs is public, which enables the attacker to lock the cell, read its contents or overwrite it.

We now give the details of the syntactic additions for public cells and the definition of observational equivalence. To let a private state cell become public, we extend the plain processes in Section 2 with a new primitive open $s.P$ Extended processes are defined as before. We extend the transitions in Fig. 1 by a new transition relation $\xrightarrow{\tau(s)}$ defined

---

[3] We write σ^* for the result of composing the substitution σ with itself repeatedly until an idempotent substitution is reached.

$$\nu\tilde{n}.(\sigma, S \cup \{s \mapsto M\}, \mathcal{P} \cup \{(\texttt{read } s \texttt{ as } x.P, L)\}) \xrightarrow{\tau(s)} \nu\tilde{n}.(\sigma, S \cup \{s \mapsto M\}, \mathcal{P} \cup \{(P\{M/x\}, L)\})$$
$$\text{if } s \notin \tilde{n} \cup L \cup locks(\mathcal{P})$$

$$\nu\tilde{n}.(\sigma, S \cup \{s \mapsto M\}, \mathcal{P} \cup \{(s := N.P, L)\}) \xrightarrow{\tau(s)} \nu\tilde{n}.(\sigma, S \cup \{s \mapsto N\}, \mathcal{P} \cup \{(P, L)\})$$
$$\text{if } s \notin \tilde{n} \cup L \cup locks(\mathcal{P})$$

$$\nu\tilde{n}.(\sigma, S \cup \{s \mapsto M\}, \mathcal{P} \cup \{(\texttt{lock } s.P, L)\}) \xrightarrow{\tau(s)} \nu\tilde{n}.(\sigma, S \cup \{s \mapsto M\}, \mathcal{P} \cup \{(P, L \cup \{s\})\})$$
$$\text{if } s \notin \tilde{n} \cup L \cup locks(\mathcal{P})$$

$$\nu\tilde{n}.(\sigma, S \cup \{s \mapsto M\}, \mathcal{P} \cup \{(\texttt{unlock } s.P, L)\}) \xrightarrow{\tau(s)} \nu\tilde{n}.(\sigma, S \cup \{s \mapsto M\}, \mathcal{P} \cup \{(P, L \setminus \{s\})\})$$
$$\text{if } s \notin \tilde{n} \cup locks(\mathcal{P}) \text{ and } s \in L$$

$$\nu\tilde{n}, s.(\sigma, S \cup \{s \mapsto M\}, \mathcal{P} \cup \{(\texttt{open } s.P, L)\}) \xrightarrow{\tau(s)} \nu\tilde{n}.(\sigma, S \cup \{s \mapsto M\}, \mathcal{P} \cup \{(P, L)\}) \text{ if } s \notin \tilde{n}$$

Fig. 3. Internal transitions for public state cells

in Fig. 3 for reasoning about public state cells. These internal transitions specify on which public state cell the operations are performed. The label $\tau(s)$ is necessary when we later define labelled bisimilarity. Note that when a public state cell is locked, we still use the rule $\xrightarrow{\tau}$ defined in Fig. 1 for reading and writing on that cell.

Let $A = \nu\tilde{n}.(\sigma, S, \mathcal{P})$ and we write $locks(A)$ for the set $locks(\mathcal{P}) \setminus \tilde{n}$. We write $\xrightarrow{\epsilon}$ for the reflexive and transitive closure of $\xrightarrow{\tau}$ and $\xrightarrow{\tau(s)}$ for any cell s. We write $A \Downarrow_a$ when $A \xrightarrow{\epsilon} \nu\tilde{n}.(\sigma, S, \mathcal{P} \cup \{(\overline{a}\langle M\rangle.P, L)\})$ with $a \notin \tilde{n}$.

Definition 4. *Observational equivalence* ($\approx$) *is the largest symmetric relation* $\mathcal{R}$ *on pairs of closed extended processes (which may contain public state cells) such that* $A \mathcal{R} B$ *implies*

(i) $locks(A) = locks(B)$, $fs(A) = fs(B)$ *and* $dom(A) = dom(B)$;
(ii) if $A \Downarrow_a$ *then* $B \Downarrow_a$;
(iii) if $A \xrightarrow{\epsilon} A'$ *then* $B \xrightarrow{\epsilon} B'$ *and* $A' \mathcal{R} B'$ *for some* B';
(iv) for all closing evaluation contexts $\mathcal{C}$, $\mathcal{C}[A] \mathcal{R} \mathcal{C}[B]$.

We stick to the original definition of observational equivalence [3] as much as possible in order to capture the intuition of indistinguishability from the attacker's point of view. The definition of observational equivalence on public state cells is similar to the one for private state cells, but the language features of public state cells are significantly different from private state cells. Moreover, the addition of public state cells increases the power of the attacker significantly, as without the name restriction νs for a state cell s, when s is unlocked, the attacker can lock the cell, read its content and overwrite it. To illustrate this point, we start by analysing several examples.

Example 4. The attacker can lock the unlocked public state cells. Assume

$$A = (\emptyset, \{s \mapsto 0\}, \{(\overline{c}\langle b\rangle, \emptyset)\})$$
$$B = (\emptyset, \{s \mapsto 0\}, \{(\texttt{read } s \texttt{ as } x. \overline{c}\langle b\rangle, \emptyset)\})$$

A and B are not observationally equivalent. Let $\mathcal{C} = (\text{-}, \text{-}, \{(0, \{s\})\} \text{-})$. The context $\mathcal{C}$ does nothing but holds the lock on cell s and it will never release the lock. So we have $\mathcal{C}[A] \Downarrow_c$ but $\mathcal{C}[B] \not\Downarrow_c$ because reading cell s in B is blocked forever by context $\mathcal{C}$.

Example 5. The attacker can read an unlocked public state cell. Assume

$$A = (\emptyset, \{s \mapsto 0\}, \{(!s := 0, \emptyset), (!s := 1, \emptyset)\})$$
$$B = (\emptyset, \{s \mapsto 1\}, \{(!s := 0, \emptyset), (!s := 1, \emptyset)\})$$

Cell s is unlocked in both A and B. Both A and B can write 0 or 1 to the cell s arbitrary number of times. The only difference between A and B is the initial values in cell s. A and B are not observationally equivalent because the context

$$C = (\text{-}, \text{-}, \{(\texttt{read } s \texttt{ as } x. \texttt{ if } x = 0 \texttt{ then } \bar{c}\langle b \rangle, \{s\})\} \text{-})$$

can distinguish them. The context C holds the lock of cell s, thus no one can change the value in s when C reads the value. We have $C[A] \Downarrow_c$ but $C[B] \not\Downarrow_c$.

In comparison, the following processes are observationally equivalent:

$$A' = (\emptyset, \{s \mapsto 0\}, \{(!s := 0, \emptyset), (!s := 1, \emptyset), (\texttt{unlock } s, \{s\})\})$$
$$B' = (\emptyset, \{s \mapsto 1\}, \{(!s := 0, \emptyset), (!s := 1, \emptyset), (\texttt{unlock } s, \{s\})\})$$

Cell s is locked in both A' and B'. When a cell is locked, the attacker cannot see its value until it is unlocked. Both A' and B' can adjust the value of cell s after $\texttt{unlock } s$. Assume

$$A' \xrightarrow{\tau(s)} (\emptyset, \{s \mapsto 0\}, \{(!s := 0, \emptyset), (!s := 1, \emptyset), (0, \emptyset)\})$$

Then B' can match this transition by first unlocking the cell s and then doing a writing $s := 0$ and evolving to exactly the same process:

$$B' \xrightarrow{\tau(s)} (\emptyset, \{s \mapsto 1\}, \{(!s := 0, \emptyset), (!s := 1, \emptyset), (0, \emptyset)\})$$
$$\xRightarrow{\tau(s)} (\emptyset, \{s \mapsto 0\}, \{(!s := 0, \emptyset), (!s := 1, \emptyset), (0, \emptyset)\})$$

Intuitively, the locked or unlocked status of a public state cell is observable by the environment. Therefore, we require $locks(A) = locks(B)$ and $fs(A) = fs(B)$ in the definition of observational equivalence. Furthermore, without this condition, this definition would not yield an equivalence relation, as transitivity does not hold in general. For example, consider the following extended processes,

$$A = (\emptyset, \{s \mapsto 0\}, \{(!s := 0, \emptyset), (!s := 1, \emptyset), (!\texttt{lock } s.\texttt{unlock } s, \emptyset)\})$$
$$B = (\emptyset, \{s \mapsto 1\}, \{(!s := 0, \emptyset), (!s := 1, \emptyset), (!\texttt{lock } s.\texttt{unlock } s, \emptyset), (\texttt{unlock } s, \{s\})\})$$
$$C = (\emptyset, \{s \mapsto 1\}, \{(!s := 0, \emptyset), (!s := 1, \emptyset), (!\texttt{lock } s.\texttt{unlock } s, \emptyset)\})$$

Without the condition, then A and B would be equivalent, as well as B and C, because the value in s can always be adjusted to be exactly the same after $\texttt{unlock } s$. But A and C are not equivalent as analysed in Example 5.

Example 6. The value in an unlocked public state cell is a part of the attacker's knowledge. Assume

$$A = \nu k.(\emptyset, \{s \mapsto k\}, \{(s := 0.a(x).\texttt{if } x = k \texttt{ then } \bar{c}\langle b \rangle, \emptyset)\})$$
$$B = \nu k.(\emptyset, \{s \mapsto k\}, \{(s := 0.a(x), \emptyset)\})$$

A and B are not observationally equivalent. Let $C = (\text{-},\text{-},\{(\text{read } s \text{ as } y.\,\overline{a}\langle y\rangle, \emptyset)\}\text{-})$. Then $C[A] \Downarrow_c$ but $C[B] \not\Downarrow_c$ because

$$C[A] \xrightarrow{\tau(s)} \nu k.\,(\emptyset, \{s \mapsto k\}, \{(\overline{a}\langle k\rangle, \emptyset), (s := 0.a(x).\text{if } x = k \text{ then } \overline{c}\langle b\rangle, \emptyset)\})$$
$$\xrightarrow{\tau(s)} \nu k.\,(\emptyset, \{s \mapsto 0\}, \{(\overline{a}\langle k\rangle, \emptyset), (a(x).\text{if } x = k \text{ then } \overline{c}\langle b\rangle, \emptyset)\})$$
$$\Longrightarrow \nu k.\,(\emptyset, \{s \mapsto 0\}, \{(\overline{c}\langle b\rangle, \emptyset)\})$$

But there is no output on channel c in $C[B]$. Hence $A \not\approx B$.

Example 7. The attacker can write an arbitrary value into an unlocked public cell. Assume two extended processes

$$A = (\emptyset, \{s \mapsto 0\}, \{(s := 0.\,s := 0, \emptyset)\})$$
$$B = (\emptyset, \{s \mapsto 0\}, \{(s := 0, \emptyset)\})$$

A and B are not observationally equivalent. Applying $C = (\text{-},\text{-},\{(s := 1.s := 1, \emptyset)\}\text{-})$ to both A and B, the interleaving of $s := 0$ and $s := 1$ can generate a sequence of values $0, 1, 0, 1, 0$ in cell s in $C[A]$, while the closest sequence generated by $C[B]$ should be $0, 1, 0, 1, 1$. So when the attacker keeps on reading the value in cell s, he would be able to notice the difference.

Instead of using the primitive open s, an alternative way for making a private state cell become public is to send cell name s on a free channel $\overline{c}\langle s\rangle.P$. The reason we choose the primitive open $s.P$ here is because sending and receiving cell names through channels is too powerful, and will lead to soundness problems when we define labelled bisimilarity later. For example, let

$$A = (\emptyset, \emptyset, \{(c(x).\text{read } x \text{ as } z.\overline{a}\langle z\rangle, \emptyset)\})$$
$$B = (\emptyset, \emptyset, \{(c(x), \emptyset)\})$$

In the presence of input and output for cell names, A and B are not observationally equivalent. Let $C = (\text{-}, \{t \mapsto 0\}\,\text{-}, \{(\overline{c}\langle t\rangle, \emptyset)\}\,\text{-})$. The context C brings his own state cell $t \mapsto 0$ and we have $C[A] \Downarrow_a$ but $C[B] \not\Downarrow_a$. That is to say, in order to define a sound labelled bisimilarity, we have to allow a process like $(\emptyset, \emptyset, \{(\text{read } t \text{ as } z.\,\overline{a}\langle z\rangle, \emptyset)\})$ to perform the reading even without a state cell $t \mapsto 0$. This requires a rather complex definition of labelled bisimilarity, while what we want is to simply free a cell which can be achieved by open $s.P$.

Now we give examples of the use of public state cells for modelling protocols and security properties. Another security concern for RFID tags is forward privacy [26]. In the following Example 8 and Example 9, we shall illustrate how to model forward privacy by public state cells. Forward privacy requires that even the attacker breaks the tag, the past events should still be untraceable. Public state cells enable us to model the compromised tags.

Example 8. We consider an improved version of the naive protocol in Example 1. Instead of simply outputting the tag's *id*, the tag generates a random number r, hashes its *id* concatenated with r and then sends both r and $h(id, r)$ to the reader for identification. This can be modelled by:

$$Q(s) = \texttt{read } s \texttt{ as } x. \, \nu r. \, \overline{a}\langle(r, h(x, r))\rangle$$

Upon receiving the value, the reader identifies the tag by performing a brute-force search of its known ids. By observing on channel a, the attacker can get the data pairs from a particular tag s: $(r_1, h(id, r_1)), (r_2, h(id, r_2)), (r_3, h(id, r_3)) \cdots$. Since the hash function is not invertible, without knowing the value of id, these data appear as just random data to the attacker. Hence this improved version satisfies the untraceability defined in Example 1. But it does not have the forward privacy. Let *RD* be process modelling the reader and back-end database. The forward privacy can be characterised by the observational equivalence

$$(\emptyset, \emptyset, \{(\,!\,\nu s, id.([s \mapsto id] \mid Q(s) \mid \texttt{open } s.\,!\,Q(s) \mid RD), \emptyset)\})$$
$$\approx (\emptyset, \emptyset, \{(\,!\,\nu s, id.([s \mapsto id] \mid !\,Q(s) \mid \texttt{open } s \mid RD), \emptyset)\})$$

The primitive open s makes the private state cell s become public. Before the cell s is broken, the attacker cannot decide how the system runs. In other words, whether the tag s is used for only once, namely $Q(s)$, or is used for arbitrary number of times, namely $!\,Q(s)$, it is out of the control of the attacker. But after the tag is broken, the attacker fully controls the tag, so he knows when and where the tag is used. Despite knowing the events that happen after the tag is broken, the attacker should still not be able to trace the past events. Therefore, in the first process, we add $!\,Q(s)$ after open s to model this scenario. Intuitively, only the events before the tag is broken may be different while the events after the tag is broken are exactly the same. Hence the above observational equivalence can capture forward privacy.

However the above equivalence does not hold which means there is no forward privacy in this protocol. The attacker can obtain the *id* from the broken tag and then verify whether the previously gathered data $(r_1, h(id, r_1))$ and $(r_2, h(id, r_2))$ refer to the same tag *id* by hashing *id* with r_1 (or r_2) and then comparing the result with $h(id, r_1)$ (or $h(id, r_2)$).

Example 9. Continuing with the OSK protocol in Example 2, we model the forward privacy by the observational equivalence:

$$(\emptyset, \emptyset, \{(\,!\,\nu s, k.([s \mapsto k] \mid T(s) \mid \texttt{open } s.\,!\,T(s) \mid RD), \emptyset)\})$$
$$\approx (\emptyset, \emptyset, \{(\,!\,\nu s, k.([s \mapsto k] \mid !\,T(s) \mid \texttt{open } s \mid RD), \emptyset)\})$$

Before the tag is broken, the attacker can obtain the data sequence $g(k), g(h(k))$, $g(h(h(k))) \cdots$ by eavesdropping on channel a. Right after each reading, the value in the tag will be updated to the hash of previous value: $h(k), h(h(k)), h(h(h(k))) \cdots$. When the tag is broken, the attacker will get from the tag a value $h^i(k)$ for some integer i. This value is not helpful for the attacker to infer whether the data $g(k), g(h(k)), \cdots$, $g(h^{i-1}(k))$ are from the same tag. Hence the OSK protocol can ensure the forward privacy.

In order to ease the verification of observational equivalence which is defined using the universal quantifier over contexts, we shall define labelled bisimilarity which replaces quantification over contexts by suitably labelled transitions. The traditional definition for labelled bisimilarity is neither sound nor complete w.r.t. observational equivalence in the presence of public state cells. We propose a novel definition for labelled bisimilarity and show how it solves all the problems caused by public state cells.

For a given cell s, we define $\overset{\tau(s)}{\Longrightarrow}$ to be the reflexive and transitive closure of $\overset{\tau}{\longrightarrow}$ and $\overset{\tau(s)}{\longrightarrow}$. We still use α to range over $\tau, a(M), \bar{a}\langle c\rangle, \nu c.\bar{a}\langle c\rangle$ and $\nu x.\bar{a}\langle x\rangle$, and use $\Longrightarrow$ for the reflexive and transitive closure of $\overset{\tau}{\longrightarrow}$, and use $\overset{\hat{\alpha}}{\Longrightarrow}$ for $\overset{\alpha}{\Longrightarrow}$ if α is not τ and $\Longrightarrow$ otherwise.

To define labelled bisimilarity, we need an auxiliary transition relation $\overset{s:=N}{\longrightarrow}$ for setting the values of public state cells:

$$\nu\widetilde{n}.(\sigma, S \cup \{s \mapsto M\}, \mathcal{P}) \overset{s:=N}{\longrightarrow} \nu\widetilde{n}.(\sigma, S \cup \{s \mapsto N\sigma\}, \mathcal{P})$$
$$\text{if } s \notin \widetilde{n} \cup locks(\mathcal{P}) \text{ and } name(N) \cap \widetilde{n} = \emptyset$$
$$\nu\widetilde{n}.(\sigma, S, \mathcal{P}) \overset{s:=N}{\longrightarrow} \nu\widetilde{n}.(\sigma, S, \mathcal{P}) \text{ if } s \in \widetilde{n} \cup locks(\mathcal{P})$$

The first rule of $\overset{s:=N}{\longrightarrow}$ represents the attacker's ability to overwrite the public state cells. The second rule does not change the value of the cell s and is just for compatibility with unlock s and open s in Definition 5. We write $A \overset{s:=N}{\longrightarrow}\overset{\tau(s)}{\Longrightarrow} A'$ for the combination of transitions $A \overset{s:=N}{\longrightarrow} B$ and $B \overset{\tau(s)}{\Longrightarrow} A'$ for some B.

Definition 5. *Labelled bisimilarity* $(\approx_l)$ *is the largest symmetric relation $\mathcal{R}$ between pairs of closed extended processes $A_i = \nu\widetilde{n}_i.(\sigma_i, S_i, \mathcal{P}_i)$ with $i = 1, 2$ such that $A_1 \mathcal{R} A_2$ implies*

1. *$locks(A_1) = locks(A_2), fs(A_1) = fs(A_2)$ and $dom(A_1) = dom(A_2)$;*
2. *Let U be the set of unlocked public state cells whose value is not already given in the substitutions of A_1 and A_2, that is*

$$U = \{ s \mid s \in fs(A_1) \setminus locks(A_1), \nexists x \in dom(\sigma_1) \text{ s.t. } S_1(s) = x\sigma_1 \text{ and } S_2(s) = x\sigma_2 \}$$

Select a fresh base variable x_s for each $s \in U$. Let

$$A_i^e = \nu\widetilde{n}_i.(\sigma_i \cup \{S_i(s)/x_s\}_{s \in U}, S_i, \mathcal{P}_i) \text{ for } i = 1, 2$$

Then

(a) *$A_1^e \approx_s A_2^e$;*
(b) *if $A_1^e \overset{s:=N}{\longrightarrow}\overset{\tau(s)}{\Longrightarrow} B_1$ with $var(N) \subseteq dom(A_1^e)$, then there exists B_2 such that $A_2^e \overset{s:=N}{\longrightarrow}\overset{\tau(s)}{\Longrightarrow} B_2$ and $B_1 \mathcal{R} B_2$;*
(c) *if $A_1^e \overset{\alpha}{\longrightarrow} B_1$ and $fv(\alpha) \subseteq dom(A_1^e)$ and $bnv(\alpha) \cap fnv(A_2^e) = \emptyset$, then there exists B_2 such that $A_2^e \overset{\hat{\alpha}}{\Longrightarrow} B_2$ and $B_1 \mathcal{R} B_2$.*

The static equivalence $A_1^e \approx_s A_2^e$ in Definition 5 is exactly the same as the one defined in Definition 2. Before we compare the static equivalence and the transitions in labelled bisimilarity, we extend A_i to A_i^e with values from unlocked public state cells. This is to reflect the fact that attacker's ability to read values from these cells.

Example 10. Consider the extended processes A and B in Example 5. As we have already shown, A and B are not observationally equivalent. Hence they are not supposed to be labelled bisimilar. We first extend A and B to A^e and B^e respectively:

$$A^e = (\{0/z\}, \{s \mapsto 0\}, \{(!s := 0, \emptyset), (!s := 1, \emptyset)\})$$
$$B^e = (\{1/z\}, \{s \mapsto 1\}, \{(!s := 0, \emptyset), (!s := 1, \emptyset)\})$$

Clearly the static equivalence between A^e and B^e does not hold, namely $A^e \not\approx_s B^e$, because the test $z = 0$ can distinguish them. Thus we have $A \not\approx_l B$.

The extension is not only for comparing the static equivalence, but also for comparing the transitions. In labelled bisimilarity, we compare the transitions starting from the extensions A^e and B^e, rather than the original processes A and B. The reason is that we need to keep a copy of the cell values, otherwise we would lose the values when someone overwrites the cells.

Example 11. Consider the extended processes A and B in Example 6. The extension A^e of A can perform the following transition:

$$A^e = \nu k.(\{k/z\}, \{s \mapsto k\}, \{(s := 0.a(x).\text{if } x = k \text{ then } \overline{c}\langle b\rangle, \emptyset)\})$$
$$\xrightarrow{\tau(s)} \nu k.(\{k/z\}, \{s \mapsto 0\}, \{(a(x).\text{if } x = k \text{ then } \overline{c}\langle b\rangle, \emptyset)\})$$
$$\xRightarrow{a(z)} \nu k.(\{k/z\}, \{s \mapsto 0\}, \{(\overline{c}\langle b\rangle, \emptyset)\})$$
$$\xrightarrow{\overline{c}\langle b\rangle} \nu k.(\{k/z\}, \{s \mapsto 0\}, \{(0, \emptyset)\})$$

But it is impossible for B's extension $B^e = \nu k.(\{k/z\}, \{s \mapsto k\}, \{(s := 0. a(x), \emptyset)\})$ to perform an output on channel c. Hence $A \not\approx_l B$.

We use $\xrightarrow{s:=N} \xrightarrow{\tau(s)}$ rather than $\xrightarrow{\tau(s)}$ in labelled bisimilarity because the attacker can set any unlocked public state cell to an arbitrary value. We shall illustrate this point by the following two examples.

Example 12. Assume

$$A = (\{0/y, 1/z\}, \{s \mapsto 0\}, \{(\text{read } s \text{ as } x. \text{ if } x = 1 \text{ then } \overline{c}\langle 0\rangle, \emptyset)\})$$
$$B = (\{0/y, 1/z\}, \{s \mapsto 0\}, \emptyset)$$

A and B are not observationally equivalent. Applying context $\mathcal{C} = (\emptyset, \emptyset, \{(s := 1, \emptyset)\})$ to A and B, we can see that $\mathcal{C}[A] \Downarrow_c$ but $\mathcal{C}[B] \not\Downarrow_c$.

Now we shall distinguish them in labelled bisimilarity. Since the current value in cell s is 0 which has already been stored in variable y, we don't need to extend A and B.

Then A can perform the following transition

$$A \xrightarrow{s:=1} \xrightarrow{\tau(s)} (\{0/y, 1/z\}, \{s \mapsto 1\}, \{(\text{if } 1 = 1 \text{ then } \overline{c}\langle a \rangle, \emptyset)\})$$

$$\xrightarrow{\overline{c}\langle a \rangle} (\{0/y, 1/z\}, \{s \mapsto 1\}, \{0, \emptyset\})$$

But there is no way for B to perform an output action. Hence $A \not\approx_l B$.

Example 13. As illustrated in Example 7, A and B are not observationally equivalent. In labelled bisimilarity, we extend A and perform the transitions $\xrightarrow{s:=1} \xrightarrow{\tau(s)}$ twice, then we will reach a process $A' = (\{0/x, 0/z\}, \{s \mapsto 0\}, \{(0, \emptyset)\})$, while the best B can do to match A is to reach a process $B' = (\{0/x, 1/z\}, \{s \mapsto 0\}, \{(0, \emptyset)\})$ and $A' \not\approx_s B'$.

Note that the transition $\xrightarrow{s:=N}$ is not included in $\xrightarrow{\alpha}$. We only need to use $\xrightarrow{s:=N}$ to change the value of the unlocked public state cell s when the processes perform some actions related to s. Comparing the combination of two transitions together ($\xrightarrow{s:=N} \xrightarrow{\tau(s)}$) in Definition 5 optimises the definition to be better suited as an assisted tool for analysing observational equivalence. Otherwise, if we follow the traditional way to define labelled bisimilarity, i.e. comparing $A_1^e \xrightarrow{s:=N} B_1^e$ and $A_1^e \xrightarrow{\tau(s)} B_1^e$ separately, the action $\xrightarrow{s:=N}$ would generate infinitely many unnecessary branches. For example, let $A = (\emptyset, \{s \mapsto 0\}, \emptyset)$. Even there is no action, A could keep on performing $\xrightarrow{s:=N}$ and would never stop: $A \xrightarrow{s:=1} (\emptyset, \{s \mapsto 1\}, \emptyset) \xrightarrow{s:=2} (\emptyset, \{s \mapsto 2\}, \emptyset) \xrightarrow{s:=3} (\emptyset, \{s \mapsto 3\}, \emptyset) \cdots$

We require $A_1^e \xrightarrow{s:=N} \xrightarrow{\tau(s)} B_1$ to be matched by $A_2^e \xrightarrow{s:=N} \xrightarrow{\tau(s)} B_2$ with the same s in the action in labelled bisimilarity. In other words, A_2^e can only match the transition of A_1^e by at most operating on the same cell s. This is equal to say the attacker holds the locks of all the unlocked public cell except cell s in A_1^e. If A_1^e does not do act on cell s, then A_2^e are not allowed to match A_1^e by operating on s.

Example 14. Extend A and B in Example 4 to $A^e = (\{0/z\}, \{s \mapsto 0\}, \{(\overline{c}\langle b \rangle, \emptyset)\})$ and $B^e = (\{0/z\}, \{s \mapsto 0\}, \{(\text{read } s \text{ as } x. \overline{c}\langle b \rangle, \emptyset)\})$. We can see that $A^e \xrightarrow{\overline{c}\langle b \rangle} (\emptyset, \{s \mapsto 0\}, \{(0, \emptyset)\})$, but there is no way for B^e to do the same output action $\overline{c}\langle b \rangle$ without going through the reading on cell s. Hence $A \not\approx_l B$.

In the presence of public state cells, labelled bisimilarity is both sound and complete with respect to observational equivalence.

Theorem 4. *In the presence of public state cells, $\approx_l = \approx$.*

5 Conclusion

We present a stateful language which is a general extension of applied pi calculus with state cells. We stick to the original definition of observational equivalence [3] as much as possible to capture the intuition of indistinguishability from the attacker's point of view, while design the labelled bisimilarity to furthest abstract observational equivalence. When all the state cells are private, we prove that observational equivalence coincides with labelled bisimilarity, which implies Abadi-Fournet's theorem in a revised version of applied pi calculus. In the presence of public state cells, we devise a labelled bisimilarity which is proved to coincide with observational equivalence. In future, we plan to develop a compiler for bi-processes with state cells to automatically verify the observational equivalence, extending the techniques of ProVerif.

References

[1] LinkedIn investigates hacking claims, http://www.guardian.co.uk/technology/2012/jun/06/linkedin-hacking
[2] Abadi, M., Cortier, V.: Deciding knowledge in security protocols under equational theories. Theor. Comput. Sci. 367(1-2), 2–32 (2006)
[3] Abadi, M., Fournet, C.: Mobile values, new names, and secure communication. In: Proc. 28th Symposium on Principles of Programming Languages (POPL 2001), pp. 104–115. ACM Press (2001)
[4] Abadi, M., Fournet, C.: Private authentication. Theor. Comput. Sci. 322(3), 427–476 (2004)
[5] Abadi, M., Gordon, A.D.: A calculus for cryptographic protocols: The spi calculus. In: 4th ACM Conference on Computer and Communications Security, pp. 36–47. ACM Press (1997)
[6] Arapinis, M., Chothia, T., Ritter, E., Ryan, M.: Analysing unlinkability and anonymity using the applied pi calculus. In: Proceedings of IEEE 23rd Computer Security Foundations Symposium, CSF 2010, pp. 107–121 (2010)
[7] Arapinis, M., Ritter, E., Ryan, M.D.: Statverif: Verification of stateful processes. In: Proceedings of IEEE 24th Computer Security Foundations Symposium, CSF 2011, pp. 33–47 (2011), http://markryan.eu/research/statverif/
[8] Backes, M., Maffei, M., Unruh, D.: Zero-knowledge in the applied pi-calculus and automated verification of the direct anonymous attestation protocol. In: IEEE Symposium on Security and Privacy, pp. 202–215 (2008)
[9] Baudet, M., Cortier, V., Delaune, S.: YAPA: A generic tool for computing intruder knowledge. ACM Transactions on Computational Logic 14 (2013)
[10] Bengtson, J., Johansson, M., Parrow, J., Victor, B.: Psi-calculi: a framework for mobile processes with nominal data and logic. Logical Methods in Computer Science 7(1) (2011)
[11] Bhargavan, K., Fournet, C., Corin, R., Zalinescu, E.: Cryptographically verified implementations for TLS. In: Proceedings of the 15th ACM Conference on Computer and Communications Security, CCS 2008, pp. 459–468. ACM (2008)
[12] Blanchet, B.: Automatic Proof of Strong Secrecy for Security Protocols. In: IEEE Symposium on Security and Privacy, pp. 86–100 (2004)
[13] Blanchet, B.: Automatic Verification of Correspondences for Security Protocols. Journal of Computer Security 17(4), 363–434 (2009)
[14] Chadha, R., Ciobâcă, Ş., Kremer, S.: Automated verification of equivalence properties of cryptographic protocols. In: Seidl, H. (ed.) ESOP 2012. LNCS, vol. 7211, pp. 108–127. Springer, Heidelberg (2012)
[15] Cheval, V., Comon-Lundh, H., Delaune, S.: Automating security analysis: Symbolic equivalence of constraint systems. In: Giesl, J., Hähnle, R. (eds.) IJCAR 2010. LNCS, vol. 6173, pp. 412–426. Springer, Heidelberg (2010)
[16] Cheval, V., Comon-Lundh, H., Delaune, S.: Trace equivalence decision: Negative tests and non-determinism. In: Proceedings of the 18th ACM Conference on Computer and Communications Security (CCS 2011), pp. 321–330 (2011)
[17] Cheval, V., Cortier, V., Delaune, S.: Deciding equivalence-based properties using constraint solving. Theoretical Computer Science 492, 1–39 (2013)

[18] Cortier, V., Delaune, S.: A method for proving observational equivalence. In: CSF 2009, pp. 266–276. IEEE Computer Society Press (July 2009)

[19] Cortier, V., Rusinowitch, M., Zalinescu, E.: Relating two standard notions of secrecy. Logical Methods in Computer Science 3, 1–29 (2007)

[20] Delaune, S., Kremer, S., Ryan, M.D.: Verifying privacy-type properties of electronic voting protocols. Journal of Computer Security (2009)

[21] Delaune, S., Kremer, S., Ryan, M.D.: Symbolic bisimulation for the applied pi calculus. Journal of Computer Security 18(2), 317–377 (2010)

[22] Delaune, S., Kremer, S., Ryan, M.D., Steel, G.: Formal analysis of protocols based on TPM state registers. In: Proc. of the 24th IEEE Computer Security Foundations Symposium (CSF 2011). IEEE Computer Society Press (2011)

[23] Dreyer, D., Neis, G., Rossberg, A., Birkedal, L.: A relational modal logic for higher-order stateful ADTs. In: Proceedings of the 37th ACM SIGPLAN-SIGACT Symposium on Principles of Programming Languages, POPL 2010, pp. 185–198 (2010)

[24] Garcia, F.D., van Rossum, P.: Modeling privacy for off-line RFID systems. In: Gollmann, D., Lanet, J.-L., Iguchi-Cartigny, J. (eds.) CARDIS 2010. LNCS, vol. 6035, pp. 194–208. Springer, Heidelberg (2010)

[25] Guttman, J.D.: Fair exchange in strand spaces. Journal of Automated Reasoning (2012)

[26] Koutarou, M.O., Suzuki, K., Kinoshita, S.: Cryptographic approach to "privacy-friendly" tags. RFID Privacy Workshop (2003)

[27] Künnemann, R., Steel, G.: YubiSecure? formal security analysis results for the Yubikey and YubiHSM. In: Jøsang, A., Samarati, P., Petrocchi, M. (eds.) STM 2012. LNCS, vol. 7783, pp. 257–272. Springer, Heidelberg (2013)

[28] Liu, J.: A proof of coincidence of labeled bisimilarity and observational equivalence in applied pi calculus. Technical Report, ISCAS-SKLCS-11-05 (2011), http://mail.ios.ac.cn/~jliu/papers/Proof.pdf

[29] Liu, J., Lin, H.: A complete symbolic bisimulation for full applied pi calculus. Theoretical Computer Science 458, 76–112 (2012)

[30] Mödersheim, S.: Abstraction by set-membership: verifying security protocols and web services with databases. In: Proc. 17th ACM Conference on Computer and Communications Security (CCS 2010), pp. 351–360. ACM (2010)

[31] Ryan, P., Schneider, S., Goldsmith, M., Lowe, G., Roscoe, B.: The Modelling and Analysis of Security Protocols. Pearson Education (2001)

[32] Sangiorgi, D., Walker, D.: The π-calculus: A Theory of Mobile Processes. Cambridge University Press, Cambridge (2001)

[33] Schmidt, B., Meier, S., Cremers, C., Basin, D.: Automated analysis of diffie-hellman protocols and advanced security properties. In: 25th Computer Security Foundations Symposium (CSF), pp. 78–94. IEEE (2012)

[34] Turon, A., Dreyer, D., Birkedal, L.: Unifying refinement and hoare-style reasoning in a logic for higher-order concurrency. In: ICFP 2013, pp. 377–390 (2013)

Computational Soundness Results for ProVerif

Bridging the Gap from Trace Properties to Uniformity

Michael Backes[1,2], Esfandiar Mohammadi[1], and Tim Ruffing[3]

[1] CISPA, Saarland University, Germany
[2] Max Planck Institute for Software Systems (MPI-SWS), Germany
[3] MMCI, Saarland University, Germany

Abstract. Dolev-Yao models of cryptographic operations constitute the foundation of many successful verification tools for security protocols, such as the protocol verifier ProVerif. Research over the past decade has shown that many of these symbolic abstractions are computationally sound, i.e., the absence of attacks against the abstraction entails the security of suitable cryptographic realizations. Most of these computational soundness (CS) results, however, are restricted to trace properties such as authentication, and the few promising results that strive for CS for the more comprehensive class of equivalence properties, such as strong secrecy or anonymity, either only consider a limited class of protocols or are not amenable to fully automated verification.

In this work, we identify a general condition under which CS for trace properties implies CS for uniformity of bi-processes, i.e., the class of equivalence properties that ProVerif is able to verify for the applied π-calculus. As a case study, we show that this general condition holds for a Dolev-Yao model that contains signatures, public-key encryption, and corresponding length functions. We prove this result in the CoSP framework (a general framework for establishing CS results). To this end, we extend the CoSP framework to equivalence properties, and we show that an existing embedding of the applied π-calculus to CoSP can be re-used for uniform bi-processes. On the verification side, as analyses in ProVerif with symbolic length functions often do not terminate, we show how to combine the recent protocol verifier APTE with ProVerif. As a result, we establish a computationally sound automated verification chain for uniformity of bi-processes in the applied π-calculus that use public-key encryption, signatures, and length functions.

1 Introduction

Manual security analyses of protocols that rely on cryptographic operations are complex and error-prone. As a consequence, research has strived for the automation of such proofs soon after the first protocols were developed. To eliminate the inherent complexity of cryptographic operations that verification tools are struggling to deal with, cryptographic operations have been abstracted as symbolic terms that obey simple cancelation rules, so-called Dolev-Yao models [1,2]. A variety of automated verification tools have been developed based on this

M. Abadi and S. Kremer (Eds.): POST 2014, LNCS 8414, pp. 42–62, 2014.

abstraction, and they have been successfully used for reasoning about various security protocols [3,4,5,6,7,8,9,10]. In particular, a wide range of these tools is capable of reasoning about the more comprehensive class of *equivalence properties*, such as strong secrecy and anonymity, which arguably is the most important class of security properties for privacy-preserving protocols.

Research over the past decade has shown that many of these Dolev-Yao models are computationally sound, i.e., the absence of attacks against the symbolic abstraction entails the security of suitable cryptographic realizations. Most of these computational soundness (CS) results against active attacks, however, have been specific to the class of trace properties [11,12,13,14,15,16,17,18,19,20,21], which is only sufficient as long as strong notions of privacy are not considered, e.g., in particular for establishing various authentication properties. Only few CS results are known for the class of equivalence properties against active attackers, which are restricted in of the following three ways: either they are restricted to a small class of simple processes, e.g., processes that do not contain private channels and abort if a conditional fails [22,23,24], or they rely on non-standard abstractions for which it is not clear how to formalize any equivalence property beyond the secrecy of payloads [25,26,27], such as anonymity properties in protocols that encrypt different signatures, or existing automated tool support is not applicable [28,29]. We are thus facing a situation where CS results, despite tremendous progress in the last decade, still fall short in comprehensively addressing the class of equivalence properties and protocols that state-of-the-art verification tools are capable to deal with. Moreover, it is unknown to which extent existing results on CS for trace properties can be extended to achieve more comprehensive CS results for equivalence properties.

Our Contribution. In this work, we close this gap by providing the first result that allows to leverage existing CS results for trace properties to CS results for an expressive class of equivalence properties: the uniformity of bi-processes in the applied π-calculus. Bi-processes are pairs of processes that differ only in the messages they operate on but not in their structure; a bi-process is uniform if for all surrounding contexts, i.e., all interacting attackers, both processes take the same branches. Blanchet, Abadi, and Fournet [7] have shown that uniformity already implies observational equivalence. Moreover, uniformity of bi-processes corresponds precisely to the class of properties that the state-of-the-art verification tool ProVerif [30] is capable to analyze, based on a Dolev-Yao model in the applied π-calculus. In contrast to previous work dealing with equivalence properties, we consider bi-protocols that use the fully fledged applied π-calculus, in particular including private channels and non-determinate processes.

To establish this main result of our paper, we first identify the following general condition for Dolev-Yao models: "whenever a computational attacker can distinguish a bi-process, there is a test in the Dolev-Yao model that allows to successfully distinguish the bi-process." We say that Dolev-Yao models with this property *allow for self-monitoring*. We show that if a specific Dolev-Yao model fulfills this property, then there is for every bi-process a so-called *self-monitor*, i.e., a process that performs all relevant tests that the attacker could perform on the two processes of the bi-process, and that raises an exception if of these tests in the symbolic model distinguishes the bi-process. We finally show that whenever a Dolev-Yao model allows for self-monitoring, CS for uniformity of bi-processes automatically holds whenever CS for trace properties has already been established. This result in particular allows for leveraging existing CS results for trace properties to more comprehensive CS results for uniformity of bi-processes, provided that the Dolev-Yao model can be proven to allow for self-monitoring.

We exemplarily show how to construct a self-monitor for a symbolic model that has been recently introduced and proven to be computationally sound for trace properties by Backes, Malik, and Unruh [31]. This symbolic model contains signatures and public-key encryption and allows to freely send and receive decryption keys. To establish that the model allows for self-monitoring, we first extend it using the common concept of a length function (without a length function, CS for uniformity of bi-processes and hence the existence of self-monitors trivially cannot hold, since encryptions of different lengths are distinguishable in general), and we show that this extension preserves the existing proof of CS for trace properties. Our main result in this paper then immediately implies that this extended model satisfies CS for uniformity of bi-processes.

We moreover investigate how computationally sound automated analyses can still be achieved in those frequent situations in which ProVerif does not manage to terminate whenever the Dolev-Yao model supports a length function. We proceed in two steps: first, we feed a stripped-down version of the protocol without length functions in ProVerif; ProVerif then yields a result concerning the uniformity of bi-processes, but only for this stripped-down protocol. Second, we analyze the original protocol using the APTE tool by Cheval, Cortier, and Plet [32], which is specifically tailored to length functions. This yields a result for the original protocol but only concerning trace equivalences. We show that both results can be combined to achieve uniformity of bi-processes for the original protocol, and thus a corresponding CS result for uniformity of bi-processes.

We present the first general framework for CS for equivalence properties, by extending the CoSP framework: a general framework for symbolic analysis and CS results for trace properties [15]. CoSP decouples the CS of Dolev-Yao models from the calculi, such as the applied π-calculus or RCF: proving x cryptographic Dolev-Yao models sound for y calculi only requires $x + y$ proofs (instead of $x \cdot y$). We consider this extension to be of independent interest. Moreover, we prove the existence of an embedding from the applied π-calculus to the extended CoSP framework that preserves the uniformity of bi-processes, using a slight variation of the already existing embedding for trace properties.

2   Equivalence Properties in the CoSP Framework

The results in this work are formulated within CoSP [15], a framework for conceptually modular CS proofs that decouples the treatment of the cryptographic primitives from the treatment of the calculi. Several calculi such as the applied π-calculus [15] and RCF [33] (a core calculus of F#) can be embedded into CoSP and combined with CS results for cryptographic primitives.

The original CoSP framework is only capable of handling CS with respect to trace properties, i.e., properties that can be formulated in terms of a single trace. Typical examples include the non-reachability of a certain "bad" protocol state, in that the attacker is assumed to have succeeded (e.g., the protocol never reveals a secret), or correspondence properties such as authentication (e.g., a user can access a resource only after proving a credential). However, many interesting protocol properties cannot be expressed in terms of a single trace. For instance, strong secrecy or anonymity are properties that are, in the computational setting, usually formulated by means of a game in which the attacker has to distinguish between several scenarios.

To be able to handle the class of equivalence properties, we extend the CoSP framework to support equivalence properties. First, we recall the basic definitions of the original framework. Dolev-Yao models are formalized as follows in CoSP.

Definition 1 (Symbolic Model). *A symbolic model* $\mathbf{M} = (\mathbf{C}, \mathbf{N}, \mathbf{T}, \mathbf{D})$ *consists of a set of constructors* $\mathbf{C}$*, a set of nonces* $\mathbf{N}$*, a message type* $\mathbf{T}$ *over* $\mathbf{C}$ *and* $\mathbf{N}$ *(with* $\mathbf{N} \subseteq \mathbf{T}$*), a set of destructors* $\mathbf{D}$ *over* $\mathbf{T}$*. We require that* $\mathbf{N} = \mathbf{N_E} \uplus \mathbf{N_P}$ *for countable infinite sets* $\mathbf{N_P}$ *of protocol nonces and attacker nonces* $\mathbf{N_E}$*.*

We write $\underline{t}$ for a list $t_1, \ldots, t_n$ if n is clear from the context. A *constructor* C/n is a symbol with (possibly zero) arity. A *nonce* N is a symbol with zero arity. A *message type* $\mathbf{T}$ *over* $\mathbf{C}$ *and* $\mathbf{N}$ is a set of terms over constructors $\mathbf{C}$ and nonces $\mathbf{N}$. A *destructor* D/n of arity n, over a message type $\mathbf{T}$ is a partial map $\mathbf{T}^n \to \mathbf{T}$. If D is undefined on $\underline{t}$, we write $D(\underline{t}) = \bot$.

To unify notation, we define for every constructor or destructor $F/n \in \mathbf{D} \cup \mathbf{C}$ and every nonce $F \in \mathbf{N}$ the partial function $eval_F : \mathbf{T}^n \to \mathbf{T}$, where $n = 0$ for a nonce, as follows: If F is a constructor, $eval_F(\underline{t}) := F(\underline{t})$ if $F(\underline{t}) \in \mathbf{T}$ and $eval_F(\underline{t}) := \bot$ otherwise. If F is a nonce, $eval_F() := F$. If F is a destructor, $eval_F(\underline{t}) := F(\underline{t})$ if $F(\underline{t}) \neq \bot$ and $eval_F(\underline{t}) := \bot$ otherwise.

Protocols. In CoSP, a protocol is represented as a tree. Each node in this tree corresponds to an action in the protocol: *computation nodes* are used for drawing fresh nonces, applying constructors, and applying destructors; *input* and *output* *nodes* are used to send and receive messages; *control nodes* are used for allowing the attacker to schedule the protocol.

Definition 2 (CoSP Protocol). *A CoSP protocol* I *is a tree of infinite depth with a distinguished root and labels on both edges and nodes. Each node has a unique identifier* ν *and one of the following types:*

- *Computation nodes are annotated with a constructor, nonce or destructor* F/n *together with the identifiers of* n *(not neeessarily distinct) nodes; we call these annotations* references, *and we call the referenced nodes* arguments. *Computation nodes have exactly two successors; the corresponding edges are labeled with* **yes** *and* **no***, respectively.*
- *Input nodes have no annotations. They have exactly one successor.*

- Output nodes *have a reference to exactly one node in their annotations. They have exactly one successor.*
- Control nodes *are annotated with a bitstring l. They have at least one and up to countably many successors; the corresponding edges are labeled with distinct bitstrings l'. (We call l the* out-metadata *and l' the* in-metadata.)

We assume that the annotations are part of the node identifier. A node ν can only reference other nodes ν' on the path from the root to ν; in this case ν' must be a computation node or input node. If ν' is a computation node, the path from ν' to ν has additionally to go through the outgoing edge of ν' with label yes.

Bi-protocols. To compare two variants of a protocol, we consider bi-protocols, which rely on the same idea as bi-processes in the applied π-calculus [7]. Bi-protocols are pairs of protocols that only differ in the messages they operate on.

Definition 3 (CoSP Bi-protocol). *A CoSP bi-protocol Π is defined like a protocol but uses bi-references instead of references. A* bi-reference *is a pair $(\nu_{\mathsf{left}}, \nu_{\mathsf{right}})$ of node identifiers of two (not necessarily distinct) nodes in the protocol tree. In the* left protocol $\mathsf{left}(\Pi)$ *the bi-references are replaced by their left components; the* right protocol $\mathsf{right}(\Pi)$ *is defined analogously.*

2.1 Symbolic Indistinguishability

In this section, we define a symbolic notion of indistinguishability. First, we model the capabilities of the symbolic attacker. Operations that the symbolic attacker can perform on terms are defined as follows, including the destruction of already known terms and the creation of new terms.[1]

Definition 4 (Symbolic Operation). *Let $\mathbf{M} = (\mathbf{C}, \mathbf{N}, \mathbf{T}, \mathbf{D})$ be a symbolic model. A* symbolic operation O/n *(of arity n) on $\mathbf{M}$ is a finite tree whose nodes are labeled with constructors from $\mathbf{C}$, destructors from $\mathbf{D}$, nonces from $\mathbf{N}$, and formal parameters x_i with $i \in \{1, \ldots, n\}$. For constructors and destructors, the children of a node represent its arguments (if any). Formal parameters x_i and nonces do not have children.*

We extend the evaluation function to symbolic operations. Given a list of terms $\underline{t} \in \mathbf{T}^n$, the evaluation function $\mathrm{eval}_O : \mathbf{T}^n \to \mathbf{T}$ recursively evaluates the tree O starting at the root as follows: The formal parameter x_i evaluates to t_i. A node with $F \in \mathbf{C} \cup \mathbf{N}_E \cup \mathbf{D}$ evaluates according to eval_F. If there is a node that evaluates to $\bot$, the whole tree evaluates to $\bot$.

A symbolic execution of a protocol is basically a valid path through the protocol tree. It induces a *view*, which contains the communication with the attacker.

---

[1] We deviate from the definition in the original CoSP framework [15], where a deduction relation describes which terms the attacker can deduce from the already seen terms. This modification is not essential; all results for trace properties that have been established in the original framework so far are compatible with our definition.

Definition 5 (Symbolic Execution). *Let a symbolic model* $\mathbf{M} = (\mathbf{C}, \mathbf{N}, \mathbf{T}, \mathbf{D})$ *and a CoSP protocol* I *be given. A* symbolic view *of the protocol* I *is a (finite) list of triples* (V_i, ν_i, f_i) *with the following conditions:*

For the first triple, we have $V_1 = \varepsilon$, ν_1 *is the root of* I, *and* f_1 *is an empty partial function, mapping node identifiers to terms. For every two consecutive tuples* (V, ν, f) *and* (V', ν', f') *in the list, let* $\tilde{\underline{\nu}}$ *be the nodes referenced by* ν *and define* $\tilde{\underline{t}}$ *through* $\tilde{t}_j := f(\tilde{\nu}_j)$. *We conduct a case distinction on* ν.

- ν *is a computation node with constructor, destructor or nonce* F. *Let* $V' = V$. *If* $m := eval_F(\tilde{\underline{t}}) \neq \perp$, ν' *is the* yes*-successor of* ν *in* I, *and* $f' = f(\nu := m)$. *If* $m = \perp$, *then* ν' *is the* no*-successor of* ν, *and* $f' = f$.
- ν *is an input node. If there exists a term* $t \in \mathbf{T}$ *and a symbolic operation* O *on* $\mathbf{M}$ *with* $eval_O(V_{Out}) = t$, *let* ν' *be the successor of* ν *in* I, $V' = V ::$ $(\mathtt{in}, (t, O))$, *and* $f' = f(\nu := t)$.
- ν *is an output node. Let* $V' = V :: (\mathtt{out}, \tilde{t}_1)$, ν' *is the successor of* ν *in* I, *and* $f' = f$.
- ν *is a control node with out-metadata* l. *Let* ν' *be the successor of* ν *with the in-metadata* l' *(or the lexicographically smallest edge if there is no edge with label* l'*),* $f' = f$, *and* $V' = V :: (\mathtt{control}, (l, l'))$.

Here, V_{Out} *denotes the list of terms in* V *that have been sent at output nodes, i.e., the terms* t *contained in entries of the form* $(\mathtt{out}, t)$ *in* V. *Analogously,* $V_{Out\text{-}Meta}$ *denotes the list of out-metadata in* V *that has been sent at control nodes.*

The set of all symbolic views of I *is denoted by* $\mathsf{SViews}(I)$. *Furthermore,* V_{In} *denotes the partial list of* V *that contains only entries of the form* $(\mathtt{in}, (*, O))$ *or* $(\mathtt{control}, (*, l'))$ *for some symbolic operation* O *and some in-metadata* l', *where the input term and the out-metadata have been masked with the symbol* $*$. *The list* V_{In} *is called* attacker strategy. *We write* $[V_{In}]_{\mathsf{SViews}(I)}$ *to denote the class of all views* $U \in \mathsf{SViews}(I)$ *with* $U_{In} = V_{In}$.

The knowledge of the attacker are the results of all the symbolic tests the attacker can perform on the messages output by the protocol. To define the attacker knowledge formally, we have to pay attention to two important details. First, we concentrate on whether a symbolic operation fails or not, i.e., if it evaluates to $\perp$ or not; we are not interested in the resulting term in case the operation succeeds. The following example illustrates why: suppose the left protocol of a bi-protocol does nothing more than sending a ciphertext c to the attacker, whereas the right protocol sends a different ciphertext c' (with the same plaintext length) to the attacker. Assume that the decryption key is kept secret. This bi-protocol should be symbolically indistinguishable. More precisely, the attacker knowledge in the left protocol should be statically indistinguishable from the attacker knowledge in the right protocol. Recall that $O = x_1$ is the symbolic operation that just returns the first message received by the attacker. If the result of O were part of the attacker knowledge, the knowledge in the left protocol (containing c) would differ from the knowledge in the right protocol (containing c'), which is not what we would like to express. On the other hand, our definition, which only cares about the failure or success of a operation, requires that the symbolic model contains an operation *equals* to be reasonable. This operation *equals* allows the attacker to test equality between terms: consider the case where the right protocol sends a publicly known term t instead of c', but still of the same length as c. In that case the attacker can distinguish the bi-protocol with the help of the symbolic operation $equals(t, x_1)$.

The second observation is that the definition should cover the fact that the attacker knows which symbolic operation leads to which result. This is essential to reason about indistinguishability: consider a bi-protocol such that the left protocol sends the pair (n, t), but the right protocol sends the pair (t, n), where t is again a publicly known term and n is a fresh protocol nonce. The two protocols do not differ in the terms that the attacker can deduce after their execution; the deducible terms are all publicly known terms as well as n. Still, the protocols are trivially distinguishable by the symbolic operation $equals(O_t, snd(x_1))$ because $equals(O_t, snd((n, t))) \neq \bot$ but $equals(t, snd((t, n))) = \bot$, where snd returns the second component of a pair and O_t is a symbolic operation that constructs t.

Definition 6 (Symbolic Knowledge). *Let $\mathbf{M}$ be a symbolic model. Given a view V with $|V_{Out}| = n$, the full symbolic knowledge function K_V is a function from symbolic operations on $\mathbf{M}$ (see Definition 4) of arity n to $\{\top, \bot\}$, defined by $K_V(O) := \bot$ if $eval_O(V_{Out}) = \bot$ and $K_V(O) := \top$ otherwise.*

Intuitively, we would like to consider two views *equivalent* if they look the same for a symbolic attacker. Despite the requirement that they have the same order of output, input and control nodes, this is the case if they agree on the out-metadata (the control data sent by the protocol) as well as the symbolic knowledge that can be gained out of the terms sent by the protocol.

Definition 7 (Equivalent Views). *Let two views V, V' of the same length be given. We denote their ith entry by V_i and V_i', respectively. V and V' are equivalent ($V \sim V'$), if the following three conditions hold:*

1. *(Same structure) V_i is of the form $(s, \cdot)$ if and only if V_i' is of the form $(s, \cdot)$ for some $s \in \{\text{out}, \text{in}, \text{control}\}$.*
2. *(Same out-metadata) $V_{Out\text{-}Meta} = V_{Out\text{-}Meta}'$.*
3. *(Same symbolic knowledge) $K_V = K_{V'}$.*

Finally, we define a bi-protocol to be symbolically indistinguishable if they lead to equivalent views when faced with the same attacker strategy.[2]

Definition 8 (Symbolic Indistinguishability). *Let $\mathbf{M}$ be a symbolic model and P be a class of bi-protocols on $\mathbf{M}$. Given an attacker strategy V_{In} (in the sense of Definition 5), a bi-protocol $\Pi \in P$ is symbolically indistinguishable under V_{In} if for all views $V_{\text{left}} \in [V_{In}]_{\text{SViews}(\text{left}(\Pi))}$ of the left protocol under V_{In}, there is a view $V_{\text{right}} \in [V_{In}]_{\text{SViews}(\text{right}(\Pi))}$ of the right protocol under V_{In} such that $V_{\text{left}} \sim V_{\text{right}}$, and vice versa.*

---

[2] For the sake of convenience, we define CS for bi-protocols. However, our definition can be easily generalized to arbitrary pairs of protocols.

A bi-protocol $\Pi \in \mathrm{P}$ is symbolically indistinguishable, *if Π is indistinguishable under all attacker strategies. We write* $\mathsf{left}(\Pi) \approx_s \mathsf{right}(\Pi)$ *for the symbolic indistinguishability of Π.*

2.2 Computational Indistinguishability

On the computational side, the constructors and destructors in a symbolic model are realized with cryptographic algorithms, formalized as follows.

Definition 9 (Computational Implementation). *Let $\mathbf{M} = (\mathbf{C}, \mathbf{N}, \mathbf{T}, \mathbf{D})$ be a symbolic model. A* computational implementation of $\mathbf{M}$ *is a family of functions $\mathbf{A} = (A_x)_{x \in \mathbf{C} \cup \mathbf{D} \cup \mathbf{N}}$ such that A_F for $F/n \in \mathbf{C} \cup \mathbf{D}$ is a partial deterministic function $\mathbb{N} \times (\{0,1\}^*)^n \to \{0,1\}^*$, and A_N for $N \in \mathbf{N}$ is a total probabilistic function with domain $\mathbb{N}$ and range $\{0,1\}^*$. The first argument of A_F and A_N represents the security parameter.*

All functions A_F have to be computable in deterministic polynomial time, and all A_N have to be computable in probabilistic polynomial time (ppt).

The computational execution of a protocol is a randomized interactive machine that runs against a ppt attacker $\mathcal{A}$. The transcript of the execution contains essentially the computational counterparts of a symbolic view.

Definition 10 (Computational Challenger). *Let $\mathbf{A}$ be a computational implementation of the symbolic model $\mathbf{M} = (\mathbf{C}, \mathbf{N}, \mathbf{T}, \mathbf{D})$ and I be a CoSP protocol. Let $\mathcal{A}$ be a ppt machine and p be a polynomial. For a security parameter k, the computational challenger $\mathsf{Exec}_{\mathbf{M}, \mathbf{A}, I, p}(k)$ is the following interactive machine:*

Initially, let ν be the root of I. Let f and n be empty partial functions from node identifiers to bitstrings and from $\mathbf{N}$ to bitstrings, respectively. Enter a loop and proceed depending on the type of ν:

- *ν is a computation node with nonce $N \in \mathbf{N}$. If $n(N) \neq \bot$, let $m' := n(N)$; otherwise sample m' according to $A_N(k)$. Let ν' be the yes-successor of ν. Let $f := f(\nu := m')$, $n := n(N := m')$, and $\nu := \nu'$.*
- *ν is a computation node with constructor or destructor F. Let $\tilde{\nu}$ be the nodes referenced by ν and $\tilde{m}_j := f(\tilde{\nu}_j)$. Then, $m' := A_F(k, \tilde{m})$. If $m' \neq \bot$, then ν' is the yes-successor of ν, if $m' = \bot$, then ν' is the no-successor of ν. Let $f := f(\nu := m')$ and $\nu := \nu'$.*
- *ν is an input node. Ask the adversary $\mathcal{A}$ for a bitstring m. Let ν' be the successor of ν. Let $f := f(\nu := m)$ and $\nu := \nu'$.*
- *ν is an output node. Send $\tilde{m}_1$ to $\mathcal{A}$. Let ν' be the successor of ν, and let $\nu := \nu'$.*
- *ν is a control node with out-metadata l. Send l to $\mathcal{A}$. Upon receiving in-metadata l', let ν' be the successor of ν along the edge labeled l' (or the lexicographically smallest edge if there is no edge with label l'). Let $\nu := \nu'$.*

Let len be the number of nodes from the root to ν plus the total length of all bitstrings in the range of f. Stop if len $> p(k)$; otherwise continue the loop. We call V the computational view *of a run.*

Definition 11 (Computational Execution). *The interaction between the challenger* $\mathsf{Exec}_{\mathbf{M},\mathbf{A},\Pi,p}(k)$ *and the adversary* $\mathcal{A}(k)$ *is called the* computational execution, *denoted by* $\langle\mathsf{Exec}_{\mathbf{M},\mathbf{A},\Pi,p}(k)|\mathcal{A}(k)\rangle$. *It stops whenever one of the two machines stops, and the output of* $\langle\mathsf{Exec}_{\mathbf{M},\mathbf{A},\Pi,p}(k)|\mathcal{A}(k)\rangle$ *is the output of* $\mathcal{A}(k)$.

Given these definitions, computational indistinguishability for bi-protocols is naturally defined. A bi-protocol is indistinguishable if its challengers are computationally indistinguishable for every ppt attacker $\mathcal{A}$.

Definition 12 (Computational Indistinguishability). *Let* Π *be an efficient[3] CoSP bi-protocol and let* $\mathbf{A}$ *be a computational implementation of* $\mathbf{M}$. Π *is computationally indistinguishable if for all ppt attackers* $\mathcal{A}$ *and for all polynomials* p, *we have that* $\langle\mathsf{Exec}_{\mathbf{A},\mathbf{M},\mathsf{left}(\Pi),p}(k)|\mathcal{A}(k)\rangle \approx_c \langle\mathsf{Exec}_{\mathbf{A},\mathbf{M},\mathsf{right}(\Pi),p}(k)|\mathcal{A}(k)\rangle$, *where* $\approx_c$ *denotes computational indistinguishability of distribution ensembles.*

Computational Soundness. Having defined symbolic and computational indistinguishability, we are finally able to relate them. The previous definitions culminate in the definition of CS for equivalence properties. It states that the symbolic indistinguishability of a bi-protocol implies its computational indistinguishability. In other words, it suffices to check the security of the symbolic bi-protocol, e.g., using mechanized protocol verifiers such as ProVerif.

Definition 13 (Computational Soundness for Equivalence Properties). *Let a symbolic model* $\mathbf{M}$ *and a class* P *of efficient bi-protocols be given. An implementation* $\mathbf{A}$ *of* $\mathbf{M}$ *is* computationally sound *for* $\mathbf{M}$ *if for every* $\Pi \in$ P, *we have that* Π *is computationally indistinguishable whenever* Π *is symbolically indistinguishable.*

3   Self-monitoring

In this section, we identify a sufficient condition for symbolic models under which CS for trace properties implies CS for equivalence properties for a class of *uniformity-enforcing protocols*, which correspond to uniform bi-processes in the applied π-calculus. We say that a symbolic model that satisfies this condition *allows for self-monitoring.* The main idea behind self-monitoring is that a symbolic model is sufficiently expressive (and its implementation is sufficiently strong) such that the following holds: whenever a computational attacker can distinguish a bi-process, there is a test in the symbolic model that allows to successfully distinguish the bi-process.

CS for Trace Properties. We first review CS for trace properties. A trace property is a prefix-closed set of node identifiers. We refer to [15] for the precise definition of computational and symbolic satisfiability. CS for trace properties states that all attacks (against trace properties) that can be excluded for the

---

[3] A (bi-)protocol is *efficient* if the size of every node identifier ν is polynomially bounded in the length of the path to the root, and ν is computable in deterministic polynomial time given all node and edge identifiers on this path.

symbolic abstraction can be excluded for the computational implementation as well. Hence, if all the symbolic traces satisfy a certain trace property, then all computational traces satisfy this property as well.

Definition 14 (Computational Soundness for Trace Properties [15]). *A symbolic model* $(\mathbf{C}, \mathbf{N}, \mathbf{T}, \mathbf{D})$ *is* computationally sound for trace properties *with respect to an implementation* $\mathbf{A}$ *for a class* P *of efficient protocols if the following holds: for each protocol* $I \in$ P *and each trace property* $\mathcal{P}$, *if* I *symbolically satisfies* $\mathcal{P}$ *then* I *computationally satisfies* $\mathcal{P}$.

Uniformity-enforcing. A bi-protocol is *uniform* if for each symbolic attacker strategy, both its variants reach the same nodes in the CoSP tree, i.e., they never branch differently.[4] Formally, we require that the bi-protocols are *uniformity-enforcing*, i.e., when the left and the right protocol of the bi-protocol Π take different branches, the attacker is informed. Since taking different branches is only visible after a control node is reached, we additionally require that computation nodes are immediately followed by control nodes.

Definition 15 (Uniformity-enforcing). *A class* P *of CoSP bi-protocols is* uniformity-enforcing *if for all bi-protocols* $\Pi \in$ P:

1. *Every control node in* Π *has unique out-metadata.*
2. *For every computation node* ν *in* Π *and for every path rooted at* ν, *a control node is reached before an output node.*

All embeddings of calculi the CoSP framework described so far, namely those of the applied π-calculus [15] and RCF [33], are formalized such that protocols written in these calculi fulfill both properties: these embeddings give the attacker a scheduling decision, using a control node, basically after every execution step.

3.1 Bridging the Gap from Trace Properties to Uniformity

The key observation for the connection to trace properties is that, given a bi-protocol Π, some computationally sound symbolic models allow to construct a self-monitor protocol Mon(Π) (not a bi-protocol!) that has essentially the same interface to the attacker as the bi-protocol Π and checks at run-time whether Π would behave uniformly. In other words, non-uniformity of bi-protocols can be formulated as a trace property **bad**, which the protocol Mon(Π) detects.

The self-monitor Mon(Π) of a bi-protocol Π behaves like one of the two variants of the bi-protocol Π, while additionally simulating the opposite variant such that Mon(Π) itself is able to detect whether Π would be distinguishable. (For instance, one approach to detect whether Π is distinguishable could consist of reconstructing the symbolic view of the attacker in the variant of Π that is not executed by Mon(Π).) At the beginning of the execution of the self-monitor, the attacker chooses if Mon(Π) should basically behave like left(Π) or like right(Π).

---

[4] We show in Lemma 1 that uniformity of bi-protocols in CoSP corresponds to uniformity of bi-processes in the applied π-calculus.

We denote the chosen variant as $b \in \{\mathsf{left}, \mathsf{right}\}$ and the opposite variant as $\bar{b}$. After this decision, $\mathsf{Mon}(\Pi)$ executes the the b-variant $b(\Pi)$ of the bi-protocol Π, however, enriched with the computation nodes and the corresponding output nodes of the opposite variant $\bar{b}(\Pi)$.[5]

The goal of the self-monitor $\mathsf{Mon}(\Pi)$ is to detect whether the execution of $b(\Pi)$ would be distinguishable from $\bar{b}(\Pi)$ at the current state. If this is the case, $\mathsf{Mon}(\Pi)$ raises the event bad, which is the disjunction of two events $\mathsf{bad\text{-}branch}$ and $\mathsf{bad\text{-}knowledge}$.

The event $\mathsf{bad\text{-}branch}$ corresponds to the case that the left and the right protocol of the bi-protocol Π take different branches. Since uniformity-enforcing protocols have a control node immediately after every computation node (see Definition 15), the attacker can always check whether $b(\Pi)$ and $\bar{b}(\Pi)$ take the same branch. We require (in Definition 17) the existence of a so-called *distinguishing subprotocol* $f_{\mathsf{bad\text{-}branch},\Pi}$ that checks whether each destructor application in $b(\Pi)$ succeeds if and only if it succeeds in $\bar{b}(\Pi)$; if not, the distinguishing subprotocol $f_{\mathsf{bad\text{-}branch},\Pi}$ raises $\mathsf{bad\text{-}branch}$.

The event $\mathsf{bad\text{-}knowledge}$ captures that the messages sent by $b(\Pi)$ and $\bar{b}(\Pi)$ (via output nodes, i.e., not the out-metadata) are distinguishable. This distinguishability is only detectable by a protocol if the constructors and destructors, which are available to both the protocol and the symbolic attacker, capture all possible tests. We require (in Definition 17) the existence of a distinguishing subprotocol $f_{\mathsf{bad\text{-}knowledge},\Pi}$ that raises $\mathsf{bad\text{-}knowledge}$ in $\mathsf{Mon}(\Pi)$ whenever a message, sent in Π, would allow the attacker to distinguish $b(\Pi)$ and $\bar{b}(\Pi)$.

Parameterized CoSP Protocols. For a bi-protocol Π, we formalize the distinguishing subprotocols $f_{\mathsf{bad\text{-}knowledge},\Pi}$ and $f_{\mathsf{bad\text{-}branch},\Pi}$ with the help of *parameterized CoSP protocols*, which have the following properties: Nodes in such protocols are not required to have successors and instead of other nodes, also formal parameters can be referenced. A parameterized CoSP protocol is intended to be plugged into another protocol; in that case the parameters references must be changed to references to nodes.

Definition 16 (Self-monitor). *Let Π be a CoSP bi-protocol. Let $f_{\mathsf{bad\text{-}knowledge},\Pi}$ and $f_{\mathsf{bad\text{-}branch},\Pi}$ be functions that map execution traces to parameterized CoSP protocols[6] whose leaves are either ok, in which case they have open edges, or nodes that raise the event $\mathsf{bad\text{-}knowledge}$, or $\mathsf{bad\text{-}branch}$ respectively. Let Π a CoSP bi-protocol.*

---

[5] This leads to the fact that whenever there is an output node in Π, there are two corresponding output nodes in $\mathsf{Mon}(\Pi)$, which contradicts the goal that the interface of Π and $\mathsf{Mon}(\Pi)$ should be the same towards the attacker. However, this technicality can be dealt with easily when applying our method. For example, in the computational proof for our case study, we use the self-monitor in an interaction with a filter machine that hides the results of the output nodes of $\bar{b}(\Pi)$ to create a good simulation towards the computational attacker, whose goal is to distinguish Π. The filter machine is then used as a computational attacker against $\mathsf{Mon}(\Pi)$.

[6] These functions are candidates for distinguishing subprotocols for $\mathsf{bad\text{-}knowledge}$ and $\mathsf{bad\text{-}branch}$, respectively, for the bi-protocol Π, as defined in Definition 17.

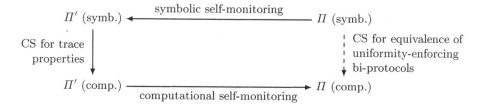

Fig. 1. Symbolic and computational self-monitoring

Recall that nodes ν of Π have bi-references (as defined in Definition 3) consisting of a left reference (to be used in the left protocol) and a right reference. We write $\mathsf{left}(\nu)$ for the node with only the left reference and $\mathsf{right}(\nu)$ analogously. Let tr be the execution trace so far, i.e., the list of node identifiers on the path from ν to the root of Π. The self-monitor $\mathsf{Mon}(\Pi)$ protocol is defined as follows:

Insert before the root node a control node with two copies of Π, called the left *branch (with $b := \mathsf{left}$) and the* right *branch (with $b := \mathsf{right}$). Apply the following modifications recursively for each node ν, starting at the root of Π:*

1. *If ν is a computation node of Π, replace ν with $f_{\texttt{bad-branch},\Pi}(b, tr)$. Append two copies $\mathsf{left}(\nu)$ and $\mathsf{right}(\nu)$ of the the computation node ν to each open edge of an ok-leaf. All left references that pointed to ν point in $\mathsf{Mon}(\Pi)$ to $\mathsf{left}(\nu)$, and all right references that pointed to ν point in $\mathsf{Mon}(\Pi)$ to $\mathsf{right}(\nu)$. The successor of $\mathsf{right}(\nu)$ is the subtree rooted at the successor of ν.*

2. *If ν is an output node of Π, replace ν with $f_{\texttt{bad-knowledge},\Pi}(b, tr)$. Append the sequence of the two output nodes $\mathsf{left}(\nu)$ (labeled with* `left`*) and $\mathsf{right}(\nu)$ (labeled with* `right`*) to each open edge of an ok-leaf. All left references that pointed to ν point in $\mathsf{Mon}(\Pi)$ to $\mathsf{left}(\nu)$, and all right references that pointed to ν point in $\mathsf{Mon}(\Pi)$ to $\mathsf{right}(\nu)$. The successor of $\mathsf{right}(\nu)$ is the subtree rooted at the successor of ν.*

Theorem 1 follows from two properties of the distinguishing subprotocols: *symbolic monitoring* and *computational monitoring* (see Figure 1). Symbolic monitoring states that whenever a bi-protocol Π is indistinguishable, the corresponding distinguishing subprotocol in $\mathsf{Mon}(\Pi)$ does not raise the event **bad**. Computational Monitoring, in turn, states that whenever the distinguishing subprotocol in $\mathsf{Mon}(\Pi)$ does not raises the event **bad**, then Π is indistinguishable.

Shortened Protocols Π_i. Since we prove Theorem 1 by induction over the nodes in a bi-protocol, we introduce a notion of *shortened protocols* in the definition of distinguishing subprotocols. For a (bi-)protocol Π, the shortened (bi-)protocol Π_i is for the first i nodes exactly like Π but that stops after the ith node that is either a control node or an output node.[7]

Definition 17 (Distinguishing Subprotocols). *Let* **M** *be a symbolic model and* **A** *a computational implementation of* **M***. Let Π be a bi-protocol and $\mathsf{Mon}(\Pi)$*

---

[7] Formally, the protocol only has an infinite chain of control nodes with single successors after this node.

its self-monitor. Let $e \in \{\texttt{bad-knowledge}, \texttt{bad-branch}\}$ *and* $n_{\texttt{bad-knowledge}}$ *denote the node type output node and* $n_{\texttt{bad-branch}}$ *denote the node type control node. Then the function* $f_{e,\Pi}(b, tr)$, *which takes as input* $b \in \{\texttt{left}, \texttt{right}\}$ *and the path to the root node, including all node and edge identifiers, is a* distinguishing subprotocol *for* e *for* Π *and* **M** *if it is computable in deterministic polynomial time, and if the following conditions hold for every* $i \in \mathbb{N}$:

1. symbolic self-monitoring: *If* Π_i *is symbolically indistinguishable,* **bad** *does symbolically not occur in* $\mathsf{Mon}(\Pi_{i-1})$, *and the ith node in* Π_i *is of type* n_e, *then the event* e *does not occur symbolically in* $\mathsf{Mon}(\Pi_i)$.

2. computational self-monitoring: *The event* e *in* $\mathsf{Mon}(\Pi_i)$ *occurs computationally with negligible probability,* Π_{i-1} *is computationally indistinguishable, and the ith node in* Π_i *is of type* n_e, *then* Π_i *is computationally indistinguishable.*

We say that a **M** *and a protocol class allows for* self-monitoring *if there are distinguishing subprotocols for* **bad-branch** *and* **bad-knowledge** *for every bi-protocol in the protocol class.*

Finally, we are ready to state our main theorem.

Theorem 1. *Let* **M** *be a symbolic model and* P *be a uniformity-enforcing class of bi-protocols. If* **M** *and* P *allow for self-monitoring (in the sense of Definition 17), then the following holds: If* **A** *is a computationally sound implementation of a symbolic model* **M** *with respect to trace properties then* **A** *is also a computationally sound implementation with respect to equivalence properties.*

4   The Applied π-calculus

In this section, we present the connection of uniform bi-processes in the applied π-calculus and our CS result in CoSP, namely that the applied π-calculus can be embedded into the extended CoSP framework. In contrast to previous work [22,23,24], we consider CS for bi-protocols from the full applied π-calculus. In particular, we also consider private channels and non-determinate processes.

We consider the variant of the applied π-calculus also used for the original CoSP embedding [15]. The operational semantics of the applied π-calculus is defined in terms of *structural equivalence* ($\equiv$) and *internal reduction* ($\rightarrow$); for a precise definition of the applied π-calculus, we refer to [7].

A uniform bi-process [30] in the applied π-calculus is the counterpart of a uniform bi-protocol in CoSP. A bi-process is a pair of processes that only differ in the terms they operate on. Formally, they contain expressions of the form *choice*$[a, b]$, where a is used in the left process and b is used in the right one. A bi-process Q can only reduce if both its processes can reduce in the same way.

Definition 18 (Uniform Bi-process). *A bi-process* Q *in the applied* π-calculus *is* uniform *if* $\mathsf{left}(Q) \rightarrow R_{\mathsf{left}}$ *implies that* $Q \rightarrow R$ *for some bi-process* R *with* $\mathsf{left}(R) \equiv R_{\mathsf{left}}$, *and symmetrically for* $\mathsf{right}(Q) \rightarrow R_{\mathsf{right}}$ *with* $\mathsf{right}(R) \equiv R_{\mathsf{right}}$.

The following lemma connects uniformity in the applied π-calculus to uniformity in CoSP. (See [34] for a proof.)

Lemma 1 (Uniformity in CoSP and the Applied π-calculus). *There is an embedding e from bi-processes in the applied π-calculus to CoSP uniformity-enforcing bi-protocols such that for every bi-process Q in the applied π-calculus, the following holds: If Q is uniform, then $\mathsf{left}(e(Q)) \approx_s \mathsf{right}(e(Q))$.*

5 Case Study: Encryption and Signatures with Lengths

We exemplify our method by proving a CS result for equivalence properties, which captures protocols that use public-key encryption and signatures. We use the CS result in [31] for trace properties, which we extend by a length function, realized as a destructor. Since encryptions of plaintexts of different length can typically be distinguished, we must reflect that fact in the symbolic model.

5.1 The Symbolic Model

Lengths in the Symbolic Model. In order to express lengths in the symbolic model, we introduce *length specifications*, which are the result of applying a special destructor $length/1$. We assume that the bitlength of every computational message m_c is of the form $|m_c| = rk$ for some natural number r, where k is the security parameter, i.e., the length of a nonce. This assumption will be made precise. With this simplification, length specifications only encode r; this can be done using Peano numbers, i.e., the constructors O (zero) and S (successor).

Even though this approach leads admittedly to rather inefficient realizations from a practical point of view,[8] the aforementioned assumption can be realized using a suitable padding. Essentially, this assumption is similar to the one introduced by Cortier and Comon-Lundh [22] for a symbolic model for symmetric encryption. The underlying problem is exactly the same: while the length of messages in the computational model, in particular the length of ciphertexts, may depend on the security parameter, there is no equivalent concept in the symbolic model. For instance, let n and m be nonces, and let ek be an encryption key. For certain security parameters in the computational model, the computational message $pair(n, m)$ may have the same length as the message $enc(ek, n)$; for other security parameters this may not be the case. Thus it is not clear if the corresponding symbolic messages should be of equal symbolic length. Comon-Lundh et al. [28] propose a different approach towards this problem, by labeling messages symbolically with an expected length and checking the correctness of these length computationally. However, it is not clear whether such a symbolic model can be handled by current automated verification tools.

Automated Verification: Combinding ProVerif and APTE. ProVerif is not able to handle recursive destructors such as *length*, e.g., $length(pair(t_1, t_2)) =$

---

[8] Consider, e.g., a payload string that should convey n bits. This message must be encoded using at least kn bits.

$length(t_1) + length(t_2)$. Recent work by Cheval and Cortier [32] extends the protocol verifier APTE, which is capable of proving trace equivalence of two processes in the applied π-calculus, to support such length functions. Since however trace equivalence is a weaker notion than uniformity, i.e., there are bi-processes that are trace equivalent but not uniform, our CS result does not carry over to APTE. Due to the lack of a tool that is able to check uniformity as well as to handle length functions properly, we elaborate and prove in [34] how APTE can be combined with ProVerif to make protocols on the symbolic model of our case study amenable to automated verification.

We consider the following symbolical model $\mathbf{M} = (\mathbf{C}, \mathbf{N}, \mathbf{T}, \mathbf{D})$.

Constructors and Nonces. We define $\mathbf{C} := \{enc/3, ek/1, dk/1, sig/3, vk/1, sk/1, string_0/1, string_1/1, emp/0, pair/2, O/0, S/1, garbageEnc/3, garbageSig/3, garbage/2, garbageInvalidLength/1\}$ and $\mathbf{N} := \mathbf{N_E} \uplus \mathbf{N_E}$ for countably infinite sets of protocol nonces $\mathbf{N_P}$ and attacker nonces $\mathbf{N_E}$. Encryption, decryption, verification, and signing keys are represented as $ek(r), dk(r), vk(r), sk(r)$ with a nonce r (the randomness used when generating the keys). The term $enc(ek(r'), m, r)$ encrypts m using the encryption key $ek(r')$ and randomness r. $sig(sk(r'), m, r)$ is a signature of m using the signing key $sk(r')$ and randomness r. The constructors $string_0$, $string_1$, and emp are used to model arbitrary strings used as payload in a protocol, e.g., a bitstring 010 would be encoded as $string_0(string_1(string_0(emp())))$. Length specifications can be constructed using O representing zero and S representing the successor of a number. $garbage$, $garbageInvalidLength$, $garbageEnc$, and $garbageSig$ are not used by the protocol; they express invalid terms the attacker may send.

Message Type. We define $\mathbf{T}$ as the set of terms M according to this grammar:

$$M ::= enc(ek(N), M, N) \mid ek(N) \mid dk(N) \mid$$
$$sig(sk(N), M, N) \mid vk(N) \mid sk(N) \mid pair(M, M) \mid S \mid N \mid L \mid$$
$$garbage(N, L) \mid garbageInvalidLength(N)$$
$$garbageEnc(M, N, L) \mid garbageSig(M, N, L)$$
$$S ::= emp() \mid string_0(S) \mid string_1(S) \qquad L ::= O() \mid S(L)$$

The nonterminals N and L represent nonces and length specifications, respectively. Note that the garbage terms carry an explicit length specification to enable the attacker to send invalid terms of a certain length.

Destructors. We define $\mathbf{D} := \{dec/2, isenc/1, isek/1, isdk/1, ekof/1, ekofdk/1, verify/2, isvk/1, issk/1, issig/1, vkofsk/1, vkof/1, unstring_0/1, unstring_1/1, fst/1, snd/1, equals/2, length/1, unS/1\}$. The destructors $isek$, $isdk$, $isvk$, $issk$, $isenc$, and $issig$ realize predicates to test whether a term is an encryption key, decryption key, verification key, signing key, ciphertext, or signature, respectively. $ekof$ extracts the encryption key from a ciphertext, $vkof$ extracts the verification key from a signature. $dec(dk(r), c)$ decrypts the ciphertext c. $verify(vk(r), s)$ verifies the signature s with respect to the verification key $vk(r)$ and returns the signed message if successful. $ekofdk$ and $vkofsk$ compute the encryption/verification key corresponding to a decryption/signing key. The destructors fst and snd are used to destruct pairs, and the destructors $unstring_0$ and $unstring_1$ allow to parse payload-strings. The destructor $length$ returns a the length of message, where the unit is the length of a nonce. The purpose of unS is destruct numbers that represent lengths. (The full description of all destructor rules is given in [34].)

Length Destructor. Our result is parametrized over the destructor $length$ that must adhere to the following restrictions:

1. Each message except for $garbageInvalidLength$ is assigned a length:
   $length(t) \neq \bot$ for all terms $t \in \mathbf{T} \setminus \{garbageInvalidLength(t') \mid t' \in \mathbf{T}\}$.
2. The length of garbage terms (constructed by the attacker) is consistent:

$$length(garbage(t, l)) = l, \qquad length(garbageEnc(t_1, t_2, l)) = l,$$
$$length(garbageSig(t_1, t_2, l)) = l, \quad length(garbageInvalidLength(t_1)) = \bot$$

3. Let $[\cdot]$ be the canonical interpretation of Peano numbers, given by $[O] = 0$ and $[S(l)] = [l] + 1$. We require the length destructor to be linear: For each constructor $C/n \in \mathbf{C} \setminus \{garbage, garbageInvalidLength, garbageEnc, garbageSig\}$ there are $a_i \in \mathbb{N}$ (where $i = 0, \ldots, n$) such that $length(t_i) = l_i$ for $i = 1, \ldots, n$ and $length(C(\underline{t})) = l$ together imply $[l] = \sum_{i=1}^{n} a_i \cdot [l_i] + a_0$.

5.2   Computational Soundness

Protocol Conditions and Implementation Conditions. For establishing CS, we require the protocols to fulfill several natural conditions regarding their use of randomness, e.g., that fresh randomness is used for key generation. Protocols that adhere to these protocol conditions are called *randomness-safe*. For the full protocol and implementation conditions, we refer to the extended version [34].

Additionally, the computational implementation needs to fulfill certain conditions, e.g., that the encryption scheme is PROG-KDM secure [35], and the signature scheme is SUF-CMA. Both protocol conditions and implementation conditions are similar to those in [31]. Requiring PROG-KDM [35] is only needed to handle protocols that send and receive decryption keys.[9]

For lengths in the computational model, we require that the computational implementation A_{length} of the destructor $length$ computes the bitlength of the corresponding bitstring. To connect the symbolic result of the destructor $length$ to bit-lengths in the computational world, we require length consistency.

Definition 19 (Length Consistency). *Let* $\mathbf{M} = (\mathbf{C}, \mathbf{N}, \mathbf{T}, \mathbf{D})$ *be a symbolic model such that there is a constructor* $length/1$ *in* $\mathbf{D}$, *and let* $[\cdot]$ *be an interpretation mapping length specifications to natural numbers.*

---

[9] In principle, our proofs do not rely on this particular security definition. For example, it would be possible to obtain a CS result for uniformity using weaker implementation conditions (IND-CCA secure public-key encryption) but a restricted protocol class, by applying our proof technique to the CS result for trace properties in [15].

Given a security parameter k, a computational variant of a message $m \in \mathbf{T}$ is obtained by implementing each constructor C and nonce N in m by the corresponding algorithm A_C or A_N, respectively. For example, for all random choices of $A_N(k)$, $A_{pair}(k, A_{string_0}(k, A_{emp}(k), A_{ek}(k, A_N(k))))$ is a computational variant of the message $pair(string_0(emp(), ek(N)))$, where $N \in \mathbf{N}$.

We say that a computational implementation $\mathbf{A}$ of $\mathbf{M}$ is length-consistent with respect to the interpretation $[\cdot]$ if for each message $m \in \mathbf{T}$ and all of its computational variants m_k under security parameter k, we have that $length(m) \neq \perp$ implies $|m_k| = [length(m)] \cdot k$.

Length specifications are ordinary messages that the protocol can process, send and receive. We require length specifications to have a length itself. Moreover, we require that the decryption algorithm A_{dec} expects a length description of the plaintext and fails if the length of the plaintexts do not match.

CS for Trace Properties with Length Functions. We extend the CS result for trace properties by Backes, Unruh, and Malik [31], which holds for signatures and public-key encryption, to lengths functions.

Theorem 2. *Let $\mathbf{A}$ be a computational implementation fulfilling the implementation conditions from above, i.e., in particular $\mathbf{A}$ is length-consistent. Then, $\mathbf{A}$ is a computationally sound implementation of the symbolic model $\mathbf{M}$ for the class of randomness-safe protocols.*

Distinguishing Subprotocols for the Symbolic Model M. In this section, we discuss the distinguishing subprotocols for the symbolic model $\mathbf{M}$. The full descriptions and proofs can be found in the extended version [34].

We construct a distinguishing subprotocol $f_{\texttt{bad-branch}, \Pi}(b, tr)$ for a computation node ν that investigates each message that has been received at an input node (in the execution trace tr of $\mathsf{Mon}(\Pi)$) by parsing the message using computation nodes. The distinguishing subprotocol then reconstructs an attacker strategy by reconstructing a possible symbolic operation for every input message. In more detail, in the symbolic execution, $f_{\texttt{bad-branch}, \Pi}(b, tr)$ parses the input message with all symbolic operations in the model $\mathbf{M}$ that the attacker could have performed as well, i.e., with all tests from the *shared knowledge*. This enables $f_{\texttt{bad-branch}, \Pi}(b, tr)$ to simulate the symbolic execution of $\bar{b}(\Pi)$ on the constructed attacker strategy. In the computational execution of the self-monitor, the distinguishing subprotocol constructs the symbolic operations (i.e., the symbolic inputs) by parsing the input messages with the implementations of all tests in the shared knowledge (i.e., lookups on output messages and implementations of the destructors). With this reconstructed symbolic inputs (i.e., symbolic operations, from messages that were intended for $b(\Pi)$, $f_{\texttt{bad-branch}, \Pi}(b, tr)$ is able to simulate the symbolic execution of $\bar{b}(\Pi)$ even in the computational execution. The distinguishing subprotocol $f_{\texttt{bad-branch}, \Pi}(b, tr)$ then checks whether this simulated symbolic execution of $\bar{b}(\Pi)$ takes in the same branch as $b(\Pi)$ would take, for the computation node ν in question. If this is not the case, the event `bad-branch` is raised.

Symbolic monitoring follows by construction because the distinguishing subprotocol reconstructs a correct attacker strategy and correctly simulates a symbolic execution. Hence, $f_{\text{bad-branch},\Pi}(b, tr)$ found a distinguishing attacker strategy for $b(\Pi)$ and $\bar{b}(\Pi)$. We show computational monitoring by applying the CS result for trace properties to conclude that the symbolic simulation of $\bar{b}(\Pi)$ suffices to check whether $b(\Pi)$ computationally branches differently from $\bar{b}(\Pi)$.

The distinguishing subprotocol $f_{\text{bad-knowledge},\Pi}(b, tr)$ for an output node ν starts like $f_{\text{bad-branch},\Pi}(b, tr)$ by reconstructing a (symbolic) attacker strategy and simulating a symbolic execution of $\bar{b}(\Pi)$. However, instead of testing the branching behavior of $\bar{b}(\Pi)$, the distinguishing subprotocol $f_{\text{bad-knowledge},\Pi}(b, tr)$ characterizes the message m that is output in $b(\Pi)$ at the output node ν in question, and then $f_{\text{bad-knowledge},\Pi}(b, tr)$ compares m to the message that would be output in $\bar{b}(\Pi)$. This characterization must honor that ciphertexts generated by the protocol are indistinguishable if the corresponding decryption key has not been revealed to the attacker so far. If a difference in the output of $b(\Pi)$ and $\bar{b}(\Pi)$ is detected, the event **bad-knowledge** is raised.

Symbolic monitoring for the distinguishing subprotocol $f_{\text{bad-knowledge},\Pi}(b, tr)$ follows by the same arguments as for $f_{\text{bad-branch},\Pi}(b, tr)$. We show computational monitoring by first applying the PROG-KDM property to prove that the computational execution of $b(\Pi)$ is indistinguishable from a *faking* setting: in the faking setting, all ciphertexts generated by the protocol do not carry any information about their plaintexts (as long as the corresponding decryption key has not been leaked). The same holds analogously for $\bar{b}(\Pi)$. We then consider all remaining real messages, i.e., all messages except ciphertexts generated by the protocol with unleaked decryption keys. We conclude the proof by showing that in the faking setting, $f_{\text{bad-knowledge},\Pi}(b, tr)$ is able to sufficiently characterize all real messages to raise the event **bad-knowledge** whenever the bi-protocol Π is distinguishable.

Lemma 2. *Let* P *be a uniformity-enforcing class of randomness-safe bi-protocols and* **A** *a computationally sound implementation of the symbolic model* **M***. For each bi-protocol* Π, $f_{\text{bad-knowledge},\Pi}$ *and* $f_{\text{bad-branch},\Pi}$ *as described above are distinguishing subprotocols (see Definition 17) for* **M** *and* P*.*

CS for Uniform Bi-processes in the Applied π-calculus. Combining our results, we conclude CS for protocols in the applied π-calculus that use signatures, public-key encryption, and corresponding length functions.

Theorem 3 (CS for Enc. and Signatures in the Applied π-calculus). *Let* **M** *be as defined in Section 5. Let* Q *be a randomness-safe bi-process in the applied π-calculus, and let* **A** *of* **M** *be an implementation that satisfies the conditions from above. Let* e *be the embedding from bi-processes in the applied π-calculus to CoSP bi-protocols. If* Q *is uniform, then* $\mathsf{left}(e(Q)) \approx_c \mathsf{right}(e(Q))$.

Proof. By Lemma 2, there are for each bi-protocol Π distinguishing subprotocols $f_{\text{bad-knowledge},\Pi}$ and $f_{\text{bad-branch},\Pi}$ for **M**. The class of the embedding of the applied π-calculus is uniformity-enforcing by Lemma 1; thus, Theorem 1 entails the claim.

6   Conclusion

In this work, we provided the first result that allows to leverage existing CS results for trace properties to CS results for uniformity of bi-processes in the applied π-calculus. Our result, which is formulated in an extension of the CoSP framework to equivalence properties, holds for Dolev-Yao models that fulfill the property that all distinguishing computational tests are expressible as a process on the model. We exemplified the usefulness of our method by applying it to a Dolev-Yao model that captures signatures and public-key encryption.

We moreover discussed how computationally sound, automated analyses can still be achieved in those frequent situations in which ProVerif does not manage to terminate whenever the Dolev-Yao model supports a length function. We propose to combine ProVerif with the recently introduced tool APTE [32].

We leave as a future work to prove for more comprehensive Dolev-Yao models (e.g., for zero-knowledge proofs) the sufficient conditions for deducing from CS results for trace properties the CS of uniformity. Another interesting direction for future work is the extension of our result to observational equivalence properties that go beyond uniformity.

Acknowledgements. This work was partially supported by the German Universities Excellence Initiative, the ERC Grant End-2-End Security, and the Center for IT-Security, Privacy and Accountability (CISPA).

References

1. Dolev, D., Yao, A.C.: On the security of public key protocols. IEEE Transactions on Information Theory 29(2), 198–208 (1983)
2. Even, S., Goldreich, O.: On the security of multi-party ping-pong protocols. In: FOCS, pp. 34–39. IEEE (1983)
3. Kemmerer, R., Meadows, C., Millen, J.: Three systems for cryptographic protocol analysis. J. of Crypt. 7(2), 79–130 (1994)
4. Backes, M., Jacobi, C., Pfitzmann, B.: Deriving cryptographically sound implementations using composition and formally verified bisimulation. In: Eriksson, L.-H., Lindsay, P.A. (eds.) FME 2002. LNCS, vol. 2391, pp. 310–329. Springer, Heidelberg (2002)
5. Delaune, S., Kremer, S., Ryan, M.: Verifying privacy-type properties of electronic voting protocols. J. Comput. Secur. 17(4), 435–487 (2009)
6. Delaune, S., Kremer, S., Ryan, M.D., Steel, G.: Formal analysis of protocols based on tpm state registers. In: CSF, pp. 66–80. IEEE (2011)
7. Blanchet, B., Abadi, M., Fournet, C.: Automated Verification of Selected Equivalences for Security Protocols. In: LICS, pp. 331–340. IEEE (2005)
8. Backes, M., Maffei, M., Unruh, D.: Zero-knowledge in the applied pi-calculus and automated verification of the direct anonymous attestation protocol. In: S&P, pp. 202–215. IEEE (2008)
9. Cortier, V., Wiedling, C.: A formal analysis of the norwegian E-voting protocol. In: Degano, P., Guttman, J.D. (eds.) POST 2012. LNCS, vol. 7215, pp. 109–128. Springer, Heidelberg (2012)
10. Backes, M., Hritcu, C., Maffei, M.: Automated verification of remote electronic voting protocols in the applied pi-calculus. In: CSF, pp. 195–209. IEEE (2008)

11. Janvier, R., Lakhnech, Y., Mazaré, L.: Completing the picture: Soundness of formal encryption in the presence of active adversaries. In: Sagiv, M. (ed.) ESOP 2005. LNCS, vol. 3444, pp. 172–185. Springer, Heidelberg (2005)
12. Micciancio, D., Warinschi, B.: Soundness of formal encryption in the presence of active adversaries. In: Naor, M. (ed.) TCC 2004. LNCS, vol. 2951, pp. 133–151. Springer, Heidelberg (2004)
13. Cortier, V., Warinschi, B.: Computationally sound, automated proofs for security protocols. In: Sagiv, M. (ed.) ESOP 2005. LNCS, vol. 3444, pp. 157–171. Springer, Heidelberg (2005)
14. Cortier, V., Kremer, S., Küsters, R., Warinschi, B.: Computationally sound symbolic secrecy in the presence of hash functions. In: Arun-Kumar, S., Garg, N. (eds.) FSTTCS 2006. LNCS, vol. 4337, pp. 176–187. Springer, Heidelberg (2006)
15. Backes, M., Hofheinz, D., Unruh, D.: CoSP: a general framework for computational soundness proofs. In: CCS, pp. 66–78. ACM (2009)
16. Backes, M., Unruh, D.: Computational soundness of symbolic zero-knowledge proofs. J. of Comp. Sec. 18(6), 1077–1155 (2010)
17. Galindo, D., Garcia, F.D., van Rossum, P.: Computational soundness of non-malleable commitments. In: Chen, L., Mu, Y., Susilo, W. (eds.) ISPEC 2008. LNCS, vol. 4991, pp. 361–376. Springer, Heidelberg (2008)
18. Cortier, V., Warinschi, B.: A composable computational soundness notion. In: CCS, pp. 63–74. ACM (2011)
19. Böhl, F., Cortier, V., Warinschi, B.: Deduction soundness: Prove one, get five for free. In: CCS, pp. 1261–1272. ACM (2013)
20. Backes, M., Bendun, F., Unruh, D.: Computational soundness of symbolic zero-knowledge proofs: weaker assumptions and mechanized verification. In: Basin, D., Mitchell, J.C. (eds.) POST 2013. LNCS, vol. 7796, pp. 206–225. Springer, Heidelberg (2013)
21. Backes, M., Maffei, M., Mohammadi, E.: Computationally sound abstraction and verification of secure multi-party computations. In: FSTTCS, Schloss Dagstuhl, pp. 352–363 (2010)
22. Comon-Lundh, H., Cortier, V.: Computational soundness of observational equivalence. In: CCS, pp. 109–118. ACM (2008)
23. Comon-Lundh, H., Cortier, V., Scerri, G.: Security proof with dishonest keys. In: Degano, P., Guttman, J.D. (eds.) POST 2012. LNCS, vol. 7215, pp. 149–168. Springer, Heidelberg (2012)
24. Canetti, R., Herzog, J.: Universally composable symbolic security analysis. J. of Crypt. 24(1), 83–147 (2011)
25. Backes, M., Pfitzmann, B., Waidner, M.: A composable cryptographic library with nested operations (extended abstract). In: CCS, pp. 220–230 (2003)
26. Backes, M., Pfitzmann, B.: Symmetric encryption in a simulatable Dolev-Yao style cryptographic library. In: CSFW, pp. 204–218. IEEE (2004)
27. Backes, M., Laud, P.: Computationally sound secrecy proofs by mechanized flow analysis. In: CCS, pp. 370–379. ACM (2006)
28. Comon-Lundh, H., Hagiya, M., Kawamoto, Y., Sakurada, H.: Computational soundness of indistinguishability properties without computable parsing. In: Ryan, M.D., Smyth, B., Wang, G. (eds.) ISPEC 2012. LNCS, vol. 7232, pp. 63–79. Springer, Heidelberg (2012)
29. Sprenger, C., Backes, M., Basin, D., Pfitzmann, B., Waidner, M.: Cryptographically sound theorem proving. In: CSFW, pp. 153–166. IEEE (2006)
30. Blanchet, B., Fournet, C.: Automated verification of selected equivalences for security protocols. In: LICS 2005, pp. 331–340. IEEE (2005)

31. Backes, M., Malik, A., Unruh, D.: Computational soundness without protocol restrictions. In: CCS, pp. 699–711. ACM (2012)
32. Cheval, V., Cortier, V., Plet, A.: Lengths may break privacy – or how to check for equivalences with length. In: Sharygina, N., Veith, H. (eds.) CAV 2013. LNCS, vol. 8044, pp. 708–723. Springer, Heidelberg (2013)
33. Backes, M., Maffei, M., Unruh, D.: Computationally sound verification of source code. In: CCS, pp. 387–398. ACM (2010)
34. Backes, M., Mohammadi, E., Ruffing, T.: Bridging the gap from trace properties to uniformity (2014),
    http://www.infsec.cs.uni-saarland.de/~mohammadi/bridge.html
35. Unruh, D.: Programmable encryption and key-dependent messages. Technical report, IACR ePrint Report 2012/423 (2012)

A Secure Key Management Interface
with Asymmetric Cryptography

Marion Daubignard[1,2], David Lubicz[2], and Graham Steel[3]

[1] ANSSI, 51 Bvd de La Tour-Maubourg, 75007 Paris, France
[2] DGA.MI, BP 57419, 35174 Bruz Cedex, France
[3] INRIA Team Prosecco, 23 Avenue d'Italie, 75013 Paris, France

Abstract. Cryptographic devices such as Hardware Security Modules are only as secure as their application programming interfaces (APIs) that offer cryptographic functionality to the outside world. Design flaws and implementation errors in security APIs have been shown to cause vulnerabilities that may leak secrets such as keys and PINs. Ideally, we would like to design such interfaces in such a way that we can formally prove security properties, even in the presence of some corrupted keys. In this work, we propose the first such provably secure interface to support asymmetric key operations for key management: Cachin and Chandran's secure token interface supports asymmetric key operations only for encrypting and signing data, but not for managing keys, while Cortier and Steel handle only symmetric keys. Due to the fact that anyone can encrypt under a public key, in order to secure integrity of the keys under management, we must consider confidentiality and integrity properties separately and provide support for classical operations of public key infrastructure (e.g. certification of public keys).

1 Introduction

In a context of constant security threats combined with increasing heterogeneity of platforms and applications, developers are turning more and more to solutions based on secure hardware, whether it be a smartcard, Trusted Platform Module (TPM), or Hardware Security Module (HSM). In a typical architecture, the secure hardware contains cryptographic keys and the ability to perform some basic crypto operations which can be leveraged to ensure security for the whole system. However, designing the application programming interface (API) of such a device is difficult: it must allow the user to manage the keys on the device and access the crypto while preventing an attacker, who may in the worst case be able to make arbitrary calls to the API, from obtaining secrets. Many attacks have been found on the APIs of contemporary devices [2,3,5]. One promising approach to solving this problem is to design APIs such that one can formally prove security properties in the presence of a suitably powerful intruder. Such an approach has been applied both in the standard cryptographic model [4] and the symbolic or Dolev-Yao model [7]. However, neither of these designs present a scheme for managing keys using asymmetric cryptography, which is widely used

M. Abadi and S. Kremer (Eds.): POST 2014, LNCS 8414, pp. 63–82, 2014.

in practice since it provides a convenient way to bootstrap security without any pre-shared secrets. This shortcoming restricts applicability of the results. The contribution of this paper is to relax this restriction by presenting the design for an API that permits key management using asymmetric keys with security proofs in the symbolic model. For the symmetric key part of the API, we adapt slightly the API designed by Cortier and Steel [7]. For the asymmetric key part, since anyone can encrypt under a public key, we have to add an explicit mechanism for assuring the integrity of keys to be imported to prevent so-called "Trojan key" attacks [6]. We add signature keys for signing encryption under public keys and also separate certification keys, the latter used to manage the public key infrastructure (PKI) of keys and certificates. We show how to adapt the security labels given to keys by Cortier and Steel to this new scenario, with separate labels for confidentiality of the private key and integrity of the corresponding public key. This allows us to account for corruption in our proof. As far as we are aware, this is the first such design to be proposed with security proofs.

In the rest of the paper, we first introduce our symbolic model and explain the features of our API design in Section 2. We describe the API rules formally in Section 3, and then give the security properties and sketch proofs in Section 4. We describe some experiments implementing protocols with the API in Section 5 and draw conclusions in Section 6. Full proofs are given in a technical report [9].

Related Work. Cortier and Steel (CS) [7] proposed an API that supports only symmetric key cryptography, but can nonetheless be used to implement any secure symmetric key exchange protocol from the Clark-Jacob corpus. The main principle is that keys are arranged in a hierarchy of levels. Each key is associated to its level and the set of agents who are allowed to use it. This association is made when storing the key on the device, by including it as metadata stored with the key, and when encrypting the key for transfer, by tagging the encrypted key with exactly this information. The API rules are designed such that keys may only be encrypted by other keys which are higher in the hierarchy, i.e. they are at least one level higher and assigned to a set of agents that is equal to or smaller than the payload key. We generalise this notion slightly in our API. The CS API includes a notion of freshness for imported keys enforced by nonces. It has also recently been extended to accommodate key revocation [8]. Although we do not include these mechanisms in our API, we do not foresee any obstacle to these generalizations if needed.

Cachin and Chandran proposed an API with a quite different design [4]. They rely on the fact that all keys are stored on a central key server. Instead of assigning security attributes such as levels and agent identifiers to keys at creation time, they allow the key's role to evolve over time by logging all operations, and then disallowing operations that would be insecure by observing the log. They allow asymmetric keys to be managed by symmetric key cryptography, but do not allow asymmetric keys to be used for key management operations like export and import.

Other work has investigated the foundations of models for secure key management APIs: Kremer, Steel and Warinschi give a model that can be interpreted in the symbolic and computational cryptography worlds [12]. They show that the possibility of key corruption requires strong assumptions to be made on the key wrapping primitives in the computational model. Recent work by Künnemann, Kremer and Steel investigates composable notions of security for key management [11]. This is an appealing idea because it allows (almost) arbitrary secure cryptographic primitives to be used with the keys under management without having to repeat the security proofs, but currently only management with symmetric keys is supported.

2   Design of the API

We present the design of our API in an abstract 'Dolev-Yao' style symbolic model. We first describe the roles assigned to keys in our API. We then give the syntax and informal semantics for the message algebra and introduce our notion of *key handles* which extends previous designs.

2.1   Key Types

In order to limit the number of key roles in the API we consider that the asymmetric keys are double keys, with one part for encryption/decryption, and one for signature/verification. This means that the same key can be used as an input of both an encryption and a signature scheme. Thus, we have encryption/verification public keys and decryption/signature private keys. It is clear that in practice a double key can simply be obtained by the concatenation of a signature and encryption key pair and that a simple key can be simulated by a double key. Thus, we do not lose generality with this simplification. Signature keys are used to sign encryptions of other keys or messages. Asymmetric public keys are certified by certification keys (with a signature algorithm). The list of key roles that we are going to manipulate is: symmetric encryption/decryption keys, encryption/verification of signature double public keys, decryption/signature double private keys, verification of certificates public keys, certification private keys.

It is possible that the algorithm used to sign the certificates is the same as the one used to sign the encrypted messages. Nonetheless, it is important to distinguish the key roles to prevent a signature algorithm from being used as a certification oracle by an adversary. The different key roles and their associated types are summarised in the table 1. $\mathcal{T}$ denotes the set of key types.

2.2   Security Levels

The set of key security levels I is a finite set together with a partial strict order relation denoted $<$. We suppose that there is a minimal element in I denoted by 0. By definition, for all $x \in I \setminus 0$, we have $0 < x$. The 0 element represents the security level of public information. We are given a partition of I in two subsets:

Key	Role	Type
Priv Double	decryption/signature private key	privDecSign
Pub Double	encryption/verification of signature public key	pubEncVerif
Sym	symmetric encryption key	symEncDec
Pub Certif	certificate verification key	pubCertVerif
Priv Certif	certificate signature key	privCertSign

Fig. 1. Table of the set of key roles and types ($\mathcal{T}$)

- the levels $I_1 \subset I$ which correspond to the keys which can only deal with regular messages;
- the levels $I_2 \subset I$ which correspond to the keys which can be used to transport keys of level I_1.

Note that for $x \in I_1$ and $y \in I_2$, if x and y are comparable with the relation $<$ then we have necessarily $x < y$. We set $I_{>0} = I_1 \sqcup I_2 = I - \{0\}$ (where $\sqcup$ denotes a disjoint union).

2.3   Message Algebra

Messages are represented by a term algebra. We suppose a given set of agents Agent, a set of nonces Nonce and a set of keys Key. We are also given a set of variables Var in which we distinguish a set of key variables VarKey and a set of nonce variables VarNonce. All these sets are countably infinite. The term algebra is given by:

$$
\begin{aligned}
\text{Keyv} &::= \text{Key} \mid \text{VarKey} \mid inv(\text{Keyv}) \\
\text{Noncev} &::= \text{Nonce} \mid \text{VarNonce} \\
\text{Msg} &::= \text{Agent} \mid \text{Keyv} \mid \text{Noncev} \mid I \mid \mathcal{T} \mid \{\!|\text{Msg}|\!\}_{\text{Keyv}} \mid \{\text{Msg}\}_{\text{Keyv}} \\
&\quad \mid \Sigma(\text{Msg}, \text{Keyv}) \mid nhdl(\text{Msg}) \mid <\text{Msg}, \text{Msg}> \\
\text{Handle} &::= h^{\alpha}_{\text{Agent}}(\text{Noncev}, \text{Noncev}, \text{Msg}, \mathcal{T}, I, \mathscr{S}, \mathscr{S}) \mid h_{\text{Agent}}(\text{Noncev}, \text{Msg})
\end{aligned}
$$

where $\mathscr{S}$ is the set of subsets of Agent.

The set Keyv represents the set of keys and variable of keys. A term of the form $inv(k)$ with $k \in$ Key represents the private key associated to the public key k. The set Noncev is the set of nonces and variable of nonces. The terms of type Msg are made of elements of Agent, Keyv, Noncev together with constructors representing encryption, signature together with sets needed to represent the attributes of the handles. More precisely,

- the term $\{\!|m|\!\}_k$ represents the symmetric encryption of the message m with the key k;
- the term $\{m\}_k$ represents the asymmetric encryption of the message m with the double key k;
- the term $\Sigma(m, k)$ represents the signature of the message m with the double key k;

- the term nhdl() allows one to encapsulate a regular message which does not correspond to the transportation of a handle (see below);
- the term $< m_1, m_2 >$ represents the pair of the two messages $m_1, m_2 \in$ Msg.

For $n > 0$, $< m_1, < m_2, < \ldots, m_n >>>$ is shortened as $m_1, \ldots, m_n$.

2.4   Handles

The purpose of a key management API is to give access to cryptographic functionalities without giving direct access to sensitive keys stored on the device. Instead, an agent can manipulate the data by calling the API commands and referring to the keys by identifiers called *handles*, of which we define two types in our API:

- *key handles* used to protect integrity and confidentiality of the data on the device. They are typically used for keys and secret nonces.
- *integrity handles* used to protect the integrity of data on the device. They are typically used for certificates that have been verified.

Identifiers are meant to be a public way of referring to keys without revealing their values. Thus, knowing an identifier does not mean knowing the cryptographic value of a key. Then, to represent that an agent *can use a key*, we write that she *owns a handle referring to that key*. Intuitively, it means that there is a part of the memory of a secure device that the agent can make use of, and that contains such a data structure. In our framework, much as in that of [7], there is no mapping between memory owned by agents and secure devices; this is totally abstracted away and translates only in the ownership of handles. As a result, if two agents a and b share a key to communicate with one another, they each own a handle referring to this key, but nothing in our model represents whether they use different physical devices. Neither do we capture that one agent has all its handles on the same physical device. It might be the case that an agent has handles spread over multiple devices. Even then, our abstraction is sound from a security point of view in the sense that we consider operations that may not be functionally possible, but do not overlook any feasible call.

Let us now formally describe the handles that we use. Key handles are terms of the form $h_a^\alpha(N_1, N_2, m, T, i, S_1, S_2)$, with:

- the agent $a \in$ Agent who owns the handle;
- the identifier $N_1 \in$ Nonce (unique in the whole system) of the handle;
- if m is a double private key, then N_2 is the identifier of the associated certificate of the double public key, else $N_2 =$ Null;
- the message $m \in$ Msg (usually m is a key or a nonce) associated to the handle;
- the type $T \in \mathcal{T}$ of the message (see table 1 for a list of possible types);
- the triple $(i, S_1, S_2) \in I \times \mathscr{S} \times \mathscr{S}$ is the security level of the handle (the security policy of the API is based on this structure); the first element i gives the role of the key (data encryption or key transport) while the second

(respectively third) element gives a set of agents who must be uncorrupted for this key's confidentiality (respectively integrity) to hold - this is explained in details below.

- the label $\alpha \in \{r, g\}$ allows to distinguish the keys which have been generated by a ($\alpha = g$) from the keys which have been received and imported ($\alpha = r$).

Integrity handles are terms of the form $h_a(N_1, m)$ with an identifier N_1 and a message $m \in$ Msg. They are meant to model the preservation of the integrity of data by a signature : given as input a valid signature of a message m, the API produces an integrity handle containing the message m. Public key certificates usually refer to some signed public information. We are more precise than this and distinguish two elements, the pre-certificate and the certificate which is a signed pre-certificate. Indeed, the outcome of the certificate verification operation is a new pre-certificate stored under an integrity handle in the device.

In the following, for clarity, we use the notation $\mathcal{C}(N_1, N_2, N_3, k, T, i, S_1, S_2)$, which is a synonym of the concatenation of the terms $N_1, N_2, N_3, k, T, i, S_1, S_2 \in$ Msg, to represent a pre-certificate of double public key. We emphasize that the notation $\mathcal{C}(N_1, N_2, N_3, k, T, i, S_1, S_2)$ does not imply requirements on the type of the fields. Nonetheless, we say that a pre-certificate is *well-formed* if its fields correspond to the following terms and types (we also give their semantics):

- the identifier $N_1 \in$ Nonce of the certificate;
- the identifier $N_2 \in$ Nonce of the associated private key;
- the identifier $N_3 \in$ Nonce of the certification public key which allows to verify the certificate;
- a double public key $k \in$ Key;
- the type $T \in \mathcal{T}$ of k ;
- the associated private key handle security level $(i, S_1, S_2) \in I \times \mathscr{S} \times \mathscr{S}$.

Thus, matching asymmetric double keys stored in a physical device are typically formalized as:

- a key handle $h^{\alpha}(N_1, N_2, k, \text{privDecSign}, i, S_1, S_2)$ for the secret part,
- an integrity handle $h_.(N_2, \mathcal{C}(N_2, N_1, N_3, k, \text{pubEncVerif}, i, S_1, S_2))$ for the certificate of the public part.

We remark that we choose to trace the association of public and private part of asymmetric key pairs via their identifiers. This requires us to have system-wide identifiers for handles, in the sense that identifiers are independent of the secure hardware they are stored in. As a result, when importing a pre-certificate, the identifier cannot be generated at random. This explains why the pre-certificate contains a field corresponding to its identifier.

It seems important to underline that we follow a *"static"* approach in the sense that we do not compute the sets of agents S_1 and S_2 dynamically, but these are imposed once and for all when the cryptographic material is generated. The reasons why we need two sets are clarified in 3.1.

2.5 API Rules

The model that we present is a transition system inspired by [7]. It represents the evolution of the knowledge of the adversary and agents with the API calls. We use a set of knowledge predicates $\mathcal{P} = \{P_a | a \in \mathsf{Agent} \cup \{\mathsf{int}\}\}$, where int is a particular element representing the attacker. For term t, $P_a(t)$ means that a knows term t.

The system is formalized as a set of rules of the general form:

$$P_{b_1}(u_1), \ldots, P_{b_k}(u_k) \overset{N_1,\ldots,N_m}{\Longrightarrow} P_{b_{k+1}}(u_{k+1}), \ldots, P_{b_l}(u_l),$$

where u_i are terms, N_i are variables, $b_i \in \mathsf{Agent}$ for $i = 1, \ldots, l$ and the P_{b_i} are predicates. The rules define how to derive knowledge predicates. They are instantiated by substituting the variables by terms of the same type. In order to explain that, let $x_1, \ldots, x_n$ be elements of Var and let $t_1, \ldots, t_n$ be a set of terms. We denote by $\{x_1 \to t_1, \ldots, x_n \to t_n\}$ the substitution σ which replaces the variables x_i by the terms t_i for $i = 1, \ldots, n$. We say that σ is well-typed if the variables x_i and the terms t_i have the same types. In the sequel, we only consider well-typed substitutions. The application of the substitution σ on the term t is denoted by $t\sigma$. Classically, given a set of rules, we say that a state $\mathcal{S}'$ is reachable from a state $\mathcal{S}$ if there exists an instantiated rule in the set allowing to transition from $\mathcal{S}$ to $\mathcal{S}'$. The state therefore represents the set of terms known to each agent (including the intruder) at a moment in time. We then generalize this reachability definition to the transitive closure of a set of rules, which we denote $\Rightarrow^*$.

We let $\mathcal{S}_b$ be the part of a state indexed by b. Then, the state of the system is given by the family $\{\mathcal{S}_b | b \in \mathsf{Agent} \cup \{\mathsf{int}\}\}$. The notations $P_b(t)$ and $t \in \mathcal{S}_b$ are equivalent. In the sequel, we provide two kinds of rules. Firstly, API rules only deal with knowledge of a given agent. As a result, such a rule has the form : $P_a(u_1), \ldots, P_a(u_k) \overset{N_1,\ldots,N_m}{\Longrightarrow} P_a(u_{k+1}), \ldots, P_a(u_l)$ for some agent a different from the intruder int. It models that the inputs provided by an agent to an API call, i.e. $u_1, \ldots, u_k$, result in the output of new terms $u_{k+1}, \ldots, u_l$, which are added to the agent's knowledge. Secondly, other rules involve the adversary : they are rules with at least one predicate $P_{\mathsf{int}}(.)$.

2.6 Adversarial Model

As is usual in Dolev-Yao style models, the adversary is assumed to have complete control of the network. We further assume that the host machines (such as a desktop computer) in which the secure device might be embedded is also under the adversary's control. Therefore the interface between our trusted platform and the attacker controlled network is just our API. It can be argued as over-pessimistic, but it is sound from a security point of view to rely only on the trust we place in the tamper-resistant devices. This modeling choice results in rules translating direct transfers from the agent knowledge to the adversary knowledge and vice versa. A consequence is that the intruder can execute any command he likes on any device and use the result (or part of it) to form a command call to any other device.

On top of network control, we empower the adversary with the ability to *statically corrupt* agents. Formally, the set of agents is partitioned once and for all into honest and dishonest agents, and every key referred to by a handle owned at some point by a dishonest agent is leaked to the adversary. This models that some keys stored on secure hardware might be lost, perhaps due to side channel attacks or other abstracted events.

These choices are illustrated in Figure 3, in which the perimeter of control of the attacker encompasses all the knowledge of honest agents, the network, and dishonest agent devices. To simplify Figure 3, we have represented one agent per device, which need not be the case in practice. However, all keys of a dishonest agent are indifferently leaked to the adversary. This quite strong corruption model could be relaxed to a key-by-key corruption model.

Our corruption model defines an order relation on the set of keys. To a key k we can associate the set S_k of devices, the corruption of which implies that of a key. A key k_1 is more secure than k_2 if $S_{k_1} \subseteq S_{k_2}$. In other words, a key that relies on the integrity of just a few agents is considered more secure than one that depends on the integrity of a large number of agents.

With such adversary capabilities, we stress that the only elements on which we can state security results are those stored in the secure devices which we have formalized. Indeed, these devices are our only source of trust and the whole point of this security API is to protect the elements stored in these secure areas from unwanted interaction with an adversary. Concretely, this means that the elements on which we can prove security results are elements under handles, and only them, i.e. key or certificate values. Of course, regular data *can* be encrypted and decrypted using our API, but it is never hosted on a secure device : no handle is created to refer to them. In our framework, regular data is thus modeled in the form of messages coming unfettered from the network, on which we do not aim to provide security guarantees. This choice to 'only' protect keys makes total sense. Firstly, there is only a limited amount of space in tamper-resistant devices so that priorities have to be attributed. Secondly, if keys are suitably protected, then so is the data that they in turn protect, because there usually *are* intermediate workstations in which data is treated and hosted.

3   Symbolic Security of the API

3.1   Security Ordering

This order relation may look complex but is in fact quite natural. The security level of a handle is given by a set of agents S such that the corruption of any member of $S = S_1 \cup S_2$ would imply the corruption of the handle. In the API, we want to guarantee that if a particular set $S = S_1 \cup S_2$ of agents are honest, then a handle cannot be corrupted. In the case of a public key API, the keys are split into a public part (the certificate), whose value is known to everyone but the integrity of which must be guaranteed, and the private part which must

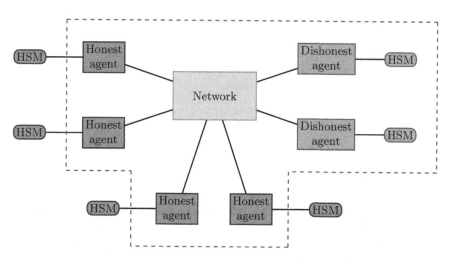

Fig. 2. Corruption model

be protected in confidentiality and integrity. The security of a key depends on both parts, but still it is important to be able to distinguish between these two aspects of security because we want to control the diffusion of the private key, while the integrity of the public part may depend on a long chain of certification.

For asymmetric keys, it may well be the case that S_1 is a rather large set (e.g. tracing a certification chain back to a root certificate) and yet we still want S_2 to be as small as possible (possibly just the agent who generated the key). Finally, it should be remarked that a key k which is wrapped by another asymmetric key k' should inherit from k' the control sets S_1 and S_2 even if k is symmetric.

Dividing the agent sets into public key and private key parts also affects our security properties. In the Cortier-Steel API, a secret key cannot be sent to an agent $a \in$ Agent outside of the control set S: indeed, it would be a violation of the security property in the case that a is a corrupt agent. In our setting, the security property guarantees the secrecy of a private key k if none of the agents of $S_1 \cup S_2$ are corrupted. We also want to ensure that no agent in $S_1 - S_2$ actually obtains the value of k, which they should not since they are not legitimate holders of the key. Both these security requirements appear in the statement of the main result of this paper (see Theorem 1). Identifying legitimate agents constitutes another important motivation for dividing the control set into two parts.

We emphasize that control sets are not to be computed dynamically, but that they are decided upon at key generation. Hence, the idea is not that a device should check integrity and secrecy of a key before using it to protect another key - that would not be possible anyway - but rather that our use of keys respect a particular security ordering, which in turn allows us to deduce which keys are impacted by the corruption of others.

Note that agent identifiers do not need to be known in advance. If identifiers come from a big enough space of possible values, one can always generate a new key referring to an agent identifier that has not been used before. The only restriction is that one cannot add the name of a new agent to the sets S of an existing key, for obvious security reasons.

3.2   The Rules of the Generic Asymmetric API

We describe the transition rules defining the security API. We recall that agents are not supposed to know key values and instead use identifiers to refer to them. However, as explained in 2.4, knowledge of an identifier N differs from ownership of a data structure pointing to a key identified by N. An agent a should not be able to use the value of a key if he does not own a handle $h(N, \dots)$ referring to it, a fact we denote as $P_a(h_a(N, \dots))$. In other words, writing $P_a(h_a(N, \dots))$ on the left-hand side of an API rule formalizes two things : the fact that agent a performs the corresponding API call with input N *and* the fact that there exists a handle $h_a(N, \dots)$ owned by agent a and identified by N. Symmetrically, writing $P_a(h_a(N, \dots))$ on the right-hand side of an API rule means that a new handle is created, owned by a and with identifier N.

When an agent wants to export a key to which he owns a handle, he provides its identifier as an input to the corresponding API function, which replaces this latter by the value of the key and its attributes when computing the real payload value to encrypt. Reciprocally, the injection functions must identify these patterns and create the appropriate handle rather than output the key value as a plaintext. Thus, we emphasize that there has to exist a distinction between handle translations and regular messages, which we materialize by the message container nhdl. Respect of the security ordering is enforced by appropriate checks when encrypting and decrypting payloads.

In the following rules, $N_i \in$ Noncev, $X_k, inv(X_k), Y_k, inv(Y_k) \in$ Keyv, $S_i \subseteq$ Agent and i (possibly indexed by an agent name) denotes an element in I.

Symmetric Key Generation. This rule allows the generation of key X_k of level i and control sets containing (S_1, S_2) by the agent e for the set of agents S_2, which is modeled by the following handle creation:

$$P_e(i), P_e(S_1), P_e(S_2) \xBybytes{N, X_k} P_e(h_e^g(N, \mathsf{Null}, X_k, \mathsf{symEncDec}, i, S_1, S_2 \cup \{e\}))$$
$$\textbf{(Sym Gen)}$$

Symmetric Encryption. This rule allows agent b to encrypt with the key X_k (to which he has a handle), a payload consisting of messages and handles $m_1, \dots, m_n$, where handles are translated into key values and attributes.

$$P_b(h_b^\alpha(N, \mathsf{Null}, X_k, \mathsf{symEncDec}, i, S_1, S_2)), P_b(m_1), \dots, P_b(m_n)$$
$$\Longrightarrow P_b(\{\!|m_1', \dots, m_n'|\!\}_{X_k}), \hspace{3cm} \textbf{(Sym Encrypt)}$$

with $b \in S_2$, $m_j, m_j' \in$ Msg and for $j = 1, \dots, n$:

- if $m_j = h_b^\alpha(N_j, N_j', X_{k,j}, T_j, i_j, S_{j,1}, S_{j,2})$ with $X_{k,j} = \mathsf{Keyv} \cup \mathsf{Noncev}$ then
    - if $i \in I_2$, $b \in \mathsf{Agent}$ and $(i_j, S_{j,1}, S_{j,2}) \prec (i, S_1, S_2)$ then we let
    $m_j' = N_j, N_j', X_{k,j}, T_j, i_j, S_{j,1}, S_{j,2}$;
    - else $m_j' = \varnothing$.
- else $m_j' = \mathsf{nhdl}(m_j)$.

Symmetric Decryption. The following rule lets agent b, provided he knows a handle pointing to key X_k, decrypt a ciphertext. Whenever a pattern consisting of a key and attributes is identified, it results in a suitable handle creation. Otherwise, the plaintext is output.

$$P_b(h_b^\alpha(N, \mathsf{Null}, X_k, \mathsf{symEncDec}, i, S_1, S_2)), P_b(\{\!|m_1, \ldots, m_n|\!\}_{X_k})$$
$$\Longrightarrow P_b(m_1'), \ldots, P_b(m_n'), \qquad\qquad\qquad \textbf{(Sym Decrypt)}$$

with $b \in S_2$, $m_j, m_j' \in \mathsf{Msg}$ and moreover for $j = 1, \ldots, n$:

- if $m_j = N_j, N_j', X_{k,j}, T_j, i_j, S_{j,1}, S_{j,2}$, then
    - if $i \in I_2$, $(i_j, S_{j,1}, S_{j,2}) \prec (i, S_1, S_2)$ then we set
    $m_j' = h_b^r(N_j, N_j', X_{k,j}, T_j, i_j, S_{j,1}, S_{j,2})$;
    - else $m_j' = \varnothing$.
- else
    - if $m_j = \mathsf{nhdl}(t_j)$ with $t_j \in \mathsf{Msg}$ then $m_j' = t_j$;
    - else $m_j' = \varnothing$.

Asymmetric Encryption/Signature Double Key Generation. The following rule allows agent e, given a certification key pair under handles[1], to generate $(X_k, inv(X_k))$ of level i_2 and control sets containing (S_1, S_2) for agent b. Note that we impose that generation and certificate issue are part of a single rule. The other possible choice is to output a handle on the public parts of the double key, and then have it certified in some certification rule. In any case, we must ensure that we only certify public keys whose integrity is ensured; in other words, we cannot write a command where the public keys are output in plaintext and resubmitted later for cetification without any integrity check.

$$P_e(h_e^\alpha(N_1, N_2, inv(Y_k), \mathsf{privCertSign}, i_1, S_{e,1}, S_{e,2})),$$
$$P_e(h_e(N_2, \mathcal{C}(N_2, N_1, N_{cert}, Y_k, \mathsf{pubCertVerif}, i_1, S_{e,1}, S_{e,2}))),$$
$$P_e(i_2), P_e(S_1), P_e(S_2), P_e(b) \overset{N_3, N_4, X_k}{\Longrightarrow}$$
$$P_e(h_e^g(N_3, N_4, inv(X_k), \mathsf{privDecSign}, i_2, S_{e,1} \cup S_{e,2} \cup S_1 \cup \{e\}, \{b, e\} \cup S_2)),$$
$$P_e(\Sigma(\mathcal{C}(N_4, N_3, N_2, X_k, \mathsf{pubEncVerif}, i_2, S_{e,1} \cup S_{e,2} \cup S_1 \cup \{e\}, \{b, e\} \cup S_2), inv(Y_k)))),$$
$$\textbf{(Asym Gen)}$$

with $e \in S_{e,2}$, $i_1, i_2 \in I_{>0}$, $\alpha \in \{r, g\}$ on condition that $i_2 < i_1$.

---

[1] We require that both parts of the certification key exist in the creating agent's secure hardware. This is not a compulsory security constraint, in the sense that a few modifications can be performed in the rules and proof to get rid of it. However, it seems reasonable in practice to perform such a verification.

Asymmetric Encryption with Signature. This API command enables an agent b, owner of a handle pointing to an asymmetric key Y_k, to encrypt and sign a payload for agents in $S_{c,2}$, provided b has an integrity handle for a public key X_k of agents in $S_{c,2}$. As in the symmetric case, handles in payload $m_1, \ldots, m_n$ are translated into real values and attributes. Encryption and signature needs to be an atomic command to enable the device to control what can be signed.

$$P_b(h_b^\alpha(N_1, N_2, inv(Y_k)), \mathrm{privDecSign}, i_b, S_{b,1}, S_{b,2}),$$
$$P_b(h_b(N_3, \mathcal{C}(N_3, N_4, N_5, X_k, \mathrm{pubEncVerif}, i_c, S_{c,1}, S_{c,2}))),$$
$$P_b(m_1), \ldots, P_b(m_n) \Longrightarrow P_b(\{m_1', \ldots, m_n'\}_{X_k}), P_b(\Sigma(\{m_1', \ldots, m_n'\}_{X_k}, inv(Y_k))),$$

(Asym SignEncrypt)

with $i_b, i_c \in I_{>0}$, $b \in S_{b,2}$, $m_j, m_j' \in \mathsf{Msg}$ and for $j = 1, \ldots, n$:

- if $m_j = h_b^\alpha(N_j, N_j', X_{k,j}, T_j, i_j, S_{j,1}, S_{j,2})$ with $X_{k,j} \in \mathsf{Keyv} \cup \mathsf{Noncev}$ then :
  - if $i_b, i_c \in I_2$, $(i_j, S_{j,1}, S_{j,2}) \prec (i_b, S_{b,1}, S_{b,2})$ and $(i_j, S_{j,1}, S_{j,2}) \prec (i_c, S_{c,1}, S_{c,2})$ then $m_j' = N_j, N_j', X_{k,j}, T_j, i_j, S_{j,1}, S_{j,2}$;
  - else $m_j' = \varnothing$.
- else $m_j' = \mathsf{nhdl}(m_j)$.

Asymmetric Decryption with Signature Verification. The following rule allows for decryption by the agent b of an authenticated ciphertext, using an integrity handle pointing to a public key Y_k to verify the signature and a handle pointing to a key $inv(X_k)$ to decrypt the ciphertext.

$$P_b(h_b(N_1, \mathcal{C}(N_1, N_2, N_3, Y_k, \mathrm{pubEncVerif}, i_c, S_{c,1}, S_{c,2}))),$$
$$P_b(h_b^\alpha(N_4, N_5, inv(X_k)), \mathrm{privDecSign}, i_b, S_{b,1}, S_{b,2})),$$
$$P_b(\{m_1, \ldots, m_n\}_{X_k}), P_b(\Sigma(\{m_1, \ldots, m_n\}_{X_k}, inv(Y_k)))$$
$$\Longrightarrow P_b(m_1'), \ldots, P_b(m_n'), \qquad\qquad \textbf{(Asym VerifDecrypt)}$$

with $i_b, i_c \in I_{>0}$, $b \in S_{b,2}$, $m_j, m_j' \in \mathsf{Msg}$ and for $j = 1, \ldots, n$:

- if $m_j = N_j, N_j', X_{k,j}, T_j, i_j, S_{j,1}, S_{j,2}$ then
  - if $i_b, i_c \in I_2$, $(i_j, S_{j,2}, S_{j,2}) \prec (i_b, S_{b,1}, S_{b,2})$ and $(i_j, S_{j,2}, S_{j,2}) \prec (i_c, S_{c,1}, S_{c,2})$ then $m_j' = h_b^r(N_j, N_j', X_{k,j}, T_j, i_j, S_{j,1}, S_{j,2})$;
  - else $m_j' = \varnothing$.
- if $m_j = \mathsf{nhdl}(t_j)$ for $t_j \in \mathsf{Msg}$ then $m_j' = t_j$.

Certification Key Generation. Given a certification key pair under handles, this rule allows agent e to generate a certification key pair $(X_k, inv(X_k))$ for agent b. As for asymmetric generation, generation and certificate issue are part of an atomic call. It eliminates the need for a certification command, for which deciding the key integrity could raise a problem.

$$P_e(h_e^\alpha(N_1, N_2, inv(Y_k)), \text{privCertSign}, i_e, S_{e,1}, S_{e,2})),$$
$$P_e(h_e(N_2, \mathcal{C}(N_2, N_1, N_{cert}, Y_k, \text{pubCertVerif}, i_e, S_{e,1}, S_{e,2}))),$$
$$P_e(i_b), P_e(S_1), P_e(S_2) \overset{N_3, N_4, X_k}{\Longrightarrow}$$
$$P_e(h_e^g(N_3, N_4, inv(X_k)), \text{privCertSign}, i_b, S_{e,1} \cup S_{e,2} \cup S_1 \cup \{e\}, \{e, b\} \cup S_2)),$$
$$P_e(\Sigma(\mathcal{C}(N_4, N_3, N_2, X_k, \text{pubCertVerif}, i_b, S_{e,1} \cup S_{e,2} \cup S_1 \cup \{e\}, \{e, b\} \cup S_2), inv(Y_k)))),$$

(Cert Gen)

with $e \in S_{e,2}$ and $i_b < i_e$.

Verification of a Certificate This rule allows an agent b, given an integrity handle pointing to a verification key and a pre-certificate signed by the matching certification key, to create the suitable integrity handle. More precisely, for $\Theta \in \{\text{EncVerif}, \text{CertVerif}\}$

$$P_b(\Sigma(\mathcal{C}(N_1, N_2, N_3, X_k, \text{pub}\Theta, i_c, S_{c,1}, S_{c,2}), inv(Y_k))),$$
$$P_b(h_b(N_3, \mathcal{C}(N_3, N_4, N_5, Y_k, \text{pubCertVerif}, i_e, S_{e,1}, S_{e,2}))) \Longrightarrow$$
$$P_b(h_b(N_1, \mathcal{C}(N_1, N_2, N_3, X_k, \text{pub}\Theta, i_c, S_{c,1}, S_{c,2}))),$$

(Cert Verif)

with $i_c, i_e \in I_{>0}$ and $(i_c, S_{c,1}, \varnothing) \prec (i_e, S_{e,1} \cup S_{e,2}, \varnothing)$.

3.3   Security Rationale

Below we will formally prove security properties for our design, but first we discuss the design features that prevent it from suffering from the kinds of attacks seen in the literature [2,3,5]. First, we maintain consistent attribute values: the attributes of a key are set once and for all when it is generated or imported onto a device, and when transporting keys, we export all attributes along with the value of the key and protect their integrity.

Second, we prevent 'Wrap and Decrypt' attacks [6, Alg.2] by the distinction between the way keys and data are tagged for encryption: either as a concatenation of key and attributes or encapsulated in a container nhdl. In an implementation of our design, a suitable tagging scheme should be used to ensure this distinction.

Key conjuring, i.e. the ability of the adversary to generate any number of (possibly related) keys on the device, is critical to a number of attacks [2]. Careful design of the decrypt command prevents this. The security proof includes an enumeration of the terms which the adversary can successfully submit to a decryption request (see **(Sign)** and **(SymEnc)**). Roughly, suitable terms are either wrapped under compromised keys or result from an honest use of the encrypt command.

Example. In Figure 3 we show the 'before' and 'after' states for three agents using the API in a typical configuration. In the 'before' state, there are no shared secrets. Alice and Bob both have accepted a copy of the CA's public

Alice

$h_A(id_2, \mathcal{C}(id_2, id_1, ., K_{CA}, \text{pubCertVerif}, 3, \{CA\}, \{CA\}))$
$h_A(id_3, \mathcal{C}(id_3, id_4, ., K_A, \text{pubCertVerif}, 3, \{A, CA\}, \{A\}))$
$h_A(id_4, id_3, inv(K_A), \text{privCertSign}, 3, \{A, CA\}, \{A\})$

CA

$h_{CA}(id_1, id_2, inv(K_{CA}), \text{privCertSign}, 3, \{CA\}, \{CA\})$
$h_{CA}(id_2, \mathcal{C}(id_2, id_1, ., K_{CA}, \text{pubCertVerif}, 3, \{CA\}, \{CA\}))$
$h_{CA}(id_3, \mathcal{C}(id_3, id_4, ., K_A, \text{pubCertVerif}, 3, \{A, CA\}, \{A\}))$
$h_{CA}(id_5, \mathcal{C}(id_5, id_6, ., K_B, \text{pubCertVerif}, 3, \{B, CA\}, \{B\}))$

Bob

$h_B(id_2, \mathcal{C}(id_2, id_1, ., K_{CA}, \text{pubCertVerif}, 3, \{CA\}, \{CA\}))$
$h_B(id_5, \mathcal{C}(id_5, id_6, ., K_A, \text{pubCertVerif}, 3, \{B, CA\}, \{A\}))$
$h_B(id_6, id_5, inv(K_A), \text{privCertSign}, 3, \{B, CA\}, \{A\})$

Before

___

After

Alice

$h_A(id_2, \mathcal{C}(id_2, id_1, ., K_{CA}, \text{pubCertVerif}, 3, \{CA\}, \{CA\}))$
$h_A(id_3, \mathcal{C}(id_3, id_4, ., K_A, \text{pubCertVerif}, 3, \{A, CA\}, \{A\}))$
$h_A(id_4, id_3, inv(K_A), \text{privCertSign}, 3, \{A, CA\}, \{A\})$
$h_A(id_5, \mathcal{C}(id_5, id_6, ., K_A, \text{pubCertVerif}, 3, \{B, CA\}, \{A\}))$
$h_A(id_7, \text{Null}, inv(K_{AB}), \text{symEncDec}, 2, \{A, B, CA\}, \{A, B\})$

CA

$h_{CA}(id_1, id_2, inv(K_{CA}), \text{privCertSign}, 3, \{CA\}, \{CA\})$
$h_{CA}(id_2, \mathcal{C}(id_2, id_1, ., K_{CA}, \text{pubCertVerif}, 3, \{CA\}, \{CA\}))$
$h_{CA}(id_3, \mathcal{C}(id_3, id_4, ., K_A, \text{pubCertVerif}, 3, \{A, CA\}, \{A\}))$
$h_{CA}(id_5, \mathcal{C}(id_5, id_6, ., K_B, \text{pubCertVerif}, 3, \{B, CA\}, \{B\}))$

Bob

$h_B(id_2, \mathcal{C}(id_2, id_1, ., K_{CA}, \text{pubCertVerif}, 3, \{CA\}, \{CA\}))$
$h_B(id_5, \mathcal{C}(id_5, id_6, ., K_A, \text{pubCertVerif}, 3, \{B, CA\}, \{A\}))$
$h_B(id_6, id_5, inv(K_A), \text{privCertSign}, 3, \{B, CA\}, \{A\})$
$h_B(id_3, \mathcal{C}(id_3, id_4, ., K_A, \text{pubCertVerif}, 3, \{A, CA\}, \{A\}))$
$h_B(id_7, \text{Null}, inv(K_{AB}), \text{symEncDec}, 2, \{A, B, CA\}, \{A, B\})$

Fig. 3. Operation of the API. See 3.3 for narration.

key certificate and placed it under an integrity handle and they have generated their own public-private keypairs. The CA has accepted public key certificates for each of these pairs. Here we are using integers to label key levels, arbitrarily assigning the long term keys the level 3.

To establish a shared secret, Alice and Bob first need to accept each others public key certificates. This can be done by requesting them from the CA. The CA uses the AsymEncryptSign command to sign the (public) message containing the certificate. Now Alice and Bob can use the certificate verification command to accept the certificates, generating new handles for them.

Now either Alice can generate a symmetric key (handle identified by id_7) and send it to Bob using AsymEncryptSign. Bob will use AsymDecryptVerify and accept the key. Alice and Bob can then exchange messages using the new symmetric key. Note that the new symmetric key is confidential between Alice and Bob, hence has a confidentiality control set S_2 containing only these identifiers, but for integrity it has inherited the dependence on the CA, hence S_1 contains the set of agents CA, Alice and Bob.

4   Security of the API in the Symbolic Model

4.1   Model of Security

In this section, we describe the capacity of the attacker in the spirit of Dolev and Yao [10], as formalized in [1].

Computation of new terms We denote by INTRUDER the set of rules which allow the attacker to build new terms from the ones that it has already. See figure 4 for a description of the rules.

The transitive reflexive closure of the preceding rules can be interpreted as the set of terms that an attacker can deduce from its knowledge at a certain state. In the following, we say that m is deducible from a set of terms T, which we denote by $T \vdash m$, if starting from the state S such that $S_{\text{int}} = T$ and for all $a \in$ Agent, $S_a = \emptyset$, there exists a state S' such that $S \Longrightarrow_{\text{INTRUDER}}^* S'$ and $m \in S'_{\text{int}}$. In the sequel, we slightly abuse notations as follows. If t is a term and S is a state, we write $t \in S$ (resp. $S \vdash t$) if $t \in \cup_{b \in \text{Agent} \cup \{\text{int}\}} S_b$ (resp. if $\cup_{b \in \text{Agent} \cup \{\text{int}\}} S_b \vdash t$).

Control of the network and corruption A couple of rules allows the intruder to control the network (see figure 4). He can intercept and forward or redirect at will messages sent over network channels. Moreover, to formalize corruption of agents (see beginning of Section 2.6), we suppose a given set H of honest agents. The device corruption rule (in figure 4) models the possibility for an adversary to open a device and retrieve all its information. A key-by-key corruption model can also be considered, as is done in [8].

4.2   Initial States

We impose a few requirements on the initial state of a device assuming they are set up in a secure environment. These requirements seem realistic in practice and

INTRUDER set of rules:

• Pair rules

$P_{\text{int}}(m_1), P_{\text{int}}(m_2) \Rightarrow P_{\text{int}}(< m_1, m_2 >)$

$P_{\text{int}}(< m_1, m_2 >) \Rightarrow P_{\text{int}}(m_1), P_{\text{int}}(m_2)$

• Symmetric cryptography

$P_{\text{int}}(X_k), P_{\text{int}}(m_1), ..., P_{\text{int}}(m_n) \Rightarrow P_{\text{int}}(\{m_1, ..., m_n\}_{X_k})$

$P_{\text{int}}(X_k), P_{\text{int}}(\{m_1, ..., m_n\}_{X_k}) \Rightarrow P_{\text{int}}(m_1), ..., P_{\text{int}}(m_n)$

• Asymmetric encryption

$P_{\text{int}}(X_k), P_{\text{int}}(m_1), ..., P_{\text{int}}(m_n) \Rightarrow P_{\text{int}}(\{m_1, ..., m_n\}_{X_k})$

$P_{\text{int}}(inv(X_k)), P_{\text{int}}(\{m_1, ..., m_n\}_{X_k})$
$\Rightarrow P_{\text{int}}(m_1), ..., P_{\text{int}}(m_n)$

• Message container

$P_{\text{int}}(m) \Rightarrow P_{\text{int}}(\text{nhdl}(m))$

$P_{\text{int}}(\text{nhdl}(m)) \Rightarrow P_{\text{int}}(m)$

• Signature

$P_{\text{int}}(\Sigma(m, X_k)) \Rightarrow P_{\text{int}}(m)$

$P_{\text{int}}(X_k), P_{\text{int}}(m)$
$\Rightarrow P_{\text{int}}(\Sigma(m, X_k))$

CONTROL set of rules:

• Control of the network

$P_a(m) \Rightarrow P_{\text{int}}(m)$

$P_{\text{int}}(m) \Rightarrow P_a(m)$

• Device corruption

$P_a(h_a^\alpha(N_1, N_2, m, T, i, S_1, S_2))$
$\Rightarrow P_{\text{int}}(m)$, where $a \notin H$

In the above rules, $m, m_i \in \text{Msg}$, $X_k \in \text{Keyv}$ and H is the set of honest agents.

Fig. 4. Rules modeling the adversary abilities

allow us to start from states compatible with the security policy. In the initial states, we assume that the attacker knows some public information like the set of key levels and the set of agents.

Definition 1. *A state S_0 is said to be* initial *if it satisfies the following hypotheses :*

1. *the set of terms known by the agents and the intruder are atomic : for all $a \in \text{Agent} \cup \{\text{int}\}$, $S_a \subseteq \text{Handle} \cup \text{Key} \cup \text{Nonce} \cup \text{Agent} \cup \mathcal{T} \cup I \cup \mathscr{S}$ and moreover $\mathcal{T} \cup I \cup \mathscr{S} \subseteq S_{\text{int}}$.*

2. *all terms stored under handles are secret : for $a \in \text{Agent}$, if $h_a^\alpha(N_1, N_2, m, T, i, S_1, S_2) \in S_a$ then for $b \in \text{Agent} \cup \{\text{int}\}$, $m \notin S_b$.*

3. *all key handles known by an agent point to an atomic element : for $a \in \text{Agent}$, if $h_a^\alpha(N_1, N_2, m, T, i, S_1, S_2) \in S_a$ then $m \in \text{Key} \cup \text{Nonce}$.*

4. *the owner of a key handle is in the set of legitimate agents for this handle. More precisely, we impose that for all $a \in \text{Agent}$, if $h_a^\alpha(N_1, N_2, m, T, i, S_1, S_2) \in S_a$ then $a \in S_2$.*

5. *any public key certificate under handle corresponds to a private key stored by a rightful agent: $\forall b \in \text{Agent}$, if $h_b(N_1, \mathcal{C}(N_1, N_2, N_3, X_k, \text{pub}\Theta, i, S_1, S_2)) \in S_b$, then there exists $a \in S_2$ so that*

$$h_a^\alpha(N_2, N_1, inv(X_k), \text{priv}\Theta', i, S_1, S_2) \in S_a,$$

with $(\Theta, \Theta') \in \{(\text{EncVerif}, \text{DecSign}), (\text{CertVerif}, \text{CertSign})\}$.

6. *the key handles form a coherent set: for all $a, a' \in \text{Agent}$, $h_a^\alpha(N_1, N_2, m, T, i, S_1, S_2) \in S_a$ and $h_{a'}^{\alpha'}(N_1', N_2', m, T', i', S_1', S_2') \in S_{a'}$ we have $N_1 = N_1', N_2 = N_2', T = T', i = i', S_1 = S_1'$ and $S_2 = S_2'$.*

We can now define the set of states for which we can prove a security property.

Definition 2. *We say that a state $\mathcal{S}$ is* accessible *from an initial state $\mathcal{S}_0$ if it is reachable by applying a finite number of times the rules of the set* API, INTRUDER *and* CONTROL *to $\mathcal{S}_0$, i.e. if $\mathcal{S}_0 \Rightarrow^*_{\mathsf{API} \cup \mathsf{CONTROL} \cup \mathsf{INTRUDER}} \mathcal{S}$.*

4.3   Security Properties and Sketch of Proof

The security of the API should entail that given a state $\mathcal{S}$, secret key values of honest agents should not be known to the intruder. But we would also like to ensure that these values are only used by rightful agents. Secret key values of honest agents are messages $m \in \mathsf{Msg}$ for which there exists a handle of the form $h^\alpha_a(.,.,m,.,.,S_1,S_2)$ with $a \in H$ and $S_1, S_2 \subseteq H$. As the set of legitimate users of m is S_2, the property that we want to prove is formalized as:

$$\forall a \in H, \forall m \in \mathsf{Msg}, \forall i \in I_{>0}, \forall \alpha \in \{r,g\}, \forall S_1, S_2 \subseteq H,$$
$$\mathcal{S} \vdash h^\alpha_a(.,.,m,.,i,S_1,S_2) \;\Rightarrow\; \mathcal{S} \nvdash m \text{ and } a \in S_2 \quad \textbf{(Sec)}$$

If this property is clearly something we want from a security API, it seems legitimate to discuss whether we should require some other security results. Other than confidentiality, security usually also comprises integrity or authenticity aspects. In our framework, this can translate into two different requirements. On one hand, integrity of the attribute values amongst various handles owned by honest agents pointing to the same key seems highly desirable. It can be formalized as :

$$\forall a \in H, \forall b \in \mathsf{Agent}, \forall m \in \mathsf{Msg},$$
$$\forall i, i' \in I_{>0}, \forall \alpha, \alpha' \in \{r,g\}, \forall S_1, S_2 \subseteq H, \forall S'_1, S'_2 \subseteq \mathsf{Agent},$$
$$\mathcal{S} \vdash h^\alpha_a(N_1, N_2, m, T, i, S_1, S_2) \wedge \mathcal{S} \vdash h^\alpha_a(N'_1, N'_2, m, T', i', S'_1, S'_2) \;\Rightarrow\;$$
$$N_1 = N'_1 \wedge N_2 = N'_2 \wedge T = T' \wedge i = i' \wedge S_1 = S'_1 \wedge S_2 = S'_2 \quad \textbf{(Intg)}$$

On the other hand, since we consider an asymmetric cryptography setting, an agent should be able to trust the value of an integrity handle he owns, on condition it points to a public key certificate whose control sets S_1 and S_2 consist of honest agents. More precisely, if S_1, S_2 contain only honest agents, then there exists a private key handle associated to this certificate the attributes of which are coherent with that of the certificate. This in turn is the meaning of the following property :

$$\forall a \in H, \forall N_1, N_2, N_3 \in \mathsf{Nonce}, \forall i \in I_{>0}, \forall S_1, S_2 \subseteq H \text{ with}$$
$$\mathcal{S} \vdash^* h_a(N_1, \mathcal{C}(N_1, N_2, N_3, X_k, \mathsf{pub}\Theta, i, S_1, S_2)) \;\Rightarrow\; \exists b \in S_2 \text{ such that}$$
$$\mathcal{S} \vdash^* h^\alpha_b(N_2, N_1, inv(X_k), \mathsf{priv}\Theta', i, S_1, S_2). \quad \textbf{(Cert)}$$

where $(\Theta, \Theta') \in \{(\mathsf{EncVerif}, \mathsf{DecSign}), (\mathsf{CertVerif}, \mathsf{CertSign})\}$.

We can now give the principal result of this paper, stating the security of our API if it is correctly initialised.

Theorem 1 (Security of the API) *Let S_0 be an initial state and S be an accessible state from S_0. Then S satisfies the properties* **Sec**, **Intg** *and* **Cert**.

Proof. We present a sketch of proof (details can be found in [9]). First we consider a more powerful attacker with access to all values stored in compromised hardware as well as to all messages m associated to handles of the form $h_a^\alpha(.,.,m,.,.,S_1,S_2)$ where $S_1, S_2 \subsetneq H$ even if a is honest. The classic adversary can learn these terms anyway, and this extension ensures stability of intruder knowledge when applying rules from INTRUDER $\cup$ CONTROL.

It yields a generalized deduction definition: we write that $S \vdash^* t$ when $\cup_{b \in \mathsf{Agent} \cup \{int\}} S_b \cup \{m, N_1, N_2 | h_a^\alpha(N_1, N_2, m, .,., S_1, S_2) \in S, S_1 \subsetneq H$ or $S_2 \subsetneq H, a \in \mathsf{Agent}\} \cup \{m, N_1, N_2 | h_a^\alpha(N_1, N_2, m, .,.,.,.) \in S, a \notin H\} \cup \{m | h_a(.,m) \in S\} \vdash t$.

We then consider a stronger version of the property (**Sec**):

$$\forall a \in H, \forall m \in \mathsf{Msg}, \forall i \in I_{>0}, \forall \alpha \in \{r, g\}, \forall S_1, S_2 \subseteq H,$$
$$S \vdash^* h_a^\alpha(.,.,m,.,i,S_1,S_2) \Rightarrow S \not\vdash^* m, a \in S_2 \text{ and } m \in \mathsf{Key} \cup \mathsf{Nonce}. \tag{Sec*}$$

Intuitively, the property (**Sec***) means that the values stored in the handles of honest agents are always of type Key or Nonce and are not deducible even with the extended deduction rule $\vdash^*$. It is clear that in order to prove the theorem, it is enough to prove the same statement with the stronger version of the property (**Sec**). In the technical report [9], we prove by induction that the property (**Sec***) is invariant under the API rules. To prove this, we introduce four invariants : the first, (**SymEnc**), states that the only well-formed symmetric encryption terms that an adversary can build are either encrypted under a compromised key, or results from an honest and well-formed request to the symmetric encryption command:

$$\forall u, k \in \mathsf{Msg}, S \vdash^* \{u\}_k \Rightarrow S \vdash^* k$$
OR $\exists S_1, S_2 \subseteq H, a \in S_2$ such that $S \vdash^* h_a(.,.,k,.,i,S_1,S_2)$ and $u = u'_1, \ldots, u'_p$
with $\quad\bullet$ either $u'_j = \mathsf{nhdl}(m_j)$
$\quad\quad\bullet$ or $u'_j = N_{j,1}, N_{j,2}, m_j, T_j, i_j, S_{j,1}, S_{j,2}, \; (i_j, S_{j,1}, S_{j,2}) \prec (i, S_1, S_2)$
$\quad\quad$ and $S \vdash^* h_a(N_{j,1}, N_{j,2}, m_j, T_j, i_j, S_{j,1}, S_{j,2})$ (**SymEnc**)

The next invariant states that all asymmetric encryption terms deducible from a reachable state have a payload deducible by the attacker or result from an honest request to the asymmetric encryption command.

$$\forall u, \quad K \in \mathsf{Msg}, \mathcal{S} \vdash^* \{u\}_K \Rightarrow \mathcal{S} \vdash^* u$$

OR $\exists S_{c,1}, S_{c,2} \subseteq H, b \in S_{c,2}$ such that

$\qquad \mathcal{S} \quad \vdash^* h_b(., \mathcal{C}(.,.,.,K, \mathsf{pubEncVerif}, i_c, S_{c,1}, S_{c,2}))$ and $u = u'_1, \dots, u'_p$

$\qquad$ with $\quad \bullet$ either $u'_j = \mathsf{nhdl}(m_j)$

$\qquad\qquad\qquad \bullet$ or $u'_j = N_{j,1}, N_{j,2}, m_j, T_j, i_j, S_{j,1}, S_{j,2}$,

$\quad (i_j, \quad S_{j,1}, S_{j,2}) \prec (i, S_{c,1}, S_{c,2})$ and $\mathcal{S} \vdash^* h_b(N_{j,1}, N_{j,2}, m_j, T_j, i_j, S_{j,1}, S_{j,2})$

$\hfill$ (**AsymEnc**)

We need a similar invariant for signed terms the adversary is able to obtain (**Sign**). The invariant here is slightly more involved since we have to deal with both the issue of certificates when generating asymmetric keys and asymmetric wrapping commands:

$$\forall\, u, k \in \mathsf{Msg}, \mathcal{S} \vdash^* \Sigma(u, k) \Rightarrow \mathcal{S} \vdash^* k$$

OR $\quad \exists S'_1, S'_2 \subseteq H, e \in S'_2$ such that

$\qquad \mathcal{S} \vdash^* h_e(.,., k, \mathsf{privCertSign}, i_1, S'_1, S'_2)$

$\qquad$ and $u = \mathcal{C}(N_4, N_3, N_2, X_k, \mathsf{pub}\Theta, i_2, S_1 \cup \{e\}, S_2 \cup \{b, e\})$

$\qquad$ with $S'_1 \cup S'_2 \subset S_1, \; e \in S'_2, i_2 < i_1, \Theta \in \{\mathsf{EncVerif}, \mathsf{CertSign}\}$

OR $\quad \exists S_{c,1}, S_{c,2} \subseteq H, b \in S_{c,2}$ such that

$\qquad \mathcal{S} \vdash^* h_b(., \mathcal{C}(.,.,.,K, \mathsf{pubEncVerif}, i_c, S_{c,1}, S_{c,2}))$ and $u = \{u'_1, \dots, u'_p\}_K$

$\qquad$ with $\quad \bullet$ either $u'_j = \mathsf{nhdl}(m_j)$

$\qquad\qquad\qquad \bullet$ or $u'_j = N_{j,1}, N_{j,2}, m_j, T_j, i_j, S_{j,1}, S_{j,2}$,

$\quad (i_j, S_{j,1}, S_{j,2}) \prec (i, S_{c,1}, S_{c,2})$ and $\mathcal{S} \vdash^* h_b(N_{j,1}, N_{j,2}, m_j, T_j, i_j, S_{j,1}, S_{j,2})$

$\hfill$ (**Sign**)

To conclude, we remark moreover that from its definition, an initial state satisfies the properties (**Sec***), (**Cert**), (**SymEnc**), (**AsymEnc**), (**Sign**).

5   Experiments

We have used our API to implement some asymmetric key protocols based on well-known examples from the Clark-Jacob corpus. Since we impose a secure encryption and signature scheme, our versions of protocols are secure even when the original is not. For example, our implementation of Needham-Schroeder public key avoids Lowe's attack because all messages are signed. Full details together with a Prolog script for generating API commands from protocols are available at http://www.lsv.ens-cachan.fr/~steel/genericapi/asym.

6   Conclusion

We have given the design for a key management API for cryptographic devices that allows the use of asymmetric keys for managing keys, together with security

properties and proofs in the Dolev Yao model. This is the first such design with
security proofs as far as we are aware. In future work we will add more flexibility
to the API. In particular it should be easy to adapt the design to other security
orderings not necessarily based on agent identifiers.

References

1. Abadi, M., Rogaway, P.: Reconciling two views of cryptography. In: van Leeuwen,
   J., Watanabe, O., Hagiya, M., Mosses, P., Ito, T. (eds.) TCS 2000. LNCS, vol. 1872,
   pp. 3–22. Springer, Heidelberg (2000)
2. Bond, M.: Attacks on cryptoprocessor transaction sets. In: Koç, Ç.K., Naccache,
   D., Paar, C. (eds.) CHES 2001. LNCS, vol. 2162, pp. 220–234. Springer, Heidelberg
   (2001)
3. Bortolozzo, M., Centenaro, M., Focardi, R., Steel, G.: Attacking and fixing
   PKCS#11 security tokens. In: Proceedings of the 17th ACM Conference on Computer and Communications Security (CCS 2010), Chicago, Illinois, USA, pp. 260–
   269. ACM Press (2010)
4. Cachin, C., Chandran, N.: A secure cryptographic token interface. In: Computer
   Security Foundations (CSF-22), Long Island, New York, pp. 141–153. IEEE Computer Society Press (2009)
5. Clulow, J.: The design and analysis of cryptographic APIs for security devices.
   Master's thesis, University of Natal, Durban (2003)
6. Clulow, J.: On the security of PKCS #11. In: Walter, C.D., Koç, Ç.K., Paar, C.
   (eds.) CHES 2003. LNCS, vol. 2779, pp. 411–425. Springer, Heidelberg (2003)
7. Cortier, V., Steel, G.: A generic security API for symmetric key management
   on cryptographic devices. In: Backes, M., Ning, P. (eds.) ESORICS 2009. LNCS,
   vol. 5789, pp. 605–620. Springer, Heidelberg (2009)
8. Cortier, V., Steel, G., Wiedling, C.: Revoke and let live: A secure key revocation
   API for cryptographic devices. In: 19th ACM Conference on Computer and Communications Security (CCS 2012), Raleigh, USA. ACM (October 2012)
9. Daubignard, M., Lubicz, D., Steel, G.: A secure key management interface with asymmetric cryptography. Technical Report RR8274, INRIA (2013),
   http://hal.inria.fr/hal-00805987
10. Dolev, D., Yao, A.C.-C.: On the security of public key protocols. IEEE Transactions
    on Information Theory 29(2), 198–207 (1983)
11. Kremer, S., Künnemann, R., Steel, G.: Universally composable key-management.
    IACR Cryptology ePrint Archive 2012, 189 (2012)
12. Kremer, S., Steel, G., Warinschi, B.: Security for key management interfaces. In:
    Proceedings of the 24th IEEE Computer Security Foundations Symposium (CSF
    2011), Cernay-la-Ville, France, pp. 266–280. IEEE Computer Society Press (June
    2011)

Abstract Channels
and Their Robust Information-Leakage Ordering

Annabelle McIver[1], Carroll Morgan[2,*], Geoffrey Smith[3], Barbara Espinoza[3],
and Larissa Meinicke[4]

[1] Macquarie University, Australia
annabelle.mciver@mq.edu.au
[2] University of New South Wales and NICTA, Australia
carrollm@cse.unsw.edu.au
[3] Florida International University, USA
{smithg,bespi009}@cis.fiu.edu
[4] University of Queensland, Australia
l.meinicke@uq.edu.au

Abstract. The observable output of a probabilistic system that processes a secret input might reveal some information about that input. The system can be modelled as an information-theoretic channel that specifies the probability of each output, given each input. Given a prior distribution on those inputs, entropy-like measures can then quantify the amount of information leakage caused by the channel. But it turns out that the conventional channel representation, as a matrix, contains structure that is redundant with respect to that leakage, such as the labeling of columns, and columns that are scalar multiples of each other. We therefore introduce *abstract channels* by quotienting over those redundancies.

A fundamental question for channels is whether one is worse than another, from a leakage point of view. But it is difficult to answer this question robustly, given the multitude of possible prior distributions and leakage measures. Indeed, there is growing recognition that different leakage measures are appropriate in different circumstances, leading to the recently proposed *g*-leakage measures, which use gain functions *g* to model the operational scenario in which a channel operates: the *strong g-leakage pre-order* requires that channel *A* never leak more than channel *B*, for any prior and any gain function. Here we show that, on abstract channels, the strong *g*-leakage pre-order is *antisymmetric*, and therefore a *partial order*.

It was previously shown [1] that the strong *g*-leakage ordering is implied by a structural ordering called *composition refinement*, which requires that $A = BR$, for some channel R; but the converse was not established in full generality, left open as the so-called *Coriaceous Conjecture*. Using ideas from [2], we here confirm the *Coriaceous Conjecture*. Hence the strong *g*-leakage ordering and composition refinement coincide, giving our partial order both structural- and leakage-testing significance.

---

* NICTA is funded by the Australian Government through the Department of Communications and the Australian Research Council through the ICT Centre of Excellence Program.

M. Abadi and S. Kremer (Eds.): POST 2014, LNCS 8414, pp. 83–102, 2014.

1 Introduction

A fundamental goal in computer security is the protection of confidential information from improper disclosure. Yet this goal often cannot be achieved perfectly, because certain leaks of confidential information are unavoidable. The importance of *quantitative information flow* is therefore that it enables us to say that certain information leaks are "small" and hence tolerable.

Consider a channel C that takes as input a secret X with *prior* probability distribution π, and produces (perhaps probabilistically) an observable output Y. If an adversary knows π and C, then its *initial uncertainty* about X will depend on π. But each separate output value y then allows it to update its knowledge about X's prior π to a *posterior* distribution $p_{X|y}$ via Bayesian reasoning. Hence its expected *remaining uncertainty* about X, after seeing the output of C, will depend on the set of possible posterior distributions on X and their probabilities. The *leakage* is the difference between the initial and final uncertainties.

This general quantitative framework is clear enough; but there is of course more than one way to measure the "uncertainty" associated with a probability distribution: popular choices include Shannon entropy [3], guessing entropy [4], min-entropy [5], and the family of g-entropies [1] each determined by its own gain function g. Each of those leakage measures has its own operational significance, which might or might not suit the operational scenario. Moreover, the leakage caused by some C will also depend on its prior π. As a result, if we consider the *leakage ordering* of two channels A and B (both taking X as input), it is difficult to give an answer that is *robust*, i.e. that does not depend on the particular prior and leakage measure. But such a robust ordering is indispensable if we aim to develop software through stepwise refinement, based on general laws that hold in *all contexts*.

There is such a robust order for *deterministic channels*, provided by the *Lattice of Information* [6]. Any deterministic channel from X to Y induces a *partition* on $\mathcal{X}$, where x_1 and x_2 belong to the same block iff they map to the same output.[1] That is, each block of the partition is the pre-image of some output y.

Definition 1 (Partition refinement). *Two deterministic channels A, B on input X are said to be in the* partition refinement *relation, written $A \sqsubseteq B$, just when the partition induced by A on $\mathcal{X}$ is refined (as a partition) by the partition induced by B: the blocks of B are formed by subdividing blocks of A.*

For example a deterministic channel A taking a secret person X to her country of birth would induce the partition in Fig. 1(a); the channel B that in some cases gives the state as well leads to Fig. 1(b).

It is intuitively clear that an adversary will *always* prefer B to A, whatever the input prior π; and this is supported by the following theorem due to Yasuoka & Terauchi, and Malacaria [7,8].

Theorem 1. *If A, B are deterministic, then $A \sqsubseteq B$ iff A never leaks more than B, on any prior π and under Shannon-entropy, min-entropy, or guessing-entropy leakage.*

---

[1] We use $\mathcal{X}$ for the set of inputs, with x being a value in $\mathcal{X}$ and X being a random variable on $\mathcal{X}$.

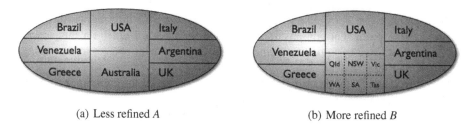

(a) Less refined A (b) More refined B

Fig. 1. Partition refinement

The "only if" direction of this theorem can be seen as expressing the partition refinement order's *soundness* with respect to the leakage order. More interestingly, the "if" direction can be seen as expressing its *completeness*, for it says that the *only* way for A to never leak more than B is for A's partition to be refined by B's.[2] Another way of understanding this result is to say that partition refinement is an order on deterministic channels with both a *structural-* and a *leakage-testing* characterization.

The main goal of this paper is to generalize these nice properties from *deterministic* to *probabilistic* channels. A first issue, however, is that the story for deterministic channels is not quite as nice as it appears, in that partition refinement is not in fact a *partial order* on deterministic channels, but only a *pre-order*. Because distinct deterministic channels can induce the same partition on X (since the particular *names* of the outputs do not matter), partition refinement is not antisymmetric. While this problem is rather obvious in the case of deterministic channels, we will see that it is more subtle for probabilistic channels, and this will lead us to introduce *abstract channels* formed by quotienting away the redundant structure of classical channel matrices.

We explore the fundamental properties of abstract channels, including their canonical representation by reduced matrices and by hyper-distributions. Turning to their robust leakage ordering, we consider a generalization of partition refinement called *composition refinement* ($\sqsubseteq_\circ$) [2,1], where $A \sqsubseteq_\circ B$ holds if A can be expressed as B followed by "post-processing". In our first major result, we show that composition refinement is antisymmetric, and therefore a partial order, on abstract channels. Next we consider the soundness and completeness of composition refinement with respect to leakage orders. It was proved in [1,9] that composition refinement implies the *strong g-leakage ordering* ($\leq_G$), where $A \leq_G B$ holds if A never leaks more than B, on any prior distribution and any gain function. The converse, however, was not proved in full generality, and was left as the *Coriaceous Conjecture*. In our second major result, we use ideas from [2] to prove the Coriaceous Conjecture. Hence composition refinement and the strong g-leakage ordering *coincide*, giving us a partial order on abstract channels that has both structural- and leakage-testing significance.

---

[2] The "if" direction is actually easy to see—for if A's partition is *not* refined by B's, then there must exist x_1 and x_2 that belong to the *same* block of B, but to *different* blocks of A. On a prior that gives non-zero probability only to x_1 and x_2, B leaks nothing about X, while A leaks everything.

In summary, our principal contributions are (1) the concept of *abstract channels*, which we argue to be the fundamental mathematical space for information-theoretic leakage; (2) the proof that composition refinement is a *partial order* on this space; and (3) the proof that composition refinement is *complete* with respect to the strong *g*-leakage ordering.

The rest of the paper is structured as follows: Section 2 presents preliminaries; Section 3 introduces abstract channels; Section 4 presents composition refinement and proves that it is a partial order on abstract channels; Section 5 proves that composition refinement implies the strong *g*-leakage ordering; Section 6 proves the converse, resolving the Coriaceous Conjecture; Section 7 gives a monadic presentation of composition refinement; Section 8 discusses limits of the information-theoretic perspective with respect to computationally-bounded adversaries; Section 9 discusses related work; and Section 10 concludes.

2 Preliminaries: Channels and Leakage Measures

We begin by recalling the basic definitions of information-theoretic channels [10]. A *channel* is a triple $(\mathcal{X}, \mathcal{Y}, C)$, where $\mathcal{X}$ and $\mathcal{Y}$ are finite sets (of secret input values and observable output values) and C is an $|\mathcal{X}| \times |\mathcal{Y}|$ *channel matrix* whose entries are between 0 and 1 and whose rows each sum to 1; the intent is that $C_{x,y}$ is the conditional probability of output y given input x. Channel C is *deterministic* if each entry of C is either 0 or 1, implying that each input row contains a single 1 which identifies its unique corresponding output.

For *prior distribution* π on $\mathcal{X}$, the *joint distribution* on $\mathcal{X} \times \mathcal{Y}$ is $p(x, y) = \pi[x] C_{x,y}$, with jointly distributed random variables X, Y whose marginal probabilities are given by $p(x) = \sum_y p(x, y)$ and $p(y) = \sum_x p(x, y)$, and whose conditional probabilities are given by $p(y|x) = p(x,y)/p(x)$ (if $p(x)$ is non-zero) and $p(x|y) = p(x,y)/p(y)$ (if $p(y)$ is non-zero). Note that p_{XY} is the *unique* joint distribution that recovers π and C, in that $p(x) = \pi[x]$ and $p(y|x) = C_{x,y}$ (if $p(x)$ is non-zero).[3]

For a given y (such that $p(y)$ is non-zero), the conditional probabilities $p(x|y)$ for each $x \in \mathcal{X}$ form the *posterior distribution* $p_{X|y}$, which is the knowledge that the adversary learns about X by seeing output y.

Example 1. Given $\mathcal{X} = \{x_1, x_2, x_3\}$, and $\mathcal{Y} = \{y_1, y_2, y_3, y_4\}$, and (the uniform) prior $\pi = (1/3, 1/3, 1/3)$, consider channel C and its associated joint matrix J as follows:

C	y_1	y_2	y_3	y_4
x_1	1	0	0	0
x_2	0	1/2	1/4	1/4
x_3	1/2	1/3	1/6	0

leads via π to the joint matrix

J	y_1	y_2	y_3	y_4
x_1	1/3	0	0	0
x_2	0	1/6	1/12	1/12
x_3	1/6	1/9	1/18	0

By summing J's columns we get the (marginal) distribution $p_Y = (1/2, 5/18, 5/36, 1/12)$ and by normalizing the columns we get the posterior distributions $p_{X|y_1} = (2/3, 0, 1/3)$, $p_{X|y_2} = (0, 3/5, 2/5)$, $p_{X|y_3} = (0, 3/5, 2/5)$ and $p_{X|y_4} = (0, 1, 0)$. □

---

[3] When necessary to avoid ambiguity, we write distributions with subscripts, e.g. p_{XY} or p_Y.

Leakage measures are defined based on various entropy-like measures of the prior distribution π and the posterior distributions $p_{X|y}$, together with their probabilities $p(y)$.

Shannon leakage is based on the Shannon entropy [3] of the prior distribution, $H(\pi) = -\sum_x \pi[x]\log\pi[x]$, and the expected Shannon entropy of the posterior distributions, $H(\pi, C) = \sum_y p(y)H(p_{X|y})$. The Shannon leakage is the difference $H(\pi) - H(\pi, C)$, which is equal to the mutual information $I(\pi, C)$.[4]

Guessing entropy leakage is based on the guessing entropy [4] of the prior distribution, $G(\pi) = \sum_i i\,\pi[x_i]$, with X indexed in non-increasing probability order, and on the expected guessing entropy of the posterior distributions $G(\pi, C) = \sum_y p(y)G(p_{X|y})$. The guessing entropy leakage is the difference $G(\pi) - G(\pi, C)$.

The operational significance of both Shannon entropy and guessing entropy can be stated in terms of the expected number of brute-force guesses that the adversary would need to find the secret.[5] But this is not really satisfactory for confidentiality, because the expected number of brute-force guesses needed to find the secret can be high even if the adversary has a high probability of guessing the secret successfully in just one try. For this reason we consider *min-entropy leakage* [5], which is based on the prior *vulnerability* of the secret to be guessed in one try $V(\pi) = \max_x \pi[x]$, and on the expected vulnerability of the posterior distributions $V(\pi, C) = \sum_y p(y)V(p_{X|y})$. The prior- and posterior min-entropies are obtained by taking the negative logarithm of the vulnerability: $H_\infty(\pi) = -\log V(\pi)$ and $H_\infty(\pi, C) = -\log V(\pi, C)$. The min-entropy leakage $\mathcal{L}(\pi, C)$ is the difference $H_\infty(\pi) - H_\infty(\pi, C)$ or, equivalently, the logarithm of the ratio of the posterior- and prior vulnerabilities, that is $\log {}^{V(\pi,C)}/_{V(\pi)}$.

While vulnerability is clearly important for confidentiality, it implicitly assumes an operational scenario in which the adversary gains only by guessing the secret *exactly*, and in *one try*. For this reason, *g-leakage* [1] generalizes vulnerability to incorporate a *gain function g*, the choice of which allows the modelling of differing operational scenarios. In each scenario, there will be some set $\mathcal{W}$ of *guesses* that the adversary could make about the secret, and for any guess w and secret value x, there will be some *gain* $g(w, x)$ that the adversary gets by having chosen w when the secret's actual value was x; gains are assumed to range from 0 (when w has no value at all) to 1 (when w is ideal). Formally, $g: \mathcal{W} \times X \to [0, 1]$, where $\mathcal{W}$ is a finite, non-empty set. Given a gain function g, the prior *g-vulnerability* is defined as the maximum expected gain over all possible guesses: that is $V_g(\pi) = \max_w \sum_x \pi[x]g(w, x)$. The posterior g-vulnerability, the g-entropy and the g-leakage are then defined as for min-entropy leakage: we have $V_g(\pi, C) = \sum_y p(y)V_g(p_{X|y})$, and $H_g(\pi) = -\log V_g(\pi)$, and $H_g(\pi, C) = -\log V(\pi, C)$ and $\mathcal{L}_g(\pi, C) = H_g(\pi) - H_g(\pi, C) = \log {}^{V_g(\pi,C)}/_{V_g(\pi)}$.

In particular, a gain function g that gives gain 1 for guessing the secret correctly and 0 otherwise makes g-leakage coincide with min-entropy leakage: it is thus a special case. But gain functions can do much more. As explained in [1], they can model a wide variety of practical operational scenarios, including those where the adversary benefits from guessing a value *close* to the secret, guessing a *part* of the secret, guessing a *property* of the secret or guessing the secret within some bounded number of tries. They can also model scenarios where there is a *penalty* for incorrect guesses.

---

[4] The more usual notation for these quantities is $H(X)$, $H(X|Y)$, and $I(X;Y)$.

[5] For Shannon entropy, this follows from a result by Massey [4].

3   Abstract Channels Capture the Essence of Leakage

For a fixed channel and prior, it can easily happen that *distinct* output values y, y' in $\mathcal{Y}$ give rise to the *same* posterior distribution on $\mathcal{X}$. In that case there is actually no benefit to the adversary from distinguishing outputs y, y', since each gives the same knowledge about X. Furthermore, the output *values* y make no difference either: all that matters for any output y is its associated posterior distribution $p_{X|y}$. This implies that the result of a channel, as far as leakage is concerned, should simply be a *distribution* on posterior distributions; following [2] we call this a *hyper-distribution*.

Example 2. Returning to channel C from Ex. 1, we notice that its outputs $y_{2,3}$ produce the same posterior distribution, i.e. that $p_{X|y_2} = p_{X|y_3}$. Hence the hyper-distribution produced by C on π has only three columns rather than four:[6]

C	$1/2$	$15/36$	$1/12$
x_1	$2/3$	0	0
x_2	0	$3/5$	1
x_3	$1/3$	$2/5$	0

In this representation the columns are normalised, and are labelled by their associated marginal probabilities: the $\mathcal{Y}$-values have been removed. Note that the probability $15/36$ of the middle posterior distribution is found by adding $p(y_2) + p(y_3)$, that is $5/18 + 5/36$.

□

We capture these two abstractions in the following definition:

Definition 2 (Abstract channel). *The leakage semantics of a channel matrix is the mapping that it gives from priors to hyper-distributions.*
    We call such a mapping an abstract channel.

The following theorem reassures us that we have not abstracted too much.

Theorem 2. *The usual leakage measures are well defined on abstract channels.*

Proof. As we saw in §2, under min-entropy leakage vulnerability is $V(\pi) = \max_x \pi[x]$, and posterior vulnerability is $V(\pi, C) = \sum_y p(y)V(p_{X|y})$. Hence the column *labels* y make no difference. Moreover, if $p_{X|y} = p_{X|y'}$ then the posterior vulnerability is unaffected by merging outputs y and y', since then

$$p(y)V(p_{X|y}) + p(y')V(p_{X|y'}) \quad = \quad p(y \vee y')V(p_{X|y}).$$

Other leakage measures, such as Shannon-based mutual information, behave similarly.

□

Taking this abstracted, semantic viewpoint makes us realise that the conventional, channel-matrix representation can contain *redundant information* as far as leakage is concerned, namely (1) *labels* on columns, (2) columns that are *all zero*, representing outputs that can never occur, and (3) *similar* columns, which are columns that are scalar multiples of each other and therefore yield the same posterior distributions.[7] By eliminating this redundant information, we obtain a well defined *reduced matrix*:

---

[6] The block representation of a hyper-distribution has probabilities in its top row, rather than $\mathcal{Y}$-values.

[7] These can be seen as analogous to redundant information in computer programs, like the names of local variables, dead code, and if-statements with identical branches. Case (2) could be seen as an instance of Case (3) with a scaling factor of zero; but then similarity would not be symmetric.

Definition 3. *The reduced matrix C^r of a channel matrix C is formed by deleting output labels and all-zero columns, then adding similar columns together, and finally ordering the resulting columns lexicographically.*

Theorem 3. *Any channel matrix C has the same leakage semantics as its reduction C^r.*

Proof. Output labels, all-zero columns, and column ordering all have no effect on the hyper-distribution. And similar columns each contribute weight to the same posterior distribution; hence merging them leaves the hyper-distribution unchanged. □

A reduced matrix hence serves as a *canonical representation* of an abstract channel.

Corollary 1. *Channels C, D represent the same abstract channel just when $C^r = D^r$.*

Example 3. Given $X = \{x_1, x_2, x_3\}$ we consider the following two channels C, D:

C	y_1	y_2	y_3
x_1	1	0	0
x_2	$1/4$	$1/2$	$1/4$
x_3	$1/2$	$1/3$	$1/6$

D	z_1	z_2	z_3
x_1	$2/5$	0	$3/5$
x_2	$1/10$	$3/4$	$3/20$
x_3	$1/5$	$1/2$	$3/10$

These channels *as matrices* are different — but *as abstract channels* they are the same. Indeed both map prior distribution $\pi = (p_1, p_2, p_3)$ to the same hyper-distribution:

	$(4p_1 + p_2 + 2p_3)/4$	$(3p_2 + 2p_3)/4$
x_1	$\dfrac{4p_1}{4p_1+p_2+2p_3}$	0
x_2	$\dfrac{p_2}{4p_1+p_2+2p_3}$	$\dfrac{3p_2}{3p_2+2p_3}$
x_3	$\dfrac{2p_3}{4p_1+p_2+2p_3}$	$\dfrac{2p_3}{3p_2+2p_3}$

To understand this, note that the second and third columns of C are *similar* (indeed column 2 is two times column 3). In the same way, columns 1 and 3 of D are similar (indeed column 1 is two-thirds times column 3). Hence A, B have the *same* reduced matrix, as shown here at right:

$$C^r = D^r = \begin{array}{c|cc} & & \\ x_1 & 1 & 0 \\ x_2 & 1/4 & 3/4 \\ x_3 & 1/2 & 1/2 \end{array}$$

□

While we have said that an abstract channel is a mapping from priors to hyper-distributions, in fact the mappings that come from channel matrices are highly constrained. Write $\lceil \pi \rceil$ for the *support* of distribution π, that is those elements (of X) to which it assigns non-zero probability. Then we have

Theorem 4. *An abstract channel C with input X is completely determined by its behaviour on any* full-support *prior π, that is one with $\lceil \pi \rceil = X$.*

Proof. If full-support π yields a certain hyper-distribution then, by scaling each of the posterior distributions with its probability, we recover the joint matrix of C^r under π. And normalizing the rows of the joint matrix gives C^r. □

It follows that we can also canonically represent an abstract channel by the hyper-distribution that it produces on (for instance) the uniform prior π_u — indeed we showed such a hyper-distribution in Ex. 2.[8]

4 Generalizing Partition Refinement to Composition Refinement

We now return our attention to the question of whether we can generalize the partition refinement $A \sqsubseteq B$ of Def. 1 in §1 from deterministic to probabilistic channels. Our criteria for success will include an investigation (in §5) of the situations in which the generalisation is *sound* in the sense that $A \sqsubseteq B$ implies that A's leakage does not exceed B's, and *complete* in that the generalisation fails only if there really is such a situation in which A leaks more than B.

In the deterministic case, A's partition is refined by B's just if we can convert from B to A by doing a "post-processing" step in which certain of B's outputs are *merged* — this corresponds to "anti-refinement" of partitions achieved by merging regions (just as federating the states of Australia takes us from Fig. 1(b) back to Fig. 1(a)). That is, we can express A as the *cascade* [12] of B and a channel R_{merge}, so that A is the *matrix product* of B and R_{merge}.[9] And, unlike partition refinement, this new formulation applies to probabilistic as well as deterministic channels.

Definition 4. *For channels A, B we say that A is composition refined by B, written $A \sqsubseteq_\circ B$, just when there exists a channel R such that $A = BR$.*

(Note that this definition appears in [1,9].)

On channel matrices, the composition-refinement relation is easily seen to be reflexive (since $C = CI$) and transitive (since $A = BR_1$ and $B = CR_2$ implies $A = (CR_2)R_1 = C(R_2R_1)$) — and so it is a preorder. But it is *not* antisymmetric, as can be seen from C, D in Ex. 3, where we have both $C \sqsubseteq_\circ D$ and $D \sqsubseteq_\circ C$:

C	y_1	y_2	y_3
x_1	1	0	0
x_2	1/4	1/2	1/4
x_3	1/2	1/3	1/6

$=$

D	z_1	z_2	z_3
x_1	2/5	0	3/5
x_2	1/10	3/4	3/20
x_3	1/5	1/2	3/10

R_1	y_1	y_2	y_3
z_1	1	0	0
z_2	0	2/3	1/3
z_3	1	0	0

and

D	z_1	z_2	z_3
x_1	2/5	0	3/5
x_2	1/10	3/4	3/20
x_3	1/5	1/2	3/10

$=$

C	y_1	y_2	y_3
x_1	1	0	0
x_2	1/4	1/2	1/4
x_3	1/2	1/3	1/6

R_2	z_1	z_2	z_3
y_1	2/5	0	3/5
y_2	0	1	0
y_3	0	1	0

However, if we restrict to *abstract channels*, we find that composition refinement is better behaved: it becomes a true partial order (Thm. 6 below). We now prove that fact, our first major result.

---

[8] In the more general setting of *Hidden Markov Models* [11], however, such functions from priors to hyper-distributions do not have the property of Thm. 4 — they are strictly more general.

[9] Indeed this equivalence was noted in Theorem 1 of [6].

Lemma 1 (**Jensen's inequality for abstract channels**). *Let $\mathcal{A}$ and $\mathcal{B}$ be abstract channels, with $(A, X, \mathcal{Z})$ and $(B, X, \mathcal{Y})$ their presentation as reduced matrices, and let F be a concave $(\frown)$ function from distributions on X to the reals. If $A = BR$ for some channel matrix R then, for any full-support prior π, we have $F(\pi, A) \geq F(\pi, B)$ where as usual $F(\pi, A) = \sum_z p(z) F(p_{X|z})$.*
Furthermore, if $\mathcal{A} \neq \mathcal{B}$ and F is strictly concave, then the inequality is strict.

Proof. Our proof relies on Jensen's inequality [10], that if $\lambda_1, \lambda_2, \ldots \lambda_N$ are coefficients in $[0, 1]$ that sum to one, and F is concave, then $\sum_n \lambda_n F(x_n) \leq F(\sum_n \lambda_n x_n)$.

We use the following matrix notation. Given matrix M with row labels X and column labels $\mathcal{Y}$, we write $M_{x,y}$ to denote the (x, y) entry and $M_{-,y}$ to denote column y. A fundamental property of matrix multiplication is that $(MN)_{-,z} = M(N_{-,z})$, i.e. that column z of MN is a linear combination of the columns of M, with column z of N as the coefficients, and thus that in fact the parentheses above are not necessary.[10]

We write D_π to denote the diagonal matrix with prior π on its diagonal, so that $D_\pi A$ is the joint matrix giving p_{XZ}. Note that because A is reduced and π is full support, the columns of $D_\pi A$ are all non-zero and non-similar; hence normalizing these columns is well defined and gives the *distinct* posterior distributions $p_{X|z} = 1/p(z) D_\pi A_{-,z}$ where $p(z)$ is the (necessarily nonzero) sum of column z. For B, similarly, the posterior distributions $p_{X|y}$ are distinct, and $p_{X|y} = 1/p(y) D_\pi B_{-,y}$.

We now show that $F(\pi, A) \geq F(\pi, B)$ under the conditions given: first we have

$$
\begin{array}{lll}
& F(\pi, A) & \\
= & \sum_z p(z) F(p_{X|z}) & \text{``defn. } F(\pi, A)\text{''} \\
= & \sum_z p(z) F(1/p(z) D_\pi A_{-,z}) & \text{``}p_{X|z} = 1/p(z) D_\pi A_{-,z}\text{''} \\
= & \sum_z p(z) F(1/p(z) D_\pi B R_{-,z}) & \text{``}A = BR\text{''} \\
= & \sum_z p(z) F(1/p(z) D_\pi (\sum_y B_{-,y} R_{y,z})) & \text{``}B R_{-,z} = \sum_y B_{-,y} R_{y,z}\text{''} \\
= & \sum_z p(z) F(\sum_y (R_{y,z} p(y)/p(z))(1/p(y) D_\pi B_{-,y})) & \text{``reorganising''} \\
= & \sum_z p(z) F(\sum_y (R_{y,z} p(y)/p(z))(p_{X|y})) & , & \text{``}p_{X|y} = 1/p(y) D_\pi B_{-,y}\text{''}
\end{array}
$$

which contains F applied to a convex combination $(\sum_y)$ whose coefficients $R_{y,z} p(y)/p(z)$ we now show are suitable for the use of Jensen. They sum to one because

$$
\begin{array}{lll}
& \sum_y R_{y,z} p(y) & \\
= & \sum_y R_{y,z} \sum_x (D_\pi B)_{x,y} & \text{``}p(y) = \sum_x (D_\pi B)_{x,y}\text{''} \\
= & \sum_{x,y} R_{y,z} (D_\pi B)_{x,y} & \text{``distributive law''} \\
= & \sum_x (D_\pi B R)_{x,z} & \text{``defn. matrix multiplication''} \\
= & \sum_x (D_\pi A)_{x,z} & \text{``}A = BR\text{''} \\
= & p(z) . & \text{``defn. } p(z)\text{''}
\end{array}
$$

With that done, we continue

$$
\begin{array}{lll}
\ldots = & \sum_z p(z) F(\sum_y (R_{y,z} p(y)/p(z))(p_{X|y})) & \text{``from above''} \\
\geq & \sum_z p(z) \sum_y (R_{y,z} p(y)/p(z)) F(p_{X|y}) & \text{``(*) Jensen wrt concave } F\text{''} \\
= & \sum_y p(y) F(p_{X|y}) \sum_z R_{y,z} & \text{``simplify''}
\end{array}
$$

---

[10] This is just associativity wrt post-multiplication by a column vector with one at row z and zeroes elsewhere.

$$=\sum_y p(y)\,F(p_{X|y})$$
$$=F(\pi, B)\ ,$$

"$\sum_z R_{y,z} = 1$"
"defn. $F(\pi, B)$"

so that $F(\pi, A) \geq F(\pi, B)$ as claimed.

Now we suppose that $\mathcal{A} \neq \mathcal{B}$ and F is strictly concave.

A strict form of Jensen's inequality is that if $\lambda_1, \lambda_2, \ldots \lambda_N$ are coefficients in $[0, 1]$ that sum to one, with at least one $\lambda_n \neq 1$, and F is strictly concave, and the x_n's are all distinct, then $\sum_n \lambda_n F(x_n) < F(\sum_n \lambda_n x_n)$. This will give strict inequality at (∗) above.

Because B is reduced, the distributions $p_{X|y}$ (the normalised columns of $D_\pi B$) are distinct; otherwise B would have similar columns. Those are the distinct x_n's for strict Jensen.

We now consider the λ_n's, showing that at least one of them is not one. No two columns of R can have a single non-zero entry in the same row, since those two columns would generate similar columns in A, contradicting A's being reduced. Thus if all columns of R have exactly one non-zero value, since those values are alone in their rows and R is a channel matrix, in fact R must be be a permutation of the identity. But that makes A a column permutation of B, impossible if A, B are reduced and distinct.

Thus channel matrix R must have some column $R_{-,\hat{z}}$ in which at least two entries are non-zero. But from $\sum_y R_{y,\hat{z}}\, p(y) = p(\hat{z})$, proved just above, plus the fact that $p(y)$ is nowhere zero, we have at least one $\hat{y}$ (in fact, two) with $R_{\hat{y},\hat{z}}\, p(\hat{y})/p(\hat{z}) \neq 1$. This $\hat{y}$ (as n) gives the $\lambda_n \neq 1$ for that $\hat{z}$, as application of strict Jensen to that $\hat{z}$ requires.

Those facts taken all together allow us to make step (∗) above strict, since for all z's (the nonstrict) Jensen applies, and for $\hat{z}$ it applies strictly.   □

A consequence of Lem. 1 is the following theorem, which is itself of interest.

Theorem 5 (Strict data-processing inequality). *Let $\mathcal{A}$ and $\mathcal{B}$ be abstract channels, and write $\mathcal{A} \sqsubset_\circ \mathcal{B}$ when $\mathcal{A} \sqsubseteq_\circ \mathcal{B}$ but $\mathcal{A} \neq \mathcal{B}$. If $\mathcal{A} \sqsubset_\circ \mathcal{B}$ then, for any full-support prior π, the mutual information leakage of $\mathcal{A}$ is strictly less than than that of $\mathcal{B}$: that is $I(\pi, \mathcal{A}) < I(\pi, \mathcal{B})$.*[11]

Proof. We appeal to the strict concavity ($\frown$) of Shannon entropy H [13, p. 85], using H for F in Lem. 1, to conclude that $H(\pi, \mathcal{A}) > H(\pi, \mathcal{B})$. Hence $I(\pi, \mathcal{A}) = H(\pi) - H(\pi, \mathcal{A}) < H(\pi) - H(\pi, \mathcal{B}) = I(\pi, \mathcal{B})$.   □

A second consequence of Lem. 1 is the partial-order property we seek.

Theorem 6 (Partial order). *Composition refinement ($\sqsubseteq_\circ$) is a partial order on abstract channels.*

Proof. Since ($\sqsubseteq_\circ$) is reflexive and transitive, we need only antisymmetry. Suppose that $\mathcal{A} \sqsubseteq_\circ \mathcal{B} \sqsubseteq_\circ \mathcal{A}$ but $\mathcal{A} \neq \mathcal{B}$. Then in fact $\mathcal{A} \sqsubset_\circ \mathcal{B} \sqsubset_\circ \mathcal{A}$ whence, from Thm. 5, we have $I(\pi, \mathcal{A}) < I(\pi, \mathcal{B}) < I(\pi, \mathcal{A})$ for any full-support prior π — which is impossible.   □

---

[11] To see that this theorem is indeed a strict version of the classic data-processing inequality [10], note that if $A = BR$, where A goes from X to Z, B goes from X to Y, and R goes from Y to Z, then for any prior π we have a Markov chain $X \to Y \to Z$. The (non-strict) data-processing inequality says that in this case $I(X; Z) \leq I(X; Y)$, which in our notation is $I(\pi, A) \leq I(\pi, B)$.

We conclude this section by completing the link with reduced channels. For channels A, B write $A \approx_\circ B$ to mean $A \sqsubseteq_\circ B \sqsubseteq_\circ A$.

Lemma 2. *For any channel C (not necessarily reduced) we have $C \approx_\circ C^r$.*

Proof. The reduced form C^r of channel C is defined in Def. 3 via a series of operations: deleting all-zero columns,[12] summing (similar) columns together, and reordering columns (lexicographically). Each of those can be effected via post-multiplication with a simple channel matrix; and so their overall effect is achieved via multiplication with the (matrix) product of all those channel matrices, again a channel matrix. Hence $C^r \sqsubseteq_\circ C$.

For the reverse direction the operations are adding an all-zero column, splitting a column into several similar columns,[13] and reordering columns. Again all of these can be achieved by post-multiplication. Hence $C \sqsubseteq_\circ C^r$, and so $C \approx_\circ C^r$ as required.   □

Theorem 7 (Quotienting). *The equivalence classes induced by the preorder $(\sqsubseteq_\circ)$ on channels are the same as induced by the kernel of reduction $(-^r)$: that is for any channels A, B we have $A \approx_\circ B$ just when $A^r = B^r$.*

Proof. If $A \approx_\circ B$ then $A^r \approx_\circ A \approx_\circ B \approx_\circ B^r$ (Lem. 2), whence $A^r \approx_\circ B^r$ by transitivity and finally $A^r = B^r$ by antisymmetry on reduced channels (Thm. 6).

If $A^r = B^r$ then $A^r \approx_\circ B^r$ (reflexivity) whence $A \approx_\circ B$ (Lem. 2 and transitivity).   □

5 Composition Refinement and Leakage Orderings

In this section we address whether $(\sqsubseteq_\circ)$ is a reasonable information order to impose; as mentioned at the beginning of §4, this is related to what we have called soundness and completeness. In §5.3 we briefly discuss compositionality.

5.1 Soundness of $(\sqsubseteq_\circ)$

The soundness condition for $(\sqsubseteq_\circ)$ concerns the situations in which $A \sqsubseteq_\circ B$ implies that A leaks no more than B. That is, given a situation in which (limiting) leakage is important, according to some leakage measure, in what sense is it *sound* to use $(\sqsubseteq_\circ)$ to reason about that system?

In fact we can argue informally that using $(\sqsubseteq_\circ)$ for our reasoning ought to be sound for any reasonable situation and associated leakage measure: if $A = BR$ for some R, then an adversary should never prefer channel A to channel B, because given channel B the adversary can always *simulate* channel A by simply post-processing the output from channel B according to channel R.

---

[12] This is where we depend on deleting only *all-zero* columns to proceed from C to C^r: although post-multiplication with a channel matrix can add an all-zero column, it cannot delete a column unless that column is all zero.

[13] This is where we depend on summing only *similar* columns to proceed from C to C^r: although post-multiplication with a channel matrix can sum any two columns, similar or not, it cannot in general decompose a column into a sum of *dissimilar* columns.

And indeed this property does hold for Shannon-entropy leakage, min-entropy leakage, and g-leakage. It is a generalized *data-processing inequality*, proved here[14] for the case of g-leakage.[15]

Theorem 8. *If $A \sqsubseteq_\circ B$ then the g-leakage of A never exceeds that of B, for any prior π and any gain function g. (We denote this by $A \leq_G B$.)*

Proof. Note first that because $\mathcal{L}_g(\pi, C) = \log V_g(\pi,C)/V_g(\pi)$ and $V_g(\pi, C)$ and $V_g(\pi)$ are positive, we have $\mathcal{L}_g(\pi, A) \leq \mathcal{L}_g(\pi, B)$ iff $V_g(\pi, A) \leq V_g(\pi, B)$.

Now

$$V_g(\pi, C) = \sum_{y \in \mathcal{Y}} \max_{w \in \mathcal{W}} \sum_{x \in \mathcal{X}} \pi[x] C_{x,y} g(w, x) \quad ,$$

and as noted in Section 4.C of [1], we can *reify* the choice of w, given y, as a probabilistic channel S from $\mathcal{Y}$ to $\mathcal{W}$ that represents the adversary's *strategy*.[16] Hence we have

$$V_g(\pi, C) = \max_S \sum_{x,y,w} \pi[x] C_{x,y} S_{y,w}\, g(w, x) = \max_S \sum_{x,w} \pi[x] (CS)_{x,w}\, g(w, x). \quad (1)$$

(It might appear that the "max" in equation (1) should actually be "sup," since there are infinitely many possible strategies. But this is not so, because the supremum is in fact realized on any strategy S such that $S_{y,w} > 0$ only if w is a best guess given output y.)

Now notice that in the case where $A = BR$, any optimal strategy S for A is *equivalent to* a strategy for B, namely RS; but of course RS might not be optimal for B — there might be a better strategy S'. This allows us to calculate

$$
\begin{array}{lll}
 & V_g(\pi, A) & \\
= & \max_S \sum_{x,w} \pi[x](AS)_{x,w} g(w, x) & \text{"Eqn. (1)"} \\
= & \max_S \sum_{x,w} \pi[x](BRS)_{x,w} g(w, x) & \text{"} A = BR \text{"} \\
\leq & \max_{S'} \sum_{x,w} \pi[x](BS')_{x,w} g(w, x) & \text{"} S' \text{ can be } RS \text{"} \\
= & V_g(\pi, B), & \text{"Eqn. (1)"}
\end{array}
$$

which gives the inequality $V_g(\pi, A) \leq V_g(\pi, B)$ that we seek.   □

5.2   Completeness of ($\sqsubseteq_\circ$)

The completeness condition we establish for ($\sqsubseteq_\circ$) is that if $A \not\sqsubseteq_\circ B$ then there exists a gain function g and a prior π for which A g-leaks strictly more than B does; this depends on a theorem we prove in §6 below. Put informally, this completeness means that if using our order ($\sqsubseteq_\circ$) we *criticise* a channel A because it does *not* satisfy $A \sqsubseteq_\circ B$, then we can *justify* our criticism by giving a π and g that shows A's inferiority in a more operational setting.

---

[14] This result first appeared as Theorem 6.2 of [1], though with a slightly different proof.

[15] Proofs for other leakage measures are similar, and indeed since min-entropy leakage is a special case of g-leakage (end §2), that in particular is a trivial corollary.

[16] This reification is reminiscent of Skolemization. Notice that it is reasonable for S to be probabilistic, since there could be more than one w that is optimal for a given y.

Surprisingly, that completeness criterion for ($\sqsubseteq_o$) does not hold wrt min-entropy leakage, even though Thm. 1 suggests that it might. This failure is shown by the following example:

$$A = \begin{array}{c|cc} x_1 & 2/3 & 1/3 \\ x_2 & 2/3 & 1/3 \\ x_3 & 1/4 & 3/4 \end{array} \qquad B = \begin{array}{c|ccc} x_1 & 1/2 & 1/2 & 0 \\ x_2 & 1/2 & 0 & 1/2 \\ x_3 & 0 & 1/2 & 1/2 \end{array}$$

Although it turns out that the min-entropy leakage of A never exceeds that of B on any prior, still $A \not\sqsubseteq_o B$.[17]

5.3 Compositionality

A more formal approach to soundness and completeness would be via compositionality, asking *given $A \sqsubseteq_o B$, for what contexts C can we be sure that also $C(A) \sqsubseteq_o C(B)$?*

In [2] a simple probabilistic programming language with hidden state is treated, with a relation ($\sqsupseteq$) there that specialises to ($\sqsubseteq_o$) here when those programs simulate channels. It is shown there that ($\sqsupseteq$) is the (unique) relation with the properties (soundness) that $A \sqsupseteq B$ implies that the min-entropy leakage of $C(A)$ *never* exceeds the min-entropy leakage of $C(B)$ for any context C in that programming language and any prior, and (completeness) that $A \not\sqsupseteq B$ implies that the min-entropy leakage of $C(A)$ *does* strictly exceed the min-entropy leakage of $C(B)$ for some context C and some prior. In this way the legitimacy of ($\sqsupseteq$) for programs, and hence of ($\sqsubseteq_o$) for channels, could be argued based on the utility of (the more restricted) min-entropy leakage, and compositionality.

The techniques for proving completeness in [2] led to the proof of Thm. 9 below.

6 The Coriaceous Property and Its Proof

We now present our second major result, the converse to Theorem 8. It says that the strong g-leakage order implies composition refinement, which intuitively means that composition refinement is not *too strong*: that is, whenever $A \not\sqsubseteq_o B$, there exists a prior π and a gain function g that causes A to leak more than B. This implication was studied in [1], but not proved in full generality—it was shown only in the case when the columns of B are linearly independent—and the general result was left as the *Coriaceous Conjecture*, which we now resolve.[18]

Theorem 9. *For any channel matrices A and B, if $A \leq_G B$ then $A \sqsubseteq_o B$.*

Proof. We argue the contrapositive, showing that if $A \not\sqsubseteq_o B$, then we can construct a gain function g and a prior π such that $V_g(\pi, A) > V_g(\pi, B)$; note that this implies that $\mathcal{L}_g(\pi, A) > \mathcal{L}_g(\pi, B)$ and hence that $A \not\leq_G B$.

---

[17] The min-entropy leakage bound can be verified using the linear-programming-based algorithm given in Section 6.F of [1]. To see that $A \not\sqsubseteq_o B$, note that because B is invertible we have $A = BR$ implies $R = B^{-1}A$—but this calculation gives an R containing negative entries.

[18] The proof is based on [14], itself extracted from the completeness proof in [2] which was, in turn, a specialisation of McIver's original proof in terms of probabilistic imperative-program fragments and their weakest preconditions [15].

Let A go from X to Z, and B from X to Y. If $A \not\sqsubseteq_\circ B$, then there exists no channel matrix R from Y to Z such that $A = BR$. If we use the abbreviation $B^\uparrow$ for the matrices $\{BR \mid R \text{ is a channel matrix from } Y \text{ to } Z\}$, then our assumption becomes $A \notin B^\uparrow$.

Because matrix A and the matrices in $B^\uparrow$ go from X to Z, they can be embedded into Euclidean space of dimension $N = |X| \times |Z|$ by gluing their columns together in order. Then $B^\uparrow$ becomes a set of points in N-space which, we observe by linearity of matrix multiplication, is both convex and closed. And A is a point in N-space that does not belong to $B^\uparrow$.

By the *Separating Hyperplane Lemma* [16] there is thus a hyperplane in N-space with point A strictly on one side, and all of the set $B^\uparrow$ strictly on the other side. If G is the normal of the hyperplane, also an N-vector thus, we have that $A \cdot G > B' \cdot G$ for all $B' \in B^\uparrow$.[19] Note that we can assume a $(>)$-separation without loss of generality, because we can negate G if necessary. Moreover we can assume without loss of generality that the elements of G are in $[0, 1]$. First, we can eliminate negative elements of G by adding a constant k to each entry; this has the effect of increasing both sides of the inequalities above by exactly $k|X|$, because with A and each B' derived from "glued" channel matrices, as vectors they all sum to the same value $|X|$. Second, we can eliminate elements of G that are greater than 1 by scaling, which simply scales both sides of $(<)$ equally.

Now by "ungluing" we can view G, a vector in N-space, as a matrix (though not necessarily a channel matrix) from X to Z. Thus we can view G as a *gain function* $g : Z \times X \to [0, 1]$, using Z as the set of guesses and defined by $g(z, x) = G_{x,z}$.[20]

It turns out that this g is precisely the gain function that causes A to leak more than B under the uniform prior π_u. For by Eqn. (1) we have

$$V_g(\pi_u, A) = \max_{S_A} \sum_{x,z} \pi_u[x](AS_A)_{x,z} g(z, x)$$

$$\text{and} \quad V_g(\pi_u, B) = \max_{S_B} \sum_{x,z} \pi_u[x](BS_B)_{x,z} g(z, x) \quad ,$$

where strategies S_A for A are channel matrices from Z to Z, and strategies S_B for B are channels matrices from Y to Z. Note then that the *identity matrix I* is a strategy for A, and that each $BS_B \in B^\uparrow$. Hence, letting S_B° denote any optimal strategy for B, we have

$$
\begin{array}{lll}
V_g(\pi_u, B) & & \\
= & \sum_{x,z} \pi_u[x](BS_B^\circ)_{x,z} g(z, x) & \text{``S_B° is optimal''} \\
= & 1/|X| \sum_{x,z} (BS_B^\circ)_{x,z} G_{x,z} & \text{``π_u is uniform over X''} \\
= & 1/|X| (BS_B^\circ) \cdot G & \text{``taking dot-product in vector form''} \\
< & 1/|X| A \cdot G & \text{``separation; $BS_B^\circ \in B^\uparrow$''} \\
= & \sum_{x,z} \pi_u[x](AI)_{x,z} g(z, x) & \text{``I is identity''} \\
\leq & \max_{S_A} \sum_{x,z} \pi_u[x](AS_A)_{x,z} g(z, x) & \text{``S_A can be I''} \\
= & V_g(\pi_u, A) \quad . & \text{``definition V_g''}
\end{array}
$$

$\square$

While Theorem 9 shows that composition refinement is no stronger than the strong g-leakage order, one might nonetheless wonder whether the gain function g constructed in the proof (using the Hyperplane Separating Lemma) represents a "practical" leakage

---

[19] We are using the vector forms here, and $(\cdot)$ is used for their dot-products.

[20] Note that this is the *transpose* of the matrix representation of gain functions used in [1].

threat, in that a "real" adversary would ever care about it. That is, perhaps the strong g-leakage ordering is itself too strong. Three comments seem relevant here. First, it seems generally prudent to make as few assumptions about the adversary as possible. Second, the partial proofs[21] in [1] show that, in the special case when $A \not\sqsubseteq_\circ B$ and the columns of B are linearly independent, there is a quite intuitive gain function g and prior π that causes A to leak more than B; g can then be a *two-block gain function*, which corresponds to the adversary wanting to guess some *property* of the secret. And finally (§5.3), with suitable definition of context it could be possible to reduce ($\sqsubseteq_\circ$) to the strong min-entropy leakage order.

7   The Mathematical Structure of Hyper-distributions

In this section, we give a monadic presentation of composition refinement which, while not necessary for the results in this paper, supports generalisation to richer settings.

7.1   Use of the Giry Monad

In Def. 2 we defined abstract channels as mappings from priors to hyper-distributions. Recall that our (finite) input space is X, and write $\mathbb{D}X$, with typical element lower-case Greek (e.g. δ, π), for the (discrete) distributions over X; in that case (discrete) *hyper*-distributions have type $\mathbb{D}^2 X$, with typical element upper-case Greek (e.g. Δ), and abstract channels have type $\mathbb{D}X \rightarrow \mathbb{D}^2 X$.[22] We now look at $\mathbb{D}^2 X$ specifically, from a monadic perspective [17].[23]

The functor $\mathbb{G}$ of the Giry monad [19] $(\mathbb{G}, \mu, \eta)$ takes a measure space to another space of measures, on the measures of that first space: this is the general technique that allows us to construct distributions $\mathbb{D}()$ "on top of" another set of distributions $\mathbb{D}X$, as in $\mathbb{D}^2 X$ (and even $\mathbb{D}^3 X$ as in §7.3 below). As part of the monad structure we have a "multiply" natural transformation μ that averages a distribution of distributions to create a single distribution again. (We see an example of this below.) Here we call it avg for "average." The "unit" natural transformation η makes a point distribution on a distribution; but we will not need it here. The functor $\mathbb{G}$ itself, acting on a mapping f e.g. from X to $\mathcal{Y}$, constructs a "lifted" mapping $\mathbb{G}f$ from $\mathbb{G}X$ to $\mathbb{G}\mathcal{Y}$, that is in our simple setting from $\mathbb{D}X$ to $\mathbb{D}\mathcal{Y}$. We call it map here.[24] Finally, we have a function exp that takes the expected value of a function from a measure space to a weighted sum based on a particular measure in that space; we see an example of that immediately below (§7.2).

---

[21] See the proofs of Lemma 6.4 and Theorems 6.5 and 6.6 of [1].

[22] Since $\mathbb{D}X$ is uncountable even for finite X, hyper-distributions are at least potentially proper measures: but when derived from matrices, as they are here, they are discrete distributions. The proper-measure case is treated in [11,17] as mentioned in §7.3 below.

[23] We keep this treatment very light: more details are found in [17], where the Kantorovich monad [18] is used in a similar style.

[24] In elementary probability it is called "push forward." Calling it map is by analogy with the use of monads in functional programming, where map "lifts" a function f between elements to a function map f between structures on those elements.

7.2 Applying g-vulnerability to Hyper-distributions Directly

We recall from §2 that a gain function $g \colon \mathcal{W} \times \mathcal{X} \to [0, 1]$ gives rise to two derived functions: the prior vulnerability V_g takes one argument, having type $\mathbb{D}\mathcal{X} \to [0, 1]$. The expected vulnerability (again) V_g of the posterior distributions takes two arguments, a prior *and* a channel; but in the mathematical presentation we consider that to be of type $\mathbb{D}^2\mathcal{X} \to [0, 1]$, i.e. to have as its *single* argument the hyper-distribution that the prior and channel jointly determine.[25] That is, with this overloading of the name "V_g" it is type-correct to write both $V_g(\delta)$ and $V_g(\Delta)$ for $\delta \colon \mathbb{D}\mathcal{X}$ and $\Delta \colon \mathbb{D}^2\mathcal{X}$.

The second form of V_g, applied to a particular hyper-distribution $\Delta \colon \mathbb{D}^2\mathcal{X}$, is then the expected value $\exp_{V_g}(\Delta)$ over Δ of the first form of V_g as a random variable on $\mathbb{D}\mathcal{X}$.[26]

7.3 Applying Composition Refinement ($\sqsubseteq_\circ$) to Hyper-distributions Directly

We now introduce *bi-hypers* on $\mathcal{X}$, that is hyper-distributions on $\mathbb{D}\mathcal{X}$ (rather than on $\mathcal{X}$ directly), that thus have type $\mathbb{D}^3\mathcal{X}$ with typical element bold upper-case Greek (e.g. $\boldsymbol{\Delta}$). The definition of composition refinement ($\sqsubseteq_\circ$) on hyper-distributions is then as follows:

Definition 5. *Given two hyper-distributions $\Delta_{A,B} \colon \mathbb{D}^2\mathcal{X}$, we say that $\Delta_A \sqsubseteq_\circ \Delta_B$ just when there is a bi-hyper $\boldsymbol{\Delta} \colon \mathbb{D}^3\mathcal{X}$ such that*

$$\Delta_A = \mathsf{map}(\mathsf{avg})(\boldsymbol{\Delta}) \quad and \quad \mathsf{avg}(\boldsymbol{\Delta}) = \Delta_B . \quad {}^{27}$$

The bi-hyper $\boldsymbol{\Delta}$ is thus a witness of the relationship ($\sqsubseteq_\circ$), just as R is a witness in the matrix setting.

This more general, abstract construction of Def. 5 is not necessary for the material (elsewhere) in this paper; but its being expressed purely in monadic terms means it applies without change to proper measures (rather than only discrete distributions). These can arise naturally in a context more general than channels, for example imperative looping programs with hidden state [11], and probabilistic- and demonic nondeterminism together [17]. In this way, the channel model can be seen to fit into this very general mathematical framework, possibly giving access to more general mathematical tools in the analysis of channels.

8 Limits of the Information-Theoretic Perspective

The perspective of abstract channels is information theoretic, concerned only with a channel's mapping from priors to hyper-distributions, and abstracting from details like the names of outputs. These choices are appropriate if we are interested only in the

---

[25] In [17] the prior vulnerability function is abstracted from any g, presented simply as a "disorder test" that is by definition some continuous, concave function in $\mathbb{D}\mathcal{X} \to [0, 1]$. Continuity requires a metric, or a topology, and that is part of what the general Giry- or Kantorovich monad structure supplies. Thus disorder tests are concave (by definition), while g-vulnerabilities are convex (by construction based on g). The latter is a just special case of the former, negated.

[26] That expected value would be written $\int V_g \, d\Delta$ or $\int_{\delta \in \mathbb{D}\mathcal{X}} V_g(\delta) \, d\Delta$ in a more mathematical setting.

[27] In the usual notation of the Giry monad that would be $\Delta_A = \mathbb{G}\mu_\mathcal{X}\boldsymbol{\Delta}$ and $\mu_{\mathbb{G}\mathcal{X}}\boldsymbol{\Delta} = \Delta_B$.

information that a channel provides to the adversary, and not in the *amount of computation* that might be required in order to exploit that information.

But if we wish to consider computationally-bounded adversaries, then we need to move to a more concrete model, one where outputs come as *strings of bits*. Also, we need to constrain the strategy-based formulation of g-vulnerability that we used in the proof of Theorem 8. For simplicity, let us restrict our attention to min-entropy leakage and (ordinary) vulnerability, whose strategy-based formulation is

$$V(\pi, C) = \max_S \sum_{x,y} \pi[x] C_{x,y} S_{y,x} \ .$$

In a computational setting, we can no longer allow S to be an arbitrary probabilistic mapping from outputs $\mathcal{Y}$ to guesses $\mathcal{X}$, but instead must require it to be efficiently computable. This in turn requires that we consider *families* of channels with respect to a "security parameter" n, so that we can consider the growth of running time as a function of n. Let us write V^c to denote the computational version of vulnerability.[28]

We can illustrate the effect of this definition by considering two channels whose input is an n-bit prime p, assumed uniformly distributed. Channel A outputs p^2, while channel B outputs pq, where q is a uniformly-distributed $(n+1)$-bit prime. Note that A and B represent the *same* abstract channel, since the reduced matrix of both is the identity matrix. Hence in the non-computational setting we have $V(\pi, A) = V(\pi, B) = 1$.

Turning next to V^c, we find that $V^c(\pi, A) = 1$, since there is an efficient strategy that maps p^2 to p by calculating the square root via binary search. In contrast, $V^c(\pi, B)$ should be smaller, since the existence of an efficient strategy that maps pq to p would contradict the standard assumptions about the difficulty of the factorization problem. Indeed, it would appear that $V^c(\pi, B) \approx V^c(\pi)$, since an efficient probabilistic strategy is believed to have a negligible probability of recovering p from pq.

Here we also have $A \sqsubseteq_\circ B$, which implies by Theorem 8 that $V(\pi, A) \leq V(\pi, B)$. Why does the same inequality not hold for V^c? Recall that the proof of Theorem 8 is based on the fact that if $A = BR$, then any strategy S for A gives rise to an equivalent strategy for B, namely RS. But notice that RS need not be efficiently computable, even if S is. Since here R is a channel that maps pq to p^2, it indeed does not give rise to an efficiently computable strategy for B. In the computational setting, however, we should be able to get a weaker version of Theorem 8 saying that if $A = BR$, where R is *efficiently computable*, then A never out-leaks B.

9   Related Work

Given the multitude of plausible ways to measure the "uncertainty" of a probability distribution and the "amount" of information leakage caused by a channel, there has long been interest in the *robustness* of such measures and the leakage orderings on channels that they give.

---

[28] There is also a technical issue that arises with *prior vulnerability*. Since now we have a family $\pi^{(n)}$ of priors, parameterized by n, it is not clear that an adversary can efficiently compute an x with maximum probability in $\pi^{(n)}$. In the example that follows, this is not in fact a problem, since there are standard techniques for efficiently generating uniformly-distributed n-bit primes. But in general, we might wish to impose constraints on $\pi^{(n)}$.

Such studies can both establish and refute relationships among measures. For instance, Massey [4] compares Shannon entropy H and guessing entropy G, showing that $G(\pi) > 2^{H(\pi)-2}$, but that there is no interesting upper bound on $G(\pi)$ in terms of $H(\pi)$. Another negative result is given by Pliam [20], who shows the incomparability of Shannon entropy and *marginal guesswork*, which is the minimum number of brute-force guesses required to guess a secret with some specified probability of success. With respect to vulnerability and min-entropy, Santhi and Vardy [21] prove a bound between posterior Shannon entropy and *Bayes risk*, which is the complement of posterior vulnerability; in our notation their bound can equivalently be written as $H(\pi, C) \geq -\log V(\pi, C) = H_\infty(\pi, C)$. Further study of similar bounds is done by Chatzikoklakis, Palamidessi, and Panangaden [22].

Turning to comparisons between channels, we have the results of Yasuoka and Terauchi [7] and Malacaria [8] described in Section 1 that establish the robustness of partition refinement in comparing *deterministic* channels. For *probabilistic channels*, Braun, Chatzikokolakis, and Palamidessi [23] compare the leakage ordering resulting from *multiplicative* and *additive* versions of min-entropy leakage—multiplicative leakage is based on the *ratio* of the posterior- and prior vulnerabilities (as in min-entropy leakage, which is just the logarithm of this ratio), while additive leakage is based on their *difference*. They show that when comparing two channels on a *given* prior, it makes no difference whether multiplicative or additive leakage is used. But when channels are compared with respect to their *capacity* (i.e. maximum leakage over all priors) then multiplicative and additive leakage can produce inconsistent results.

Finally, Sabelfeld and Sands [24] describe a "PER" model of security specifications, based on partitions of the hidden-value space; and there are some similarities between their treatment of partitions and ours: in particular, refining a PER that specifies a program's input could be construed as allowing the program to be less secure; and refining an output PER would require the program to be more secure. Their extension to probability, however, does not seem to lead to the same relation between channels as our does.

10   Conclusion

This paper can be seen as an exploration of the mathematical foundations of quantitative information flow. We have argued that, from the information-theoretic perspective, it is *abstract channels* that are the fundamental objects of study: for when we consider the information-theoretic leakage caused by a channel C, the essential fact is precisely the mapping that C gives from priors to hyper-distributions—and any of the multitude of possible leakage measures can be seen as simply *summarizing* this mapping. Concretely, then, we have seen that classical channel matrices contain structural redundancies which ought to be quotiented away, leading to *reduced matrices*. The utility of the abstract-channel framework is further clarified by our study of *composition refinement*, which is only a pre-order on channel matrices, but which we have proved is a *partial order* on abstract channels. And, by our proof that composition refinement coincides with the *strong g-leakage ordering*, it is a partial order with both structural- and leakage-testing significance—and is therefore a compelling generalization (from deterministic to probabilistic channels) of *partition refinement* in the Lattice of Information. Finally, we have discussed the limits of the information-theoretic perspective, pointing out that the abstract channels framework is not suitable for addressing computationally-bounded adversaries.

We have shown that channels can be regarded as functions from priors to hyper-distributions and sketched in §7 how they can be formalised using general mathematical machinery; in future work we will investigate this abstraction further in its relation to channels. The characterisation of hypers within the general type of functions would be the first step towards determining which program contexts preserve the order. For example, the Coriaceous result establishes how to show that two channels are not related by ($\sqsubseteq_\circ$) by finding a refuting gain function g; an interesting result would be to determine whether this g can be used to produce the precise conditions under which e.g. min-entropy testing would fail, in the style of program testing "in context" [2]. Another interesting question is whether two programs with an abstract channel denotation can be proved to be in the ($\sqsubseteq_\circ$) relation based on examining the way in which they were constructed. Similar ideas have been discussed in [25] for the specific case of preserving a particular threshold of leakage with respect to a single entropy measurement.

More generally, since particular leakage measures are appropriate for particular applications, we can define a family of weaker pre-orders on abstract channels for a fixed leakage measure m: we say $\mathcal{A} \leq_m \mathcal{B}$ iff the m-leakage of $\mathcal{A}$ never exceeds that of $\mathcal{B}$, for any prior π. What we do not know is whether these are *partial orders* for important choices of m, such as Shannon-, guessing-, or min-entropy leakage. Nor do we know whether they are *strictly weaker* than ($\sqsubseteq_\circ$), though we do know this for $\leq_{min-entropy}$ by the example in §5.2.

Finally, our preliminary investigations suggest that ($\sqsubseteq_\circ$) is not a lattice [26]; future work will reveal other general properties and how to exploit them in channel analysis.

Acknowledgments. Geoffrey Smith and Barbara Espinoza were partially supported by the National Science Foundation under grant CNS-1116318. McIver and Morgan were supported by the Australian Research Council under grant DP120101413. Finally, this paper builds on work [1] done jointly with Mário Alvim, Kostas Chatzikokolakis, and Catuscia Palamidessi, to whom we are deeply appreciative.

References

1. Alvim, M.S., Chatzikokolakis, K., Palamidessi, C., Smith, G.: Measuring information leakage using generalized gain functions. In: Proc. 25th IEEE Computer Security Foundations Symposium (CSF 2012), pp. 265–279 (June 2012)
2. McIver, A., Meinicke, L., Morgan, C.: Compositional closure for Bayes risk in probabilistic noninterference. In: Abramsky, S., Gavoille, C., Kirchner, C., Meyer auf der Heide, F., Spirakis, P.G. (eds.) ICALP 2010. LNCS, vol. 6199, pp. 223–235. Springer, Heidelberg (2010)
3. Shannon, C.E.: A mathematical theory of communication. Bell System Technical Journal 27, 379–423, 623–656 (1948)
4. Massey, J.L.: Guessing and entropy. In: Proc. 1994 IEEE International Symposium on Information Theory, p. 204 (1994)
5. Smith, G.: On the foundations of quantitative information flow. In: de Alfaro, L. (ed.) FOSSACS 2009. LNCS, vol. 5504, pp. 288–302. Springer, Heidelberg (2009)

6. Landauer, J., Redmond, T.: A lattice of information. In: Proc. 6th IEEE Computer Security Foundations Workshop (CSFW 1993), pp. 65–70 (June 1993)
7. Yasuoka, H., Terauchi, T.: Quantitative information flow — verification hardness and possibilities. In: Proc. 23rd IEEE Computer Security Foundations Symposium (CSF 2010), pp. 15–27 (2010)
8. Malacaria, P.: Algebraic foundations for information theoretical, probabilistic and guessability measures of information flow. CoRR abs/1101.3453 (2011)
9. McIver, A., Meinicke, L., Morgan, C.: Compositional closure for Bayes risk in probabilistic noninterference. CoRR abs/1007.1054 (2010) (Draft full version of [2] with appendices)
10. Cover, T.M., Thomas, J.A.: Elements of Information Theory, 2nd edn. John Wiley & Sons, Inc. (2006)
11. McIver, A., Meinicke, L., Morgan, C.: Hidden-Markov program algebra with iteration. At arXiv:1102.0333v1 (2011) (To appear in Mathematical Structures in Computer Science in 2012)
12. Desoer, C.A.: Communication through channels in cascade. PhD thesis, Massachusetts Institute of Technology (1953)
13. Gallager, R.G.: Information Theory and Reliable Communication. John Wiley & Sons, Inc. (1968)
14. McIver, A., Meinicke, L., Morgan, C.: Draft proof of the Coriaceous Conjecture (November 2012), http://www.dagstuhl.de/mat/index.en.phtml?12481
15. McIver, A., Morgan, C.: Abstraction, Refinement and Proof for Probabilistic Systems. Technical Monographs in Computer Science. Springer, New York (2005)
16. Trustrum, K.: Linear Programming. Library of Mathematics. Routledge and Kegan Paul, London (1971)
17. McIver, A., Meinicke, L., Morgan, C.: A Kantorovich-monadic powerdomain for information hiding, with probability and nondeterminism. In: Proc. 27th IEEE Symposium on Logic in Computer Science (LICS 2012), pp. 461–470 (2012)
18. van Breugel, F.: The metric monad for probabilistic nondeterminism (2005), Draft available at http://www.cse.yorku.ca/~franck/research/drafts/monad.pdf
19. Giry, M.: A categorical approach to probability theory. In: Categorical Aspects of Topology and Analysis. Lecture Notes in Mathematics, vol. 915, pp. 68–85. Springer (1981)
20. Pliam, J.O.: On the incomparability of entropy and marginal guesswork in brute-force attacks. In: Roy, B., Okamoto, E. (eds.) INDOCRYPT 2000. LNCS, vol. 1977, pp. 67–79. Springer, Heidelberg (2000)
21. Santhi, N., Vardy, A.: On an improvement over Rényi's equivocation bound. In: 44th Annual Allerton Conference on Communication, Control, and Computing (2006)
22. Chatzikokolakis, K., Palamidessi, C., Panangaden, P.: On the Bayes risk in information-hiding protocols. Journal of Computer Security 16(5), 531–571 (2008)
23. Braun, C., Chatzikokolakis, K., Palamidessi, C.: Quantitative notions of leakage for one-try attacks. In: Proc. 25th Conference on Mathematical Foundations of Programming Semantics (MFPS 2009). ENTCS, vol. 249, pp. 75–91 (2009)
24. Sabelfeld, A., Sands, D.: A PER model of secure information flow. Higher-Order and Symbolic Computation 14(1), 59–91 (2001)
25. Braun, C., Chatzikokolakis, K., Palamidessi, C.: Compositional methods for information-hiding. In: Amadio, R.M. (ed.) FOSSACS 2008. LNCS, vol. 4962, pp. 443–457. Springer, Heidelberg (2008)
26. McIver, A., Morgan, C., Meinicke, L., Smith, G., Espinoza, B.: Abstract channels, gain functions and the information order. In: FCS 2013 Workshop on Foundations of Computer Security (2013), http://prosecco.gforge.inria.fr/personal/bblanche/fcs13/fcs13proceedings.pdf

Quantitative Information Flow in Boolean Programs

Rohit Chadha[1], Dileep Kini[2], and Mahesh Viswanathan[2]

[1] University of Missouri, USA
[2] University of Illinois, Urbana-Champaign, USA

Abstract. The *quantitative information flow bounding problem* asks, given a program P and threshold q, whether the information leaked by P is bounded by q. When the amount of information is measured using mutual information, the problem is known to be PSPACE-hard and decidable in EXPTIME. We show that the problem is in fact decidable in PSPACE, thus establishing the exact complexity of the quantitative information flow bounding problem. Thus, the complexity of bounding quantitative information flow in programs has the same complexity as safety verification of programs. We also show that the same bounds apply when comparing information leaked by two programs.

1 Introduction

A *non-interferent* program [13,20] ensures that *low-security observations* by an adversary of an execution of the program is independent of its *high-security* inputs, thus preserving confidentiality of its inputs. While non-interference is desirable, explicit outputs of a program often violate non-interference. For example, the winning bid in an anonymous auction *reveals* information about all other bids, namely an upper bound on other bids. Therefore, others (e.g [12,14,19,22]) propose to quantify the amount of information leaked by a program in order to evaluate security of programs. In these quantitative approaches, a program is seen as a *transformation* of a random variable taking values from the set of inputs into a random variable taking values from the set of observations. The amount of information leaked by the program is modeled as the difference between the initial uncertainty and the uncertainty remaining in the secret inputs given the observations an adversary makes about the execution of the program. In order to measure uncertainty, information-theoretic measures such as Shannon's entropy [12,14,19] and min-entropy [22] are employed. The appropriate measure of information usually depends on the application. Min-entropy, for example, is used to measure vulnerability to being guessed in one try and is useful for measuring information leaked by password-checkers. However, note that this is inappropriate for voting protocols which publish vote tallies as an unanimous election always reveals how each voter voted and min-entropy based measure will say that *all* information is leaked for such protocols. Thus, min-entropy will not be able to distinguish a secure electronic protocol from an insecure protocol protocol such as one which outputs a list of voters along with their voting

M. Abadi and S. Kremer (Eds.): POST 2014, LNCS 8414, pp. 103–119, 2014.

preferences. Using Shannon entropy to measure information leaked is more appropriate for such protocols.

We consider the complexity of evaluating the amount of information leaked by a program when the uncertainty is measured using Shannon's entropy [21] as has been proposed in [12,14,19]. In this case, the amount of information leaked by a program is mutual information between the inputs and outputs. We start by considering the complexity of *quantitative information flow bounding problem* [25,27]: given a program P with uniformly distributed inputs, and a rational number q, check if the information leaked by the program does not exceed q.[1] The quantitative information flow bounding problem was first considered in [25,27] who study complexity of the quantitative information flow problem for (deterministic) imperative Boolean programs. They show that the problem is PP-hard for loop-free Boolean programs. The class PP is the class of decision problems solvable by a probabilistic Turing machine in polynomial time, with an error probability of less than $\frac{1}{2}$. This implies, in particular, that the quantitative information flow bounding problem is harder than reachability in loop-free Boolean programs as the latter is NP-complete and the complexity class PP contains the complexity class NP. Intuitively, the hardness of problem comes from the fact that one has to compute, for each possible output, how many inputs lead to that particular output. For reachability, we only have to guess one input which leads to the reachable state.

For Boolean programs (with loops), the quantitative information flow problem was shown to PSPACE-hard in [25,27]. However, no upper bounds are given in [25,27]. The problem was shown to be in EXPTIME in [5]. They also show that the problem is PSPACE-complete when the number of outputs is *logarithmic* in the size of the program.

We briefly recall the strategy used in [5] to establish that the quantitative information flow bounding problem is in PSPACE when the number of outputs is *logarithmic* in the size of the program. The proof therein relies on a recent result on straight-line programs (SLPs). An SLP is a sequence of assignments to integer variables in which the operations allowed are addition, subtraction and multiplication (no division). The value of the variable last assigned to is said to be the number defined by SLP. A recent result shows that the problem of checking whether an SLP defines a strictly positive number is decidable in counting hierarchy [2], which is contained in PSPACE. Now, [5] show that for each program P and rational number q there is an SLP $prog_{(P,q)}$ such that the information leaked by the program by program P does not exceed q iff the number defined by $prog_{(P,q)}$ is strictly positive. The program $prog_{(P,q)}$ is polynomial in a size of P and q if the number of outputs of P is logarithmic in the size of the program (and can be constructed in polynomial time). However, if there is no restriction on number of outputs then the size of $prog_{(P,q)}$ can be exponential in the size of P. Therefore, they have to restrict the number of outputs to achieve the PSPACE upper bound.

---

[1] Uniformly distributed inputs is a commonly used assumption. For arbitrary input distributions, the same complexity bounds will apply for Boolean programs.

Contributions. Our first contribution is to show that the quantitative information flow bounding problem is in PSPACE which matches the PSPACE lower bound without any restrictions on the number of outputs, thus establishing the *exact* complexity of quantitative information flow. This is surprising since checking safety of Boolean programs (or reachability in Boolean programs) is also PSPACE-complete. This shows that the problem of bounding quantitative information flow is (complexity-theoretically) as easy as safety verification of Boolean programs.

For the upper bound, we cannot directly use the construction of the SLP $prog_{(P,q)}$ outlined in [5] as the size of $prog_{(P,q)}$ is exponential in the size of P. Instead, we establish a new result about PSPACE-SLP generators. A PSPACE-SLP generator F is an algorithm that outputs an SLP on its input w, using only a polynomially-bounded work-tape (note the output can still be exponential in $|w|$, the length of w). We give sufficient conditions that ensure that the problem of checking whether, given w, the number defined by the SLP $F(w)$ is strictly positive can be decided in PSPACE (even when the output $F(w)$ is exponential in length of w). We then show that there is a PSPACE-SLP generator f that a) satisfies the above conditions and b) given a program P and a rational number q computes the SLP $prog_{(P,q)}$.

We then consider the *quantitative information flow comparison problem*: given programs P_1 and P_2 check if information leaked by program P_1 is less than the information leaked by P_2. The *quantitative information flow comparison problem* was first studied in [26], where they show that the comparison problem is #P-hard for loop-free Boolean programs.[2] We show that the *quantitative information flow comparison problem* is also PSPACE-complete by using methods similar to the quantitative information flow bounding problem.

Finally, we are able to conclude PSPACE-completeness for quantitative information flow bounding problem and the quantitative information flow comparison problem when the observations of the adversary are not explicit outputs, but implicitly derived from the timing behavior of an execution of a program. Following [5], we abstract the timing behavior as the number of steps of the execution of a program. The conclusion follows from the observation that a Boolean program takes at most an exponential number of steps[3] and hence can be encoded by a binary counter.

The rest of the paper is organized as follows. We introduce relevant notation and definitions in Section 2. We establish our result on SLP-generators in Section 4. The results on quantitative information flow bounding problem and quantitative information flow comparison problem are presented in Section 5. We conclude in Section 6.

---

[2] Note #P is a class of function problems and not decision problems. The precise statement of #P-hardness in [26] is that the function class #P is as hard as the class of function problems solvable in polynomial time with an oracle for comparing quantitative information flow in loop-free Boolean programs.

[3] We only consider terminating programs.

Related Work. In the recent years, several automated approaches from model-checking [3,18,7,8], static analysis [9,10,11,3] and statistical analysis [18,6] have been employed to compute the information leaked by a program. The *complexity* of computing the amount of leakage was only considered recently [26,25,27,24,5]. The problem was first tackled in [26], where quantitative information flow comparison problem is studied. The PSPACE lower bound for non-interference was shown in [27] which implies the lower bound for both the quantitative information flow bounding problem and for the quantitative information flow comparison problem. A PSPACE upper and lower bound for programs for measures based on min-entropy and guessing entropy was established in [27]. However, an exact upper bound was not known for the case when the information is measured using Shannon's entropy.

Non-interference and quantitative information flow bounding problem when programs are modeled abstractly as nondeterministic transition systems are considered in [23] and [24] respectively. In this setting, the problems are shown to be PSPACE-complete.[4] However, this only implies an EXPSPACE-upper bound because the translation into an explicit state description causes an exponential blowup. For example, the following program with three variables x, y, z:

$$x := x \lor (y \land z); \text{ end}$$

is represented in [24] as a state machine with 16 states. (The factor of 2 is due to the program counter).

As discussed above, the best known upper bound for quantitative information flow bounding problem was EXPTIME [5] which follows from EXPTIME-completeness of quantitative information flow problem in recursive Boolean programs [5]. The EXPTIME upper bound improves to PSPACE when the number of outputs variables are logarithmic in the size of the program [5].

The proof of the PSPACE-upper bound in [5] is established by reducing the quantitative information flow bounding problem in PSPACE to checking whether an SLP defines a positive integer. The restriction on the number of outputs ensures that the constructed program is polynomial in length. Then the recent result of [2] is invoked which shows that the problem of checking whether an SLP defines a positive integer is in counting hierarchy and hence in PSPACE. Since we are not restricting the number of outputs, the reduction yields an SLP which is exponential in input size. Thus, we cannot use [2] and have to establish our result on SLP generators.

Attacks based on implicit observations of program execution, such as timing behavior, are hard to protect against and can lead to serious breaches of confidentiality (see for example, [4] which exhibits a practical timing attack against OpenSSL which allows the adversary to obtain private RSA keys.) Hence, several approaches have been proposed in the literature to counteract timing leaks (see [1,17] for example).

---

[4] Even though the partial program model defined in [24] is a Boolean program, the complexity results are reported in terms of the size of the explicit nondeterministic transition system, which is exponentially larger than the size of partial program.

2   Preliminaries

We recall some standard definitions and establish some notations. Note that for a set X, the set of all boolean valued functions with domain X shall be denoted as 2^X. Please note that our notations closely follow [5].

2.1   Boolean Programs

Syntax: The programs that we consider have input variables, output variables and local variables. Input variables can be either *high-security input variables*, meaning that the adversary cannot observe their values, or *low-security input variables*, meaning that their values are known to the adversary. The output variables will be *low-security variables*, i.e., their values shall be observable to the adversary. The values of local variables will not be observable to the adversary.[5]

Formally, we assume a countable set Vars of variables which can take Boolean values $\top$ (true) and $\bot$ (false). The set Exps of Boolean expressions is generated by the following BNF grammar ($x \in$ Vars):

$$\phi ::= \top \mid \bot \mid x \mid \neg\phi \mid (\phi \vee \phi) \mid (\phi \wedge \phi).$$

A program can manipulate its variables using statements. The set of statements, Stmts, is defined by the following BN F grammar ($x \in$ Vars, $\phi \in$ Exps):

$$
\begin{aligned}
s ::= \ &\textbf{skip} &&\text{(Skip)}\\
\mid\ &x \leftarrow \phi &&\text{(Assignment)}\\
\mid\ &\textbf{if } \phi \textbf{ then } s \textbf{ else } s \textbf{ end} &&\text{(Conditional)}\\
\mid\ &\textbf{while } \phi \textbf{ do } s \textbf{ end} &&\text{(Iteration)}\\
\mid\ &s; s &&\text{(Sequential composition)}
\end{aligned}
$$

As usual we say that $\text{Vars}(s)$ is the set of variables occurring in s.

A *program* P is of the form

$$\textbf{high } \overrightarrow{h}; \textbf{ low } \overrightarrow{l}; \textbf{ out } \overrightarrow{o}; \textbf{ local } \overrightarrow{z}; s$$

where s is a statement and $\overrightarrow{h}, \overrightarrow{l}, \overrightarrow{o}, \overrightarrow{z}$ are vectors of variables such that $\text{Vars}(s) \subseteq \overrightarrow{h} \cup \overrightarrow{l} \cup \overrightarrow{o} \cup \overrightarrow{z}$.

Semantics: Recall that a transition system, T, is a tuple $(Q, \rightarrow)$ where the set Q is a finite set of *configurations* and $\rightarrow \subseteq Q \times Q$ is a set of transitions. T is said to be *deterministic* if $c \rightarrow c_1$ and $c \rightarrow c_2$ implies that $c_1 = c_2$. A *computation* from a configuration c_0 is a sequence $c_0 \rightarrow \cdots \rightarrow_m$. We say that $c \overset{m}{\Rightarrow} c'$ if there exists a computation $c_0 \rightarrow \cdots \rightarrow c_m$ with $c_0 = c$ and $c_m = c'$, and we write $c \Rightarrow c'$ if $c \overset{m}{\Rightarrow} c'$ for some $m \in \mathbb{N}$.

---

[5] Note that high-security output variables can always be modeled as local variables.

We give an informal description of the semantics of programs. The operational semantics of a program P can be given in terms of a deterministic transition system $(\text{Conf}_P, \rightarrow_P, c_0)$ of size exponential in the size of P. A configuration $c \in \text{Conf}_P$ keeps track of the "current line number" and the "values" of the variables of the program P. A transition in $\rightarrow_P$ represents one execution step of P. The program P *terminates* on inputs $\vec{h}_0, \vec{l}_0$ if there is a computation from a configuration in which the "current line number" is the line of the first statement of P, the input variables are set to $\vec{h}_0, \vec{l}_0$, and the local and output variables are set to $\bot$ that reaches the configuration with the "current line number" corresponding to line number of the last statement of the program. If P terminates, we define the output of P to be the values of the output variables upon termination.

Therefore, P can be seen as a partial function $F_P : H \times L \to O$ where $H = 2^{\vec{h}}, L = 2^{\vec{l}}$ and $O = 2^{\vec{o}}$. $F_P(\vec{h}_0, \vec{l}_0)$ is defined iff P terminates on $\vec{h}_0, \vec{l}_0$, and is the value output by P on $\vec{h}_0, \vec{l}_0$. From now on, we will confuse P with the function F_P. We will only consider terminating programs. One could possibly model non-termination as an explicit observation and our complexity results will not change in that case. This is because nontermination on an input can be decided for while programs in PSPACE.

3   Mutual Information

We recall some standard definitions. Let $\mathcal{X}$ be a discrete random variable with values taken from a finite set X. If μ is the probability distribution of $\mathcal{X}$, the *Shannon entropy* of μ, written $H_\mu(\mathcal{X})$, is defined as

$$H_\mu(\mathcal{X}) = - \sum_{x \in X} \mu(\mathcal{X} = x) \cdot \log \mu(\mathcal{X} = x).$$

If $\mathcal{X}$ and $\mathcal{Y}$ are discrete random variables taking values from finite sets X and Y with joint probability distribution μ, the *conditional entropy* of $\mathcal{X}$ given $\mathcal{Y}$, written $H_\mu(\mathcal{X} \mid \mathcal{Y})$, is defined as

$$H_\mu(\mathcal{X} \mid \mathcal{Y}) = \sum_{y \in Y} \mu(\mathcal{Y} = y) \cdot H_\mu(\mathcal{X} \mid \mathcal{Y} = y).$$

The *mutual information* of $\mathcal{X}$ and $\mathcal{Y}$, written $I_\mu(\mathcal{X}; \mathcal{Y})$, is defined as

$$I_\mu(\mathcal{X}; \mathcal{Y}) = H_\mu(\mathcal{X}) - H_\mu(\mathcal{X} \mid \mathcal{Y}).$$

We have $I_\mu(\mathcal{X}; \mathcal{Y}) \geq 0$.

3.1   Quantitative Information Flow in Programs

We use conditional mutual information to quantify the amount of information leaked by the program as has been proposed in [12,14,19]. We assume that the reader is familiar with information theory and in particular conditional mutual information. As discussed above, the semantics of a Boolean program P is a function $P : H \times L \to O$. Assume now that the inputs are sampled from a distribution μ. Let $\mathcal{H}$ be the random variable taking values in H and $\mathcal{L}$ be the random variable taking values in L according to the distribution μ. μ can be extended to a joint probability distribution on H, L and O as follows

$$\mu(\mathcal{O} = o \mid \mathcal{H} = h, \mathcal{L} = l) = \begin{cases} 1 & \text{if } P(h,l) = o \\ 0 & \text{otherwise} \end{cases}.$$

The *information leaked by the program* P is then defined to be

$$\mathrm{SE}_\mu(P) := \mathrm{I}_\mu(\mathcal{H}; \mathcal{O} \mid \mathcal{L}).$$

In case there are no low-security inputs, the information leaked by the function F is just the mutual information between $\mathcal{H}$ and $\mathcal{O}$:

$$\mathrm{SE}_\mu(P) = \mathrm{I}_\mu(\mathcal{H}; \mathcal{O}).$$

A program P is *non-interferent* iff $\mathrm{SE}_\mu(P) = 0$ for all μ.[6]

We now recall a result proved in [5] that will allow us to restrict our attention to programs that have only high-security inputs. Given a program P with high-security input variables $\overrightarrow{h}$, low-security input variables $\overrightarrow{l}$ and low-security output variables $\overrightarrow{o}$, let the program $P_{nolowinp}$ be defined as follows. For each variable $l \in \overrightarrow{l}$, pick a new variable l_{new}. $P_{nolowinp}$ has high-security input variables $\overrightarrow{h}, \overrightarrow{l}$ and no low-security input variables. The output variables of $P_{nolowinp}$ are $\overrightarrow{o}$ and $\overrightarrow{l_{new}}$. The program $P_{nolowinp}$ initially copies the values $\overrightarrow{l}$ into $\overrightarrow{l_{new}}$ and then behaves exactly like P. The following is shown in [5]:

Proposition 1. $\mathrm{SE}_\mu(P_{nolowinp}) = \mathrm{SE}_\mu(P) + \mathrm{H}_\mu(\mathcal{L})$.

Note that when μ is U, the uniform distribution on $H \times L$, we have that $\mathrm{H}_\mu(\mathcal{L}) = \log |\mathcal{L}|$. Thus, it follows that if P has r low-security input variables, we get that

Proposition 2. $\mathrm{SE}_\mathsf{U}(P_{nolowinp}) = \mathrm{SE}_\mathsf{U}(P) + r$.

Thus, for uniformly distributed inputs, we shall only need to consider programs with no low-security inputs. We shall make use of the following theorem proved in [3,16]:

Theorem 1. *Let* $F_P \colon H \to O$ *be the semantics of a program* P *with no low-security inputs. Then*

$$\mathrm{SE}_\mathsf{U}(P) = \log |H| - \frac{1}{|H|} \sum_{o \in O} |F^{-1}(o)| \log |F^{-1}(o)|.$$

---

[6] It can be shown that this definition is equivalent to the standard definition of non-interference: for any low-input $l \in L$ and high inputs $h, h' \in H$, we have that $P(h,l) = P(h',l)$.

3.2   Decision Problems for Quantitative Information Flow

The quantitative information flow bounding problem: The *quantitative informa-tion flow bounding problem* asks, given a program P and a rational number $q \geq 0$, whether the information leaked by P does not exceed q, i.e., whether $\mathsf{SE_U}(P) \leq q$. The input to the decision problem is the program P and q (with numerator and denominator given in binary). The size of input problem is the size of P and the size of numerator and denominator q.

The quantitative information flow comparison problem: The *quantitative infor-mation flow comparison problem* asks, given programs P and P', whether the information leaked by P exceeds the information leaked by P', i.e., whether $\mathsf{SE_U}(P') < \mathsf{SE_U}(P)$. The input to the decision problem are the programs P and P'.

3.3   Straight-line Programs (SLP)s

Let Var be a countable set of variables. A (division-free) *straight-line program (SLP)* is a finite sequence of statements of the form $x \leftarrow 0$ or $x \leftarrow 1$ or $x \leftarrow Y \odot Z$, where $\odot \in \{+, -, \cdot\}$, $x \in Var$ and $Y, Z \in Var \cup \{0, 1\}$. are taken from a countable set of variables.

An SLP p is said to be *closed* if each variable that appears on the right-hand side of a statement also appears on the left-hand side of a preceding statement. The semantics for any such program is the usual where $\leftarrow$ corresponds to as-signment and the operators $+, -, \cdot$ are addition, subtraction and multiplication over the set of integers, $\mathbb{Z}$. The value of a closed SLP p denoted by $val(p)$ is the value of the last variable assigned in its last statement. The problem PosSLP is to decide, given a closed SLP p, whether $val(p) > 0$. It is shown in [2] that PosSLP is in counting hierarchy.

The standard square-and-multiply algorithm for exponentiation gives us the following.

Proposition 3. *Given a natural number $N > 0$ in binary with k bits, there is a closed SLP p_N of length $O(k)$ using only one variable such that $val(p_N) = N$. Given numbers $N_1, N_2 > 0$ in binary with k_1 and k_2 bits respectively, there is a closed SLP $p_{N_1^{N_2}}$ of length $O(k_1 + k_2)$ and using only 2 variables such that $val(p_{N_1^{N_2}}) = N_1^{N_2}$.*

4   SLP Generators

Given a finite set of variables V, we will say that a *SLP generator compatible with V* is an algorithm that outputs a closed SLP which uses variables in V. We shall be interested in special kinds of SLP generators:

Definition 1. *An SLP generator f compatible with V is said to be a good SLP-generator if:*

- f is a function computable in **PSPACE**, i.e., for any input w, $f(w)$ is computed using polynomially bounded workspace.
- For any input w, if the SLP $f(w)$ were to be executed then for each $x \in V$ at any point, the value of the variable x is $\geq -2^{2^{|w|}}$ and is $< 2^{2^{|w|}}$, where $|w|$ is the length of w.

Please note that the output $f(w)$ generated using a good SLP-generator f can be exponentially long (in terms of $|w|$), as will be the case when we apply our results in Theorem 2. We will be interested in deciding whether for a given w, the value of the program $f(w) > 0$. Since, $f(w)$ is exponentially long, we cannot directly apply result of [2] which says that PosSLP is in counting hierarchy and hence in **PSPACE**. However, the conditions of being a good SLP generator will allow us to adapt the proof of PosSLP being in counting hierarchy to establish the following result, whose proof has been moved to the Appendix for the sake of the flow of the paper.

Lemma 1. *Given a good SLP generator f compatible with V, the following language is* **PSPACE***:*

$$\{w \mid val(f(w)) > 0\}.$$

5 Complexity of Quantitative Information Flow

We will now consider the quantitative information flow bounding problem and the quantitative information flow comparison problem, showing both of them to be **PSPACE**-complete. Since non-interference in Boolean programs is **PSPACE**-hard [27], these two problems are easily seen to be **PSPACE**-hard. We only need to show the upper bounds.

We start by first considering the quantitative information flow bounding problem. We shall need one Lemma.

Lemma 2. *Let P be a program with $\overrightarrow{h}$ as high-security input variables, no low-security input variables and $\overrightarrow{o}$ as the output variables. If n is the number of high-security input variables and $O = 2^{\overrightarrow{o}}$ then*

$$\prod_{o \in O} |P^{-1}(o)|^{|P^{-1}(o)|} \leq 2^{n \cdot 2^n}.$$

Proof. Since mutual information is always positive, we have that $\mathrm{SE}_\mathsf{U}(P) \geq 0$. Thus, by Theorem 1, we get that

$$n - \frac{1}{2^n} \log \prod_{o \in O} |P^{-1}(o)|^{|P^{-1}(o)|} \geq 0.$$

Therefore,

$$\log \prod_{o \in O} |P^{-1}(o)|^{|P^{-1}(o)|} \leq n2^n.$$

The claim follows by exponentiating both sides. $\square$

Theorem 2. *The quantitative information flow bounding problem is* PSPACE-*complete for Boolean programs.*

Proof. We only need to prove the upper bound. Thanks to Proposition 2, we only need to consider programs with no low-security inputs.

Let P be a program with high input variables $\overrightarrow{h}$ and low-security output variables $\overrightarrow{o}$. Let the number of input variables be n and the number of output variables be m. Let $H = 2^{\overrightarrow{h}}$ and $O = 2^{\overrightarrow{o}}$. Let q be a rational number. We have $|H| = 2^n$.

Theorem 1 implies that $\mathrm{SE}_\mathsf{U}(P)$, the information leaked by P, is

$$n - \frac{1}{2^n} \log \prod_{o \in O} |P^{-1}(o)|^{|P^{-1}(o)|}.$$

Thus,

$$\mathrm{SE}_\mathsf{U}(P) \leq q \Leftrightarrow \log \prod_{o \in O} |P^{-1}(o)|^{|P^{-1}(o)|} \geq 2^n(n - q).$$

Observe that the number $2^n(n - q)$ is polynomial in the size of the program P and rational number q and can be computed in polynomial time. Thus it suffices to show that for any given positive rational number $\frac{r}{s}$, we can decide if

$$\log \prod_{o \in O} |P^{-1}(o)| \log |P^{-1}(o)| \geq \frac{r}{s}$$

in polynomial space (r can be taken to be positive as a program never leaks more than n bits). Note that since

$$\log \prod_{o \in O} |P^{-1}(o)|^{|P^{-1}(o)|} \geq \frac{r}{s} \Leftrightarrow \prod_{o \in O} |P^{-1}(o)|^{|P^{-1}(o)| \cdot s} \geq 2^r,$$

it suffices to show that we can decide if

$$\prod_{o \in O} |P^{-1}(o)|^{|P^{-1}(o)| \cdot s} - 2^r \geq 0$$

in polynomial space.

In order to show this, we will construct a good SLP generator f that given a program P and natural numbers r and s, constructs a SLP program with 6 variables[7] S such that

$$val(S) = \prod_{o \in O} |P^{-1}(o)|^{|P^{-1}(o)| \cdot s} - 2^r + 1.$$

The result will then follow from Lemma 1.

Let k be the size of s. We make a few observations before we show how to construct f.

---

[7] Since there are exponentially many outputs, program S itself will turn out to be exponential in length.

(a) $|P^{-1}(o)| \leq 2^n$. Hence $|P^{-1}(o)|$ can be represented as a binary number of size $n + 1$. The number $|P^{-1}(o)|s$ can be represented as a number of size $n + k + 1$ and computed in polynomial time given $|P^{-1}(o)|$ and s.

(b) Given $|P^{-1}(o)|$ and $|P^{-1}(o)|s$, we can construct in polynomial time (and hence in polynomial space) a SLP S_o whose value is $|P^{-1}(o)|^{|P^{-1}(o)| \cdot s}$ using two variables (See Proposition 3).

(c) By Lemma 2,

$$\prod_{o \in O} |P^{-1}(o)|^{|P^{-1}(o)| \cdot s} \leq 2^{s \cdot n \cdot 2^n}$$

and hence

$$\prod_{o \in O} |P^{-1}(o)|^{|P^{-1}(o)| \cdot s} \leq 2^{n \cdot 2^{n+k}}.$$

(d) P has m output variables. Let us fix an enumeration $o_1, \ldots, o_m$ of these variables. Hence each possible output $o \in O$ can be uniquely identified with a m-bit binary natural number whose ℓ-th bit is 1 iff o_ℓ is 1. We will henceforth confuse elements of O with the m-bit binary numbers representing them. We will use j to range over the m-bit binary natural numbers representing elements of O. Similarly, each input of P can be identified with a n-bit natural number.

(e) For any output j, $|P^{-1}(j)|$ can be computed using a work-tape polynomial in the size of P as follows. We initialize $|P^{-1}(j)|$ as 0. Recall that every input can be represented as a n-bit integer. We utilize this to iterate over all inputs as follows. We initialize a n-bit integer k as 0. At the 1-st iteration, we take all inputs to be zero, run the program P on this (which can be done in polynomial space) and check whether the output of P is j or not. If the output is j then we increment $|P^{-1}(j)|$ otherwise we leave $|P^{-1}(j)|$ unchanged. In either case, we increment k. At $k + 1$-st iteration, we take the input corresponding to k, run the program P on this input and check whether the output of P is j or not. Once again, if the output is j we increment $|P^{-1}(j)|$ otherwise we leave $|P^{-1}(j)|$. In either case, we increment k. The iterations stop when k becomes 2^n.

Now, we describe how the good SLP generator f is constructed. f will use six variables $\{z, x_0, y_0, x_1, y_1, res\}$ and its input tape will have a definition of P along with natural numbers r and s written on it. We give the psuedo-code for f in Figure 1 and describe f in detail. The PSLP f uses two integers j and k. j is used to iterate over outputs. In each iteration, the integer $count$ is used to compute the number of inputs that lead to the output j. The computation of $count$ is done by iterating over all inputs (k is used for this iteration).

At the first step f will output the assignment $z \leftarrow 1$. Now, f will do 2^m iterations numbered $0, 1, \ldots, 2^{m-1}$. At iteration j, f first computes $|P^{-1}(j)|$. Note that as observed above in (e), $|P^{-1}(j)|$ can be computed using polynomial workspace by iterating over all possible inputs, running program P for each input. After computing $|P^{-1}(j)|$, f computes $|P^{-1}(j)|s$ and f outputs the SLP computing $|P^{-1}(j)|^{|P^{-1}(j)| \cdot s}$ using variables x_0 and y_0. Without loss of generality,

---

Input: P, r, s where

  P is a program, r and s are natural numbers.
  Let $h_0, h_1, \cdots, h_n$ be the input variables of P and
  $o_0, o_1, \cdots, o_m$ be the output variables of P.

```
{
int k,j,count,power;
Output("z ← 1");
for (j := 0, j < 2^m, j + +)
  {
      count := 0;
      for (k := 0, k < 2^n, k + +)
        {
            h_0 := k[0]; h_1 := k[1]; ···; h_n := k[n];
            P(h⃗);
            if (o_0 = j[0]) ∧ (o_1 = j[1]) ∧ ··· ∧ (o_m = j[m])
            then count := count + 1
        }
      power := count × s;
      Output(expSLP(count, power, x_0, y_0));
      Output("z ← z · y_0");
  }
Output(expSLP(2, r, x_1, y_1));
Output("y_1 ← y_1 − 1");
Output("res ← z − y_1");
}
```

Fig. 1. Psuedo-code for the good SLP generator f. The ℓ-th bit of j (k, respectively) is represented by $j[\ell]$ ($k[\ell]$, respectively). The command Output(str) outputs the string str. $expSLP(t, u, x, y)$ is the SLP computing t^u using variables x, y with result being stored in y (See Proposition 3).

we can assume that the variable assigned to in the last statement of the program for $|P^{-1}(j)|^{|P^{-1}(j)|s}$ is y_0. After outputting the SLP defining $|P^{-1}(j)|^{|P^{-1}(j)|s}$, f outputs the assignment $z \leftarrow z \cdot y_0$. Using observations (a) and (b) above, it is easy to see all these 2^m iterations can be done using polynomially bounded space.

  After the 2^m iterations are over, it is easy to see the SLP output thus far has value $\prod_{o \in O} |P^{-1}(o)|^{|P^{-1}(o)|\cdot s}$ and that the variable last assigned to is z. f next outputs the SLP for 2^r using variables x_1 and y_1 with y_1 being the variable assigned to in the last statement of the SLP for 2^r. f then outputs the assignment $y_1 \leftarrow y_1 - 1$.

  Next, f outputs the statement $res = z - y_1$ and then terminates. It is easy to see using observation (c) above that f is a good SLP generator. and that if S is the SLP output by f then $val(S) = \prod_{o \in O} |P^{-1}(o)|^{|P^{-1}(o)|\cdot s} - 2^r + 1$. The result follows from Lemma 1. □

Similarly we can show that the quantitative information flow comparison problem is PSPACE-complete.

Corollary 1. *The quantitative information flow comparison problem is PSPACE-complete for Boolean programs.*

Proof. First, we make an observation that we will allow us to assume that the programs being compared have the same number of input variables. If P is a program with n inputs, let $P_{moreinputs}$ be the program with $n + k$ inputs which is constructed from P as follows. $P_{moreinputs}$ has exactly the same set of low-security input variables and the same set of output variables as P. $P_{moreinputs}$ also has each high-security input variable that has P has. In addition P has k new high security inputs $o_{new}^1, o_{new}^2, \ldots, o_{new}^k$. The body of the program $P_{moreinputs}$ is exactly the body of the program P (in other words, $o_{new}^1, o_{new}^2, \ldots, o_{new}^k$ are never utilized in the program). Then using Theorem 1 and Proposition 2, it follows that $\mathrm{SE}_\mathsf{U}(P) = \mathrm{SE}_\mathsf{U}(P_{moreinputs})$.

As observed above, we only need to show the upper bound. Now, let P and P' be two programs with the same number of input variables m and with O and O' as the set of outputs respectively. If r_1 and r_2 are the number of low-security input variables of P_1 and P_2 respectively then it is easy to see using Theorem 1 and Proposition 2 that

$$\mathrm{SE}_\mathsf{U}(P) < \mathrm{SE}_\mathsf{U}(P')$$

iff

$$m - \tfrac{1}{2^m} \log(\textstyle\prod_{o \in O} |P^{-1}(o)|^{|P^{-1}(o)|}) - r_1 < \\ m - \tfrac{1}{2^m} \log(\textstyle\prod_{o' \in O'} |P'^{-1}(o')|^{|P'^{-1}(o')|}) - r_2$$

iff

$$\log(\textstyle\prod_{o \in O} |P^{-1}(o)|^{|P^{-1}(o)|}) > \\ \log(\textstyle\prod_{o' \in O'} |P'^{-1}(o')|^{|P'^{-1}(o')|}) + (r_2 - r_1)2^m$$

iff

$$\prod_{o \in O} |P^{-1}(o)|^{|P^{-1}(o)|} > 2^{(r_2 - r_1)2^m} \prod_{o' \in O'} |P'^{-1}(o')|^{|P'^{-1}(o')|}.$$

Note that 2^m is representable by a m-bit integer. The result follows by observing that we can check if

$$\prod_{o \in O} |P^{-1}(o)|^{|P^{-1}(o)|} > 2^{(r_2 - r_1)2^m} \prod_{o' \in O'} |P'^{-1}(o')|^{|P'^{-1}(o')|}.$$

in PSPACE in a fashion similar to the proof of Theorem 2. □

5.1   Information Leaked from Timing Behavior

We now turn our attention to the problem of estimating the information leaked by a program by its timing behavior. [5] propose using the number of steps taken by a program as an abstraction of timing behavior. Thus, in order to measure the information leaked by a program by its timing behavior, we can consider P as function from its inputs to natural numbers and define the amount of information leaked by the timing behavior as in Section 3.1. More precisely, given a program P, with high input variables $\overrightarrow{h}$ and low input variables $\overrightarrow{l}$, let $\text{Steps}_P : 2^{\overrightarrow{h}} \times 2^{\overrightarrow{l}} \to \mathbb{N}$ be the function such that $\text{Steps}_P(\overrightarrow{h}_0, \overrightarrow{l}_0)$ is the number of steps in the computation of $P(\overrightarrow{h}_0, \overrightarrow{l}_0)$. Now, we can define $\text{SE}_\mu(\text{Steps}_P)$ in a manner analogous to the definition of $\text{SE}_\mu(P)$.

Definition 2. $\text{SE}_\mathsf{U}(\text{Steps}_P)$ *is the* information leaked by the timing behavior *of P.*

A terminating while program takes at most $c2^t$ steps, where c is the number of statements in the program and t is the total number of variables of the program. The number of steps can be represented as a natural number whose (binary) size is polynomial in the size of program. It is easy to see that the proofs of Theorem 2 and Corollary 1 can be modified to show the following (the lower bounds follow from [5]):

Corollary 2. *The problem of bounding information leaked by the timing behavior of a Boolean program is* PSPACE-*complete. The problem of comparing information leaked by timing behavior of Boolean programs is* PSPACE-*complete.*

6   Conclusions and Future Work

We have shown that the quantitative information flow bounding problem and the quantitative information flow comparison problem for Boolean programs are PSPACE-complete. Surprisingly, this matches the PSPACE-completeness of safety verification of Boolean programs. The same bounds apply when the adversary observes the number of executions steps and not explicit outputs.

The PSPACE-upper bound result implies that the quantitative information flow bounding problem is reducible to safety verification of Boolean programs. While we have not given this direct reduction, one can be obtained by composing the reductions in the proofs of Lemma 1 and Theorem 2. Thus, in order to check if the information leaked by a program is less than q we can reduce the problem to the safety verification problem of Boolean programs and then use an off-the-shelf verification tool. We are currently investigating this approach.

In order to establish the upper bound, we establish a new result on SLP generators. In particular, we give sufficient restrictions that ensures that the problem of checking whether the number defined by the output of an SLP generator F on input w is strictly positive can be decided in PSPACE. This result may be of independent interest.

Acknowledgements. Work by Rohit Chadha was supported by the National Science Foundation under Grant No. TWC-1314338. Work by Dileep Kini was supported by the National Science Foundation under Grant No. SHF-1016989. Work by Mahesh Viswanathan was supported by the National Science Foundation under Grant No. TWC-1314485.

References

1. Agat, J.: Transforming out timing leaks. In: POPL 2000, pp. 40–53 (2000)
2. Allender, E., Bürgisser, P., Kjeldgaard-Pedersen, J., Miltersen, P.B.: On the complexity of numerical analysis. SIAM Journal on Computing 38(5), 1987–2006 (2009)
3. Backes, M., Köpf, B., Rybalchenko, A.: Automatic discovery and quantification of information leaks. In: IEEE Symposium on Security and Privacy, pp. 141–153 (2009)
4. Brumley, D., Boneh, D.: Remote timing attacks are practical. Computer Networks 48(5), 701–716 (2005)
5. Chadha, R., Ummels, M.: The complexity of quantitative information flow in recursive programs. In: FSTTCS, pp. 534–545 (2012)
6. Chatzikokolakis, K., Chothia, T., Guha, A.: Statistical measurement of information leakage. In: Esparza, J., Majumdar, R. (eds.) TACAS 2010. LNCS, vol. 6015, pp. 390–404. Springer, Heidelberg (2010)
7. Chatzikokolakis, K., Palamidessi, C., Panangaden, P.: Probability of error in information-hiding protocols. In: CSF 2007, pp. 341–354 (2007)
8. Chatzikokolakis, K., Palamidessi, C., Panangaden, P.: Anonymity protocols as noisy channels. Information and Computation 206(2-4) (2008)
9. Clark, D., Hunt, S., Malacaria, P.: Quantified interference for a while language. Electronic Notes in Theoretical Computer Science (Proc. QAPL 2004) 112, 49–166 (1984)
10. Clark, D., Hunt, S., Malacaria, P.: Quantitative information flow, relations and polymorphic types. Journal of Logic Computation 15(2), 181–199 (2005)
11. Clark, D., Hunt, S., Malacaria, P.: A static analysis for quantifying information flow in a simple imperative language. Journal of Computer Security 15(3), 321–371 (2007)
12. Denning, D.E.R.: Cryptography and Data Security. Addison-Wesley (1982)
13. Goguen, J.A., Meseguer, J.: Security policies and security models. In: IEEE Symposium on Security and Privacy, pp. 11–20 (1982)
14. Gray III, J.W.: Toward a mathematical foundation for information flow security. In: IEEE Symposium on Security and Privacy, pp. 21–35 (1991)
15. Hesse, W., Allender, E., Mix Barrington, D.A.: Uniform constant-depth threshold circuits for division and iterated multiplication. Journal of Computing Systems and Sciences 65(4), 695–716 (2002)
16. Köpf, B., Basin, D.A.: An information-theoretic model for adaptive side-channel attacks. In: ACM Conference on Computer and Communications Security, pp. 286–296 (2007)
17. Köpf, B., Dürmuth, M.: A provably secure and efficient countermeasure against timing attacks. In: CSF 2009, pp. 324–335 (2009)
18. Köpf, B., Rybalchenko, A.: Approximation and randomization for quantitative information-flow analysis. In: CSF 2010, pp. 3–14 (2010)
19. Millen, J.K.: Covert channel capacity. In: IEEE Symposium on Security and Privacy, pp. 60–66 (1987)
20. Reynolds, J.C.: Syntactic control of interference. In: POPL 1978, pp. 39–46 (1978)
21. Shannon, C.: A mathematical theory of communication. The Bell System Technical Journal 27, 379–423, 623–656 (1948)
22. Smith, G.: On the foundations of quantitative information flow. In: de Alfaro, L. (ed.) FOSSACS 2009. LNCS, vol. 5504, pp. 288–302. Springer, Heidelberg (2009)

23. van der Meyden, R., Zhang, C.: Algorithmic verification of noninterference properties. Electronic Notes in Theoretical Computer Science 168, 61–75 (2007)
24. Černý, P., Chatterjee, K., Henzinger, T.A.: The complexity of quantitative information flow problems. In: CSF 2011, pp. 205–217 (2011)
25. Yasuoka, H., Terauchi, T.: On bounding problems of quantitative information flow. In: Gritzalis, D., Preneel, B., Theoharidou, M. (eds.) ESORICS 2010. LNCS, vol. 6345, pp. 357–372. Springer, Heidelberg (2010)
26. Yasuoka, H., Terauchi, T.: Quantitative information flow - verification hardness and possibilities. In: CSF 2010, pp. 15–27 (2010)
27. Yasuoka, H., Terauchi, T.: Quantitative information flow as safety and liveness hyperproperties. In: QAPL 2012, pp. 77–91 (2012)

A   Proof of Lemma 1

We recall a couple of definitions before we give the proof of the lemma.

Chinese Remainders: First we recall the the idea of Chinese Remainder Representation, CRR, of a number: An m-bit number can be uniquely represented using its residue modulo polynomially many primes each of which is $O(\log m)$ bits.[8]. More precisely, if we are given the residues of a number modulo all primes $p < m^2$ then there is a unique such number among those with less than m-bits. By the (p, j)-th bit of a CRR of a number N, we will mean the jth bit of the residue with respect to prime p.

Dlogtime-uniform threshold circuits: A *majority gate* is one which outputs the value which occurs in most of its inputs. Boolean Circuits built using majority gates in addition to the boolean gates are called *threshold* circuits. The uniformity condition of Dlogtime essentially says that the connection between gates of the circuit can be determined in logarithmic time.

Let f be a good SLP-generator and let w be an input word of length n. Now, for SLP $f(w)$, we know that the integers to which the variables evaluate to are always between -2^{2^n} to $2^{2^n} - 1$. So if we define an SLP X_w which computes $2^{2^n} + val(f(w))$ then $val(X_w) \geq 0$. Furthermore, $val(f(w)) > 0$ iff the most significant bit of $val(X_w)$ and some other bit of $val(X_w)$ is 1. Also note that X_w uses 2 extra variables (first compute 2^{2^n} using two new variables, then follow it by the SLP $f(w)$, and finally add the result of 2^{2^n} to $f(w)$). We can of course fix the two extra variables (i.e., the same extra two variables will work for all w).

Now we are ready to state the crucial result from [15] which we shall use in the proof:

Theorem 3. *There are Dlogtime-uniform threshold circuits D_m of polynomial size and constant depth that compute the following transformation:*

Input: *A number Y, between 0 and 2^m in Chinese Remainder Representation (CRR) using all primes $p < m^2$.*

---

[8] A residue of a number N modulo a prime p is the remainder when N is divided by p

Output: *The m bits in the binary representation of Y.*

We will apply the Theorem for the case $m = 2^n + 1$. Thus $m^2 = (2^n + 1)^2$.

First, we observe any bit of the CRR of $val(X_w)$ can be computed in space polynomial in n. To obtain the bit (p, j) we maintain for each variable in X_w its residue modulo p and update it according to the statements of X_w. The residue is a number less than 2^{2n+2} and hence requires $O(n)$ space, and the calculation for each statement can be done in $O(n)$ time. We also know that the statements of $f(w)$ can be generated in polynomial space. So altogether any bit in the CRR of $val(X_w)$ can be computed in PSPACE.

The idea now is to use the circuit D_{2^n+1} to translate the CRR of $val(X_w)$ to its binary representation and show that any bit in the binary representation of $val(X_w)$ can be calculated in polynomial space. We show this by showing that the output of any gate of D_{2^n+1} (when the input is CRR of $val(X_w)$) can be computed in polynomial space. This is done by inducting on the height of the gates present in the circuit. For the base case, we have seen that the input gates can be computed in PSPACE. For the inductive step, consider any gate G at height $h + 1$. We can iterate over all gates G' of D_{2^n+1} and identify if G' is a child of G in polynomial space because the circuit D_{2^n+1} is from a Dlogtime-uniform family. The children (of which there can be exponentially many) are all at height h or less and hence output of each one can be computed in PSPACE. If G is a NOT gate, output of G can be easily computed from its child. If G is a majority gate, we need only compare the number of children which evaluate to 1 against the number of those that evaluate to 0 which can be done in polynomial space by maintaining these numbers in binary counters.

In summary, to determine if $val(f(w)) > 0 \in L(f)$ we need to identify the value of two bits in the binary representation of $val(X_w)$ (one most significant bit and some other guessed bit). Even though $f(w)$ (and hence X_w) can be exponentially long, the good SLP conditions ensure that we can calculate the residues of the result in polynomial space. Using this along with Theorem 3 as above gives us the complete proof of our lemma.

When Not All Bits Are Equal:
Worth-Based Information Flow

Mário S. Alvim[1], Andre Scedrov[2], and Fred B. Schneider[3]

[1] Universidade Federal de Minas Gerais, Brazil
[2] University of Pennsylvania, USA
[3] Cornell University, USA

Abstract. Only recently have approaches to quantitative information flow started to challenge the presumption that all leaks involving a given number of bits are equally harmful. This paper proposes a framework to capture the semantics of information, making quantification of leakage independent of the syntactic representation of secrets. Secrets are defined in terms of fields, which are combined to form structures; and a *worth assignment* is introduced to associate each structure with a worth (perhaps in proportion to the harm that would result from disclosure). We show how worth assignments can capture inter-dependence among structures within a secret, modeling: (i) secret sharing, (ii) information-theoretic predictors, and (iii) computational (as opposed to information-theoretic) guarantees for security. Using non-trivial worth assignments, we generalize Shannon entropy, guessing entropy, and probability of guessing. For deterministic systems, we give a lattice of information to provide an underlying algebraic structure for the composition of attacks. Finally, we outline a design technique to capture into worth assignments relevant aspects of a scenario of interest.

1 Introduction

Quantitative information flow (QIF) is concerned with measuring how much secret information leaks to an adversary through a system. The adversary is presumed to have *a priori information* about the secrets before execution starts and to access *public observables* as execution proceeds. By combining a priori information and public observables, the adversary achieves *a posteriori information* about the secrets. The *leakage* from an execution is the difference between a posteriori and a priori information.

This definition of leakage depends on how information is measured. Cachin [1] advocates that information measures not only include a way to calculate some numeric value but also offer an *operational interpretation*, which describes what aspect of interest is being quantified. Popular information measures include: *Shannon entropy* [2–8], which measures how much information is leaked per guess; *guessing entropy* [9, 10], which measures how many tries are required before the secret is correctly guessed; and *probability of guessing* [11,12], which measures how likely it is that a secret is correctly inferred in a certain number of tries.

M. Abadi and S. Kremer (Eds.): POST 2014, LNCS 8414, pp. 120–139, 2014.

These measures are best suited to sets of monolithic and equally valuable secrets, so researchers have recently begun to consider richer scenarios. The *g-leakage* framework [13] of Alvim et al. makes use of gain functions to quantify the benefit of different guesses for the secret. However, identifying sufficiently expressive yet not over-complicated gain-functions is often a challenge. Moreover, that framework generalizes probability of guessing, but not Shannon entropy or guessing entropy. Finally, it is not suitable to infinitely risk-averse adversaries. In this paper we propose an approach that addresses these limitations; a detailed comparison with *g*-leakage is given in Section 6.

We model a secret as being partitioned into *fields*, which are combined to form *structures*. Since disclosure of different structures might cause different harms, a *worth assignment* is introduced to associate a *worth* with each structure. For instance, the secret corresponding to a client's bank account might comprise two 10-digit structures: a pincode and a telephone number. Leaking the pincode has the potential to cause considerable harm, so that structure would be assigned high worth; the telephone number is public information, so this structure would be assigned low worth.

Assuming that all structures have equal worth can lead to misleading comparisons between systems that leak structures with different worths but the same numbers of bits. Conversely, ignoring the structure of secrets may lead to a deceptive estimate of the harm from leaking different numbers of bits. Consider two systems that differ in the way they represent a house address. In system C_1, standard postal addresses are used (i.e., a number, street name, and zip-code); system C_2 uses GPS coordinates (i.e., a latitude and a longtitude, each a signed 10-digit number). Under Shannon entropy with plausible sizes[1] for address fields, C_1 requires 129 bits to represent a location that C_2 represents using 69 bits. Yet the same content is revealed whether C_1 leaks its 129 bits or C_2 leaks its 69 bits. (The a priori information for addresses in C_1 is not zero, since certain values for a house number, street name, and zip-code can be ruled out. And a similar argument can be made for C_2, given knowledge of habitable terrain. Accounting for idiosyncrasies in the syntactic representation of secrets, however, can be a complicated task, hence an opportunity for error. Worth assignments avoid some of that complexity.)

When secrets are not modeled as monolithic, distinct structures within a given secret may be correlated. A clever adversary, thus, might infer information about a structure with more worth (and presumably better protected) by attacking a correlated structure with less worth (and presumably less well protected). For instance, the location of a neighborhood is often correlated to the political preferences of its residents, so an adversary may target a person's house address to infer information about what political party they support. Worth assignments can model such correlations and adjust the relative worth of structures. Moreover, they can capture the computational complexity of inferring one structure from the other, which is a common limitation of information theoretical

---

[1] Specifically, assume a 5-digit house number, a 20-character alphabetic street name, and a 5-digit zip-code.

approaches to QIF. As an example, a public RSA key is a perfect predictor, in an information theoretical sense, for the corresponding private key. In practice, however, the public key should not be assigned the same worth as the private key because a realistic adversary is not expected to retrieve the latter from the former in viable time.

In this paper, we propose *measures of information worth* that incorporate the structure and worth of secrets. As in other QIF literature, we assume the adversary performs attacks, controlling the low input to a probabilistic system execution and observing the low outputs. An attack induces a probability distribution on the space of secrets according to what the adversary observes. This characterization admits measures of information worth for the information contained in each distribution; leakage is then defined as the difference in information between distributions. Our approach generalizes probability of guessing, guessing entropy, and Shannon entropy to admit non-trivial worth assignments. Yet our work remains consistent with the Lattice of Information [14] for deterministic systems, which is an underlying algebraic structure for sets of system executions.

The main contributions of this paper are:

- We propose a framework of structures and worth assignments to capture the semantics of information, making the quantification of leakage independent of the particular representation chosen for secrets.
- We show how to use worth assignments to model the inter-dependence among structures within a given secret, capturing practical scenarios including: (i) secret sharing, (ii) information-theoretic predictors, and (iii) computational (as opposed to information-theoretic) guarantees for security.
- We generalize Shannon entropy and guessing entropy to incorporate worth explicitly, and we introduce other measures without traditional equivalents. We show that our theory of measures of information worth and the g-leakage framework are not comparable in general, although they do overlap.
- We prove that our measures of information worth are consistent with the Lattice of Information for deterministic systems, which allows sound reasoning about the composition of attacks in such systems.
- We outline a design technique for worth assignments that capture the following aspects of the scenario of interest: (i) *secrecy requirements* that determine what structures are intrinsically sensitive, and by how much, (ii) *consistency requirements* that ensure the adequacy of the worth assignment, and (iii) the *adversarial knowledge* that may be of help in attacks.

The paper is organized as follows. Section 2 describes our model for the structure and worth of secrets in probabilistic systems. Section 3 uses worth assignments to propose measures of information worth. Section 4 shows that the proposed measures are consistent with respect to the Lattice of Information for deterministic systems under composite attacks. Section 5 outlines a technique for designing adequate worth assignments for a scenario of interest. Finally, Section 6 discusses related work, and Section 7 concludes the paper. Full proofs can be found in the Appendix of the corresponding technical report [15].

2   Modeling the Structure and Worth of Secrets

We decompose secrets into elementary units called *fields*, each a piece of information with a domain. Let $\mathcal{F} = \{f_1, \ldots, f_m\}$ denote the (finite) set of fields in some scenario of interest, and for $1 \leq i \leq m$, let $domain(f_i)$ be the domain of values for field f_i. A *structure* is a subset $\mathfrak{f} \subseteq \mathcal{F}$, and if $\mathfrak{f} = \{f_{i_1}, \cdots, f_{i_k}\}$, its domain is given by $domain(\mathfrak{f}) = domain(f_{i_1}) \times \cdots \times domain(f_{i_k})$. The set of all possible structures is the power set $\mathcal{P}(\mathcal{F})$ of fields, and the structure $\mathfrak{f} = \mathcal{F}$ containing all fields is called the *maximal structure*.

A *secret* s is a mapping from the maximal structure to values, i.e., $s = \langle s[f_1], \ldots, s[f_m] \rangle$, where $s[f_i] \in domain(f_i)$ is the value assumed by field f_i. Hence the set $\mathcal{S}$ of possible secrets is $\mathcal{S} = domain(\mathcal{F})$. Given a secret s and a (not necessarily maximal) structure $\mathfrak{f} \subseteq \mathcal{F}$, we call a *sub-secret* $s[\mathfrak{f}]$ the projection of s on the domain of $\mathfrak{f}$, and the set of all possible sub-secrets associated with that structure is $\mathcal{S}[\mathfrak{f}] = domain(\mathfrak{f})$.

Structures may carry some valuable piece of information on their own. A *worth assignment* attributes to each structure a non-negative, real number. Worth may be seen as the utility obtained by an adversary who learns the contents of the structure, or it may be seen as the damage suffered should the contents of the structure become known to that adversary.

Definition 1 (Worth assignment). *A worth* assignment *is a function* $\omega : \mathcal{P}(\mathcal{F}) \to \mathbb{R}$ *from the set of structures to reals, satisfying for all* $\mathfrak{f}, \mathfrak{f}' \in \mathcal{P}(\mathcal{F})$: (i) *non-negativity:* $\omega(\mathfrak{f}) \geq 0$, *and* (ii) *monotonicity:* $\mathfrak{f} \subseteq \mathfrak{f}' \implies \omega(\mathfrak{f}) \leq \omega(\mathfrak{f}')$.

We require non-negativity of ω because the knowledge of the contents of a structure should not carry a negative amount of information, and we require monotonicity because every structure should be at least as sensitive as any of its parts. Note that monotonicity implies that the worth of the maximal structure, $\omega(\mathcal{F})$, is an upper bound for the worth of every structure.

Expressiveness of Worth Assignments. The worth of a structure should appropriately represent the sensitivity of that structure in a scenario of interest. Consider a medical database where a secret is a patient's entire record, and structures are sub-sets of that record (e.g., a patient's name, age, smoking habits). The worth assigned to an individual's smoking habits should reflect: (i) how much the *protector* (i.e., the party interested in keeping the secret concealed) cares about hiding whether an individual is a smoker, (ii) how much an adversary would benefit from learning whether an individual is a smoker, and, more subtly, (iii) how effective (information-theoretically and/or computationally) a predictor an individual's smoking habits are for other sensitive structures (for instance, heavy smokers are more likely to develop lung cancer, and insurance companies may deny them coverage based on that). Worth assignments can capture these aspects, modeling also:

a) **Semantic-based leakage.** Worth assignments provide a natural means to abstract from syntactic idiosyncrasies and treat structures according to meaning. In the bank system of Section 1, for instance, we would assign higher worth to the 10-digit pincode than to the 10-digit telephone number, thus distinguishing among eventual 10-digit leaks according to relevance:

$$\omega(\{\text{pin-code}\}) > \omega(\{\text{telephone number}\}).$$

Conversely, structures with equivalent meanings should be assigned the same worth, regardless of representation. For instance, the worth of all structures corresponding to an address should be the same, whether it is represented in GPS coordinates or in the standard postal address format:

$$\omega(\{\text{GPS address}\}) = \omega(\{\text{postal address}\}).$$

b) **Secret sharing.** The combination of two structures may convey more worth than the sum of their individual worths. In *secret sharing*, for instance, different persons retain distinct partial secrets (i.e., structures) that in isolation give no information about the secret as a whole (i.e., the maximal structure), but that reveal the entire secret when combined. As another example, a decryption key without any accompanying ciphertext is of little worth, so each corresponding structure should have, in isolation, a worth close to zero. When combined, however, the benefit to the adversary exceeds the sum of their individual worths:

$$\omega(\{\text{ciphertext}, \text{decryption key}\}) \gg \omega(\{\text{ciphertext}\}) + \omega(\{\text{decryption key}\}).$$

c) **Correlation of structures.** Knowledge of a particular structure may imply knowledge of another (e.g., if the adversary has access to tax files, learning someone's tax identification number implies learning their name as well), or it may increase the probability of learning another structure (recall the correlation between smoking habits and lung cancer). An adversary might exploit correlations between different structures within a given secret to obtain information about a more important (and presumably better protected) structure through a less important (and presumably less well protected) structure. By considering the distribution on secrets and the capabilities of the adversary, we can adjust the relative worth of one structure with respect to any other, thus avoiding potentially harmful loopholes. In particular, worth assignments can model:

  (i) **Information-theoretic predictors.** The worth of a structure should reflect the worth it carries, via correlation, from other structures. For instance, when an individual's identity can be recovered with 60% probability from the combination of the zip-code, date of birth, and gender [16], we might enforce $\omega(\{\text{zip-code}, \text{date of birth}, \text{gender}\})$ to be at least as great as 60% of the worth $\omega(\{\text{identity}\})$. More generally, given any two structures $f, f' \in \mathcal{P}(\mathcal{F})$, the requirement

$$\omega(f) \geq correlation(f, f') \cdot \omega(f')$$

might be imposed on a worth assignment ω. Here $correlation(f, f')$ is a function representing how well f predicts f'.

(ii) **Computational effort.** Even perfect information-theoretic correlations among structures may not be of practical use for the adversary (e.g., the correlation of public and private RSA keys). Worth assignments can reflect this. We can impose, on any two structures $\mathfrak{f}, \mathfrak{f}' \in \mathcal{P}(\mathcal{F})$, the requirement

$$w(\mathfrak{f}) > w(\mathfrak{f}')/cost(\mathfrak{f}, \mathfrak{f}'),$$

where $cost(\mathfrak{f}, \mathfrak{f}')$ is a function of the computational effort needed to obtain $\mathfrak{f}'$ from $\mathfrak{f}$.

2.1 A Worth-Based Approach to QIF

We adopt a probabilistic version of the model of deterministic systems and attacks proposed by Köpf and Basin [17]. Let $\mathcal{S}$ be a finite set of *secrets*, $\mathcal{A}$ be a finite set of adversary-controlled inputs or *attacks*, and $\mathcal{O}$ be a finite set of *observables*. A *(probabilistic computational) system* is a family $C = \{(\mathcal{S}, \mathcal{O}, C_a)\}_{a \in \mathcal{A}}$ of *(information-theoretic) channels* parametrized by the adversary-chosen

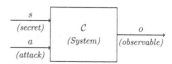

Fig. 1. A system with one high input, one low input, and one low output

input $a \in \mathcal{A}$. Each $(\mathcal{S}, \mathcal{O}, C_a)$ is a channel in which $\mathcal{S}$ is the *channel input*, $\mathcal{O}$ is the *channel output*, and C_a is a $|\mathcal{S}| \times |\mathcal{O}|$ matrix of conditional probability distributions called the *channel matrix*. Each entry $C_a(s, o)$ in the matrix represents the probability of the system producing observable o when the secret is s and the adversary-chosen low input is a. Given a probability distribution p_S on $\mathcal{S}$, the behavior of the system under attack a is described by the joint distribution $p_a(s, o) = p_S(s) \cdot C_a(s, o)$, with marginal $p_a(o) = \sum_s p_a(s, o)$, and conditional distribution $p_a(s|o) = p_a(s, o)/p_a(o)$ whenever $p_a(o) > 0$ (and similarly for $p_a(s)$ and $p_a(o|s)$).

As is usual in QIF, assume that the adversary knows the probability distribution p_S on the set of secrets and the family of channel matrices C describing the system's behavior. By controlling the low input, the adversary can launch an attack as follows: pick $a \in \mathcal{A}$ so the channel matrix is set to C_a, thereby manipulating the behavior of the system. The adversary's goal is to infer as much information as possible from the secret, given knowledge about how the system works, the attack fed to the system, and the observations made as the system executes.

Let Ω be the set of all possible worth assignments for the structures of $\mathcal{S}$, $Pr(S)$ be the set of all probability distributions on $\mathcal{S}$, and $\mathcal{C}_\mathcal{A}$ be the set of channel matrices induced by attacks $a \in \mathcal{A}$. A *measure of information worth* is a function $\nu : \Omega \times Pr(\mathcal{S}) \times \mathcal{C}_\mathcal{A} \to \mathbb{R}^+$. The quantity $\nu(w, p_S, C_a)$ represents the *a posteriori* information with respect to S revealed by attack $C_a \in \mathcal{C}_\mathcal{A}$, given probability distribution $p_S \in Pr(\mathcal{S})$ on secrets and worth assignment $w \in \Omega$. Before any attack is performed, the adversary has some *a priori* information about the secret due to knowledge of p_S and w only, and we represent this information by

$\nu(\omega, p_S)$. Because the attack is expected to disclose secret information to the adversary, the leakage from an attack C_a is defined as the difference[2], between the a posteriori and a priori information associated with C_a.

Before discussing measures of information, we will fix some additional notation. For any $S' \subseteq S$ we denote by $p_S(\cdot|S')$ the normalization of p_S with respect to S', i.e., for every $s \in S$, $p_S(s|S') = p_S(s)/p_S(S')$ if $s \in S'$, and $p_S(s|S') = 0$ otherwise. The support of a distribution p_S is denoted $supp(p_S)$. A set $\mathsf{P} = \{S_1, \dots, S_n\}$ is a *partition* on S iff: (i) $\bigcup_{S_i \in \mathsf{P}} S_i = S$, and (ii) for $1 \le i \ne j \le n$, $S_i \cap S_j = \emptyset$. Each $S_i \in \mathsf{P}$ is called a *block* in the partition. We denote the set of all partitions in S by $\mathsf{LoI}(S)$ [3]. Following [10], any partition $\mathsf{P}_a = \{S_{o_1}, \dots, S_{o_n}\}$ on S induced by the attack a can be seen as a random variable with carrier $\{S_{o_1}, \dots, S_{o_n}\}$ and probability distribution $p_S(S_{o_i}) = \sum_{s \in S_{o_i}} p_S(s)$.

3   Measures of Information Worth

3.1   Operational Interpretation of Measures Revisited

One of Shannon's greatest insights, which ultimately led to the creation of the field of information theory, can be formulated as: *information is describable in terms of answers to questions*. The more information the adversary has about a random variable, the fewer questions of a certain type that must be asked in order to infer its value, and the smaller the Shannon entropy of this random variable.

Formally, the *Shannon entropy* of a probability distribution p_S is defined as $SE(p_S) = -\sum_s p_S(s) \log p_S(s)$, and the *conditional Shannon entropy* of p_S given a channel C_a is defined as $SE(p_S, C_a) = \sum_{o \in \mathcal{O}} p_a(o) SE(p_a(\cdot|o))$. A possible operational interpretation of this measure is: The adversary can pose questions *Does $S \in S'$?*, for some $S' \subseteq S$, to an oracle, and Shannon entropy quantifies the expected minimum number of guesses needed to infer the entire secret with certainty. A decrease in the Shannon entropy of the secret space caused by a system can be seen as the leakage from the system. This question-and-answer interpretation has an algorithmic equivalent: S is seen as a search space, and by repeatedly asking questions *Does $S \in S'$?*, the adversary is performing a binary search on the space of secrets. Now, Shannon entropy corresponds to the average height of the optimal binary search tree.

However, Shannon entropy is not the unique meaningful measure of information. Guessing entropy allows the adversary to pose a different type of question; whereas probability of guessing quantifies a different aspect of the scenario of

---

[2] Braun et al. [12] make a distinction between this definition of leakage, called *additive leakage*, and *multiplicative leakage*, where the ratio (rather than the difference) of the a posteriori and a priori information is taken. Divisions by zero avoided, the results of this paper apply to both definitions. For simplicity, we adopt the first.

[3] LoI stands for *Lattice of Information*. The reason for this nomenclature is clarified in Section 4.1.

Table 1. Operational interpretation for three traditional information-flow measures, and a new measure. The question mark indicates the value of measure.

Measure	d1: Type of question	d2: Num. questions in attack	d3: Prob. of attack successful
Shannon entropy $SE(p_S)$	*Does $S \in S'$?*	?	S is inferred with prob. 1
Guessing entropy $NG(p_S)$	*Is $S = s$?*	?	S is inferred with prob. 1
Prob. of guessing $PG_n(p_S)$	*Is $S = s$?*	n guesses allowed	?
Prob. of guessing under $\in$ $PG_n^{\in}(p_S)$	*Does $S \in S'$?*	n guesses allowed	?

interest. Yet, the operational interpretation of these measures also can be described in terms of questions and answers as follows.

For simplicity, assume that elements of S are ordered by decreasing probabilities, i.e., if $1 \leq i < j \leq |S|$ then $p_S(s_i) \geq p_S(s_j)$. The *guessing entropy* of p_S is defined as $NG(p_S) = \sum_{i=1}^{|S|} i \cdot p_S(s_i)$, and the *conditional guessing entropy* of p_S given a channel C_a is defined as $NG(p_S, C_a) = \sum_{o \in \mathcal{O}} p_a(o) NG(p_a(\cdot|o))$. An operational interpretation of guessing entropy is: The adversary can pose questions *Is $S = s$?*, for some $s \in S$, to an oracle, and guessing entropy quantifies the expected number of guesses needed to learn the entire secret. Algorithmically, guessing entropy is the expected number of steps needed for the adversary to find the secret using linear search on the space of secrets.

Still assuming that the elements of S are in decreasing order of probabilities, the *probability of guessing* the secret in n tries is defined as $PG_n(p_S) = \sum_{i=1}^{n} p_S(s_i)$. The *conditional probability of guessing* of p_S in n tries given a channel C_a is defined as $PG_n(p_S, C_a) = \sum_{o \in \mathcal{O}} p_a(o) PG_n(p_a(\cdot|o))$. An operational interpretation of probability of guessing in n tries is: The adversary can pose questions *Is $S = s$?*, for some $s \in S$, and the measure quantifies the probability of guessing the entire secret in n tries. Algorithmically, the probability of guessing is the chance of success by an adversary performing a linear search on the space of secrets, after n steps.

Note that the landscape of these measures is covered by varying three dimensions of their operational interpretation:

d1: the *type of question* the adversary is allowed to pose;
d2: the *number of questions (guesses)* the adversary is allowed to pose;
d3: the *probability of success*, i.e., that of the adversary inferring the secret.

Table 1 summarizes the operational interpretation of Shannon entropy, guessing entropy and probability of guessing in terms of dimensions **d1**, **d2**, and **d3**. The type of question is fixed for each measure; the other two dimensions have a dual behavior: one is fixed and the other one is quantified. In particular, Shannon entropy and guessing entropy fix the probability of guessing the secret to be 1 and quantify the number of questions necessary to do so; probability of guessing fixes the number of guesses to be n and quantifies the probability of the secret being guessed.

We add a fourth row to Table 1 for a measure whose operational interpretation is: The adversary can pose questions *Does $S \in \mathcal{S}'$?*, for some $\mathcal{S}' \subseteq \mathcal{S}$, to an oracle, and the measure quantifies the probability of guessing the entire secret in n tries. Algorithmically, this measure is analogous to the probability of guessing but allowing the adversary to perform a binary (rather than linear) search on the space of secrets. The *probability of guessing under $\in$*, in n tries, of a distribution p_S is defined as $PG_n^\in(p_S) = \max_{\mathsf{P} \in \mathtt{LoI}(\mathcal{S}), |\mathsf{P}| \leq 2^n} \sum_{\mathcal{S}' \in \mathsf{P}, |\mathcal{S}'| = 1} p_S(\cdot | \mathcal{S}')$. The *conditional probability of guessing under $\in$*, in n tries, of p_S given a channel C_a is defined as $PG_n^\in(p_S, C_a) = \sum_{o \in \mathcal{O}} p_a(o) PG_n^\in(p_a(\cdot | o))$.

Worth as a New Dimension. The traditional measures in Table 1 presume secrets are monolithic and equally sensitive. We relax this restriction by introducing a new dimension to the operational interpretation of measures:

d4: the *worth* the adversary extracts from a guess.

We can enrich the landscape of measures of information with new definitions that exploit the extra freedom allowed by the new dimension **d4**. As with the traditional case, for each measure we fix the type of question the adversary is allowed to pose and vary the role played by the other three dimensions. Hence we classify the measures into three groups:

- *W*-**measures** quantify the worth extracted from an attack when the following dimensions are fixed: (i) the number of questions that can be posed, and (ii) the required probability of success.
- *N*-**measures** quantify the number of guesses the adversary needs in order to succeed when the following dimensions are fixed: (i) the required probability of success, and (ii) a minimum worth-threshold to extract as measured according to a *W*-measure ν modeling the adversary's preferences.
- *P*-**measures** quantify the probability of an attack being successful when the following dimensions are fixed: (i) the number of questions that can be posed, and (ii) a minimum worth-threshold to extract as measured according to a *W*-measure ν modeling the adversary's preferences.

According to this classification, Shannon entropy and guessing entropy are *N*-measures, and probability of guessing is a *P*-measure (all of them implicitly using a trivial worth assignment). Table 2 organizes the measures of information worth we propose in this paper. The new table subsumes Table 1 of traditional measures.

W-measures are used to specify the fixed worth-threshold necessary to fully define *P*-measures and *N*-measures, and hence we will start our discussion with them. First we introduce a few conventions.

Assume that the set $\mathcal{S}$ of secrets follows a probability distribution p_S, and that its fields are given by set $\mathcal{F}$. Assume also that an appropriate worth assignment

Table 2. Operational interpretation for measures of information worth. The question mark indicates the value of the measure.

W-measures: quantifying worth	d1: Type of question	d2: Num. questions in attack	d3: Prob. of attack successful	d4: Worth of payoff to attacker
Worth of certainty $WCER(\omega, p_S)$	Does $S \in S'$?	1 guess allowed	success with prob. 1	?
W-vulnerability $WV(\omega, p_S)$	Does $S \in S'$?	1 guess allowed	? (product prob. $\times$ worth)	
Worth of exp. = $WEXP_{n,\nu}^=(\omega, p_S)$	Is $S = s$?	n guesses allowed	success with prob. 1	? (using W-measure ν)

N-measures: quantifying number of guesses	d1: Type of question	d2: Num. questions in attack	d3: Prob. of attack successful	d4: Worth of payoff to attacker
W-guessing entropy $WNG_{w,\nu}(\omega, p_S)$	Is $S = s$?	?	success with prob. 1	extracted worth w (using W-measure ν)
W-Shannon entropy $WSE_{w,\nu}(\omega, p_S)$	Does $S \in S'$?	?	success with prob. 1	extracted worth w (using W-measure ν)

P-measures: quantifying prob. of success	d1: Type of question	d2: Num. questions in attack	d3: Prob. of attack successful	d4: Worth of payoff to attacker
W-prob. of guessing $WPG_{w,n,\nu}^\in(\omega, p_S)$	Does $S \in S'$?	n guesses allowed	?	extracted worth w (using W-measure ν)

ω is provided. For an attack C_a producing observables in a set $\mathcal{O}$, the information conveyed by each $o \in \mathcal{O}$ is the information contained in the probability distribution $p_a(\cdot|o)$ that o induces on secrets. A measure of information worth is *composable* if the value of an attack can be calculated as a function of information conveyed by each observable: $\nu(\omega, p_S, C_a) = \sum_{o \in \mathcal{O}} p_a(o)\nu(\omega, p_S(\cdot|o))$. All measures we propose in this paper are composable, but they easily extend to worst-case versions. Finally, define the *worth of a secret* $s \in S$ to be the worth of learning all of its fields, i.e., $\omega(s) = \omega(\mathcal{F})$.

3.2 W-measures

Worth of Certainty. Consider a risk-averse adversary who is allowed to guess any part of the secret—as opposed to the secret as a whole—but who will do so only when absolutely certain the guess will succeed. To model this scenario, we note that a field is deducible with certainty from p_S if its contents is the same in every secret in the support of the distribution. Formally, the *deducible fields* from p_S are defined as $ded(p_S) = \mathcal{F} \setminus \{f \in \mathcal{F} \mid \exists s', s'' \in supp(p_S) : s'[f] \neq s''[f]\}$. For an attack C_a producing observables in a set $\mathcal{O}$, the deducible fields from each $o \in \mathcal{O}$ are those that can be inferred from the probability distribution $ded(p_a(\cdot|o))$ that o induces on secrets. The information contained in a probability distribution is defined as the worth of its deducible fields.

Definition 2 (Worth of certainty). *The* worth of certainty *of p_S is defined as $WCER(\omega, p_S) = \omega(ded(p_S))$. The* worth of certainty *of an attack C_a is a W-measure defined as $WCER(\omega, p_S, C_a) = \sum_{o \in \mathcal{O}} p_a(o) WCER(\omega, p_a(\cdot|o))$.*

W-vulnerability. Consider an adversary who can guess a less likely structure, provided that this structure is worth enough to yield a higher overall expected gain. Formally, for every structure $\mathfrak{f} \subseteq \mathcal{F}$, we define $p_S(\mathfrak{f})$ to be the probability that $\mathfrak{f}$ can be deduced by an adversary knowing the distribution p_S: $p_S(\mathfrak{f}) = \max_{x \in S[\mathfrak{f]}} \sum_{s \in S, s[\mathfrak{f}]=x} p_S(s)$. A rational adversary maximizes the product of probability and worth, so we define W-vulnerability as follows.

Definition 3 (W-vulnerability). *The W-vulnerability of p_S is defined as $WV(\omega, p_S) = \max_{\mathfrak{f} \subseteq \mathcal{F}} (p_S(\mathfrak{f})\omega(\mathfrak{f}))$. The W-vulnerability of an attack C_a is a W-measure defined as $WV(\omega, p_S, C_a) = \sum_{o \in \mathcal{O}} p_a(o) WV(\omega, p_a(\cdot|o))$.*

Worth of expectation under =. Consider an adversary who can explore the space of secrets using brute force, i.e., by guessing the possible values of the secret, one by one. Assume that this adversary is allowed $n \geq 0$ tries. The aim is to extract as much worth as possible according to some W-measure ν modeling the adversary's preferences. This leads to the following measure.

Definition 4 (Worth of expectation under =). *Let $n \geq 0$ be the maximum number of tries allowed for the adversary. The* worth of expectation under = *of p_S is $WEXP_{n,\nu}^{=}(\omega, p_S) = \max_{\mathcal{S}' \subseteq \mathcal{S}, |\mathcal{S}'| \leq n} (p_S(\mathcal{S}')\omega(\mathcal{F}) + p_S(\bar{\mathcal{S}}')\nu(\omega, p_S(\cdot|\bar{\mathcal{S}}')))$, where $\bar{\mathcal{S}}' = \mathcal{S} \backslash \mathcal{S}'$. The* worth of expectation under = *of an attack C_a is a W-measure defined as $WEXP_{n,\nu}^{=}(\omega, p_S, C_a) = \sum_{o \in \mathcal{O}} p_a(o) WEXP_{n,\nu}^{=}(\omega, p_a(\cdot|o))$.*

3.3   N-measures

W-guessing entropy. Consider an adversary who can ask questions *Is $S = s$?* but who, instead of having to guess the secret as a whole, can fix a minimum worth $0 \leq \mathsf{w} \leq \omega(\mathcal{F})$ to obtain according to some W-measure ν modeling the adversary's preferences. A generalized version of guessing entropy quantifies the expected number of questions to obtain a minimum worth w from such attacks.

Definition 5 (W-guessing entropy). *Let $0 \leq \mathsf{w} \leq \omega(\mathcal{F})$ be a worth threshold quantified according to a W-measure ν. The W-guessing entropy of p_S is $WNG_{\mathsf{w},\nu}(\omega, p_S) = \min_{\mathcal{S}' \subseteq \mathcal{S}, \nu(\omega, p_S(\cdot|\bar{\mathcal{S}}')) \geq \mathsf{w}} (p_S(\bar{\mathcal{S}}')NG(p_S(\cdot|\bar{\mathcal{S}}')) + p_S(\mathcal{S}')(|\bar{\mathcal{S}}'| + 1))$, where $\bar{\mathcal{S}}' = \mathcal{S} \backslash \mathcal{S}'$. The W-guessing entropy of an attack C_a is a N-measure defined as $WNG_{\mathsf{w},\nu}(\omega, p_S, C_a) = \sum_{o \in \mathcal{O}} p_a(o) WNG_{\mathsf{w},\nu}(\omega, p_a(\cdot|o))$.*

W-Shannon entropy. Consider an adversary who is allowed to ask questions of the type *Does $S \in \mathcal{S}'$?* but who, instead of having to guess the entire secret, can fix a minimum worth-threshold $0 \leq \mathsf{w} \leq \omega(\mathcal{F})$ to extract according to a W-measure ν. A generalized version of Shannon entropy quantifies the expected number of questions necessary to obtain worth w from the attacks.

Definition 6 (*W*-Shannon entropy). *Let* $0 \leq \mathsf{w} \leq \omega(\mathcal{F})$ *be a worth threshold quantified according to a W-measure* ν*. The W-Shannon entropy of* p_S *is defined as* $WSE_{\mathsf{w},\nu}(\omega, p_S) = \min_{\mathsf{P} \in LoI(S), \forall S' \in \mathsf{P}} \nu(\omega, p_S(\cdot | S')) \geq \mathsf{w} SE(p_\mathsf{P})$*. The W-Shannon entropy of the distribution* p_S*, given an attack* C_a*, is a N-measure defined as* $WSE_{\mathsf{w},\nu}(\omega, p_S, C_a) = \sum_{o \in \mathcal{O}} p_a(o) WSE_{\mathsf{w},\nu}(\omega, p_a(\cdot | o))$*.*

3.4   *P*-measures

***W*-Probability of Guessing.** Consider an adversary allowed to pose n questions of the type *Does* $S \in S'$*?*. The following measure quantifies the chances of extracting worth $0 \leq \mathsf{w} \leq \omega(\mathcal{F})$, as measured by some *W*-measure ν, from an attack. Given n questions, at most 2^n blocks can be inspected, which leads to the following mathematical definition.

Definition 7 (*W*-probability of Guessing). *Let* $0 \leq \mathsf{w} \leq \omega(\mathcal{F})$ *be a worth threshold quantified according to a W-measure* ν*, and* $n \geq 0$ *be the maximum number of tries allowed for the adversary. The W-probability of guessing of* p_S *is* $WPG_{\mathsf{w},n,\nu}^{\in}(\omega, p_S) = \max_{\mathsf{P} \in LoI(S), |\mathsf{P}| \leq 2^n} \sum_{S' \in \mathsf{P}, \nu(\omega, p_S(\cdot | S')) \geq \mathsf{w}} p_S(S')$*. The W-probability of guessing of an attack* C_a *is a P-measure defined as follows:* $WPG_{\mathsf{w},n,\nu}^{\in}(\omega, p_S, C_a) = \sum_{o \in \mathcal{O}} p_a(o) WPG_{\mathsf{w},n,\nu}^{\in}(\omega, p_a(\cdot | o))$*.*

3.5   Mathematical Properties of Measures of Information Worth

The proposed measures of information worth by definition always yield nonnegative values. It is a subtler matter, however, to show that they also always yield non-negative values for leakage. Theorem 1 below shows that non-negativity of leakage holds for our measures of information worth under certain conditions. Because *N*-measures and *P*-measures have a *W*-measure as an input parameter to model the preferences of the adversary, we restrict consideration to *W*-measures presenting a consistent behavior with respect to the number of possible values for the secret. Intuitively, whenever some secret value is ruled out from the search space, the adversary's information about the secret, according to the measure, does not decrease. Formally:

Definition 8 (Monotonicity with respect to blocks). *Given a set* S *of secrets, a W-measure* ν *is said to be* monotonic with respect to blocks *if, for every worth assignment* ω*, every probability distribution* p_S *on* S*, and all subsets (i.e., blocks)* S', S'' *of* S *such that* $S' \subseteq S''$*, it is the case that* $\nu(\omega, p_S(\cdot | S')) \geq \nu(\omega, p_S(\cdot | S''))$*. When* ν *quantifies uncertainty, the inequality is reversed.*

At first it might seem that monotonicity with respect to blocks would hold for every *W*-measure. But this is not the case. It does hold for worth of certainty, for instance, but it does not hold for *W*-vulnerability, as shown in the following example.

Example 1. The vulnerability of a probability distribution p_S is calculated as $V(p_S) = max_s \, p(s)$. Consider the block $S' = \{s_1, s_2, s_3, s_4\}$ of secrets, where

$p(s_1) = 1/2$ and $p(s_2) = p(s_3) = p(s_4) = 1/6$. Then $V(S') = 1/2$. Suppose that S' is split into blocks $S'' = \{s_1\}$ and $S''' = \{s_2, s_3, s_4\}$. Hence, even if $S''' \subseteq S'$, we have $V(S''') = 1/3 < V(S')$. Since traditional vulnerability is a particular case of W-vulnerability (Theorem 2), the example is also valid for the former.

In probabilistic systems, the adversary's knowledge is not tied to blocks of secrets but to probability distributions induced by observations. The concept of monotonicity is generalized accordingly.

Definition 9 (Monotonicity with respect to observations). *Given a set S of secrets, a measure of information worth ν is said to be* monotonic with respect to observations *if for every worth assignment ω, every probability distribution p_S on S, and all observables $o \in \mathcal{O}$: $\nu(\omega, p_S(\cdot|o)) \geq \nu(\omega, p_S(\cdot))$. When ν quantifies uncertainty, then the inequality is reversed.*

From Example 1 it follows that W-vulnerability is not monotonic with respect to observations. It is easy to see, however, that worth of uncertainty is.

The following theorem establishes the non-negativity of leakage by showing that the adversary's information after an attack is never smaller than the a priori information.

Theorem 1. *Let S be a set of secrets composed by the fields in $\mathcal{F}$ and let C_a be an attack. Let ν be a W-measure that is monotonic with respect to observations, $n \geq 0$ be the number of guesses allowed for the adversary, and $0 \leq w \leq \omega(\mathcal{F})$. For every distribution p_S on S and every worth assignment ω:*

$$WCER(\omega, p_S, C_a) \geq WCER(\omega, p_S) \tag{1}$$
$$WV(\omega, p_S, C_a) \geq WV(\omega, p_S) \tag{2}$$
$$WEXP^=_{n,\nu}(\omega, p_S, C_a) \geq WEXP^=_{n,\nu}(\omega, p_S) \tag{3}$$
$$WNG_{w,\nu}(\omega, p_S, C_a) \leq WNG_{w,\nu}(\omega, p_S) \tag{4}$$
$$WSE_{w,\nu}(\omega, p_S, C_a) \leq WSE_{w,\nu}(\omega, p_S) \tag{5}$$
$$WPG^\in_{w,n,\nu}(\omega, p_S, C_a) \geq WPG^\in_{w,n,\nu}(\omega, p_S) \tag{6}$$

3.6 Relation with Traditional Measures

We now substantiate our claim that Shannon entropy, guessing entropy, and probability of guessing (and, in particular, vulnerability) are measures of information that ignore the worth of structures. Define the *binary worth assignment* ω_{bin} that attributes zero worth to any proper structure, i.e., $\omega_{bin}(\mathfrak{f}) = 1$ if $\mathfrak{f} = \mathcal{F}$, $\omega_{bin}(\mathfrak{f}) = 0$ if $\mathfrak{f} \subset \mathcal{F}$. Theorem 2 asserts that the traditional measures implicitly use ω_{bin} as a worth assignment, which means that only the maximal structure is deemed to be conveying relevant information. For instance, the theorem states that Shannon entropy is the particular case of W-Shannon entropy in which the adversary must perform a binary search to the maximum level of granularity, i.e., until the secret is unequivocally identified.

Theorem 2. *Let S be a set of secrets distributed according to p_S, and let C_a be an attack. Then the following hold:*

$$SE(p_S, C_a) = WSE_{1,WCER}(\omega_{bin}, p_S, C_a) \tag{7}$$
$$NG(p_S, C_a) = WNG_{1,WCER}(\omega_{bin}, p_S, C_a) \tag{8}$$
$$PG_n(p_S, C_a) = WEXP^{=}_{n,\nu_{null}}(\omega_{bin}, p_S, C_a) \qquad (\forall n \geq 0) \tag{9}$$
$$V(p_S|C_a) = WV(\omega_{bin}, p_S, C_a) \tag{10}$$

where ν_{null} is a W-measure such that $\nu_{null}(\omega, p_S) = 0$ for every ω and p_S.

4 Algebraic Structure for Measures of Information Worth in Deterministic Systems

4.1 Deterministic Systems and Attack Sequences

In a deterministic system $\mathcal{C}$, for each pair of high input $s \in S$ and and low input $a \in \mathcal{A}$, a single output $o \in \mathcal{O}$ is produced with probability 1. Therefore each attack $a \in \mathcal{A}$ induces a partition P_a on the set of secrets, where each block $S_{a,o} \in \mathsf{P}_a$ contains all secrets mapped to o when the low input to the system is a, i.e., $S_{a,o} = \{s \in S | \mathcal{C}(s, a) = o\}$. When the attack is clear from the context, we write S_o for $S_{a,o}$. An attack step can be described mathematically as $\mathcal{C}(s, a) \in \mathsf{P}_a$, which is a two-phase process: (i) the adversary chooses a partition P_a on S, corresponding to attack $a \in \mathcal{A}$, and (ii) the system responds with the block $S_o \in \mathsf{P}_a$ that contains the secret.

The adversary may perform multiple attack steps for the same secret. The adversary combines information acquired in an *attack sequence* $\hat{a} = a_{t_1}, \ldots, a_{t_k}$ of k steps by intersecting the partitions corresponding to each step in the sequence, thereby obtaining a refined partition[4] $\mathsf{P}_{\hat{a}} = \bigcap_{a \in \hat{a}} \mathsf{P}_a$. Hence an attack sequence $\hat{a}$ can be modeled as a single attack where the adversary chooses the partition $\mathsf{P}_{\hat{a}}$ as the low input to the system and obtains as an observable the block to which the secret s belongs. Formally, $\mathcal{C}(s, \hat{a}) \in \mathsf{P}_{\hat{a}}$ holds.

4.2 The Lattice of Information and the Leakage from Attack Sequences

The set of all partitions on a finite set S forms a *complete lattice* called the *Lattice of Information* (LoI) [14]. The order on lattice elements is the *refinement order* $\sqsubseteq$ on partitions: $\mathsf{P} \sqsubseteq \mathsf{P}'$ iff for every $S_j \in \mathsf{P}'$ there exists $S_i \in \mathsf{P}$ such that $S_j \subseteq S_i$. The relation $\sqsubseteq$ is a partial order on the set of all partitions on S. The *join* $\sqcup$ of two elements in the LoI is the intersection of partitions, and their *meet* $\sqcap$ is the transitive closure union of partitions. Given two partitions P and P', both $\mathsf{P} \sqcup \mathsf{P}'$ and $\mathsf{P} \sqcap \mathsf{P}'$ are partitions as well. We fix the deterministic system and let the elements in the LoI model possible executions. By controlling the

---

[4] The intersection of partitions is defined as $\mathsf{P} \cap \mathsf{P}' = \bigcup_{S_o \in \mathsf{P}, S_{o'} \in \mathsf{P}'} S_o \cap S_{o'}$.

low input to the system, the adversary chooses among executions, so the LoI serves as an algebraic representation of the partial order on the attack sequences the adversary can perform. Each attack sequence $\hat{a}$ corresponds to one element $P_{\hat{a}}$—i.e., the partition it induces—in the LoI for $\mathcal{S}$.

An attack sequence can be seen as a path in the LoI. Each attack sequence is mapped to an element in the lattice, and by performing an attack step the adversary may obtain a finer partition on the space of secrets, therefore moving up in the lattice to a state with more information. The leakage of information from an attack sequence is, thus, the difference in the measures of information worth between the initial and final partition in the path. This definition of leakage encompasses the traditional definitions for Shannon entropy, guessing entropy, and probability of guessing.

4.3   Consistency with Respect to the LoI

The Lattice of Information has been used as an underlying algebraic structure for deterministic systems, and it provides an elegant way to reason about leakage under composition of attacks. Yasuoka and Terauchi [18] showed that orderings based on probability of guessing, guessing entropy, and Shannon entropy are all equivalent, and Malacaria [10] showed that they coincide with the refinement order in the LoI. These results establish that the traditional measures behave well with respect to the LoI: the finer a partition is, the more information (or the less uncertainty) the measures attribute to it.

All measures of information worth proposed in Section 3 behave in a similar way. That is, they are *consistent with respect to the LoI*. This is formally established in the following theorem.

Theorem 3. *Let $\mathcal{S}$ be a set of secrets composed by the fields in $\mathcal{F}$. For all P and P' in the LoI for $\mathcal{S}$, the following are equivalent:*

$$P \sqsubseteq P' \tag{11}$$

$$\forall \omega \ \forall p_S \quad WCER(\omega, p_S, P) \leq WCER(\omega, p_S, P') \tag{12}$$

$$\forall \omega \ \forall p_S \ WV(\omega, p_S, P) \leq WV(\omega, p_S, P') \tag{13}$$

$$\forall n \ \forall \nu \ \forall \omega \ \forall p_S \quad WEXP_{n,\nu}^{=}(\omega, p_S, P) \leq WEXP_{n,\nu}^{=}(\omega, p_S, P') \tag{14}$$

$$\forall w \ \forall \nu \ \forall \omega \ \forall p_S \quad WNG_{w,\nu}(\omega, p_S, P) \geq WNG_{w,\nu}(\omega, p_S, P') \tag{15}$$

$$\forall w \ \forall \nu \ \forall \omega \ \forall p_S \quad WSE_{w,\nu}(\omega, p_S, P) \geq WSE_{w,\nu}(\omega, p_S, P') \tag{16}$$

$$\forall w \ \forall n \ \forall \nu \ \forall \omega \ \forall p_S \ WPG_{w,n,\nu}^{\in}(\omega, p_S, P) \leq WPG_{w,n,\nu}^{\in}(\omega, p_S, P') \tag{17}$$

where $n \geq 0$; $0 \leq w \leq \omega(\mathfrak{f})$, and ν ranges over all composable W-measures that are consistent with respect to the LoI plus the worth of certainty measure WCER. In (15) and (16) ν is restricted to be monotonic with respect to blocks.

5   A Design Technique for Worth Assignments

We now outline a general technique to capture into worth assignments relevant aspects of some given scenario of interest.

The domain of worth assignments is the power set $\mathcal{P}(\mathcal{F})$ of the set $\mathcal{F}$ of fields. By endowing $\mathcal{P}(\mathcal{F})$ with the set-inclusion ordering, we obtain a (complete) *lattice of structures* $\mathsf{L}_{\mathcal{F}}$. For every structure $\mathfrak{f} \in \mathcal{P}(\mathcal{F})$ there is a partition $\mathsf{P}_{\mathfrak{f}}$, belonging to the LoI, distinguishing structure $\mathfrak{f}$. Formally, $\mathsf{P}_{\mathfrak{f}} = \{\mathcal{S}_{s[\mathfrak{f}]=x} \mid x \in \mathcal{S}[\mathfrak{f}]\}$ where to every $x \in \mathcal{S}[\mathfrak{f}]$ corresponds the block $\mathcal{S}_{s[\mathfrak{f}]=x} = \{s \in \mathcal{S} \mid s[\mathfrak{f}] = x\}$. Proposition 1

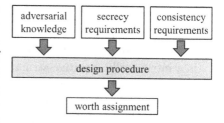

Fig. 2. Scheme of a design technique for worth assignments

shows that the set-inclusion ordering on structures coincides with the refinement relation on the corresponding partitions, thereby establishing that the space of structures is a sub-lattice of the LoI.

Proposition 1. *For every* $\mathfrak{f}, \mathfrak{f}' \in \mathcal{P}(\mathcal{F})$: $\mathfrak{f} \subseteq \mathfrak{f}'$ *iff* $\mathsf{P}_{\mathfrak{f}} \sqsubseteq \mathsf{P}_{\mathfrak{f}'}$.

Hence, the space of structures $\mathsf{L}_{\mathcal{F}}$ is isomorphic to the complete lattice formed by all partitions $\mathsf{P}_{\mathfrak{f}}$ for $\mathfrak{f} \subseteq \mathcal{F}$, ordered by the refinement relation $\sqsubseteq$.

Figure 2 depicts our design technique, which constructs a worth assignment having as input the following three parameters describing a scenario of interest.

a) **Adversarial knowledge** is any relevant information the adversary knows from sources external to the system (e.g., newspapers, common-sense, other systems). As usual in QIF and privacy, adversarial knowledge is modeled as a probability distribution on the space of secrets [19–21].

b) **Secrecy requirements** reflect the protector's (i.e., the party interested in hiding the secret) interests, specifying which structures are *intrinsically sensitive* and which are only *contingently sensitive*, that is, sensitive only to the extent they possibly reveal information about other intrinsically sensitive structures. (E.g., a patient's lung cancer status may be considered intrinsically sensitive, whereas smoking habits may be considered sensitive only to the extent that they reveal information about the patient's cancer status.) Secrecy requirements are represented as a partial function from the space of structures to non-negative reals that associates every intrinsically sensitive structures with an appropriate, a priori, worth.

c) **Consistency requirements** are mathematical properties imposed on worth assignments. Non-negativity and monotonicity are considered *syntactic* consistency requirements—they depend only on the representation of secrets, not on their meaning. Syntactic requirements alone are not sufficient to guarantee the consistency of worth assignments. Often semantic requirements also need to be considered, such as the adjustments for information-theoretic predictors and computational cost from Section 2. Other examples are (i) *inclusion-exclusion consistency:* the worth of the composition of two structures is equal to the sum of their individual worths, minus the worth they share: $\omega(\mathfrak{f} \sqcup \mathfrak{f}') = \omega(\mathfrak{f}) + \omega(\mathfrak{f}') - \omega(\mathfrak{f} \sqcap \mathfrak{f}')$, and (ii) *independence:* statistically independent structures add their worth; so if $\mathsf{P}_{\mathfrak{f}'}$ and $\mathsf{P}_{\mathfrak{f}'}$ are independent then $\omega(\mathfrak{f} \sqcup \mathfrak{f}') = \omega(\mathfrak{f}) + \omega(\mathfrak{f}')$.

Once the inputs are provided, a design proceeds as follows:

1. Construct the complete lattice $L_{\mathcal{F}}$ of structures.
2. Use secrecy requirements to annotate each element P_f in $L_{\mathcal{F}}$, where $f \in \mathcal{P}(\mathcal{F})$ is a intrinsically sensitive structure, with the appropriate a priori worth in accordance to the protector's interests.
3. Using the adversarial knowledge, derive a probability distribution p_S. Partitions in the LoI can be seen as random variables, so use p_S to derive the probability distribution in the elements of $L_{\mathcal{F}}$.
4. Take some well established measure of information ν (e.g., guessing entropy), and for every structure $f' \in \mathcal{P}(\mathcal{F})$, update its worth according to $w(f') = \max_{f \in \mathcal{P}(\mathcal{F})} \nu(P_{f'}|P_f)$. Repeat until all structures respect the consistency requirements.

This design technique captures the adversarial knowledge into the worth assignment, and the worth of structures will inherit the operational interpretation of the measure ν chosen in step 4. However, because the procedure depends on the probability distribution on the elements of $L_{\mathcal{F}}$, certain semantic requirements only can be approximated. An example is the inclusion-exclusion principle: if it were to be preserved for all probability distributions p_S, then it would be a valuation on the lattice, which is known not to exist [22].

6   Related Work

Relation with g-leakage. We start by reviewing g-leakage [13]. Given a set S of possible secrets and a finite, nonempty set Z of allowable guesses, a *gain function* is a function $g : Z \times S \to [0,1]$. Given a gain function g, the *prior g-vulnerability* of a probability distribution p_S is defined as $V_g(p_S) = \max_{z \in Z} \sum_{s \in S} p_S(s)g(z,s)$. Given also a channel C_a from secrets in S to observables in $\mathcal{O}$, the *posterior g-vulnerability* is $V_g(p_S, C_a) = \sum_{o \in \mathcal{O}} p(o)V_g(p_a(\cdot|o))$. The g-vulnerability is converted into g-entropy by taking its logarithm: $H_g(p_S) = -\log V_g(p_S)$ and $H_g(p_S, C_a) = -\log V_g(p_S, C_a)$. Finally, g-leakage is the difference between prior and posterior g-entropies: $\mathcal{L}_g(p_S, C_a) = H_g(p_S) - H_g(p_S, C_a)$. Comparing our work with g-leakage, two main points are noteworthy:

(i) g-leakage as defined in [13] cannot capture scenarios where the worth of a structure depends on the probability of that structure. Hence worth of certainty and W-Shannon entropy cannot be modeled using g-leakage.

Proposition 2. *Given a set of secrets S and a set of guesses Z, there is no gain function $g : Z \times S \to \mathbb{R}^+$ such that, for all priors p_S on S, and all partitions P on the LoI for S, it is the case that: (i) $V_g(p_S) = WCER(\omega, p_S)$, or (ii) $V_g(p_S) = SE(p_S)$, or (iii) $H_g(p_S) = SE(p_S)$.*

(ii) g-leakage and measures of information worth coincide in some scenarios, and when it happens, our approach can give practical operational interpretations to gain functions—in fact, a common criticism of the g-leakage framework concerns the challenge of identifying adequate functions for a scenario of interest. Take guessing entropy, as an example. Take an allowable guess z to be an ordered list $\Lambda(\mathcal{S}')$ of the secret elements of a subset $\mathcal{S}' \subseteq \mathcal{S}$ of secrets. A guess $\Lambda(\mathcal{S}')$ means that the adversary believes that the secret belongs to the set $\mathcal{S}'$. Moreover, in a brute-force attack the adversary would guess secrets in that same order they appear in that list. Then, for the binary worth assignment ω_{bin}[5], define a gain function $g_{\omega_{bin}}(\Lambda(\mathcal{S}'), s) = -\Lambda(\mathcal{S}')(s)$ if $s \in \mathcal{S}'$, and $g_{\omega_{bin}}(\Lambda(\mathcal{S}'), s) = -(|\bar{\mathcal{S}}'| + 1)$ otherwise. It can be shown that the W-guessing entropy captures the g-vulnerability of an adversary guided by the gain function $g_{\omega_{bin}}$, i.e., that $WNG_{1, WCER}(\omega_{bin}, p_S) = V_{g_{\omega_{bin}}}(p_S)$. However, $g_{\omega_{bin}}$ ranges over negative values, which is not allowed by the original g-vulnerability framework.[6] Fortunately we do not run into the same type of problem when using W-vulnerability, worth of expectation under $=$, and W-probability of guessing to provide operational interpretations for g-functions.

Other Related Work. Köpf and Basin [17] proposed the model for deterministic systems we extended in this paper. Shannon [23] points out the independence of the information contents with respect to its representation, and gives the first steps in trying to understand how Shannon entropy would behave in a lattice of partitions. The Lattice of Information is introduced by Landauer and Redmond [14]. Yasuoka and Terauchi [18] show the equivalence of the ordering on traditional measures, and Malacaria [10] uses the LoI as an algegraic foundation to unify all these orderings. Backes, Köpf and Rybalchenko [24], and Heusser and Malacaria [25] use model checkers and sat-solvers to determine the partitions induced by deterministic programs. Adão et al. [26] relax the assumption of perfect cryptography by allowing the adversary to infer a key at some (possibly computational) cost, and introduce a quantitative extension of the usual Dolev-Yao intruder model to analyze implementations of security protocols. Their work focuses on cryptography, whereas ours is applied to QIF. Askarov et al. [27] show that the possibly unbouded leakage of termination-insensitive noninterference can be mitigated by making the secret sufficiently random and large. Demange and Sands [28] point out that secrets can not always be chosen to fulfill such requirements, and they develop a framework in which "small" secrets are handled more carefully than "big" ones. They focus on preventing leakage, whereas we aim at providing rigorous information-theoretic measures for quantifying leakage.

7 Conclusion and Future Work

This paper proposed a framework to incorporate the worth of structures—possibly representing their sensitivity—into information-flow measures. We

---

[5] The procedure can be generalized to worth assignments other than ω_{bin}.

[6] If we try to capture W-guessing entropy using g-entropy instead of g-vulnerability, the situation becomes even worse: no gain function exists, even with negative values.

generalized Shannon entropy, guessing entropy and probability of guessing, and we proved that the generalizations are consistent with respect to the Lattice of Information for deterministic systems. We also outlined a design technique for worth assignments that captures important aspects of a scenario of interest.

We are currently refining the design technique for worth assignments to make it fully automated. We are also investigating scenarios where every attack incurs some *cost*. The resulting theory would enable the study of the trade-off between the information yielded by an attack versus cost.

Acknowledgments. The authors would like to thank Geoffrey Smith and Santosh S. Venkatesh for helpful discussions. Mário S. Alvim was a postdoctoral research associate at the Mathematics Department of the University of Pennsylvania when much of this research was performed. Support for Mário S. Alvim and Andre Scedrov comes in part from the AFOSR MURI "Science of Cyber Security: Modeling, Composition, and Measurement" as AFOSR grant FA9550-11-1-0137. Additional support for Scedrov comes from NSF grant CNS-0830949 and from ONR grant N00014-11-1-0555. Fred Schneider is supported in part by AFOSR grant F9550-06-0019, by the AFOSR MURI "Science of Cyber Security: Modeling, Composition, and Measurement" as AFOSR grant FA9550-11-1-0137, by NSF grants 0430161, 0964409, and CCF-0424422 (TRUST), by ONR grants N00014-01-1-0968 and N00014-09-1-0652, and by grants from Microsoft.

References

1. Cachin, C.: Entropy Measures and Unconditional Security in Cryptography. PhD thesis, ETH Zürich (1997) Reprint as of ETH Series in Information Security and Cryptography, vol. 1. Hartung-Gorre Verlag, Konstanz (1997) ISBN 3-89649-185-7
2. Clark, D., Hunt, S., Malacaria, P.: Quantitative information flow, relations and polymorphic types. J. of Logic and Computation 18(2), 181–199 (2005)
3. Malacaria, P.: Assessing security threats of looping constructs. In: Hofmann, M., Felleisen, M. (eds.) Proceedings of the 34th ACM SIGPLAN-SIGACT Symposium on Principles of Programming Languages, POPL 2007, pp. 225–235. ACM (2007)
4. Malacaria, P., Chen, H.: Lagrange multipliers and maximum information leakage in different observational models. In: Proc. of the 2008 Workshop on Programming Languages and Analysis for Security (PLAS 2008), pp. 135–146. ACM (June 2008)
5. Moskowitz, I.S., Newman, R.E., Syverson, P.F.: Quasi-anonymous channels. In: Proc. of CNIS, pp. 126–131, IASTED (2003)
6. Moskowitz, I.S., Newman, R.E., Crepeau, D.P., Miller, A.R.: Covert channels and anonymizing networks. In: Jajodia, S., Samarati, P., Syverson, P.F. (eds.) Workshop on Privacy in the Electronic Society 2003, pp. 79–88. ACM (2003)
7. Chatzikokolakis, K., Palamidessi, C., Panangaden, P.: Anonymity protocols as noisy channels. Inf. and Comp. 206(2-4), 378–401 (2008)
8. Alvim, M.S., Andrés, M.E., Palamidessi, C.: Information Flow in Interactive Systems. In: Gastin, P., Laroussinie, F. (eds.) CONCUR 2010. LNCS, vol. 6269, pp. 102–116. Springer, Heidelberg (2010)
9. Massey: Guessing and entropy. In: Proceedings of the IEEE International Symposium on Information Theory, p. 204. IEEE (1994)

10. Malacaria, P.: Algebraic foundations for information theoretical, probabilistic and guessability measures of information flow. CoRR abs/1101.3453 (2011)
11. Smith, G.: On the foundations of quantitative information flow. In: de Alfaro, L. (ed.) FOSSACS 2009. LNCS, vol. 5504, pp. 288–302. Springer, Heidelberg (2009)
12. Braun, C., Chatzikokolakis, K., Palamidessi, C.: Quantitative notions of leakage for one-try attacks. In: Proceedings of the 25th Conf. on Mathematical Foundations of Programming Semantics. Electronic Notes in Theoretical Computer Science, vol. 249, pp. 75–91. Elsevier B.V. (2009)
13. Alvim, M.S., Chatzikokolakis, K., Palamidessi, C., Smith, G.: Measuring information leakage using generalized gain functions. In: Proceedings of the 25th IEEE Computer Security Foundations Symposium (CSF), pp. 265–279 (2012)
14. Landauer, J., Redmond, T.: A lattice of information. In: Proc. Computer Security Foundations Workshop VI, pp. 65–70 (June 1993)
15. Alvim, M.S., Scedrov, A., Schneider, F.B.: When not all bits are equal: Worth-based information flow. Technical report (2013),
    http://ecommons.library.cornell.edu/handle/1813/33124
16. Sweeney, L.: Uniqueness of simple demographics in the U.S. population, Carnegie Mellon University, Laboratory for International Data Privacy (2000)
17. Köpf, B., Basin, D.: Automatically deriving information-theoretic bounds for adaptive side-channel attacks. J. Comput. Secur. 19(1), 1–31 (2011)
18. Yasuoka, H., Terauchi, T.: Quantitative information flow — verification hardness and possibilities. In: Proc. 23rd IEEE Computer Security Foundations Symposium (CSF 2010), pp. 15–27 (2010)
19. Dwork, C.: Differential privacy. In: Bugliesi, M., Preneel, B., Sassone, V., Wegener, I. (eds.) ICALP 2006, part II. LNCS, vol. 4052, pp. 1–12. Springer, Heidelberg (2006)
20. Ghosh, A., Roughgarden, T., Sundararajan, M.: Universally utility-maximizing privacy mechanisms. In: Proceedings of the 41st Annual ACM Symposium on Theory of Computing, STOC 2009, pp. 351–360. ACM, New York (2009)
21. Alvim, M.S., Andrés, M.E., Chatzikokolakis, K., Palamidessi, C.: On the relation between differential privacy and quantitative information flow. In: Aceto, L., Henzinger, M., Sgall, J. (eds.) ICALP 2011, Part II. LNCS, vol. 6756, pp. 60–76. Springer, Heidelberg (2011)
22. Nakamura, Y.: Entropy and semivaluations on semilattices. Kodai Mathematical Seminar Reports 22(4), 443–468 (1970)
23. Shannon, C.: The lattice theory of information. IRE Professional Group on Information Theory 1(1), 105–107 (1953)
24. Backes, M., Köpf, B., Rybalchenko, A.: Automatic discovery and quantification of information leaks. In: IEEE Symposium on Security and Privacy, pp. 141–153 (2009)
25. Heusser, J., Malacaria, P.: Quantifying information leaks in software. In: Proceedings of the 26th Annual Computer Security Applications Conference, ACSAC 2010, pp. 261–269. ACM, New York (2010)
26. Adão, P., Mateus, P., Viganò, L.: Protocol insecurity with a finite number of sessions and a cost-sensitive guessing intruder is np-complete. Theoretical Computer Science (2013) ISSN 0304-3975,
    http://www.sciencedirect.com/science/article/pii/S0304397513006956,
    doi:http://dx.doi.org/10.1016/j.tcs.2013.09.015
27. Askarov, A., Hunt, S., Sabelfeld, A., Sands, D.: Termination-insensitive noninterference leaks more than just a bit. In: Jajodia, S., Lopez, J. (eds.) ESORICS 2008. LNCS, vol. 5283, pp. 333–348. Springer, Heidelberg (2008)
28. Demange, D., Sands, D.: All secrets great and small. In: Castagna, G. (ed.) ESOP 2009. LNCS, vol. 5502, pp. 207–221. Springer, Heidelberg (2009)

Leakage Resilience against Concurrent Cache Attacks

Gilles Barthe[1], Boris Köpf[1], Laurent Mauborgne[2], and Martín Ochoa[3]

[1] IMDEA Software Institute, Spain
[2] AbsInt GmbH, Germany
[3] TU Munich, Germany

Abstract. In this paper we show how to engineer proofs of security for software implementations of leakage-resilient cryptosystems on execution platforms with concurrency and caches. The proofs we derive are based on binary executables of the cryptosystem and on simple but realistic models of microprocessors.

1 Introduction

The sharing of hardware resources is fundamental for the cost-effective implementation of concurrency in processors, operating systems, and the cloud. Unfortunately, sharing of hardware between conflicting parties introduces side channels that breach the isolation between processes and virtual machines. Typical goals of side-channel attacks are the recovery of cryptographic keys [20] and private information about users [22]; shared resources that have been exploited to this end are processor caches [7], branch prediction units [3], and main memory [14].

Leakage resilient cryptosystems [10, 26] offer formal security guarantees even if the underlying hardware reveals partial information about the internal state of the computation. In today's leakage resilient cryptosystems, the modeling of leakage focuses on physical characteristics such as power consumption or electromagnetic radiation. So far, there has been little focus on applying leakage resilient cryptography to other forms of leakage that arise in the setting of modern computing platforms, and in particular to leakage through cache.

In this paper we show how to engineer proofs of security for software implementations of leakage-resilient cryptosystems on execution platforms with concurrency and caches. Our proofs are based on binary executables of the cryptosystem and on simple but realistic models of microprocessors. We obtain them by tackling the following technical challenges:

– We propose a novel notion of leakage that caters for concurrent access-based adversaries [13, 20]. This notion of leakage characterizes an adversary that can choose an inital cache state and observe the final cache state, for each time slice of a concurrently running computation. We specialize this notion of leakage to pseudorandom generators, and propose a new security definition in which the adversary can freely interleave request queries, that leak information about keys, with test queries, that output a real or random output according to a secret bit b.

M. Abadi and S. Kremer (Eds.): POST 2014, LNCS 8414, pp. 140–158, 2014.

Then, we prove leakage-resilience of a PRF-based PRG in this model. Our proof goes beyond the one from [26] in that it allows leakage functions to be adaptively chosen and makes weaker assumptions on locality of leakage. These relaxations are essential for dealing with concurrent access-based adversaries as considered in this paper. We cast our proof in terms of games, for future certification using automated tools [5].

– We propose a novel program analysis technique that allows us to statically derive upper bounds on the range of *all* leakage functions that a concurrent access-based adversary can apply to the state of the cipher. These upper bounds can be used for instantiating the parameters of the cryptographic proof. Our technique is based on an algorithm that efficiently maintains a compact representation of a superset of the set of observations that any concurrent cache adversary can make. We cast this algorithm as an abstract domain [8], which we plug into CacheAudit [9], a framework for the automatic, static analysis of cache side-channels of binary executables.

We perform a case study where we use our analysis techniques for certifying the security of a binary executable of a leakage-resilient pseudorandom generator that is based on a library implementation of the AES block cipher. Using our novel abstract domain, we derive bounds for the side-channel leakage of this implementation to concurrent cache adversaries, which we use to instantiate the cryptographic proof. For example, we can show that the advantage of an adversary for distinguishing the output of the PRG from random is upper-bounded by $\frac{1}{2^{94}}$ for an 8KB cache with 128B line size for AES-256. We stress that on several modern CPUs, AES is either implemented in hardware [1] or can be implemented in software without cache side channels [15]. Here, we use AES as a simple yet realistic example for demonstrating the feasibility of platform-based security proofs.

In summary, our contributions are to show how existing cryptosystems can be connected to a notion of leakage that captures caches and concurrency, and to develop program analysis techniques that enable us to statically deliver leakage bounds based on executable code.

Related Work. Leakage resilient cryptography (e.g. [10,19]) provides models for expressing the security of cryptosystems against adversaries that can obtain partial information about the internal state of the computation. Yu et al. [26] specialize these models to match engineering experience in power analysis attacks. In particular, they account for an adversary who chooses the leakage functions a priori, i.e. before the attack. Moreover, their model requires that each leakage function is applied only to the inputs and outputs of a particular round. Based on these assumptions, they prove the security of a simple pseudorandom generator.

Our leakage model is inspired by that of Yu et al. [26], but it differs in the following two aspects. First, we allow the adversary to adaptively choose leakage functions between rounds, from a fixed set of leakage functions. This accounts for the fact that, in concurrent cache attacks, the adversary can partially influence the leakage during the attack by interacting with the cache and the scheduler.

Second, instead of applying a leakage function to the inputs and outputs of a round, we apply it to *all* previously sampled keys. This accounts for the fact that, in cache attacks, keys might persist in the cache beyond the rounds in which they are used.

On the static analysis side, we base our work on CacheAudit [9], a framework for the automatic, static analysis of cache-based side-channels. CacheAudit makes use of the fact that one can obtain upper bounds for the information leaked through the cache by abstract interpretation and model counting [17,18].

An alternative, language-based approach by Zhang et al. [27] is to mitigate timing side channels based on systematic addition of delays. Another approach by Stefan et al. [24] uses typing and restrictive scheduling to close cache timing leaks. Our adversary model differs from theirs in that we consider access-based adversaries, i.e. those that can probe the cache. Finally, two recent approaches rely on the operating system making sure that caches are flushed upon context switches [4] or that security-relevant blocks are never evicted from the cache [16]. In contrast, our approach focuses on the security of the client program and makes only weak assumptions on the operating system.

Organization of this paper. In Section 2 we formalize a leakage model for concurrent cache adversaries and in Section 3 we present a proof of cryptographic security against this leakage model. In Section 4 we present algorithms to compute bounds on the leakage based on binary code, which we put to work in a case study in Section 5. We conclude in Section 6.

2   Leakage to Concurrent Cache Adversaries

In this section we express the information that is leaked to a cache side-channel adversary in terms of program semantics, where we consider a scenario in which the adversary and the victim are concurrent processes that share the same processor cache. Upon a context switch the adversary partially *observes* the final cache state of the victim's computation.[1] The adversary can further *choose* the initial state of the cache of the victim's subsequent time slice. Early instances of this kind of attack against AES can be found in [7,20], a more recent and highly effective one is [13].

2.1   Programs, Computations, Caches

A *program* $P = (\Sigma, I, \mathcal{T})$ consists of the following components

- Σ - a set of *states*
- $I \subseteq \Sigma$ - a set of *initial* states
- $\mathcal{T} \subseteq \Sigma \times \Sigma$ - a *transition relation*

---

[1] In practice, the adversary performs memory accesses and measures the corresponding latencies, thereby learning which memory blocks are loaded in, or have been evicted from, the cache (but not their content).

For reasoning about cache side channels, we consider a program state that consists of logical memories (representing values of memory locations and registers) in $\mathcal{M}$ and a cache state in $\mathcal{C}$ (representing the memory blocks that are currently loaded, but *not* their content), i.e., $\Sigma = \mathcal{M} \times \mathcal{C}$. The *memory update* $upd_{\mathcal{M}}$ is a function $upd_{\mathcal{M}}: \mathcal{M} \to \mathcal{M}$ that is determined by the instruction set semantics. The *cache update* is a function $upd_{\mathcal{C}}: \mathcal{M} \times \mathcal{C} \to \mathcal{C}$ that is determined by the cache replacement strategy. For a formal description of the LRU replacement strategy, see Appendix A.1. We obtain the global transition relation $\mathcal{T} \subseteq \Sigma \times \Sigma$ as

$$\mathcal{T} = \{((m_1, c_1), (m_2, c_2)) \mid m_2 = upd_{\mathcal{M}}(m_1) \ \wedge \ c_2 = upd_{\mathcal{C}}(c_1, m_1)\}$$

which formally captures the asymmetric relationship between logical memories and caches.

A *computation* of P is a sequence of states and $\sigma_0 \sigma_1 \ldots \sigma_n \in \Sigma^*$ such that $\sigma_0 \in I$ and that for all $i \in \{0, \ldots, n-1\}$, $(\sigma_i, \sigma_{i+1}) \in \mathcal{T}$. The set of all computations is the *trace collecting semantics* $Col(P)$. We further denote the projection of all computations to logical memories by $Col^{\mathcal{M}}(P)$.

2.2   Leakage to Concurrent Adversaries

We assume that our program runs concurrently with the adversary, where we make the worst-case assumption that the adversary can probe and set the cache state at each context switch. For formalizing this adversary we assume a given set of *context switches* $A \subseteq \mathbb{N}$. A *concurrent computation for A* is a sequence of states $(m_0, c_0), \ldots, (m_n, c_n) \in \Sigma^*$ such that

1. for all $i \in \{0, \ldots, n-1\}$: $m_{i+1} = upd_{\mathcal{M}}(m_i)$, i.e. the logical memory is always updated according to the program semantics;
2. for all $i \in \{0, \ldots, n-1\} \setminus A$: $c_{i+1} = upd_{\mathcal{C}}(c_i, m_i)$, i.e. without a context switch the cache is updated according to the program semantics;
3. for all $i \in A \cup \{0\}$: $c_{i+1} = upd_{\mathcal{C}}(c_i^*, m_i)$, i.e. at each context switch and initially, the cache can be set to an arbitrary state c_i^* by the adversary.

That is, the adversary's *choices* can be expressed as a tuple $a \in \mathcal{C}^{A \cup \{0\}}$ of cache states. They define a mapping

$$adv_{A,a}: Col^{\mathcal{M}}(P) \to Col_A(P)$$

where $Col_A(P)$ denotes the set of all concurrent computations for A.

Likewise, we can express the *observations* an adversary can make at context switches in A as a function $\pi_A: Col_A(P) \to \mathcal{C}^A$ that projects concurrent computations to sub-sequences of cache states with indices in A. The composition of both functions defines a *leakage function*

$$\Lambda^{A,a} = \pi_A \circ adv_{A,a}$$

that maps internal states of the computation to cache observations at A. Notice that cache states in our model only track *which* memory blocks are loaded, but not their content. Observing a cache state models leakage about accesses to memory space that is shared between victim and adversary, as in [13]. For modeling disjoint memory spaces, we consider observations that only reveal *how many* memory blocks are loaded in each cache set [17].

Leakage about a Key. For expressing the leakage about keys in round-based constructions, we assume that the key of round j can only affect the cache between positions $\alpha(j)$ and $\omega(j)$ of each computation. As a consequence, information about the key is observable at context switches between those positions. Moreover, information about the key may also persist in the cache state beyond $\omega(j)$ and be observable at the subsequent context switch. We account for this by defining $A_{\alpha(j),\omega(j)} = A \cap \{\alpha(j), \dots, \omega(j)\} \cup \min\{i \in A \mid i \geq \omega(j)\}$. For given (A, a), the leakage about the key of round j can then be over-approximated by the following function:

$$\Lambda_j^{A,a} = \pi_{A_{\alpha(j),\omega(j)}} \circ adv_{A,a}$$

Schedulers. Without any restrictions on when context switches can occur, we cannot hope to obtain meaningful security guarantees.[2] To model such restrictions, we introduce the notion of a *scheduler* $S \subset \mathcal{P}(\mathbb{N})$ that describes all permitted sets of context switches A. For a given scheduler, we can completely characterize the set of functions $\mathcal{L}_j$ the adversary can apply to a round key by

$$\mathcal{L}_j = \bigcup_{\substack{A \in S \\ a}} \Lambda_j^{A,a}$$

This class of leakage function will provide the interface between the cryptographic proofs and the guarantees derived by the static analysis.

3   Leakage Resilient PRG

Stateful pseudo-random number generators (PRGs) that depend on a secret key can be used as the basis for stream ciphers. Such constructions have been proposed as a means to provide leakage resilient cryptographic primitives [10, 21, 25, 26]. In this section, we prove the security of a stateful pseudo-random number generator based on a pseudo-random function (PRF), assuming partial leakages $\mathcal{L}_j$ on round keys as discussed in the previous section. Our proof is given in terms of bounds on the advantage of distinguishing the PRG from a truly random generator, depending on the computational power of the adversary and the maximal leakage per key.

---

[2] This is demonstrated by an attack that successfully recovers the secret key in such a setting [13].

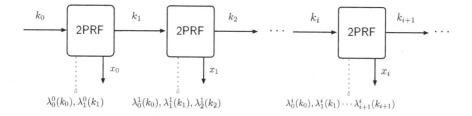

Fig. 1. Stateful PRG. Leakage is depicted by dotted arrows.

3.1 A Leakage Resilient PRG

The construction is depicted in Figure 1, and is based on a pseudorandom function $2PRF \colon \{0,1\}^n \to \{0,1\}^{n+m}$ that takes as input a round key k_i of n bits and returns as output a pseudorandom string of $n+m$ bits [3]. The first n bits of this string are used as a key k_{i+1} for the next round, and the last m bits are output. The sequence $x_0 x_1 \ldots$ is the output of the pseudorandom generator.

Our security proof is inspired from [26], and follows the spirit of so-called *practical* leakage-resilient cryptography, where bounds are obtained assuming leakage functions that match engineering practice. In particular, we make the assumption that leakage does not reveal information about future computations; for concurrent access-based cache attacks, this assumption is perfectly natural, since caches only hold information about *past* computations made by the victim. Our proof is based on the random oracle model; extending the proof to the standard model as done e.g. in [26] is left for further work.

The security of the pseudorandom generator is expressed in terms of a cryptographic game where, in each round i, the adversary can do one of the following:

- choose a list of leakage functions $\lambda_0^i, \ldots, \lambda_{i+1}^i$ and observe the values of $\lambda_0^i(k_0), \ldots, \lambda_{i+1}^i(k_{i+1})$ together with the legitimate output x_i of the 2PRF at round i. This is called a **request** query.
- test the round, and get the legitimate output x_i or a random output, according to a secret bit b sampled uniformly at the onset of the game. This is called a **test** query.

Moreover, the adversary has access to an oracle $2PRF_{adv}$ which he can query for the output of the 2PRF, for a chosen key. After p rounds of this game, the adversary is asked to guess the bit b. The adversary wins if his guess $\bar{b}$ is correct, i.e. $b = \bar{b}$. In summary, this game captures the notion that outputs of the 2PRF should be indistinguishable from random.

The game is formally defined in Figure 2. We use K_{adv} to store the keys queried by the adversary to the $2PRF_{adv}$ oracle and $K_{reqtest}$ to store the round

---

[3] Such a function can be constructed for instance by choosing an $IV \in \{0,1\}^{n-1}$ and defining $2PRF(k) = (BC_k(0\|IV), BC_k(1\|IV))$ given an n-bit block-cipher BC as we will do in Sect. 5.

Game G_{real} :	**Proc** 2PRF$(k : \{0,1\}^n)$:	**Oracle** request$(\lambda_0^i : \mathcal{L}_0^i, \ldots,$
$S \leftarrow [];$	if $k \notin \text{dom } S$ then	$\quad\quad\quad\quad \lambda_{i+1}^i : \mathcal{L}_{i+1}^i)$:
$K_{adv} \leftarrow \epsilon;$	$\quad k' \xleftarrow{\$} \{0,1\}^n;$	$(k_{i+1}, x) \leftarrow 2PRF(k_i);$
$i \leftarrow 0;$	$\quad x' \xleftarrow{\$} \{0,1\}^m;$	$K_{reqtest} \leftarrow k_{i+1} :: K_{reqtest};$
$k_0 \xleftarrow{\$} \{0,1\}^n;$	$\quad S[k] \leftarrow (k', x');$	$\ell \leftarrow (\lambda_0^i(k_0), \ldots, \lambda_{i+1}^i(k_{i+1}));$
$K_{reqtest} \leftarrow [k_0];$	return $S[k];$	$i \leftarrow i + 1;$
$b \xleftarrow{\$} \{0,1\};$		return $(x, \ell);$
$\bar{b} \leftarrow \mathcal{A}();$		
return $b = \bar{b};$		

	Oracle 2PRF$_{adv}(k : \{0,1\}^n)$:	**Oracle** test :
	$K_{adv} \leftarrow k :: K_{adv};$	$(k_{i+1}, x) \leftarrow 2PRF(k_i);$
	return 2PRF$(k);$	$K_{reqtest} \leftarrow k_{i+1} :: K_{reqtest};$
		if b then $x \xleftarrow{\$} \{0,1\}^m;$
		$i \leftarrow i + 1;$
		return $x;$

Fig. 2. Initial game G_{real}

keys of the stateful PRG. We store the values sampled by 2PRF in the array S. Note that, at each round i, the leakage functions are chosen from sets $\mathcal{L}_0^i, \ldots, \mathcal{L}_{i+1}^i$. Then $\mathcal{L}_j = \prod_i \mathcal{L}_j^i$ is the set of functions that the adversary can apply to the key of round j.

We now present the main theorem of this section, which quantifies the advantage of any adversary from distinguishing the PRG from a truly random number generator, given that he makes at most q queries to the 2PRF$_{adv}$ oracle, sees at most p outputs of the PRG and that the total leakage per key is bounded by a constant d.

Theorem 1. *Let $\mathcal{A}$ be an adversary that makes at most p queries to request or test, and at most q queries to 2PRF$_{adv}$. If for all $\Lambda_i \in \mathcal{L}_i$, $0 \le i < p$, it holds $|\text{ran}(\Lambda_i)| \le d$ then:*

$$\Pr[G_{real} : b = \bar{b}] \le \frac{1}{2} + \frac{p\,(p-1) + q\,p\,(d+1)}{2^n}$$

Proof. The idea of the proof is to bound the adversary's advantage by the probability of the following events: 1) there is a cycle in the PRG, due to a repetition of a round key, 2) the adversary guesses a round key that was already used in a previous round and 3) the adversary guesses a round key before it is used. These are precisely the cases in which an adversary could distinguish the PRG from a truly random generator, as we show using a game reduction and Shoup's Lemma [23]: Starting from the original game as depicted in Figure 2, we defined a transformed version G_1, where we modify the oracles 2PRF and 2PRF$_{adv}$ so that only adversary queries are stored in the map S, whereas queries originating from request and test are always answered with fresh random values. This only makes a difference if there is a collision between secret keys, i.e. $k_i = k_{i'}$ for distinct i and i' (we call this event bad_{RR}), or if the adversary calls the 2PRF_{adv} oracle with a secret key, i.e. $k_i \in K_{\text{adv}}$ for some i; we distinguish the case where the adversary queries 2PRF_{adv} with k_i before the ith round (we call this event bad_{AR}) from the case where the adversary query occurs after the ith round (and call this event bad_{RA}). We introduce bad flags to capture these events and modify the code of the oracles as follows:

Proc $2\text{PRF}(k : \{0,1\}^n)$:	**Oracle** $2\text{PRF}_{\text{adv}}(k : \{0,1\}^n)$:	**Oracle** test :
if $k \in K_{\text{reqtest}}$ then	if $k \in K_{\text{reqtest}}$ then	$k_{i+1} \xleftarrow{\$} \{0,1\}^n$;
$\quad \text{bad}_{RR} \leftarrow$ true;	$\quad \text{bad}_{RA} \leftarrow$ true;	$x \xleftarrow{\$} \{0,1\}^m$;
if $k \in K_{\text{adv}}$ then	$K_{\text{adv}} \leftarrow k :: K_{\text{adv}}$;	$K_{\text{reqtest}} \leftarrow k_{i+1} :: K_{\text{reqtest}}$;
$\quad \text{bad}_{AR} \leftarrow$ true;	if $k \notin \text{dom } S$ then	$i \leftarrow i+1$;
$k' \xleftarrow{\$} \{0,1\}^n$;	$\quad k' \xleftarrow{\$} \{0,1\}^n$;	return x;
$x' \xleftarrow{\$} \{0,1\}^m$;	$\quad x' \xleftarrow{\$} \{0,1\}^m$;	
return (k', x');	$\quad S[k] \leftarrow (k', x')$;	
	return $S[k]$;	

The two games are equivalent up to bad. It follows from Shoup's Lemma [23] that

$$\left| \Pr[\mathsf{G}_{\text{real}} : b = \bar{b}] - \Pr[\mathsf{G}_1 : b = \bar{b}] \right| \leq \Pr[\mathsf{G}_1 : \text{bad}_{RR}] + \Pr[\mathsf{G}_1 : \text{bad}_{AR}] + \Pr[\mathsf{G}_1 : \text{bad}_{RA}]$$

Moreover, the key k_i is always a freshly sampled value and $|K_{\text{reqtest}}| \leq p$, therefore the event $k_i \in K_{\text{reqtest}}$ (bad_{RR}) is a standard birthday event and has a probability of at most $\frac{p\,(p-1)}{2^n}$. Also, the probability of the event $k_i \in K_{\text{adv}}$ (bad_{AR}) for a given freshly uniformly sampled k_i key is upper bounded by $\frac{q}{2^n}$. There are at most p rounds, i.e. $0 \leq i < p$, thus the probability of a collision between k_i and a key in K_{adv} is upper bounded by $\frac{q\,p}{2^n}$. Finally, the value x output by the test oracle is a fresh uniformly sampled value for each round, and hence the probability of the adversary $\mathcal{A}$ guessing the bit b correctly in G_1 is $\frac{1}{2}$. Summarizing, we have

$$\left| \Pr[\mathsf{G}_{\text{real}} : b = \bar{b}] - \frac{1}{2} \right| \leq \frac{p\,(p-1)}{2^n} + \frac{q\,p}{2^n} + \Pr[\mathsf{G}_1 : \text{bad}_{RA}]$$

Next, we introduce a game G_2 in which a fresh key k is sampled uniformly at the onset of the game, and an adversary $\mathcal{A}'$ can observe at each round i the value of $\lambda^i(k)$, for a leakage function λ^i drawn from a set $\mathcal{L}^i$. The adversary wins if he guesses correctly the key. The game is formalized as follows:

Game G_2 :	**Oracle** leak$(\lambda^i : \mathcal{L}^i)$:
$i \leftarrow 0$;	$\ell \leftarrow \lambda^i(k)$;
$k \xleftarrow{\$} \{0,1\}^n$;	$i \leftarrow i+1$;
$\bar{k} \leftarrow \mathcal{A}'()$;	return ℓ;
return $k = \bar{k}$;	

One can prove that for every adversary $\mathcal{A}$ against G_1 making at most p queries to the request oracle and q queries to the $\mathsf{2PRF}_{\mathrm{adv}}$ oracle, there exists an adversary $\mathcal{A}'$ against G_2 such that $\Pr[\mathsf{G}_1 : \mathsf{bad}_{RA}] \leq q\,p\,\Pr[\mathsf{G}_2 : k = \bar{k}]$.

Finally, $\Pr[\mathsf{G}_2 : k = \bar{k}]$ is upper-bounded by $\frac{d}{2^n}$, given the assumption that the total range of his observations is upper bounded by d, i.e. $\prod_{i=0}^{p} |\mathsf{ran}(\lambda^i)| \leq d$. This last step follows from Theorem 1 of [9], which we reproduce in Appendix A.3.

4   Computing Bounds on the Leakage

For computing the range of the leakage functions that a concurrent cache-based adversary can apply to the internal state of a concrete program, one needs to consider *all* possible computations, which is infeasible in most cases. Abstract interpretation [8] overcomes this fundamental problem by resorting to an approximation of the state space and the transition relation. In this section, we present corresponding approximations for concurrent cache-based adversaries. We proceed by reducing the problem in two steps to the problem of computing numbers of reachable cache states, for which static analysis techniques are in place [9, 17]. Throughout the section we rely on the notation introduced in Section 2.

4.1   Reduction to Empty Initial Cache States

In the first reduction step, we show how to soundly abstract from the adversary's choices of cache states. The result is a generalization of a result from [9] to concurrent computations.

Let $a_\emptyset \in \mathcal{C}^{A \cup \{0\}}$ be the mapping that takes each $i \in A \cup \{0\}$ to the empty cache state.

Lemma 1. *For the LRU replacement strategy and all A and $a \in \mathcal{C}^{A \cup \{0\}}$,*

$$\left| \mathsf{ran}(\Lambda^{A,a}) \right| \leq \left| \mathsf{ran}(\Lambda^{A,a_\emptyset}) \right|$$

Proof. With LRU replacement, each cache set (seen as a list of memory blocks) of the final cache state of the time slice of a computation with initial cache state $a_\emptyset(i)$ is a prefix of the corresponding cache set of the same computation, performed with initial cache state $a(i)$. The remaining lines of each set are determined by $a(i)$. This correspondence defines, for each a, a surjective mapping from $\mathsf{ran}(\Lambda^{A,a_\emptyset})$ to $\mathsf{ran}(\Lambda^{A,a})$, from which the assertion follows.

4.2   Abstract Interpretation

Reachability problems on programs can be cast as finding fixpoints of the transition relation, because reaching a fixpoint means that no new states can be discovered. Abstract interpretation [8] computes such fixpoints based on approximations of the statespace and the transition relation. The relationship between the abstract and the concrete statespace is given by a *concretization function* γ that maps abstract states to sets of concrete states. A static analysis is *(globally) sound* if the concretization of an abstract fixpoint contains a concrete fixpoint.

In our case, the goal is to define such an abstract domain $\mathcal{T}^{\sharp}$ whose fixpoints $t^* \in \mathcal{T}^{\sharp}$ satisfy

$$Col_S^C(P) \subseteq \gamma_{\mathcal{T}}(t^*) \tag{1}$$

CacheAudit [9] is an abstract interpretation framework that enables computing such abstract fixpoints t^* based on binary executables and concrete cache models. For framing a sound cache analysis within CacheAudit, an abstract domain needs to satisfy the following local soundness condition, where $\mathcal{B}$ denotes the set of all memory blocks:

$$\forall t^{\sharp} \in \mathcal{T}^{\sharp}, M \subseteq \mathcal{B} \ : \ upd_{\mathcal{T}}(\gamma_{\mathcal{T}}(t^{\sharp}), M) \subseteq \gamma_{\mathcal{T}}(upd_{\mathcal{T}^{\sharp}}(t^{\sharp}, M)) \ , \tag{2}$$

This statement captures that the abstract cache update function $upd_{\mathcal{T}^{\sharp}}$ computes a superset of the concrete cache update function $upd_{\mathcal{T}}$. Computing the set of reachable observations w.r.t. $upd_{\mathcal{T}^{\sharp}}$ is hence necessarily a superset of $upd_{\mathcal{T}}$. The global soundness then follows from the fact that CacheAudit updates the abstract cache with a superset of the set of possible memory blocks that are accessed at each program point.

Theorem 2. *Local soundness implies global soundness, i.e.* $(2) \Rightarrow (1)$

This theorem from [9] is a specialization of a result of [8] to the way in which abstract domains are combined in CacheAudit.

We present our new abstract domain in two steps: in the first step we abstract sets of cache traces by traces of sets of cache states, while keeping enough information about the history of computation to obtain reasonably precise bounds. In the second step we further abstract to obtain finite representations. Since in abstract interpretation, abstract domains compose, it is enough to prove soundness of each step to have the soundness of the whole abstraction process.

4.3   An Abstract Domain for Concurrent Computations

One of the main reason for the intractability of computing leakage functions is the need to keep track of sets of traces. The first step we propose is to abstract such sets into a single (possibly infinite) trace of abstract states abstracting sets of caches and possible interruption choices of the adversary. For that purpose, we assume a given abstract domain for cache *states* such as the one from [11], whose elements we denote by $c^{\sharp}$. The concretization of an abstract cache is a set of caches, i.e.

$$\gamma_C(c^{\sharp}) \subseteq \mathcal{C} \ .$$

In addition, we assume that this abstract domain is equipped with a join $\sqcup$ that soundly over-approximates unions of sets of caches.

We define the abstract domain $\mathcal{T}^{\sharp}$ that groups together cache states with the same concurrent access history as follows: Each element $t^{\sharp} \in \mathcal{T}^{\sharp}$ consists of a partial map of pairs of nonnegative integers to abstract cache states. We denote this map by $t^\# = (c_{i,j}^\#)$. Here $(c_{i,j}^\#)$ represents the set of possible cache states at position j when the last context switch happened i steps ago. During the analysis we will maintain $(c_{i,j}^\#)$ for $1 \leq i \leq j \leq n$, where n is the current program point. That is, our abstract state is of the form

$$
\begin{array}{cccc}
c_{1,1}^\# & c_{1,2}^\# & \cdots & c_{1,n}^\# \\
& c_{2,2}^\# & \cdots & c_{2,n}^\# \\
& & \ddots & \vdots \\
& & & c_{n,n}^\#
\end{array}
$$

For convenience of notation we further define $c_{0,j}^\# = c_\emptyset^\#$ (with $\gamma_C(c_\emptyset^\#) = \{c_\emptyset\}$) for all $j \geq 0$.

Concretization Function We first define the concretization of an abstract state $(c_{i,j}^\#)$, with $0 \leq i \leq j \leq n$, w.r.t. given (ordered) set of context switches $A = \{i_1, \ldots, i_k\}$ with $i_k \leq n$ by:

$$
\begin{aligned}
\gamma_A(c_{i,j}^\#) = \quad & \gamma_C(c_{0,0}^\#) \quad \cdots \quad \gamma_C(c_{i_1,i_1}^\#) \\
& \cdot \gamma_C(c_{1,i_1+1}^\#) \cdots \gamma_C(c_{i_2-i_1,i_2}^\#) \\
& \vdots \qquad\qquad\qquad \vdots \\
& \cdot \gamma_C(c_{1,i_k+1}^\#) \cdots \gamma_C(c_{n-i_k,n}^\#)
\end{aligned}
$$

The result is a set of traces built from a trace of sets using the Cartesian product $\cdot$, where the end of each line corresponds to the states that can be observed at a context switch.

For a scheduler S, we then define the concretization of an abstract state as the union of the concretizations w.r.t. all sets of context switches in S, i.e.

$$
\gamma_T(c_{i,j}^\#) = \bigcup_{A \in S_n} \gamma_A(c_{i,j}^\#)
$$

where $S_n = \{A \cap \{1, \ldots n\} \mid A \in S\}$ denotes the sets of context switches that are truncated at position n.

Abstract Transition Function We define an abstract transition function $upd_{T^\#}(c_{0 \leq i \leq j \leq n}^\#, M) = (c_{0 \leq i \leq j \leq n+1}^\#)$ that maps a set of memory blocks M and a state representing traces of length n to a state representing traces of length $n+1$, where

$$
c_{i+1,n+1}^\# = upd_{C^\#}(c_{i,n}^\#, M) \quad \text{for } 0 \leq i \leq n
$$

The case $i > 1$ describes the scenario in which *no* context switch happens at position n. The case $i = 0$ describes the scenario in which a context switch happens, where we only need to consider the empty initial state due to Lemma 1 (recall that $c_{0,n}^\# = c_\emptyset^\#$). The entries $c_{i,j}^\#$ with $j \leq n$ remain unchanged.

The following lemma states the local soundness of our abstract domain. Together with Theorem 2, it ensures the global soundness of our analysis.

Lemma 2. $upd_{\mathcal{T}}(\gamma_{\mathcal{T}}(t^{\sharp}), M) \subseteq \gamma_{\mathcal{T}}(upd_{\mathcal{T}^{\sharp}}(t^{\sharp}, M))$

The proof of Lemma 2 is given in Appendix A.2; it proceeds by a simple unfolding of definitions and a reduction to the soundness of $upd_{\mathcal{C}^{\sharp}}$.

4.4 Compact Representations of Infinite Computations

With the abstraction described above we can represent cache observations up to a moment n in time. We now propose a further abstraction that enables us to finitely represent and compute cache observations for *all* points in time, using fixpoint techniques of abstract interpretation.

Our current abstract domain for concurrent computations grows in two directions, both of which have to be bounded in a meaningful way: (1) the number of instructions since the beginning of the computation, and (2) the number of instructions since the last context switch happenend.

For bounding (1) we assume that the computation of the individual rounds of the PRG is performed in one main loop whose body takes exactly ℓ steps to execute. We leverage this knowledge to fold the abstract states corresponding to the same number of instructions inside the loop body. Technically, we will abstract each program point $n \in \mathbb{N}$ with the unique $j \in \{0, \ldots \ell - 1\}$ such that $j \equiv n \mod \ell$, and we write $j = [n]$. In this way we only need to maintain elements $c^{\sharp}_{i,[n]}$ instead of all $c^{\sharp}_{i,n}$.

For bounding (2), we impose a threshold s on the length of the history we track about the last context switch. To achieve soundness, we modify the update function such that the last element $c^{\sharp}_{s,j}$ aggregates all possible cache states $c^{\sharp}_{i,j}$ with $i \geq s$.

Our new abstract state, which we denote by $(d^{\sharp}_{i,j})$, for $0 \leq i \leq s$ and $0 \leq j < \ell$ is updated using the following transition function

$$d^{\sharp}_{i+1,[n+1]} = upd_{\mathcal{C}^{\sharp}}\left(d^{\sharp}_{i,[n]}, M\right) \qquad \text{if } 0 \leq i < s - 1$$

$$d^{\sharp}_{s,[n+1]} = upd_{\mathcal{C}^{\sharp}}\left(d^{\sharp}_{s,[n]}, M\right) \sqcup d^{\sharp}_{s-1,[n+1]}$$

Since the second subscript is an equivalence class, the update functions define a set of fixpoint equations. The transfer function for this set of equations is obviously monotonic, so we can iterate from a matrix entirely filled with empty caches to compute this fixpoint. In addition, we can use program points to store columns of this matrix and use the fixpoint iteration techniques already developed for CacheAudit.

Even though $c^{\sharp}_{i,j}$ with $i > s$ of the abstract state defined in Section 4.3 are not explicitly represented in the above state, we define their concretization by

$$\gamma_{\mathcal{T}}(c^{\sharp}_{i,n}) = \gamma_{\mathcal{T}}(d^{\sharp}_{\min\{i,s\},[n]}) \tag{3}$$

The definition of $(d^{\sharp}_{i,j})$ and the corresponding update function ensures that the thus defined $\gamma_{\mathcal{T}}(c^{\sharp}_{i,n})$ is always a superset of the concretization of the explicit representation. We obtain the following corollary for the compactly represented abstract state.

Corollary 1. $upd_T(\gamma_T(t^{\sharp}), M) \subseteq \gamma_T(upd_{T^{\sharp}}(t^{\sharp}, M))$

Proof. Follows from the proof of the previous lemma and by monotonicity of the new update function.

4.5   Computing Bounds on the Leakage

We now present an algorithm for upper-bounding counting the range of the leakage function based on a fixpoint $(d^{\sharp}_{i,j})$ with $i \leq s$ and $j \leq \ell - 1$ of the abstract domain described above. For convenience of notation we describe the algorithm in terms of $(c^{\sharp}_{i,j})$ and explicit indices, which can be immediately translated using Equation (3).

Recall from Section 2 that $A_{\alpha,\omega} = A \cap \{\alpha, \dots, \omega\} \cup \min\{i \in A \mid i \geq \omega\}$ is the set of context switches at which the adversary can make observations about a secret that is present in logical memory from position α to position ω. The leakage about such secrets can hence be described by the function $\Lambda^{A,a}_{\alpha,\omega} = \pi_{A_{\alpha,\omega}} \circ adv_{A,a}$. We obtain an upper bound on the size of the range of $\Lambda^{A,a}_{\alpha,\omega}$ as follows

$$
\begin{aligned}
\left| \Lambda^{A,a}_{\alpha,\omega}(Col^{\mathcal{M}}(P)) \right| &\overset{(*)}{\leq} \left| \Lambda^{A,c_{\emptyset}}_{\alpha,\omega}(Col^{\mathcal{M}}(P)) \right| \\
&= \left| \pi_{A_{\alpha,\omega}}(adv_{A,c_{\emptyset}}(Col^{\mathcal{M}}(P))) \right| \\
&\overset{(**)}{\leq} \left| \pi_{A_{\alpha,\omega}}(\gamma_A(c^{\sharp}_{i,j})) \right| \\
&= \left| \gamma_C(c^{\sharp}_{i_1-\alpha,i_1}) \right| \left| \gamma_C(c^{\sharp}_{i_2-i_1,i_2}) \right| \cdots \left| \gamma_C(c^{\sharp}_{i_{k+1}-i_k,i_{k+1}}) \right|
\end{aligned}
$$

where $(*)$ follows from Lemma 1, $(**)$ follows from Theorem 2, and $A_{\alpha,\omega} = \{i_1, \dots i_{k+1}\}$. We can instantiate this upper bound by applying existing procedures for counting concretizations of abstract cache states [17] to the elements of $(c^{\sharp}_{i,j})$.

For upper-bounding the leakage for a given scheduler S, we need to maximize the above expression over all $A \in S$. We show how this can be done for a very general class of schedulers, whose only requirement is a lower bound f on the number of instructions processed by the victim between two interruptions by the adversary.

$$
S_f = \{A \subseteq \mathbb{N} \mid i = j \vee |i - j| \geq f\} \tag{4}
$$

For bounding the leakage w.r.t. to S_f, we first give a recursive formula that expresses the maximal number of observation that an adversary can make at and between context switches at positions x and y

$$
R_{x,y} = \max_{x \leq j \leq y-f} R_{x,j} \left| \gamma_C \left(c^{\sharp}_{y-j,y} \right) \right| \qquad \text{if } y \geq x + f \tag{5}
$$

where we adopt the convention that $R_{x,y} = 1$ whenever $y < x + f$.

Observe that it is *not* sufficient to use $R_{\alpha,\omega}$ for upper-bounding the leakage of a secret that is present in logical memory between positions α and ω because (1) α does not necessarily coincide with a context switch, and (2) the final context switch may happen an indefinite number of steps after ω. To account for this fact we define

$$L_{\alpha,\omega} = \max \left\{ \max_{\substack{r \leq \alpha \\ \omega \leq t}} \left| \gamma_C(c^{\sharp}_{t-r,t}) \right|, \ \max_{\substack{r \leq \alpha < x \\ y < \omega \leq t}} \left| \gamma_C(c^{\sharp}_{x-r,x}) \right| R_{x,y} \left| \gamma_C(c^{\sharp}_{t-y,t}) \right| \right\}$$

The left term in the definition of $L_{\alpha,\omega}$ captures the case where no context switch happens between α and ω. The second term captures the case where at least one context switch happens; in this case x is the position of the first, and y is the position of the last context switch between α and ω. For readability we omit further constraints on the minimal distance f between each two context switches.

The following lemma states that $L_{\alpha,\omega}$ describes an upper bound on the information that is leaked about the logical memory between positions α and ω.

Lemma 3

$$\max_{A \subseteq S} \left| \mathsf{ran}(\Lambda^{A,a}_{\alpha,\omega}) \right| \leq L_{\alpha,\omega}$$

The correctness of $R_{x,y}$ follows by a simple induction on y using the bound on $\Lambda^{A,a}_{\alpha,\omega}$ described above. The correctness of $L_{\alpha,\omega}$ follows by construction. Equation (5) immediately suggests an implementation of the algorithm using dynamic programming.

4.6 Leakage Per Key

For deriving bounds on the leakage *per key* for the PRG described in Section 3, we also assume that k_i is part of the internal state of rounds i and $i+1$. If each round can be computed in ℓ commands, the leakage about k_i is hence upper-bounded by $L_{i\ell,(i+2)\ell-1}$ As we identify all i modulo ℓ in (5), we immediately obtain that $L_{0,2\ell-1}$ is an upper bound for the leakage about each round key.

Corollary 2. *For all $j \in \mathbb{N}$ we have*

$$\forall \Lambda \in \mathcal{L}_j : |\mathsf{ran}(\Lambda)| \leq L_{0,2\ell-1}$$

5 Case Study

In this section we report on a case study where we use our techniques to derive formal security guarantees against concurrent cache-based adversaries for binary executable of the leakage-resilient pseudorandom number generator from [26].

Implementation of Abstract Domain and Counting. We implement a special case of the abstract domain presented in Section 4. Namely, we use a fixed history threshold of $s = 1$, thereby trading precision for efficiency of the analysis. We connect this abstract domain to the CacheAudit platform [9]. CacheAudit takes as input a (32 bit) x86 binary executable, reconstructs the control flow, and uses abstract interpretation to compute an over-approximation of the set of program states (which comprise the cache) that are reachable. The local soundness of our novel domain (stated in Lemma 2), together with the correctness of CacheAudit (stated in Theorem 2) ensures that our analysis soundly over-approximates the set of all concurrent computations.

We further choose f such that the scheduler interrupts *at most once* per round of the pseudorandom number generator. With Corollary 2 we see that the leakage *per key* exceeds the leakage *per round* by a factor of at most three. We can hence obtain a leakage bound by maximising over the number of concretizations of abstract cache states that appear in the fixpoint, which is how we avoid implementing the concurrent counting procedure from Section 4.5 in full generality. We perform the counting of individual cache states using the techniques described in [17].

Implementation of the PRG. We implement the 2PRF by concatenating two blocks produced by a block cipher $\mathsf{BC}\colon \{0,1\}^n \times \{0,1\}^n \to \{0,1\}^n$. More precisely, for an initialization vector $IV \in \{0,1\}^{n-1}$ we compute

$$2\mathsf{PRF}(k) = (\mathsf{BC}_k(0\|IV), \mathsf{BC}_k(1\|IV)) \ .$$

For our implementation, we instantiate BC with the AES implementation from the PolarSSL library [2], where we use a keylength of 256 bits. We put the key schedule and the two calls to the block cipher in an infinite loop and use gcc to compile this program to a 32-bit x86 executable, which is the artifact we analyze using the techniques developed in this paper.

Experimental Results. We perform the analysis of the executable on a set-associative cache with LRU replacement strategy, where we consider different cache sizes, line sizes, and associativities. The results of our analysis are given in Table 1.

Columns 5 and 6, respectively, present bounds on the leakage to an concurrent cache adversary per round and per key. Our data show that leakage increases with the cache size and decreases with the line size. The first effect occurs because a larger cache size means that the table is spread out into more cache sets, which increases the resolution with which the adversary can observe the memory accesses of the victim. The second effect occurs because a larger line size decreases the adversary's resolution. Finally, our data shows that greater associativities lead to better bounds.

The entries of Column 6 can be used to instantiate the parameters in Theorem 1, where we consider an adversary with $q = 2^{50}$ and set the amount of observable data with the same IV to be 1GB, thus $p \leq 2^{25}$. The cryptographic

Table 1. Leakage about the 2PRF based on the PolarSSL AES 256 implementation, for different cache sizes, line sizes, and associativities. The entries of columns 5 and 6 represent the range of the leakage functions per round and per key, respectively. The entries of column 7 represent bits of security computed using Theorem 1.

Cache size	Line size	Ways	Possible cache observations (bits)	Leakage per round (bits)	Leakage per key (bits)	Security (bits)
2KB	64B	4	18.6	18.3	54.9	126.1
4KB	64B	4	37.2	36.8	110.4	70.6
8KB	64B	4	74.3	55.2	165.6	15.4
16KB	64B	4	148.6	70.2	210.6	0
32KB	64B	4	297.2	73.1	219.3	0
64KB	64B	4	594.41	75.0	225	0
8KB	**32B**	4	148.6	109.5	328.5	0
8KB	**64B**	4	74.3	55.2	165.5	15.4
8KB	**128B**	4	37.2	28.8	86.4	94.6
8KB	64B	**2**	101.4	68.1	204.3	0
8KB	64B	**4**	74.3	55.2	165.6	15.4
8KB	64B	**8**	50.7	39.9	119.7	61.3

security guarantees we obtain with these parameters are given in column 7; they range from very strong (e.g. 126.1 bits for a 2KB cache with 64B line size) to non-existent (e.g. 8KB cache with 32B line size).

Discussion. Column 4 presents an absolute, *program-independent* bound on the number of cache states an adversary can observe in each context switch. Throughout the case study, we consider an adversary whose memory space is disjoint from the victim's, i.e. one who can observe how many memory blocks are loaded in each cache set, but not which. For the example of an 8KB cache with 4 ways and lines of 64B, this number amounts to $(4+1)^{8192/(4*64)}$, where the basis denotes the number of observations per set (0-4 blocks have been loaded into that set by the victim) and the exponent denotes the number of (independent) cache sets.

A comparison between columns 4 and 5 sheds light on the scope of our technique. For caches up to 4KB, the entries in both columns almost coincide. This is due to the fact that the 4KB+256B of tables in the PolarSSL AES implementation entirely fill such small caches, and that the static analysis can only predict that each of the corresponding memory blocks can either be loaded or not. The small difference in leakage stems from the fact that the static analysis *can* predict that the memory blocks containing local variables will be loaded. For caches of 8KB or more the static analysis can moreover determine that the memory access patterns of the executable only affect the memory blocks in which the tables and the local variables reside, hence the bounds obtained by static analysis are significantly better than those obtained by pure combinatorics.

Finally, we remark that there are several timing-relevant features of hardware our approach does not cover (and make assertions about) yet, including out-of-order execution, pipelines, TLBs, and multiple levels of caches. Likewise, implementations of instruction-based scheduling [24] are not yet widely deployed. From a practical perspective, it is currently still wise to rely on implementations that entirely avoid secret-dependent memory lookups, e.g. [1, 6, 15].

6   Conclusions

We have presented the first proof of resilience against side-channel attacks by concurrent cache-based adversaries. To achieve this, we extended existing leakage-resilient cryptosystems to a notion of leakage that captures caches and concurrency, and we developed program analysis techniques for statically deriving formal security guarantees based on executable code.

Acknowledgments. This work was partially funded by European Project FP7-256980 NESSoS, by the Spanish Project TIN2012-39391-C04-01 StrongSoft, and by the Madrid Regional Project S2009TIC-1465 PROMETIDOS. This work was partially developed while Martín Ochoa was affiliated with Siemens AG.

References

1. Intel Advanced Encryption Standard (AES) Instructions Set, http://software.intel.com/file/24917
2. PolarSSL, http://polarssl.org/
3. Acıiçmez, O., Koç, Ç.K., Seifert, J.-P.: Predicting secret keys via branch prediction. In: Abe, M. (ed.) CT-RSA 2007. LNCS, vol. 4377, pp. 225–242. Springer, Heidelberg (2006)
4. Barthe, G., Betarte, G., Campo, J.D., Luna, C.: Cache-Leakage Resilient OS Isolation in an Idealized Model of Virtualization. In: CSF. IEEE (2012)
5. Barthe, G., Grégoire, B., Heraud, S., Béguelin, S.Z.: Computer-aided security proofs for the working cryptographer. In: Rogaway, P. (ed.) CRYPTO 2011. LNCS, vol. 6841, pp. 71–90. Springer, Heidelberg (2011)
6. Bernstein, D.: Salsa20, http://cr.yp.to/snuffle.html
7. Bernstein, D.J.: Cache-timing attacks on AES. Technical report (2005)
8. Cousot, P., Cousot, R.: Abstract interpretation: a unified lattice model for static analysis of programs by construction of approximation of fixpoints. In: ACM (ed.) POPL (1977)
9. Doychev, G., Feld, D., Köpf, B., Mauborgne, L., Reineke, J.: CacheAudit: A Tool for the Static Analysis of Cache Side Channels. In: USENIX Security Symposium (2013)
10. Dziembowski, S., Pietrzak, K.: Leakage-Resilient Cryptography. In: FOCS. IEEE (2008)
11. Ferdinand, C., Martin, F., Wilhelm, R., Alt, M.: Cache behavior prediction by abstract interpretation. Science of Computer Programming 35(2), 163–189 (1999)
12. Grund, D.: Static Cache Analysis for Real-Time Systems – LRU, FIFO, PLRU. PhD thesis, Saarland University (2012)
13. Gullasch, D., Bangerter, E., Krenn, S.: Cache Games - Bringing Access-Based Cache Attacks on AES to Practice. In: S&P. IEEE (2011)

14. Jana, S., Shmatikov, V.: Memento: Learning secrets from process footprints. In: S&P. IEEE (2012)

15. Käsper, E., Schwabe, P.: Faster and timing-attack resistant AES-GCM. In: Clavier, C., Gaj, K. (eds.) CHES 2009. LNCS, vol. 5747, pp. 1–17. Springer, Heidelberg (2009)

16. Kim, T., Peinado, M., Mainar-Ruiz, G.: StealthMem: System-level protection against cache-based side channel attacks in the cloud. In: 19th USENIX Security Symposium. USENIX (2012)

17. Köpf, B., Mauborgne, L., Ochoa, M.: Automatic Quantification of Cache Side-Channels. In: Madhusudan, P., Seshia, S.A. (eds.) CAV 2012. LNCS, vol. 7358, pp. 564–580. Springer, Heidelberg (2012)

18. Köpf, B., Rybalchenko, A.: Approximation and Randomization for Quantitative Information-Flow Analysis. In: CSF. IEEE (2010)

19. Micali, S., Reyzin, L.: Physically observable cryptography. In: Naor, M. (ed.) TCC 2004. LNCS, vol. 2951, pp. 278–296. Springer, Heidelberg (2004)

20. Osvik, D.A., Shamir, A., Tromer, E.: Cache Attacks and Countermeasures: The Case of AES. In: Pointcheval, D. (ed.) CT-RSA 2006. LNCS, vol. 3860, pp. 1–20. Springer, Heidelberg (2006)

21. Pietrzak, K.: A leakage-resilient mode of operation. In: Joux, A. (ed.) EURO-CRYPT 2009. LNCS, vol. 5479, pp. 462–482. Springer, Heidelberg (2009)

22. Ristenpart, T., Tromer, E., Shacham, H., Savage, S.: Hey, you, get off of my cloud: exploring information leakage in third-party compute clouds. In: CCS. ACM (2009)

23. Shoup, V.: Sequences of games: a tool for taming complexity in security proofs. Cryptology ePrint Archive, Report 2004/332 (2004)

24. Stefan, D., Buiras, P., Yang, E.Z., Levy, A., Terei, D., Russo, A., Mazières, D.: Eliminating cache-based timing attacks with instruction-based scheduling. In: Crampton, J., Jajodia, S., Mayes, K. (eds.) ESORICS 2013. LNCS, vol. 8134, pp. 718–735. Springer, Heidelberg (2013)

25. Yu, Y., Standaert, F.-X.: Practical leakage-resilient pseudorandom objects with minimum public randomness. In: Dawson, E. (ed.) CT-RSA 2013. LNCS, vol. 7779, pp. 223–238. Springer, Heidelberg (2013)

26. Yu, Y., Standaert, F.-X., Pereira, O., Yung, M.: Practical leakage-resilient pseudo-random generators. In: CCS. ACM (2010)

27. Zhang, D., Askarov, A., Myers, A.C.: Language-based control and mitigation of timing channels. In: PLDI. ACM (2012)

A   Appendix

A.1   Example Formalization Cache Update Function

We formally describe upd_C only for the LRU strategy and a single cache set; see [12] for formalizations of other replacement strategies. Upon a cache miss, LRU replaces the least-recently-used memory block. To this end, it tracks the ages of memory blocks within the cache, where the youngest block has age 0 and the oldest cached block has age $k - 1$. Thus, the state of the cache can be modeled as a function that assigns an age to each memory block $b \in \mathcal{B}$, where non-cached blocks are assigned age k:

$$\mathcal{C} := \{c \in \mathcal{B} \to A \mid \forall a, b \in \mathcal{B} : c(a) \neq c(b) \lor c(a) = c(b) = k\},$$

where $A := \{0, ..., k-1, k\}$ is the set of ages. The constraint encodes that no two blocks can have the same age. For readability we omit the additional constraint that blocks of non-zero age are preceded by other blocks, i.e. that caches do not contain "holes". The cache update for LRU is then given by

$$upd_C(c, b) := \lambda b' \in \mathcal{B}. \begin{cases} 0 & : b' = b \\ c(b') + 1 & : c(b') < c(b) \\ c(b') & : c(b') > c(b) \end{cases}$$

A.2   Local Soundness of Cache Trace Domain

Lemma 2

$$upd_\mathcal{T}(\gamma_\mathcal{T}(t^\sharp), M) \subseteq \gamma_\mathcal{T}(upd_{\mathcal{T}^\sharp}(t^\sharp, M)),$$

Proof.

$$upd_\mathcal{T}(\gamma_\mathcal{T}(c^\sharp_{i,j}), M) =$$

$$= \bigcup_{A \in S_n} upd_\mathcal{T}(\gamma_A(c^\sharp_{i,j}, M))$$

$$= \bigcup_{n \notin A} \gamma_C(c^\sharp_{0,0}) \ldots \gamma_C(c^\sharp_{n-i_k,n}) upd_C(\gamma(c^\sharp_{n-i_k,n}), M)$$

$$\cup \bigcup_{n \in A} \gamma_A(c^\sharp_{i,j}) upd_C(c_\emptyset, M)$$

$$\overset{(*)}{\subseteq} \bigcup_{n \notin A} \gamma_C(c^\sharp_{0,0}) \ldots \gamma_C(c^\sharp_{n-i_k,n}) \gamma_C(upd_{C^\sharp}(c^\sharp_{n-i_k,n}), M)$$

$$\cup \bigcup_{n+1 \in A} \gamma_A(c^\sharp_{i,j}) upd_{C^\sharp}(c^\sharp_\emptyset, M)$$

$$= \gamma_\mathcal{T}(upd_{\mathcal{T}^\sharp}(t^\sharp, M)) ,$$

where $(*)$ follows from the local soundness of the cache state abstract domain $C^\sharp$.

A.3   Bounded Range Leakage and Guessing

We recall the following result (see [9] for a proof):

Lemma 4. *Let $X \to Y \to \hat{X}$ be a Markov Chain. Then*

$$\Pr[X = \hat{X}] \leq \max_x \Pr[X = x] \, |\mathsf{ran}(Y)|$$

In particular, if X returns uniformly random n-bit strings, $\Pr[X = \hat{X}] \leq \frac{1}{2^n} |\mathsf{ran}(Y)|$

In the context of G_2 in Theorem 1, the key k is a uniformly chosen random n-bit string, and $\Lambda(k)$ the vector of observations of k given to the adversary, corresponding to the variable Y. Therefore, the probability of an adversary of outputting k' such that $k = k'$ is upper bounded by $\frac{1}{2^n} |\mathsf{ran}(\Lambda)| \leq \frac{d}{2^n}$.

Information Flow Control in WebKit's JavaScript Bytecode

Abhishek Bichhawat[1], Vineet Rajani[2], Deepak Garg[2], and Christian Hammer[1]

[1] Saarland University, Germany
[2] MPI-SWS, Germany

Abstract. Websites today routinely combine JavaScript from multiple sources, both trusted and untrusted. Hence, JavaScript security is of paramount importance. A specific interesting problem is information flow control (IFC) for JavaScript. In this paper, we develop, formalize and implement a dynamic IFC mechanism for the JavaScript engine of a production Web browser (specifically, Safari's WebKit engine). Our IFC mechanism works at the level of JavaScript *bytecode* and hence leverages years of industrial effort on optimizing both the source to bytecode compiler and the bytecode interpreter. We track both explicit and implicit flows and observe only moderate overhead. Working with bytecode results in new challenges including the extensive use of unstructured control flow in bytecode (which complicates lowering of program context taints), unstructured exceptions (which complicate the matter further) and the need to make IFC analysis permissive. We explain how we address these challenges, formally model the JavaScript bytecode semantics and our instrumentation, prove the standard property of termination-insensitive non-interference, and present experimental results on an optimized prototype.

Keywords: Dynamic information flow control, JavaScript bytecode, taint tracking, control flow graphs, immediate post-dominator analysis.

1 Introduction

JavaScript (JS) is an indispensable part of the modern Web. More than 95% of all websites use JS for browser-side computation in Web applications [1]. Aggregator websites (e.g., news portals) integrate content from various mutually untrusted sources. Online mailboxes display context-sensitive advertisements. All these components are glued together with JS. The dynamic nature of JS permits easy inclusion of external libraries and third-party code, and encourages a variety of code injection attacks, which may lead to integrity violations. Confidentiality violations like information stealing are possible wherever third-party code is loaded directly into another web page [2]. Loading third-party code into separate iframes protects the main frame by the same-origin policy, but hinders interaction that mashup pages crucially rely on and does not guarantee absence of attacks [3]. *Information flow control* (IFC) is an elegant solution for such

M. Abadi and S. Kremer (Eds.): POST 2014, LNCS 8414, pp. 159–178, 2014.

problems. It ensures security even in the presence of untrusted and buggy code. IFC for JS differs from traditional IFC as JS is extremely dynamic [3,1], which makes sound static analysis difficult.

Therefore, research on IFC for JS has focused on dynamic techniques. These techniques may be grouped into four broad categories. First, one may build an IFC-enabled, custom interpreter for JS source [4,5]. This turns out to be extremely slow and requires additional code annotations to handle semi-structured control flow like exceptions, return-in-the-middle, break and continue. Second, we could use a black-box technique, wherein an off-the-shelf JS interpreter is wrapped in a monitor. This is nontrivial, but doable with only moderate overhead and has been implemented in secure multi-execution (SME)[6,7]. However, because SME is a black-box technique, it is not clear how it can be generalized beyond *non-interference* [8] to handle *declassification* [9,10]. Third, some variant of inline reference monitoring (IRM) might inline taint tracking with the client code. Existing security systems for JS with IRM require subsetting the language in order to prevent dynamic features that can invalidate the monitoring process. Finally, it is possible to instrument the runtime system of an existing JS engine, either an interpreter or a just-in-time compiler (JIT), to monitor the program on-the-fly. While this requires adapting the respective runtime, it incurs only moderate overhead because it retains other optimizations within the runtime and is resilient to subversion attacks.

In this work, we opt for the last approach. We instrument a production JS engine to track taints dynamically and enforce *termination-insensitive non-interference* [11]. Specifically, we instrument the bytecode interpreter in WebKit, the JS engine used in Safari and other open-source browsers. The major benefit of working in the bytecode interpreter as opposed to source is that we retain the benefits of these years of engineering efforts in optimizing the production interpreter and the source to bytecode compiler.

We describe the key challenges that arise in dynamic IFC for JS bytecode (as opposed to JS source), present our formal model of the bytecode, the WebKit JS interpreter and our instrumentation, present our correctness theorem, and list experimental results from a preliminary evaluation with an optimized prototype running in Safari. In doing so, our work significantly advances the state-of-the-art in IFC for JS. Our main contributions are:

- We formally model WebKit's bytecode syntax and semantics, our instrumentation for IFC analysis and prove non-interference. As far as we are aware, this is the first formal model of bytecode of an in-production JS engine. This is a nontrivial task because WebKit's bytecode language is large (147 bytecodes) and we built the model through a careful and thorough understanding of approximately 20,000 lines of actual interpreter code.[1]

---

[1] Unlike some prior work, we are not interested in modeling semantics of JS specified by the ECMAScript standard. Our goal is to remain faithful to the production bytecode interpreter. Our formalization is based on WebKit build #r122160, which was the last build when we started our work.

- Using ideas from prior work [12], we use on-the-fly intra-procedural static analysis of immediate post-dominators to restrict overtainting, even with bytecode's pervasive unstructured conditional jumps. We extend the prior work to deal with exceptions. Our technique covers all unstructured control flow in JS (including break and continue), without requiring additional code annotations of prior work [5] and improves permissiveness.
- To make IFC execution more permissive, we propose and implement a byte-code-specific variant of the *permissive-upgrade* check [13].
- We implement our complete IFC mechanism in WebKit and observe moderate overheads.

Limitations. We list some limitations of our work to clarify its scope. Although our instrumentation covers all WebKit bytecodes, we have not yet instrumented or modeled native JS methods, including those that manipulate the Document Object Model (DOM). This is ongoing work, beyond the scope of this paper. Like some prior work [4], our sequential non-interference theorem covers only single invocations of the JS interpreter. In reality, JS is reactive. The interpreter is invoked every time an event (like a mouse click) with a handler occurs and these invocations share state through the DOM. We expect that generalizing to *reactive non-interference* [14] will not require any instrumentation beyond what we already plan to do for the DOM. Finally, we do not handle JIT-compilation as it is considerably more engineering effort. JIT can be handled by inlining our IFC mechanism through a bytecode transformation.

Due to lack of space, several proofs and details of the model have been omitted from this paper. They can be found in a technical appendix available from the authors' homepages.

2   Related Work

Three classes of research are closely related to our work: formalization of JS semantics, IFC for dynamic languages, and formal models of Web browsers. Maffeis et al. [15] present a formal semantics for the entire ECMA-262 specification, the foundation for JS 3.0. Guha et al. [16] present the semantics of a core language which models the essence of JS and argue that all of JS 3.0 can be translated to that core. S5 [17] extends [16] to include accessors and eval. Our work goes one step further and formalizes the core language of a production JS engine (WebKit), which is generated by the source-to-bytecode compiler included in WebKit. Recent work by Bodin et al. [18] presents a Coq formalization of ECMAScript Edition 5 along with an extracted executable interpreter for it. This is a formalization of the English ECMAScript specification whereas we formalize the JS bytecode implemented in a real Web browser.

Information flow control is an active area of security research. With the widespread use of JS, research in dynamic techniques for IFC has regained momentum. Nonetheless, static analyses are not completely futile. Guarnieri et al. [19] present a static abstract interpretation for tracking taints in JS. However, the omnipresent eval construct is not supported and this approach does not take implicit flows into account. Chugh et al. propose a staged information flow approach for JS [20]. They perform server-side static policy checks on statically available code and generate residual policy-checks that must be applied to dynamically loaded code. This approach is limited to certain JS constructs excluding dynamic features like dynamic field access or the with construct.

Austin and Flanagan [21] propose purely dynamic IFC for dynamically-typed languages like JS. They use the no-sensitive-upgrade (NSU) check [22] to handle implicit flows. Their permissive-upgrade strategy [13] is more permissive than NSU but retains termination-insensitive non-interference. We build on the permissive-upgrade strategy. Just et al. [12] present dynamic IFC for JS bytecode with static analysis to determine implicit flows precisely even in the presence of semi-unstructured control flow like break and continue. Again, NSU is leveraged to prevent implicit flows. Our overall ideas for dealing with unstructured control flow are based on this work. In contrast to this paper, there was no formalization of the bytecodes, no proof of correctness, and implicit flow due to exceptions was ignored.

Hedin and Sabelfeld propose a dynamic IFC approach for a language which models the core features of JS [4], but they ignore JS's constructs for semi-structured control flow like break and continue. Their approach leverages a dynamic type system for JS source. To improve permissiveness, their subsequent work [23] uses testing. It detects security violations due to branches that have not been executed and injects annotations to prevent these in subsequent runs. A further extension introduces annotations to deal with semi-structured control flow [5]. Our approach relies on analyzing CFGs and does not require annotations.

Secure multi-execution (SME) [6] is another approach to enforcing non-interference at runtime. Conceptually, one executes the same code once for each security level (like low and high) with the following constraints: high inputs are replaced by default values for the low execution, and low outputs are permitted only in the low execution. This modification of the semantics forces even unsafe scripts to adhere to non-interference. FlowFox [7] demonstrates SME in the context of Web browsers. Executing a script multiple times can be prohibitive for a security lattice with multiple levels. Further, all writes to the DOM are considered publicly visible output, while tainting allows persisting a security label on DOM elements. It is also unclear how declassification may be integrated into SME. Austin and Flanagan [24] introduce a notion of faceted values to simulate multiple executions in one run. They keep n values for every variable corresponding to n security levels. All the values are used for computation as the program proceeds but the mechanism enforces non-interference by restricting the leak of high values to low observers.

Browsers work reactively; input is fed to an event queue that is processed over time. Input to one event can produce output that influences the input to a subsequent event. Bohannon et al. [14] present a formalization of a reactive system and compare several definitions of reactive non-interference. Bielova et al. [25] extend reactive non-interference to a browser model based on SME. This is currently the only approach that supports reactive non-interference for JS. We will extend our work to the reactive setting as the next step.

Finally, Featherweight Firefox [26] presents a formal model of a browser based on a reactive model that resembles that of Bohannon et al. [14]. It instantiates the consumer and producer states in the model with actual browser objects like window, page, cookie store, mode, connection, etc. Our current work entirely focuses on the formalization of the JS engine and taint tracking to monitor information leaks. We believe these two approaches complement each other and plan to integrate such a model into our future holistic enforcement mechanism spanning JS, the DOM and other browser components.

3   Background

We provide a brief overview of basic concepts in dynamic enforcement of information flow control (IFC). In dynamic IFC, a language runtime is instrumented to carry a security label or taint with every value. The taint is an element of a pre-determined lattice and is an upper bound on the security levels of all entities that have influenced the computation that led to the value. For simplicity of exposition, we use throughout this paper a three-point lattice $\{L, H, \star\}$ (L = low or public, H = high or secret, $\star$ = partially leaked secret), with $L \sqsubseteq H \sqsubseteq \star$ [13]. For now, readers may ignore $\star$. Our instrumentation works over a more general powerset lattice, whose individual elements are Web domains. We write r^ℓ for a value r tagged with label ℓ.

Information flows can be categorized as *explicit* and *implicit* [27]. Explicit flows arise as a result of variables being assigned to others, or through primitive operations. For instance, the statement x = y + z causes an explicit flow from values in both z and y to x. Explicit flows are handled in the runtime by updating the label of the computed value (x in our example) with the least upper bound of the labels of the operands in the computation (y, z in our example).

Implicit flows arise from control dependencies. For example, in the program 1 = 0; if (h) {1 = 1;}, there is an implicit flow from h to the final value of 1 (that value is 1 iff h is 1). To handle implicit flows, dynamic IFC systems maintain the so-called *pc* label (program-context label), which is an upper bound on the labels of values that have influenced the control flow thus far. In our last example, if the value in h has label H, then *pc* will be H within the if branch. After 1 = 1 is executed, the final value of 1 inherits not only the label of 1 (which is L), but also of the *pc*; hence, that label is also H. This alone does not prevent information leaks: When h = 0, 1 ends with 0^L; when h = 1, 1 ends with 1^H. Since 0^L and 1^H can be distinguished by a public attacker, this program leaks the value of h despite correct propagation of implicit taints. Formally, the instrumented semantics so far fail the standard property of *non-interference* [8].

This problem can be resolved through the well-known *no-sensitive-upgrade* (NSU) check [22,21], which prohibits assignment to a low-labeled variable when *pc* is high. This recovers non-interference if the adversary cannot observe program termination (*termination-insensitive non-interference*). In our example, when h = 0, the program terminates with $1 = 0^L$. When h = 1, the instruction 1 = 1 gets stuck due to NSU. These two outcomes are deemed observationally equivalent for the low adversary, who cannot determine whether or not the program has terminated in the second case. Hence, the program is deemed secure.

Roughly, a program is termination-insensitive non-interferent if any two terminating runs of the program starting from low-equivalent heaps (i.e., heaps that look equivalent to the adversary) end in low-equivalent heaps. Like all sound dynamic IFC approaches, our instrumentation renders any JS program termination-insensitive non-interferent, at the cost of modifying semantics of programs that leak information.

4   Design, Challenges, Insights and Solutions

We implement dynamic IFC for JS in the widely used WebKit engine by instrumenting WebKit's bytecode interpreter. In WebKit, bytecode is generated by a source-code compiler. Our goal is to not modify the compiler, but we are forced to make slight changes to it to make it compliant with our instrumentation. The modification is explained in Section 6. Nonetheless, almost all our work is limited to the bytecode interpreter.

WebKit's bytecode interpreter is a rather standard stack machine, with several additional data structures for JS-specific features like scope chains, variable environments, prototype chains and function objects. Local variables are held in registers on the call stack. Our instrumentation adds a label to all data structures, including registers, object properties and scope chain pointers, adds code to propagate explicit and implicit taints and implements a more permissive variant of the NSU check. Our label is a word size bit-set (currently 64 bits); each bit in the bit-set represents taint from a distinct domain (like google.com). Join on labels is simply bitwise or.

Unlike the ECMAScript specification of JS semantics, the actual implementation does *not* treat scope chains or variable environments like ordinary objects. Consequently, we model and instrument taint propagation on all these data structures separately. Working at the low-level of the bytecode also leads to several interesting conceptual and implementation issues in taint propagation as well as interesting questions about the threat model, all of which we explain in this section. Some of the issues are quite general and apply beyond JS. For example, we combine our dynamic analysis with a bit of static analysis to handle unstructured control flow and exceptions.

Threat model and compiler assumptions. We explain our high-level threat model. Following standard practice, our adversary may observe all low-labeled values in the heap (more generally, an adversary at level ℓ in a lattice can observe all heap values with labels $\leq \ell$). However, we do not allow the adversary to directly observe internal data structures like the call stack or scope chains. This is consistent with actual interfaces in a browser that third-party scripts can access. In our non-interference proofs we must also show low-equivalence of these internal data structures across two runs to get the right induction invariants, but assuming that they are inaccessible to the adversary allows more permissive program execution, which we explain in Section 4.1.

The bytecode interpreter executes in a shared space with other browser components, so we assume that those components do not leak information over side channels, e.g., they do not copy heap data from secret to public locations. This also applies to the compiler, but we do not assume that the compiler is functionally correct. Trivial errors in the compiler, e.g., omitting a bytecode could result in a leaky program even when the source code has no information leaks. Because our IFC works on the compiler's output, such compiler errors are not a concern. Formally, we assume that the compiler is an unspecified deterministic function of the program to compile and of the call stack, but not of the heap. This assumption also matches how the compiler works within WebKit: It needs access to the call stack and scope chain to optimize generated bytecode. However, the compiler never needs access to the heap. We ignore information leaks due to other side channels like timing.

4.1   Challenges and Solutions

IFC for JS is known to be difficult due to JS's highly dynamic nature. Working with bytecode instead of source code makes IFC harder. Nonetheless, solutions to many JS-specific IFC concerns proposed in earlier work [4] also apply to our instrumentation, sometimes in slightly modified form. For example, in JS, every object has a fixed parent, called a prototype, which is looked up when a property does not exist in the child. This can lead to implicit flows: If an object is created in a high context (when the pc is high) and a field missing from it, but present in the prototype, is accessed later in a low context, then there is an implicit leak from the high pc. This problem is avoided in both source- and bytecode-level analysis in the same way: The "prototype" pointer from the child to the parent is labeled with the pc where the child is created, and the label of any value read from the parent after traversing the pointer is joined with this label. Other potential information flow problems whose solutions remain unchanged between source- and bytecode-level analysis include implicit leaks through function pointers and handling of `eval` [12,4].

Working with bytecode both leads to some interesting insights, which are, in some cases, even applicable to source code analysis and other languages, and poses new challenges. We discuss some of these challenges and insights.

Unstructured control flow and CFGs. To avoid overtainting pc labels, an important goal in implicit flow tracking is to determine when the influence of a control construct has ended. For block-structured control flow limited to `if` and `while` commands, this is straightforward: The effect of a control construct ends with its lexical scope, e.g., in (`if (h) {l = 1;}; l = 2`), h influences the control flow at `l = 1` but not at `l = 2`. This leads to a straightforward pc upgrading and downgrading strategy: One maintains a *stack* of pc labels [22]; the effective pc is the top one. When entering a control flow construct like `if` or `while`, a new *pc* label, equal to the join of labels of all values on which the construct's guard depends with the previous effective *pc*, is pushed. When exiting the construct, the label is popped.

Unfortunately, it is unclear how to extend this simple strategy to non-block-structured control flow constructs such as exceptions, `break`, `continue` and `return`-in-the-middle for functions, all of which occur in JS. For example, consider the program `l = 1; while(1) {... if (h) {break;}; l = 0; break;}` with h labeled H. This program leaks the value of h into l, but no assignment to l appears in a block-scope guarded by h. Indeed, the *pc* upgrading and downgrading strategy just described is ineffective for this program. Prior work on source code IFC either omits some of these constructs [4,28], or introduces additional classes of labels to address these problems — a label for exceptions [4], a label for each loop containing `break` or `continue` and a label for each function [5]. These labels are more restrictive than needed, e.g., the code indicated by dots in the example above is executed irrespective of the condition h in the first iteration, and thus there is no need to raise the *pc* before checking that condition. Further, these labels are programmer annotations, which we cannot support as we do not wish to modify the compiler.

Importantly, unstructured control flow is a *very serious* concern for us, because WebKit's bytecode has completely unstructured branches like jump-if-false. In fact, all control flow, except function calls, is unstructured in bytecode.

To solve this problem, we adopt a solution based on static analysis of generated bytecode [29,12]. We maintain a control flow graph (CFG) of known bytecodes and for each branch node, compute its immediate post-dominator (IPD). The IPD of a node is the first instruction that will definitely be executed, no matter which branch is taken. Our *pc* upgrading and downgrading strategy now extends to arbitrary control flow: When executing a branch node, we push a new *pc* label on the stack *along with* the node's IPD. When we actually reach the IPD, we pop the *pc* label. In [30,31], the authors prove that the IPD marks the end of the scope of an operation and hence the security context of the operation, so our strategy is sound. In our earlier example, the IPD of `if(h)` ... is the end of the `while` loop because of the first `break` statement, so when h == 0, the assignment `l = 1` fails due to the NSU check and the program is termination-insensitive non-interference secure.

JS requires dynamic code compilation. We are forced to extend the CFG and to compute IPDs whenever code for either a function or an `eval` is compiled. Fortunately, the IPD of a node in the CFG lies either in the same function as the node or some function earlier in the call-chain (the latter may happen due to exceptions), so extending the CFG does not affect computation of IPDs of earlier nodes. This also relies on the fact that code generated from `eval` cannot alter the CFG of earlier functions in the call stack [12]. In the actual implementation, we optimize the calculation of IPDs further by working only intra-procedurally, as explained below. At the end, our IPD-based solution works for all forms of unstructured control flow, including unstructured branches in the bytecode, and semi-structured `break`, `continue`, `return`-in-the-middle and exceptions in the source code.

Exceptions and synthetic exit nodes. Maintaining a CFG in the presence of exceptions is expensive. An exception-throwing node in a function that does not catch that exception should have an outgoing control flow edge to the next exception handler in the call-stack. This means that (a) the CFG is, in general, inter-procedural, and (b) edges going out of a function depend on its calling context, so IPDs of nodes in the function must be computed *every time the function is called*. Moreover, in the case of recursive functions, the nodes must be replicated for every call. This is rather expensive. Ideally, we would like to build the function's CFG once when *the function is compiled* and work intra-procedurally (as we would had there been no exceptions). We explain how we attain this goal in the sequel.[2]

In our design, every function that may throw an unhandled exception has a special, *synthetic exit node* (SEN), which is placed after the regular return node(s) of the function. Every exception-throwing node, whose exception will not be caught within the function, has an outgoing edge to the SEN, which is traversed when the exception is thrown. The semantics of SEN (described below) correctly transfer control to the appropriate exception handler. By doing this, we eliminate all cross-function edges and our CFGs become intra-procedural. The CFG of a function can be computed when the function is compiled and is never updated. (In our implementation, we build two variants of the CFG, depending on whether or not there is an exception handler in the call stack. This improves efficiency, as we explain later.)

Control flows to the SEN when the function returns normally or when an exception is thrown but not handled within the function. If no unhandled exception occurred within the function, then the SEN transfers control to the caller (we record whether or not an unhandled exception occurred). If an unhandled exception occurred, then the SEN triggers a special mechanism that searches the call stack backward for the first appropriate exception handler and transfers control to it. (In JS, exceptions are indistinguishable, so we need to find only the first exception handler.) Importantly, we pop the call-stack up to the frame that contains the first exception handler but do *not* pop the *pc*-stack, which ensures that all code up to the exception handler's IPD executes with the same *pc* as the SEN, which is indeed the semantics one would expect if we had a CFG with cross-function edges for exceptions. This prevents information leaks.

If a function does not handle a possible exception but there is an exception handler on the call stack, then all bytecodes that could potentially throw an exception have the SEN as one successor in the CFG. Any branching bytecode will thus need to push to the *pc*-stack according to the security label of its condition. However, we do *not* push a new *pc*-stack entry if the IPD of the current node is the same as the IPD on the top of the *pc*-stack (this is just an optimization) or if the IPD of the current node is the SEN, as in this case the *real* IPD, which is outside of this method, is already on the *pc*-stack. These semantics emulate the effect of having cross-function exception edges.

---

[2] This problem and our solution are not particular to JS; they apply to dynamic IFC analysis in all languages with exceptions and functions.

For illustration, consider the following two functions f and g. The ◇ at the end of g denotes its SEN. Note that there is an edge from throw 9 to ◇ because throw 9 is not handled within g. □ denotes the IPD of the handler catch(e) { l = 1; }.

```
function f() = {                          function g() = {
  l = 0;                                    if (h) {throw 9;}
  try { g(); } catch(e) { l = 1; }          return 7;
  □ return l;                             } ◇
}
```

It should be clear that in the absence of instrumentation, when f is invoked with $pc = L$, the two functions together leak the value of h (which is assumed to have label H) into the return value of f. We show how our SEN mechanism prevents this leak. When invoking g() we do not know if there will be an exception in this function. Depending on the outcome of this method call, we will either jump to the exception handler or continue at □. Based on that branch, we push the current pc and IPD $(L, \square)$ on the pc-stack. When executing the condition if (h) we do *not* push again, but merely update the top element to $(H, \square)$. If h == 0, control reaches ◇ without an exception but with $pc = H$ because the IPD of if (h) is ◇. At this point, ◇ returns control to f, thus $pc = H$, but at □, pc is lowered to L, so f ends with the return value 0^L. If h == 1, control reaches ◇ with an unhandled exception. At this point, following the semantics of SEN, we find the exception handler catch(e) { l = 1; } and invoke it with the same pc as the point of exception, i.e., H. Consequently, NSU prevents the assignment l = 1, which makes the program termination-insensitive non-interferent.

Because we do not wish to replicate the CFG of a function every time it is called recursively, we need a method to distinguish the same node corresponding to two different recursive calls on the pc-stack. For this, when pushing an IPD onto the pc-stack, we pair it with a pointer to the current call-frame. Since the call-frame pointer is unique for each recursive call, the CFG node paired with the call-frame identifies a unique merge point in the real control flow graph.

In practice, even the intra-procedural CFG is quite dense because many JS bytecodes can potentially throw exceptions and, hence, have edges to the SEN. To avoid overtainting, we perform a crucial common-case optimization: When there is no exception handler on the call stack we do not create the SEN and the corresponding edges from potentially exception-throwing bytecodes at all. This is safe as a potentially thrown exception can only terminate the program instantly, which satisfies termination-insensitive non-interference if we ensure that the exception message is not visible to the attacker. Whether or not an exception handler exists is easily tracked using a stack of Booleans that mirrors the call-stack; in our design we overlay this stack on the pc-stack by adding an extra Boolean field to each entry of the pc-stack. In summary, each entry of our pc-stack is a quadruple containing a security label, a node in the intraprocedural CFG, a call-frame pointer and a Boolean value. In combination with SENs, this design allows us to work only with intraprocedural CFGs that are computed when a function is compiled. This improves efficiency.

Permissive-upgrade check, with changes. The standard NSU check halts program execution whenever an attempt is made to assign a variable with a low-labeled value in a high *pc*. In our earlier example, 1 = 0; if (h) {1 = 1;}, assuming that h stores a *H*-labeled value, program execution is halted at the command 1 = 1. As Austin and Flanagan (AF in the sequel) observe [13], this may be overly restrictive when 1 will not, in fact, have observable effects (e.g., 1 may be overwritten by a constant immediately after if (h) {1 = 1;}). So, they propose propagating a special taint called ⋆ into 1 at the instruction 1 = 1 and halting a program when it tries to *use* a value labeled ⋆ in a way that will be observable (AF call this special taint *P* for "partially leaked"). This idea, called the *permissive-upgrade* check, allows more program execution than NSU would, so we adopt it. In fact, this additional permissiveness is absolutely essential for us because the WebKit compiler often generates dead assignments within branches, so execution would pointlessly halt if standard NSU were used.

We differ from AF in *what* constitutes a use of a value labeled ⋆. As expected, AF treat occurrence of ⋆ in the guard of a branch as a use. Thus, the program 1 = 0; if (h) {1 = 1;}; if (1) {1' = 2} is halted at the command if (1) when h == 1 because 1 obtains taint ⋆ at the assignment 1 = 1 (if the program is not halted, it leaks h through 1'). However, they allow ⋆-tainted values to flow into the heap. Consider the program 1 = 0; if (h) {1 = 1;}; obj.a = 1. This program is insecure in our model: The heap location obj.a, which is accessible to the adversary, ends with 0^L when h == 0 and with $1^⋆$ when h == 1. AF deem the program secure by assuming that any value with label ⋆ is low-equivalent to any other value (in particular, 0^L and $1^⋆$ are low-equivalent). However, this definition of low-equivalence for dynamic analysis is virtually impossible to enforce if the adversary has access to the heap outside the language: After writing 0^L to obj.a (for h == 0), a dynamic analysis cannot determine that the alternate execution of the program (for h == 1) *would have* written a ⋆-labeled value and, hence, cannot prevent the adversary from seeing 0^L.

Consequently, in our design, we use a modified permissive-upgrade check, which we call the *deferred NSU check*, wherein a program is halted at any construct that may potentially flow a ⋆-labeled value into the heap. This includes all branches whose guard contains a ⋆-labeled value and any assignments whose target is a heap location and whose source is ⋆-labeled. However, we do not constrain flow of ⋆-labeled values in data structures that are invisible to the adversary in our model, e.g., local registers and variable environments. This design critically relies on treating internal data structures differently from ordinary JS objects, which is not the case, for instance, in the ECMAScript specification.

5   Formal Model and IFC

We formally model WebKit's JS bytecode and the semantics of its bytecode interpreter with our instrumentation of dynamic IFC. We prove termination-insensitive non-interference for programs executed through our instrumented interpreter. We do not model the construction of the CFG or computation of

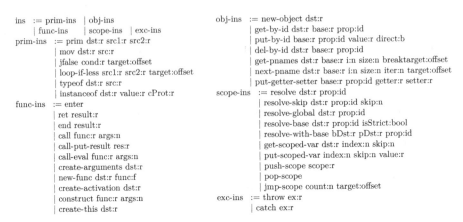

Fig. 1. Instructions

IPDs; these are standard. To keep presentation accessible, we present our formal model at a somewhat high-level of abstraction. Details are resolved in our technical appendix.

5.1   Bytecode and Data Structures

The version of WebKit we model uses a total of 147 bytecodes or instructions, of which we model 69. The remaining 78 bytecodes are redundant from the perspective of formal modeling because they are *specializations* or wrappers on other bytecodes to improve efficiency. The syntax of the 69 bytecodes we model is shown in Fig. 1. The bytecode `prim` abstractly represents 34 primitive binary and unary (with just the first two arguments) operations, all of which behave similarly. For convenience, we divide the bytecodes into primitive instructions (prim-ins), instructions related to objects and prototype chains (obj-ins), instructions related to functions (func-ins), instructions related to scope chains (scope-ins) and instructions related to exceptions (exc-ins). A bytecode has the form ⟨*inst_name list_of_args*⟩. The arguments to the instruction are of the form ⟨var⟩:⟨type⟩, where *var* is the variable name and *type* is one of the following: r, n, bool, id, prop and offset for register, constant integer, constant Boolean, identifier, property name and jump offset value, respectively.

In WebKit, bytecode is organized into code blocks. Each code block is a sequence of bytecodes with line numbers and corresponds to the instructions for a function or an `eval` statement. A code block is generated when a function is created or an `eval` is executed. In our instrumentation, we perform control flow analysis on a code block when it is created and in our formal model we abstractly represent a code block as a CFG, written ζ. Formally, a CFG is a directed graph, whose nodes are bytecodes and whose edges represent possible control flows. There are no cross-function edges. A CFG also records the IPD of each node. IPDs are computed using an algorithm by Lengauer and Tarjan [32] when the CFG is created. If the CFG contains uncaught exceptions, we also create a SEN. For a CFG ζ and a non-branching node $\iota \in \zeta$, $Succ(\zeta, \iota)$ denotes ι's unique successor. For a conditional branching node ι, $Left(\zeta, \iota)$ and $Right(\zeta, \iota)$ denote successors when the condition is true and false, respectively.

The bytecode interpreter is a standard stack machine, with support for JS features like scope chains and prototype chains. The state of the machine (with our instrumentation) is a quadruple $\langle \iota, \theta, \sigma, \rho \rangle$, where ι represents the current node that is being executed, θ represents the heap, σ represents the call-stack and ρ is the pc-stack.

We assume an abstract, countable set $\mathcal{A} = \{a, b, \ldots\}$ of heap locations, which are references to objects. The heap θ is a partial map from locations to objects. An object O may be:

- An ordinary JS object $N = (\{p_i \mapsto v_i\}_{i=0}^n, \_\_proto\_\_ \mapsto a^{\ell_p}, \ell_s)$, containing properties named $p_0, \ldots, p_n$ that map to labeled values $v_0, \ldots, v_n$, a prototype field that points to a parent at heap location a, and two labels ℓ_p and ℓ_s. ℓ_p records the pc where the object was created. ℓ_s is the so-called structure label, which is an upper bound on all pcs that have influenced which fields exist in the object.[3]
- A function object $F = (N, \zeta, \Sigma)$, where N is an ordinary object, ζ is a CFG, which corresponds to the the function stored in the object, and Σ is the scope chain (closing context) of the function.

A labeled value $v = r^\ell$ is a value r paired with a security label ℓ. A value r in our model may be a heap location a or a JS primitive value n, which includes integers, Booleans, regular expressions, arrays, strings and the special JS values `undefined` and `null`.

The call-stack σ contains one call-frame for each incomplete function call. A call-frame μ contains an array of registers for local variables, a CFG ζ for the function represented by the call-frame, the return address (a node in the CFG of the previous frame), and a pointer to a scope-chain that allows access to variables in outer scopes. Additionally, each call-frame has an exception table which maps each potentially exception-throwing bytecode in the function to the exception handler within the function that surrounds the bytecode; when no such exception handler exists, it points to the SEN of the function (we conservatively assume that any unknown code may throw an exception, so bytecodes `call` and `eval` are exception-throwing for this purpose). $|\sigma|$ denotes the size of the call-stack and $!\sigma$ its top frame. Each register contains a labeled value.

A scope chain, Σ, is a sequence of scope chain nodes (SCNs), denoted S, paired with labels. In WebKit, a scope chain node S may either be an object or a variable environment V, which is an array of labeled values. Thus, $\Sigma ::= (S_1, \ell_1) : \ldots : (S_n, \ell_n)$ and $S ::= O \mid V$ and $V ::= v_1 : \ldots : v_n$.

Each entry of the pc-stack ρ is a triple (ℓ, ι, p), where ℓ is a security label, ι is a node in a CFG, and p is a pointer to some call-frame on the call stack

---

[3] The $\_\_proto\_\_$ field is the parent of the object; it is not the same as the prototype field of a function object, which is an ordinary property. Also, in our actual model, fields p_i map to more general property descriptors that also contain attributes along with labeled values. We elide attributes here to keep the presentation simple.

σ. (For simplicity, we ignore a fourth Boolean field described in Section 4.1 in this presentation.) When we enter a new control context, we push the new pc ℓ together with the IPD ι of the entry point of the control context and a pointer p to current call-frame. The pair (ι, p) uniquely identifies where the control of the context ends; p is necessary to distinguish the same branch point in different recursive calls of the function [12]. In our semantics, we use the meta-function $isIPD$ to pop the stack. It takes the current instruction, the current pc-stack and the call stack σ, and returns a new pc-stack.

$$isIPD(\iota, \rho, \sigma) := \begin{cases} \rho.pop() & \text{if } !\rho = (\_, \iota, !\sigma) \\ \rho & \text{otherwise} \end{cases}$$

As explained in Section 4.1, as an optimization, we push a new node (ℓ, ι, σ) onto ρ only when (ι, σ) (the IPD) differs from the corresponding pair on the top of the stack and, to handle exceptions correctly, we also require that ι not be the SEN. Otherwise, we just join ℓ with the label on the top of the stack. This is formalized in the function $\rho.push(\ell, \iota, \sigma)$, whose obvious definition we elide.

If x is a pair of any syntactic entity and a security label, we write $\Upsilon(x)$ for the entity and $\Gamma(x)$ for the label. In particular, for $v = r^\ell$, $\Upsilon(v) = r$ and $\Gamma(v) = \ell$.

5.2 Semantics and IFC with Intra-procedural CFGs

We now present the semantics, which faithfully models our implementation using intra-procedural CFGs with SENs. The semantics is defined as a set of state transition rules that define the judgment: $\langle \iota, \theta, \sigma, \rho \rangle \rightsquigarrow \langle \iota', \theta', \sigma', \rho' \rangle$. Fig. 2 shows rules for selected bytecodes. For reasons of space we omit rules for other byte-codes and formal descriptions of some meta-function like $opCall$ that are used in the rules. $C \Rightarrow A \diamond B$ is shorthand for a meta-level (if (C) then A else B).

prim reads the values from two registers **src1** and **src2**, performs a binary operation generically denoted by $\oplus$ on the values and writes the result into the register **dst**. **dst** is assigned the join of the labels in **src1**, **src2** and the head of the pc-stack ($!\rho$). To implement deferred NSU (Section 4.1), the existing label in **dst** is compared with the current pc. If the label is lower than the pc, then the label of **dst** is joined with $\star$. Note that the premise $\rho' = isIPD(\iota', \rho, \sigma)$ pops an entry from the pc-stack if its IPD matches the new program node ι'. This premise occurs in all semantic rules.

jfalse is a conditional jump. It skips **offset** number of successive nodes in the CFG if the register **cond** contains **false**, else it falls-through to the next node. Formally, the node it branches to is either $Right(\zeta, \iota)$ or $Left(\zeta, \iota)$, where ζ is the CFG in $!\sigma$. In accordance with deferred NSU, the operation is performed only if **cond** is not labeled $\star$. **jfalse** also starts a new control context, so a new node is pushed on the top of the pc-stack with a label that is the join of $\Gamma(\text{cond})$ and the current label on the top of the stack (unless the IPD of the branch point is already on top of the stack or it is the SEN, in which case we join the new label with the previous). Traversed from bottom to top, the pc-stack always has monotonically non-decreasing labels.

$$\text{prim:} \frac{\begin{array}{c} \iota = \text{``op-prim dst:r src1:r src2:r''}, \\ \mathcal{L} := \Gamma(!\sigma(src1)) \sqcup \Gamma(!\sigma(src2)) \sqcup \Gamma(!\rho), \\ \mathcal{V} := \Upsilon(!\sigma(src1)) \oplus \Upsilon(!\sigma(src2)) \\ (\Gamma(!\sigma(dst)) \geq \Gamma(!\rho)) \implies (\mathcal{L} := \mathcal{L}) \diamond (\mathcal{L} := \star) \\ \sigma' := \sigma\left[\begin{array}{c} \Upsilon(!\sigma(dst)) := \mathcal{V} \\ \Gamma(!\sigma(dst)) := \mathcal{L} \end{array}\right], \\ \iota' := Succ(!\sigma'.CFG, \iota), \ \rho' := isIPD(\iota', \rho, \sigma') \end{array}}{\iota, \theta, \sigma, \rho \rightsquigarrow \iota', \theta, \sigma', \rho'}$$

$$\text{push-scope:} \frac{\begin{array}{c} \iota = \text{``op-push-scope scope:r''}, \\ \sigma' := pushScope(\Gamma(!\rho), \sigma, scope), \\ \iota' := Succ(!\sigma'.CFG, \iota), \ \rho' := isIPD(\iota', \rho, \sigma') \end{array}}{\iota, \theta, \sigma, \rho \rightsquigarrow \iota', \theta, \sigma', \rho}$$

$$\text{jfalse:} \frac{\begin{array}{c} \iota = \text{``op-jfalse cond:r target:offset''}, \\ \Gamma(!\sigma(cond)) \neq \star, \ \mathcal{L} := \Gamma(!\sigma(cond)) \sqcup \Gamma(!\rho), \\ \Upsilon(!\sigma(cond)) = false \implies \iota' := Left(!\sigma.CFG, \iota) \\ \diamond \iota' := Right(!\sigma.CFG, \iota), \\ \rho'' := \rho.push(\mathcal{L}, IPD(\iota), CF(\iota)), \ \rho' := isIPD(\iota', \rho'', \sigma) \end{array}}{\iota, \theta, \sigma, \rho \rightsquigarrow \iota', \theta, \sigma, \rho'}$$

$$\text{call:} \frac{\begin{array}{c} \iota = \text{``op-call func:r args:n''}, \\ \Gamma(func) \neq \star, \ (\iota', \sigma', \ell_f) := opCall(\sigma, \iota, func, args), \\ \mathcal{L} := \ell_f \sqcup \Gamma(!\sigma(func)) \sqcup \Gamma(!\rho), \\ \rho'' := \rho.push(\mathcal{L}, IPD(\iota), CF(\iota)), \ \rho' := isIPD(\iota', \rho'', \sigma') \end{array}}{\iota, \theta, \sigma, \rho \rightsquigarrow \iota', \theta, \sigma', \rho}$$

$$\text{ret:} \frac{\begin{array}{c} \iota = \text{``op-ret res:r''}, \\ (\iota', \sigma', \gamma) := opRet(\sigma, res), \ \rho' := isIPD(\iota', \rho, \sigma') \end{array}}{\iota, \theta, \sigma, \rho \rightsquigarrow \iota', \theta, \sigma', \rho'}$$

$$\text{put-by-id:} \frac{\begin{array}{c} \iota = \text{``op-put-by-id base:r prop:id value:r direct:b''}, \\ \Gamma(!\sigma(value)) \neq \star, \ direct = true \implies \\ \theta' := putDirect(\Gamma(!\rho), \sigma, \theta, base, prop, value) \diamond \\ \theta' := putIndirect(\Gamma(!\rho), \sigma, \theta, base, prop, value), \\ \iota' := Succ(!\sigma.CFG, \iota), \ \rho' := isIPD(\iota', \rho, \sigma) \end{array}}{\iota, \theta, \sigma, \rho \rightsquigarrow \iota', \theta', \sigma, \rho'}$$

$$\text{throw:} \frac{\begin{array}{c} \iota = \text{``op-throw ex:r''}, \ excValue := \Upsilon(!\sigma(ex)), \\ (\sigma', \iota') := throwException(\sigma, \iota), \ \rho' := isIPD(\iota', \rho, \sigma') \end{array}}{\iota, \theta, \sigma, \rho \rightsquigarrow \iota', \theta, \sigma', \rho'}$$

Fig. 2. Semantics, selected rules

put-by-id updates the property **prop** in the object pointed to by register **base**. As explained in Section 4.1, we allow this only if the value to be written is not labeled $\star$. The flag **direct** states whether or not to traverse the prototype chain in finding the property; it is set by the compiler as an optimization. If the flag is **true**, then the chain is not traversed (meta-function $putDirect$ handles this case). If **direct** is **false**, then the chain is traversed (meta-function $putIndirect$). Importantly, when the chain is traversed, the resulting value is labeled with the join of prototype labels ℓ_p and structure labels ℓ_s of all traversed objects. This is standard and necessary to prevent implicit leaks through the ___proto___ pointers and structure changes to objects.

push-scope, which corresponds to the start of the JS construct **with(obj)**, pushes the object pointed to by the register **scope** into the scope chain. Because pushing an object into the scope chain can implicitly leak information from the program context later, we also label all nodes in the scope-chain with the pc's at which they were added to the chain. Further, deferred NSU applies to the scope chain pointer in the call-frame as it does to all other registers.

call invokes a function of the target object stored in the register **func**. Due to deferred NSU, the call proceeds only if $\Gamma(\text{func})$ is not $\star$. The call creates a new call-frame and initializes arguments, the scope chain pointer (initialized with the function object's Σ field), CFG and the return node in the new frame. The CFG in the call-frame is copied from the function object pointed to by **func**. All this is formalized in the meta-function $opCall$, whose details we omit here. Call is a branch instruction and it pushes a new label on the pc-stack which is the join of the current pc, $\Gamma(\text{func})$ and the structure label ℓ_f of the function object (unless the IPD of the current node is the SEN or already on the top of the pc-stack, in which case we join the new pc-label with the previous). **call** also initializes the new registers' labels to the new pc. A separate bytecode, not shown here and executed first in the called function, sets register values to undefined. eval is similar to call but the code to be executed is also compiled.

ret exits a function. It returns control to the caller, as formalized in the meta-function *opRet*. The return value is written to an interpreter variable (γ).

throw throws an exception, passing the value in register ex as argument to the exception handler. Our *pc*-stack push semantics ensure that the exception handler, if any, is present in the call-frame pointed to by the *top* of the *pc*-stack. The meta-function *throwException* pops the call-stack up to this call-frame and transfers control to the exception handler, by looking it up in the exception table of the call-frame. The exception value in the register ex is transferred to the handler through an interpreter variable.

Correctness of IFC. We prove that our IFC analysis guarantees termination-insensitive non-interference [11]. Intuitively, this means that if a program is run twice from two states that are observationally equivalent for the adversary and both executions terminate, then the two final states are also equivalent for the adversary. To state the theorem formally, we formalize equivalence for various data structures in our model. The only nonstandard data structure we use is the CFG, but graph equality suffices for it. A well-known complication is that low heap locations allocated in the two runs need not be identical. We adopt the standard solution of parametrizing our definitions of equivalence with a partial bijection β between heap locations. The idea is that two heap locations are related in the partial bijection if they were created by corresponding allocations in the two runs. We then define a rather standard relation $\langle \iota_1, \theta_1, \sigma_1, \rho_1 \rangle \sim_\ell^\beta \langle \iota_2, \theta_2, \sigma_2, \rho_2 \rangle$, which means that the states on the left and right are equivalent to an observer at level ℓ, up to the bijection β on heap locations. We defer details to the appendix.

Theorem 1 (Termination-insensitive non-interference) *Suppose:*
(1) $\langle \iota_1, \theta_1, \sigma_1, \rho_1 \rangle \sim_\ell^\beta \langle \iota_2, \theta_2, \sigma_2, \rho_2 \rangle$, *(2)* $\langle \iota_1, \theta_1, \sigma_1, \rho_1 \rangle \rightsquigarrow^* \langle \mathbf{end}, \theta_1', [], [] \rangle$, *and*
(3) $\langle \iota_2, \theta_2, \sigma_2, \rho_2 \rangle \rightsquigarrow^* \langle \mathbf{end}, \theta_2', [], [] \rangle$. *Then,* $\exists \beta' \supseteq \beta$ *such that* $\theta_1' \sim_\ell^{\beta'} \theta_2'$.

6   Implementation

We instrumented WebKit's JS engine (JavaScriptCore) to implement the IFC semantics of the previous section. Before a function starts executing, we generate its CFG and calculate IPDs of its nodes by static analysis of its bytecode. We modify the source-to-bytecode compiler to emit a slightly different, but functionally equivalent bytecode sequence for finally blocks; this is needed for accurate computation of IPDs. For evaluation purposes, we label each source script with the script's domain of origin; each seen domain is dynamically allocated a bit in our bit-set label. In general, our instrumentation terminates a script that violates IFC. However, for the purpose of evaluating overhead of our instrumentation, we ignore IFC violations in all experiments described here.

We also implement and evaluate a variant of *sparse labeling* [21] which optimizes the common case of computations that mostly use local variables (registers

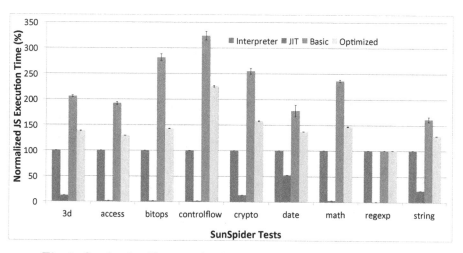

Fig. 3. Overheads of basic and optimized IFC in SunSpider benchmarks

in the bytecode). Until a function reads a value from the heap with a label different from the pc, we propagate taints only on heap-writes, but not on in-register computations. Until that point, all registers are assumed to be implicitly tainted with pc. This simple optimization reduces the overhead incurred by taint tracking significantly in microbenchmarks. For both the basic and optimized version, our instrumentation adds approximately 4,500 lines of code to WebKit.

Our baseline for evaluation is the uninstrumented interpreter with JIT disabled. For comparison, we also include measurements with JIT enabled. Our experiments are based on WebKit build #r122160 running in Safari 6.0. The machine has a 3.2GHz Quad-core Intel Xeon processor with 8GB RAM and runs Mac OS X version 10.7.4.

Microbenchmark. We executed the standard SunSpider 1.0.1 JS benchmark suite on the uninstrumented interpreter with JIT disabled and JIT enabled, and on the basic and the optimized IFC instrumentations with JIT disabled. Results are shown in Figure 3. The x-axis ranges over SunSpider tests and the y-axis shows the average execution time, normalized to our baseline (uninstrumented interpreter with JIT disabled) and averaged across 100 runs. Error bars are standard deviations. Although the overheads of IFC vary from test to test, the average overheads over our baseline are 121% and 45% for basic IFC and optimized IFC, respectively. The test *regexp* has almost zero overhead because it spends most time in native code, which we have not yet instrumented. We also note that, as expected, the JIT-enabled configuration performs extremely well on the SunSpider benchmarks.

Macrobenchmarks. We measured the execution time of the intial JS on 9 popular English language Websites. We load each Website in Safari and measure the total time taken to *execute* the JS code without user interaction. This excludes time for network communication and internal browser events and establishes a

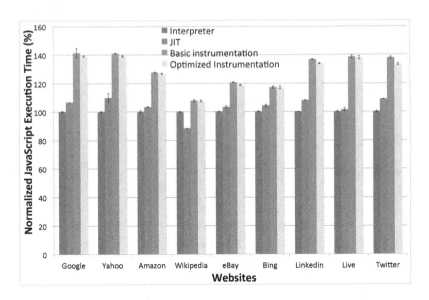

Fig. 4. Overheads of basic and optimized IFC in real websites

very conservative baseline. The results, normalized to our baseline, are shown in Fig. 4. Our overheads are all less than 42% (with an average of around 29% in both instrumentations). Interestingly, we observe that our optimization is less effective on real websites indicating that real JS accesses the heap more often than the SunSpider tests. When compared to the amount of time it takes to fetch a page over the network and to render it, these overheads are negligible. Enabling JIT worsens performance compared to our baseline indicating that, for the code executed here, JIT is not useful. We also experimented with JS-Bench [33], a sophisticated benchmark derived from JS code in the wild. The average overhead on all JSBench tests (a total 23 iterations) is approximately 38% for both instrumentations. Details are present in our technical appendix.

7   Conclusion and Future Work

We have explored dynamic information flow control for JS bytecode in WebKit, a production JS engine. We formally model the bytecode, its semantics, our instrumentation and prove the latter correct. We identify challenges, largely arising from pervasive use of unstructured control flow in bytecode, and resolve them using very limited static analysis. Our evaluation indicates only moderate overheads in practice.

In ongoing work, we are instrumenting the DOM and other native JS methods. We also plan to generalize our model and non-interference theorem to take into account the reactive nature of Web browsers. Going beyond non-interference, the design and implementation of a policy language for representing allowed information flows looks necessary.

Acknowledgments. This work was funded in part by the Deutsche Forschungsgemeinschaft (DFG) grant "Information Flow Control for Browser Clients" under the priority program "Reliably Secure Software Systems" (RS3) and the German Federal Ministry of Education and Research (BMBF) within the Centre for IT-Security, Privacy and Accountability (CISPA) at Saarland University.

References

1. Richards, G., Hammer, C., Burg, B., Vitek, J.: The eval that men do – a large-scale study of the use of eval in JavaScript applications. In: Mezini, M. (ed.) ECOOP 2011. LNCS, vol. 6813, pp. 52–78. Springer, Heidelberg (2011)

2. Jang, D., Jhala, R., Lerner, S., Shacham, H.: An empirical study of privacy-violating information flows in JavaScript web applications. In: Proc. 17th ACM Conference on Computer and Communications Security, pp. 270–283 (2010)

3. Richards, G., Hammer, C., Zappa Nardelli, F., Jagannathan, S., Vitek, J.: Flexible access control for Javascript. In: Proc. 2013 ACM SIGPLAN International Conference on Object Oriented Programming Systems Languages & Applications, OOPSLA 2013, pp. 305–322 (2013)

4. Hedin, D., Sabelfeld, A.: Information-flow security for a core of JavaScript. In: Proc. 25th IEEE Computer Security Foundations Symposium, pp. 3–18 (2012)

5. Hedin, D., Birgisson, A., Bello, L., Sabelfeld, A.: JSFlow: Tracking information flow in JavaScript and its APIs. In: Proc. 29th ACM Symposium on Applied Computing (2014)

6. Devriese, D., Piessens, F.: Noninterference through secure multi-execution. In: Proc. 2010 IEEE Symposium on Security and Privacy, pp. 109–124 (2010)

7. De Groef, W., Devriese, D., Nikiforakis, N., Piessens, F.: Flowfox: a web browser with flexible and precise information flow control. In: Proc. 2012 ACM Conference on Computer and Communications Security, pp. 748–759 (2012)

8. Goguen, J.A., Meseguer, J.: Security policies and security models. In: Proc. 1982 IEEE Symposium on Security and Privacy, pp. 11–20 (1982)

9. Myers, A.C., Liskov, B.: A decentralized model for information flow control. In: Proc. 16th ACM Symposium on Operating Systems Principles, pp. 129–142 (1997)

10. Zdancewic, S., Myers, A.C.: Robust declassification. In: Proc. 14th IEEE Computer Security Foundations Workshop, pp. 15–23 (2001)

11. Volpano, D., Irvine, C., Smith, G.: A sound type system for secure flow analysis. J. Comput. Secur. 4(2-3), 167–187 (1996)

12. Just, S., Cleary, A., Shirley, B., Hammer, C.: Information flow analysis for Java-Script. In: Proc. 1st ACM SIGPLAN International Workshop on Programming Language and Systems Technologies for Internet Clients, pp. 9–18 (2011)

13. Austin, T.H., Flanagan, C.: Permissive dynamic information flow analysis. In: Proc. 5th ACM SIGPLAN Workshop on Programming Languages and Analysis for Security, pp. 3:1–3:12 (2010)

14. Bohannon, A., Pierce, B.C., Sjöberg, V., Weirich, S., Zdancewic, S.: Reactive non-interference. In: Proc. 16th ACM Conference on Computer and Communications Security, pp. 79–90 (2009)

15. Maffeis, S., Mitchell, J.C., Taly, A.: An operational semantics for JavaScript. In: Ramalingam, G. (ed.) APLAS 2008. LNCS, vol. 5356, pp. 307–325. Springer, Heidelberg (2008)

16. Guha, A., Saftoiu, C., Krishnamurthi, S.: The essence of JavaScript. In: D'Hondt, T. (ed.) ECOOP 2010. LNCS, vol. 6183, pp. 126–150. Springer, Heidelberg (2010)
17. Politz, J.G., Carroll, M.J., Lerner, B.S., Pombrio, J., Krishnamurthi, S.: A tested semantics for getters, setters, and eval in JavaScript. In: Proceedings of the 8th Dynamic Languages Symposium, pp. 1–16 (2012)
18. Bodin, M., Chargueraud, A., Filaretti, D., Gardner, P., Maffeis, S., Naudziuniene, D., Schmitt, A., Smith, G.: A trusted mechanised Javascript specification. In: Proc. 41st ACM SIGPLAN-SIGACT Symposium on Principles of Programming Languages (2014)
19. Guarnieri, S., Pistoia, M., Tripp, O., Dolby, J., Teilhet, S., Berg, R.: Saving the world wide web from vulnerable javascript. In: Proc. 2011 International Symposium on Software Testing and Analysis, ISSTA 2011, pp. 177–187 (2011)
20. Chugh, R., Meister, J.A., Jhala, R., Lerner, S.: Staged information flow for Java-Script. In: Proc. 2009 ACM SIGPLAN Conference on Programming Language Design and Implementation, pp. 50–62 (2009)
21. Austin, T.H., Flanagan, C.: Efficient purely-dynamic information flow analysis. In: Proc. ACM SIGPLAN Fourth Workshop on Programming Languages and Analysis for Security, pp. 113–124 (2009)
22. Zdancewic, S.A.: Programming Languages for Information Security. PhD thesis, Cornell University (August 2002)
23. Birgisson, A., Hedin, D., Sabelfeld, A.: Boosting the permissiveness of dynamic information-flow tracking by testing. In: Foresti, S., Yung, M., Martinelli, F. (eds.) ESORICS 2012. LNCS, vol. 7459, pp. 55–72. Springer, Heidelberg (2012)
24. Austin, T.H., Flanagan, C.: Multiple facets for dynamic information flow. In: Proc. 39th Annual ACM SIGPLAN-SIGACT Symposium on Principles of Programming Languages, pp. 165–178 (2012)
25. Bielova, N., Devriese, D., Massacci, F., Piessens, F.: Reactive non-interference for a browser model. In: 5th International Conference on Network and System Security (NSS), pp. 97–104 (2011)
26. Bohannon, A., Pierce, B.C.: Featherweight Firefox: formalizing the core of a web browser. In: Proc. 2010 USENIX Conference on Web Application Development, WebApps 2010, pp. 11–22 (2010)
27. Denning, D.E.: A lattice model of secure information flow. Commun. ACM 19(5), 236–243 (1976)
28. Dhawan, M., Ganapathy, V.: Analyzing information flow in JavaScript-based browser extensions. In: Proc. 2009 Annual Computer Security Applications Conference, ACSAC 2009, pp. 382–391 (2009)
29. Robling Denning, D.E.: Cryptography and Data Security. Addison-Wesley Longman Publishing Co., Inc., Boston (1982)
30. Xin, B., Zhang, X.: Efficient online detection of dynamic control dependence. In: Proc. 2007 International Symposium on Software Testing and Analysis, pp. 185–195 (2007)
31. Masri, W., Podgurski, A.: Algorithms and tool support for dynamic information flow analysis. Information & Software Technology 51(2), 385–404 (2009)
32. Lengauer, T., Tarjan, R.E.: A fast algorithm for finding dominators in a flowgraph. ACM Trans. Program. Lang. Syst. 1(1), 121–141 (1979)
33. Richards, G., Gal, A., Eich, B., Vitek, J.: Automated construction of JavaScript benchmarks. In: Proceedings of the 2011 ACM International Conference on Object Oriented Programming Systems Languages and Applications, pp. 677–694 (2011)

A Separation Logic for Enforcing Declarative Information Flow Control Policies

David Costanzo and Zhong Shao

Yale University, New Haven, USA

Abstract. In this paper, we present a program logic for proving that a program does not release information about sensitive data in an unintended way. The most important feature of the logic is that it provides a formal security guarantee while supporting "declassification policies" that describe precise conditions under which a piece of sensitive data can be released. We leverage the power of Hoare Logic to express the policies and security guarantee in terms of state predicates. This allows our system to be far more specific regarding declassification conditions than most other information flow systems.

The logic is designed for reasoning about a C-like, imperative language with pointer manipulation and aliasing. We therefore make use of ideas from Separation Logic to reason about data in the heap.

1 Introduction

Information Flow Control (IFC) is a field of computer security concerned with tracking the propagation of information through a system. A primary goal of IFC reasoning is to formally prove that a system does not inadvertently leak high-security data to a low-security observer. A major challenge is to precisely define what "inadvertently" should mean here.

A simple solution to this challenge, taken by many IFC systems (e.g., [7,8,14,19,23]), is to define an information-release policy using a lattice of security labels. A *noninterference* property is imposed: information cannot flow down the lattice. Put another way, any data that the observer sees can only have been influenced by data with label less than or equal to the observer's label in the lattice. This property is sometimes called *pure noninterference.*

Purely-noninterfering systems are unfortunately not very useful. Almost all real-world systems need to violate noninterference sometimes. For example, consider one of the most standard security-sensitive situations: password authentication. In order for a password to be useful, there must be a way for a user to submit a guess at the password. If the guess is incorrect, then the user will be informed as such. However, the information that the guess was incorrect is dependent on the password itself; the user (who might be a malicious attacker) learns that the password is definitely *not* the one that was guessed. This represents a flow of information (albeit a minor one) from the high-security password to the low-security user, thus violating noninterference. In a purely noninterfering system, sensitive data has no way whatsoever of affecting the outcome of a

M. Abadi and S. Kremer (Eds.): POST 2014, LNCS 8414, pp. 179–198, 2014.

computation, and so the situation is essentially equivalent to the data not being present in the system at all.

There have been numerous attempts at refining the notion of inadvertent information release beyond the rules of a strict lattice structure. IFC systems commonly allow for some method of *declassification*, a term used to describe an information leak (i.e., an information flow moving down the security lattice) that is understood to be in some way "acceptable" or "purposeful" (as opposed to "inadvertent"). These declassifications violate the pure noninterference property described above. Ideally, an IFC system should still provide some sort of security guarantee even in the presence of declassification. It is quite rare, however, for a system to have a satisfactory formal guarantee. Those that do usually must make significant concessions that limit the generality or practicality of the system.

Our primary goal is to leverage the strengths of a program logic to devise a powerful IFC system that provides formal security guarantees even in the presence of declassification. A secondary goal is to avoid relational reasoning, which is usually required for the more expressive IFC reasoning systems (e.g., [15]) due to the nature of noninterference, but can be very difficult to use in practice.

We achieve these goals by using unary state predicates to refine the pure noninterference property into one that cleanly describes exactly how a piece of high-security data could affect observable output. Instead of simply saying that an observer cannot distinguish between any values of the high-security data, we say that the observer cannot distinguish between any values among a particular set — the set described by the state predicate. This method of refining pure noninterference to express a semantic notion of declassification appears in many previous IFC reasoning systems (e.g., [3],[15],[20]), though we take a rather unique approach toward designing a system that establishes the property. Our contributions in this paper are as follows:

- We define a novel, security-aware semantics for a simple imperative language with pointer arithmetic and aliasing. The semantics instruments state with security labels, and tracks information flow through propagation of these labels. We show that this semantics is sensible and overhead-free by relating its executions back to a standard small-step operational semantics without labels.
- We present a program logic for formally verifying the safety of a program under the security-aware semantics. The logic builds upon Hoare Logic [9] and Separation Logic [16,17], and uses a unary predicate language syntax that has the ability to refer to security labels in the program state. Note that our choice of Separation Logic is somewhat arbitrary — we need to reason about low-level pointer manipulation, but a different pointer-analysis logic may be just as suitable.
- We prove a strong, termination-insensitive security guarantee for any program that is verified using our program logic. This guarantee generalizes traditional pure noninterference to account for semantic declassification.
- All of the technical work in this paper is fully formalized and proved in the Coq proof assistant. The Coq development can be found at [6].

The remainder of this paper is organized as follows: Section 2 informally discusses how our system works and highlights contributions; Section 3 defines our language, state model, and operational semantics; Section 4 describes the program logic and its soundness theorem relative to the operational semantics; Section 5 describes the noninterference-based security guarantee provided by the program logic; Section 6 describes related work; and Section 7 concludes.

2   Informal Discussion

In this section, we will describe our system informally in order to provide some high-level motivation. We pick a starting point of a C-like, imperative language with pointer arithmetic and aliasing, as we would like our logic to be applicable to low-level systems code. The main operations of our language are variable assignment $x := E$, heap dereference/load $x := [E]$, and heap dereference/store $[E] := E'$. The expressions E can be any standard mathematical expressions on program variables, so pointer arithmetic is allowed. Aliasing is also clearly allowed since $[x]$ and $[y]$ refer to the same heap location if x and y contain the same value.

2.1   Security Labels

Our instrumented language semantics will track information flow by attaching a *security label* to every value in the program state. For simplicity of presentation, we will assume that the only labels are Lo and Hi (a more general version of our system allows labels to be any set of elements that form a lattice structure). Unlike many static IFC reasoning systems, we attach the label to the *value* rather than the *location*. This means that a program is allowed to, for example, overwrite some Lo data stored in variable x with some other Hi data. Many other systems would instead label the location x as Lo, meaning that Hi data could never be written into it. Supporting label overwrites allows our system to verify a wider variety of programs.

Label propagation is done in a mostly obvious way. If we have a direct assignment such as $x := y$, then the label of y's data propagates into x along with the data itself. We compute the composite label of an expression such as $2 * x + z$ to be the least upper bound of the labels of its constituent parts (for the two-element lattice of Lo and Hi, this will be Lo if and only if each constituent label is Lo). For the heap-read command $x := [E]$, we must propagate both the label of E and the label of the data located at heap address E into x. In other words, if we read some low-security data from the heap using a high-security pointer, the result must be tainted as high security in order for our information flow tracking to be accurate. Similarly, the heap-write command $[E] := E'$ must propagate both the label of E' and the label of pointer E into the location E in the heap. As a general rule for any of these atomic commands, we compute the composite label of the entire read-set, and propagate that into all locations in the write-set.

2.2   Noninterference

As discussed in Section 1, the ultimate goal of our IFC system is to prove a formal security guarantee that holds for any verified program. The standard security guarantee is noninterference, which says that the initial values of Hi data have no effect on the "observable behavior" of a program's execution. We choose to define observable behavior in terms of a special output channel. We include an output command in our language, and an execution's observable behavior is defined to be exactly the sequence of values that the execution outputs.

The standard way to express this noninterference property formally is in terms of two executions: a program is deemed to be noninterfering if two executions of the program from *observably equivalent* initial states always yield identical outputs. Two states are defined to be observably equivalent when only their high-security values differ. Thus this property describes what one would expect: changing the value of any high-security data in the initial state will cause no change in the program's output.

We refine this noninterference property by requiring a precondition to hold on the initial state of an execution. That is, we alter the property to say that two executions will yield identical outputs if they start from two observably equivalent states that both satisfy some state predicate P. This weakening of noninterference is interesting for two reasons. First, it provides a link between information flow security and Hoare Logic (a program logic that derives pre/postconditions as state predicates). Second, this property describes a certain level of dependency between high-security inputs and low-security outputs, rather than the complete independence of pure noninterference. This means that a program that satisfies this weaker noninterference may be semantically declassifying data. In this sense, we can use this property as an interesting security guarantee for a program that may declassify some data. To better understand this weaker version of noninterference, let us consider a few examples.

Public Parity. Suppose we have a variable x that contains some high-security data. We wish to specify a *declassification policy* which says that only the parity of the Hi value can be released to the public. We will accomplish this by verifying the security of some program with a precondition P that says "x contains high data, y contains low data, and $y = x\%2$". Our security property then says that if we have an execution from some state satisfying P, then changing the value of x will not affect the output as long as the new state also satisfies P. Since y is the parity of x and is unchanged in the two executions, this means that as long as we change x to some other value *that has the same parity*, the output will be unchanged. Indeed, this is exactly the property that one would expect to have with a policy that releases only the parity of a secret value: only the secret's parity can influence the observable behavior.

Public Average. Suppose we have three secrets stored in x, y, and z, and we are only willing to release their average as public (e.g., the secrets are employee salaries at a particular company). This is similar to the previous example, except that we now have multiple secrets. The precondition P will say that x, y, and z all contain Hi data, a contains Lo data, and $a = (x + y + z)/3$. In this situation, noninterference will say that we can change the value of the *set* of secrets from any triple to any other triple, and the output will be unaffected as long as the average of the three values is unchanged.

Public Zero. Suppose we have a secret stored in x, and we are only willing to release it if it is zero. We could take the approach of the previous two examples and store a public boolean in another variable which is true if and only if x is 0. However, there is an even simpler way to represent the desired policy without using an extra variable. Our precondition P will say that either x is 0 and its label is Lo, or x is nonzero and its label is Hi. This is an example of a *conditional label*: a label whose value depends on some state predicate. If x is 0, then noninterference says nothing since there is no high-security data in the state. If x is nonzero, then noninterference says that changing its value (but *not* its label) will have no effect on the output as long as P still holds; in order for P to still hold, we must be changing x to some other *nonzero* value. Hence all nonzero values of x will look the same to an observer. Conditional labels are a novelty of our system; we will see in Section 4 how they can be a powerful tool for verifying the security of a program.

3   Language and Semantics

Our programming language is defined as follows:

$$
\begin{array}{lll}
\text{(Exp)} & E & ::= x \mid c \mid E + E \mid \cdots \\
\text{(BExp)} & B & ::= \texttt{false} \mid E = E \mid B \wedge B \mid \cdots \\
\text{(Cmd)} & C & ::= \texttt{skip} \mid \texttt{output}\,E \mid x := E \mid x := [E] \mid [E] := E \mid C; C \\
& & \mid \texttt{if}\,B\,\texttt{then}\,C\,\texttt{else}\,C \mid \texttt{while}\,B\,\texttt{do}\,C
\end{array}
$$

Valid code includes variable assignment, heap load/store, if statements, while loops, and output. Our model of a program state, consisting of a variable store and a heap, is given by:

$$
\begin{array}{lll}
\text{(Lbl)} & L & ::= \texttt{Lo} \mid \texttt{Hi} \\
\text{(Val)} & V & ::= \mathbb{Z} \times \text{Lbl} \\
\text{(Store)} & s & ::= \text{Var} \rightarrow \text{option Val} \\
\text{(Heap)} & h & ::= \mathbb{N} \rightarrow \text{option Val} \\
\text{(State)} & \sigma & ::= \text{Store} \times \text{Heap}
\end{array}
$$

Given a variable store s, we define a denotational semantics $[\![E]\!]s$ that evaluates an expression to a pair of integer and label, with the label being the least upper bound of the labels of the constituent parts. The denotation of an expression also may evaluate to None, indicating that the program state does not contain the necessary resources to evaluate. We have a similar denotational semantics for boolean expressions. The formal definitions of these semantics are omitted here

$$\frac{[\![E]\!]s = \mathrm{Some}\ (n, l)}{\langle(s, h),\ x := E,\ K\rangle \xrightarrow[l']{} \langle(s[x \mapsto (n, l \sqcup l')], h),\ \mathrm{skip},\ K\rangle} \ \text{(ASSGN)}$$

$$\frac{[\![E]\!]s = \mathrm{Some}\ (n_1, l_1) \qquad h(n_1) = \mathrm{Some}\ (n_2, l_2)}{\langle(s, h),\ x := [E],\ K\rangle \xrightarrow[l']{} \langle(s[x \mapsto (n_2, l_1 \sqcup l_2 \sqcup l')], h),\ \mathrm{skip},\ K\rangle} \ \text{(READ)}$$

$$\frac{[\![E]\!]s = \mathrm{Some}\ (n_1, l_1) \qquad h(n_1) \neq \mathrm{None} \qquad [\![E']\!]s = \mathrm{Some}\ (n_2, l_2)}{\langle(s, h),\ [E] := E',\ K\rangle \xrightarrow[l']{} \langle(s, h[n_1 \mapsto (n_2, l_1 \sqcup l_2 \sqcup l')]),\ \mathrm{skip},\ K\rangle} \ \text{(WRITE)}$$

$$\frac{[\![E]\!]\sigma = \mathrm{Some}\ (n, \mathrm{Lo})}{\langle\sigma,\ \mathrm{output}\ E,\ K\rangle \xrightarrow[\mathrm{Lo}]{[n]} \langle\sigma,\ \mathrm{skip},\ K\rangle} \ \text{(OUTPUT)}$$

$$\frac{[\![B]\!]\sigma = \mathrm{Some}\ (\mathrm{true}, l) \qquad l \sqsubseteq l'}{\langle\sigma,\ \mathrm{if}\ B\ \mathrm{then}\ C_1\ \mathrm{else}\ C_2,\ K\rangle \xrightarrow[l']{} \langle\sigma,\ C_1,\ K\rangle} \ \text{(IF-TRUE)}$$

$$\frac{[\![B]\!]\sigma = \mathrm{Some}\ (\mathrm{false}, l) \qquad l \sqsubseteq l'}{\langle\sigma,\ \mathrm{if}\ B\ \mathrm{then}\ C_1\ \mathrm{else}\ C_2,\ K\rangle \xrightarrow[l']{} \langle\sigma,\ C_2,\ K\rangle} \ \text{(IF-FALSE)}$$

$$\frac{\begin{array}{c}[\![B]\!]\sigma = \mathrm{Some}\ (\_, \mathrm{Hi})\\ \langle\mathrm{mark\_vars}(\sigma, \mathrm{if}\ B\ \mathrm{then}\ C_1\ \mathrm{else}\ C_2),\ \mathrm{if}\ B\ \mathrm{then}\ C_1\ \mathrm{else}\ C_2,\ []\rangle \xrightarrow[\mathrm{Hi}]{}_n \langle\sigma', \mathrm{skip}, []\rangle\end{array}}{\langle\sigma,\ \mathrm{if}\ B\ \mathrm{then}\ C_1\ \mathrm{else}\ C_2,\ K\rangle \xrightarrow[\mathrm{Lo}]{} \langle\sigma', \mathrm{skip}, K\rangle} \ \text{(IF-HI)}$$

$$\frac{[\![B]\!]\sigma = \mathrm{Some}\ (\mathrm{true}, l) \qquad l \sqsubseteq l'}{\langle\sigma,\ \mathrm{while}\ B\ \mathrm{do}\ C,\ K\rangle \xrightarrow[l']{} \langle\sigma,\ C; \mathrm{while}\ B\ \mathrm{do}\ C,\ K\rangle} \ \text{(WHILE-TRUE)}$$

$$\frac{[\![B]\!]\sigma = \mathrm{Some}\ (\mathrm{false}, l) \qquad l \sqsubseteq l'}{\langle\sigma,\ \mathrm{while}\ B\ \mathrm{do}\ C,\ K\rangle \xrightarrow[l']{} \langle\sigma,\ \mathrm{skip},\ K\rangle} \ \text{(WHILE-FALSE)}$$

$$\frac{\begin{array}{c}[\![B]\!]\sigma = \mathrm{Some}\ (\_, \mathrm{Hi})\\ \langle\mathrm{mark\_vars}(\sigma, \mathrm{while}\ B\ \mathrm{do}\ C),\ \mathrm{while}\ B\ \mathrm{do}\ C,\ []\rangle \xrightarrow[\mathrm{Hi}]{}_n \langle\sigma', \mathrm{skip}, []\rangle\end{array}}{\langle\sigma,\ \mathrm{while}\ B\ \mathrm{do}\ C,\ K\rangle \xrightarrow[\mathrm{Lo}]{} \langle\sigma', \mathrm{skip}, K\rangle} \ \text{(WHILE-HI)}$$

$$\frac{}{\langle\sigma,\ C_1; C_2,\ K\rangle \xrightarrow[l]{} \langle\sigma,\ C_1,\ C_2 :: K\rangle} \ \text{(SEQ)}$$

$$\frac{}{\langle\sigma,\ \mathrm{skip},\ C :: K\rangle \xrightarrow[l]{} \langle\sigma,\ C,\ K\rangle} \ \text{(SKIP)} \qquad \frac{}{\langle\sigma,\ C,\ K\rangle \xrightarrow[l]{}_0 \langle\sigma,\ C,\ K\rangle} \ \text{(ZERO)}$$

$$\frac{\langle\sigma,\ C,\ K\rangle \xrightarrow[l]{o} \langle\sigma', C', K'\rangle \qquad \langle\sigma', C', K'\rangle \xrightarrow[l]{o'}_n \langle\sigma'', C'', K''\rangle \qquad n > 0}{\langle\sigma,\ C,\ K\rangle \xrightarrow[l]{o + o'}_{n+1} \langle\sigma'', C'', K''\rangle} \ \text{(SUCC)}$$

Fig. 1. Security-Aware Operational Semantics

as they are standard and straightforward. Note that we will sometimes write $[\![E]\!]\sigma$ as shorthand for $[\![E]\!]$ applied to the store of state σ.

Figure 1 defines our operational semantics. The semantics is security-aware, meaning that it keeps track of security labels on data and propagates these labels throughout execution in order to track which values might have been influenced by some high-security data. The semantics operates on machine configurations, which consist of program state, code, and a list of commands called the continuation stack (we use a continuation-stack approach solely for the purpose of simplifying some proofs). The transition arrow of the semantics is annotated with a *program counter label*, which is a standard IFC construct used to keep track of information flow resulting from the control flow of the execution. Whenever an execution enters a conditional construct, it raises the pc label by the label of the boolean expression evaluated; the pc label then taints any assignments that are made within the conditional construct. The transition arrow is also annotated with a list of outputs (equal to the empty list when not explicitly written) and the number of steps (equal to 1 when not explicitly written).

Note. Two rules of our semantics are omitted here, but can be found in the Coq development [6]. These rules make sure that a low-context execution will diverge safely (rather than get stuck) when it attempts to run a high-context execution that diverges. These rules are necessary for technical reasons, but they ultimately have no significant bearing on our end-to-end noninterference guarantee, since that guarantee only ever mentions terminating executions.

Two of the rules for conditional constructs make use of a function called mark_vars. The function mark_vars(σ, C) alters σ by setting the label of each variable in modifies(C) to Hi, where modifies(C) is a standard syntactic function returning an overapproximation of the store variables that may be modified by C. Thus, whenever we raise the pc label to Hi, our semantics taints all store variables that appear on the left-hand side of an assignment or heap-read command within the conditional construct, even if some of these commands do not actually get executed. Note that regardless of which branch of an if statement is taken, the semantics taints all the variables in *both* branches. This is required for noninterference, due to the well-known fact that the *lack* of assignment in a branch of an if statement can leak information about the branching expression. Consider, for example, the following program:

```
1    y := 1;
2    if (x = 0) then y := 0 else skip;
3    if (y = 0) then skip else output 1;
```

Suppose x contains Hi data initially, while y contains Lo data. If x is 0, then y will be assigned 0 at line 2 and tainted with a Hi label (by the pc label). Then nothing happens at line 3, and the program produces no output. If x is nonzero, however, nothing happens at line 2, so y still has a Lo label at line 3. Thus the output command at line 3 executes without issue. Therefore the output of this program depends on the Hi data in x, even though our instrumented semantics executes safely. We choose to resolve this issue by using the mark_vars function in the semantics. Then y will be tainted at line 2 regardless of the value of x, and so the semantics will get stuck at line 3 when x is nonzero. In other words, we would only be able to verify this program with a precondition saying that $x = 0$ — the program is indeed noninterfering with respect to this precondition (according to our generalized noninterference definition described in Section 2).

The operational semantics presented here is mixed-step and manipulates security labels directly. In order to make sense of such a non-standard semantics, we relate it to a standard one that erases labels. We omit the formal definition of this erasure semantics here since it is exactly the expected small-step operational semantics for a simple imperative language. The definition can be found in the technical report and Coq development [6].

The erasure semantics operates on states without labels, and it does not use continuation stacks. Given a state σ with labels, we write $\bar{\sigma}$ to represent the same state with all labels erased from both the store and heap. We will also use τ to range over states without labels. Then the following two theorems hold:

Theorem 1. *Suppose* $\langle \sigma, C, [] \rangle \xrightarrow{o}_* \langle \sigma', \text{skip}, [] \rangle$ *in the instrumented seman-*

tics. Then, for some τ, $\langle \bar{\sigma}, C \rangle \xrightarrow{o}_* \langle \tau, \text{skip} \rangle$ *in the standard semantics.*

Theorem 2. *Suppose* $\langle \bar{\sigma}, C \rangle \xrightarrow{o}_* \langle \tau, \text{skip} \rangle$ *in the standard semantics, and suppose* $\langle \sigma, C, [] \rangle$ *never gets stuck when executed in the instrumented semantics. Then, for some* σ', $\langle \sigma, C, [] \rangle \xrightarrow{o}_* \langle \sigma', \text{skip}, [] \rangle$ *in the instrumented semantics.*

These theorems together guarantee that the two semantics produce identical observable behaviors (outputs) on terminating executions, as long as the instrumented semantics does not get stuck. Our program logic will of course guarantee that the instrumented semantics does not get stuck in any execution satisfying the precondition.

4   The Program Logic

In this section, we will present the logic that we use for verifying the security of a program. A logic judgment takes the form $l \vdash \{P\} C \{Q\}$. P and Q are the pre- and postconditions, C is the program to be executed, and l is the pc label under which the program is verified. P and Q are *state assertions*, whose syntax and semantics are given in Figure 2.

Note. We allow assertions to contain logical variables, but we elide the details here to avoid complicating the presentation. In Figure 2, we claim that the type of $\llbracket P \rrbracket$ is a set of states — in reality, the type is a function from logical variable environments to sets of states. In an assertion like $E \mapsto (n, l)$, the n and l may be logical variables rather than constants, and E may itself contain logical variables. The full details of logical variables can be found in the technical report and Coq development [6].

$$P, Q ::= \text{emp}_s \mid \text{emp}_h \mid E \mapsto \_ \mid E \mapsto (n, l) \mid B \mid x.\text{lbl} = l$$
$$\mid x.\text{lbl} \sqsubseteq l \mid \text{lbl}(E) = l \mid \exists X \; . \; P \mid P \wedge Q \mid P \vee Q \mid P * Q$$

$$[\![P]\!] \; : \; \mathcal{P}(\text{state})$$

$$(s, h) \in [\![\text{emp}]\!] \iff h = \emptyset$$

$$(s, h) \in [\![E \mapsto \_]\!] \iff \exists a, n, l \; . \; [\![E]\!]s = \text{Some } a \wedge h = [a \mapsto (n, l)]$$

$$(s, h) \in [\![E \mapsto (E', l)]\!] \iff \exists a, b \; . \; [\![E]\!]s = \text{Some } a \wedge [\![E']\!]s = \text{Some } b \wedge h = [a \mapsto (b, l)]$$

$$(s, h) \in [\![B]\!] \iff [\![B]\!]s = \text{Some true}$$

$$(s, h) \in [\![x.\text{lbl} = l]\!] \iff \exists n \; . \; s(x) = \text{Some } (n, l)$$

$$(s, h) \in [\![x.\text{lbl} \sqsubseteq l]\!] \iff \exists n, l' \; . \; s(x) = \text{Some } (n, l') \text{ and } l' \sqsubseteq l$$

$$(s, h) \in [\![\text{lbl}(E) = l]\!] \iff \bigsqcup_{x \in \text{vars}(E)} \text{snd}(s(x)) = l$$

$$(s, h) \in [\![\exists X \; . \; P]\!] \iff \exists v \in \mathbb{Z} + \text{Lbl} \; . \; (s, h) \in [\![P[v/X]]\!]$$

$$(s, h) \in [\![P \wedge Q]\!] \iff (s, h) \in [\![P]\!] \cap [\![Q]\!]$$

$$(s, h) \in [\![P \vee Q]\!] \iff (s, h) \in [\![P]\!] \cup [\![Q]\!]$$

$$(s, h) \in [\![P * Q]\!] \iff \begin{pmatrix} \exists h_0, h_1 \; . \; h_0 \uplus h_1 = h \\ \text{and } (s, h_0) \in [\![P]\!] \\ \text{and } (s, h_1) \in [\![Q]\!] \end{pmatrix}$$

Fig. 2. Assertion Syntax and Semantics

Definition 1 (Sound judgment). *We say that a judgment* $l \vdash \{P\} \, C \, \{Q\}$ *is sound if, for any state* $\sigma \in [\![P]\!]$, *the following two properties hold:*

1. *The operational semantics cannot get stuck when executed from initial configuration* $\langle \sigma, C, [] \rangle$ *under context* l.
2. *If the operational semantics executes from initial configuration* $\langle \sigma, C, [] \rangle$ *under context* l *and terminates at state* σ', *then* $\sigma' \in [\![Q]\!]$.

Selected inference rules for our logic are shown in Figure 3. The rules make use of two auxiliary syntactic functions, $\text{vars}(P)$ and $\text{no\_lbls}(P, S)$ (S is a set of store variables). The first function returns the set of all store variables that appear somewhere in P, while the second checks that for each variable $x \in S$, $x.\text{lbl}$ does not appear anywhere in P.

The (IF)/(WHILE) rules may look rather complex, but almost all of that is just describing how to reason about the mark_vars function that gets applied at the beginning of a conditional construct when the pc label increases. An additional complexity present in the (IF) rule involves the labels l_t and l_f. In fact, these labels describe a novel and interesting feature of our system: when verifying an if statement, it might be possible to reason that the pc label gets raised by l_t in one branch and by l_f in the other, based on the fact that B holds in one branch but not in the other. This is interesting if l_t and l_f are different

$$\texttt{mark\_vars}(P,S,l,l') \triangleq \begin{cases} P & , \quad \text{if } l \sqsubseteq l' \\ P \wedge \left(\bigwedge_{x \in S} l \sqcup l' \sqsubseteq x.\texttt{lbl} \right) & , \quad \text{otherwise} \end{cases}$$

$$\frac{}{l \vdash \{\texttt{emp}\}\,\texttt{skip}\,\{\texttt{emp}\}}\ (\text{SKIP})$$

$$\frac{}{\texttt{Lo} \vdash \{\texttt{lbl}(E) = \texttt{Lo} \wedge \texttt{emp}\}\,\texttt{output}\,E\,\{\texttt{lbl}(E) = \texttt{Lo} \wedge \texttt{emp}\}}\ (\text{OUTPUT})$$

$$\frac{x \notin \texttt{vars}(E')}{l \vdash \{E = E' \wedge \texttt{lbl}(E) = l' \wedge \texttt{emp}\}\,x := E\,\{x = E' \wedge x.\texttt{lbl} = l' \sqcup l \wedge \texttt{emp}\}}\ (\text{ASSIGN})$$

$$\frac{x \notin \texttt{vars}(E_1) \cup \texttt{vars}(E_2)}{l \vdash \{x = E_1 \wedge \texttt{lbl}(E) = l_1 \wedge E \mapsto (E_2, l_2)\}\,x := [E]\,\{x = E_2 \wedge x.\texttt{lbl} = l_1 \sqcup l_2 \sqcup l \wedge E[E_1/x] \mapsto (E_2, l_2)\}}\ (\text{READ})$$

$$\frac{}{l \vdash \{\texttt{lbl}(E) = l_1 \wedge \texttt{lbl}(E') = l_2 \wedge E \mapsto \_\}\,[E] := E'\,\{E \mapsto (E', l_1 \sqcup l_2 \sqcup l)\}}\ (\text{WRITE})$$

$$\frac{\begin{array}{c} P \Rightarrow B \vee \neg B \qquad B \wedge P \Rightarrow \texttt{lbl}(B) = l_t \\ \neg B \wedge P \Rightarrow \texttt{lbl}(B) = l_f \qquad S = \texttt{modifies}(\texttt{if } B \texttt{ then } C_1 \texttt{ else } C_2) \\ l_t \sqcup l_f \not\sqsubseteq l \Rightarrow \texttt{no\_lbls}(P, S) \qquad l_t \sqcup l \vdash \{B \wedge \texttt{mark\_vars}(P, S, l_t, l)\}\,C_1\,\{Q\} \\ l_f \sqcup l \vdash \{\neg B \wedge \texttt{mark\_vars}(P, S, l_f, l)\}\,C_2\,\{Q\} \end{array}}{l \vdash \{P\}\,\texttt{if } B \texttt{ then } C_1 \texttt{ else } C_2\,\{Q\}}\ (\text{IF})$$

$$\frac{\begin{array}{c} P \Rightarrow \texttt{lbl}(B) = l' \\ S = \texttt{modifies}(\texttt{while } B \texttt{ do } C) \qquad l' \not\sqsubseteq l \Rightarrow \texttt{no\_lbls}(P, S) \\ l' \sqcup l \vdash \{B \wedge \texttt{mark\_vars}(P, S, l', l)\}\,C\,\{\texttt{mark\_vars}(P, S, l', l)\} \end{array}}{l \vdash \{P\}\,\texttt{while } B \texttt{ do } C\,\{\neg B \wedge \texttt{mark\_vars}(P, S, l', l)\}}\ (\text{WHILE})$$

$$\frac{l \vdash \{P\}\,C_1\,\{Q\} \qquad l \vdash \{Q\}\,C_2\,\{R\}}{l \vdash \{P\}\,C_1;C_2\,\{R\}}\ (\text{SEQ})$$

$$\frac{P' \Rightarrow P \qquad Q \Rightarrow Q' \qquad l \vdash \{P\}\,C\,\{Q\}}{l \vdash \{P'\}\,C\,\{Q'\}}\ (\text{CONSEQ})$$

$$\frac{l \vdash \{P_1\}\,C\,\{Q_1\} \qquad l \vdash \{P_2\}\,C\,\{Q_2\}}{l \vdash \{P_1 \wedge P_2\}\,C\,\{Q_1 \wedge Q_2\}}\ (\text{CONJ})$$

$$\frac{l \vdash \{P\}\,C\,\{Q\} \qquad \texttt{modifies}(C) \cap \texttt{vars}(R) = \emptyset}{l \vdash \{P * R\}\,C\,\{Q * R\}}\ (\text{FRAME})$$

Fig. 3. Selected Inference Rules for the Logic

```
1   i := 0;
2   while (i < 64) do
3       x := [A+i];
4       if (x = 0)
5           then
6                   output i
7           else
8                   skip;
9       i := i+1
```

Fig. 4. Example: Alice's Private Calendar

labels. In every other static-analysis IFC system we are aware of, a particular pc label must be determined at the entrance to the conditional, and this pc label will propagate to both branches. We will provide an example program later in this section that illustrates this novelty.

Given our logic inference rules, we can prove the following theorem:

Theorem 3 (Soundness). *If* $l \vdash \{P\} C \{Q\}$ *is derivable according to our inference rules, then it is a* sound *judgment, as defined in Definition 1.*

We will not go over the proof of this theorem here since there is not really anything novel about it in regards to security. The proof is relatively straightforward and not significantly different from soundness proofs in other Hoare/separation logics. The primary theorem in this work is the one that says that any verified program satisfies our noninterference property — this will be discussed in detail in Section 5.

4.1   Example: Alice's Calendar

In the remainder of this section, we will show how our logic can be used to verify an interesting example. Figure 4 shows a program that we would like to prove is secure. Alice owns a calendar with 64 time slots beginning at some location designated by constant A. Each time slot is either 0 if she is free at that time, or some nonzero value representing an event if she is busy. Alice decides that all free time slots in her calendar should be considered low security, while the time slots with events should be secret. This policy allows for others to schedule a meeting time with her, as they can determine when she is available. Indeed, the example program shown here prints out all free time slots.

Figure 5 gives an overview of the verification, omitting a few trivial details. In between each line of code, we show the current pc label and a state predicate that currently holds. The program is verified with respect to Alice's policy, described by the precondition P defined in the figure. This precondition is the iterated separating conjunction of 64 calendar slots; each slot's label is Lo if its value is 0 and Hi otherwise. A major novelty of this verification regards the conditional statement at lines 4-8. As mentioned earlier, in other IFC systems, the label of

$$P \triangleq \overset{63}{\underset{i=0}{*}} \; (A + i \mapsto (n_i, l_i) \wedge n_i = 0 \iff l_i = \mathsf{Lo})$$

Lo ⊢ {P}

1 i := 0;

   Lo ⊢ {P ∧ 0 ≤ i ∧ i.lbl = Lo}

2 while (i < 64) do

      Lo ⊢ {P ∧ 0 ≤ i < 64 ∧ i.lbl = Lo}

3   x := [A+i];

      Lo ⊢ {P ∧ 0 ≤ i < 64 ∧ i.lbl = Lo ∧
              (x = 0 ⟺ x.lbl = Lo)}

4   if (x = 0)

5   then

         Lo ⊢ {P ∧ 0 ≤ i < 64 ∧ i.lbl = Lo ∧
                x = 0 ∧ x.lbl = Lo}

6   output i

         Lo ⊢ {P ∧ 0 ≤ i < 64 ∧ i.lbl = Lo ∧
                x = 0 ∧ x.lbl = Lo}

         Lo ⊢ {P ∧ 0 ≤ i < 64 ∧ i.lbl = Lo}

7   else

         Hi ⊢ {P ∧ 0 ≤ i < 64 ∧ i.lbl = Lo ∧
                x ≠ 0 ∧ x.lbl = Hi}

8   skip;

         Hi ⊢ {P ∧ 0 ≤ i < 64 ∧ i.lbl = Lo ∧
                x ≠ 0 ∧ x.lbl = Hi}

         Hi ⊢ {P ∧ 0 ≤ i < 64 ∧ i.lbl = Lo}

      Lo ⊢ {P ∧ 0 ≤ i < 64 ∧ i.lbl = Lo}

9   i := i+1

      Lo ⊢ {P ∧ 0 ≤ i ∧ i.lbl = Lo}

Lo ⊢ {P ∧ i ≥ 64 ∧ 0 ≤ i ∧ i.lbl = Lo}

Fig. 5. Calendar Example Verification

the boolean expression "$x = 0$" would have to be determined at the time of entering the conditional, and its label would then propagate into both branches via the pc label. In our system, however, we can reason that the expression's label (and hence the resulting pc label) will be different depending on which branch is taken. If the "true" branch is taken, then we know that x is 0, and hence we know from the state assertion that its label is Lo. This means that the pc label is Lo, and so the output statement within this branch will not leak high-security data. If the "false" branch is taken, however, then we can reason that the pc label will be Hi, meaning that an output statement could result in a leaky program (e.g., if the value of x were printed). This program does not attempt to output anything within this branch, so it is still valid.

Since the program is verified with respect to precondition P, the noninterference guarantee for this example says that if we change any high-security event in Alice's calendar to any other high-security event (i.e., nonzero value), then the output will be unaffected. In other words, an observer cannot distinguish between any two events occurring at a particular time slot. This seems like exactly the property Alice would want to have, given that her policy specifies that all free slots are Lo and all events are Hi.

5   Noninterference

In this section, we will discuss the method for formally proving our system's security guarantee. Much of the work has already been done through careful design of the security-aware semantics and the program logic. The fundamental idea is that we can find a bisimulation relation for our Lo-context instrumented semantics. This relation will guarantee that two executions operate in lock-step, always producing the same program continuation and output.

The bisimulation relation we will use is called *observable equivalence*. It intuitively says that the low-security portions of two states are identical; the relation is commonly used in many IFC systems as a tool for proving noninterference. In our system, states σ_1 and σ_2 are observably equivalent if: (1) they contain equal values at all locations that are present and Lo in both states; and (2) the presence and labels of all store variables are the same in both states. This may seem like a rather odd notion of equivalence (in fact, it is not even transitive, so "equivalence" is a misnomer here) — two states can be observably equivalent even if some heap location contains Hi data in one state and Lo data in the other. To see why we need to define observable equivalence in this way, consider a heap-write command $[x] := E$ where x is a Hi pointer. If we vary the value of x, then we will end up writing to two different locations in the heap. Suppose we write to location 100 in one execution and location 200 in the other. Then location 100 will contain Hi data in the first execution (as the Hi pointer taints the value written), but it may contain Lo data in the second since we never wrote to it. Thus we design observable equivalence so that this situation is allowed.

The following definitions describe observable equivalence formally:

Definition 2 (Observable Equivalence of Stores). *Suppose s_1 and s_2 are variable stores. We say that they are observably equivalent, written $s_1 \sim s_2$, if, for all program variables x:*

- *If $s_1(x) = $ None, then $s_2(x) = $ None.*
- *If $s_1(x) = $ Some (v_1, Hi), then $s_2(x) = $ Some (v_2, Hi) for some v_2.*
- *If $s_1(x) = $ Some (v, Lo), then $s_2(x) = $ Some (v, Lo).*

Definition 3 (Observable Equivalence of Heaps). *Suppose h_1 and h_2 are heaps. We say that they are observably equivalent, written $h_1 \sim h_2$, if, for all natural numbers n:*

- *If $h_1(n) = $ Some (v_1, Lo) and $h_2(n) = $ Some (v_2, Lo), then $v_1 = v_2$.*

We say that two states are observably equivalent (written $\sigma_1 \sim \sigma_2$) when both their stores and heaps are observably equivalent. Given this definition, we define a convenient relational denotational semantics for state assertions as:

$$(\sigma_1, \sigma_2) \in \llbracket P \rrbracket^2 \iff \sigma_1 \in \llbracket P \rrbracket \wedge \sigma_2 \in \llbracket P \rrbracket \wedge \sigma_1 \sim \sigma_2$$

In order to state noninterference cleanly, it helps to define a "bisimulation semantics" consisting of the following single rule (the side condition will be discussed below):

$$\frac{\langle \sigma_1, C, K \rangle \xrightarrow[\text{Lo}]{o} \langle \sigma_1', C', K' \rangle \qquad \langle \sigma_2, C, K \rangle \xrightarrow[\text{Lo}]{o} \langle \sigma_2', C', K' \rangle \quad \text{(side condition)}}{\langle \sigma_1, \sigma_2, C, K \rangle \longrightarrow \langle \sigma_1', \sigma_2', C', K' \rangle}$$

This bisimulation semantics operates on configurations consisting of a *pair* of states and a program. As two executions progress step-by-step, the bisimulation semantics makes sure that the executions continue to produce identical outputs and step to identical programs. The semantics requires a Lo program counter label because two executions from observably equivalent states may in fact step to different programs when the program counter label is Hi.

With this definition of a bisimulation semantics, we can split noninterference into the following progress and preservation properties.

Theorem 4 (Progress). *Suppose we derive* Lo $\vdash \{P\} \, C \, \{Q\}$ *using our program logic. For any $(\sigma_1, \sigma_2) \in \llbracket P \rrbracket^2$, suppose we have*

$$\langle \sigma_1, \sigma_2, C, K \rangle \longrightarrow_* \langle \sigma_1', \sigma_2', C', K' \rangle,$$

where $\sigma_1' \sim \sigma_2'$ and $(C', K') \neq (\text{skip}, [])$. Then there exist σ_1'', σ_2'', C'', K'' such that

$$\langle \sigma_1', \sigma_2', C', K' \rangle \longrightarrow \langle \sigma_1'', \sigma_2'', C'', K'' \rangle$$

Theorem 5 (Preservation). *Suppose we have $\sigma_1 \sim \sigma_2$ and $\langle \sigma_1, \sigma_2, C, K \rangle \longrightarrow \langle \sigma_1', \sigma_2', C', K' \rangle$. Then $\sigma_1' \sim \sigma_2'$.*

For the most part, the proofs of these theorems are relatively straightforward. Preservation requires proving the following two simple lemmas about Hi-context executions:

1. Hi-context executions never produce output.
2. If the initial and final values of some location differ across a Hi-context execution, then the location's final value must have a Hi label.

There is one significant difficulty in the proof that requires discussion. If C is a heap-read command $x := [E]$, then Preservation does not obviously hold. The reason for this comes from our odd definition of observable equivalence; in particular, the requirements for a heap location to be observably equivalent are weaker than those for a store variable. Yet the heap-read command is copying directly from the heap to the store. In more concrete terms, the heap location pointed to by E might have a Hi label in one state and Lo label in the other; but this means x will now have different labels in the two states, violating the definition of observable equivalence for the store.

We resolve this difficulty via the side condition in the bisimulation semantics. The side condition says that the situation we just described does not happen. More formally, it says that if C has the form $x := [E]$, then the heap location pointed to by E in σ_1 has the same label as the location pointed to by E in σ_2.

This side condition is sufficient for proving Preservation. However, we still need to show that the side condition holds in order to prove Progress. This fact comes from induction over the specific inference rules of our logic. For example, consider the (READ) rule from Section 4. In order to use this rule, the precondition requires us to show that $E \mapsto (n, l_2)$. Since both states σ_1 and σ_2 satisfy the precondition, we see that the heap locations pointed to by E both have label l_2, and so the side condition holds. Note that the side condition holds even if l_2 is a logical variable rather than a constant.

In order to prove that the side condition holds for *every* verified program, we need to show it holds for all inference rules involving a heap-read command. In particular, this means that no heap-read rule in our logic can have a precondition that only implies $E \mapsto \_$.

Now that we have the Progress and Preservation theorems, we can easily combine them to prove the overall noninterference theorem for our instrumented semantics:

Theorem 6 (Noninterference, Instrumented Semantics). *Suppose we derive* Lo $\vdash \{P\} C \{Q\}$ *using our program logic. Pick any state $\sigma_1 \in \llbracket P \rrbracket$, and consider changing the values of any Hi data in σ_1 to obtain some $\sigma_2 \in \llbracket P \rrbracket$. Suppose, in the instrumented semantics, we have*

$$\langle \sigma_1, C, [] \rangle \xrightarrow[\text{Lo}]{o_1}{}_* \langle \sigma_1', \text{skip}, [] \rangle \qquad and \qquad \langle \sigma_2, C, [] \rangle \xrightarrow[\text{Lo}]{o_2}{}_* \langle \sigma_2', \text{skip}, [] \rangle.$$

Then $o_1 = o_2$.

Finally, we can use the results from Section 3 along with the safety guaranteed by our logic to prove the final, end-to-end noninterference theorem:

Theorem 7 (Noninterference, Erasure Semantics). *Suppose we derive* Lo $\vdash \{P\} \, C \, \{Q\}$ *using our program logic. Pick any state* $\sigma_1 \in \llbracket P \rrbracket$, *and consider changing the values of any* Hi *data in* σ_1 *to obtain some* $\sigma_2 \in \llbracket P \rrbracket$. *Suppose, in the erasure semantics, we have*

$$\langle \bar{\sigma}_1, C \rangle \xrightarrow{o_1}_* \langle \tau_1, \text{skip} \rangle \qquad and \qquad \langle \bar{\sigma}_2, C \rangle \xrightarrow{o_2}_* \langle \tau_2, \text{skip} \rangle.$$

Then $o_1 = o_2$.

6   Related Work

There are many different systems for reasoning about information flow. We will briefly discuss some of the more closely-related ones here.

Some IFC systems with declassification, such as HiStar [26], Flume [11], and RESIN [25], reason at the operating system or process level, rather than the language level. These systems can support complex security policies, but their formal guarantees suffer due to how coarse-grained they are.

On the language-level side of IFC [18], there are many type systems and program logics that share similarities with our logic.

Amtoft et al. [1] develop a program logic for proving noninterference of a program written in a simple object-oriented language. They use relational assertions of the form "x is independent from high-security data." Such an assertion is equivalent to saying that x contains Lo data in our system. Thus their logic can be used to prove that the final values of low-security data are independent from initial values of high-security data — this is pure noninterference. Note that, unlike our system, theirs does not attempt to reason about declassification. Some other differences between these IFC systems are:

– We allow pointer arithmetic, while they disallow it by using an object-oriented language. Pointer arithmetic adds significant complexity to information flow reasoning. In particular, their system uses a technique similar to our mark_vars function for reasoning about conditional constructs, except that they syntactically check for all locations in both the store and heap that might be modified within the conditional. With the arbitrary pointer arithmetic of our system, it is not possible to syntactically bound which heap locations will be written to, so we require the additional semantic technique described in Section 5 that involves enforcing a side condition on the bisimulation semantics.

– Our model of observable behavior provides some extra leniency in verification. Our system allows bad leaks to happen within the program state, so long as these leaks are not made observable via an output command. In their system (and most other IFC systems), the enforcement mechanism must prevent those leaks within program state from happening in the first place.

Banerjee et al. [3] develop an IFC system that specifies declassification policies through state predicates in basically the same way that we do. For example, they might have a (relational) precondition of "$A(x \geq y)$," saying that two states agree on the truth value of $x \geq y$. This corresponds directly to a precondition of "$x \geq y$" in our system, and security guarantees for the two systems are both stated relative to the precondition. The two systems have very similar goals, but there are a number of significant differences in the basic setup that make the systems quite distinct:

- Their system does not attempt to reason about the program heap at all. They have some high-level discussions about how one might support pointers in their setup, but there is nothing formal.
- Their system enforces noninterference primarily through a type system (rather than a program logic). The declassification policies, specified by something similar to a Hoare triple, are only used at specific points in the program where explicit "declassify" commands are executed. A type system enforces pure noninterference for the rest of the program besides the declassify commands. Their end-to-end security guarantee then talks about how the knowledge of an observer can only increase at those points where a declassify command is executed (a property known in the literature as "gradual release"). Thus their security guarantee for individual declassification commands looks very similar to our version of noninterference, but their end-to-end security guarantee looks quite different. We do not believe that there is any comparable notion of gradual release in our system, as we do not have explicit program points where declassification occurs.
- Because they use a type system, their system must statically pick security labels for each program variable. This means that there is no notion of dynamically propagating labels during execution, nor is there any way to express our novel concept of conditional labels. As a result, the calendar example program of Section 4 would not be verifiable in their system.

Delimited Release [19] is an IFC system that allows certain prespecified expressions (called *escape hatches*) to be declassified. For example, a declassification policy for high-security variable h might say that the expression $h\%2$ should be considered low security. Relaxed Noninterference [12] uses a similar idea, but builds a lattice of semantic declassification policies, rather than syntactic escape hatches — e.g., h would have a policy of $\lambda x \, . \, x\%2$. Our system can easily express any policy from these systems, using a precondition saying that some low-security data is equal to the escape hatch function applied to the secret data. Our strong security guarantee is identical to the formal guarantees of both of these systems, saying that the high-security value will not affect the observable behavior as long as the escape hatch valuation is unchanged.

Relational Hoare Type Theory (RHTT) [15] is a logic framework for verifying information-flow properties. It is based on a highly general relational logic. The system can be used to reason about a wide variety of security-related notions, including declassification, information erasure, and state-dependent access control. While RHTT can be extremely expressive, it seems to achieve different goals than our system. We began with a desire to formally reason about the propagation of security labels through a system, and to specify declassification policies in terms of these labels. Thus the natural choice for us was to use a syntactic representation for labels and explicitly add them into program state. Ideally, we could use these labels to represent different principals, and thus be able to specify interesting policies in a decentralized setting. RHTT, on the other hand, is built around a semantic notion of security labels. Instead of saying that x is Lo, one says that in two corresponding states, x has the same value. This allows policies to be highly expressive, but also can make it quite difficult to understand what a given policy is saying. It is unclear how one should go about representing a decentralized setting in RHTT, where there is interaction between the data of various principals.

Intransitive noninterference [13] is a declassification mechanism whereby certain specific downward flows are allowed in the label lattice. The system formally verifies that a program obeys the explicitly-allowed flows. These special flows are intransitive — e.g., we might allow Alice to declassify data to Bob and Bob to declassify to Charlie, but that does not imply that Alice is allowed to declassify to Charlie. The intransitive noninterference system is used to verify simple imperative programs; their language is basically the same as ours, except without the heap-related commands. One idea for future work is to generalize our state predicate P into an action G that precisely describes the transformation that a program is allowed to make on the state. If we implemented this idea, it would be easy to embed the intransitive noninterference system. The action G would specify exactly which special flows are allowed (e.g., the data's label can be changed from Alice to Bob or from Bob to Charlie, but not from Alice to Charlie directly). Ideally, we would have a formal noninterference theorem in terms of G that would give the same result as the formal guarantee in [13].

Another related system is Chong and Myers' lambda calculus with downgrading policies [5]. This system shares a similar goal to ours: to provide an end-to-end security guarantee relative to declassification policies. In their system, the language contains explicit declassify commands, and certain conditions (specified via the policy syntax) must be verified at the point of declassification. The actual method for verifying these conditions is left as a parameter of the system. While both of our systems prove an end-to-end guarantee, these guarantees seem to be rather different. Theirs provides a road map describing how a Hi piece of data may end up affecting observable behavior, while ours specifies which values that piece of data could have in order to affect observable behavior. It is unclear how either guarantee would be described in the other system.

Self-composition [4] is an approach to noninterference reasoning that essentially converts relational predicates into unary ones. The fundamental idea is that we can prove a program C is noninterfering by making a copy of it, C', giving all variables in C' a fresh name, and then executing the composed program $C; C'$. A pre/postcondition for $C; C'$ of $x = x'$, for example, will then effectively say that x is a low-security location. Our system, just like the self-composition approach, is based on the desire to deal with unary predicates rather than relational ones. Unlike the self-composition approach, however, we use a syntactic notion of labels, and we do not perform any syntactic translations on the program. Additionally, it is unclear whether the self-composition approach can be used for programs that do odd things with pointer arithmetic and aliasing. Indeed, in [4], there is an explicitly-stated assumption that the address values of pointers do not affect the control flow of programs.

All of the language-based IFC systems mentioned so far, including our own system, use static reasoning. There are also many dynamic IFC systems (e.g., [2,10,22,24]) that attempt to enforce security of a program during execution. Because dynamic systems are analyzing information flow at runtime, they will incur some overhead cost in execution time. Static IFC systems need not necessarily incur extra costs. Indeed, our final noninterference theorem uses the erasure semantics, meaning that there is no overhead whatsoever.

Finally, Sabelfeld and Sands [21] define a road map for analyzing declassification policies in terms of four dimensions: *who* can declassify, *what* can be declassified, *when* can declassification occur, and *where* can it occur. Our notion of declassification can talk about any of these dimensions if we construct the precondition in the right way. The *who* dimension is most naturally handled via the label lattice, but one could also imagine representing principals explicitly in the program state and reasoning about them in the logic. The *what* dimension is handled by default, as the program state contains all of the data to be declassified. The *when* dimension can easily be reasoned about by including a time field in the state. Similarly, the *where* dimension can be reasoned about by including an explicit program counter in the state.

7   Conclusion

In this paper, we described a novel program logic for reasoning about information flow in a low-level language with pointer arithmetic. Our system uses an instrumented operational semantics to statically reason about the propagation of syntactic labels. Our logic can reason about labels conditioned on state predicates — as far as we are aware, the example program of Section 4 cannot be verified in any other IFC system that uses syntactic labels.

In the future, we hope to extend our work to handle termination-sensitivity, dynamic memory allocation, nondeterminism, and concurrency. We also plan to develop some automation and apply our logic to actual operating system code.

References

1. Amtoft, T., Bandhakavi, S., Banerjee, A.: A logic for information flow in object-oriented programs. In: POPL, pp. 91–102 (2006)
2. Austin, T.H., Flanagan, C.: Efficient purely-dynamic information flow analysis. In: PLAS, pp. 113–124 (2009)
3. Banerjee, A., Naumann, D.A., Rosenberg, S.: Expressive declassification policies and modular static enforcement. In: IEEE Symposium on Security and Privacy, pp. 339–353 (2008)
4. Barthe, G., D'Argenio, P.R., Rezk, T.: Secure information flow by self-composition. In: CSFW, pp. 100–114 (2004)
5. Chong, S., Myers, A.C.: Security policies for downgrading. In: ACM Conference on Computer and Communications Security, pp. 198–209 (2004)

6. Costanzo, D., Shao, Z.: A separation logic for enforcing declarative information flow control policies. Technical report, Dept. of Computer Science, Yale University, New Haven, CT (January 2014), http://flint.cs.yale.edu/publications/ddifc.html
7. Denning, D.E., Denning, P.J.: Certification of programs for secure information flow. Commun. ACM 20(7), 504–513 (1977)
8. Heintze, N., Riecke, J.G.: The slam calculus: Programming with secrecy and integrity. In: POPL, pp. 365–377 (1998)
9. Hoare, C.A.R.: An axiomatic basis for computer programming. Commun. ACM 12(10), 576–580 (1969)
10. Hritcu, C., Greenberg, M., Karel, B., Pierce, B.C., Morrisett, G.: All your ifcexception are belong to US. In: IEEE Symposium on Security and Privacy, pp. 3–17 (2013)
11. Krohn, M.N., Yip, A., Brodsky, M.Z., Cliffer, N., Kaashoek, M.F., Kohler, E., Morris, R.: Information flow control for standard os abstractions. In: SOSP, pp. 321–334 (2007)
12. Li, P., Zdancewic, S.: Downgrading policies and relaxed noninterference. In: POPL, pp. 158–170 (2005)
13. Mantel, H., Sands, D.: Controlled declassification based on intransitive noninterference. In: Chin, W.-N. (ed.) APLAS 2004. LNCS, vol. 3302, pp. 129–145. Springer, Heidelberg (2004)
14. Myers, A.C., Liskov, B.: A decentralized model for information flow control. In: SOSP, pp. 129–142 (1997)
15. Nanevski, A., Banerjee, A., Garg, D.: Verification of information flow and access control policies with dependent types. In: IEEE Symposium on Security and Privacy, pp. 165–179 (2011)
16. O'Hearn, P.W., Reynolds, J.C., Yang, H.: Local reasoning about programs that alter data structures. In: Fribourg, L. (ed.) CSL 2001. LNCS, vol. 2142, pp. 1–19. Springer, Heidelberg (2001)
17. Reynolds, J.C.: Separation logic: A logic for shared mutable data structures. In: LICS, pp. 55–74 (2002)
18. Sabelfeld, A., Myers, A.C.: Language-based information-flow security. IEEE Journal on Selected Areas in Communications 21(1), 5–19 (2003)
19. Sabelfeld, A., Myers, A.C.: A model for delimited information release. In: Futatsugi, K., Mizoguchi, F., Yonezaki, N. (eds.) ISSS 2003. LNCS, vol. 3233, pp. 174–191. Springer, Heidelberg (2004)
20. Sabelfeld, A., Sands, D.: A per model of secure information flow in sequential programs. In: Swierstra, S.D. (ed.) ESOP 1999. LNCS, vol. 1576, pp. 40–58. Springer, Heidelberg (1999)
21. Sabelfeld, A., Sands, D.: Declassification: Dimensions and principles. Journal of Computer Security 17(5), 517–548 (2009)
22. Stefan, D., Russo, A., Mitchell, J.C., Mazières, D.: Flexible dynamic information flow control in haskell. In: Haskell, pp. 95–106 (2011)
23. Volpano, D.M., Smith, G.: A type-based approach to program security. In: Bidoit, M., Dauchet, M. (eds.) CAAP 1997, FASE 1997, and TAPSOFT 1997. LNCS, vol. 1214, pp. 607–621. Springer, Heidelberg (1997)
24. Yang, J., Yessenov, K., Solar-Lezama, A.: A language for automatically enforcing privacy policies. In: POPL, pp. 85–96 (2012)
25. Yip, A., Wang, X., Zeldovich, N., Kaashoek, M.F.: Improving application security with data flow assertions. In: SOSP, pp. 291–304 (2009)
26. Zeldovich, N., Boyd-Wickizer, S., Kohler, E., Mazières, D.: Making information flow explicit in histar. In: OSDI, pp. 263–278 (2006)

Defining and Enforcing Referential Security

Jed Liu and Andrew C. Myers

Department of Computer Science
Cornell University
Ithaca, New York, United States
{liujed,andru}@cs.cornell.edu

Abstract. Referential integrity, which guarantees that named resources can be accessed when referenced, is an important property for reliability and security. In distributed systems, however, the attempt to provide referential integrity can itself lead to security vulnerabilities that are not currently well understood. This paper identifies three kinds of *referential security* vulnerabilities related to the referential integrity of distributed, persistent information. Security conditions corresponding to the absence of these vulnerabilities are formalized. A language model is used to capture the key aspects of programming distributed systems with named, persistent resources in the presence of an adversary. The referential security of distributed systems is proved to be enforced by a new type system.

1 Introduction

To make programming manageable, distributed systems are increasingly being implemented using high-level languages and libraries that present distributed resources as language-level objects. This approach goes back to research platforms such as Argus [14], Emerald [4], and Network Objects [3], but is now applied widely in commercial programming using middleware platforms such as CORBA [19], in more recent object-relational mapping (ORM) systems such as Hibernate [10] and other Java Persistence API (JPA) [6] implementations, and in modern JavaScript ORM libraries [5].

Distributed systems naturally cross trust domains; it is often why they are distributed in the first place. Running a program on a federated platform composed of differently trusted distributed nodes creates security vulnerabilities that are not immediately apparent at the high level of abstraction at which the programmer is operating. Some of these vulnerabilities have been addressed by prior work; for example, the Fabric system [15] provides a high-level, Java-like abstraction for distributed programming, while using information-flow control to enforce both confidentiality and integrity properties.

In this paper, we identify three new security goals relating to the security of references that cross trust domains. Cross-domain references are a common feature not only of high-level distributed programming models, but of distributed systems in general. For example, web pages hyperlink to other pages, and relational-database tuples can contain foreign keys referring to other tuples. Regardless of the kind of system, security and reliability vulnerabilities are created when references cross trust boundaries, because they introduce dependencies between different parts of the system. This paper identifies some of these *referential vulnerabilities,* formally characterizes them, and explores a language-based approach to modeling, analyzing, and preventing them.

M. Abadi and S. Kremer (Eds.): POST 2014, LNCS 8414, pp. 199–219, 2014.

The first goal is *referential integrity*. A system has referential integrity if a reference can be relied upon to continue pointing to the same object. Referential integrity fails when that object is deleted while the reference still exists, resulting in a *dangling reference*, or when the reference points to a different object altogether.

Referential integrity appears in many guises. We use the term in a more general sense than in the database literature, where referential integrity is an important aspect of the relational model [7]. For example, the web lacks referential integrity: the referent of a hyperlink can be deleted, leading to the familiar "404" error. Referential integrity is also an important property for programming languages. In languages such as C that lack referential integrity, dangling pointers are a serious problem. In other languages, automatic garbage collection reclaims memory while preserving referential integrity.

While absolute referential integrity sounds ideal, it cannot be achieved in a federated system: referential integrity is necessarily limited by the trustworthiness of the node (or nodes) storing the referent object. Therefore, this paper generalizes referential integrity to systems where nodes are partially trusted.

Our second goal is *intentional persistence*. With referential integrity, a reference to an object is a promise that the object will not move or disappear: it must be persistent. Therefore, reachability implies persistence, as in various object-oriented databases (e.g., [1, 17]) and in marshaling mechanisms such as Java serialization. However, if all reachable objects are persistent, objects can become *accidentally persistent* because they are unexpectedly reachable. This can inflate resource consumption, leading to poor performance and system failure. This problem is familiar to those who have used Java serialization. Intentional persistence entails the absence of accidental persistence.

The third goal of this paper is immunity against *storage attacks*. Referential integrity prevents discarding reachable objects. But this gives an adversary a means to mount a denial-of-service attack. The adversary creates references to objects intended to be discarded, preventing reclamation and perhaps exhausting available storage space.

This paper formalizes these three goals as *referential security properties*, corresponding to the absence of referential vulnerabilities. This is done in the context of a simple programming language that captures the key elements of distributed programming in a federated system with persistent information and pointers. A novel type system is defined and is proved to enforce these security properties. Details of these proofs are found in an accompanying technical report [16].

The rest of this paper is structured as follows. Section 2 describes the language model. Section 3 presents security policies for reasoning about the three vulnerabilities. Section 4 introduces the programming language $\lambda_{persist}$, which abstractly describes distributed programming with persistence and distrust. The language is defined formally in Sections 5 and 6. Section 7 defines the adversary model. Section 8 formalizes the desired security conditions, and sketches the proofs that the type system of $\lambda_{persist}$ soundly enforces them. Related work is discussed in Section 9, and Section 10 concludes.

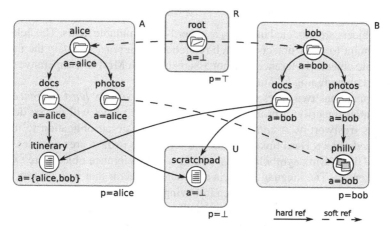

Fig. 1. Directory example

2   Language Model

2.1   Modeling Distributed Computing as a Language

We model distributed computing using a core programming language that we call $\lambda_{persist}$. In $\lambda_{persist}$, persistence, distribution, and communication are implicit but are constrained by policy annotations. Programs in $\lambda_{persist}$ are assumed to be mapped onto distributed host nodes in some way that agrees with these annotations. This mapping could be done manually by the programmer, or automatically by a compiler, à la Jif/split [23].

This implicit translation to a distributed implementation means that some apparently ordinary source-level operations may be implemented using distributed communication and computation. For example, function application may be implemented as a remote procedure call. Similarly, following references at the language level may involve communication between nodes to fetch referenced objects.

Although the concrete mapping from source-level constructs onto host nodes is left implicit, we can nevertheless faithfully evaluate the security of source-level computations. The key is to ensure that the system is secure under *any* possible concrete mapping that is consistent with the policy annotations in the source program. That is, any given computation or information might be located on any host that satisfies the source-level security constraints. A technical contribution of this paper is to develop an effective system of such source-level constraints, expressed as a type system.

Although we refer to $\lambda_{persist}$ as a source language, little attempt is made to make it congenial to actual programming. In particular, the type annotations introduced would be onerous in practice. They could be inferred automatically using standard constraint-solving techniques for inequations over $\mathcal{L}$, but we leave this to future work. One can view the type system as describing a program (or system) analysis, and the formal results of this paper as a demonstration that this analysis achieves its security goals.

2.2   Objects and References

Persistent objects are modeled in $\lambda_{persist}$ as records with mutable fields. The fields of an object can point to other objects through references. References contain the names of these mutable objects. References are not assignable as in ML [18]; imperative updates are achieved by assigning to mutable fields.

The language has two types of references: hard and soft. A *hard reference* is one with referential integrity: a promise that the referenced object will not be destroyed if its host is trustworthy. A *soft reference* does not create an obligation to maintain the referenced object. Hard links in Unix and references in Java are examples of hard references. URLs, Unix symbolic links, and Java SoftReference objects are examples of soft references. The language models a garbage collector that may destroy objects reachable only via soft references. When following a soft reference or an untrusted hard reference, a program must be prepared to handle a failure in case the referenced object no longer exists.

This simple data model can represent many different kinds of systems, such as distributed objects, databases, and the web. The shared directory structure shown in Figure 1 serves as a running example. Alice and Bob are traveling together and are using the system to share photos and itineraries. The root directory is kept on a host R. Alice and Bob keep their directory objects on their own hosts, A and B, respectively. To share sightseeing ideas, they use a common scratchpad stored on host U. Solid arrows in the figure represent hard references, and dashed arrows are soft references. The a and p annotations are policies, which we now explain.

3   Policies for Persistent Programming

3.1   Persistence Policies

In a federated system, referential integrity cannot be absolute, because the referenced object may be located on an untrusted, perhaps maliciously controlled, host machine. Therefore, referential integrity must be constrained by the degree of trust in the referenced host. This constraint is expressed by assigning each object a *persistence policy* describing how much it can be trusted to remain in existence.

The precise form of the persistence policy is left abstract in this paper. Persistence policies p are assumed to be drawn from a bounded lattice $(\mathcal{L}, \preccurlyeq, \perp, \top)$ of *policy levels*. If $p_1 \preccurlyeq p_2$ for two persistence policies p_1 and p_2, then p_2 describes objects that are at least as persistent as those described by p_1.

Persistence policies have a simple, concrete interpretation. Absent replication, objects are located only on host nodes that are trusted to enforce their persistence policies, so a persistence policy p corresponds to a set of sufficiently trusted host nodes H_p. Therefore, if $p_1 \preccurlyeq p_2$, then p_2 must be enforceable by a smaller set of hosts: $H_{p_1} \supseteq H_{p_2}$. In fact, it is reasonable to think of a policy p as simply a set of hosts.

In Figure 1, the root directory has persistence policy $\top$, which only host R is trusted to enforce. Alice has a user directory and a persistence policy alice. While R is trusted to enforce this policy, she has chosen to use her own host A. Similarly, Bob's directory is on host B. The shared scratchpad is kept on an untrusted host U, which can only enforce the persistence policy $\perp$.

Persistence policies are integrated into the type system of $\lambda_{persist}$. The type of an object reference includes a lower bound on the persistence policy of its referent; the type system ensures that the persistence of an object is always at least as high as that of any reference pointing to it. Programs can therefore use the persistence of a reference to determine whether the reference can be trusted to be intact. This rule enables sound reasoning about persistence and referential integrity as the graph of objects is traversed.

For example, in Figure 1, while Alice and Bob both have a hard reference to the scratchpad, they must be prepared for a persistence failure when using the references. The type system of $\lambda_{persist}$ will ensure their code handles such a failure. Any reference to the scratchpad must have a type with $\perp$ persistence, because it can be no higher than the $\perp$ persistence of the scratchpad itself.

Whether a hard reference can be trusted to be intact depends on context. In Figure 1, Alice and Bob both have a hard reference to the itinerary. Because Alice trusts her own persistence level, if either reference is typed with alice persistence, then she can use it without worrying about a persistence failure. However, unless Bob trusts Alice, he would need to be prepared for such a failure when using the references.

Soft references also have types with persistence levels, and hence might be trusted. Trusted soft references can be promoted to trusted hard references. Therefore, soft references are distinct from untrusted hard references.

In $\lambda_{persist}$, persistence is defined not by reachability, but by policy. This resolves by fiat one of the three problems identified earlier: accidental persistence. Accidents are avoided by allowing programmers to express their intention explicitly. An object that is not intended to be persistent is prevented from being treated as a persistent object.

3.2   Characterizing the Adversary

Security involves an adversary, and is always predicated on assumptions about the power of the adversary. In the kind of decentralized, federated system under consideration, the adversary is assumed to control some of the nodes in the system.

Different participants in a distributed system may have their own viewpoints about who the adversary is, yet all participants need security assurance. Therefore, a given adversary is modeled as a point α in the lattice of persistence policy levels. In the host-set interpretation of persistence policies, α defines the set of trusted hosts that the adversary does not control. The adversary is assumed to have the power to delete (i.e., violate the persistence of) an object if its persistence is not α or higher (i.e., $\alpha \not\sqsubseteq p$), because the object might be stored at a host node controlled by the adversary. Other actions by the adversary are modeled by special evaluation rules (see Section 7).

The formal results for the security properties enforced by $\lambda_{persist}$ treat the adversary as an arbitrary parameter. Therefore, these properties hold for any adversary.

3.3   Storage Attacks and Authority Policies

We introduce the idea of *storage attacks*, in which a malicious adversary tries to prevent reclamation of object storage by exploiting the enforcement of referential integrity. For example, in Figure 1, Bob has shared with Alice an album containing the photos he has so far taken during their trip. Bob does not consider the album to be private, so others may create references to his album, as Alice has done. However, an adversary that creates a hard reference to this album can prevent Bob from reclaiming its storage.

To prevent such storage attacks, we ensure that hard references can be created only in sufficiently trusted code. We introduce *creation authority* to abstractly define this power to create new references. This is the only action requiring some form of authority in this paper, so for brevity, we refer to creation authority simply as *authority*.

Like persistence policies, authority policies a are assumed to be drawn from a bounded lattice $(\mathcal{L}, \preccurlyeq)$ of policy levels. Without loss of expressive power, they are assumed to be drawn from the same lattice as persistence policies. Authority prevents storage attacks because hard references can only be created to objects whose authority policy a is less than or equal to the authority a_p of the process; that is, $a \preccurlyeq a_p$.

A hard reference is a reference that should have referential integrity, so creating hard references requires authority. The adversary is assumed to have some ability to create hard references, described by its authority level α. Soft references do not keep an object alive, so no creation authority is required to create a soft reference.

In Figure 1, the root directory has the authority policy $\bot$, so anyone can create a hard reference to it. Bob's philly album is large, so he has given it the authority policy bob; only he can create hard references that prevent the album from being deleted. Therefore, Alice's reference to the album must be soft. Alice has drafted an itinerary, giving it the authority policy {alice, bob} to indicate she will persist the document for as long as Bob requires. Bob's reference to the itinerary, therefore, can be hard.

It may sound odd to posit control over creation of references. But a reference with referential integrity is a contract between the referrer and the referent. For example, the node containing the referent is obligated to notify the referrer if the object moves. Entering into a contract requires agreement by both parties, so it is reasonable for the node containing the referent to refuse the creation of a reference.

3.4 Integrity

Thus far, the powers of the adversary include creating references to low-authority objects and destroying objects with low persistence. Because the adversary may control some nodes, the adversary can also change the state of objects located at these nodes. This may in turn affect code running on nodes not controlled by the adversary, if the adversary supplies inputs to that code, or if it affects the decision to run that code.

Integrity policies describe limitations on these effects of the adversary. Integrity policies w are drawn from a bounded lattice $(\mathcal{L}, \preccurlyeq)$ of policy levels; without loss of expressive power, it is assumed to be the same lattice as for persistence and authority policies. In fact, we can think of the persistence and authority levels of an object as the integrity of other, implicit attributes of the object. For persistence, this implicit attribute is the existence of the object itself. For authority, the attribute is the set of incoming references to the object. This unifying view of different policies as different aspects of integrity explains why all three kinds of policies can come from the same lattice.

The ordering $\preccurlyeq$ corresponds to increasing integrity. If $w_1 \preccurlyeq w_2$, an information flow from level w_2 to w_1 would be secure: more-trusted information would be affecting

		Integrity	Authority	Persistence	Set of hosts
$\top$ "High"		Trusted, Untainted: No one can affect data	"superuser": No one can make a hard reference	Persistent: No one can delete object	No host nodes
$\bot$ "Low"		Untrusted, Tainted: Anyone can affect data	"anyone": Anyone can make a hard reference	Transient: Anyone can delete object	All host nodes

Fig. 2. Interpretations of the extremal policy labels

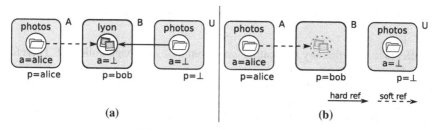

(a)   **(b)**

Fig. 3. Authority affects integrity of dereferences. Alice is following her soft reference to the lyon album. An adversary can affect the outcome of the dereference, because the album has low authority. (a) The untrusted host U has a hard reference preventing lyon from being garbage collected; Alice's dereference succeeds. (b) Host U has removed its hard reference, allowing lyon to be garbage collected; Alice's dereference fails.

less-trusted information.[1] In $\lambda_{persist}$, each variable and each field of an object has an associated integrity level describing how trusted it is, and hence how powerful an adversary must be to damage it. The integrity of a reference is the integrity of the field or variable it was read from.

Figure 2 summarizes the interpretation of the three kinds of policies.

3.5   Integrity of Dereferences and Garbage Collection

An adversary can directly affect the result of a dereference in two ways. First, if the reference has low integrity, the adversary can alter it to point to a different object. Second, if the referent has low persistence, the adversary can delete it. Therefore, the integrity of any dereference can be no higher than the integrity and persistence annotations on the reference. In Figure 1, if Alice follows the reference from her docs directory to the scratchpad, she obtains an untrusted result; the untrusted host U influences the result by choosing whether to delete the scratchpad object.

More subtly, the adversary can manipulate hard references to influence the garbage collector, and thereby *indirectly* affect the result of a dereference. For example, in Figure 3a, Alice is following her soft reference to Bob's lyon album. Bob has marked lyon as only requiring low authority, allowing the untrusted, adversarial host U to create a

---

[1] This ordering is the opposite of the "upside-down" ordering typically seen in work on information-flow security [2].

Variables x, y $\in$ Var		Policy levels	$w, a, p, \ell \in \mathcal{L}$
Memory locations m $\in$ Mem		PC labels	$pc ::= w$
Labeled record types $S ::= \{\overrightarrow{x_i : \tau_i}\}_s$		Storage labels	$s ::= (a, p)$
Labeled ref types $R ::= \{\overrightarrow{x_i : \tau_i}\}_r$		Reference labels	$r ::= (a^+, a^-, p)$
Base types $b ::= \text{bool} \mid \tau_1 \xrightarrow{pc} \tau_2 \mid R \mid \text{soft } R$		Types	$\tau ::= b_w \mid \mathbf{1}$

$$\text{Values } v, u ::= x \mid \text{true} \mid \text{false} \mid * \mid m^S \mid \text{soft } m^S \mid \lambda(x : \tau)[pc].e \; (\mid \bot_p)$$
$$\text{Terms } e ::= v \mid v_1\, v_2 \mid \text{if } v_1 \text{ then } e_2 \text{ else } e_3 \mid \{\overrightarrow{x_i = v_i}\}^S \mid v.x$$
$$\mid v_1.x := v_2 \mid \text{soft } e \mid e_1 \parallel e_2 \mid \text{exists } v \text{ as } x : e_1 \text{ else } e_2 \mid \text{let } x = e_1 \text{ in } e_2$$

Fig. 4. Syntax of $\lambda^0_{persist}$. Parenthesized productions only appear at run time.

hard reference, and thereby preventing lyon from being garbage-collected. Therefore, Alice's dereference must succeed.

However, in Figure 3b, the adversary U has removed its reference. Subsequently, lyon has been garbage-collected, and Alice's dereference fails. The adversary has indirectly affected the outcome of the dereference. To account for this, the integrity of Alice's dereference must be no higher than the authority required by lyon.

4   Types for Persistent Programming

To formalize the ideas presented in the previous section, we introduce the $\lambda_{persist}$ language, an extension to the simply typed lambda calculus. Figure 4 gives part of the formal syntax of $\lambda_{persist}$. Its type system prevents referential vulnerabilities by integrating policies for persistence, authority, and integrity into types. Accidental persistence is prevented because persistence is determined by policies expressing the programmer's intent, rather than by reachability. Referential integrity is maintained by a $\lambda_{persist}$ program with respect to a particular adversary if following hard references whose persistence and integrity are above the level of the adversary never leads to an object that has been destroyed by the adversary or garbage-collected. Storage attacks are prevented if the adversary is unable to change the set of high-authority objects that are reachable through hard references.

4.1   Labels

We assume a bounded lattice $(\mathcal{L}, \leqslant, \bot, \top)$ of *policy levels*, from which integrity (w), authority (a), and persistence policies (p) are drawn.

Objects and reference values are annotated with *storage labels* consisting of a creation authority policy and a persistence policy. All non-unit types τ consist of a base type b along with an integrity policy annotation w; fields and variables thereby acquire integrity policies, because they are part of their types. Objects do not have their own integrity labels because all of their state is in their fields, which do have labels.

The program-counter label pc [9] is an integrity level indicating the degree to which the program's control flow has been tainted by untrusted data. This label restricts the side effects of code.

4.2 Example

Suppose we want to create a hierarchical, distributed directory structure, such as in Figure 1. Each directory maps names to either strings, representing ordinary files, or to other directories, and contains a reference to its parent directory (elided in the figure). To faithfully model ordinary filesystems, directories higher in the hierarchy should be more persistent: if they are destroyed, so is everything below.

A fully general directory structure would require augmenting $\lambda_{persist}$ with recursive and dependent types; for simplicity, these features have been omitted from $\lambda_{persist}$ because they do not appear to add interesting issues. However, we can capture the security of a general directory structure by using $\lambda_{persist}$ records to build a fixed-depth directory structure with a fixed set of entry names for each directory.

4.3 Modeling Objects and References

The security policies of $\lambda_{persist}$ are about objects and references to them. Therefore, $\lambda_{persist}$ extends the lambda calculus with records that represent the content of objects. The record $\{\overrightarrow{x_i = v_i}\}$ comprises a set of fields $\overrightarrow{x_i}$ with corresponding values $\overrightarrow{v_i}$. Records are not values in the language; instead, they are accessed via references m^S, where m is the identity of the object and $S = \{\overrightarrow{x_i : \tau_i}\}_s$ gives its base record type. The *storage label* s is a pair (a, p). The *authority label* a is an upper bound on the authority required to create a new reference to the referent object.

References to objects have labeled reference types $\{\overrightarrow{x_i : \tau_i}\}_r$. A reference label r is a triple (a^+, a^-, p) that gives upper and lower bounds on the authority required by the referent, and a lower bound on the persistence of the referent. The *upper authority label* a^+ restricts reference copying to prevent storage attacks. The *lower authority label* a^- prevents the adversary from exploiting garbage collection to damage integrity (Section 3.5), by tainting the integrity of dereferencing soft references.

4.4 Modeling Distributed Systems

The goal of the $\lambda_{persist}$ language is to model a distributed system in which code is running at different host nodes. A single program written in $\lambda_{persist}$ is intended to represent such a system. The key to modeling distributed, federated computation faithfully is that different parts of the program can be annotated with different integrity labels, representing the trust that has been placed in that part of the code. To model a set of computations (subprograms $\overrightarrow{e_i}$) executing at different nodes, the individual computations are composed in parallel ($e_1 \parallel \cdots \parallel e_n$) into a single $\lambda_{persist}$ program.

From the viewpoint of a given principal in the system, code with a low integrity label, relative to that principal, can be replaced by any code at all. For the purposes of evaluating the security of the system, this code is in effect erased and replaced by the adversary. Therefore the single-program representation faithfully models a distributed system containing an adversary.

5   Accidental Persistence and Storage Attacks

We present $\lambda_{persist}$ in two phases. In this section, we present $\lambda^0_{persist}$, a simplified subset of $\lambda_{persist}$ that prevents accidental persistence and storage attacks.

5.1   Syntax of $\lambda^0_{persist}$

Figure 4 gives the syntax of $\lambda^0_{persist}$. The names x and y range over variable names Var; m ranges over a space of memory addresses Mem; w, a, p, and ℓ range over the lattice $\mathcal{L}$ of policy levels; and s and r range over the space of storage labels $\mathcal{L}^2$ and reference labels $\mathcal{L}^3$, respectively.

Types in $\lambda^0_{persist}$ consist of base types with an integrity label (b_w), and the unit type $\mathbf{1}$. Base types include booleans, functions, and two kinds of references to mutable records: hard (R) and soft (soft R). The metavariable R denotes a labeled reference type.

The type $\tau_1 \xrightarrow{pc} \tau_2$ is a function type with a pc annotation that is a lower bound on the pc label of the caller. It gives an upper bound on the authority level of references the function creates and on the authority level of references held in the closure environment.

Values include variables x, booleans true and false, the unit value $*$, record-typed memory locations (references) m^S, soft references soft m^S, and functions $\lambda(x{:}\tau)[pc].e$. The pc component of a function $\lambda(x{:}\tau)[pc].e$ has the same meaning as that in function types. At run time, p-persistence failures $\perp_p$ can also appear as values.

Most terms are standard. The unusual features are record constructors $\{\overrightarrow{x_i = v_i}\}^S$, soft references soft e, parallel composition $e_1 \parallel e_2$, and soft-reference tests exists v as x: e_1 else e_2.

5.2   Example

Returning to the directory example in Figure 1, Bob can add to the itinerary with the code below. It starts at the root of the directory structure, traverses down to the itinerary, and invokes an add method to add a museum.

```
let home = root.bob
in exists home as bob:
        let docs = bob.docs
        in docs.itinerary.add "Rodin Museum"
      else:  ...
```

The garbage collector may have snapped the soft reference home to Bob's home directory, so exists is used to determine whether the reference is still valid. If so, the body of the exists is evaluated with bob bound to a hard reference to the home directory.[2] (This reference can be created because the pc label at this point has sufficient creation authority.) The second select expression, bob.docs, dereferences the hard reference.

---

[2] To avoid a race with the garbage collector, an implementation of exists should first optimistically create the hard reference, then check its validity before exposing it to the program.

$$[\text{LET}] \quad \frac{\forall p.\ v \neq \bot_p}{\langle \text{let } x = v \text{ in } e, M\rangle \xrightarrow{e} \langle e\{v/x\}, M\rangle}$$

$$[\text{CREATE}] \quad \frac{m = \text{newloc}(M)}{\left\langle \{\overrightarrow{x_i = v_i}\}^S, M\right\rangle \xrightarrow{e} \left\langle m^S, M[m^S \mapsto \{\overrightarrow{x_i = v_i}\}]\right\rangle}$$

$$\begin{bmatrix}\text{PARALLEL-}\\\text{RESULT}\end{bmatrix} \quad \langle v_1 \| v_2, M\rangle \xrightarrow{e} \langle *, M\rangle \qquad [\text{SELECT}] \quad \frac{M(m^S) = \{\overrightarrow{x_i = v_i}\}}{\left\langle m^S.x_c, M\right\rangle \xrightarrow{e} \langle v_c, M\rangle}$$

$$[\text{ASSIGN}] \quad \frac{M(m^S) \neq \bot \qquad \forall p.\ v \neq \bot_p}{\left\langle m^S.x_c := v, M\right\rangle \xrightarrow{e} \left\langle *, M[m^S.x_c \mapsto v]\right\rangle}$$

$$\begin{bmatrix}\text{DANGLE-}\\\text{SELECT}\end{bmatrix} \frac{M(m^S) = \bot \quad p = \text{persist}(m^S)}{\left\langle m^S.x_c, M\right\rangle \xrightarrow{e} \langle \bot_p, M\rangle} \quad \begin{bmatrix}\text{DANGLE-}\\\text{ASSIGN}\end{bmatrix} \frac{M(m^S) = \bot \quad p = \text{persist}(m^S)}{\left\langle m^S.x_c := v, M\right\rangle \xrightarrow{e} \langle \bot_p, M\rangle}$$

$$\begin{bmatrix}\text{EXISTS-}\\\text{TRUE}\end{bmatrix} \frac{M(m^S) \neq \bot}{\left\langle \text{exists soft } m^S \text{ as } x : e_1 \text{ else } e_2, M\right\rangle \xrightarrow{e} \left\langle e_1\{m^S/x\}, M\right\rangle}$$

$$\begin{bmatrix}\text{EXISTS-}\\\text{FALSE}\end{bmatrix} \frac{M(m^S) = \bot}{\left\langle \text{exists soft } m^S \text{ as } x : e_1 \text{ else } e_2, M\right\rangle \xrightarrow{e} \langle e_2, M\rangle}$$

Evaluation contexts

$E ::= \text{soft } [\cdot] \mid \text{let } x = [\cdot] \text{ in } e \mid [\cdot] \| e \mid e \| [\cdot]$

$$\begin{bmatrix}\text{FAIL-}\\\text{PROP}\end{bmatrix} \quad \begin{array}{c}\langle F[\bot_p], M\rangle \xrightarrow{e} \langle \bot_p, M\rangle \\ F ::= \text{soft } [\cdot] \mid \text{let } x = [\cdot] \text{ in } e\end{array}$$

$$[\text{PROG-STEP}] \quad \frac{\langle e, M\rangle \xrightarrow{e} \langle e', M'\rangle}{\langle e, M\rangle \rightarrow \langle e', M'\rangle} \qquad [\text{GC}] \quad \frac{\text{gc}(G, \langle e, M\rangle)}{\langle e, M\rangle \rightarrow \langle e, M[G \mapsto \bot]\rangle}$$

Fig. 5. Small-step operational semantics for nonadversarial execution of $\lambda^0_{persist}$. Rules that are standard have been elided.

$$[\text{S1}] \quad \frac{n > m}{\vdash \{x_1 : \tau_1, \ldots, x_n : \tau_n\}_r \leq \{x_1 : \tau_1, \ldots, x_m : \tau_m\}_r} \qquad [\text{S2}] \quad \frac{\vdash R_1 \leq R_2}{\vdash \text{soft } R_1 \leq \text{soft } R_2}$$

$$[\text{S3}] \quad \frac{\vdash b_1 \leq b_2 \quad \vdash w_2 \preccurlyeq w_1}{\vdash (b_1)_{w_1} \leq (b_2)_{w_2}} \quad [\text{S4}] \quad \frac{\vdash \tau_2 \leq \tau_1 \quad \vdash \tau_1' \leq \tau_2' \quad \vdash pc_1 \preccurlyeq pc_2}{\vdash \tau_1 \xrightarrow{pc_1} \tau_1' \leq \tau_2 \xrightarrow{pc_2} \tau_2'}$$

$$[\text{S5}] \quad \frac{\vdash a_1^+ \preccurlyeq a_2^+ \quad \vdash a_2^- \preccurlyeq a_1^- \quad \vdash p_2 \preccurlyeq p_1}{\vdash \{\overrightarrow{x_i : \tau_i}\}_{(a_1^+, a_1^-, p_1)} \leq \{\overrightarrow{x_i : \tau_i}\}_{(a_2^+, a_2^-, p_2)}}$$

Fig. 6. Subtyping rules for $\lambda^0_{persist}$

5.3 Operational Semantics of $\lambda^0_{persist}$

Figure 5 gives the small-step operational semantics of $\lambda^0_{persist}$, omitting standard rules. The notation $e\{v/x\}$ denotes capture-avoiding substitution of value v for variable x in expression e. A failed or garbage-collected memory location contains value $\bot$. Most of the operational semantics rules are straightforward, but a few deserve more explanation.

Let M represent a memory: a finite partial map from typed memory locations m^S to closed record values. Let $\langle e, M\rangle$ be a system configuration. A small evaluation step is a transition from $\langle e, M\rangle$ to another configuration $\langle e', M'\rangle$, written $\langle e, M\rangle \rightarrow \langle e', M'\rangle$.

Let $\mathsf{locs}(e)$ represent the set of locations appearing explicitly in e. A memory M is well-formed only if every address m appears at most once in $\mathsf{dom}(M)$, and for any location m^S in $\mathsf{dom}(M)$, $\mathsf{locs}(M(m^S)) \subseteq \mathsf{dom}(M)$. A configuration $\langle e, M \rangle$ is well-formed only if M is well-formed, $\mathsf{locs}(e) \subseteq \mathsf{dom}(M)$, and e has no free variables.

Though the operational semantics refer to complete record types, only their persistence labels are needed at run time. These labels are only used to determine the level of persistence failure that occurs when dereferencing a dangling reference (rules DANGLE-SELECT and DANGLE-ASSIGN), so run-time overhead should be small.

The record constructor $\{\overrightarrow{x_i = v_i}\}^S$ (rule CREATE) creates a new memory location m^S to hold the record. The component S specifies the base type and storage label of the record. The storage label governs at what nodes the object can be created. The function $\mathsf{newloc}(M)$ deterministically generates a fresh memory location.

The field-selection expression $v.x$ (rules SELECT and DANGLE-SELECT) evaluates v to a memory location m^S. If the location has not failed, the result of the selection is the value of the field x of the record at that location. Otherwise, a p-persistence failure occurs, where p is the persistence level of m^S, written $p = \mathsf{persist}(m^S)$.

The field-assignment expression $v_1.x := v_2$ evaluates v_1 to a memory location m^S (rules ASSIGN and DANGLE-ASSIGN) If the location has not failed, v_2 is assigned into the field x of the record at that location; otherwise, a p-persistence failure occurs (where $p = \mathsf{persist}(m^S)$). The notation $M[m^S.x_c \mapsto v]$ denotes the memory resulting from updating with value v the field x_c of the record at location m^S.

Persistence failures propagate outward dynamically (FAIL-PROP) until the whole program fails. The production F gives the contexts from which persistence failures propagate. The full $\lambda_{persist}$ language, defined in Section 6, can handle these failures.

The soft-reference expression $\mathsf{soft}\ e$ evaluates e to a hard reference and turns it into a soft reference. The soft-reference test $(\mathsf{exists}\ v\ \mathsf{as}\ x : e_1\ \mathsf{else}\ e_2)$ promotes the soft reference v (if valid) to a hard reference bound to x and evaluates e_1. If the reference is invalid, e_2 is evaluated instead.

In rule GC, the notation $\mathsf{gc}(G, \langle e, M \rangle)$ means that G is a set of locations that is *collectible*. G is considered collectible if it has no GC roots (i.e., hard references in e), and no location outside G has a hard reference into G.

5.4   Subtyping in $\lambda_{persist}^0$

The subtyping judgment $\vdash \tau_1 \leq \tau_2$ states that any value of type τ_1 can be treated as a value of type τ_2. Subtyping in $\lambda_{persist}^0$ is the least reflexive and transitive relation consistent with the rules given in Figure 6.

Subtyping on soft references is covariant (rule S2). While hard references may be soundly used as soft references, this is omitted for simplicity. Rule S3 gives contravariant subtyping on integrity labels. Rule S4 gives standard subtyping on functions; the additional pc component is covariant. Rule S5 gives subtyping for labeled reference types. It ensures the bounds specified by the reference label of the subtype are at least as precise as those of the supertype.

[T-Bool]
$$\frac{b \in \{\text{true}, \text{false}\}}{\Gamma; pc \vdash b : \text{bool}_\top}$$

[T-Unit]
$$\Gamma; pc \vdash * : \mathbf{1}$$

[T-Var]
$$\frac{\Gamma(x) = \tau}{\Gamma; pc \vdash x : \tau}$$

[T-Bot]
$$\frac{p \neq \top}{\Gamma; pc \vdash \bot_p : \tau}$$

[T-Loc]
$$\frac{\vdash_{wf} S : \text{rectype} \qquad S = \{\overrightarrow{x_i : \tau_i}\}_{(a,p)}}{\Gamma; pc \vdash m^S : (\{\overrightarrow{x_i : \tau_i}\}_{(a,a,p)})_\top}$$

[T-Soft]
$$\frac{\Gamma; pc \vdash e : R_w}{\Gamma; pc \vdash \text{soft } e : (\text{soft } R)_w}$$

[T-If]
$$\frac{\begin{array}{c}\Gamma; pc \vdash v : \text{bool}_w \\ \Gamma; pc \sqcap w \vdash e_i : \tau^{(\forall i)} \\ \vdash \text{auth}^+(\tau) \preccurlyeq pc \sqcap w\end{array}}{\Gamma; pc \vdash \text{if } v \text{ then } e_1 \text{ else } e_2 : \tau \sqcap w}$$

[T-Pll]
$$\frac{\begin{array}{c}\Gamma; pc \vdash e_i : \tau_i^{(\forall i)} \\ \vdash \text{auth}^+(\tau_i) \preccurlyeq pc^{(\forall i)}\end{array}}{\Gamma; pc \vdash e_1 \| e_2 : \mathbf{1}}$$

[T-Abs]
$$\frac{\begin{array}{c}\Gamma, x : \tau'; pc' \vdash e : \tau \\ \vdash_{wf} (\tau' \xrightarrow{pc'} \tau)_\top : \text{type} \qquad \vdash pc' \preccurlyeq pc\end{array}}{\Gamma; pc \vdash \lambda(x : \tau')[pc'].e : (\tau' \xrightarrow{pc'} \tau)_\top}$$

[T-App]
$$\frac{\begin{array}{c}\Gamma; pc \vdash v_1 : (\tau' \xrightarrow{pc'} \tau)_w \\ \Gamma; pc \vdash v_2 : \tau' \\ \vdash pc' \preccurlyeq pc \sqcap w\end{array}}{\Gamma; pc \vdash v_1\, v_2 : \tau \sqcap w}$$

[T-Rec]
$$\frac{\vdash_{wf} S : \text{rectype} \qquad S = \{\overrightarrow{x_i : \tau_i}\}_{(a,p)} \qquad \Gamma; pc \vdash v_i : \tau_i'^{(\forall i)}}{\Gamma; pc \vdash \{\overrightarrow{x_i = v_i}\}^S : (\{\overrightarrow{x_i : \tau_i}\}_{(a,a,p)})_\top} \quad \begin{array}{l}\vdash \tau_i' \leq \tau_i^{(\forall i)} \quad \vdash \text{auth}^+(\tau_i') \preccurlyeq pc^{(\forall i)} \quad \vdash \text{integ}(\tau_i) \preccurlyeq pc^{(\forall i)} \quad \vdash p \preccurlyeq pc\end{array}$$

[T-Sel]
$$\frac{\begin{array}{c}\Gamma; pc \vdash v : (\{\overrightarrow{x_i : \tau_i}\}_r)_w \\ \vdash \text{auth}^+(r) \preccurlyeq pc \\ w' = w \sqcap \text{persist}(r)\end{array}}{\Gamma; pc \vdash v.x_c : \tau_c \sqcap w'}$$

[T-Asgn]
$$\frac{\begin{array}{c}\Gamma; pc \vdash v_1 : (\{\overrightarrow{x_i : \tau_i}\}_r)_w \\ \vdash \text{auth}^+(r) \preccurlyeq pc \\ \Gamma; pc \vdash v_2 : \tau \\ \vdash \tau \sqcap pc \sqcap w \leq \tau_c \\ \vdash \text{auth}^+(\tau) \preccurlyeq pc \sqcap w\end{array}}{\Gamma; pc \vdash v_1.x_c := v_2 : \mathbf{1}}$$

[T-Exists]
$$\frac{\begin{array}{c}\Gamma; pc \vdash v : (\text{soft } \{\overrightarrow{x_i : \tau_i}\}_r)_w \qquad \vdash \text{auth}^+(r) \preccurlyeq pc \sqcap w \\ w' = \text{auth}^-(r) \sqcap \text{persist}(r) \sqcap w \qquad \Gamma, x : (\{\overrightarrow{x_i : \tau_i}\}_r)_w; pc \sqcap w' \vdash e_1 : \tau \\ \Gamma; pc \sqcap w' \vdash e_2 : \tau \qquad \vdash \text{auth}^+(\tau) \preccurlyeq pc \sqcap w'\end{array}}{\Gamma; pc \vdash \text{exists } v \text{ as } x : e_1 \text{ else } e_2 : \tau \sqcap w'}$$

[T-Let]
$$\frac{\begin{array}{c}\Gamma; pc \vdash e_1 : \tau' \qquad \vdash \text{auth}^+(\tau') \preccurlyeq pc \\ w = \text{integ}(\tau') \qquad pc' = pc \sqcap w \\ \Gamma, x : \tau'; pc' \vdash e_2 : \tau \qquad \vdash \text{auth}^+(\tau) \preccurlyeq pc'\end{array}}{\Gamma; pc \vdash \text{let } x = e_1 \text{ in } e_2 : \tau \sqcap w}$$

[T-Sub]
$$\frac{\Gamma; pc \vdash e : \tau' \qquad \vdash \tau' \leq \tau}{\Gamma; pc \vdash e : \tau}$$

Fig. 7. Typing rules for $\lambda^0_{persist}$

$$[\text{WT1}] \quad \vdash_{wf} \text{bool}_w : \text{type} \qquad [\text{WT2}] \quad \frac{\vdash pc \leq w \qquad \vdash_{wf} \tau_1 : \text{type} \qquad \vdash_{wf} \tau_2 : \text{type} \qquad \vdash \text{auth}^+(\tau_1) \sqcup \text{auth}^+(\tau_2) \leq pc}{\vdash_{wf} (\tau_1 \xrightarrow{pc} \tau_2)_w : \text{type}}$$

$$[\text{WT3}] \quad \vdash_{wf} \mathbf{1} : \text{type} \qquad [\text{WT4}] \quad \frac{\vdash_{wf} (\{\overrightarrow{x_i : \tau_i}\}_{(a,a,p)})_T : \text{type} \qquad \vdash \text{integ}(\tau_i) \leq p \ ^{(\forall i)}}{\vdash_{wf} \{\overrightarrow{x_i : \tau_i}\}_{(a,p)} : \text{rectype}}$$

$$[\text{WT5}] \quad \frac{\vdash_{wf} R_T : \text{type}}{\vdash_{wf} (\text{soft } R)_w : \text{type}} \qquad [\text{WT6}] \quad \frac{\vdash_{wf} \tau_i : \text{type} \ ^{(\forall i)} \qquad \vdash \text{auth}^+(\tau_i) \leq a^+ \ ^{(\forall i)} \qquad \vdash a^+ \leq w \sqcap p \qquad \vdash a^- \leq a^+}{\vdash_{wf} (\{\overrightarrow{x_i : \tau_i}\}_{(a^+,a^-,p)})_w : \text{type}}$$

Fig. 8. Well-formedness of types

5.5 Static Semantics of $\lambda^0_{persist}$

Typing rules for $\lambda^0_{persist}$ are given in Figure 7. The notation $\text{auth}^+(r)$ and $\text{auth}^-(r)$ give the upper (a^+) and lower (a^-) authority component of a reference label r, respectively. The notation $\text{auth}^+(\tau)$, defined below, gives the authority level needed to create a hard reference to a value of type τ. The integrity of τ is written $\text{integ}(\tau)$, and $\tau \sqcap \ell$ denotes the type obtained by tainting (meeting) the integrity of τ with ℓ.

$$\text{auth}^+(\text{bool}) = \text{auth}^+(\mathbf{1}) = \text{auth}^+(\text{soft } R) = \bot$$
$$\text{auth}^+(\tau_1 \xrightarrow{pc} \tau_2) = pc \qquad \text{auth}^+(\{\overrightarrow{x_i : \tau_i}\}_s) = \text{auth}^+(s)$$

The typing context includes a *type assignment* Γ and the program-counter label pc. We write $x : \tau \in \Gamma$ and $\Gamma(x) = \tau$ interchangeably. The typing assertion $\Gamma; pc \vdash e : \tau$ means that the expression e has type τ under type assignment Γ with program-counter label pc.

Most of the typing rules are standard rules, extended to ensure that the pc is sufficiently high to obtain any hard references that may result from evaluating subexpressions (e.g., premise $\vdash \text{auth}^+(\tau) \leq pc$ in Rule T-IF), and that the pc is suitably tainted.

Rule T-REC checks the creation of records. The pc must be high enough to create any hard references that appear in the fields, and to write to the fields themselves.

When using a hard reference v_1, the pc must have sufficient authority to possess v_1 (premise $\vdash \text{auth}^+(r) \leq pc$ in rules T-SEL and T-ASGN). When assigning through v_1, hard references contained in the assigned value v_2 also require authority. Since the integrity and persistence of v_1 can affect whether the assignment succeeds, we taint the pc with these labels before comparing with the authority requirement of v_2.

Rule T-EXISTS checks soft-reference validity tests. It ensures that the pc has the authority to promote the reference from soft to hard (premise $\vdash \text{auth}^+(r) \leq pc$).

The rules for determining the well-formedness of types are given in Figure 8. In rule WT6, a reference type $(\{\overrightarrow{x_i : \tau_i}\}_{(a^+,a^-,p)})_w$ is well-formed only if the upper authority label a^+ is an upper bound on the authority levels of the field types τ_i. This ensures that the upper authority label is an accurate summary of the authority required by the fields. We also require a^+ be bounded from above by the integrity w of the reference, since low-integrity data should not influence the creation of high-authority references. To ensure hosts are able to create hard references to the objects they store, we also require $\text{auth}^+(r)$ to be bounded from above by the persistence level p of the record.

6   Ensuring Referential Integrity

In a distributed system, references can span trust domains, so to be secure and reliable, program code must in general be ready to encounter a dangling reference, one perhaps created by the adversary. Therefore, we extend $\lambda^0_{persist}$ with *persistence-failure handlers* to obtain the full $\lambda_{persist}$ language (see [16] for its full syntax). The type system of $\lambda_{persist}$ forces the programmer to be aware of and to handle all potential failures.

We might consider an approach in which failures must be handled immediately upon encountering a broken reference. However, because low-persistence references may be used frequently, this would likely result in much duplication of failure-handling code.

Instead, $\lambda_{persist}$ factors out failure-handling code from ordinary code by treating failures as a kind of exception. The value of (try e_1 catch p: e_2) is the value of evaluating e_1. If a dangling reference at persistence level p or higher is encountered, the failure handler e_2 is evaluated instead. A try expression creates a context (e_1) in which the programmer can write simpler code under the assumption that certain persistence failures are impossible, yet without sacrificing the property that all failures are handled.

6.1   Persistence Handler Levels

To track the failures that the current context can handle, a *set* of persistence levels $\mathcal{H}$ is used.[3] It provides lower bounds on the persistence levels of hard references that may be directly dereferenced. Functions $\lambda(x{:}\tau)[pc;\mathcal{H}].e$ and function types $\tau_1 \xrightarrow{pc,\mathcal{H}} \tau_2$ are extended with an $\mathcal{H}$ component, which is an upper bound on the $\mathcal{H}$ levels of the caller.

6.2   Example

Returning to the directory example in Figure 1, Alice can add a place to the list of sightseeing ideas with the code below. This code starts at Alice's docs directory, traverses the reference to the scratchpad, and invokes an add method to add a museum.

```
let pad = docs.scratchpad
in try pad.add "Rodin Museum" catch ⊥: ...
```

The expression pad.add follows a hard reference to the scratchpad. Despite the hard reference, a try is needed because Alice does not trust host U to persist the scratchpad.

6.3   Static and Dynamic Semantics of $\lambda_{persist}$

The small-step operational semantics of $\lambda_{persist}$ extends that of $\lambda^0_{persist}$ with the rules at the top of Figure 9. Failures propagate outward dynamically (TRY-ESC) until either they are handled by a failure handler (TRY-CATCH), or the whole program fails. See [16] for the full operational semantics for $\lambda_{persist}$.

The subtyping rules are the same as for $\lambda^0_{persist}$, except that function subtyping is also contravariant on the $\mathcal{H}$ component. Full subtyping rules are also in [16].

---

[3] Formally, $\mathcal{H}$ is drawn from the upper powerdomain [22] of persistence levels.

$$\begin{bmatrix} \text{TRY-} \\ \text{VAL} \end{bmatrix} \quad \frac{\forall p'.\ v \neq \bot_{p'}}{\langle \text{try } v \text{ catch } p\colon e, M \rangle \xrightarrow{e} \langle v, M \rangle} \quad \begin{bmatrix} \text{TRY-} \\ \text{CATCH} \end{bmatrix} \quad \frac{p \preccurlyeq p'}{\langle \text{try } \bot_{p'} \text{ catch } p\colon e, M \rangle \xrightarrow{e} \langle e, M \rangle}$$

$$\begin{bmatrix} \text{TRY-} \\ \text{ESC} \end{bmatrix} \quad \frac{p \not\preccurlyeq p'}{\langle \text{try } \bot_{p'} \text{ catch } p\colon e, M \rangle \xrightarrow{e} \langle \bot_{p'}, M \rangle} \qquad E ::= \dots \mid \text{try } [\cdot] \text{ catch } p\colon e$$

$$\begin{bmatrix} \text{T-SOFT-} \\ \text{SELECT} \end{bmatrix} \quad \frac{\Gamma; pc; \mathcal{H} \vdash v : (\text{soft } \{\overrightarrow{x_i : \tau_i}\}_r)_w, \top \qquad \vdash \text{auth}^+(\tau_c) \preccurlyeq pc}{p = \text{auth}^-(r) \sqcap \text{persist}(r) \sqcap w \qquad \vdash \mathcal{H} \preccurlyeq p}{\Gamma; pc; \mathcal{H} \vdash v.x_c : \tau_c \sqcap p, p}$$

$$\begin{bmatrix} \text{T-SOFT-} \\ \text{ASSIGN} \end{bmatrix} \quad \frac{\Gamma; pc; \mathcal{H} \vdash v_1 : (\text{soft } \{\overrightarrow{x_i : \tau_i}\}_r)_w, \top \qquad p = \text{auth}^-(r) \sqcap \text{persist}(r) \sqcap w}{\Gamma; pc; \mathcal{H} \vdash v_2 : \tau, \top \qquad \vdash \tau \sqcap pc \sqcap p \preccurlyeq \tau_c \qquad \vdash \text{auth}^+(\tau) \preccurlyeq pc \sqcap p \qquad \vdash \mathcal{H} \preccurlyeq p}{\Gamma; pc; \mathcal{H} \vdash v_1.x_c := v_2 : \mathbf{1}, p}$$

$$[\text{T-TRY}] \quad \frac{\Gamma; pc; \mathcal{H}, p \vdash e_1 : \tau, \mathcal{X}_1 \qquad w = \bigsqcap_{p' \in \mathcal{X}_1} (p \sqcup p')}{\Gamma; pc \sqcap w \sqcap \text{integ}(\tau); \mathcal{H} \vdash e_2 : \tau, \mathcal{X}_2 \qquad \vdash \text{auth}^+(\tau) \preccurlyeq pc}{\Gamma; pc; \mathcal{H} \vdash \text{try } e_1 \text{ catch } p\colon e_2 : \tau \sqcap w, (\mathcal{X}_1/p) \sqcap \mathcal{X}_2}$$

Fig. 9. Additional small-step evaluation and typing rules for $\lambda_{persist}$

The typing rules for $\lambda_{persist}$ extend those for $\lambda^0_{persist}$. They augment the typing context with a *handler environment* $\mathcal{H}$, indicating the set of persistence failures the evaluation context can handle. Typing judgments additionally produce an effect $\mathcal{X}$, which is a set indicating the persistence failures that can occur during evaluation.

The typing rules for $\lambda^0_{persist}$ are converted straightforwardly to thread $\mathcal{H}$ and $\mathcal{X}$ through typing judgments. Rules T-SEL and T-ASGN gain premises to ensure the context has a suitable handler in case dereferences fail. See [16] for the converted rules.

The bottom of Figure 9 gives three new typing rules. T-SOFT-SELECT and T-SOFT-ASSIGN check direct uses of soft references. They taint the integrity of the dereference with $\text{auth}^-(r)$ because the result of the dereference is affected by those able to pin the referent in memory by creating a hard reference (Section 3.5). Rule T-TRY checks try expressions. To reflect the installation of a p-persistence handler, p is added to the handler environment $\mathcal{H}$ when checking e_1. The value w in the typing rule is a conservative summary of the persistence errors that can occur while evaluating e_1 and are not handled by the p-persistence handler. Because evaluation of e_2 depends on the result of e_1, the pc label for evaluating e_2 is tainted by w. In this rule, the notation $\mathcal{X}/p$ denotes the subset of persistence errors $\mathcal{X}$ not handled by p.

7   The Power of the Adversary

Possible actions of the adversary are modeled by extending the operational semantics of Figure 5 with more transitions. To support reasoning about what an adversary may have affected in a partially evaluated program, $\lambda_{persist}$ is also augmented to include bracketed expressions, resulting in the language $[\lambda_{persist}]$. The term $[e]$ represents an expression e that may have been influenced by the adversary, and $[v]$ is an influenced value. The

$$m = \mathsf{newloc}(M) \qquad \varnothing; \top; \top \vdash \overrightarrow{\{x_i = [v_i]\}}^S : R_\top, \top$$

[α-CREATE]
$$\frac{\vdash^\alpha_{[wf]} M[m^S \mapsto \overrightarrow{\{x_i = [v_i]\}}] \qquad \alpha \not\leqslant \mathsf{persist}(S)}{\langle e, M \rangle \leadsto_\alpha \left(e, M[m^S \mapsto \overrightarrow{\{x_i = [v_i]\}}] \right)}$$

[α-ASSIGN]
$$\frac{\begin{array}{c} m^S \in \mathsf{dom}(M) \qquad M(m^S) \neq \bot \\ S = \{\overrightarrow{x_i : \tau_i}\}_s \qquad \varnothing; \top; \top \vdash [v] : \tau_c, \top \\ \vdash^\alpha_{[wf]} M[m^S.x_c \mapsto [v]] \end{array}}{\langle e, M \rangle \leadsto_\alpha \left(e, M[m^S.x_c \mapsto [v]] \right)}$$

[α-FORGET]
$$\frac{\begin{array}{c} m^S \in \mathsf{dom}(M) \\ \alpha \not\leqslant \mathsf{persist}(S) \end{array}}{\langle e, M \rangle \leadsto_\alpha \left(e, M[m^S \mapsto \bot] \right)}$$

Fig. 10. Effects caused by the α-adversary

operational semantics is extended by adding rules that propagate these brackets in the obvious manner. (Doubly bracketed values are considered expressions, not values.)

The rule for typing bracketed expressions is as follows:

[T-BRACKET]
$$\frac{\Gamma; pc \sqcap \ell; \mathcal{H} \vdash e : \tau, \mathcal{X} \qquad \alpha \not\leqslant \ell \qquad \vdash \mathsf{auth}^+(\tau) \leqslant pc \sqcap \ell}{\Gamma; pc; \mathcal{H} \vdash [e] : \tau \sqcap \ell, \mathcal{X}}$$

The adversary is powerful, as shown by the transitions defined in Figure 10. Adversaries may create new records (rule α-CREATE), modify existing records (rule α-ASSIGN), or remove records from memory altogether (rule α-FORGET), but their ability is bounded by an integrity label $\alpha \in \mathcal{L}$. Such an *α-adversary* has all creation authority except α and higher, can modify any record field except those with α (or higher) integrity, and can delete any record except those with α (or higher) persistence. A small evaluation step taken in the presence of an α-adversary is written $\langle e, M \rangle \to_\alpha \langle e', M' \rangle$.

It is important to know that any evaluation of a program in the original language can be simulated in the augmented language, which amounts to showing that the rules cover all the ways that brackets can appear. This is proved straightforwardly by induction on the evaluation rules.

The adversary's transitions embody a simplifying assumption that the adversary can only create well-typed values. While it is reasonable to allow the adversary to create ill-typed values, an implementation with run-time type checking can catch ill-typed values when they cross between hosts and replace them with well-typed default values.

8 Results

The goal of $\lambda_{persist}$ is to prevent accidental persistence and to ensure that the adversary cannot damage referential integrity or cause storage attacks. Accidental persistence is prevented by the use of persistence policies. We now show how to formalize the other security properties and sketch the proof that they are enforced.

8.1 Soundness and Well-Formedness

We have proved [16] the [$\lambda_{persist}$] type system sound with the usual method, via preservation and progress. A well-formed $\lambda_{persist}$ memory M, written $\vdash_{wf} M$, maps typed locations to record values with the same type. In a $\lambda_{persist}$ configuration that is well-formed with respect to an α-adversary (written $\vdash_{wf}^{\alpha} \langle e,M \rangle$), no noncollectible high-persistence location is deleted. $\lambda_{persist}$ configurations are well-formed in a nonadversarial setting ($\vdash_{wf} \langle e,M \rangle$) if they are well-formed with respect to the $\bot$-adversary.

Corresponding well-formedness conditions are defined similarly for $[\lambda_{persist}]$ and is written with brackets around the wf subscript. Well-formed $[\lambda_{persist}]$ memories additionally require that values appearing in low-integrity record fields must be bracketed.

8.2   Security Relation

The key to proving both referential integrity and immunity to storage attacks is to show that the adversary cannot meaningfully influence the high-integrity parts of the program and memory. To do this, we define a *security relation* and show that each configuration $\langle e_1, M_1 \rangle$ reached via the language augmented by adversarial transitions must be related to some configuration $\langle e_2, M_2 \rangle$ reachable by purely nonadversarial execution. This security property is possibilistic, which is problematic for confidentiality properties [21] but is acceptable for integrity.

Because the two executions being compared operate on different heaps, with the adversary behaving differently in the two executions, the addresses chosen during record allocation may differ. However, the structure of the high-integrity part of the heap should still correspond. A *high-integrity homomorphism* ϕ is used to relate corresponding locations in the two heaps that are high-integrity or high-persistence. High-integrity homomorphisms are injective, preserve location types, and are isomorphisms on both high-integrity and high-persistence locations. This is defined formally in [16].

An expression e_1 is considered to be related to e_2 via a high-integrity homomorphism ϕ, written $e_1 \approx_{\alpha}^{\phi} e_2$, if e_1 is equal to e_2 (modulo bracketed expressions) when the memory locations in e_1 are transformed via ϕ.

We also define a security relation on memories: M_1 and M_2 are related via ϕ, written $M_1 \approx_{\alpha}^{\phi} M_2$, if two conditions hold for each location $m^S \in \text{dom}(\phi)$. If m^S is not deleted, then $\phi(m^S)$ maps to a related record. Otherwise, if m^S is deleted, high-authority, and high-persistence, then so is $\phi(m^S)$. The formal definition is given in [16]. These two security relations induce a security relation on configurations:

$$\langle e_1, M_1 \rangle \approx_{\alpha}^{\phi} \langle e_2, M_2 \rangle \overset{def.}{\Longleftrightarrow} e_1 \approx_{\alpha}^{\phi} e_2 \wedge M_1 \approx_{\alpha}^{\phi} M_2.$$

A $[\lambda_{persist}]$ program has limited adversary influence if related initial configurations produce related final configurations. We now see that the language $[\lambda_{persist}]$ enforces security, because all well-formed programs do have limited adversary influence.

8.3   Referential Integrity

Theorem 1 formalizes the referential integrity result, showing that the adversary has limited influence on program execution: execution in the presence of an adversary is ϕ-related to a nonadversarial execution.

For the remainder of this paper, assume $\langle e_1, M_1 \rangle$ is a well-formed configuration and $\langle e_2, M_2 \rangle$ is a well-formed, nonadversarial, ϕ-related configuration, such that e_1 and e_2 have type τ and M_2 is well-formed:

$$\vdash_{[wf]}^{\alpha} \langle e_1, M_1 \rangle \ \wedge \ \vdash_{[wf]} \langle e_2, M_2 \rangle \ \wedge \ \langle e_1, M_1 \rangle \approx_{\alpha}^{\phi} \langle e_2, M_2 \rangle$$
$$\wedge \ \varnothing; pc; \mathcal{H} \vdash e_1 : \tau, \mathcal{X} \ \wedge \ \varnothing; pc; \mathcal{H} \vdash e_2 : \tau, \mathcal{X} \ \wedge \ \vdash_{[wf]}^{\alpha} M_2$$

Theorem 1 (Referential integrity). *Suppose* $\langle e_1, M_1 \rangle$ *takes some number of steps in the presence of an adversary to another configuration* $\langle e_1', M_1' \rangle$. *Then either* $\langle e_2, M_2 \rangle$ *diverges, or it can take some number of steps in the absence of an adversary to another configuration* $\langle e_2', M_2' \rangle$ *and there exists a high-integrity homomorphism* ϕ' *from* M_1' *to* M_2' *that extends* ϕ, *such that* $\langle e_1', M_1' \rangle$ *is related to* $\langle e_2', M_2' \rangle$ *via* ϕ':

$$\langle e_1, M_1 \rangle \rightarrow_{\alpha}^{*} \langle e_1', M_1' \rangle \wedge \neg \langle e_2, M_2 \rangle \Uparrow$$
$$\Rightarrow \exists e_2', M_2', \phi'. \ \langle e_2, M_2 \rangle \rightarrow^{*} \langle e_2', M_2' \rangle \wedge \langle e_1', M_1' \rangle \approx_{\alpha}^{\phi'} \langle e_2', M_2' \rangle \wedge \phi = \phi'|_{\mathrm{dom}(\phi)}$$

Proof: Induction on the derivation of $\langle e_1, M_1 \rangle \rightarrow_{\alpha} \langle e_1', M_1' \rangle$.

8.4 Storage Attacks

To formalize immunity to storage attacks, we first show that the adversary cannot cause more high-persistence locations to be allocated. Theorem 1 captures this via the security relation, since all high-persistence locations are mapped by the homomorphism.

We now show that the adversary cannot cause more high-authority locations to become *noncollectible*; that is, reachable through hard references. Lemma 1 says that this is also implied by Theorem 1. (We write $nc(m^S, \langle e, M \rangle)$ to mean m^S is noncollectible in $\langle e, M \rangle$. The formal, inductive definition is in [16].)

Lemma 1. *If* m^S *is a high-authority, noncollectible location in* $\langle e_1, M_1 \rangle$, *then* $\phi(m^S)$ *is also noncollectible in* $\langle e_2, M_2 \rangle$.

$$\vdash \alpha \preccurlyeq \mathsf{auth}^{+}(S) \wedge nc(m^S, \langle e_1, M_1 \rangle) \Rightarrow nc(\phi(m^S), \langle e_2, M_2 \rangle)$$

Proof: By induction on the derivation of $nc(m^S, \langle e_1, M_1 \rangle)$.

9 Related Work

This paper identifies and addresses a new problem, referential security. As a result, little prior work is closely related.

Some prior work has tried to improve referential integrity through system mechanisms, for example improving the referential integrity of web hyperlinks [8, 11]. Systems mechanisms for improving referential integrity (and other aspects of trustworthiness) are orthogonal to the language model presented here, but could be used to justify assigning persistence, integrity, and authority levels to nodes.

Liblit and Aiken [12] develop a type system for distributed data structures. Its explicit two-level hierarchy distinguishes between local pointers that are meaningful only to a single processor, and global pointers that are valid everywhere. The type system ensures that local pointers do not leak into a global context. This work was extended in [13] to add types for dealing with private vs. shared data. However, this line of work does not consider security properties that require defense against an adversary.

Riely and Hennessey study type safety in a distributed system of partially trusted mobile agents [20] but do not consider referential security.

This paper builds on prior work on language-based information-flow security, much of which is summarized by [21]. The Fabric system [15] is programmed in a high-level language that includes integrity annotations and abstracts away the locations of objects, as $\lambda_{persist}$ does. Its type system does not enforce referential security, however, so adding the features described here is an obvious next step.

10   Conclusions

Complex distributed information systems are being integrated across different organizations with only partial trust, often in the context of cloud computing. But the security properties that are desirable in distributed computing are poorly understood, and the options for enforcing security are murkier still. In fact, the desirable referential security properties are actually in tension with each other. The result is that programmers have little guidance in designing distributed systems to be secure and reliable.

This paper makes several contributions that aid in resolving this situation. The paper newly identifies and formalizes some important referential security properties. It introduces a high-level language for modeling referential security issues in a distributed system. The language introduces a way to express referential security requirements through label annotations for persistence and creation authority, which can be viewed as different aspects of integrity. The paper demonstrates how to enforce referential security, through static analysis expressed as a type system in the language. The type system is validated by formal proofs that $\lambda_{persist}$ programs enforce the new security properties.

While this paper is a useful first step, clearly there is more to be done. The type system could be enriched with more features such as parametric polymorphism, recursive and dependent types. With such extensions, an implementation would then help evaluate how well these types guide programmers designing distributed computing systems.

Acknowledgments. This research was supported in part by ONR Grants N00014-09-1-0652 and N00014-13-1-0089; by MURI grant FA9550-12-1-0400, administered by the U.S. Air Force; by NSF Grants 0541217, 0627649, and 0964409; and by a grant from Microsoft Corporation. The views and conclusions here are those of the authors and do not necessarily reflect those of ONR, the Navy, the Air Force, NSF, or Microsoft. The U.S. Government is authorized to reproduce and distribute reprints for Government purposes, notwithstanding any copyright annotation thereon.

We also thank Aslan Askarov, Danfeng Zhang, Owen Arden, Barbara Liskov, Mike George, and David Schulz for their suggestions about this work or its presentation.

References

1. Atkinson, M., Bancilhon, F., DeWitt, D., Dittrich, K., Maier, D., Zdonik, S.: The object-oriented database system manifesto. In: Proc. International Conference on Deductive Object Oriented Databases, Kyoto, Japan (December 1989)
2. Biba, K.J.: Integrity considerations for secure computer systems. Technical Report ESD-TR-76-372, USAF Electronic Systems Division, Bedford, MA (April 1977)
3. Birrell, A., Nelson, G., Owicki, S., Wobber, E.: Network objects. In: SOSP 1993, pp. 217–230 (December 1993)
4. Black, A., Hutchinson, N., Jul, E., Levy, H.: Object structure in the Emerald system. In: OOPSLA 1986, pp. 78–86 (November 1986)
5. Breeze (2013), http://www.breezejs.com
6. Böck, H.: Java Persistence API. Springer (2011)
7. Codd, E.F.: Extending the database relational model to capture more meaning. ACM Transactions on Database Systems (TODS) 4(4), 397–434 (1979)
8. Davis, H.C.: Referential integrity of links in open hypermedia systems. In: Proc. 9th ACM Conference on Hypertext and Hypermedia, pp. 207–216 (1998)
9. Denning, D.E.: Cryptography and Data Security. Addison-Wesley, Reading (1982)
10. Hibernate, http://www.hibernate.org
11. Kappe, F.: A scalable architecture for maintaining referential integrity in distributed information systems. Journal of Universal Computer Science 1(2) (1995)
12. Liblit, B., Aiken, A.: Type systems for distributed data structures. In: POPL, pp. 199–213 (January 2000)
13. Liblit, B., Aiken, A., Yelick, K.A.: Type systems for distributed data sharing. In: Cousot, R. (ed.) SAS 2003. LNCS, vol. 2694, pp. 273–294. Springer, Heidelberg (2003)
14. Liskov, B.H.: The Argus language and system. In: Alford, M.W., Hommel, G., Schneider, F.B., Ansart, J.P., Lamport, L., Mullery, G.P., Zhou, T.H., et al. (eds.) Distributed Systems. LNCS, vol. 190, pp. 343–430. Springer, Heidelberg (1985)
15. Liu, J., George, M.D., Vikram, K., Qi, X., Waye, L., Myers, A.C.: Fabric: A platform for secure distributed computation and storage. In: SOSP, pp. 321–334 (2009)
16. Liu, J., Myers, A.C.: A language for securely referencing persistent information in a federated system. Technical Report 1813-35150, Computing and Information Science Department, Cornell University (January 2014)
17. Maier, D., Stein, J.: Development and implementation of an object-oriented DBMS. In: Shriver, B., Wegner, P. (eds.) Research Directions in Object-Oriented Programming. MIT Press (1987)
18. Milner, R., Tofte, M., Harper, R.: The Definition of Standard ML. MIT Press, Cambridge (1990)
19. OMG: The Common Object Request Broker: Architecture and Specification, OMG TC Document Number 91.12.1, Revision 1.1 (December 1991)
20. Riely, J., Hennessy, M.: Trust and partial typing in open systems of mobile agents. In: POPL 1999, pp. 93–104 (1999)
21. Sabelfeld, A., Myers, A.C.: Language-based information-flow security. IEEE Journal on Selected Areas in Communications 21(1), 5–19 (2003)
22. Smyth, M.B.: Power domains. Journal of Computer and System Sciences 16(1), 23–36 (1978)
23. Zheng, L., Chong, S., Myers, A.C., Zdancewic, S.: Using replication and partitioning to build secure distributed systems. In: Proc. IEEE Symp. on Security and Privacy, pp. 236–250 (May 2003)

Extending and Applying a Framework for the Cryptographic Verification of Java Programs

Ralf Küsters[1], Enrico Scapin[1], Tomasz Truderung[1], and Jürgen Graf[2]

[1] University of Trier, Germany
[2] Karlsruhe Institute of Technology, Germany
{kuesters,scapin,truderung}@uni-trier.de, graf@kit.edu

Abstract. In our previous work, we have proposed a framework which allows tools that can check standard noninterference properties but a priori cannot deal with cryptography to establish cryptographic indistinguishability properties, such as privacy properties, for Java programs. We refer to this framework as the CVJ framework (Cryptographic Verification of Java Programs) in this paper.

While so far the CVJ framework directly supports public-key encryption (without corruption and without a public-key infrastructure) only, in this work we further instantiate the framework to support, among others, public-key encryption and digital signatures, both with corruption and a public-key infrastructure, as well as (private) symmetric encryption. Since these cryptographic primitives are very common in security-critical applications, our extensions make the framework much more widely applicable.

To illustrate the usefulness and applicability of the extensions proposed in this paper, we apply the framework along with the tool Joana, which allows for the fully automatic verification of noninterference properties of Java programs, to establish cryptographic privacy properties of a (non-trivial) cloud storage application, where clients can store private information on a remote server.

1 Introduction

In [24], a framework has been proposed which allows tools that can check standard noninterference properties but cannot deal with cryptography directly, in particular probabilities and polynomially bounded adversaries, to establish cryptographic indistinguishability properties, such as privacy properties, for Java programs. In this paper, we refer to this framework as the CVJ framework (Cryptographic Verification of Java programs). The framework combines techniques from program analysis and cryptography, more specifically, universal composability [9,19,27,29], a well-established concept in cryptography. The idea is to first check noninterference properties for the Java program to be analyzed where cryptographic operations (such as encryption) are performed within so-called ideal functionalities. Such functionalities typically provide guarantees even in the face of unbounded adversaries and can often be formulated without probabilistic operations. Therefore, such analysis can be carried out by tools that a priori cannot deal with cryptography (probabilities, polynomially bounded adversaries). Theorems shown within the framework now imply that the Java program enjoys strong cryptographic indistinguishability properties when the ideal functionalities are replaced by their realizations, i.e., the actual cryptographic operations.

M. Abadi and S. Kremer (Eds.): POST 2014, LNCS 8414, pp. 220–239, 2014.

The theorems proved within the CVJ framework are very general in that they guarantee that any ideal functionality can be replaced by its realization. In particular, they are not tailored to specific cryptographic operations. However, to make the framework directly applicable to a wide range of cryptographic software, i.e., software that uses cryptographic operations (such as asymmetric and symmetric encryption, digital signatures, MACs, etc.), it is necessary to provide a rich set of ideal functionalities along with their realizations written in Java. So far, in [24] only an ideal functionality for public-key encryption has been proposed and it has been shown that this functionality can be realized by any IND-CCA2-secure public-key encryption scheme, a standard security notion for such schemes (see, e.g., [4]). This functionality does not support reasoning about corruption and also it does not support a public-key infrastructure (PKI).

Contribution of This Paper. The main goal and the main contribution of this work is therefore to instantiate the CVJ framework with further (and more suitable) ideal functionalities which commonly occur in cryptographic applications, and to provide realizations of such functionalities based on standard cryptographic assumptions. We note that similar functionalities as the once introduced in this work have been considered in the cryptographic literature based on Turing machine models (see, e.g., [9, 26, 29]) before. The new contribution here is that we provide formulations in *Java* (more precisely, in a rich fragment of Java) such that these functionalities can actually be used to analyze Java programs. Designing such functionalities and carrying out the proofs (w.r.t. programming language semantics) is non-trivial and requires some care since the interaction between different classes is much more complex than between Turing machines, where in the former case we have to deal, for example, with exceptions, inheritance, references to potential complex objects that can be exchanged, and hence, the manipulation of one object can affect many other objects. Also, since the ideal functionalities we propose will be part of the (Java) programs to be analyzed, they should be formulated in a "tool friendly" way. For example, for this reason, in our functionalities corruption is modeled in a quite different way than it is typically done in the Turing machine models.

More concretely, in this work we propose ideal functionalities, written in Java, for public-key encryption, digital signatures, (private) symmetric encryption, and nonce generation.

The functionalities for public-key encryption and digital signatures support static corruption and a public-key infrastructure. The latter means that parties can register their public encryption and verification keys using the functionalities. Other parties can then use the functionalities to encrypt messages and verify signatures by simply providing the name of the intended recipient of the message/the alleged signer of the message. The functionality then guarantees that the correct public-key is used for encryption/verification. As for static corruption, the adversary can register his own (possibly dishonestly generated) public keys which then can be used by other (honest) parties just like honestly generated and registered keys. We show that both functionalities, public-key encryption and digital signatures, can be realized using standard cryptographic schemes and assumptions (IND-CCA2-secure public-key encryption schemes and UF-CMA-secure digital signature schemes).

The functionality for private symmetric encryption allows a user to encrypt messages (using a symmetric encryption scheme) for herself. She does not share the symmetric key with other parties. This is useful, for example, to store confidential information on an untrusted medium. Again, this functionality is realized using a standard symmetric encryption scheme, based on standard cryptographic assumptions (IND-CCA2 security).

Finally, the ideal functionality for nonce generation that we propose guarantees that nonces are always fresh. That is, this functionality prevents collisions of nonces. It is realized in the obvious way, by choosing nonces (of the length of the security parameter) uniformly at random.

We illustrate the usefulness and applicability of these functionalities in a case study. We apply the CVJ framework, along with the tool Joana [16, 17], which allows for the fully automatic verification of noninterference properties of Java programs, to establish cryptographic privacy properties of a non-trivial cloud storage application, where clients can store private information on a remote server. The cloud storage system makes use of all cryptographic primitives considered in this paper, and hence, the code of these functionalities is included in the verified program. We note that, except for a much simpler Java program analyzed in [24], there has been no other verification effort that establishes cryptographic security guarantees of Java programs.

Related Work. Obtaining cryptographic guarantees for programs written in real-world programming languages is a challenging and quite recent research field (see also [24] for a discussion of related work). Many approaches in this field carry out symbolic (Dolev-Yao style) analysis, without computational/cryptographic guarantees (see, e.g., [5, 11, 15]). Most, of the very few, approaches that aim at cryptographic guarantees follow one of the following approaches: i) They rely on symbolic analysis and then apply computational soundness results (see, e.g., [1]), ii) they derive formal models from the source code and analyze these models using specialized tools for cryptographic verification, such as the tool CryptoVerif [7] (see, e.g., [2]), or iii) they derive source code from formal specifications (see, e.g., [8]). The CVJ framework, in contrast, aims at using existing program analysis tools and techniques to directly obtain cryptographic security guarantees. It is the only approach for the cryptographic analysis of Java programs, other approaches aim at C or F# code. Also, unlike most other approaches, it considers cryptographic indistinguishability properties, rather than trace properties, such as authentication and weak secrecy. An approach similar to the approach taken in the CVJ framework is the one by Fournet et al. [6, 12]. However, they consider F# and focus on the use of refinement types.

Structure of This Paper. In Section 2, we first briefly recall the CVJ framework. In the four subsequent sections, we present the ideal functionalities for public-key encryption, digital signatures, private symmetric encryption, and nonce generation, respectively, including their realizations. In Section 7, we turn to the case study. Further details are provided in the extended version of this paper [22].

2   The CVJ Framework

We briefly recall the framework from [24]. The definitions and theorems stated here are somewhat simplified and informal, but should suffice to follow the rest of the paper. We refer the reader to [24] for full details.

As already mentioned in the introduction, in order to establish cryptographic indistinguishability properties for a Java program, by the CVJ framework it suffices to prove that the program enjoys a (standard) noninterference property when the cryptographic operations are replaced by so-called ideal functionalities, which in our case will model cryptographic primitives, such as encryption and digital signatures. The CVJ framework then ensures that the Java program enjoys the desired cryptographic indistinguishability properties when the ideal functionalities are replaced by their realizations, i.e., the actual cryptographic operations. Since ideal functionalities often do not involve probabilistic operations and are secure even for unbounded adversaries, the noninterference properties can be verified by tools that a priori cannot deal with cryptography (probabilities, polynomially bounded adversaries). Without the ideal functionalities, the tools would, for example, consider a secret message that is sent encrypted over a network controlled by the adversary to be an information leakage, because an unbounded adversary can break the encryption.

Jinja+. The CVJ framework is stated and proven for a Java-like language called *Jinja+*. Jinja+ is based on *Jinja* [18] and extends this language with some useful additional features, such as arrays and randomness. Jinja+ covers a rich subset of Java, including classes, inheritance, (static and non-static) fields and methods, the primitive types `int`, `boolean`, and `byte` (with the usual operators for these types), arrays, exceptions, and field/method access modifiers, such as `public`, `private`, and `protected`. It also includes the primitive `randomBit()` which returns a random bit each time it is called.

A (Jinja+) *program/system* is a set of class declarations. A class declaration consists of the name of the class, the name of its direct superclass, a list of field declarations, and a list of method declarations. A program/system is *complete* if it uses only classes/methods/fields declared in the program itself.

All Java programs considered in this paper, including the systems considered in our case study as well as the functionalities fall into the Jinja+ fragment. While the syntax of Jinja+ and Java differ, their is a straightforward translation from Jinja+ to Java, which is why we use Java syntax throughout this paper.

Indistinguishability. An *interface I* is defined like a (Jinja+) system but where (i) all private fields and private methods are dropped and (ii) method bodies as well as static field initializers are dropped. A system S *implements* an interface I, written $S : I$, if I is a subinterface of the public interface of S, i.e. the interface obtained from S by dropping method bodies, initializers of static fields, private fields, and private methods. We say that *a system S uses an interface I*, written $I \vdash S$, if, besides its own classes, S uses at most classes/methods/fields declared in I. We write $I_0 \vdash S : I_1$ for $I_0 \vdash S$ and $S : I_1$. We also say that two interfaces are *disjoint* if the sets of class names declared in these interfaces are disjoint.

For two systems S and T we denote by $S \cdot T$ the *composition* of S and T which, formally, is the union of (declarations in) S and T. Clearly, for the composition to make sense, we require that there are no name clashes in the declarations of S and T. Of course, S may use classes/methods/fields provided in the public interface of T, and vice versa.

A system E is called an *environment* if it declares a distinct private static variable `result` of type `boolean` with initial value `false`. Given a system $S : I$, we call E an

I-environment for S if there exists an interface I_E disjoint from I such that $I_E \vdash S : I$ and $I \vdash E : I_E$. Note that $E \cdot S$ is a complete program. The value of the variable result at the end of the run of $E \cdot S$ is called the *output* of the program $E \cdot S$; the output is false for infinite runs. If $E \cdot S$ is a deterministic program, we write $E \cdot S \rightsquigarrow$ true if the output of $E \cdot S$ is true. If $E \cdot S$ is a randomized program, we write $\mathrm{Prob}\{E \cdot S \rightsquigarrow \mathrm{true}\}$ to denote the probability that the output of $E \cdot S$ is true.

We assume that all systems have access to a security parameter (modeled as a public static variable of a class SP). We denote by $P(\eta)$ a program P running with security parameter η.

To define computational equivalence and computational indistinguishability between (probabilistic) systems, we consider systems that run in (probabilistic) polynomial time in the security parameter. We omit the details of the runtime notions used in the CVJ framework here, but note that the runtimes of systems and environments are defined in such a way that their composition results in polynomially bounded programs.

Let P_1 and P_2 be (complete, possibly probabilistic) programs. We say that P_1 and P_2 are *computationally equivalent*, written $P_1 \equiv_{\mathsf{comp}} P_2$, if $|\mathrm{Prob}\{P_1(\eta) \rightsquigarrow \mathrm{true}\} - \mathrm{Prob}\{P_2(\eta) \rightsquigarrow \mathrm{true}\}|$ is a negligible function in the security parameter η.[1]

Let S_1 and S_2 be probabilistic polynomially bounded systems. Then S_1 and S_2 are *computationally indistinguishable w.r.t. I*, written $S_1 \approx_{\mathsf{comp}}^{I} S_2$, if $S_1 : I$, $S_2 : I$, both systems use the same interface, and for every polynomially bounded I-environment E for S_1 (and hence, S_2) we have that $E \cdot S_1 \equiv_{\mathsf{comp}} E \cdot S_2$.

Simulatability and Universal Composition. We now define what it means for a system to realize another system, in the spirit of universal composability, a well-established approach in cryptography. Security is defined by an ideal system F (also called an ideal functionality), which, for instance, models ideal encryption, signatures, MACs, key exchange, or secure message transmission. A real system R (also called a real protocol) realizes F if there exists a simulator S such that no polynomially bounded environment can distinguish between R and $S \cdot F$. The simulator tries to make $S \cdot F$ look like R for the environment (see the subsequent sections for examples).

More formally, let F and R be probabilistic polynomially bounded systems which implement the same interface I_{out} and use the same interface I_E, except that in addition F may use some interface I_S provided by a simulator. Then, we say that R *realizes F w.r.t. I_{out}*, written $R \leq^{I_{out}} F$ or simply $R \leq F$, if there exists a probabilistic polynomially bounded system S (the simulator) such that $R \approx_{\mathsf{comp}}^{I_{out}} S \cdot F$. As shown in [24], $\leq$ is reflexive and transitive.

A main advantage of defining security of real systems by the realization relation $\leq$ is that systems can be analyzed and designed in a modular way: The following theorem implies that it suffices to prove security for the systems R_0 and R_1 separately in order to obtain security of the composed system $R_0 \cdot R_1$.

Theorem 1 (Composition Theorem (simplified) [24]). *Let I_0 and I_1 be disjoint interfaces and let R_0, F_0, R_1, and F_1 be probabilistic polynomially bounded systems such*

---

[1] As usual, a function f from the natural numbers to the real numbers is *negligible*, if for every $c > 0$ there exists η_0 such that $f(\eta) \leq \frac{1}{\eta^c}$ for all $\eta > \eta_0$.

that $R_0 \leq^{I_0} F_0$ and $R_1 \leq^{I_1} F_1$. Then, $R_0 \cdot R_1 \leq^{I_0 \cup I_1} F_0 \cdot F_1$, where $I_0 \cup I_1$ is the union of the class, method and field names declared in I_0 and I_1.

Noninterference. The (standard) noninterference notion for confidentiality [13] requires the absence of information flow from high to low variables within a program. Here, we define noninterference for a deterministic (Jinja+) program P with some static variables $\vec{x}$ of primitive types that are labeled as high. Also, some other static variables of primitive types are labeled as low. We say that $P[\vec{x}]$ is a *program with high variables* $\vec{x}$ (and low variables). By $P[\vec{a}]$ we denote the program P where the high variables $\vec{x}$ are initialized with values $\vec{a}$ and the low variables are initialized as specified in P.

Now, noninterference for a deterministic program is defined as follows: Let $P[\vec{x}]$ be a program with high variables. Then, $P[\vec{x}]$ *has the noninterference property* if the following holds: for all $\vec{a}_1$ and $\vec{a}_2$ (of appropriate type), if $P[\vec{a}_1]$ and $P[\vec{a}_2]$ terminate, then at the end of their runs, the values of the low variables are the same. Note that this defines *termination-insensitive* noninterference.

The above notion of noninterference deals with complete programs (closed systems). This notion is generalized to open systems as follows: Let I be an interface and let $S[\vec{x}]$ be a (not necessarily closed) deterministic system with a security parameter and high variables $\vec{x}$ such that $S : I$. Then, $S[\vec{x}]$ is *I-noninterferent* if for every deterministic I-environment E for $S[\vec{x}]$ and every security parameter η, noninterference holds for the system $E \cdot S[\vec{x}](\eta)$, where the variable result declared in E is considered to be the only low variable. Note that here neither E nor S are required to be polynomially bounded.

Tools for checking noninterference often consider only a single closed program. However, I-noninterference is a property of a potentially open system $S[\vec{x}]$, which is composed with an arbitrary I-environment. Therefore, in [24] a technique has been developed which reduces the problem of checking I-noninterferent to checking noninterference for a single (almost) closed system. More specifically, it was shown that to prove I-noninterference for a system $S[\vec{x}]$ with $I_E \vdash S : I$ it suffices to consider a single environment $\tilde{E}_{\vec{u}}^{I,I_E}$ (or $\tilde{E}_{\vec{u}}$, for short) only, which is parameterized by a sequence $\vec{u}$ of values. The output produced by $\tilde{E}_{\vec{u}}$ to $S[\vec{x}]$ is determined by $\vec{u}$ and is independent of the input it gets from $S[\vec{x}]$. To keep $\tilde{E}_{\vec{u}}$ simple, the analysis technique assumes some restrictions on interfaces between $S[\vec{x}]$ and E. In particular, $S[\vec{x}]$ and E should interact only through primitive types, arrays, exceptions, and simple objects. Moreover, E is not allowed to call methods of S directly (formally, we require I to be $\emptyset$). However, since S can call methods of E, this is not an essential limitation.

Theorem 2 (simplified, [24]). *Let $S[\vec{x}]$ be a deterministic program with a restricted interface to its environment, as mentioned above, and let $I = \emptyset$. Then, I-noninterference holds for $S[\vec{x}]$ if and only if for all sequences $\vec{u}$ noninterference holds for $\tilde{E}_{\vec{u}} \cdot S[\vec{x}]$.*

Automatic analysis tools, such as Joana [16, 17], often ignore or can ignore specific values encoded in a program, such as an input sequence $\vec{u}$. Hence, such an analysis of $E_{\vec{u}} \cdot S[\vec{x}]$ implies noninterference for all sequences $\vec{u}$, and by the theorem, this implies I-noninterference for $S[\vec{x}]$.

From I-Noninterference to Computational Indistinguishability. The central theorem that immediately follows from (the more general) results proven within the CVJ framework is the following.

Theorem 3 (simplified, [24]). *Let I and J be disjoint interfaces. Let F, R, $P[\vec{x}]$ be systems such that $R \leq^J F$, $P[\vec{x}] \cdot F$ is deterministic, and $P[\vec{x}] \cdot F : I$ (and hence, $P[\vec{x}] \cdot R : I$). Now, if $P[\vec{x}] \cdot F$ is I-noninterferent, then, for all $\vec{a}_1$ and $\vec{a}_2$ (of appropriate type), we have that $P[\vec{a}_1] \cdot R \approx^I_{comp} P[\vec{a}_2] \cdot R$.*

The intuition and the typical use of this theorem is that the cryptographic operations that P needs to perform are carried out using the system R (e.g., a cryptographic library). The theorem now says that to prove cryptographic privacy of the secret inputs ($\forall\ \vec{a}_1, \vec{a}_2 : P[\vec{a}_1] \cdot R \approx^I_{comp} P[\vec{a}_2] \cdot R$) it suffices to prove I-noninterference for $P[\vec{x}] \cdot F$, i.e., the system where R is replaced by the ideal counterpart F (the ideal cryptographic library). The ideal functionality F, which in our case will model cryptographic primitives in an ideal way, can typically be formulated without probabilistic operations and also the ideal primitives specified by F will be secure even in presence of unbounded adversaries. Therefore, the system $P[\vec{x}] \cdot F$ can be analyzed by standard tools that a priori cannot deal with cryptography (probabilities and polynomially bounded adversaries).

As mentioned before, F relies on the interface $I_E \cup I_S$ (which, for example, might include an interface to a network library) provided by the environment and the simulator, respectively. This means that when checking noninterference for the system $P[\vec{x}] \cdot F$ the code implementing this library does not have to be analyzed. Being provided by the environment/simulator, it is considered completely untrusted and the security of $P[\vec{x}] \cdot F$ does not depend on it. In other words, $P[\vec{x}] \cdot F$ provides noninterference for all implementations of the interface. Similarly, R relies on the interface I_E provided by the environment. Hence, $P[\vec{x}] \cdot R$ enjoys computational indistinguishability for all implementations of I_E. This has two advantages: i) one obtains very strong security guarantees and ii) the code to be analyzed in order to establish noninterference/computational indistinguishability is kept small, considering the fact that libraries tend to be very big.

3   Public-Key Encryption with a Public Key Infrastructure

We now propose an ideal functionality Ideal-PKIEnc, formulated in Java (Jinja+), for public-key encryption with a public-key infrastructure (PKI). This functionality is an extension of a more restricted public-key encryption functionality proposed in [24]. First, the functionality proposed here allows a user to encrypt messages for a given party based on the identifier of this party. The functionality uses the included public key infrastructure to obtain the public key of the party registered under the given identifier. In contrast, to encrypt a message, the user of the functionality in [24] had to provide a public-key herself, and hence, take care of the correct binding of public keys to parties herself. Second, in the functionality proposed here, as opposed to the one in [24], we model static corruption, including dishonestly generated keys. For this, special care was needed to make sure that the resulting functionality is "tool-friendly".

We also provide an implementation (realization) of this ideal functionality, denoted by Real-PKIEnc, in Java (Jinja+) and prove, within the CVJ framework, that this implementation realizes the ideal functionality Ideal-PKIEnc under standard cryptographic assumptions.

As already mentioned in the introduction, the design of such functionalities and the realization proofs pose additional challenges compared to the Turing machine based formulations proposed in the cryptographic literature.

In the rest of this section, we first provide the interface for Ideal-PKIEnc, and hence, Real-PKIEnc. Then, the actual ideal functionality and its realization are presented, along with a realization theorem.

3.1   The Interface for Public-Key Encryption

In this section, we present the interface I_{PKIEnc} of the ideal functionality Ideal-PKIEnc and its implementation Real-PKIEnc and discuss the intended way of using it. The interface I_{PKIEnc} is specified as follows:

```
 1  public class Encryptor {
 2    public Encryptor(byte[] publicKey);
 3    public byte[] encrypt(byte[] message);
 4    public byte[] getPublicKey();
 5  }
 6  public final class Decryptor {
 7    public Decryptor();
 8    public byte[] decrypt(byte[] message);
 9    public Encryptor getEncryptor();
10  }
11  public class RegisterEnc {
12    public static void registerEncryptor(int id, Encryptor encryptor,
13                         byte[] pki_domain) throws PKIError, NetworkError;
14    public static Encryptor getEncryptor(int id, byte[] pki_domain)
15                                         throws PKIError, NetworkError;
16  }
```

Typical Usage. The intended way for an honest user with identifier ID_A to create and register her keys is the following:

```
17  Decryptor decryptor = new Decryptor();
18  Encryptor encryptor = decryptor.getEncryptor();
19  try {
20      RegisterEnc.registerEncryptor(ID_A, encryptor, PKI_DOMAIN);
21  }
22  catch (PKIError e) {}      // registration failed: id already claimed
23  catch (NetworkError e) {} // network problems
```

Intuitively, an object of class Decryptor encapsulates a public/private key pair, generated when the object is created (line 17 above). This object provides access to the method decrypt. The owner of this object (that is, the party who has created it) is not supposed to share it with any other parties. Instead, the owner of the decryptor shares an associated encryptor (obtained in line 18), which, intuitively, encapsulates only the public key. More precisely, to make her public key available within a PKI to other parties, the user registers the encryptor she has obtained (line 20). That is, she registers her encryptor under her identifier (ID_A) and what we call a PKI domain (which is a publicly known identifier used to distinguish keys registered for different purposes/applications). This step may result in an error: i) if some key has been registered already under this identifier and PKI domain (exception PKIError), or ii) if some network failure occurred, e.g., the registration server was unavailable (exception NetworkError). We emphasize that we

do not require the party who wants to register a public key to provide a proof of possession (PoP) of the private key corresponding to the public key.[2] After an encryptor has
been registered, it can be used by other parties as follows:

```
24  try {
25      Encryptor encryptor = RegisterEnc.getEncryptor(ID_A, PKI_DOMAIN);
26      encryptor.encrypt(message);
27  } catch(PKIError e) {}      // id has not been successfully registered
28      catch(NetworkError e) {} // network problems
```

The encryptor of the party registered under ID_A and PKI_DOMAIN is obtained in line 25
and used in line 26 to encrypt a message. Note that a user can also obtain the public key
encapsulated in the encryptor, using the method getPublicKey.

Corruption. To model (static) corruption, we allow encryptors also to be created directly, without creating associated decryptors, simply by providing an arbitrary bitstring
pubk as the public key:

```
29  Encryptor enc = new Encryptor(pubk);
30  try {
31      RegisterEnc.registerEncryptor(ID, enc, PKI_DOMAIN);
32  } catch (PKIError | NetworkError e) {}
```

By this, a dishonest party (the adversary) can register any bitstring pubk as a public
key, including dishonestly generated keys. This key can then be used by any other party
(honest and dishonest) to encrypt messages for the dishonest party, just like public keys
of honest parties. Note that since we do not require PoPs, a dishonest party can register
any public key of another (possibly honest) party under his identity. (As mentioned
before, the literature on PKIs recommends that applications should not rely on PoPs
being performed [3].)

An encryptor created in the above way is called *corrupted*. There is no corresponding
(corrupted) decryptor, because the adversary can run the decryption algorithm himself.
For messages encrypted with a corrupted encryptor (public key), no security guarantees are provided. (Jumping ahead to Section 3.2, the functionality will hand the message to be encrypted with a corrupted encryptor directly to the environment/adversary/
simulator.)

We note that, as expected, when some party obtains an encryptor by the method
RegisterEnc.getEncryptor, the party does not know a priori whether the obtained
encryptor is corrupted (it has been generated directly) or uncorrupted (it has been generated via Decryptor).

3.2   The Ideal Functionality for Public-Key Encryption

We now present the ideal functionality for public-key encryption, Ideal-PKIEnc. This
functionality provides the interface I_{PKIEnc}, introduced above, to its users (parties, environment) with ideal implementations of the methods declared in I_{PKIEnc}.

---

[2] In most applications, PoPs are not necessary and as argued in the literature (see, e.g., [3]),
applications should be designed in such a way that their security does not depend on the assumption of such proofs being performed.

The functionality Ideal-PKIEnc is defined on top of the interface $I_{\text{CryptoLibEnc}}$ which contains methods for key generation, encryption, and decryption:

```
33  public class CryptoLib {
34    public static KeyPair pke_generateKeyPair();
35    public static byte[] pke_encrypt(byte[] message, byte[] publicKey);
36    public static byte[] pke_decrypt(byte[] ciphertext, byte[] privKey);
37  }
```

So Ideal-PKIEnc expects the above methods to be implemented outside of Ideal-PKIEnc. In the analysis of a system $P[\vec{x}]$ which uses Ideal-PKIEnc (i.e., in the analysis of the system $P[\vec{x}] \cdot$ Ideal-PKIEnc), such methods have to be provided by the environment, and thus, are completely untrusted. In particular, in the analysis of $P[\vec{x}] \cdot$ Ideal-PKIEnc the code for CryptoLib, which would typically be very large, does not have to be analyzed. This tremendously simplifies the analysis of $P[\vec{x}] \cdot$ Ideal-PKIEnc (see also the explanation in Section 2 following Theorem 3).

The basic idea of the implementation of Ideal-PKIEnc is that if a message m is to be encrypted with an (uncorrupted) public key, then not m but a sequence of zeros of the same length as m is encrypted instead, using method pke_encrypt of CryptoLib. By this, it is guaranteed that the resulting ciphertext c does not depend on m, except for the length of m. The functionality stores the pair (m, c) for later decryption. If some ciphertext c' is to be decrypted, the functionality first checks whether there exists a pair of the form (m', c') (the functionality guarantees that there is at most one such pair). Then, m' is returned as the plaintext. If no such pair exists (and hence, c' was not created using the functionality), c' is decrypted using method pke_decrypt of CryptoLib, and the resulting plaintext is returned. More specifically, Ideal-PKIEnc works as follows.

On initialization of an object of the class Decryptor, a public/private key pair is created by calling the key generation method of the class CryptoLib. At this point, the decryptor object also creates an (initially empty) list of message/ciphertext pairs. This list is used as a look-up table for decryption by the method decrypt of class Decryptor as sketched above.

Encryptors returned by the method getEncryptor of class Decryptor are objects of the class UncorruptedEncryptor (which is a subclass of the class Encryptor). An encryptor object contains the same public-key as the associated decryptor and shares (a reference to) the list of message/ciphertext pairs with the associated decryptor. When method encrypt of such an encryptor is called with a message m, the encryption method of class CryptoLib is called to encrypt a sequence of zeros of the same length as m, resulting in a ciphertext c (ciphertexts seen before are rejected). Then, the pair (m, c) is stored in the list and the ciphertext c is returned as the result of the encryption.

In contrast, a corrupted encryptor (i.e., an encryptor object created directly as in line 29 above, rather than being derived from a decryptor) implements encryptions simply by calling the encryption method of the class CryptoLib using the bitstring (the public key) it has been provided with upon creation. Note that in this case, no security guarantees are provided; the original message instead of zeros is encrypted.

The methods for registering and obtaining encryptors in class RegisterEnc are implemented in a straightforward way by Ideal-PKIEnc, using a list of registered encryptors along with associated identifiers and domains.

The most important part of the code of Ideal-PKIEnc is listed in the extended version of this paper [22]; for the full code see [23].

3.3   The Realization of Ideal-PKIEnc

We now provide the realization Real-PKIEnc of the ideal functionality Ideal-PKIEnc presented above.

The functionality Real-PKIEnc builds on a public key infrastructure. A public-key infrastructure is a trusted public key registry, where i) users can register their public keys under their identifiers and (PKI) domains (in the sense of Section 3.1) and ii) users can obtain other users' public keys by providing the identifiers and domains of these users. The interface I_{PKI} for the public key infrastructure used by Real-PKIEnc is the following:

```
38   public class PKI {
39     static void register(int id, byte[] domain, byte[] pubKey)
40                                     throws PKIError, NetworkError;
41     static byte[] getKey(int id, byte[] domain)
42                                     throws PKIError, NetworkError;
43   }
```

The method register is supposed to throw PKIError if the provided user identifier and domain pair has been claimed already, i.e., some other party has registered a key for the same identifier and domain pair before. The same exception is supposed to be thrown by the method getKey if the given identifier id has not been registered. Registering or fetching a public key typically involves to contact a public-key server. If this fails, the NetworkError is thrown. When proving that Real-PKIEnc realizes Ideal-PKIEnc we will assume that I_{PKI} is properly implemented (see Section 3.4 for details).

Now, based on I_{PKI}, the different classes and methods provided by Real-PKIEnc are implemented as presented next.

The methods registerEncryptor and getEncryptor of the class RegisterEnc work as follows. When an encryptor is to be registered by the method registerEncryptor, its public key is registered in the PKI using the method register. The method getEncryptor uses the method getKey to fetch the corresponding public key and wraps it into an encryptor which is then returned.

The classes Encryptor and Decryptor of Real-PKIEnc are implemented in a straightforward way using an encryption scheme: messages are simply encrypted/decrypted directly using such a scheme. Note that whether an encryptor was obtained from a decryptor (using the method getEncryptor) or whether it was created directly (as in line 29) leads to the same implementation, namely, invoking the encryption function of the encryption scheme. The only difference is that in one case the public/private key pair was created (honestely) within the class Decryptor of Real-PKIEnc and in the other case the public key was created outside of Real-PKIEnc (possibly in some dishonest way).

The most important part of the code of Real-PKIEnc is listed in [22]; see [23] for the full code.

3.4   Realization Result

We now show that Real-PKIEnc realizes Ideal-PKIEnc, provided that i) the encryption scheme used in the implementation of Real-PKIEnc is IND-CCA2-secure [4] and ii) that the public-key infrastructure used by Real-PKIEnc works "properly".

As for i), we note that IND-CCA2-security is a standard and widely used security notion for public-key encryption schemes. Similarly to ideal functionality for public-key encryption proposed in the cryptographic literature, it has been shown that IND-CCA2-security is necessary to realize Ideal-PKIEnc (see, e.g., [9, 26]).

As for ii), the behavior of a "proper public-key infrastructure" is formalized by an ideal functionality Ideal-PKI, which operates in the obvious way: It maintains a list of registration records, each consisting of an identifier, a domain, and a key (the code is given in [22]). The adversary (simulator) is informed about registration requests and requests for obtaining public-keys and can schedule when these requests are answered by Ideal-PKI (because in a realization such requests typically involve communication over a network controlled by the adversary). We assume the existence of some public-key infrastructure Real-PKI that realizes Ideal-PKI. Note that there are various ways of realizing Ideal-PKI and that all of them will require certain trust assumptions. For example, one could assume the existence of one or more honest certificate authorities and that parties are provided with the (authentic) public keys of these authorities. Typically, one would use some existing public-key infrastructure (with appropriate assumptions) to realize Ideal-PKI. However, this is not the focus of this work. (In fact, proving the security of a full-fledged PKI would be a challenging task by itself.). In our case study (see Section 7), we consider a simple realization which involves a single certificate authority, the assumption being that it in fact realizes Ideal-PKI.

With this, we can now state our main theorem for public-key encryption.

Theorem 4. *If* Real-PKIEnc *uses an IND-CCA2-secure public-key encryption scheme and* Real-PKI $\leq^{I_{PKI}}$ Ideal-PKI, *then* Real-PKIEnc · Real-PKI $\leq^{I_{PKIEnc}}$ Ideal-PKIEnc.

The proof of Theorem 4 is given in [22]. The proof is highly modular and leverages such properties of the realization relation as the composition theorem, reflexivity, and transitivity. In the proof, we split Ideal-PKIEnc and Real-PKIEnc into two parts: one providing encryption and decryption and one providing key registration and retrieving. For the former part, we generalize the result of [24] for public-key functionality without corruption and without PKI to the case with corruption.

4   Digital Signatures with a Public Key Infrastructure

In this section, we propose an ideal functionality Ideal-Sig, formulated in Java (Jinja+), for digital signatures with a public key infrastructure, where, again, we model corruption. We also provide a real implementation Real-Sig of this functionality in Java (Jinja+) and prove, in the CVJ framework, that it realizes Ideal-Sig. Just as for public key encryption, similar functionalities for digital signatures have been proposed in the cryptographic literature before (see, e.g., [10, 26]). But again, the new contribution here is that we provide a formulation in Java, instead of the (simpler) Turing machine models, such that these functionalities can actually be used to analyze Java programs. This is non-trivial and needs some care. We first present the public interface of Ideal-Sig and Real-Sig.

4.1 The Interface for Digital Signatures

The public interface I_{PKISig} of Ideal-Sig and Real-Sig (both have the same public interface) is as follows:

```
1  public final class Signer {
2    public Signer();
3    public byte[] sign(byte[] message);
4    public Verifier getVerifier();
5  }
6  public class Verifier {
7    public Verifier(byte[] verifKey);
8    public boolean verify(byte[] signature, byte[] message);
9    public byte[] getVerifKey();
10 }
11 public class RegisterSig {
12   public static void registerVerifier(int id, Verifier verifier,
13                      byte[] pki_domain) throws PKIError, NetworkError;
14   public static Verifier getVerifier(int id, byte[] pki_domain)
15                              throws PKIError, NetworkError;
16 }
```

Typical Usage. Similarly to public-key encryption, the intended way for an honest user with identifier ID_A to create and register her keys is the following:

```
17 Signer sig = new Signer();
18 Verifier ver = sig.getVerifier();
19 try {
20     SigEnc.registerVerifier(ID_A, ver, PKI_DOMAIN);
21 } catch (PKIError e) {}       // registration failed: id already claimed
22   catch (NetworkError e) {} // network problems
```

Intuitively, an object of the class Signer encapsulates a verification/signing key pair, which is generated when the object is created (line 17). It allows a party who owns such an object to sign messages (this requires the signing key), using the method sign (of the class Signer). This party can also obtain a Verifier object (line 18), which encapsulates the related verification key and can be used (by other parties) to verify signatures via the method verify. Similarly to the case of public-key encryption, such a verifier can be registered in the public-key infrastructure (line 20) in order to make the verification key available to other parties. Again, we do not require a proof of possession of the corresponding signing key.

After a verifier has been registered, it can be used by other parties to check whether a signature signature is valid for a message message w.r.t. the verification key of (ID_A, PKI_DOMAIN) encapsulated in verifier:

```
23  try {
24      Verifier verifier = RegisterSig.getVerifier(ID_A, PKI_DOMAIN);
25      verifier.verify(signature, message);
26  } catch(PKIError e) {}       // id has not been successfully registered
27    catch(NetworkError e) {} // network problems
```

Corruption. To model (static) corruption, analogously to the case of public-key encyrption we allow verifiers to be created directly, without creating associated signers, simply by providing an arbitrary bitstring verif_key as the public key:

```
28  Verifier ver = new Verifier(verif_key);
29  try {
30      RegisterSig.registerVerifier(ID, ver, PKI_DOMAIN);
31  } catch (PKIError | NetworkError e) {}
```

By this, a dishonest party (the adversary) can register any bitstring verif_key he wants as a verification key, including dishonestly generated keys. This key can then be used by any other party (honest and dishonest) to verify messages signed by the dishonest party, just like with verification keys of honest parties. Note that since we do not require PoPs, a dishonest party can register any verification key of another (possibly honest) party under his identity. A verifier created in such a way is called *corrupted*. A corresponding signing object is not necessary as the adversary can directly sign messages by himself using the matching signing key (if this key is known to the adversary). Note that, given a verifier object, other parties cannot tell a priori whether this verifier object is corrupted or not.

4.2   The Ideal Functionality for Digital Signatures

We now present the ideal functionality for digital signatures, Ideal-Sig. This functionality provides the interface I_{PKISig}, introduced above, to its users (parties, environment) with ideal implementations of the methods declared in I_{PKISig}.

The functionality is defined on top of the interface $I_{CryptoLibSig}$ which contains methods for key generation, signing, and verification. Analogously to the interface $I_{CryptoLibEnc}$ for public-key encryption, these methods are supposed to be provided by the environment, and hence, are completely untrusted. In particular, in the analysis of a system that uses Ideal-Sig, they do not have to be analyzed, which, again, greatly simplifies the analysis task.

Now, Ideal-Sig works as follows. On initialization of an object of class Signer, a verification/signing key pair is created by calling the key generation operation of the interface $I_{CryptoLibSig}$. A signer object also creates an (initially empty) list of signed messages; this list will be shared with all associated verifiers (objects returned by getVerifier). When the method sign is called to sign a message m, the signing procedure of $I_{CryptoLibSig}$ is called to sign m using the encapsulated signing key. Before this signature is returned, the signed message m is added to the list of signed messages.

A verifier object returned by the method getVerifier belongs to the class UncorruptedVerifier (a subclass of the class Verifier) and it implements ideal verification as follows: the method verify when called to verify a signature s on a message m first uses the verification procedure of $I_{CryptoLibSig}$ to check if s is a valid signature on m w.r.t. the verification key encapsulated in the verifier object. If this is the case, it additionally checks if m is in the list of signed messages (this list, as mentioned before, is shared with the associated signer object). If this is true as well, the method returns 'true'. The idea behind this procedure is that, independently of how the signing and verification algorithms work, the verification of a signature on some message succeeds only if this message has been signed before (and hence, logged) using Ideal-Sig.

A (corrupted) verifier object created directly implements the verification procedure simply by calling the verification method of $I_{\mathsf{CryptoLibSig}}$.

The methods for registering and obtaining verifiers in class RegisterSig are implemented in a straightforward way by Ideal-PKIEnc, using a list of registered verifiers along with associated identifiers and domains.

The most important part of the code of Ideal-Sig is listed in [22]; see [23] for the full code.

4.3   The Realization of Ideal-Sig

The classes Verifier and Signer of the realization Real-Sig of the ideal functionality Ideal-Sig are implemented in a straightforward way using a digital signature scheme: messages are simply signed/verified directly using such a scheme. Analogously to the methods in EncPKI, the methods registerVerifier and getVerifier of the class RegisterSig are based on the interface I_{PKI} introduced in Section 3.3.

The most important part of the code of Real-Sig is listed in [22]; see [23] for the full code.

4.4   Realization Result

We prove that Real-PKISig realizes Ideal-PKISig, provided that i) the signature scheme used in the implementation of Real-PKISig is UF-CMA-secure [14] and ii) that, analogously to the case of public-key encryption, the public-key infrastructure used by Real-PKISig realizes the ideal functionality Ideal-PKI (see Section 3.4). Again, it has been shown that UF-CMA-security is necessary to realize Ideal-PKIEnc (see, e.g., [26]).

Theorem 5. *If* Real-PKISig *uses an UF-CMA-secure signature scheme and* Real-PKI $\leq^{I_{PKI}}$ Ideal-PKI, *then* Real-PKISig · Real-PKI $\leq^{I_{PKIEnc}}$ Ideal-PKISig.

The proof of this theorem is again highly modular and leverages such properties of the realization relation as the composition theorem, reflexivity, and transitivity. The basic structure of the proof is analogous to the one for public-key encryption. We split Ideal-PKISig and Real-PKISig into two parts: i) signing and verification and ii) key registration and retrieving of verification keys. The most involved part is to show that the real component for signing and verification realizes the corresponding ideal component. Here we make use of an existing results in the cryptographic literature, in particular [26], and reduce the statement to a corresponding statement in the Turing machine model. We refer to the extended version of this paper [22] for details.

5   Private Symmetric Encryption

In this section, we present an ideal functionality for what we call *private symmetric encryption* and a realization of this functionality. Private symmetric encryption allows a user to encrypt messages (using a symmetric encryption scheme) just for herself. She does not share the symmetric key with other parties. This is useful, for example, to store confidential information on an untrusted medium. Since keys do not have to be shared between parties, the functionality can be kept quite simple.

The public interface I_{SymEnc} of this functionality and its realization consists of only one class SymEnc with two methods: encrypt and decrypt. These methods use a symmetric key generated when an object of this class is created.

In the ideal functionality Ideal-SymEnc for private symmetric encryption, encryption and decryption work analogously to the case of public-key encryption: a sequence of zeros is encrypted instead of the given plaintext and the ciphertext obtained in this way is logged along with the plaintext, which enables the functionality to recover this plaintext when the ciphertext is to be decrypted. The realization Real-SymEnc simply uses the encapsulated key to encrypt and decrypt messages using a symmetric encryption scheme. Clearly, there is no need to model (static) corruption here: a dishonest party can simply perform private symmetric encryption by himself. We refer the reader to the extended version of this paper [22], as well as [23] for the full code of Ideal-SymEnc and Real-SymEnc.

We obtain the following result. We omit the proof here because it closely follows the one for public-key encryption only that it is much simpler now, as we neither need to consider a public-key infrastructure nor corruption (see [21] for a corresponding result in a Turing machine model).

Theorem 6. *If* Real-SymEnc *uses an IND-CCA2-secure symmetric encryption scheme, then* Real-SymEnc $\leq^{I_{PKIEnc}}$ Ideal-SymEnc.

6   Nonce Generation

In this section, we propose an ideal functionality and its realization for nonce generation, formulated in Java (Jinja+). The property that the ideal functionality is supposed to provide is nonce freshness, i.e., nonces returned by the functionality should always be different to the nonce that have been returned so far (no collisions); unguessability of nonces is not intended to be modeled by this functionality.

The public interface I_{Nonce} for this functionality consists of one class NonceGen with one method newNonce only, which is supposed to return a fresh nonce.

The ideal functionality Ideal-Nonce for nonce generation works as follows. The functionality maintains an, initially empty, collection (formally, a static list) of nonces that have been returned so far. When the method newNonce is called, the environment/simulator is asked to provide a bitstring; more precisely, the method CryptoLib.newNonce(), which is supposed to be provided by the environment is called. Then, the method newNonce checks whether the returned bitstring is fresh, i.e., whether it does not already belong to the collection of returned nonces. If the nonce is indeed fresh, the nonce is added to the collection and returned to the caller of the method. Otherwise, the above process is repeated until a fresh nonce is returned by the environment/simulator. This guarantees that Ideal-Nonce always outputs a fresh nonce.

In the realization Real-Nonce of Ideal-Nonce, if the method newNonce is called, a bitstring of the length of the security parameter is picked uniformly at random and then returned to the caller. More precisely, we assume the method `CryptoLib.newNonce()` called by Real-Nonce to work in this way.

We refer the reader to the extended version [22] for the most important part of the code of Ideal-Nonce and Real-Nonce; see [23] for the full code. Now, it is easy to prove that Real-Nonce realizes Ideal-Nonce.

Theorem 7. Real-Nonce $\leq^{I_{Nonce}}$ Ideal-Nonce.

To prove this theorem, we let the simulator S work just like Real-Nonce, i.e., when asked to provide a new nonce by Ideal-Nonce, it picks a bitstring of the length of the security parameter uniformly at random and returns this bitstring to Ideal-Nonce. Now, Real-Nonce cannot be distinguished by any (polynomial bounded) environment from $S \cdot$ Ideal-Nonce unless Real-Nonce produces a collision, which, however, happens with negligible probability only.

7 The Case Study

As a case study of the results obtained in this paper, we now describe the verification of a cloud storage system implemented in Java. This system illustrates how the ideal functionalities we have developed and presented in this paper can be used to analyze an interesting and non-trivial Java program. As already mentioned in the introduction, except for the work in [24], where only a much simpler Java program has been considered, there has been no other work on establishing cryptographic (indistinguishability) properties for Java programs.

In what follows, we first provide a brief description of the cloud storage system program. Then we state the (cryptographic) security property that we verify and, finally, report on the verification process carried out using the tool Joana [16, 17], which, as already mentioned, allows for the fully automatic verification of noninterference properties of Java programs.

Description of the Cloud Storage System. We have implemented a cloud storage system that allows a user (through her client application) to store data on a remote server such that confidentiality of the data stored on the server is guaranteed even if the server is untrusted: data stored on the server is encrypted using a symmetric key known only to the client.

More specifically, data is stored (encrypted with the symmetric key of a user) on the server along with a label and a counter (a version number). When data is to be stored under some label, a new (higher) counter is chosen and the data is stored under the label and the new counter; old data is still preserved (under smaller counters). Different users can have data repositories on one server. These repositories are strictly separated. The system can be used to securely store any kind of data. A user may use our cloud storage system, for example, to store her passwords remotely on a server such that she has access to them on different devices.

Communication between a client and a server is secured and authenticated using functionalities for public-key encryption and digital signatures. Moreover, the functionality for nonce generation is essential to prevent replay attacks (when the client and the server run a sub-protocol to synchronize counter values for labels). The extended version of this paper [22] gives a more detailed description of our application; see [23] for the full code of the system.

The Security Property. As mentioned, the most fundamental security property of the cloud storage system is confidentiality of the stored data. This property is supposed to be guaranteed even if the server and all clients of other users may be dishonest and cooperate with an active adversary.

To formulate this confidentiality property, we provide (besides the code of the client and the server) a setup class with the method main, which gets a secret bit secret_bit as input. This method models the interaction between the program of an honest client and the active adversary (the environment). The adversary has full control over the network and subsumes the server and all dishonest clients. The adversary also controls the actions taken by the honest client. In particular, he determines the label and data items the honest client is supposed to store on the server. More precisely, in every request, the adversary provides a pair of data items. The secret bit secret_bit determines which of the two items the client actually asks the server to store (see [22] for a more detailed explanation of the setup class and [23] for the full code).

The security property now requires that no (probabilistic polynomial-time) adversary should be able to determine the secret bit secret_bit, and hence, whether the data items in the first or in the second component of the item pairs provided by the adversary are sent by the client. This specifies a strong cryptographic privacy property, common in cryptography. Formally, this indistinguishability property is state as follows:

$$\mathsf{CS}_R[\mathtt{false}] \approx^{\emptyset}_{\mathsf{comp}} \mathsf{CS}_R[\mathtt{true}] \tag{1}$$

where $\mathsf{CS}_R[b]$ denotes the described system, consisting of the setup class and the client class, with secret_bit set to b. The index R indicates that in this system the cryptographic operations are carried out using the real cryptographic schemes (rather than ideal functionalities).

We note that the computational indistinguishability relation in (1) uses the empty interface $I = \emptyset$. This means that the adversary (environment) cannot directly call methods of the client object. As explained before, by the definition of the setup class, the environment can nonetheless determine which actions are taken and when. We also point out that CS_R is an open system which uses some classes not defined within CS_R, such as a network library. These classes are provided by the environment and, therefore, are untrusted. Thus, property (1) implies confidentiality of the stored messages no matter how such untrusted libraries are implemented.

Verification of the Security Property. In order to prove (1), by Theorem 3 it suffices to show that

$$\mathsf{CS}_I[b] \text{ is } I\text{-noninterferent,} \tag{2}$$

where CS_I denotes the system which coincides with CS_R except that the real cryptographic schemes are replaced by their ideal counterparts (ideal functionalities), i.e., Ideal-PKEnc, Ideal-Sig, Ideal-SymEnc, and Ideal-Nonce. Since, as can easily been seen, $\mathsf{CS}_I[b]$ satisfies the conditions of Theorem 2, we can further reduce checking (2) to checking the following property:

$$\tilde{E}_{\vec{u}} \cdot \mathsf{CS}_I[b] \text{ is noninterferent for all } \vec{u}, \tag{3}$$

where the family of systems $\tilde{E}_{\vec{u}}$, parameterized by a finite sequence of integers $\vec{u}$, is as described in Section 2. This system can be automatically generated from $CS_l[b]$. Also note that by "noninterference" we mean standard termination-insensitive noninterference (see Section 2). Altogether it suffices to prove (3) in order to obtain (1).

Joana was easily able to establish property (3). It took about 17 seconds on a standard PC (Core i5 2.3GHz, 8GB RAM) to finish the analysis of the program (with a size of 950 LoC). Note that the actual running code of the distributed system is much bigger than what Joana needed to analyze, because the code of the distributed system includes untrusted libraries, such as the standard Java library for networking, which do not need to be analyzed, as already mentioned above.

Acknowledgment. This work was partially supported by *Deutsche Forschungsgemeinschaft* (DFG) under Grant KU 1434/6-2 within the priority programme 1496 "Reliably Secure Software Systems – RS^3".

References

1. Aizatulin, M., Gordon, A.D., Jürjens, J.: Extracting and verifying cryptographic models from C protocol code by symbolic execution. In: Proceedings of the 18th ACM Conference on Computer and Communications Security (CCS 2011). ACM (2011)
2. Aizatulin, M., Gordon, A.D., Jürjens, J.: Computational verification of C protocol implementations by symbolic execution. In: ACM Conference on Computer and Communications Security (CCS 2012). ACM (2012)
3. Asokan, N., Niemi, V., Laitinen, P.: On the Usefulness of Proof-of-Possession. In: Proceedings of the 2nd Annual PKI Research Workshop (2003)
4. Bellare, M., Desai, A., Pointcheval, D., Rogaway, P.: Relations among Notions of Security for Public-Key Encryption Schemes. In: Krawczyk, H. (ed.) CRYPTO 1998. LNCS, vol. 1462, pp. 26–45. Springer, Heidelberg (1998)
5. Bhargavan, K., Fournet, C., Gordon, A.D.: Modular verification of security protocol code by typing. In: Proceedings of the 37th ACM SIGPLAN-SIGACT Symposium on Principles of Programming Languages (POPL 2010). ACM (2010)
6. Bhargavan, K., Fournet, C., Kohlweiss, M., Pironti, A., Strub, P.-Y.: Implementing TLS with verified cryptographic security. In: IEEE Symposium on Security & Privacy, Oakland (2013)
7. Blanchet, B.: A Computationally Sound Mechanized Prover for Security Protocols. In: IEEE Symposium on Security and Privacy (S&P 2006). IEEE Computer Society (2006)
8. Cadé, D., Blanchet, B.: Proved Generation of Implementations from Computationally Secure Protocol Specifications. In: Basin, D., Mitchell, J.C. (eds.) POST 2013. LNCS, vol. 7796, pp. 63–82. Springer, Heidelberg (2013)
9. Canetti, R.: Universally Composable Security: A New Paradigm for Cryptographic Protocols. In: Proceedings of the 42nd Annual Symposium on Foundations of Computer Science (FOCS 2001). IEEE Computer Society (2001)
10. Canetti, R.: Universally Composable Signature, Certification, and Authentication. In: Proceedings of the 17th IEEE Computer Security Foundations Workshop (CSFW-17 2004). IEEE Computer Society (2004)
11. Chaki, S., Datta, A.: ASPIER: An automated framework for verifying security protocol implementations. In: Proceedings of the 22nd IEEE Computer Security Foundations Symposium (CSF 2009). IEEE Computer Society (2009)
12. Fournet, C., Kohlweiss, M., Strub, P.-Y.: Modular code-based cryptographic verification. In: Proceedings of the 18th ACM Conference on Computer and Communications Security (CCS 2011). ACM (2011)

13. Goguen, J.A., Meseguer, J.: Security Policies and Security Models. In: Proceedings of IEEE Symposium on Security and Privacy (1982)

14. Goldwasser, S., Micali, S., Rivest, R.L.: A digital signature scheme secure against adaptive chosen-message attacks. SIAM Journal on Computing 17(2), 281–308 (1988)

15. Goubault-Larrecq, J., Parrennes, F.: Cryptographic protocol analysis on real C code. In: Cousot, R. (ed.) VMCAI 2005. LNCS, vol. 3385, pp. 363–379. Springer, Heidelberg (2005)

16. Graf, J., Hecker, M., Mohr, M.: Using JOANA for Information Flow Control in Java Programs - A Practical Guide. In: Proceedings of the 6th Working Conference on Programming Languages (ATPS 2013). Lecture Notes in Informatics (LNI), vol. 215. Springer, Heidelberg (2013)

17. Hammer, C., Snelting, G.: Flow-Sensitive, Context-Sensitive, and Object-sensitive Information Flow Control Based on Program Dependence Graphs. International Journal of Information Security 8(6), 399–422 (2009)

18. Klein, G., Nipkow, T.: A Machine-Checked Model for a Java-Like Language, Virtual Machine, and Compiler. ACM Trans. Program. Lang. Syst. 28(4), 619–695 (2006)

19. Küsters, R.: Simulation-Based Security with Inexhaustible Interactive Turing Machines. In: Proceedings of the 19th IEEE Computer Security Foundations Workshop (CSFW-19 2006). IEEE Computer Society (2006)

20. Küsters, R., Tuengerthal, M.: Joint State Theorems for Public-Key Encryption and Digital Signature Functionalities with Local Computation. Technical Report 2008/006, Cryptology ePrint Archive (2008), http://eprint.iacr.org/2008/006

21. Küsters, R., Tuengerthal, M.: Universally Composable Symmetric Encryption. In: Proceedings of the 22nd IEEE Computer Security Foundations Symposium (CSF 2009). IEEE Computer Society (2009)

22. Küsters, R., Scapin, E., Truderung, T., Graf, J.: Extending and Applying a Framework for the Cryptographic Verification of Java Programs. Cryptology ePrint Archive, Report 2014/038 (2014), http://eprint.iacr.org/2014/038

23. Küsters, R., Scapin, E., Truderung, T., Graf, J.: A Java Implementation of a Cloud Storage System (2013), http://infsec.uni-trier.de/publications/software/CloudStorage.zip

24. Küsters, R., Truderung, T., Graf, J.: A Framework for the Cryptographic Verification of Java-like Programs. In: IEEE Computer Security Foundations Symposium, CSF 2012. IEEE Computer Society (2012)

25. Küsters, R., Truderung, T., Graf, J.: A Framework for the Cryptographic Verification of Java-like Programs. Cryptology ePrint Archive, Report 2012/153 (2012), http://eprint.iacr.org/2012/153

26. Küsters, R., Tuengerthal, M.: Joint State Theorems for Public-Key Encryption and Digital Signature Functionalities with Local Computation. In: Proceedings of the 21st IEEE Computer Security Foundations Symposium (CSF 2008). IEEE Computer Society (2008)

27. Küsters, R., Tuengerthal, M.: The IITM Model: a Simple and Expressive Model for Universal Composability. Technical Report 2013/025, Cryptology ePrint Archive (2013), http://eprint.iacr.org/2013/025

28. Nipkow, T., von Oheimb, D.: Java$_{light}$ is Type-Safe — Definitely. In: POPL (1998)

29. Pfitzmann, B., Waidner, M.: A Model for Asynchronous Reactive Systems and its Application to Secure Message Transmission. In: IEEE Symposium on Security and Privacy. EEE Computer Society (2001)

Compiling CAO: From Cryptographic Specifications to C Implementations*

Manuel Barbosa, David Castro, and Paulo F. Silva

HASLab/INESC TEC — Universidade do Minho, Portugal
{mbb,dcastro,paufil}@di.uminho.pt

Abstract. We present a compiler for CAO, an imperative DSL for the cryptographic domain. The tool takes high-level cryptographic algorithm specifications and translates them into C implementations through a series of security-aware transformations and optimizations. The compiler back-end is highly configurable, allowing the targeting of very disparate platforms in terms of memory requirements and computing power.

1 Introduction

The development of cryptographic software poses a set of challenges that differ from general-purpose software. Producing cryptographic code requires a set of skills related to mathematics, electrical engineering and computer science. Moreover, performance is usually critical and aggressive optimizations must be performed without altering the security semantics. It is common to find cryptographic software directly implemented in assembly because this permits a more efficient implementation, whilst ensuring that low-level security policies are satisfied. Hence, the development of cryptographic software is often an error-prone and time consuming task that only experts can be trusted to carry out.

The CAO language [1] aims to change this. It is a domain specific language (DSL) tailored for the implementation of cryptographic software. In this paper we present a tool for compiling CAO programs into C libraries, i.e., cryptographic components that can then be integrated into more complex software projects. Although at the high-level it appears similar to that of a standard compiler, the architecture of the CAO compiler has been tailored to cater for the widely different scenarios for which cryptographic code may need to be produced, with two main design goals: i. to create a compilation tool that is flexible and configurable enough to permit targeting a wide range or computing platforms, from powerful servers to embedded microcontrollers; and ii. to incorporate, whenever possible, domain-specific transformations and optimizations early on in the compilation process, avoiding platform-specific variants of these transformation stages. One example of this is the generation of indistinguishable operations needed in the deployment of countermeasures against side-channel attacks.

* This work was supported by Project Best Case, which is co-financed by the North Portugal Regional Operational Programme (ON.2 – O Novo Norte), under the National Strategic Reference Framework (NSRF), through the European Regional Development Fund (ERDF).

M. Abadi and S. Kremer (Eds.): POST 2014, LNCS 8414, pp. 240–244, 2014.
© Springer-Verlag Berlin Heidelberg 2014

CAO Language. CAO is an imperative language that supports high-level cryptographic concepts as first-class features, allowing the programmer to focus on implementation aspects that are critical for security and efficiency. In particular, CAO has call-by-value semantics and does not provide any language construct to dynamically allocate memory nor input/output support, as it is targeted at implementing the core components of cryptographic libraries. The native types and operators in the language are highly expressive. The CAO native types are: booleans, arbitrary precision integers, machine integers, signed/unsigned bit strings of a given length, rings or fields defined by an integer, extension fields defined by a type and a polynomial, vectors of elements of a type and a given length and matrices of elements of a type and a given size. There is a number of built-in operators and expressions which deal with values of these types. The operators include: arithmetic binary/unary operators, operators for comparing elements, bitwise operators for bit-strings and shift, rotate and concatenation operations on bit-strings. CAO is strongly typed, and the type system provides a powerful mechanism for implementing templates of cryptographic programs by using *symbolic constants* and a limited form of dependent types. A detailed description of (an earlier version of) the CAO language, type checking rules and a proof of their soundness can be found in [1].

In addition to the CAO compiler described in this paper, CAO is supported by two other tools: the CAO interactive interpreter and the CAOVerif tool [3], a deductive verification tool inspired by the Frama-C platform.

2   Compiler Architecture

The CAO compiler is logically divided in classical *front-end*, *middle-end* and *back-end* structure. The front-end parses the input file and produces an abstract representation, or *Abstract Syntax Tree* (AST), which is then checked against the typing rules of the language. This results in an annotated AST which is used in subsequent stages. The most distinctive parts of our compiler are the middle-end and the back-end which we will describe in more detail in the following.

2.1   Middle-End

In addition to generating C code, the CAO compiler is also intended to perform meaningful CAO-to-CAO transformations. The middle-end takes the annotated AST and applies a sequence of such transformations towards a CAO format suitable for easy translation to C. The most interesting steps are the following.

Expansion. This optional transformation follows from the fact that most cryptographic algorithms use iterative structures with statically determined bounds. The body of the iteration is unrolled and the loop variables are instantiated.

Evaluation. This transformation evaluates the statically computable expressions, possibly instantiated in the previous step. Operator properties such as idempotence and cancellation are also used to simplify expressions.

Simplification. This transformation is in charge of reducing the mismatch between CAO and C. Compilers that generate assembly code traditionally use an intermediate representation known as three-address code, in which every instruction is in its simpler form with two operand addresses and one result address. Our format shares some of the same principles and, looking ahead, it is consistent with the syntax adopted in the construction of the supporting static libraries.

Optimization. At this stage, the *Control Flow Graph* (CFG) of the CAO code is inferred and transformations to and from *Static Single Assignment* (SSA) form are implemented using adaptations of the algorithms described in [4] and [5]. We provide a set of functions to manipulate the CFG (and CFG in SSA form), to ease the task of implementing (domain-specific) optimization passes.

Side-Channel Countermeasures. The CAO compiler incorporates a popular software countermeasure against side-channel attacks [2]. The compiler ensures that the code generated for two potentially vulnerable functions (specified by the user) is indistinguishable: both functions execute the same sequence of native CAO operations. To this end, it reorders instructions and, if necessary, introduces dummy operations. The resulting code is kept as efficient as possible by heuristic optimization. This is done after the optimization stage, since optimization could break this security-critical protection. We note that such countermeasures do not guarantee security against side-channel attacks, but are commonly used to increase the resilience of implementations.

2.2   Back-End

Targeting a language like C poses different challenges than translating code to assembly. One of the reasons for this is that the design space is much larger and the C code can be compiled to very disparate platforms. We tackle this problem using a two-layer approach: the CAO code is translated to a specific C format, which is then linked with a static library where the semantics of the CAO operations is implemented and the data types are defined. This allows adjusting the C data type definitions and the implementation of the operations to the characteristics of the target platform. We identified the following variants of static library implementations that may be preferable depending on the target:

- native variable declarations versus complex declarations using C macros;
- automatic static allocation of memory versus explicit dynamic allocation;
- implementing operations using C functions versus using C macros;
- returning results by value versus returning results by reference;
- calling a function by passing values versus passing references;
- translating literals to constants versus initializing auxiliary variables;
- implement operators so as to preserve the input values in arguments versus unsafe implementations.

For each target platform, our back-end takes a configuration file that describes the specific implementation choices adopted for the static library and generates the C code accordingly with the definitions. For example, in the case of variables of a given type use explicit allocation, the compiler will know to call a memory allocation routine. Similarly, if operations over a given type take parameters by reference, then the code generator will make sure the routine receives a pointer to the input parameter.

An important point is that the target platform specification also declares which operations are defined in the static library allowing for incomplete implementations. Therefore, the compilation may fail with an error when the translation is not possible because an operation or data type is not supported.

3   Conclusions and Directions for Future Work

The CAO compiler has been successfully used to implement different cryptographic functions and algorithms, targeting both powerful computational platforms and constrained embedded devices. Example implementations include the SHA family of hash functions, HMAC authentication algorithms, RSA-OAEP encryption and Rabin-Williams signatures. The compiler code is reasonably stable and the current release can be used in real-world contexts. It is available from http://crypto.di.uminho.pt/CAO and will soon be published as an open-source project in the Hackage repository.

So far we have only preliminary results regarding a comparative analysis of the tradeoff between the reduction in development time and the performance penalty incurred by using the CAO compiler. Future work will include a more detailed analysis of these trade-offs. Nevertheless, these results indicate that a highly optimized CAO back-end can lead to C implementations with analogous performance to those offered by open-source off-the-shelf cryptographic packages. This is because the output of the CAO compiler is essentially a sequence of calls to an underlying static library, which can incorporate state-of-the-art optimizations, with the extra advantage that these can be transparently reused from one CAO program to another.

Additional directions for future work include improving the compiler efficiency, supporting additional countermeasures against side-channel attacks, and supporting novel cryptographic constructions, namely those based on lattices.

References

1. Barbosa, M., Moss, A., Page, D., Rodrigues, N.F., Silva, P.F.: Type checking cryptography implementations. In: Arbab, F., Sirjani, M. (eds.) FSEN 2011. LNCS, vol. 7141, pp. 316–334. Springer, Heidelberg (2012)
2. Barbosa, M., Page, D.: On the automatic construction of indistinguishable operations. In: Smart, N.P. (ed.) Cryptography and Coding 2005. LNCS, vol. 3796, pp. 233–247. Springer, Heidelberg (2005)
3. Barbosa, M., Pinto, J., Filliâtre, J.C., Vieira, B.: A deductive verification platform for cryptographic software. Electronic Communications of the EASST 33 (2010)

4. Cytron, R., Ferrante, J., Rosen, B.K., Wegman, M.N., Zadeck, F.K.: Efficiently computing static single assignment form and the control dependence graph. ACM Trans. Program. Lang. Syst (TOPLAS) 13(4), 451–490 (1991)
5. Sreedhar, V.C., Ju, R.D.-C., Gillies, D.M., Santhanam, V.: Translating out of static single assignment form. In: Cortesi, A., Filé, G. (eds.) SAS 1999. LNCS, vol. 1694, pp. 194–210. Springer, Heidelberg (1999)

Decentralized Composite Access Control

Petar Tsankov, Srdjan Marinovic, Mohammad Torabi Dashti, and David Basin

Institute of Information Security, ETH Zurich, Switzerland
{ptsankov,srdanm,torabidm,basin}@inf.ethz.ch

Abstract. Formal foundations for access control policies with both authority delegation and policy composition operators are partial and limited. Correctness guarantees cannot therefore be formally stated and verified for decentralized composite access control systems, such as those based on XACML 3. To address this problem we develop a formal policy language BELLOG that can express both delegation and composition operators. We illustrate, through examples, how BELLOG can be used to specify practical policies. Moreover, we present an analysis framework for reasoning about BELLOG policies and we give decidability and complexity results for policy entailment and policy containment in BELLOG.

1 Introduction

We present the first formal language for specifying and reasoning about *decentralized composite* access control policies, which are policies that require both authority delegation and policy compositions. Below, we illustrate these concepts, and motivate the need for their formal study.

Consider a simple grid system. The grid owner allows *privileged* clients to issue access control policies for the grid's storage space by delegating the authority over the storage resources to them. Privileged clients issue policies, and may also further delegate this authority. To decide who can access storage resources, the grid owner composes the collected policies using different composition operators, such as permit-override (permit if at least one client grants access), majority voting (permit if most clients grant access), etc. This example demonstrates how modern access control systems require both authority delegation and policy composition features, hence going beyond composition-only systems, e.g. those based on XACML 2, and delegation-only systems, such as KeyNote 2 [1]. Real-world examples include grid resource sharing systems [2], electronic health record management [3] and highly distributed Web services [4]. To cater for such decentralized composite access control systems, the industry has recently released the XACML 3 standard.

The need for a formal foundation is evident: Without it, one cannot precisely define how existing and future decentralized composite access control systems should behave (e.g. the ones built upon XACML 3 implementations). Furthermore, formal guarantees about the correctness of decentralized composite policies, e.g. by answering policy entailment and containment questions, cannot be derived. The existing formal access control languages fall short in this regard.

M. Abadi and S. Kremer (Eds.): POST 2014, LNCS 8414, pp. 245–264, 2014.

They either express authority delegation or policy composition, but not both together; see the related work.

Contributions. We are the first to address the problem of formally specifying and reasoning about decentralized composite policies. We develop a novel logic programming language, dubbed BELLOG, for constructing decentralized composite policy languages. BELLOG is an extension of Datalog [5], where the truth values come from Belnap's four-valued logic [6]. All delegation languages based on Datalog can therefore be mapped to BELLOG. Furthermore, BELLOG is more expressive than the existing multi-valued policy algebras, such as PBel [7] and PTaCL [8].

Through examples, we illustrate how decentralized composite policies can be encoded in BELLOG. We also present syntactic extensions of BELLOG that ease the specification of common policy composition and authority delegation idioms, for instance: permit-override, only-one-applicable, agreement, hand-off trust application, transitive delegation, etc.

We present a policy analysis framework for verifying policies written in BELLOG, and demonstrate how different policy analysis questions are used to reason about a policy's behavior in some or all system configurations. We show that verifying BELLOG policies for a given system configuration is in PTIME, and verification for all possible system configurations of a finite domain of subjects and objects is in CO-NP-COMPLETE. We furthermore identify a useful fragment of BELLOG where verification for all possible system configurations for infinitely many subjects and objects belongs to CO-NEXP.

Finally, BELLOG can be used as a four-valued logic programming language for reasoning with inconsistent and incomplete knowledge. BELLOG and its decision procedures are therefore of independent interest.

Related Work. The closest related works to BELLOG are policy algebras, formal delegation languages, and XACML 3, which is an informal policy language.

Policy algebras—such as PBel [7], PTaCL [8], and D-Algebra [9]—are languages for composing a set of policies. A composite policy is a tree, where the internal nodes are composition operators, and the leaf nodes are core policies. Existing policy algebras cannot express arbitrarily long delegation chains and therefore cannot be used for decentralized composite access control. Moreover, they lack operators for composing *intensionally* defined policy sets, i.e. policy sets that are not fixed at the policy specification time; see §4.

Delegation languages—such as KeyNote2 [1], DKAL [10], SecPAL [11], RT [12], GP [13], and DCC [14]—allow a policy writer to delegate to other principals authority over attributes and policy decisions. In contrast to BELLOG, these languages support only the permit-override operator for composing policies. Although the permit-override operator is sufficient in their access control setup, this is not the case for decentralized composite policies. Most existing delegation languages are founded on logic programming. We remark that although many-valued extensions for logic programming exist [15–17], they also cannot express

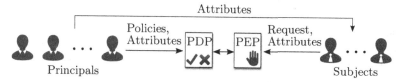

Fig. 1. The system model with the Policy Enforcement Point (PEP), Policy Decision Point (PDP), principals, subjects, requests, and attributes

all composition operators found in policy algebras, e.g. the only-one-applicable operator; that is, they are functionally incomplete.

XACML 3 is currently the only access control language supporting decentralized composite access control. Similarly to BELLOG, XACML 3 has four policy decisions and operators for encoding delegation and policy composition. In contrast to BELLOG, XACML is informal and some aspects are underspecified; for example, loop handling in delegation chains is left to implementations. Moreover, XACML 3 has a fixed set of composition operators and new operators cannot be added as syntactic extensions. Kolovski et al. [18] give a formalization of XACML 3 which focuses on delegations and supports only three composition operators. BELLOG, in contrast, supports all finitary composition operators.

Finally, we remark that BELLOG is not meant to be an all-encompassing policy specification language. For example, the constraint-based conditions of [11] are not expressible in BELLOG.

Organization. In §2, we introduce our system model. In §3, we define our logic programming language BELLOG and define the main decision problems for BELLOG programs. In §4, we illustrate the specification of decentralized composite policies in BELLOG. In §5, we present our policy analysis framework. We conclude the paper in §6. Note that proofs and technical details can be found in the extended version of the paper [19].

2   System Model and the Running Example

A Policy Decision Point (PDP) maps access requests to policy decisions and a Policy Enforcement Point (PEP) enforces the policy decisions made by the PDP. We consider an open distributed system, as illustrated in Figure 1, where there are multiple principals that may issue policies and attributes and store them at the PDP. One principal is designated as the PDP's administrator. The administrator writes the policy against which all requests are evaluated.

Subject and object attributes are issued and signed by principals. Authority over attributes can be delegated to other principals. An attribute issued by a principal is either stored at the PDP, or given to the subject, who may provide it to the PDP together with a request. Attributes that are not explicitly communicated to the PDP are assumed not to have been issued, as is the case in other decentralized systems [1]. A policy domain database contains the identifiers of objects such as roles, file names, etc. Both the administrator and authorized principals can extend this database.

To illustrate our system model, consider a grid system that stores files for multiple research projects. Each project has one or more project leaders. The grid system has one PDP that decides access for all files. The PDP's policy, inspired by policies in the Swedish Grid Initiative (SweGrid) system [2], is:

R1: A project leader controls access to the project's files and folders, and can delegate these rights.

R2: If there is a conflicting decision among the project leaders for a given request, then grant access only to requests made by the project leaders.

R3: If no policy applies to a given request, then grant the request if its target is a public project folder, otherwise deny it.

R4: Access rights are recursively extended to sub-folders.

This policy exemplifies the tight coupling between the use of delegation and composition in decentralized composite policies. The PDP must first compute the delegations for each folder according to R1, then compose the access rights for each folder according to R2 and R3, and finally extend the policy decisions to sub-folders according to R4. Note that R4 can be encoded as delegation from a parent folder to its children. Such couplings of delegation and composition idioms prevent the decentralized composite policies from being split into and evaluated as two independent, delegation and composition, parts.

3 BELLOG

In this section, we define the syntax and semantics of BELLOG and study the time complexity of its decision problems. BELLOG builds upon the syntax and semantics of stratified Datalog [5], and extends it over a four-valued truth space. We see BELLOG as a foundation for constructing high-level access control languages, and we therefore present BELLOG as a generic many-valued logic programming language. In §4, we illustrate how BELLOG can be used to specify practical access control policies.

Syntax. We fix a finite set $\mathcal{P}$ of predicate symbols, where $\mathcal{D}_4 = \{\mathsf{f}_4, \bot_4, \top_4, \mathsf{t}_4\} \subseteq \mathcal{P}$, along with a countably infinite set $\mathcal{C}$ of constants, and a countably infinite set $\mathcal{V}$ of variables. The sets $\mathcal{P}$, $\mathcal{C}$, and $\mathcal{V}$ are pairwise disjoint. Each predicate symbol $p \in \mathcal{P}$ is associated with an arity and we may write p^n to emphasize that p's arity is n. The predicate symbols in $\mathcal{D}_4$ have zero arity. As a convention, we write P to denote a BELLOG program and use the remaining uppercase letters to denote variables. Predicate and constant symbols are written using lowercase *italic* and sans font respectively.

A *domain* Σ is a nonempty finite set of constants. We associate a domain Σ with a set of *atoms* $\mathcal{A}_{\Sigma(\mathcal{V})} = \{p^n(t_1, \cdots, t_n) \mid p^n \in \mathcal{P}, \{t_1, \cdots, t_n\} \subseteq \Sigma \cup \mathcal{V}\}$. A *literal* is either a, $\neg a$, or $\sim a$, for $a \in \mathcal{A}_{\Sigma(\mathcal{V})}$, and $\mathcal{L}_{\Sigma(\mathcal{V})}$ denotes the set of literals over Σ. We refer to $\neg a$ as *negative literals* and to a and $\sim a$ as *non-negative literals*. The function $vars : \mathcal{A}_{\Sigma(\mathcal{V})} \mapsto 2^{\mathcal{V}}$ maps atoms to the set of variables appearing in them. An atom a is *ground* iff $vars(a) = \emptyset$, and $\mathcal{A}_{\Sigma(\emptyset)}$ denotes the set of ground atoms. We extend $vars$ to literals in the standard way.

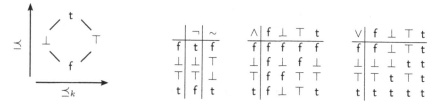

Fig. 2. BELLOG's truth space   **Fig. 3.** Truth tables of BELLOG's operators

A BELLOG program, defined over the domain Σ, is a finite set of *rules* of the form:

$$p \leftarrow q_1, \ldots, q_n \, ,$$

where $n > 0$, $p \in \mathcal{A}_{\Sigma(V)}$, $\{q_1, \cdots, q_n\} \subseteq \mathcal{L}_{\Sigma(V)}$, and $vars(p) \subseteq \bigcup_{1 \leq i \leq n} vars(q_i)$. We refer to p as the rule's head and to $q_1, \ldots, q_n$ as the rule's body.

The predicate symbols in a BELLOG program P are partitioned into intensionally defined predicates, denoted idb_P, and extensionally defined predicates, denoted edb_P. The set idb_P contains all predicate symbols that appear in the heads of P's rules, and the set edb_P contains the remaining predicate symbols. We write $\mathcal{A}_{\Sigma(V)}^{edb_P}$ ($\mathcal{L}_{\Sigma(V)}^{edb_P}$) and $\mathcal{A}_{\Sigma(V)}^{idb_P}$ ($\mathcal{L}_{\Sigma(V)}^{idb_P}$) to denote the sets of atoms (literals) constructed from predicate symbols in edb_P and idb_P respectively.

A rule $p \leftarrow q_1, \cdots, q_n$ is ground iff all the literals in its body are ground. The *grounding* of a BELLOG program P is the finite set of ground rules, denoted by $P^{\downarrow}$, obtained by substituting all variables in P's rules with constants from Σ in all possible ways.

A BELLOG program P is *stratified* iff the rules in P can be partitioned into sets $P_0, \cdots, P_n$ called strata, such that: (1) for every predicate symbol p, all rules with p in their heads are in one stratum P_i; (2) if a predicate symbol p occurs as a non-negative literal in a rule of P_i, then all rules with p in their heads are in a stratum P_j with $j \leq i$; (3) if a predicate symbol p occurs as a negative literal in a rule's body in P_i, then all rules with p in their heads are in a stratum P_j with $j < i$. The given definition of stratified BELLOG extends with non-negative literals that of stratified Datalog [20].

Semantics. The truth space of BELLOG is the lattice $(\mathcal{D}, \preceq, \wedge, \vee)$, where $\mathcal{D} = \{f, \bot, \top, t\}$, $\preceq$ is the partial truth ordering on $\mathcal{D}$, and $\wedge$ and $\vee$ are the meet and join operators. Figure 2 shows the lattice's Hasse diagram, where $\preceq$ is depicted upwards. We adopt the meaning of the non-classical truth values $\bot$ and $\top$ from Belnap's four-valued logic [6]: $\bot$ denotes *missing information* and $\top$ denotes *conflicting information*. We define the partial knowledge ordering on $\mathcal{D}$, denoted with $\preceq_k$, and depict it in Figure 2 rightwards. We denote the meet and join operators on the lattice $(\mathcal{D}, \preceq_k)$ by $\otimes$ and $\oplus$, respectively. The truth tables of the unary operators $\neg$ and $\sim$ are given in Figure 3, where we also depict the truth tables for the operators $\wedge$ and $\vee$ for convenience.

An *interpretation* I, over a domain Σ, is a function $I : \mathcal{A}_{\Sigma(\emptyset)} \to \mathcal{D}$, mapping ground atoms to truth values, where $I(f_4) = f$, $I(\bot_4) = \bot$, $I(\top_4) = \top$, and $I(t_4) = t$. Fix a domain Σ, and let $\mathcal{I}$ be the set of all interpretations over Σ.

We define a partial ordering $\sqsubseteq$ on interpretations: given $I_1, I_2 \in \mathcal{I}$, $I_1 \sqsubseteq I_2$ iff $\forall a \in \mathcal{A}_{\Sigma(\emptyset)}$. $I_1(a) \preceq I_2(a)$. We define the meet $\sqcap$ and join $\sqcup$ operators on $\mathcal{I}$ as: $I_1 \sqcap I_2 = \lambda a.\ I_1(a) \wedge I_2(a)$ and $I_1 \sqcup I_2 = \lambda a.\ I_1(a) \vee I_2(a)$. The structure $(\mathcal{I}, \sqsubseteq, \sqcap, \sqcup, I_f, I_t)$ is a complete lattice where $I_f = \lambda a.f$ is the least element and $I_t = \lambda a.t$ is the greatest element. Given a continuous function $\Phi : \mathcal{I} \to \mathcal{I}$, we write $\lceil \Phi \rceil$ for the least fixed point of Φ. The interpretation $\lceil \Phi \rceil$ is calculated, using the Kleene fixed point theorem, as M^{ω} where $M^0 = I_f$, and $M^{i+1} = \Phi(M^i)$ for $i \geq 0$.

We extend interpretations over the operators $\neg$ and $\sim$ as $I(\neg a) = \neg I(a)$ and $I(\sim a) = \sim I(a)$ respectively, where $a \in \mathcal{A}_{\Sigma(\emptyset)}$. We also extend interpretations over vectors of literals as $I(\boldsymbol{l}) = I(l_1) \wedge \cdots \wedge I(l_n)$ where $\boldsymbol{l} = l_1, \cdots, l_n$ and $\{l_1, \cdots, l_n\} \subseteq \mathcal{L}_{\Sigma(\emptyset)}$. We write $\bigvee \{v_1, \cdots v_n\}$ for $v_1 \vee \cdots \vee v_n$. For the empty set we put $\bigvee \{\} = f$.

An interpretation I is a *model* of a given program P iff $\forall (a \leftarrow \boldsymbol{l}) \in P^{\downarrow}$. $I(a) \succeq I(\boldsymbol{l})$. A model therefore, for every rule, assigns to the head a truth value no smaller, in $\preceq$, than the truth value assigned to the body. A model I is *supported* iff $\forall a \in \mathcal{A}_{\Sigma(\emptyset)}$. $I(a) = \bigvee \{I(\boldsymbol{l}) \mid (a \leftarrow \boldsymbol{l}) \in P^{\downarrow}\}$. Note that the definition of supported models for BELLOG programs extends that of stratified Datalog. Intuitively, a model I is supported if it does not over-assign truth values to head atoms. In contrast to stratified Datalog, BELLOG's truth values are not totally ordered; therefore, a supported model I of a BELLOG program P does not guarantee that for an atom a there is a rule $(a \leftarrow \boldsymbol{l}) \in P^{\downarrow}$ such that $I(a) = I(\boldsymbol{l})$. For example, for the program $P = \{a \leftarrow \top_4, a \leftarrow \bot_4\}$ the interpretation $I = \{a \mapsto t\}$ is a supported model; note that $\{a \mapsto \bot\}$ and $\{a \mapsto \top\}$ are not models of P.

We associate a BELLOG program P with the operator $T_P : \mathcal{I} \mapsto \mathcal{I}$:

$$T_P(J)(a) = \bigvee \{J(\boldsymbol{l}) \mid (a \leftarrow \boldsymbol{l}) \in P^{\downarrow}\}$$

Lemma 1. *Given a* BELLOG *program P, an interpretation I is a supported model iff $T_P(I) = I$.*

The proof follows immediately from the definition of T_P.

In general, a program P may have multiple supported models. For instance, any interpretation is a supported model for the program $\{p \leftarrow p\}$. For BELLOG's semantics we choose a minimal supported model: a supported model I is *minimal* iff there does not exist another supported model I' such that $I' \sqsubset I$. For a program P where only non-negative literals are in its rules, T_P is monotone, hence continuous due to the finiteness of $\mathcal{I}$, and has a unique minimal supported model. In contrast, if a program P contains negative literals in its rules, then the operator T_P is not monotone, and there could be multiple minimal supported models. For example, the program $P = \{a \leftarrow \neg b\}$ has more than one minimal supported models, e.g. $\{a \mapsto f, b \mapsto t\}$ and $\{a \mapsto t, b \mapsto f\}$.

For a stratified BELLOG program P, we construct one minimal supported model by computing, for each strata of P, the minimal supported model that contains the model of the previous stratum. This construction is analogous to that of stratified Datalog given in [21]. To define the model construction, we introduce the following notation. We write $(P^{\downarrow}) \triangleleft I$ for the program obtained by replacing all literals in $P^\downarrow$ constructed with edb_P predicate symbols with their truth values according to I. Formally,

$$(P^\downarrow) \triangleleft I \;=\; \{p \leftarrow q'_1, \cdots, q'_n \mid (p \leftarrow q_1, \cdots, q_n) \in P^\downarrow,$$

$$q'_i = I(q_i) \text{ if } q_i \in \mathcal{L}^{\mathsf{edb}_P}_{\Sigma(\emptyset)}, \text{otherwise } q'_i = q_i\} \;.$$

Note that all negative literals in a stratum P_i of a stratified BELLOG program are constructed with predicate symbols in edb_{P_i}. Given an interpretation I, the program $P_i^\downarrow \triangleleft I$ therefore contains only non-negative literals, and the operator $T_{P_i^\downarrow \triangleleft I}$ is monotone.

We now define the model semantics of a stratified BELLOG program:

Definition 1. *Given a stratified* BELLOG *program P, with strata $P_0, \cdots, P_n$, the model of P, denoted $[\![P]\!]$, is the interpretation M_n, where $M_{-1} = I_f$, and $M_i = \lceil T_{P_i^\downarrow \triangleleft M_{i-1}} \rceil \sqcup M_{i-1}$ for $0 \le i \le n$.*

Each M_i, for $0 \le i \le n$, is well-defined because the operators $T_{P_i^\downarrow \triangleleft M_{i-1}}$ are monotone, and therefore continuous because the lattice $(\mathcal{I}, \sqsubseteq, \sqcap, \sqcup)$ is finite.

Theorem 1. *Given a stratified* BELLOG *program P, $[\![P]\!]$ is a minimal supported model.*

For the previous example $P = \{a \leftarrow \neg b\}$, the given construction results in $[\![P]\!] = \{a \mapsto \mathsf{t}, b \mapsto \mathsf{f}\}$. For details on our choice of semantics see [19].

We remark that a BELLOG program P that does not use the predicates $\top_4$, $\bot_4$, and the operator $\sim$ in its rules is a syntactically valid stratified Datalog program. Furthermore, stratified BELLOG subsumes stratified Datalog; see [19]. In particular, this means that BELLOG can express all policy languages based on stratified Datalog.

The *input* to a BELLOG program P is an interpretation $I \in \mathcal{I}$, where all atoms from $\mathcal{A}^{\mathsf{idb}_P}_{\Sigma(\emptyset)}$ are mapped to f. For a program P and the input I, we write $[\![P]\!]_I$ as a shorthand for $[\![P \cup P']\!]$, where $P' = \{a \leftarrow v_4 \mid I(a) = v\}$ and $v \in \mathcal{D}$.

From the definition of stratification, it is immediate that given a stratified program P with strata $P_0, \cdots, P_n$, and an input I, the program $P \cup P'$ can be stratified into strata $P', P_0, \cdots, P_n$.

We finally remark that the semantics of a BELLOG program is independent of the given stratification. The proof can be found in [19].

Decision Problems. We define BELLOG's decision problems. In §5, we reduce the decision problems within our policy analysis framework to BELLOG's decision problems.

Let P be a stratified BELLOG program, Σ be a domain of constants, and q be a ground atom. For a given input I, the *query entailment* decision problem, denoted $P \models^I_\Sigma q$, asks whether $[\![P]\!]_I(q) = \mathsf{t}$. The general case of $[\![P]\!]_I(q) = v$, with $v \in \mathcal{D}$, is immediately reducible to the query entailment problem. The *query validity* decision problem, denoted $P \models_\Sigma q$, asks whether for all inputs I defined over Σ, $P \models^I_\Sigma q$. Similarly to the *data* complexity of Datalog [22], we study the complexity of the given decision problems when the maximum arity of predicates in P and the set of variables that appear in P are fixed. The input size for BELLOG's decision problems is thus determined by the number of predicate symbols in $\mathcal{P}$, the number of rules in P, and the number of constants in the domain Σ.

Theorem 2. *The query entailment problem and the query validity problem belong, respectively, to the complexity classes* PTIME *and* CO-NP-COMPLETE.

We next consider a generalization of the query validity problem. Let Σ_P denote the set of constants that appear in P. The *all-domains query validity* decision problem, denoted $P \models q$, asks whether $P \models_{\Sigma'} q$ for all domains $\Sigma' \subseteq \mathcal{C}$ that contain Σ_P and the constants in q; recall that $\mathcal{C}$ is the infinite set of constants. The problem of all-domains query validity is in general undecidable for BELLOG programs, because the problem of query validity in Datalog, which is undecidable [23], can be reduced to this problem. We show, however, that all-domains query validity is decidable for any stratified BELLOG program P that has only unary predicate symbols in edb$_P$. We call those *unary-edb programs*. We show in §5 that the unary-edb BELLOG programs capture a useful class of policies. Namely, those policies where the set of principals is finite.

Theorem 3. *The all-domains query validity problem for a unary-edb* BELLOG *program belongs to the complexity class* CO-NEXP.

Note that the input for the all-domains query validity problem is determined only by the number of predicate symbols in $\mathcal{P}$ and the number of rules in the program P.

Syntactic Extensions. We now present a set of syntactic extension to BEL-LOG to ease the specification of complex rules. In §4, we use them for writing decentralized composite policies.

We extend the syntax for writing policy rules to

$$rule ::= p \leftarrow body$$
$$body ::= q_1, \cdots, q_n \mid \neg body \mid {\sim} body \mid body \wedge body \ ,$$

where $n > 0$, $p \in \mathcal{A}_{\Sigma(\mathcal{V})}$, and $\{q_1, \cdots, q_n\} \subseteq \mathcal{L}_{\Sigma(\mathcal{V})}$. We call the rules of the form $p \leftarrow q_1, \cdots, q_n$ *basic rules* and the remaining rules *composite rules*. Similarly to basic rules, we require that for any composite rule $p \leftarrow body$, $vars(p) \subseteq vars(body)$.

We define the translation function $\mathcal{T}$ that maps a basic rule r to the set $\{r\}$:

$$\mathcal{T}(p \leftarrow q_1, \cdots, q_n) = \{p \leftarrow q_1, \cdots, q_n\} \ ,$$

and maps a composite rule $p \leftarrow body$ to a set of basic rules:

$$\mathcal{T}(p \leftarrow \neg body) = \{p \leftarrow \neg p_{\mathsf{fresh}}(\boldsymbol{X})\} \cup \mathcal{T}(p_{\mathsf{fresh}}(\boldsymbol{X}) \leftarrow body)$$
$$\mathcal{T}(p \leftarrow {\sim} body) = \{p \leftarrow {\sim} p_{\mathsf{fresh}}(\boldsymbol{X})\} \cup \mathcal{T}(p_{\mathsf{fresh}}(\boldsymbol{X}) \leftarrow body)$$
$$\mathcal{T}(p \leftarrow body_1 \wedge body_2) = \{p \leftarrow p_{\mathsf{fresh1}}(\boldsymbol{X}_1), p_{\mathsf{fresh2}}(\boldsymbol{X}_2)\}$$
$$\cup \mathcal{T}(p_{\mathsf{fresh1}}(\boldsymbol{X}_1) \leftarrow body_1) \cup \mathcal{T}(p_{\mathsf{fresh2}}(\boldsymbol{X}_2) \leftarrow body_2)$$

$$p \lor q := \neg(\neg p \land \neg q)$$
$$p \oplus q := (p \land \top) \lor (q \land \top) \lor (p \land q)$$
$$p = \mathsf{f} := \neg(p \lor \sim p)$$
$$p = \top := (p \neq \mathsf{f}) \land (p \neq \mathsf{t}) \land ((p \lor \bot) = \mathsf{t})$$

$$p \otimes q := (p \land \bot) \lor (q \land \bot) \lor (p \land q)$$
$$p = \mathsf{t} := p \land \sim p$$
$$p = \bot := (p \neq \mathsf{f}) \land (p \neq \mathsf{t}) \land ((p \lor \top) = \mathsf{t})$$
$$p \neq v := \neg(p = v)$$

Fig. 4. Derived connectives for combining composite rule bodies. Here p, q, and c denote rule bodies and $v \in \mathcal{D}$.

In these rules p_{fresh}, p_{fresh1}, p_{fresh2} are predicate symbols that do not appear in $\mathcal{P}$, $\boldsymbol{X} = vars(body)$ and $\boldsymbol{X}_i = vars(body_i)$ for $i \in \{1, 2\}$. Note that the recursive function $\mathcal{T}$ terminates for any composite rule and yields a set of basic rules; see [19]. The size of the set is linear in the number of nested *bodies* in the composite rule.

The meaning of a BELLOG program P with composite rules is that of the BELLOG program $P' = \bigcup_{r \in P}(\mathcal{T}(r))$. For example, consider the composite rule:

$$p(X) \leftarrow \neg\sim q(X, Y) \ .$$

The function $\mathcal{T}$ translates this composite rule into a set of basic rules:

$$\{p(X) \leftarrow \neg p_{\mathsf{fresh}}(X, Y), \ p_{\mathsf{fresh}}(X, Y) \leftarrow \sim q(X, Y)\} \ .$$

A BELLOG program P with composite rules is *well-formed* iff its rules can be partitioned into sets $P_0, \cdots, P_n$ such that: (1) for every predicate symbol p, all rules with p in their heads are in one stratum P_i; (2) if a predicate symbol p occurs as a non-negative literal in a basic body in P_i, then all rules with p in their heads are in a stratum P_j with $j \leq i$; and (3) if a predicate symbol p occurs in the body of a composite rule in P_i or as a negative literal in a basic rule in P_i, then all rules with p in their heads are in a stratum P_j with $j < i$. Note that well-formed BELLOG extends stratified BELLOG with the condition that if a predicate symbol p occurs in the body of a composite rule in P_i, then all rules with p in their heads are in a stratum P_j with $j < i$. This is a sufficient but not necessary condition that any composite rule of a well-formed program is translated into a stratified set of basic rules.

Theorem 4. *The translation of a well-formed* BELLOG *program with composite rules is a stratified* BELLOG *program.*

In Figure 4, we derive additional connectives using syntactic combinations of $\neg$, $\sim$, and $\land$. The binary connective $\_ \lor \_$ corresponds to the join operator on the lattice $(\mathcal{D}, \preceq)$, and the binary connectives $\_ \otimes \_$ and $\_ \oplus \_$ correspond to the meet and join operators on the lattice $(\mathcal{D}, \preceq_k)$, respectively; for details see [6]. The unary connective $\_ = v$, where $v \in \mathcal{D}$, indicates whether the truth value assigned to the atom is v. The result of $p = v$ is t if p's result is v, and f otherwise. The composition $p \neq v$ returns t only if p's result is not v, otherwise it returns f. Furthermore, we formally establish that BELLOG can represent any n-ary operator $D^n \to D$:

Theorem 5. *Given an operator* $g : D^n \to D$ *and a list of* n *rule bodies* $q_1, \cdots, q_n$, *there exists a* body *expression* ϕ *for a* BELLOG *composite rule* $p \leftarrow \phi$ *such that*

$$\llbracket P \rrbracket_I(p) = g(\llbracket P \rrbracket_I(q_1), \ldots, \llbracket P \rrbracket_I(q_n)) ,$$

for all inputs I, *and programs* P *where* $\{p \leftarrow \phi\} \subseteq P$ *and* p *is not the head of any other rule.*

4   Decentralized Composite Policies in BELLOG

We first introduce the basic building blocks, namely attributes and delegations, and then we demonstrate how to encode decentralized composite policies in BEL-LOG, including the grid policy from §2. We conclude with a discussion of BEL-LOG's more intricate features for policy specifications.

We assume that the PDP's domain database contains all constants that appear in the policies, attributes, and access requests, as well as any other additional constants which may denote roles, file names, etc.

Attributes and Delegations. We represent attributes with *attribute_name*(·) predicate symbols. We take the first argument of an attribute as the issuing principal's identifier. For example, $hr(\text{ann}, \text{fred})$ denotes that, according to Ann, Fred works in the Human Resources department. To highlight the attribute's issuer, we may write $hr(\text{fred})@\text{ann}$ instead of $hr(\text{ann}, \text{fred})$.

The truth value of an attribute a is t if it is either stored at the PDP or provided by the subject; otherwise it is f. In short, the attributes are by default assumed not to exist if they are not present. For some policies it may however be more appropriate to assume that a given attribute (e.g. an attribute that is provided by the subject) is missing ($\bot$) rather than non-existent (f). BELLOG can accommodate for such policies too. For example, given an attribute a, we can define its *assume-missing* counterpart $a_\bot$ with the rule $a_\bot \leftarrow a \vee \bot$.

Attribute delegations are specified with BELLOG rules where the rule's head is the delegated attribute and the rule body is the delegation condition. For example, with the rule

$$researcher(S)@\text{ann} \leftarrow hr(S')@\text{ann}, labcard(S)@S' ,$$

Ann asserts that a subject S is a researcher if a subject S' with the attribute hr asserts that S is a researcher. That is, Ann delegates the attribute *researcher* to subjects that have the attribute hr. For example, if Fred has the attribute hr and issues $labcard(\text{dave})@\text{fred}$, then the PDP derives $researcher(\text{dave})@\text{ann}$.

Delegations may require non-monotonic operators. Imagine that Ann stores at the PDP a list of revoked subjects, and she will not accept delegations of the attribute *researcher* for revoked subjects. We extend her delegation rule as

$$researcher(S)@\text{ann} \leftarrow hr(S')@\text{ann}, labcard(S)@S', \neg revoked(S)@\text{ann} .$$

Non-monotonic operators must be used with caution when applied to the attributes that subjects supply. This is because a subject may gain access if she can withhold the attribute *revoked* from the PDP; cf. [8]. In §5, we return to this issue and show how one can verify whether a policy is monotone with respect to the attributes provided by the subject.

BELLOG's composite rules can be used to express more complex delegation conditions. In our grid example, the administrator may for instance require two project leaders—Ann and Fred—to agree on the *pub* file attribute, denoting that a file is public. This is written as

$$pub\_agree(F)@\mathsf{admin} \leftarrow pub(F)@\mathsf{ann} \oplus pub(F)@\mathsf{fred} \; ,$$

where $\oplus$ is the maximal agreement operator. Note that the administrator derives a conflict if the principals disagree whether a file is public, because $\mathsf{f} \oplus \mathsf{t} = \top$.

As illustrated, BELLOG can specify standard attribute delegations, as well as non-monotonic delegation idioms which cannot be captured in existing Datalog-based languages. There are other delegation idioms that BELLOG can express, but we omit their presentation due to space constraints. For example, the hand-off idiom [14], where a principal delegates authority over all attributes, can be expressed in BELLOG by representing attributes with a predicate *says* where one of the arguments denotes an attribute name.

Policy Decisions. We take the $\mathsf{t}, \mathsf{f}, \bot,$ and $\top$ elements as, respectively, *grant*, *deny*, *gap*, and *conflict* policy decisions. The *gap* decision indicates that a policy neither grants nor denies a request, and *conflict* indicates that a policy can both grant and deny a request. The partial ordering $\preceq$ in Figure 2 defines the *permissiveness* of policy decisions. The meet $\wedge$ and join $\vee$ operators on the lattice $(\mathcal{D}, \preceq)$ correspond to the standard *deny-override* and *permit-override* operators for composing policy decisions. The meet $\otimes$ and join $\oplus$ operators on the lattice $(\mathcal{D}, \preceq_k)$ correspond to the *maximal agreement* and *minimal agreement* composition operators; see [15].

Policies. A principal can issue multiple policies for different subjects and resources; we insist however that each principal has one designated root policy. A root policy combines all of the principal's sub-policies and possibly other principals' policies. In our grid scenario, we use the atom $pol\_name(Sub, File)@Prin$ to denote the decision of the policy *name*, issued by *Prin*, for *Sub* accessing *File*. We fix the atom $pol(Sub, File)@Prin$ to denote *Prin*'s root policy. For example, when the PDP derives t for the atom $pol(\mathsf{fred}, \mathsf{foo.txt})@\mathsf{piet}$, the PDP interprets this as "Piet's root policy grants Fred access to the file foo.txt". Principals may choose any other predicate symbols to denote decisions of their sub-policies.

Policies are encoded as BELLOG rules where the head of a policy rule is a policy name atom. For example, the project leader Piet may issue the policy

$$pol(S, F)@\mathsf{piet} \leftarrow researcher(S)@\mathsf{piet}, prj\_file(F)@\mathsf{piet} \; ,$$

which grants his researchers S access to any project files F. Similarly, Ann, who is a project leader, may issue the policy

$$pol(\mathsf{ann}, F)@\mathsf{ann} \leftarrow prj\_file(F)@\mathsf{ann}$$
$$pol(S, F)@\mathsf{ann} \leftarrow pol(S', F)@\mathsf{ann}, give\_access(S, F)@S' \; ,$$

$$p \triangleleft c \triangleright q := ((c = \mathsf{t}) \wedge p) \vee ((c \neq \mathsf{t}) \wedge q) \qquad p \overset{v}{\mapsto} q := q \triangleleft (p = v) \triangleright p$$
$$p \bowtie q := p \triangleleft (q = \bot) \triangleright (q \triangleleft (p = \bot) \triangleright \bot) \qquad p \blacktriangleright q := q \triangleleft (p = \mathsf{t}) \triangleright \bot$$

Fig. 5. Conditional and override policy composition operators

where the first rule grants Ann access to any project file F, and the second rule states that any subject S' with access to F may delegate this access to any subject S by issuing a *give_access* attribute. Then, Ann may provide access to Fred by issuing *give_access*(fred, foo.txt)@ann; Fred too may issue *give_access*(dave, foo.txt)@fred to further delegate to Dave access to foo.txt.

A policy can also combine the decisions of a set of sub-policies; we call these *composite* policies. A composite policy encoded with a basic BELLOG rule, for example, implicitly combines the sub-policies' decisions using the deny-override $\wedge$ operator. Composite policies that combine their sub-policies' decisions with more complex composition operators, such as the gap- and conflict-override operators, are encoded with BELLOG composite rules.

In addition to $\wedge$, BELLOG's operators $\neg$, $\sim$, $\vee$, $\otimes$, $\oplus$ can also be employed as composition operators. To complement these operators, in Figure 5 we define further conditional and override operators for composing policies. The ternary operator $\_ \triangleleft \_ \triangleright \_$ is the *if-then-else* operator. The result of the composition $p \triangleleft c \triangleright q$ is p's decision only if c's result is t, otherwise q's decision is taken.

The binary operator $\_ \overset{v}{\mapsto} \_$ represents the *v-override operator*, where $v \in \mathcal{D}$. The result of the composition $p \overset{v}{\mapsto} q$ is q if p's decision is v, otherwise it results in p's decision. The operators $\overset{\bot}{\mapsto}$ and $\overset{\top}{\mapsto}$ correspond to the *gap-override* and *conflict-override* operators, respectively. Given a list of policies $p_1, \cdots, p_n$, we encode the operator *first-applicable* as $p_1 \overset{\bot}{\mapsto} (p_2 \overset{\bot}{\mapsto} (\cdots \overset{\bot}{\mapsto} p_n))$, i.e. the composition takes the decision of the first policy in the list whose decision is not $\bot$.

The binary operator $\_ \bowtie \_$ is the *only-one-applicable* operator, i.e. the composition $p \bowtie q$ results in $\bot$ if both policy decisions are not $\bot$ or both decisions are $\bot$, otherwise the result is the policy decision that is not $\bot$.

The binary operator $\_ \blacktriangleright \_$ is the *on-permit-apply-second*[1] operator. The composition $p \blacktriangleright q$ returns q only if the decision of p is t, otherwise it returns $\bot$. The operator $\blacktriangleright$ is useful for specifying policies that either (1) grant or provide no decision, or (2) deny or provide no decision. For example, the policy *researcher*(Sub) $\blacktriangleright$ t grants access only if the subject Sub is a researcher; otherwise, the policy returns $\bot$. In contrast, the policy *revoked*(Sub) $\blacktriangleright$ f denies access if the subject Sub is revoked, and provides no decision otherwise. We also use the operator $\blacktriangleright$ for specifying policies with policy targets, which define the requests that are applicable to a policy. Given a policy p and its target p_{target}, $p_{\text{target}} \blacktriangleright p$ results in $\bot$ if p_{target} does not evaluate to t, otherwise it results in p's decision.

---

[1] The on-permit-apply-second operator has been recently proposed as an additional operator for the XACML 3 standard. See [24] for full description.

We finally remark that BELLOG can express any four-valued policy composition language, such as PBel [7]. This is a corollary of Theorem 5.

Grid Policy. We now exercise these operators in our grid scenario. The administrator may compose the policies issued by the project leaders Piet and Ann with the maximal agreement operator:

$$pol\_leaders(S, F)@\text{admin} \leftarrow pol(S, F)@\text{piet} \oplus pol(S, F)@\text{ann} .$$

For brevity, we have not specified the policies of Piet and Ann. The composition of their policies may result in conflicts and gaps. According to requirements R2 and R3 (see §2), the administrator must resolve conflicts by granting requests made by project leaders, and resolve gaps by granting access only to public folders. The pol_root policy encodes these requirements:

$$pol\_root(S, F)@\text{admin} \leftarrow$$

$$(pol\_leaders(S, F)@\text{admin} \overset{\top}{\mapsto} prj\_leader(S)@\text{admin}) \overset{\bot}{\mapsto} pub(F)@\text{admin} .$$

The composite policy $pol\_leaders$ considers the decisions of Piet's and Ann's policies for all requests. The administrator may, however, want to consider the decisions of Piet's policy only for the files contained in the folder prj1. This can be encoded by defining a policy with an explicit policy target:

$$pol\_piet(S, F)@\text{admin} \leftarrow contains(\text{prj1}, F)@\text{admin} \blacktriangleright pol(S, F)@\text{piet} ,$$

where the attribute $contains(F_1, F_2)@\text{admin}$ indicates that the folder F_1 contains F_2. The attribute is transitively assigned to sub-folders:

$$contains(F_1, F_2)@\text{admin} \leftarrow subfolder(F_1, F_2)@\text{fs} ,$$

$$contains(F_1, F_3)@\text{admin} \leftarrow contains(F_1, F_2)@\text{admin}, contains(F_2, F_3)@\text{admin} ,$$

where the attribute $subfolder(F_1, F_2)@\text{fs}$ is provided by the file system fs and indicates that F_1 is directly contained in F_2. Note that the policy pol_piet results in $\bot$ for any request to a file not contained in the folder prj1.

The administrator must also encode the requirement R4, which states that any access right to a folder is transitively extended to sub-folders. Namely

$$pol\_root(S, F)@\text{admin} \leftarrow contains(F', F)@\text{admin}, pol\_root(S, F')@\text{admin} .$$

Note that the policy decision for a folder is extended to sub-folders with the permit-override operator. This is because instantiating the variable F' results in multiple rules with the same head atom, which are combined with the operator $\vee$ according to BELLOG's semantics. To illustrate this, consider the folder f_3, where f_3 is contained in f_2, which in turn is contained in f_1. Instantiating the variable F' and simplifying the instantiated rules result in the following rule:

$$pol\_root(S, f_3)@\text{admin} \leftarrow pol\_root(S, f_1)@\text{admin} \vee pol\_root(S, f_2)@\text{admin} .$$

Alternatively, the administrator may want to combine the instantiated rule bodies with deny-override, maximal agreement, or minimal agreement. We show how this can be done with BELLOG's intensional operators, defined below.

Intensional Compositions. So far, we have presented *extensional* policy composition operators that compose a fixed, explicitly given list of sub-policies. For example, we used

$$pol\_leaders(S, F)@\mathsf{admin} \leftarrow pol(S, F)@\mathsf{piet} \oplus pol(S, F)@\mathsf{ann}$$

to combine policies of two project leaders, one from Piet and one from Ann, with the maximal agreement operator. Such extensional encodings are tediously "static", because if new project leaders are added to or removed from the PDP, then the administrator must explicitly change the policy rule. Alternatively, the administrator may write a rule that composes the policies that are issued by any principal who is a project leader. One attempt to do this is:

$$pol\_leaders(S, F)@\mathsf{admin} \leftarrow pol(S, F)@P, prj\_leader(P)@\mathsf{admin} \ ,$$

where the set of composed policies is *intensionally* defined as those issued by project leaders. This attempt however fails because the project leaders' policies are implicitly combined with the permit-override operator, instead of the maximal agreement operator $\oplus$. This is because BELLOG's semantics, much like other logic programs, uses the join operator $\vee$ when combining rule bodies with the same head atom.

We extend BELLOG's syntax with additional operators to account for intensional compositions:

$$rule ::= p \leftarrow [\ \bigvee\ |\ \bigwedge\ |\ \bigoplus\ |\ \bigotimes\ ]\ body \ ,$$

where $p \in \mathcal{A}_{\Sigma(V)}$, $body$ is a composite rule body, as defined in §3, and $vars(p) \subseteq vars(body)$. We refer to the operators written in front of $body$ as *intensional* composition operators. Intuitively, the intensional operator $\bigoplus$ combines all grounded bodies of rules with the same head atom with the $\oplus$ operator. For example, grounding the simple rule $p(\mathsf{a}) \leftarrow \bigoplus q(X)$ over the domain $\Sigma = \{\mathsf{a}, \mathsf{b}\}$ results in two grounded bodies, $q(\mathsf{a})$ and $q(\mathsf{b})$, with the same head atom $p(\mathsf{a})$. The grounded bodies are combined with $\oplus$; the meaning of $p(\mathsf{a}) \leftarrow \bigoplus q(X)$ is therefore $p(\mathsf{a}) \leftarrow q(\mathsf{a}) \oplus q(\mathsf{b})$. Other operators behave similarly with respect to their syntactic counterparts. The formal translation of the intensional operators to BELLOG's core syntax is given in [19]. We remark that the intensional operators $\bigwedge, \bigoplus$, and $\bigotimes$ cannot have the head atom appear in the rule body because their encoding uses composite rules.

We can now encode the intensional composition of the project leaders' policies with the maximal agreement operator as

$$pol\_leaders(S, F)@\mathsf{admin} \leftarrow \bigoplus(pol(S, F)@P \lhd prj\_leader(P)@\mathsf{admin} \rhd \bot) \ .$$

Note that the policies that are *not* issued by a project leader are replaced with $\bot$, and the composition "ignores" such policies, because $v \oplus \bot = v$ for any $v \in \mathcal{D}$.

Intensional compositions are also useful for specifying policies that propagate policy decisions over hierarchically structured data, such as file systems, role hierarchies, etc. To illustrate, we extend our grid example with Piet's policy that by default permits a subject S to access a folder F, unless Piet issues the attribute $deny(S, F)$. In contrast to the requirement R4, he uses the deny-override operator to propagate deny decisions over the sub-folders:

$$pol\_fold(S, F)@\mathsf{piet} \leftarrow \neg deny(S, F)@\mathsf{piet}$$

$$pol(S, F)@\mathsf{piet} \leftarrow \bigwedge(pol\_fold(S, F')@\mathsf{piet} \vartriangleleft contains(F', F)@\mathsf{admin} \vartriangleright \mathsf{t}) \ .$$

The last rule replaces the policy decisions for folders F' that do not contain F with t, since for any $v \in \mathcal{D}$ we have $v \wedge \mathsf{t} = v$.

We summarize the key difference between intensional and extensional operators as follows. The intensional operators reflect changes in the domain (e.g. addition and removal of principals, files, etc.) through changes in the policy input. The extensional operators require explicit modification of the policy rules to reflect such changes.

5 Analysis

Writing a correct policy, i.e. one that grants and denies requests as intended by the policy writer, is often challenging in practice. This is both because policies are often initially given informally and imprecisely and because the policy writer can err in their formalization. In particular, a policy writer must foresee all possible policy inputs, understand how the delegation rules, the sub-policies, and their compositions influence the policy's behavior, and verify that the policy does not exhibit any unintended decisions. As a first step towards verifying the policy's behavior, the policy writer specifies the high-level requirements as formal policy analysis questions. Second, a decision procedure is used to check, in an automated manner, whether the analysis questions are answered positively, or not.

Below we present our framework for analyzing policies written in BELLOG. A *policy set* is a set of delegations and policies, which are encoded as BELLOG rules and collectively define a BELLOG program. Every policy set has a designated *root policy*. The decision of a policy set for a given request is the decision of the policy set's root policy. We fix the predicate $pol(Subject, Object)$ to denote a root policy's decisions. For brevity, we omit writing the issuer of policies and attributes. We use the terms *input* and *(policy) context* interchangeably.

Policy Entailment. Policy entailment answers whether a policy set entails a given permission in a given policy context.

Definition 2. *(Policy Entailment) Given a policy set P and a policy context I, P entails the request $pol(S, O)$ iff $P \models^I_\Sigma pol(S, O)$.*

Policy entailment analysis is akin to software testing in that the policy writer checks the policy set for unintended grants and denies in specific policy contexts (i.e. test scenarios). Although limited in its scope, since the policy writer must give a specific context, determining policy entailment scales with the size of the domain, unlike the policy containment problem which we define shortly. Note that policy entailment can also be used for constructing PDPs.

To illustrate policy entailment, consider the following policy set P:

$$\{ \, pol(S, O) \leftarrow (pol\_leaders(S, O) \overset{\top}{\mapsto} prj\_leader(S)) \overset{\bot}{\mapsto} pub(O) \, \} \, .$$

For simplicity we do not specify the policy $pol\_leaders$. One requirement for P, which is derived from the requirement R2 given in §2, may be to deny access to subjects who are not project leaders whenever the policy $pol\_leaders$ returns a conflict. To check this property, we may ask whether the policy set entails the permission $pol(\mathsf{fred}, \mathsf{foo.txt})$ in the context:

$$I = \{ pol\_leaders(\mathsf{fred}, \mathsf{foo.txt}) \mapsto \top, prj\_leader(\mathsf{fred}) \mapsto \mathsf{f} \} \, ,$$

where the remaining atoms are mapped to f. For this context the policy set does not entail the permission, as expected.

Because the guarantees provided by entailment analysis are limited to the context provided by the policy writer, the requirement may not hold for other policy contexts. For example, the given policy set P violates its requirement for

$$I' = \{ pol\_leaders(\mathsf{fred}, \mathsf{foo.txt}) \mapsto \top, prj\_leader(\mathsf{fred}) \mapsto \bot, pub(\mathsf{foo.txt}) \mapsto \mathsf{t} \} \, ,$$

because the policy set entails $pol(\mathsf{fred}, \mathsf{foo.txt})$, although $pol\_leaders$ results in a conflict and the PDP does not know whether Fred is a project leader.

Deciding policy entailment is reducible to query entailment; see §3. Policy entailment can be therefore decided in time polynomial in the size of the context.

Policy Containment. Policy containment thoroughly analyzes a policy set against all policy contexts. It can be used to answer questions such as: "*Do all requests in **all** policy contexts evaluate to a conclusive policy decision, i.e. grant or deny?*" Containment analysis is done either for a particular policy domain or for all possible policy domains. In more detail, the domain policy containment answers whether a policy set P_1 is more permissive than another policy set P_2 for all policy contexts for *a given domain*. The all-domains policy containment answers whether a policy set P_1 is more permissive than another policy set P_2 for all policy contexts for *all possible domains*. Even though all-domains evaluations imply those for one domain, checking for all domains is decidable only for a fragment of BELLOG, as we later show.

Many analysis questions require that only specific subsets of policy contexts and requests are considered for comparisons. For example, to verify that the policy set P correctly encodes our requirement derived from R2, the policy writer may ask whether P denies all requests made by subjects who are not project leaders, for all contexts where the policy $pol\_leaders$ results in a conflict. We encode such analysis questions with a condition that constraints the contexts and requests where the policy sets are compared. Formally, the syntax for writing containment questions is

$$cond \Rightarrow P_1 \preceq P_2 \, .$$

The symbols P_1 and P_2 are policy sets and $cond$ is inductively defined as

$$cond ::= \forall X.cond \mid attr \preceq v \mid v \preceq attr \mid \neg cond \mid cond \wedge cond \mid \mathsf{t}$$
$$v ::= \bot \mid \top \, ,$$

where $X \in V$, $attr \in \mathcal{A}^{edb_P}_{\Sigma(V)}$, i.e. $attr$ is an input attribute. Note that the attributes in a condition may contain variables. We write $fv(cond)$ for the set of variables in $cond$ that are not in the scope of $\forall$. We fix the variables S and O to denote the subject and the object in the request $pol(S, O)$. A policy containment question $cond \Rightarrow P_1 \preceq P_2$ is well-formed iff $fv(cond) \subseteq \{S, O\}$.

We define the satisfaction relation $\Vdash_\Sigma$ between a policy context I, a condition $cond$ of a well-formed policy containment question, and a policy domain Σ:

$$I \Vdash_\Sigma t$$

$$
\begin{array}{lll}
I \Vdash_\Sigma q \preceq v & \text{if} & I(q) \preceq v \\
I \Vdash_\Sigma v \preceq q & \text{if} & v \preceq I(q) \\
I \Vdash_\Sigma \neg cond & \text{if} & I \not\Vdash_\Sigma cond \\
I \Vdash_\Sigma cond_1 \wedge cond_2 & \text{if} & I \Vdash_\Sigma cond_1 \text{ and } I \Vdash_\Sigma cond_2 \\
I \Vdash_\Sigma \forall X.cond(X) & \text{if} & \forall X \in \Sigma. \ I \Vdash_\Sigma cond(X)
\end{array}
$$

As a shorthand, in the following we write $q = v$ for $(q \preceq v) \wedge (v \preceq q)$ where $v \in \{\bot, \top\}$, $q = f$ for $(q \preceq \bot) \wedge (q \preceq \top)$, and $q = t$ for $\neg(q \preceq \bot) \wedge \neg(q \preceq \top)$. Given two conditions c_1 and c_2 we define their disjunction $c_1 \vee c_2$ in the standard way as $\neg(\neg c_1 \wedge \neg c_2)$. To compare the truth values of any two attributes p and q, we write $p = q$ as a shorthand for $(p = f \wedge q = f) \vee (p = \bot \wedge q = \bot) \vee (p = \top \wedge q = \top) \vee (p = t \wedge q = t)$.

Definition 3. *(Domain Policy Containment) Given a question $cond \Rightarrow P_1 \preceq P_2$, and a domain Σ, then P_1 is contained in P_2 for all policy contexts over Σ that satisfy $cond$, denoted by $\Vdash_\Sigma cond \Rightarrow P_1 \preceq P_2$, iff*

$$\forall I \in \mathcal{I}, \forall S, O \in \Sigma. \ (I \Vdash_\Sigma cond) \rightarrow (\llbracket P_1 \rrbracket_I(pol(S, O)) \preceq \llbracket P_2 \rrbracket_I(pol(S, O))) \ ,$$

where $\mathcal{I}$ is the set of all policy contexts defined over the domain Σ.

Note that we overload the relation $\Vdash_\Sigma$.

In practice, the policy domain may change over time, e.g. subjects and objects are added to and removed from the system. After changes to Σ, domain policy containment may no longer hold. As mentioned, a stronger policy containment guarantee is thus to verify that P_1 is contained in P_2 for *all* domains Σ'.

Definition 4. *(All-domains Policy Containment) Given a question $cond \Rightarrow P_1 \preceq P_2$, P_1 is contained in P_2 for all policy contexts in all policy domains, denoted $\Vdash cond \Rightarrow P_1 \preceq P_2$, iff $\Vdash_\Sigma cond \Rightarrow P_1 \preceq P_2$ holds for all domains Σ.*

To illustrate how containment questions are specified and used, we start with the previously given question: "*Do all requests in **all** policy contexts evaluate to a conclusive policy decision*". To encode this question for the policy set P, we construct a policy set P' by first renaming the predicate symbol pol in P to pol' and then adding the rule

$$pol(S, O) \leftarrow (pol'(S, O) \overset{\top}{\mapsto} f) \overset{\bot}{\mapsto} f \ .$$

By construction, the policy set P' denies all requests that are evaluated to gap or conflict by the policy set P. Therefore, $\models_\Sigma t \Rightarrow P \preceq P'$ holds iff the policy set P is conclusive. We set the condition to t because we must check containment for all requests and for all policy contexts.

As a second example, we use policy containment to encode the requirement that the policy set P denies access to subjects who are not project leaders whenever the policy $pol\_leaders$ results in a conflict:

$$(pol\_leaders(S, O) = \top) \wedge \neg(prj\_leader(S) = t) \Rightarrow P \preceq P_f ,$$

where P_f is the policy set that denies all requests. This asks whether P denies $pol(S, O)$ in all contexts where the policy $pol\_leaders$ results in a conflict for the request $pol(S, O)$ ($pol\_leaders(S, O) = \top$) and the subject S is not a project leader ($\neg(prj\_leader(S) = t)$). Both domain and all-domains containment evaluations give negative answers; see the counterexample above. The policy set, however, satisfies the requirement if the attribute prj_leader is either t or f. We can easily encode this assumption as

$$(pol\_leaders(S, O) = \top) \wedge (prj\_leader(S) = f) \Rightarrow P \preceq P_f .$$

Domain and all-domains containment evaluations answer this question positively.

Policy containment is also useful for comparing a policy set's behavior in one context to its behavior in a different policy context. Consider a scenario where a subject can push some attributes to the PDP. An important property for the policy set is that a subject cannot influence the policy set to grant a request by withholding attributes. We refer to such policy sets as *push-monotonic*: whenever a subject provides fewer attributes to the PDP, the policy set results in a less permissive decision. Consider the policy set P:

$$\{ \quad pol(S, O) \leftarrow researcher(S), prj\_file(O)$$
$$researcher(S) \leftarrow hr(S'), labcard(S', S), \neg revoked(S) \}$$

The policy writer may formulate the question: "*Is the policy set more restrictive when the subject provides fewer (pushed) attributes?*" To answer this question, one must compare the policy set to itself in all policy contexts that are identical except for the attributes pushed by the subject. To encode this question, we first construct a policy set P' by renaming every predicate symbol p that appears in edb_P to p', where $\mathsf{edb}_P = \{revoked(\cdot), labcard(\cdot, \cdot), hr(\cdot), revoked(\cdot), prj\_file(\cdot)\}$. Suppose the attribute $revoked$ is locally stored at the PDP and the remaining attributes are pushed by the subject. The analysis question is encoded as

$$\forall X. (revoked(X) = revoked'(X)) \wedge \forall X, Y. (labcard(X, Y) \preceq labcard'(X, Y))$$
$$\wedge \forall X. (hr(X) \preceq hr'(X)) \wedge \forall X. (prj\_file(X) \preceq prj\_file'(X)) \Rightarrow P \preceq P' .$$

This analysis problem asks whether P is less permissive than P' in all policy contexts that are identical for the stored attribute and all pushed attributes to P are also pushed to P'. The question indeed holds for the policy set P.

The problems of deciding domain and all-domains policy containment are reducible to domain and all-domains query validity, respectively.

Theorem 6. *Policy containment is polynomially reducible to query validity.*

Table 1. Complexity of BELLOG's policy analysis problems

Analysis problem	Entailment	Domain containment	All-domains containment	All-domains containment*
Complexity	PTIME	CO-NP-COMPLETE	UNDECIDABLE	CO-NEXP

⋆ For policies that belong to the unary-edb BELLOG fragment.

Corollary 1. *The problem of domain policy containment belongs to the complexity class* CO-NP-COMPLETE. *The problem of all-domains policy containment for unary-edb policy sets belongs to the complexity class* CO-NEXP.

If a policy set has attributes associated to a single user, group, resource, etc. and there are finitely many principals, then the policy set can be written in the unary-edb fragment. This is because all attributes have the form $attr\_name(Issuer, Object)$ can be re-encoded as $attr\_name_{Issuer}(Object)$ since there are finitely many principals.

6   Conclusions

In this paper we present BELLOG, a formal language for specifying access control policies that require both authority delegation and policy composition. This sets BELLOG apart from the existing formal access control languages, which support either authority delegation or policy composition. BELLOG can therefore specify decentralized composite policies, which thus far have lacked formal semantics; examples include policies based on the XACML 3 standard [25] and policies for large-scale distributed systems, such as [2–4, 26]. We present an analysis framework for reasoning about BELLOG policies and give complexity bounds for deciding policy entailment and policy containment in BELLOG, summarized in Table 1.

We see BELLOG as a foundation for constructing high-level policy languages for decentralized composite access control, much like Datalog is the foundation for delegation languages such as RT [12] and SecPAL [11]. We plan to build implementations of BELLOG and apply them in practice. In particular we will focus on algorithms for fast evaluation of practically-relevant policies, and sound approximation techniques for deciding the policy analysis problems efficiently.

References

1. Blaze, M., Feigenbaum, J., Ioannidis, J., Keromytis, A.: The KeyNote Trust-Management System Version 2. RFC 2704 (Informational) (September 1999)
2. SNIC: SweGrid: e-Infrastructure for Computing and Storage, http://www.snic.vr.se/projects/swegrid/
3. Axiomatics: Policy Decision Points (September 2013)
4. Armbrust, M., Fox, A., Griffith, R., Joseph, A.D., Katz, R., Konwinski, A., Lee, G., Patterson, D., Rabkin, A., Stoica, I., Zaharia, M.: A View of Cloud Computing. Commun. ACM 53(4), 50–58 (2010)
5. Ceri, S., Gottlob, G., Tanca, L.: What You Always Wanted to Know About Datalog (And Never Dared to Ask). IEEE Trans. on Knowl. and Data Eng., 146–166 (1989)

6. Belnap, N.D.: A Useful Four-Valued Logic. In: Modern Uses of Multiple-Valued Logic. D. Reidel (1977)
7. Bruns, G., Huth, M.: Access Control via Belnap Logic: Intuitive, Expressive, and Analyzable Policy Composition. ACM Trans. Inf. Syst. Secur., 1–27 (2011)
8. Crampton, J., Morisset, C.: PTaCL: A Language for Attribute-Based Access Control in Open Systems. In: Degano, P., Guttman, J.D. (eds.) POST 2013. LNCS, vol. 7215, pp. 390–409. Springer, Heidelberg (2012)
9. Ni, Q., Bertino, E., Lobo, J.: D-Algebra for Composing Access Control Policy Decisions. In: Proceedings of the 4th International Symposium on Information, Computer, and Communications Security, ASIACCS 2009, pp. 298–309. ACM (2009)
10. Gurevich, Y., Neeman, I.: DKAL: Distributed-Knowledge Authorization Language. Computer Security Foundations Symposium, 149–162 (2008)
11. Becker, M.Y., Fournet, C., Gordon, A.D.: SecPAL: Design and semantics of a decentralized authorization language. Journal of Computer Security, 619–665 (2010)
12. Li, N., Mitchell, J., Winsborough, W.: Design of a Role-based Trust-management Framework. In: IEEE Symposium on Security and Privacy, pp. 114–130 (2002)
13. Garg, D., Pfenn, F.: Non-Interference in Constructive Authorization Logic. In: Proceedings of the 19th IEEE Workshop on Computer Security Foundations, CSFW 2006, pp. 283–296. IEEE Computer Society, Washington, DC (2006)
14. Abadi, M.: Access Control in a Core Calculus of Dependency. Electronic Notes in Theoretical Computer Science 172, 5–31 (2007)
15. Fitting, M.: Bilattices in Logic Programming. In: Proceedings of the Twentieth International Symposium on Multiple-Valued Logic, pp. 238–246 (1990)
16. Marinovic, S., Craven, R., Ma, J., Dulay, N.: Rumpole: A Flexible Break-glass Access Control Model. In: Symposium on Access Control Models and Technologies, SACMAT 2011, pp. 73–82. ACM (2011)
17. Dong, C., Dulay, N.: Shinren: Non-monotonic Trust Management for Distributed Systems. In: Nishigaki, M., Jøsang, A., Murayama, Y., Marsh, S. (eds.) IFIPTM 2010, vol. 321, pp. 125–140. Springer, Heidelberg (2010)
18. Kolovski, V., Hendler, J., Parsia, B.: Analyzing Web Access Control Policies. In: Proceedings of the 16th International Conference on WWW, pp. 677–686. ACM (2007)
19. Tsankov, P., Marinovic, S., Dashti, M.T., Basin, D.: Decentralized Composite Access Control. Technical report, ETH Zurich (2014), http://dx.doi.org/10.3929/ethz-a-010045530
20. Apt, K.R., Blair, H.A., Walker, A.: Towards a Theory of Declarative Knowledge. In: Minker, J. (ed.) Foundations of Deductive Databases and Logic Programming, pp. 89–148. Morgan Kaufmann Publishers Inc. (1988)
21. Abiteboul, S., Hull, R., Vianu, V.: Foundations of Databases. Addison-Wesley (1995)
22. Vardi, M.Y.: The Complexity of Relational Query Languages (Extended Abstract). In: Proceedings of the Fourteenth Annual ACM Symposium on Theory of Computing, STOC 1982, pp. 137–146. ACM, New York (1982)
23. Shmueli, O.: Decidability and Expressiveness Aspects of Logic Queries. In: Proceedings of the ACM Symposium on Principles of Database Systems. ACM (1987)
24. Rissanen, E.: XACML 3.0 Additional Combining Algorithms Profile Version 1.0. Technical report, Axiomatics
25. OASIS: eXtensible Access Control Markup Language, http://docs.oasis-open.org/xacml/3.0/xacml-3.0-core-spec-os-en.html
26. Seitz, L., Rissanen, E., Sandholm, T., Firozabadi, B.S., Mulmo, O.: Policy Administration Control and Delegation Using XACML and Delegent. In: Proceedings of the International Workshop on Grid Computing, pp. 49–54. IEEE (2005)

Temporal Logics for Hyperproperties

Michael R. Clarkson[1], Bernd Finkbeiner[2], Masoud Koleini[1],
Kristopher K. Micinski[3], Markus N. Rabe[2], and César Sánchez[4]

[1] George Washington University, USA
[2] Universität des Saarlandes, Germany
[3] University of Maryland, College Park, USA
[4] IMDEA Software Institute, Spain

Abstract. Two new logics for verification of hyperproperties are proposed. Hyperproperties characterize security policies, such as noninterference, as a property of sets of computation paths. Standard temporal logics such as LTL, CTL, and CTL* can refer only to a single path at a time, hence cannot express many hyperproperties of interest. The logics proposed here, HyperLTL and HyperCTL*, add explicit and simultaneous quantification over multiple paths to LTL and to CTL*. This kind of quantification enables expression of hyperproperties. A model checking algorithm for the proposed logics is given. For a fragment of HyperLTL, a prototype model checker has been implemented.

1 Introduction

Trace properties, which developed out of an interest in proving the correctness of programs [32], characterize correct behavior as properties of individual execution traces. Although early verification techniques specialized in proving individual correctness properties of interest, such as mutual exclusion or termination, temporal logics soon emerged as a general, unifying framework for expressing and verifying trace properties. Practical model checking tools [11, 16, 28] based on those logics now enable automated verification of program correctness.

Verification of security is not directly possible with such tools, because some important security policies cannot be characterized as properties of individual execution traces [38]. Rather, they are properties of sets of execution traces, also known as *hyperproperties* [15]. Specialized verification techniques have been developed for particular hyperproperties [5, 27, 41, 43], as well as for *2-safety* properties [52], which are properties of pairs of execution traces. But a unifying program logic for expressing and verifying hyperproperties could enable automated verification of a wide range of security policies.

In this paper, we propose two such logics. Both are based, like hyperproperties, on examining more than one execution trace at a time. Our first logic, *HyperLTL*, generalizes linear-time temporal logic (LTL) [44]. LTL implicitly quantifies over only a single execution trace of a system, but HyperLTL allows explicit quantification over multiple execution traces simultaneously, as well as propositions that stipulate relationships among those traces. For example, HyperLTL can express

M. Abadi and S. Kremer (Eds.): POST 2014, LNCS 8414, pp. 265–284, 2014.

information-flow policies such as *observational determinism* [37,46,61], which requires programs to behave as (deterministic) functions from low-security inputs to low-security outputs. The following two programs do not satisfy observational determinism, because they leak the value of high-security variable h through low-security variable l, thus making the program behave nondeterministically from a low-security user's perspective:

$$(1) \quad l := h \qquad\qquad (2) \quad \textbf{if } h = 0 \textbf{ then } l := 1 \textbf{ else } l := 0$$

Other program logics could already express observational determinism or closely related policies [7,30,41]. Milushev and Clarke [40–42] have even proposed other logics for hyperproperties, which we discuss in Section 8. But HyperLTL provides a simple and unifying logic in which many information-flow security policies can be directly expressed.

Information-flow policies are not one-size-fits-all. Different policies might be needed depending on the power of the adversary. For example, the following program does not satisfy observational determinism, but the program might be acceptable if nondeterministic choices, denoted [], are resolved such that the probability distribution on output value l is uniform:

$$(3) \quad l := h \;[]\; l := 0 \;[]\; l := 1$$

On the other hand, if the adversary can influence the resolution of nondeterministic choices, program (3) could be exploited to leak information. Similarly, the following program does satisfy observational determinism, but the program might be unacceptable if adversaries can monitor execution time:

$$(4) \quad \textbf{while } h > 0 \textbf{ do } \{h := h - 1\}$$

In Section 3, we show how policies appropriate for the above programs, as well as other security policies, can be formalized in HyperLTL.

Our second logic, *HyperCTL**, generalizes a branching-time temporal logic, CTL* [18]. Although CTL* already has explicit trace quantifiers, only one trace is ever in scope at a given point in a formula (see Section 5.1), so CTL* cannot directly express hyperproperties. But HyperCTL* can, because it permits quantification over multiple execution traces simultaneously. HyperLTL and HyperCTL* enjoy a similar relationship to that of LTL and CTL*: HyperLTL is the syntactic fragment of HyperCTL* containing only formulas in *prenex* form—that is, formulas that begin exclusively with quantifiers and end with a quantifier-free formula. HyperCTL* is thus a strict generalization of HyperLTL. HyperCTL* also generalizes a related temporal logic, SecLTL [17], and subsumes epistemic temporal logic [19,54] (see Section 5).

Having defined logics for hyperproperties, we investigate model checking of those logics. In Section 6, we show that for HyperCTL* the model checking problem is decidable by reducing it to the satisfiability problem for quantified propositional temporal logic (QPTL) [50]. Since HyperCTL* generalizes Hyper-LTL, we immediately obtain that the HyperLTL model checking problem is also decidable. We present a hierarchy of fragments, which allows us to precisely characterize the complexity of the model checking problem in the number quantifier alternations. The lowest fragment, which disallows any quantifier alternation, can be checked by a space-efficient polynomial-time algorithm (NLOGSPACE in the number of states of the program).

We also prototype a model checker that can handle an important fragment of HyperLTL, including all the examples from Section 3. The prototype implements a new model checking algorithm based on a well-known LTL algorithm [58,59] and on a self-composition construction [7,52]. The complexity of our algorithm is exponential in the size of the program and doubly exponential in the size of the formula—impractical for real-world programs, but at least a demonstration that model checking of hyperproperties formulated in our logic is possible.

This paper contributes to theoretical and foundational aspects of security by:

- defining two new program logics for expressing hyperproperties,
- demonstrating that those logics are expressive enough to formulate important information-flow policies,
- proving that the model checking problem is decidable, and
- prototyping a new model checking algorithm and using it to verify security policies.

The rest of the paper is structured as follows. Section 2 defines the syntax and semantics of HyperLTL. Section 3 provides several example formulations of information-flow policies. Section 4 defines the syntax and semantics of HyperCTL*. Section 5 compares our two logics with other temporal and epistemic logics. Section 6 obtains a model checking algorithm for HyperCTL*. Section 7 describes our prototype model checker. Section 8 reviews related work, and Section 9 concludes.

2   HyperLTL

HyperLTL extends propositional linear-time temporal logic (LTL) [44] with explicit quantification over *traces*. A *trace* is an infinite sequence of sets of *atomic propositions*. Let AP denote the set of all atomic propositions. The set TR of all traces is therefore $(2^{\mathsf{AP}})^\omega$.

We first define some notation for manipulating traces. Let $t \in \mathsf{TR}$ be a trace. We use $t[i]$ to denote element i of t, where $i \in \mathbb{N}$. Hence, $t[0]$ is the first element of t. We write $t[0, i]$ to denote the prefix of t up to and including element i, and $t[i, \infty]$ to denote the infinite suffix of t beginning with element i.

Syntax. Let π be a *trace variable* from an infinite supply $\mathcal{V}$ of trace variables. Formulas of HyperLTL are defined by the following grammar:

$$
\begin{aligned}
\psi &::= \exists \pi.\, \psi \mid \forall \pi.\, \psi \mid \varphi \\
\varphi &::= a_\pi \mid \neg \varphi \mid \varphi \vee \varphi \mid \mathbf{X} \varphi \mid \varphi \mathbf{U} \varphi
\end{aligned}
$$

Connectives $\exists$ and $\forall$ are universal and existential trace quantifiers, read as "along some traces" and "along all traces." For example, $\forall \pi_1.\, \forall \pi_2.\, \exists \pi_3.\, \psi$ means that for all traces π_1 and π_2, there exists another trace π_3, such that ψ holds on those three traces. (Since branching-time logics also have explicit path quantifiers, it is natural to wonder why one of them does not suffice to formulate hyperproperties. Section 5.1 addresses that question.) A HyperLTL formula is *closed* if all occurrences of trace variables are bound by a trace quantifier.

An atomic proposition a, where $a \in \mathsf{AP}$, expresses some fact about states. Since formulas may refer to multiple traces, we need to disambiguate which trace the proposition refers to. So we annotate each occurrence of an atomic proposition with a trace variable π. Boolean connectives $\neg$ and $\vee$ have the usual classical meanings. Implication, conjunction, and bi-implication are defined as syntactic sugar: $\varphi_1 \rightarrow \varphi_2 \equiv \neg\varphi_1 \vee \varphi_2$, and $\varphi_1 \wedge \varphi_2 \equiv \neg(\neg\varphi_1 \vee \neg\varphi_2)$, and $\varphi_1 \leftrightarrow \varphi_2 \equiv (\varphi_1 \rightarrow \varphi_2) \wedge (\varphi_2 \rightarrow \varphi_1)$. True and false, written true and false, are defined as $a_\pi \vee \neg a_\pi$ and $\neg\mathsf{true}$.

Temporal connective $\mathrm{X}\,\varphi$ means that φ holds on the next state of every quantified trace. Likewise, $\varphi_1 \mathrm{U} \varphi_2$ means that φ_2 will eventually hold of the states of all quantified traces that appear at the same index, and until then φ_1 holds. The other standard temporal connectives are defined as syntactic sugar: $\mathrm{F}\,\varphi \equiv \mathsf{true}\,\mathrm{U}\,\varphi$, and $\mathrm{G}\,\varphi \equiv \neg\mathrm{F}\,\neg\varphi$, and $\varphi_1 \mathrm{W} \varphi_2 \equiv (\varphi_1 \mathrm{U} \varphi_2) \vee \mathrm{G}\,\varphi_1$, and $\varphi_1 \mathrm{R} \varphi_2 \equiv \neg(\neg\varphi_1 \mathrm{U} \neg\varphi_2)$.

We also introduce syntactic sugar for comparing traces. Given a set P of atomic propositions, $\pi[0] =_P \pi'[0] \equiv \bigwedge_{a \in P} a_\pi \leftrightarrow a_{\pi'}$. That is, $\pi[0] =_P \pi'[0]$ holds whenever the first state in both π and π' agree on all the propositions in P. And $\pi =_P \pi' \equiv \mathrm{G}(\pi[0] =_P \pi'[0])$, that is, all the positions of π and π' agree on P. The analogous definitions hold for $\neq$.

Semantics. The validity judgment for HyperLTL formulas is written $\Pi \models_T \psi$, where T is a set of traces, and $\Pi : \mathcal{V} \rightarrow \mathsf{TR}$ is a *trace assignment* (i.e., a *valuation*), which is a partial function mapping trace variables to traces. Let $\Pi[\pi \mapsto t]$ denote the same function as Π, except that π is mapped to t. We write trace set T as a subscript on $\models$, because T propagates unchanged through the semantics; we omit T when it is clear from context. Validity is defined as follows:

$$
\begin{array}{lll}
\Pi \models_T \exists\pi.\,\psi & \text{iff} & \text{there exists } t \in T : \Pi[\pi \mapsto t] \models_T \psi \\
\Pi \models_T \forall\pi.\,\psi & \text{iff} & \text{for all } t \in T : \Pi[\pi \mapsto t] \models_T \psi \\
\Pi \models_T a_\pi & \text{iff} & a \in \Pi(\pi)[0] \\
\Pi \models_T \neg\varphi & \text{iff} & \Pi \not\models_T \varphi \\
\Pi \models_T \varphi_1 \vee \varphi_2 & \text{iff} & \Pi \models_T \varphi_1 \text{ or } \Pi \models_T \varphi_2 \\
\Pi \models_T \mathrm{X}\,\varphi & \text{iff} & \Pi[1, \infty] \models_T \varphi \\
\Pi \models_T \varphi_1 \mathrm{U} \varphi_2 & \text{iff} & \text{there exists } i \geq 0 : \Pi[i, \infty] \models_T \varphi_2 \\
& & \text{and for all } 0 \leq j < i \text{ we have } \Pi[j, \infty] \models_T \varphi_1
\end{array}
$$

Trace assignment *suffix* $\Pi[i, \infty]$ denotes the trace assignment $\Pi'(\pi) = \Pi(\pi)[i, \infty]$ for all π. If $\Pi \models_T \varphi$ holds for the empty assignment Π, then T *satisfies* φ.

We are interested in whether programs satisfy formulas, so we first derive a set T of traces from a program, first using *Kripke structures* as a unified representation of programs. A Kripke structure K is a tuple $(S, s_0, \delta, \mathsf{AP}, L)$

comprising a set of *states* S, an *initial state* $s_0 \in S$, a transition function $\delta : S \to 2^S$, a set of *atomic propositions* AP, and a labeling function $L : S \to 2^{\mathsf{AP}}$. To ensure that all traces are infinite, we require that $\delta(s)$ is nonempty for every state s.

The set $\mathsf{Traces}(K)$ of traces of K is the set of all sequences of labels produced by the state transitions of K starting from initial state. Formally, $\mathsf{Traces}(K)$ contains trace t iff there exists a sequence $s_0 s_1 \ldots$ of states, such that s_0 is the initial state, and for all $i \geq 0$, it holds that $s_{i+1} \in \delta(s_i)$; and $t[i] = L(s_i)$. A Kripke structure K *satisfies* φ, denoted by $K \models \varphi$, if $\mathsf{Traces}(K)$ satisfies φ.

It will later be technically convenient to consider enlarging the set AP of atomic propositions permitted by a Kripke structure to a set AP$'$, such that AP $\subset$ AP$'$. We extend $\mathsf{Traces}(K)$ into the set of traces $\mathsf{Traces}(K, \mathsf{AP}')$ that is agnostic about whether each new proposition holds at each state. A trace $(P_0 \cup P_0')(P_1 \cup P_1') \ldots \in \mathsf{Traces}(K, \mathsf{AP}')$ whenever $P_0 P_1 \ldots \in \mathsf{Traces}(K)$, and for all $i \geq 0$: $P_i' \subseteq \mathsf{AP}' \setminus \mathsf{AP}$. The final conjunct requires every possible set of new atomic propositions to be included in the traces.

3   Security Policies in HyperLTL

We now put HyperLTL into action by formulating several *information-flow security policies*, which stipulate how information may propagate from inputs to outputs. Information-flow is a very active field in security; see [20,48] for surveys.

Noninterference. A program satisfies *noninterference* [23] when the outputs observed by low-security users are the same as they would be in the absence of inputs submitted by high-security users. Since its original definition, many variants with different execution models have been named "noninterference." For clarity of our examples, we choose a simple *state-based* synchronous execution model in which atomic propositions of the traces contain the values of program variables, and in which progress of time corresponds to execution steps in the model. We also assume that the variables are partitioned into input and output variables, and into two security levels, *high* and *low*. (We could handle lattices of security levels by conjoining several formulas that stipulate noninterference between elements of the lattice.)

Noninference [38] is a variant of noninterference that can be stated in our simple system model. Noninference stipulates that, for all traces, the low-observable behavior must not change when all high inputs are replaced by a dummy input λ, that is, when the high input is removed. Noninference, a *liveness hyperproperty* [15], can be expressed in HyperLTL as follows:

$$\forall \pi. \exists \pi'. \; (\mathrm{G}\, \lambda_{\pi'}) \; \wedge \; \pi =_L \pi' \tag{5}$$

where $\lambda_{\pi'}$ expresses that all of the high inputs in the current state of π' are λ, and $\pi =_L \pi'$ expresses that all low variables in π and π' have the same values.

Nondeterminism. Noninterference was introduced for use with deterministic programs. Nonetheless, nondeterminism naturally arises when program specifications abstract from implementation details, so many variants of noninterference have been developed for nondeterministic programs. We formalize two variants here.

A (nondeterministic) program satisfies *observational determinism* [61] if every pair of traces with the same initial low observation remain indistinguishable for low users. That is, the program appears to be deterministic to low users. Programs that satisfy observational determinism are immune to *refinement attacks* [61], because observational determinism is preserved under refinement. Observational determinism, a *safety hyperproperty* [15], can be expressed in HyperLTL as follows:

$$\forall \pi. \forall \pi'. \; \pi[0] =_{L,\text{in}} \pi'[0] \; \rightarrow \; \pi =_{L,\text{out}} \pi' \tag{6}$$

where $\pi =_{L,\text{in}} \pi'$ and $\pi =_{L,\text{out}} \pi'$ express that both traces agree on the low input and low output variables, respectively.

Generalized noninterference (GNI) [35] permits nondeterminism in the low-observable behavior, but stipulates that low-security outputs may not be altered by the injection of high-security inputs. Like noninterference, GNI was original formulated for event-based systems, but it can also be formulated for state-based systems [38]. GNI is a liveness hyperproperty and can be expressed as follows:

$$\forall \pi. \forall \pi'. \exists \pi''. \; \pi =_{H,\text{in}} \pi'' \; \wedge \; \pi' =_L \pi'' \tag{7}$$

The trace π'' in (7) is an *interleaving* of the high inputs of the first trace and the low inputs and outputs of the second trace. Other security policies based on interleavings, such as *restrictiveness* [36], *separability* [38], and *forward correctability* [39] can similarly be expressed in HyperLTL.

Declassification. Some programs need to reveal secret information to fulfill functional requirements. For example, a password checker must reveal whether the entered password is correct or not. The noninterference policies we have examined so far prohibit such behavior. More flexible security policies have been designed to permit *declassification* of information; see [49] for a survey.

With HyperLTL, we easily specify customized declassification policies. For example, suppose that a system inputs a password in its initial state, then declassifies whether that password is correct in the next state. The following policy (a safety hyperproperty) stipulates that leaking the correctness of the password is permitted, but that otherwise observational determinism must hold:

$$\forall \pi. \forall \pi'. (\pi[0] =_{L,\text{in}} \pi'[0] \; \wedge \; X(pw_\pi \leftrightarrow pw_{\pi'})) \rightarrow \pi =_{L,\text{out}} \pi' \tag{8}$$

where atomic proposition pw expresses that the entered password is correct.

Quantitative noninterference. Quantitative information-flow policies [12, 14, 24, 31] permit leakage of information at restricted rates. One way to measure leakage is with *min-entropy* [51], which quantifies the amount of information an attacker can gain given the answer to a single guess about the secret. The *bounding problem* [60] for min-entropy is to determine whether that amount is bounded from above by a constant n. Assume that the program whose leakage is being quantified is deterministic, and assume that the secret input to that program is uniformly distributed. The bounding problem then reduces to determining that there is no tuple of $2^n + 1$ low-distinguishable traces [51,60] (a safety hyperproperty). We can express that as follows:

$$\neg \exists \pi_0. \ldots . \exists \pi_{2^n}. \left(\bigwedge_i \pi_i =_{L,\text{in}} \pi_0 \right) \wedge \bigwedge_{i \neq j} \pi_i \neq_{L,\text{out}} \pi_j \tag{9}$$

The initial negation can pushed inside to obtained a proper HyperLTL formula.

Quantitative flow and entropy naturally bring to mind probabilistic systems. We haven't yet explored extending our logics to enable specification of policies that involve probabilities. Perhaps techniques previously used with epistemic logic [25] could be adapted; we leave this as future work.

Event-based systems. Our examples above use a synchronous state-based execution model. Many formulations of security policies, including the original formulation of noninterference [23], instead use an *event-based* system model, in which input and output events are not synchronized and have no relation to time. HyperLTL can express policies for asynchronous execution models, too. For example, HyperLTL can express the original definition of noninterference [23] and observational determinism; the companion technical report [13] shows how. The key idea is to allow the system to stutter and to quantify over all stuttered versions of the executions. We characterize the correct *synchronization* of a pair of traces as having updates to low variables only at the same positions. We then add an additional antecedent to the policy formula to require that only those pairs of traces that are synchronized correctly need to fulfill the security condition.

4   HyperCTL*

HyperLTL was derived from LTL by extending the models of formulas from single traces to sets of traces. However, like LTL, HyperLTL is restricted to linear time and cannot express branching-time properties (e.g., all states that succeed the current state satisfy some proposition). We show now that a branching-time logic for hyperproperties could be derived from a branching-time logic for trace properties, such as CTL* [18]. We call this logic HyperCTL*. The key idea is again to use sets instead of singletons as the models of formulas.

Syntax. HyperCTL* generalizes HyperLTL by allowing quantifiers to appear anywhere within a formula. Quantification in HyperCTL* is over *paths* through a Kripke structure. A path p is an infinite sequence of pairs of a state and a set of atomic propositions. Hence, a path differs from a trace by including a state of the Kripke structure in each element. Formally, $p \in (S \times 2^{\text{AP}})^\omega$, where S is the states of the Kripke structure. As with traces, $p[i]$ denotes the element i of

p, and $p[i, \infty]$ denotes the suffix of p beginning with element i. We also define a new notation: let $p(i)$ be the state in element i of p.

In HyperCTL*, π is a *path variable* and $\exists \pi$ is a *path quantifier*. Formulas of HyperCTL* are defined by the following grammar:

$$\varphi ::= a_\pi \mid \neg\varphi \mid \varphi \vee \varphi \mid X\,\varphi \mid \varphi \,U\, \varphi \mid \exists\pi.\,\varphi$$

We introduce all the syntactic sugar for derived logical operators, as for HyperLTL. The universal quantifier can now be defined as syntactic sugar, too: $\forall\pi.\,\varphi \equiv \neg\exists\pi.\,\neg\varphi$. A HyperCTL* formula is *closed* if all occurrences of some path variable π are in the scope of a path quantifier. A HyperCTL* *specification* is a Boolean combination of closed HyperCTL* formulas each beginning with a quantifier (or its negation).

Semantics. The validity judgment for HyperCTL* formulas is written $\Pi \models_K \varphi$, where K is a Kripke structure, and $\Pi : \mathcal{V} \to (S \times 2^{\mathsf{AP}})^\omega$ is a *path assignment*, which is a partial function mapping path variables to paths. We write K as a subscript on $\models$, because K propagates unchanged through the semantics; we omit K when it is clear from context. Validity is defined as follows:

$$
\begin{aligned}
\Pi &\models_K a_\pi & &\text{iff} & &a \in L\big(\Pi(\pi)(0)\big) \\
\Pi &\models_K \neg\varphi & &\text{iff} & &\Pi \not\models_K \varphi \\
\Pi &\models_K \varphi_1 \vee \varphi_2 & &\text{iff} & &\Pi \models_K \varphi_1 \text{ or } \Pi \models \varphi_2 \\
\Pi &\models_K X\,\varphi & &\text{iff} & &\Pi[1, \infty] \models_K \varphi \\
\Pi &\models_K \varphi_1 \,U\, \varphi_2 & &\text{iff} & &\text{there exists } i \geq 0 : \Pi[i, \infty] \models_K \varphi_2 \\
& & & & &\text{and for all } 0 \leq j < i \text{ we have } \Pi[j, \infty] \models_K \varphi_1 \\
\Pi &\models_K \exists\pi.\,\varphi & &\text{iff} & &\text{there exists } p \in \mathsf{Paths}(K, \Pi(\pi')(0)) : \Pi[\pi \mapsto p] \models_K \varphi
\end{aligned}
$$

In the clause for existential quantification, π' denotes the path variable most recently added to Π (i.e., closest in scope to π). If Π is empty, let $\Pi(\pi')(0)$ be the initial state of K. It would be straightforward but tedious to further formalize this notation, so we omit the details. That clause uses another new notation, $\mathsf{Paths}(K, s)$, which is the set of paths produced by Kripke structure K beginning from state s. Formally, $\mathsf{Paths}(K, s)$ contains path p, where $p = (s_0, P_0)(s_1, P_1) \ldots$ and $P_i \in 2^{\mathsf{AP}}$, iff exists a sequence $s_0 s_1 \ldots$ of states, such that s_0 is s, and for all $i \geq 0$, it holds that $s_{i+1} \in \delta(s_i)$ and $P_i = L(s_i)$.

Like with Traces in HyperLTL, we define $\mathsf{Paths}(K, s, \mathsf{AP}')$ as follows: We have $(s_0, P_0 \cup P_0')(s_1, P_1 \cup P_1') \ldots \in \mathsf{Paths}(K, s, \mathsf{AP}')$ iff $(s_0, P_0)(s_1, P_1) \ldots \in \mathsf{Paths}(K, s)$, and for all $i \geq 0$, it holds that $P_i' \subseteq \mathsf{AP}' \setminus \mathsf{AP}$.

We say that a Kripke structure K *satisfies* a HyperCTL* specification φ, denoted by $K \models \varphi$, if $\Pi \models_K \varphi$ holds true for the empty assignment. The *model checking problem* for HyperCTL* is to decide whether a given Kripke structure satisfies a given HyperCTL* specification.

HyperCTL vs. HyperLTL.* LTL can be characterized as the fragment of CTL* containing formulas of the form $A\,\varphi$, where A is the CTL* universal path quantifier and φ contains no quantifiers. Formula $A\varphi$ is satisfied in CTL* by a Kripke structure iff φ is satisfied in LTL by the traces of the Kripke structure.

A similar relationship holds between HyperLTL and HyperCTL*: HyperLTL can be characterized as the fragment of HyperCTL* containing formulas in *prenex* form—that is, a series of quantifiers followed by a quantifier-free formula. A formula φ in prenex form is satisfied in HyperCTL* by a Kripke structure iff φ is satisfied in HyperLTL by the traces of the Kripke structure. HyperCTL* is a strict generalization of HyperLTL, which extends HyperLTL with the capability to use quantified formulas as subformulas in the scope of temporal operators. For example, consider the program $(l := 0 \ [\!] \ l := 0) \ [\!] \ (l := 1 \ [\!] \ l := 1)$. A low-observer can infer which branch of the center-most nondeterministic choice is taken, but not which branch is taken next. This is expressed by HyperCTL* formula $\forall \pi. \ X \, \forall \pi'. \ X \, (l_\pi \leftrightarrow l_{\pi'})$. There is no equivalent HyperLTL formula.

As we show in Subsection 5.3, the temporal logic SecLTL [17] can be encoded in HyperCTL*, but not in HyperLTL. This provides further examples that distinguish HyperLTL and HyperCTL*.

5   Related Logics

We now examine the expressiveness of HyperLTL and HyperCTL* compared to several existing temporal logics: LTL, CTL*, QPTL, ETL, and SecLTL. There are many other logics that we could compare to in future work; some of those are discussed in Section 8.

5.1   Temporal Logics

HyperCTL* is an extension of CTL* and therefore subsumes LTL, CTL, and CTL*. Likewise, HyperLTL subsumes LTL. But temporal logics LTL, CTL, and CTL* cannot express information-flow policies. LTL formulas express properties of individual execution paths. All of the noninterference properties of Section 3 are properties of sets of execution paths [15, 38]. Explicit path quantification does enable their formulation in HyperLTL.

Even though CTL and CTL* have explicit path quantifiers, information-flow security policies, such as observational determinism (6), cannot be expressed with them. Consider the following fragment of CTL* semantics:

$$s \models A \, \varphi \ \text{ iff for all } p \in \mathsf{Paths}(K, s): \ p \models \varphi$$
$$p \models \Phi \quad \text{ iff } p(0) \models \Phi$$

Path formulas φ are modeled by paths p, and *state* formulas Φ are modeled by states s. State formula $A \, \varphi$ holds at state s when all paths proceeding from s satisfy φ. Any state formula Φ can be treated as a path formula, in which case Φ holds of the path iff Φ holds in the first state on that path. Using this semantics, consider the meaning of $AA \, \varphi$, which is the form of observational determinism (6):

$$s \models AA \, \varphi$$
$$= \text{for all } p \in \mathsf{Paths}(K, s): \ p \models A\varphi$$
$$= \text{for all } p \in \mathsf{Paths}(K, s) \text{ and } p' \in \mathsf{Paths}(K, s): \ p' \models \varphi$$

Note how the meaning of AA φ is ultimately determined by the meaning of φ, where φ is modeled by the single path p'. Path p is ignored in determining the meaning of φ; the second universal path quantifier causes p to "leave scope." Hence φ cannot express correlations between p and p', as observational determinism requires. So CTL* path quantifiers do not suffice to express information-flow policies. Neither do CTL path quantifiers, because CTL is a sub-logic of CTL*. In fact, even the modal μ-calculus does not suffice to express some information-flow properties [2].

By using the self-composition construction [7,52], it is possible to express relational noninterference in CTL [7] and observational determinism in CTL* [30]. Those approaches resemble HyperCTL*, but HyperCTL* formulas express policies directly over the original system, rather than over a self-composed system. Furthermore, the self-composition approach does not seem capable of expressing policies that require both universal and existential quantifiers over infinite executions, like noninference (5) and generalized noninterference (7). It is straightforward to express such policies in our logics.

QPTL. Quantified propositional temporal logic (QPTL) [50] extends LTL with quantification over propositions, whereas HyperLTL extends LTL with quantification over traces. Quantification over traces is more powerful than quantification over propositions, as we now show.

QPTL formulas are generated by the following grammar, where $a \in \mathsf{AP}$:

$$\psi ::= a \mid \neg\psi \mid \psi \vee \psi \mid \mathrm{X}\,\psi \mid \mathrm{F}\,\psi \mid \exists a.\,\psi$$

All QPTL connectives have the same semantics as in LTL, except for propositional quantification:

$$p \models \exists a.\psi \quad \text{iff} \quad \text{there exists } p' \in (2^{\mathsf{AP}})^\omega : p =_{\mathsf{AP}\setminus a} p' \text{ and } p' \models \psi\,.$$

Theorem 1. *HyperLTL subsumes QPTL, but QPTL does not subsume HyperLTL.*

Proof sketch. To express a QPTL formula in HyperLTL, rewrite the formula to prenex form, and rename all bound propositions with unique fresh names from a set AP'. These propositions act as free variables, which are unconstrained because they do not occur in the Kripke structure. Replace each propositional quantification $\exists a$ in the QPTL formula by a path quantification $\exists \pi_a$ in the HyperLTL formula. And replace each occurrence of a by a_{π_a}. The result is a HyperLTL formula that holds iff the original QPTL formula holds.

But not all HyperLTL formulas can be expressed in QPTL. For example, QPTL cannot express properties that require the existence of paths, such as $\exists\pi.\,\mathrm{X}\,a_\pi$. $\qquad\qquad\square$

In Section 6, we exploit the relationship between HyperLTL and QPTL to obtain a model checking algorithm for HyperLTL.

5.2   Epistemic Logics

HyperLTL and HyperCTL* express information-flow policies by explicit quantification over multiple traces or paths. Epistemic temporal logic has also been used to express such policies [4, 10, 26, 55] by implicit quantification over traces or paths with the *knowledge* connective K of epistemic logic [19]. We do not yet know which is more powerful, particularly for information-flow policies. But we do know that HyperLTL subsumes a common epistemic temporal logic.

Define ETL (epistemic temporal logic) to be LTL with the addition of K under its perfect recall semantics [4, 19, 54]. The model of an ETL formula is a pair (K, Agts) of a Kripke structure K and a set Agts of equivalence relations on AP, called the *agents*; each relation models the knowledge of an agent. (*Interpreted systems*, rather than Kripke structures, are often used to model ETL formulas [19, 54]. Interpreted systems differ in style but can be translated to our formulation.) In the *asynchronous* semantics of ETL, $\mathsf{K}_A\psi$ holds on state i of trace $t \in \mathsf{Traces}(K)$, denoted $t, i \models \mathsf{K}_A\varphi$, iff

$$\text{for all } t' \in \mathsf{Traces}(K) : \ t[0, i] \approx_A t'[0, i] \text{ implies } t', i \models \varphi,$$

where $\approx_A$ denotes stutter-equivalence on finite traces with respect to A. In the *synchronous* semantics of ETL, stutter-equivalence is replaced by stepwise-equivalence.

The following two theorems show that HyperLTL subsumes ETL:

Theorem 2. *In the synchronous semantics, for every ETL formula ψ and every set Agts of agents, there exists a HyperLTL formula φ such that for all Kripke structures K, we have $(K, \mathsf{Agts}) \models \psi$ iff $K \models \varphi$.*

Theorem 3. *In the asynchronous semantics, for every ETL formula ψ and every set Agts of agents, there exists a HyperLTL formula φ such that for all asynchronous Kripke structures K, we have $(K, \mathsf{Agts}) \models \psi$ iff $K \models \varphi$.*

Proofs of both theorems appear in the companion technical report [13]. Theorem 3 requires an additional assumption that K is an *asynchronous* Kripke structure, i.e. that it can always stutter in its current state and that it is indicated in an atomic proposition whether the last state was a stuttering step.

HyperLTL and ETL have the same worst-case complexity for model checking, which is non-elementary. But, as we show in Section 6, the complexity of our model checking algorithm on the information-flow policies of Section 3 is much better—only NLOGSPACE (for observational determinism, declassification, and quantitative noninterference for a fixed number of bits) or PSPACE (for noninference and generalized noninterference) in the size of the system. For those policies in NLOGSPACE, that complexity, unsurprisingly, is as good as algorithms based on self-composition [7]. This ability to use a general-purpose, efficient HyperLTL model checking algorithm for information flow seems to be an improvement over encodings of information flow in ETL.

5.3 SecLTL

SecLTL [17] extends temporal logic with the *hide* modality $\mathcal{H}$, which allows to express information flow properties such as noninterference [23]. The semantics of SecLTL is defined in terms of labeled transition system, where the edges are labeled with valuations of the set of variables. The formula $\mathcal{H}_{H,O}\varphi$ specifies that the current valuations of a subset H of the input variables I are kept secret from an attacker who may observe variables in O until the release condition φ becomes true. The semantics is formalized in terms of a set of *alternative paths* to which the *main path* is compared:

$$\mathsf{AltPaths}(p, H) = \{p' \in \mathsf{Paths}(K_M, p[0]) \mid p[1] =_{I \setminus H} p'[1] \text{ and } p[2, \infty] =_I p'[2, \infty]\}$$

where K_M is the equivalent Kripke structure for the labeled transition system M (we will explain the translation later in this section.) A path p satisfies the SecLTL formula $\mathcal{H}_{H,O}\varphi$, denoted by $p \models \mathcal{H}_{H,O}\varphi$, iff

$$\forall p' \in \mathsf{AltPaths}(p, H).\ \big(p =_O p',\ \text{or there exists } i \geq 0 :$$
$$p[i, \infty] \models_K \varphi \text{ and } p[1, i-1] =_O p'[1, i-1]\big)$$

A labeled transition system M satisfies a SecLTL formula ψ, denoted by $M \models \psi$, if every path p starting in the initial state satisfies ψ.

SecLTL can express properties like the dynamic creation of secrets discussed in Section 4, which cannot be expressed by HyperLTL. However, SecLTL is subsumed by HyperCTL*. To encode the hide modality in HyperCTL*, we first translate M into a Kripke structure K_M, whose states are labeled with the valuation of the variables on the edge leading into the state. The initial state is labeled with the empty set. In the modified system, $L(p[1])$ corresponds to the current labels. We encode $\mathcal{H}_{H,O}\varphi$ as the following HyperCTL* formula:

$$\forall \pi'.\ \pi[1] =_{I \setminus H} \pi'[1] \wedge \mathrm{X}\left(\pi[1] =_O \pi'[1]\ \mathrm{W}\ (\pi[1] \neq_I \pi'[1] \vee \varphi)\right)$$

Theorem 4. *For every SecLTL formula ψ and transition system M, there is a HyperCTL* formula φ such that $M \models \psi$ iff $K_M \models \varphi$.*

The model checking problem for SecLTL is PSPACE-hard in the size of the Kripke structure [17]. The encoding of SecLTL specifications in HyperCTL* implies that the model checking problem for HyperCTL* is also PSPACE-hard (for a fixed specification of alternation depth ≥ 1), as claimed in Theorem 6.

6   Model Checking and Satisfiability

In this section we exploit the connection between HyperCTL* and QPTL to obtain a model checking algorithm for HyperCTL* and study its complexity. We identify a hierarchy of fragments of HyperCTL* characterized by the number of quantifier alternations. This hierarchy allows us to give a precise characterization of the complexity of the model checking problem. The fragment of formulas with quantifier alternation depth 0 includes already many formulas of interest and our result provides an NLOGSPACE algorithm in the size of the Kripke structure.

Definition 1 (Alternation Depth). *A HyperCTL* formula φ in NNF has alternation depth 0 plus the highest number of alternations from existential to universal and universal to existential quantifiers along any of the paths of the formula's syntax tree starting in the root. Occurrences of U and R count as an additional alternation.*

Theorem 5. *The model checking problem for HyperCTL* specifications φ with alternation depth k on a Kripke structure K is complete for $NSPACE(g_c(k, |\varphi|))$ and it is in $NSPACE(g_c(k-1, |K|))$ for some $c > 0$.*

The function $g_c(x, y)$ denotes a tower of exponentials of height x with argument y: $g_c(0, y) = y$ and $g_c(x, y) = c^{g(x-1,y)}$. $NSPACE(g_c(x, y))$ denotes the class of languages accepted by a Turing machine bounded in space by $O(g_c(x, y))$. Abusing notation, we define $g_c(-1, y) = \log y$ and $NSPACE(\log y) = $ NLOGSPACE in y.

Proof. Both directions, the lower bound and the upper bound, are based on the complexity of the satisfiability problem for QPTL formulas φ in prenex normal form and with alternation depth k, which is complete for $NSPACE(g(k, |\varphi|))$ [50].

For the upper bound on the HyperCTL* model checking complexity, we first translate until operators $\psi \, \mathsf{U} \, \psi'$ as $\exists t. \, t \wedge \mathsf{G}(t \to \psi' \vee (\psi \wedge \mathsf{X}\,t)) \wedge \neg \mathsf{G}\,t$. Let $\psi(K, \mathsf{AP}')$ encode a Kripke structure K, where $K = (S, s_0, \delta, \mathsf{AP}, L)$, as a QPTL formula (cf. [33]) using the set of atomic propositions AP', which must contain atomic propositions replacing those of AP and additional atomic propositions to describe the states S. The formula $\psi(K, \mathsf{AP}')$ is linear in $|K|$ and does not require additional quantifiers.

HyperCTL* path quantifiers $\exists \pi. \varphi$ and $\forall \pi. \varphi$ are then encoded as $\exists \mathsf{AP}_\pi. \, \psi$ $(K, \mathsf{AP}_\pi) \wedge \varphi_{\mathsf{AP}_\pi}$ and $\forall \mathsf{AP}_\pi. \psi(K, \mathsf{AP}_\pi) \to \varphi_{\mathsf{AP}_\pi}$, where AP_π is a set of *fresh* atomic propositions including a copy of AP and additional atomic propositions to describe the states S. The formula $\varphi_{\mathsf{AP}_\pi}$ is obtained from φ by replacing all atomic propositions referring to path π by their copies in AP_π. Atomic propositions in the formula that are not in AP (i.e. their interpretation is not fixed in K) need to be added to the sets AP_π accordingly.

For the lower bound, we reduce the satisfiability problem for a given QPTL formula φ in prenex normal form to a model checking problem $K \models \varphi'$ of HyperCTL*. We assume, without loss of generality, that φ is closed (if a free proposition occurs in φ, we bind it with an existential quantifier) and each quantifier in φ introduces a different proposition.

The Kripke structure K consists of two states $S = \{s_0, s_1\}$, is fully connected $\delta(s) = S$ for all $s \in S$, and has a single atomic proposition $\mathsf{AP} = \{p\}$. The states are labeled as follows: $L(s_0) = \emptyset$ and $L(s_1) = \{p\}$. Essentially, paths in K can encode all sequences of valuations of a variable in QPTL. To obtain the HyperCTL* formula, we now simply replace every quantifier in the QPTL formula with a path quantifier. The only technical problem left is that quantification in QPTL allows to choose freely the value of p in the current state, while path quantification in HyperCTL* only allows the path to differ in the next state. We solve the issue by shifting the propositions using a next operator. $\square$

Lower bounds in $|K|$. An NLOGSPACE *lower* bound in the size of the Kripke structure for fixed specifications with alternation depth 0 follows from the non-emptiness problem of non-deterministic Büchi automata. For alternation depth 1 and more we can derive PSPACE hardness in the size of the Kripke structure from the encoding of the logic SecLTL into HyperCTL* (see Subsection 5.3).

The result can easily be transferred to HyperLTL, since in the SecLTL formula that is used to prove PSPACE hardness, the Hide operator does not occur in the scope of temporal operators and hence the translation yields a HyperLTL formula.

Theorem 6. *For HyperLTL formulas the model checking problem is hard for PSPACE in the size of the system.*

A Remark on Efficiency The use of the standard encoding of the until operator in QPTL with an additional quantifier shown above is, in certain cases, wasteful. The satisfiability of QPTL formulas can be checked with an automata-theoretic construction, where we first transform the formula into prenex normal form, then generate a nondeterministic Büchi automaton for the quantifier-free part of the formula, and finally apply projection and complementation to handle the existential and universal quantifiers. In this way, each quantifier alternation, including the alternation introduced by the encoding of the until operators, causes an exponential blow-up. However, if an until operator occurs in the quantifier-free part, the standard transformation of LTL formulas to nondeterministic Büchi automata handle this until operator without requiring a quantifier elimination, resulting in an exponential speedup.

Using this insight, the model checking complexity for many of the formulas presented above and in Section 3 can be reduced by one exponent. Additionally, the complexity with respect to the size of the system reduces to NLOGSPACE for HyperCTL* formulas where the leading quantifiers are all of the same type and are followed by some quantifier-free formula which may contain until operators without restriction. Observational determinism and the declassification policy discussed in Section 3 are examples for specifications in this fragment. This insight was used for the prototype implementation described in Section 7 and it avoids an additional complementation step for noninference (5).

Satisfiability. The positive result regarding the model checking problem for HyperCTL* does not carry over to the satisfiability problem. The *finite-state satisfiability problem* consists of the existence of a finite model, while the *general satisfiability problem* asks for the existence of a possibly infinite model.

Theorem 7. *For HyperCTL*, finite-state satisfiability is hard for Σ_1^0 and general satisfiability is hard for Σ_1^1.*

In the proof, located in the companion technical report [13], we reduce the LTL synthesis problem of distributed systems to the satisfiability problem of HyperCTL*.

7   Prototype Model Checker

The results of the previous section yield a model checking algorithm for all of HyperCTL*. But most of our information-flow policy examples do not require the full expressiveness of HyperCTL*. In fact, we have been able implement a prototype model checker for an expressive fragment of the logic mostly using off-the-shelf components.

Define *HyperLTL$_2$* as the fragment of HyperLTL (and of HyperCTL*) in which the series of quantifiers at the beginning of a formula may involve at most one alternation. Every formula in HyperLTL$_2$ thus may begin with at most two (whence the name) kinds of quantifiers—a sequence of $\forall$'s followed by a sequence of $\exists$'s, or vice-versa. For example, $\exists\pi.\psi$ and $\forall\pi_1.\forall\pi_2.\exists\pi_3.\psi$ are allowed, but $\forall\pi_1.\exists\pi_2.\forall\pi_3.\psi$ is not. HyperLTL$_2$ suffices to express all the security policies formulated in Section 3. (Another logic for hyperproperties, $\mathcal{IL}_\mu^k$ [41], similarly restricts fixpoint operator alternations with no apparent loss in expressivity for security policies.)

Our model checking algorithm for HyperLTL$_2$, detailed in the companion technical report [13], is based on algorithms for LTL model checking [21,22,57]. Those LTL algorithms determine whether a Kripke structure satisfies an LTL formula by performing various automata constructions and by checking language containment. Our algorithm likewise uses automata constructions and language containment, as well as self composition [7,52] and a new *projection* construction.

We prototyped this algorithm in about 3,000 lines of OCaml code. Our prototype accepts as input a Kripke structure and a HyperLTL$_2$ formula, then constructs the automata required by our algorithm, and outputs a countermodel if the formula does not hold of the structure. For automata complementation, our prototype outsources to GOAL [53], an interactive tool for manipulating Büchi automata. We have used the prototype to verify noninference (5), observational determinism (6), and generalized noninterference (7) for small Kripke structures (up to 10 states); running times were about 10 seconds or less.

Since our algorithm uses automata complementation, the worst-case running time is exponential in the size of the Kripke structure's state space and doubly exponential in the formula size. So as one might expect, our prototype currently does not scale to medium-sized Kripke structures (up to 1,000 states). But our purpose in building this prototype was to demonstrate a proof-of-concept for model checking of hyperproperties. We conjecture that practical symbolic model checking algorithms, such as BMC and IC3, could be used to scale up our approach to real-world systems.

8   Related Work

McLean [38] formalizes security policies as closure with respect to *selective interleaving functions*. He shows that trace properties cannot express security policies such as noninterference and average response time, because those are not properties of single execution traces. Mantel [34] formalizes security policies with *basic security predicates*, which stipulate *closure conditions* for trace sets.

Clarkson and Schneider [15] introduce *hyperproperties*, a framework for expressing security policies. Hyperproperties are sets of trace sets, and are able to formalize security properties such as noninterference, generalized noninterference, observational determinism and average response time. Clarkson and

Schneider use second-order logic to formulate hyperproperties. That logic isn't verifiable, in general, because it cannot be effectively and completely axiomatized. Fragments of it, such as HyperLTL and HyperCTL*, can be verified.

Alur et al. [2] show that modal μ-calculus is insufficient to express all *opacity* policies [9], which prohibit observers from discerning the truth of a predicate. (Alur et al. [2] actually write "secrecy" rather than "opacity.") Simplifying definitions slightly, a trace property P is *opaque* iff for all paths p of a system, there exists another path p' of that system, such that p and p' are low-equivalent, and exactly one of p and p' satisfies P. Noninference (5) is an opacity policy [47] that HyperLTL can express.

Huisman et al. reduce observational-determinism properties to properties in CTL* [30] and in modal μ-calculus [29] on a self-composed system. Barthe et al. use self composition to verify observational determinism [7] and noninterference [6] on terminating programs. Van der Meyden and Zhang [56] reduce a broader class of information-flow policies to safety properties on a self-composed system expressible in standard linear and branching time logics, and use model checking to verify noninterference policies. Their methodology requires customized model checking algorithms for each security policy, whereas this work proposes a single algorithm for all policies.

Balliu et al. [4] use a linear-time temporal epistemic logic to specify many declassification policies derived from noninterference. Their definition of noninterference, however, seems to be that of observational determinism (6). They do not consider any information-flow policies involving existential quantification, such as noninference. They also do not consider systems that accept inputs after execution has begun. Halpern and O'Neill [26] use a similar temporal epistemic logic to specify *secrecy* policies, which subsume many definitions of noninterference; they do not pursue model checking algorithms.

Alur et al. [1] discuss branching-time logics with *path equivalences* that are also able to express certain security properties. The authors introduce operators that resemble the knowledge operator of epistemic logics. As the logics build on branching-time logics they are not subsumed by HyperLTL. The relationship to HyperCTL* is still open.

Milushev and Clarke [40–42] propose three logics for hyperproperties:

- *Holistic hyperproperty logic* $\mathcal{HL}$, which is based on coinductive predicates over streams. Holistic hyperproperties "talk about whole traces at once; their specifications tend to be straightforward, but they are difficult to reason about, exemplified by the fact that no general approach to verifying such hyperproperties exists" [40]. HyperLTL and HyperCTL* are logics that talk about whole traces at once, too; and they have straightforward specifications as well as a general approach to verification.
- *Incremental hyperproperty logic* $\mathcal{IL}$ is a fragment of *least fixed-point logic* [8]. There is a manual verification methodology for $\mathcal{IL}$ [40], but no automated decision procedure.
- Another incremental hyperproperty logic $\mathcal{IL}_\mu^k$, a fragment of polyadic modal μ-calculus [3] that permits at most one quantifier alternation (a greatest

fixed-point followed by a least fixed-point). There is an automated model checking technique [41] for $\mathcal{IL}_\mu^k$ based on *parity games*. That technique has been prototyped and applied to a few programs.

All these logics suffice to express security policies such as noninterference and generalized noninterference. Like our logics, the exact expressive limitation is still an open problem.

As the preceding discussion makes clear, the expressiveness of HyperLTL and HyperCTL* versus several other logics is an open question. It's possible that some of those logics will turn out to be more expressive or more efficiently verifiable than HyperLTL or HyperCTL*. It's also possible that it will turn out to be simply a matter of taste which style of logic is more suitable for hyperproperties. The purpose of this paper was to explore one design option: a familiar syntax, based on widely-used temporal logics, that can straightforwardly express well-known hyperproperties.

9 Concluding Remarks

In designing a logic for hyperproperties, starting with HyperLTL was natural, because hyperproperties are sets of trace sets, and LTL uses trace sets to model programs. From HyperLTL, the extension to HyperCTL* was also natural: we simply removed the restrictions on where quantifiers could appear. The curtailment to HyperLTL$_2$ was also natural, because it was the fragment needed to express information-flow security policies. HyperLTL$_2$ permits up to one quantifier alternation, but what about hyperproperties with more? We do not yet know of any security policies that are examples. As Rogers [45] writes, "The human mind seems limited in its ability to understand and visualize beyond four or five alternations of quantifier. Indeed, it can be argued that the inventions... of mathematics are devices for assisting the mind in dealing with one or two additional alternations of quantifier." For practical purposes, we might not need to go much higher than one quantifier alternation.

Acknowledgements. Fred B. Schneider suggested the name "HyperLTL." We thank him, Rance Cleaveland, Rayna Dimitrova, Dexter Kozen, José Meseguer, and Moshe Vardi for discussions about this work. Adam Hinz worked on an early prototype of the model checker. This work was supported in part by AFOSR grant FA9550-12-1-0334, NSF grant CNS-1064997, the German Research Foundation (DFG) under the project SpAGAT within the Priority Program 1496 "Reliably Secure Software Systems — RS^3," and Spanish Project "TIN2012-39391-C04-01 STRONGSOFT."

References

1. Alur, R., Černý, P., Chaudhuri, S.: Model checking on trees with path equivalences. In: Grumberg, O., Huth, M. (eds.) TACAS 2007. LNCS, vol. 4424, pp. 664–678. Springer, Heidelberg (2007)

2. Alur, R., Černý, P., Zdancewic, S.: Preserving secrecy under refinement. In: Bugliesi, M., Preneel, B., Sassone, V., Wegener, I. (eds.) ICALP 2006. LNCS, vol. 4052, pp. 107–118. Springer, Heidelberg (2006)

3. Andersen, H.R.: A polyadic modal mu-calculus. Technical Report 1994-145, Technical University of Denmark, DTU (1994)

4. Balliu, M., Dam, M., Guernic, G.L.: Epistemic temporal logic for information flow security. In: Proc. Workshop on Programming Languages and Analysis for Security (June 2011)

5. Banerjee, A., Naumann, D.A.: Stack-based access control and secure information flow. Journal of Functional Programming 15(2), 131–177 (2005)

6. Barthe, G., Crespo, J.M., Kunz, C.: Beyond 2-safety: Asymmetric product programs for relational program verification. In: Artemov, S., Nerode, A. (eds.) LFCS 2013. LNCS, vol. 7734, pp. 29–43. Springer, Heidelberg (2013)

7. Barthe, G., D'Argenio, P.R., Rezk, T.: Secure information flow by self-composition. In: Proc. IEEE Computer Security Foundations Workshop, pp. 100–114 (June 2004)

8. Bradfield, J., Stirling, C.: Modal mu-calculi. In: Handbook of Modal Logic, pp. 721–756. Elsevier, Amsterdam (2007)

9. Bryans, J.W., Koutny, M., Mazaré, L., Ryan, P.Y.A.: Opacity generalised to transition systems. In: Dimitrakos, T., Martinelli, F., Ryan, P.Y.A., Schneider, S. (eds.) FAST 2005. LNCS, vol. 3866, pp. 81–95. Springer, Heidelberg (2006)

10. Chadha, R., Delaune, S., Kremer, S.: Epistemic logic for the applied pi calculus. In: Lee, D., Lopes, A., Poetzsch-Heffter, A. (eds.) FMOODS 2009. LNCS, vol. 5522, pp. 182–197. Springer, Heidelberg (2009)

11. Cimatti, A., Clarke, E., Giunchiglia, F., Roveri, M.: NuSMV: A new symbolic model verifier. In: Halbwachs, N., Peled, D.A. (eds.) CAV 1999. LNCS, vol. 1633, pp. 495–499. Springer, Heidelberg (1999)

12. Clark, D., Hunt, S., Malacaria, P.: Quantified interference for a while language. Electronic Notes in Theoretical Computer Science 112, 149–166 (2005)

13. Clarkson, M.R., Finkbeiner, B., Koleini, M., Micinski, K.K., Rabe, M.N., Sánchez, C.: Temporal logics for hyperproperties (January 2014), http://arxiv.org/abs/1401.4492

14. Clarkson, M.R., Myers, A.C., Schneider, F.B.: Quantifying information flow with beliefs. Journal of Computer Security 17(5), 655–701 (2009)

15. Clarkson, M.R., Schneider, F.B.: Hyperproperties. Journal of Computer Security 18(6), 1157–1210 (2010)

16. Cook, B., Koskinen, E., Vardi, M.: Temporal property verification as a program analysis task. In: Gopalakrishnan, G., Qadeer, S. (eds.) CAV 2011. LNCS, vol. 6806, pp. 333–348. Springer, Heidelberg (2011)

17. Dimitrova, R., Finkbeiner, B., Kovács, M., Rabe, M.N., Seidl, H.: Model checking information flow in reactive systems. In: Kuncak, V., Rybalchenko, A. (eds.) VMCAI 2012. LNCS, vol. 7148, pp. 169–185. Springer, Heidelberg (2012)

18. Emerson, E.A., Halpern, J.Y.: "Sometimes" and "not never" revisited: On branching versus linear time temporal logic. Journal of the ACM 33(1), 151–178 (1986)

19. Fagin, R., Halpern, J.Y., Moses, Y., Vardi, M.Y.: Reasoning About Knowledge. MIT Press, Cambridge (1995)

20. Focardi, R., Gorrieri, R.: Classification of security properties (Part I: Information flow. In: Focardi, R., Gorrieri, R. (eds.) FOSAD 2000. LNCS, vol. 2171, pp. 331–396. Springer, Heidelberg (2001)

21. Gastin, P., Oddoux, D.: Fast LTL to Büchi automata translation. In: Berry, G., Comon, H., Finkel, A. (eds.) CAV 2001. LNCS, vol. 2102, pp. 53–65. Springer, Heidelberg (2001)
22. Gerth, R., Peled, D., Vardi, M.Y., Wolper, P.: Simple on-the-fly automatic verification of linear temporal logic. In: Proc. Protocol Specification, Testing and Verification, pp. 3–18 (June 1995)
23. Goguen, J.A., Meseguer, J.: Security policies and security models. In: Proc. IEEE Symposium on Security and Privacy, pp. 11–20 (April 1982)
24. Gray III, J.W.: Toward a mathematical foundation for information flow security. In: Proc. IEEE Symposium on Security and Privacy, pp. 210–234 (May 1991)
25. Gray III, J.W., Syverson, P.F.: A logical approach to multilevel security of probabilistic systems. Distributed Computing 11(2), 73–90 (1998)
26. Halpern, J.Y., O'Neill, K.R.: Secrecy in multiagent systems. ACM Transactions on Information and System Security 12(1), 5:1–5:47 (2008)
27. Hammer, C., Snelting, G.: Flow-sensitive, context-sensitive, and object-sensitive information flow control based on program dependence graphs. International Journal of Information Security 8(6), 399–422 (2009)
28. Holzmann, G.J.: The model checker SPIN. IEEE Transactions on Software Engineering 23, 279–295 (1997)
29. Huisman, M., Blondeel, H.-C.: Model-checking secure information flow for multi-threaded programs. In: Mödersheim, S., Palamidessi, C. (eds.) TOSCA 2011. LNCS, vol. 6993, pp. 148–165. Springer, Heidelberg (2012)
30. Huisman, M., Worah, P., Sunesen, K.: A temporal logic characterisation of observational determinism. In: Proc. IEEE Computer Security Foundations Workshop, pp. 3–15 (July 2006)
31. Köpf, B., Basin, D.: An information-theoretic model for adaptive side-channel attacks. In: Proc. ACM Conference on Computer and Communications Security, pp. 286–296 (October 2007)
32. Lamport, L.: Proving the correctness of multiprocess programs. IEEE Transactions on Software Engineering 3(2), 125–143 (1977)
33. Manna, Z., Pnueli, A.: The Temporal Logic of Reactive and Concurrent Systems: Specification. Springer, New York (1992)
34. Mantel, H.: Possibilistic definitions of security—an assembly kit. In: Proc. IEEE Computer Security Foundations Workshop, pp. 185–199 (July 2000)
35. McCullough, D.: Noninterference and the composability of security properties. In: Proc. IEEE Symposium on Security and Privacy, pp. 177–186 (April 1988)
36. McCullough, D.: A hookup theorem for multilevel security. Proc. IEEE Transactions on Software Engineering 16(6), 563–568 (1990)
37. McLean, J.: Proving noninterference and functional correctness using traces. Journal of Computer Security 1(1), 37–58 (1992)
38. McLean, J.: A general theory of composition for trace sets closed under selective interleaving functions. In: Proc. IEEE Symposium on Security and Privacy, pp. 79–93 (April 1994)
39. Millen, J.K.: Unwinding forward correctability. In: Proc. IEEE Computer Security Foundations Workshop, pp. 2–10 (June 1994)
40. Milushev, D., Clarke, D.: Towards incrementalization of holistic hyperproperties. In: Degano, P., Guttman, J.D. (eds.) POST 2012. LNCS, vol. 7215, pp. 329–348. Springer, Heidelberg (2012)
41. Milushev, D., Clarke, D.: Incremental hyperproperty model checking via games. In: Riis Nielson, H., Gollmann, D. (eds.) NordSec 2013. LNCS, vol. 8208, pp. 247–262. Springer, Heidelberg (2013)

42. Milushev, D.V.: Reasoning about Hyperproperties. PhD thesis, Katholieke Universiteit Leuven (June 2013)
43. Myers, A.C.: JFlow: Practical mostly-static information flow control. In: Proc. ACM Symposium on Principles of Programming Languages, pp. 228–241 (1999)
44. Pnueli, A.: The temporal logic of programs. In: Proc. Foundations of Computer Science, pp. 46–57 (September 1977)
45. Rogers, H.: Theory of Recursive Functions and Effective Computability. MIT Press, Cambridge (1987)
46. Roscoe, A.W.: CSP and determinism in security modelling. In: Proc. IEEE Symposium on Security and Privacy, pp. 114–127 (May 1995)
47. Ryan, P.Y.A., Peacock, T.: Opacity—further insights on an information flow property. Technical Report CS-TR-958, Newcastle University (April 2006)
48. Sabelfeld, A., Myers, A.C.: Language-based information-flow security. IEEE Journal on Selected Areas in Communications 21(1), 5–19 (2003)
49. Sabelfeld, A., Sands, D.: Dimensions and principles of declassification. In: Proc. IEEE Computer Security Foundations Workshop, pp. 255–269 (2005)
50. Sistla, A.P., Vardi, M.Y., Wolper, P.: The complementation problem for Büchi automata with appplications to temporal logic. Theoretical Computer Science 49, 217–237 (1987)
51. Smith, G.: On the foundations of quantitative information flow. In: de Alfaro, L. (ed.) FOSSACS 2009. LNCS, vol. 5504, pp. 288–302. Springer, Heidelberg (2009)
52. Terauchi, T., Aiken, A.: Secure information flow as a safety problem. In: Hankin, C., Siveroni, I. (eds.) SAS 2005. LNCS, vol. 3672, pp. 352–367. Springer, Heidelberg (2005)
53. Tsay, Y.-K., Chen, Y.-F., Tsai, M.-H., Wu, K.-N., Chan, W.-C.: GOAL: A graphical tool for manipulating Büchi automata and temporal formulae. In: Grumberg, O., Huth, M. (eds.) TACAS 2007. LNCS, vol. 4424, pp. 466–471. Springer, Heidelberg (2007)
54. van der Meyden, R.: Axioms for knowledge and time in distributed systems with perfect recall. In: Proc. IEEE Symposium on Logic in Computer Science, pp. 448–457 (1993)
55. van der Meyden, R., Wilke, T.: Preservation of epistemic properties in security protocol implementations. In: Proc. ACM Conference on Theoretical Aspects of Rationality and Knowledge, pp. 212–221 (2007)
56. van der Meyden, R., Zhang, C.: Algorithmic verification of noninterference properties. Electronic Notes in Theoretical Computer Science 168, 61–75 (2007)
57. Vardi, M.Y.: An automata-theoretic approach to linear temporal logic. In: Moller, F., Birtwistle, G. (eds.) Logics for Concurrency. LNCS, vol. 1043, pp. 238–266. Springer, Heidelberg (1996)
58. Vardi, M.Y., Wolper, P.: Reasoning about infinite computations. Information and Computation 115(1), 1–37 (1994)
59. Wolper, P.: Constructing automata from temporal logic formulas: A tutorial. In: Brinksma, E., Hermanns, H., Katoen, J.-P. (eds.) FMPA 2000. LNCS, vol. 2090, pp. 261–277. Springer, Heidelberg (2001)
60. Yasuoka, H., Terauchi, T.: On bounding problems of quantitative information flow. In: Gritzalis, D., Preneel, B., Theoharidou, M. (eds.) ESORICS 2010. LNCS, vol. 6345, pp. 357–372. Springer, Heidelberg (2010)
61. Zdancewic, S., Myers, A.C.: Observational determinism for concurrent program security. In: Proc. IEEE Computer Security Foundations Workshop, pp. 29–43 (June 2003)

Time-Dependent Analysis of Attacks

Florian Arnold[1], Holger Hermanns[2], Reza Pulungan[3], and Mariëlle Stoelinga[1]

[1] Formal Methods & Tools Group, Department of Computer Science
University of Twente, P.O. Box 217, 7500 AE Enschede, The Netherlands
{f.arnold,m.i.a.stoelinga}@utwente.nl
[2] Dependable Systems and Software, Saarland University,
66123 Saarbrücken, Germany
hermanns@cs.uni-saarland.de
[3] Jurusan Ilmu Komputer dan Elektronika, Universitas Gadjah Mada, Indonesia
pulungan@ugm.ac.id

Abstract. The success of a security attack crucially depends on time: the more time available to the attacker, the higher the probability of a successful attack; when given enough time, any system can be compromised. Insight in time-dependent behaviors of attacks and the evolution of the attacker's success as time progresses is therefore a key for effective countermeasures in securing systems.

This paper presents an efficient technique to analyze attack times for an extension of the prominent formalism of attack trees. If each basic attack step, *i.e.*, each leaf in an attack tree, is annotated with a probability distribution of the time needed for this step to be successful, we show how this information can be propagated to an analysis of the entire tree. In this way, we obtain the probability distribution for the entire system to be attacked successfully as time progresses. For our approach to be effective, we take great care to always work with the best possible compression of the representations of the probability distributions arising. This is achieved by an elegant calculus of acyclic phase type distributions, together with an effective compositional compression technique. We demonstrate the effectiveness of this approach on three case studies, exhibiting orders of magnitude of compression.

1 Introduction

Computer security attacks on traditional IT-systems as well as on modern IT-enabled systems, such as cars, pacemakers, or power grid infrastructure, are on the rise. Successful attacks have a certain structure and timing, and one of the dominant problems in preventing attacks is that the security engineers fail to properly predict the potential angle and timing of an attack.

In a recent article [1] Basin and Capkun argue that there is a lot to learn from the study of successful attacks. In particular, it can help in refining the attacker model, so as to understand the potential attack angles better, and thus arrive at ever more effective countermeasures. In this context, security engineers and product managers are facing the practical challenge of limited resources. In the

M. Abadi and S. Kremer (Eds.): POST 2014, LNCS 8414, pp. 285–305, 2014.

end, decisions have to be made about how much to spend on security, and where to invest their budget. Making well-informed choices requires insight in attacks: which attacks seem more likely than others? How much time might they take to succeed?

There is a growing awareness that the mathematical foundations of such quantitative aspects of security are worth to be better investigated [2]. Concretely, the quantitative analysis of attacks can yield valuable insights in aspects like (1) system parameters: which parameters influence attack times and probabilities most? (2) what-if scenarios, e.g., what if attack probabilities increase with two orders of magnitude? (3) design alternatives. This paper contributes to this research strand, and it does so in the context of a prominent practical attack modelling formalism, attack trees.

Attack trees (AT) were coined by Schneier [3], as a means to describe, document, brainstorm, and analyze system security. Over the last decades indeed a wide range of techniques have been developed to analyze costs, probability, effort, etc., associated to a successful attack [4–7].

This paper studies the probability of a successful attack as time advances, i.e., the probability distribution of attack times: given a time bound t, what is the probability that the system is successfully compromised within time t? Our probabilistic timed analysis of attacks is conservatively extending earlier time-abstract analyses [3,5,7,8]. The latter only considered the probability whether or not an attack eventually could take place, while we evaluate the success probability as a function of time.

To represent probabilistic timed behaviour, we use *acyclic phase-type* (APH) distributions. APH distributions are a distingushed class of probability distributions, as they can be used to approximate any other probability distribution with arbitrary precision; and—as we fruitfully exploit in this paper—allow for very compact representations. Furthermore, effective fitting techniques exist to derive APH distributions from statistical data [9,10]. We therefore assume that each leaf of an attack tree is annotated with an APH distribution representing the time needed for this step to be successful. Of course, one may argue that it is difficult to get realistic data about the timing of these attack steps—apart from the attacker anyway behaving notoriously unpredictably—and that therefore, the outcomes of this quantitative security analyses should not be trusted. Still, the benefit of the approach we propose lies in the possibility to easily pose and effectively evaluate 'what if' questions, understand system parameters, and to study design alternatives at the push of a button. Especially the 'what if' approach gives a way to understand the sensitivity of the system with respect to different leaf distributions.

At the core of the paper's contribution lies a compositional attack tree semantics that maps on APH distributions, together with a compositional compression algorithm. Here, compositionality refers to the possibility to weave the compression into the compositional construction of the APH distribution associated with the entire graph. This keeps the representations as small as possible. The compression exploits Laplace domain properties in a symbolic and effective manner.

Three case studies exemplify the effectiveness of this approach, among them a study of the Stuxnet attack, and a novel and large industrial case. The case studies are carried out with a full-fledged implementation of the approach we present.

Related Work. Weiss's threat logic trees [11] and Amoroso's threat trees [12] were the first formal models to represent attacks for security analysis. In 1999, Schneier introduced the notion of attack trees [3]. Since then a colorful variety of new formalisms has evolved. These variations can be classified in *static* models, which do not take the evolution of time into account, and *dynamic* models which can express timed behavior such as sequencing. A more detailed overview and classification can be found in [13].

Static models have been rigorously formalized by Mauw and Oostdijk [14]. Multi-parameter attack trees [4] were introduced to process different parameters in parallel. The idea to shift the focus from the attacker's to the defender's point of view was captured by the introduction of defense trees [15], [16] and attack-countermeasure trees [6]. While these tree-based models are evaluated by a bottom-up analysis [5], graph-based formalisms suggested by Sheyner et al. [17] can be analyzed with model checking.

In the field of dynamic attack models, most formalisms are graph-based, for instance compromise graphs developed by McQueen [18]. Distinct attacker preferences were introduced in [19]. More expressive approaches use Petri nets to model intrusion detection as attack nets [20]. A tree-based formalism has only recently been introduced by Piètre-Cambacédès and Bouissou [21,22] which enables the modeling of sequences within complex attack scenarios.

2 Preliminaries

Random Variables. A real-valued *random variable* is a function $X : \Omega \rightarrow \mathbb{R}$ that assigns a real value to each outcome of a stochastic experiment; in our case, X describes the time it takes until a system is successfully attacked. Then $\mathbb{P}(X \leq t)$ denotes the probability that X has a value less than or equal to t; in our case the probability that a successful attack occurs within time t. The function $F : \mathbb{R} \rightarrow [0, 1]$ given by

$$F(t) = \mathbb{P}(X \leq t)$$

is called the *cumulative distribution function (CDF)* of X; and $X \sim F$ denotes that X has CDF F. (Note that, in many cases, $\mathbb{P}(X = t) = 0$. Therefore one considers the cumulative probability $\mathbb{P}(X \leq t)$.) We denote by $\mathcal{F}$ the class of all cumulative distribution functions.

Well-known examples are the (negative) exponential distribution whose CDF is given by

$$\mathbb{P}(X \leq t) = 1 - e^{-\lambda t}, \quad \text{for any } t \in \mathbb{R}^+.$$

This distribution has a parameter $\lambda > 0$, called rate, which determines the "speed" with which the probability grows. We write $X \sim \exp(\lambda)$ if X has an exponential distribution.

Apart from its CDF, a random variable can also be characterized by its *probability density function (PDF, or density for short)* f, which is the derivative of the CDF

$$\mathbb{P}(X \le t) = \int_{-\infty}^{t} f(x)dx.$$

Thus, the PDF of the exponential distribution is given by $f(t) = \lambda e^{-\lambda t}$.

Furthermore, it is important to realize that, given a real-valued random variable X, and a real-valued function $f : \mathbb{R} \to \mathbb{R}$, $f(X)$ is again a random variable. Given several random variables $X_1, X_2, \ldots X_n$ and a function $g : \mathbb{R}^2 \to \mathbb{R}$, we have by repetitive application that $g(X_1, g(X_2, \ldots, g(X_{n-1}, X_n)))$ is a random variable. Below, we will heavily consider random variables $X_1 + X_2 + \ldots + X_n$, $\max(X_1, X_2, \ldots X_n)$, and $\min(X_1, X_2, \ldots X_n)$. If we take the sum of k independent random variables each governed by an exponential distribution with parameter λ, then we obtain the *Erlang distribution* with parameters k, λ. Its density $f(x) = \frac{\lambda^k}{(k-1)!}x^{k-1}e^{-\lambda x}$ is the so-called *convolution* of the PDFs of exponential distributions. We write $X \sim \mathrm{erl}(k, \lambda)$ if X is Erlang-distributed.

Acyclic Phase-Type Distributions. Phase-type distributions are represented by the time needed to reach a final state in a *continuous-time Markov chain* (CTMC). If this Markov chain is acyclic, then we speak about an *acyclic phase-type distribution (APH)*. APHs consitute a very prominent class of probability distributions: they subsume the exponential and Erlang distributions. Notably, APH distributions are topologically dense [23]. This implies that any continuous distribution can be approximated arbitrarily closely by an APH distribution or a PH distribution. Very effective tools exist that compute tight approximations of arbitrary distributions by small APH distributions or fit an APH distribution to measurements, *i.e.*, given a set of empirical data, they can compute the APH distribution that matches most closely [9, 10, 24]. Moreover, as we show below, APH distributions are closed under summation, maximum, and minimum and allow for drastic compression techniques. All this makes the APH distributions a suitable class to model time-dependent behavior of attack trees.

A CTMC is a tuple $\mathcal{M} = (\mathcal{S}, \mathbf{Q}, \boldsymbol{\pi})$, where $\mathcal{S} = \{s_1, s_2, \cdots, s_n, s_{n+1}\}$ is a countable set of states, $\mathbf{Q} : (\mathcal{S} \times \mathcal{S}) \to \mathbb{R}$ is a so-called infinitesimal *generator matrix*, and $\boldsymbol{\pi} : \mathcal{S} \to [0, 1]$ is the initial probability distribution on $\mathcal{S}$. Intuitively, for any two states $s, s' \in \mathcal{S}$, $\mathbf{Q}(s, s')$ specifies the *rate* of the transition from s to s'. This means that the probability that a state change occurs from s to s' within t time units is $1 - \exp(-\mathbf{Q}(s, s')t)$. By definition $\mathbf{Q}(s, s') \ge 0$ for all $s \ne s'$, and $\mathbf{Q}(s, s) = -\sum_{s \ne s'} \mathbf{Q}(s, s')$. The negative of the diagonal value, $E(s) = -\mathbf{Q}(s, s)$, is called the *exit rate* of state s.

If state s_{n+1} is absorbing (*i.e.*, $E(s_{n+1}) = 0$) and all other states s_i, for $1 \le i \le n$, are transient (*i.e.*, there is a nonzero probability that s_i will never be visited once it is left), the generator matrix of the CTMC can be written as

$$\mathbf{Q} = \begin{bmatrix} \mathbf{A} & \mathbf{A} \\ \mathbf{0} & \mathbf{0} \end{bmatrix}.$$

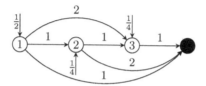

Fig. 1. An acyclic PH distribution

Fig. 2. Graphical representation of (a) an exponential distribution and (b) an Erlang distribution with 3 phases

In this paper we consider CTMCs with acyclic graph structure, or, from the matrix perspective, with $\mathbf{A}$ being an upper triangular matrix. Fig. 1 shows an example of such an acyclic CTMC. The probability distribution of the time until the absorbing state is reached in such a CTMC is called an APH distribution [25]. Together with the initial probability vector at transient states α, matrix $\mathbf{A}$ completely characterizes the APH distribution under consideration. The pair $(\alpha, \mathbf{A})$ is called the *representation* of the APH distribution. The CDF of the APH distribution, which represents the probability distribution of the time to absorption mentioned above, is given by

$$F(t) = \mathbb{P}(X \le t) = 1 - \alpha e^{\mathbf{A}t}\mathbf{1}, \tag{1}$$

where $\mathbf{1}$ is a vector of proper size whose components are all 1.

The simplest APH distributions are formed by the family of exponential and Erlang distributions; see Fig. 2 for their graph-based APH representations.

Three Stochastic Operations. We consider three operations on continuous probability distributions, since they have very intuitive correspondences with the operators on attack trees. Let X_1 and X_2 be two independent random variables with distribution functions $F_1(t)$ and $F_2(t)$, respectively; and let the random variables $X_{\text{con}} = X_1 + X_2$, $X_{\max} = \max\{X_1, X_2\}$, and $X_{\min} = \min\{X_1, X_2\}$ be the summation (convolution), maximum, and minimum, respectively, of X_1 and X_2. The random variables X_{con}, $X_{\max}$, and $X_{\min}$, have CDFs $F_{\text{con}}(t) = \int_0^t F_1(t - x)F_2(x)dx$, $F_{\max}(t) = F_1(t)F_2(t)$, and $F_{\min}(t) = 1 - (1 - F_1(t))(1 - F_2(t))$, respectively.

Acyclic phase-type distributions are closed under these three operations. Given APH distributions PH_1 and PH_2, we use $\text{con}(\text{PH}_1, \text{PH}_2)$, $\max(\text{PH}_1, \text{PH}_2)$, and $\min(\text{PH}_1, \text{PH}_2)$ to denote the convolution, maximum, and respectively minimum of the two APH distributions. The following theorem provides the recipe to obtain the representation of the convolution, maximum, and minimum, given the representations of the two constituent APH distributions.

Theorem 1. *[25, Theorem 2.2.9] Let $(\alpha, \mathbf{A})$ and $(\beta, \mathbf{B})$ be the representations of PH distributions $F(t)$ and $G(t)$ of size m and n, respectively. Then*

(a) their convolution *is a PH distribution with representation $(\delta, \mathbf{D})$ of size $m + n$, where*

$$\delta = [\alpha, \alpha_{m+1}\beta] \quad and \quad \mathbf{D} = \begin{bmatrix} \mathbf{A} & \mathbf{A}\beta \\ 0 & \mathbf{B} \end{bmatrix}.$$

(b) their maximum *is a PH distribution with representation $(\delta, \mathbf{D})$ of size $mn + m + n$, where[1]*

$$\delta = \begin{bmatrix} \alpha \otimes \beta, & \beta_{n+1}\alpha, & \alpha_{m+1}\beta \end{bmatrix} \quad and \quad \mathbf{D} = \begin{bmatrix} \mathbf{A} \oplus \mathbf{B} & \mathbf{I}_A \otimes \mathbf{B} & \mathbf{A} \otimes \mathbf{I}_B \\ 0 & \mathbf{A} & 0 \\ 0 & 0 & \mathbf{B} \end{bmatrix}.$$

(c) their minimum *is a PH distribution with representation $(\delta, \mathbf{D})$ of size mn, where*

$$\delta = \alpha \otimes \beta \quad and \quad \mathbf{D} = \mathbf{A} \oplus \mathbf{B}.$$

3   Attack Trees

Attack trees establish an intuitive model to systematically describe possible attack scenarios on a system and thereby form the basis for a threat analysis.

Attack Tree Syntax. The graphical representation of an AT is a tree. The root node of the tree identifies the goal of the attacker within the considered scenario. This goal can be achieved by executing a series of basic attack steps (BAS) which are encoded as leaves of the AT. A BAS describes one action of the attacker to exploit the system's vulnerabilities which can not be refined into finer steps. Complex attack scenarios are described by composing the involved BASs. The syntactic tool to express this composition in an AT are so-called gates. Most AT formalisms use AND gates and OR gates to describe conjunctive and disjunctive composition respectively [3,14]. Additionally, we introduce SEQ gates to model time dependencies between BASs. This gate is described in more detail in the sequel. We use the standard distinctive shapes to visualize AND gates and OR gates. The graphical representation of an SEQ gate is an AND gate with a horizontal arrow pointing in the direction of progressing time.

The syntax and semantics of ATs allow the leaves to be annotated with any CDF in $\mathcal{F}$, but our analysis techniques exploit the fact that we work with APH distributions.

Definition 1 (AT gates and elements). *An AT gate is one of AND, OR or SEQ. We denote by $\mathcal{G}$ the set of gates. An AT element is either a gate, or a CDF. The set of AT elements $\mathcal{E}$ is given by $\mathcal{E} = \mathcal{G} \cup \mathcal{F}$.*

---

[1] $\otimes$ and $\oplus$ denote the Kronecker product and sum operators, respectively. See for instance [25].

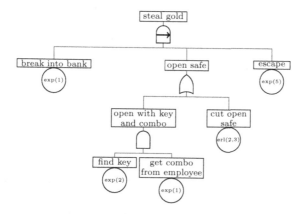

Fig. 3. Attack tree for the scenario 'steal gold from a bank'

In the sequel, given a set X, we let X^* denote the set of all sequences, also called lists, over X. For a list $x \in X^*$, let $|x|$ denote its length; $(x)_i$ is the i-th element of x. Informally, an attack tree is a directed acyclic graph whose leaves are labeled by an element of $\mathcal{F}$; all other nodes are gates, being either AND, OR or SEQ.

Definition 2 (Attack tree syntax). *An attack tree $\mathcal{A}$ is a graph (V, child, r, l), where*

- V *is a finite set of* vertices.
- child $: V \to V^*$ *assigns to each vertex a list of* input vertices.
- *We define the set of* edges *of $\mathcal{A}$ by $E_\mathcal{A} = \{(v, w) \in V^2 \mid \exists i \,.\, w = (\text{child}(v))_i\}$. We require that $(V, E_\mathcal{A})$ is acyclic with a single root $r \in V$. All vertices have to reach r.*
- *We denote by L the* leaves *of $(V, E_\mathcal{A})$, so that $L = \{v \in V \mid |\text{child}(v)| = 0\}$.*
- $\ell : V \to \mathcal{E}$ *is a labeling function that assigns to each vertex an AT element such that*
  - *Each leaf in A is annotated with a CDF: $\ell(v) \in \mathcal{F}$, for all $v \in L$;*
  - *All other vertices are annotated with gates: $\ell(v) \in \mathcal{G}$ for all $v \in V \backslash L$.*

Example 1. The attack tree in Fig. 3 models the attack scenario to rob gold from a bank. To do so, the attacker first has to get into the bank before he can try to open the safe. This time dependency is modeled with a SEQ gate. The attacker has two possible ways to open the safe; he can either unlock it or cut it open; hence, the OR gate. To unlock the safe, the attacker needs to find a key and obtain the access combo from an employee. As there is no time dependency between these two steps, we compose them with an AND gate. After opening the safe, the attacker has to make for a safe escape with his booty. The distribution of the time to execute each BAS is modeled as exponential or Erlang distribution.

Timed Probabilistic Semantics of Attack Trees. In this section we define the semantics of the AT elements. We aggregate the CDFs of the BASs along the gates to obtain a single CDF for an AT $\mathcal{A}$, making use of the operators introduced above. Therefore, the semantics of each AT element, denoted by $[\![.]\!]$, is a CDF. We aim to derive $[\![r]\!]$ for the root node r. We further define $[\![\mathcal{A}]\!] = [\![r]\!]$. Let in the following $v \in V(A)$ be a node of $\mathcal{A}$ with inputs $v_1, \ldots, v_n$.

BAS. Let v be a leaf, so $\ell(v) \in \mathcal{F}$. It is then annotated with a CDF that represents the distribution of the time to execute this attack step. We formalize this interpretation by defining the semantics of a leaf node as its annotated CDF, i.e., $[\![v]\!] = L(v)$.

AND gate. Let vertex v be labeled with AND, $\ell(v) = \text{AND}$. Then the attack step represented by v is completed by the attacker, once each of the steps represented by its input vertices are completed. This corresponds to the latest time a step represented by the input vertices is completed which in turn is expressed by the maximum over the CDFs of its inputs, in other words $[\![\text{AND}(v_1, \ldots, v_n)]\!] = \max\{[\![v_1]\!], \ldots, [\![v_n]\!]\}$.

OR gate. Let $\ell(v) = \text{OR}$. Then the attack step represented by vertex v is completed, when at least one of the steps represented by its input vertices is completed. This corresponds to the earliest time at which an attack step represented by any of the input vertices is completed. Analogous to the AND gate we thus define its semantics using the minimum of the CDFs: $[\![\text{OR}(v_1, \ldots, v_n)]\!] = \min\{[\![v_1]\!], \ldots, [\![v_n]\!]\}$.

SEQ gate. Finally, let $\ell(v) = \text{SEQ}$. The semantics of a SEQ gate is similar to that of an AND gate in the sense that the attack step represented by it is only achieved if all the steps represented by its input vertices are completed. In addition, it expresses a causal dependency of BASs that induces a temporal order: attack steps can only be executed in succession: A step commences at the moment another step is successfully completed. The time at which the step represented by vertex v is achieved corresponds to the sum of the times required to complete each of the attack steps represented by its input vertices. As these times are random variables distributed according to CDFs, we use the convolution operation to define the semantics of the SEQ gate as $[\![\text{SEQ}(v_1, \ldots, v_n)]\!] = \text{con}\{[\![v_1]\!], \ldots, [\![v_n]\!]\}$. The SEQ gate is a novelty in attack modeling, its semantics is inspired by the 'trigger' element in [21].

The CDF $[\![\mathcal{A}]\!]$ corresponding to the entire attack tree $\mathcal{A}$ is derived by composing the CDFs in the leaves with maximum, minimum, and convolution operations along the tree structure.

4   Efficient Analysis of Attack Trees

This section shows how we can efficiently analyze attack times for ATs whose leaves are annotated with APH distributions, based on clever representations of these. In general, the CTMC representation of an APH distribution is not unique, and two representations of one APH distribution can differ drastically in size. In practice, there is a need to have the smallest possible representation. This holds in particular when applying the minimum, maximum and sum operators, since these yield exponential blow ups of the CTMC representations. To tackle this problem, we discuss two important representations: the ordered bidiagonal representation, and the Cox representation.

APH Representations. The size of an APH representation is the dimension of $\mathbf{A}$. Notably, any APH distribution has infinitely many representations of different sizes. An *(acyclic) minimal representation* of an APH distribution is an APH representation with the least possible number of states.

There are two different canonical forms of APH representations, ordered bidiagonal and Cox forms, each with a simple and easy-to-understand structure. Each of them is "canonical" in the sense that it (if viewed as a graph) is unique up to isomorphism. Every APH representation can be transformed into either of them without altering its stochastic behavior, *i.e.*, its distribution.

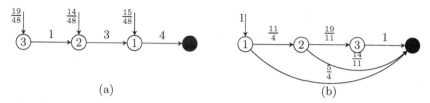

(a)   (b)

Fig. 4. (a) An ordered bidiagonal and (b) a Cox representations of the APH representation from Fig. 1

Ordered Bidiagonal. Fig. 4(a) depicts an *ordered bidiagonal representation*. Such representation has a simple structure: the states are ascendingly ordered by their exit rates, each of them has only one transition to its neighbour, and the initial distributions spans the entire state space. An efficient algorithm, called the *spectral polynomial algorithm* (SPA) [26], can be used to construct the ordered bidiagonal representation of any given APH representation. SPA has complexity $\mathcal{O}(n^3)$, where n is the size of the given APH representation.

Cox. A *Dirac* distribution is a probability distribution that assigns full probability to a single outcome. Consider the representation depicted in Fig. 4(b). Here, every state, apart from the absorbing state, has a transition to the next state, possibly a transition to the absorbing state, and no other transitions. If the representation has descending exit rates and a Dirac initial distribution to the highest exit rate state, then it is called a *Cox representation*. The name is due to David R. Cox [27], who coined this representation.

Once an ordered bidiagonal representation is obtained, transforming it to the associated Cox representation can be performed with complexity $\mathcal{O}(n)$ [28], where n is the number of states in the resulting representation.

Size Compression. Given the three operations introduced in Section 2, Theorem 1 is the basis for constructing complex APH representations from simpler ones. However, in practice we often face an explosion in size, especially rooted in the fact that the maximum and minimum are basically cross-product constructions. Hence, they grow as the product of their component sizes, while the convolution grows as their sum. This phenomenon is not uncommon especially for concurrent system representations. Luckily, we have an effective means to compress the resulting sizes considerably in almost all cases. This is rooted in a polynomial-time algorithm [29] that compresses the size of any APH representations. Due to space constraints, we only provide a brief summary of the functioning of this algorithm below. For an exhaustive discussion of the algorithm and its properties, the interested reader is referred to [29].

Given an arbitrary APH representation $(\boldsymbol{\alpha}, \mathbf{A})$ as input, the algorithm returns an ordered bidiagonal representation, denoted $\mathsf{Red}(\boldsymbol{\alpha}, \mathbf{A})$, having the same PH distribution, with a representation size being at most the size of the original one. The compression achievable goes beyond concepts like lumpability [30], since the algorithm exploits properties of the Laplace-Stieltjes transform. In very brief terms, the algorithm checks, for each matrix row and column certain dependencies in the matrix of its ordered bidiagonal representation of the distribution (obtained by running the SPA algorithm a priori). These dependencies are expressible in terms of linear equation systems. If satisfied, a state can be identified as being removable, and is subsequently removed from the representation. This process is then iterated until no further state is identified as being removable.

Overall, the algorithm has complexity $\mathcal{O}(n^3)$, where n is the number of states of the original representation. It can be applied to arbitrary APH distributions. In fact, this can turn an exponential growth (in the number of composed components) of the matrix size into a linear growth which is almost certainly a minimal APH representation [29].

Implementation. We have implemented a tool to generate and manipulate APH representations, together with the compression algorithm in a toolsuite called APHzip. The tool accepts as input an expression written in a prefix notation The expressions follow the grammar

$$P ::= \exp(\lambda) \mid \mathsf{erl}(k, \lambda) \mid \mathsf{con}(P, P) \mid \max(P, P) \mid \min(P, P) \mid \mathsf{cox}(\mu, \lambda, P),$$

where $\lambda \in \mathbb{R}_+$ and $\mu \in \mathbb{R}_{\geq 0}$ are *rates*, and $k \in \mathbb{Z}_+$. Here, $\exp(\lambda)$ and $\mathsf{erl}(k, \lambda)$ represent exponential and Erlang distributions; these are the building blocks of more complex APHs constructed by using operators convolution (con), maximum (max), and minimum (min). $\mathsf{cox}(\mu, \lambda, P)$ is an operator used to produce Cox representations. This operator semantically works as follows: given an APH P, $\mathsf{cox}(\mu, \lambda, P)$ is a new APH obtained by adding a new state having a transition with rate μ to the absorbing state and a transition with rate λ to P. Repeated application of this operator enables us to produce any Cox representation, and hence represent any APH distribution (and hence approximate any distribution with arbitrary precision) as APHzip expressions.

The user-perceived functionality of APHzip is simple. It takes an expression, compresses it, and returns the resulting compressed APH representation, either as a nested cox($\cdot$)-expression, or as a file containing the result as a simple list of transitions. For end users experimenting with attack trees and similar formalisms, APHzip is wrapped in a web-based interface accessible at the address http://depend.cs.uni-saarland.de/tools/aphzip.

Phase-Type Fitting for a Basic Attack Step. Generally, there are two ways to obtain the CDF for a BAS: 1) with historical data; or 2) on the basis of expert opinion. If empirical data is available, that data is provided as input to a fitting tool, preferably G-Fit [10]. G-Fit then produces the best matching CDF, represented by a hyper-Erlang distribution. Since hyper-Erlang distributions are a subset of the family of APH, we already have a convenient input format for our analysis. A second possibility is that experts estimate the mean time t to execute this BAS and then use $\exp(1/t)$ as APH representation. This is justified by the fact that the exponential distribution is the "most random" of all distributions with a given mean, in the sense that it has maximal entropy. Indeed, other attack models use the exponential distribution as a default choice [21, 31].

Time-Dependent Analysis. In this section we use the above concepts to evaluate a given attack tree $\mathcal{A}$ with respect to the total time required by the attacker to reach the root node. In a first step, the CDFs of the leaves are obtained as APH distributions from fitting algorithms [9, 10]. We then compress the APH distribution $[\![\mathcal{A}]\!]$ of $\mathcal{A}$ with the tool APHzip. For this purpose, we need to transform $\mathcal{A}$ into an expression which follows the grammar of APHzip. This can be done by traversing $\mathcal{A}$ in a depth-first manner: the labels of all nodes are listed in the order the nodes occur this traversal. Additionally, we have to take care of nested brackets and the fact that $\text{con}(\cdot)$, $\max(\cdot)$ and $\min(\cdot)$ are binary operators in APHzip (for efficiency reasons).

Example 2. Consider the AT in Fig. 3. Starting at the root, we order the nodes according to their occurrence in a depth-first manner and put the corresponding *APH* operations in place, keeping track of nested brackets. This yields

$$\text{con}(\exp(1), \min(\max(\exp(2), \exp(1)), \text{erl}(2,3)), \exp(5)).$$

As $\text{con}(\cdot)$ above has three parameters, we need to nest another $\text{con}(\cdot)$ expression with the latter two parameters to obtain a valid APHzip expression.

The CDF of such a compressed APH distribution can then be derived numerically on the basis of Equation (1): Given a set of time-points T and a PH representation $(\boldsymbol{\alpha}, \mathbf{A})$, we compute the probabilities $F(t)$ that the absorbing state is hit within t time-units, for each $t \in T$. To calculate these probabilities, we have implemented a postprocessing tool which uses the uniformization technique [32] and the Fox-Glynn algorithm [33]. Alternatively, several stochastic model checkers such as PRISM [34] or MRMC [35] can be employed as postprocessing tools.

The time-dependent analysis is a powerful tool since it basically performs a static analysis for any point in time. As an example, we fix the time horizon $t = 1$ and calculate the probability to reach the root of the model in Fig.3 with a static bottom-up evaluation. As there is no correspondence for the SEQ gate in static models, we treat it as an AND gate. At first, we define random variable X_1 which corresponds to the BAS 'break into bank' and is distributed according to $\exp(1)$, so $X_1 \sim \exp(1)$. Similarly, define $X_2 \sim \exp(2)$, $X_3 \sim \exp(5)$ and $X_4 \sim \text{erl}(2,3)$ to represent the other BASs. We have $\mathbb{P}(X_1 \leq 1) = 0.63$, $\mathbb{P}(X_2 \leq 1) = 0.87$, $\mathbb{P}(X_1 \leq 3) = 0.99$ and $\mathbb{P}(X_4 \leq 1) = 0.8$. In a static evaluation, the probability to reach an AND gate is the product of the probabilities of its inputs. An OR gate with input probabilities c_1 and c_2 is reached with probability $1 - (1 - v_1)(1 - v_2)$. The probability to steal the gold in this static interpretation is thus calculated by

$$\mathbb{P}(\text{steal gold}) = 0.63 \cdot (1 - (1 - 0.87 \cdot 0.63) \cdot (1 - 0.8)) \cdot 0.99 = 0.57.$$

Evaluating the random variable C which is distributed according to the APH distribution in Example 2 after one time unit yields the same result with our tool chain: $\mathbb{P}(C \leq 1) = 0.57$.

Conservative Extension. The above example illustrates that time-dependent analysis conservatively extends the conventional static and thus untimed interpretation. To make this precise, we restrict to attack trees without SEQ gates (which are dynamic in nature), and relate to the conventional static probabilistic semantics [14].

We assume that each BAS vertex v has a probability p_v associated to it. Then the conventional static probabilistic semantics for a BAS is $[\![v]\!] = p_v$, for an AND gate it is $[\![\text{AND}(v_1, \ldots, v_n)]\!] = \prod_1^n [\![v_i]\!]$, and for an OR gate it is $[\![\text{OR}(v_1, \ldots, v_n)]\!] = 1 - \prod_1^n (1 - [\![v_i]\!])$. This induces a static probabilistic semantics $[\![\mathcal{A}]\!]$ of any attack tree $\mathcal{A}$ (without SEQ gates), provided each BAS has a probability associated to it. It gives the probability to succesfully carry out the attack represented by the tree.

For a given attack tree $\mathcal{A}$ and time $t \in \mathbb{R}^+$, we now use $\mathcal{A}_t$ to refer to the attack tree where each BAS v gets the static probability $p_v = F_v(t)$ associated, where $F_v = L(v)$ is the CDF labelling vertex v. So we look at each BAS at time t and ask for the probability that the basic attack step represented by it is already completed. On the other hand, we can also take the timed interpretation $[\![\mathcal{A}]\!]$ of the entire tree, which by the semantics in Section 3 is some CDF $F_{\mathcal{A}}$ and look at the probability of successfully having completed the attack by time t by evaluating $F_{\mathcal{A}}(t)$. We refer to this value as $[\![\mathcal{A}]\!]_t$ in the theorem below.

Theorem 2. *Let $\mathcal{A}$ be an attack tree without SEQ gates. For any time point $t \in \mathbb{R}^+$, $[\![\mathcal{A}]\!]_t = [\![\mathcal{A}_t]\!]$.*

Thus, the time-dependent analysis conservatively extends static attack tree modelling. The proof uses the semantic interpretation of AND and OR gates as maximum and minimum operations, respectively (Section 3), the definition of the stochastic operations maximum and minimum (Section 2) and their properties, and the fact that as long as the underlying model has a tree structure, all nodes on the same level are stochastically independent.

5   Implications for System Security

Our analysis technique describes a system's vulnerabilities in a temporal context, but the results still need to be interpreted in terms of security. Generally, the analysis provides the user with a temporal dimension for possible attack vectors and associated risks expressed by success probabilities—can attacks be successfully executed in hours, days or rather months? More specific findings for security practitioners can be generated by elaborating on the primary results.

Lower Bound Analysis. In some cases the attacker has only a little time frame to execute an attack. An example for such a time-dependent vulnerability is the roll-out or update of an operating system. Once it is on the market, many hackers will try to find and exploit unknown vulnerabilities before they are found and fixed by the developers. In this race, the starting point of an attack is quite predictable. Thus, the analysis of $\mathbb{P}(0 < X < u)$ is of interest to answer the question 'How much time does the attacker need to succeed with a certain percentage'. The result gives an idea about how fast one has to react to fix vulnerabilities.

Cost-Benefit Analysis of Countermeasures. Security officers often face the problem to determine the benefits of investments into the existing security landscape. If more than one countermeasure might be beneficial but the budget is limited, a cost-benefit analysis is the classical tool to arrive at a decision. Our analysis framework helps to argue from a temporal perspective: 'Given countermeasures A, B and C, which one is most effective in reducing the risk of a successful attack within 1 day?'. This question can be answered by performing a separate analysis for each countermeasure option. We adapt the original attack tree by removing all subtrees and leaves that are prevented by the respective countermeasure and analyze the resulting model. The results can then be compared with respect to the desired properties.

Impact of Individual BASs. Naturally, one wants to identify the most serious vulnerabilities in a system. Therefore, a typical question which follows from the formation of an attack tree is the following: 'Which BAS has the most impact in the attack tree?'. In the context of our temporal analysis this question reads as 'The execution time of which BAS impacts the total execution time of the whole attack scenario most significantly?'. We can answer this by performing a sensitivity analysis. We perform $k + 1$ experiments, where k is the number of BASs. Initially, we analyse the original attack tree, and in each subsequent analysis we change the input distribution of one BAS, leaving the others fixed; *i.e.*, we adapt the parameters of the distribution of the considered BAS in such a way that the expected execution time of this BAS doubles. We can then determine in how far this change reflects in the execution time of the whole attack scenario. By comparing the results we can rank the BASs with respect to their impact on the total execution time of a successful attack. Moreover one can answer the question 'If the system is to be protected for one month, against which BAS it is

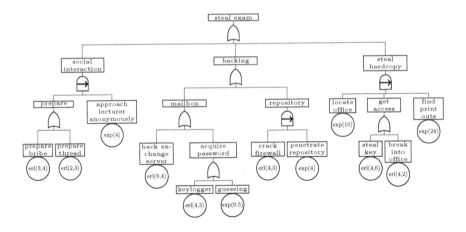

Fig. 5. Attack tree for the case study 'Steal exam'

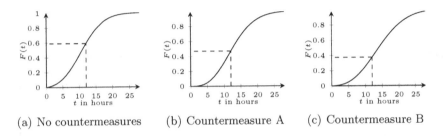

(a) No countermeasures   (b) Countermeasure A   (c) Countermeasure B

Fig. 6. CDFs of the time to steal the exam with respect to different countermeasures

most important to protect?'. On the downside, this kind of sensitivity analysis requires $k + 1$ times more resources.

6   Case Studies

In this section we highlight the effectiveness of our approach by means of several case studies. They demonstrate that the algorithm implemented in APHzip yields significant state space compressions so that even complex scenarios can be analyzed efficiently, as presented in Table 2.

Steal Exam. This case study models a student who wants to get hold of a forthcoming exam. Within this scenario we consider three different types of attacks: social engineering, hacking and physical intrusion. Each attack type consists of various possible attack paths. To obtain a digital version of the exam via hacking, the student can, for instance, try to find a copy of the exam on either the mailbox server or the repository. Both possible attack paths can be refined in several BASs. For instance, the student could either hack the exchange server externally

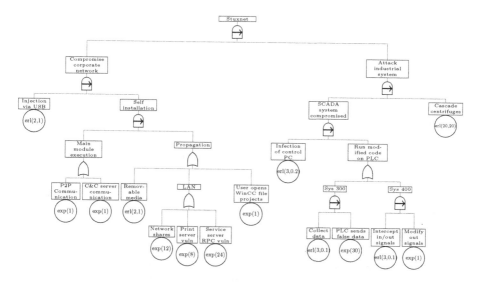

Fig. 7. Attack tree for the case study 'Stuxnet'

or try to acquire the account data by either using a keylogger or simply guessing the password. To each BAS we assign an exponential or an Erlang-distibution as estimates of the time required by the attacker to successfully execute this step.

The school wants to decrease the risk of such a theft, since it would heavily damage its reputation. The school management has the options to either acquire safe deposit boxes (countermeasure A) in which exams can be stored, or to apply a policy which forbids to send exams via email (countermeasure B). The first option would prevent the BAS 'steal key', since the lockers are password-protected. The second option would prevent the subtree 'mailbox'. We assume that the countermeasures block the corresponding BAS in their entirety. The school management wants to find the option which minimizes the risk of an attack within the opening time of the school (12 hours). We evaluated the attack scenario in the original set-up, and with respect to the two countermeasures. The results are displayed in Fig. 6. The attack tree without countermeasures applied is presented in Fig. 5.

The results clearly show that countermeasure B is more effective than countermeasure A. It reduces the risk of a successful attack within the given time by a third. The introduction of a policy is in this case more effective than an investment into the physical infrastructure. Of course, the application of both countermeasures would reduce the probability of a successful theft even more. This example highlights the strength of a timed analysis. It allows the security practitioner to evaluate the system security with respect to crucial time intervals.

Stuxnet. The second case study considers the Stuxnet attack, a sophisticated cyber attack which targeted industrial installations in 2010 and arouse great interest in media and among security experts. The model is based on [36]. To

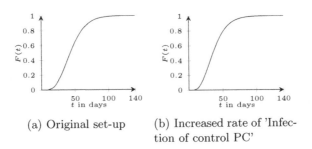

(a) Original set-up   (b) Increased rate of 'Infection of control PC'

Fig. 8. CDFs of the time to successfully execute the Stuxnet attack

Table 1. Sensitivity analysis of the 'Stuxnet' case study. The table shows the increase in the probability of success of the whole attack after 20, 40 and 60 days, if the rate of the respective step is doubled.

BAS	after 20 days	after 40 days	after 60 days
Injection via USB	+1.0 %	+2.3 %	+1.2 %
P2P Communication	+0.2 %	+0.3 %	+0.1 %
C&C server communication	+0.2 %	+0.3 %	+0.1 %
Removable media	+0.1 %	+0.2 %	+0.1 %
Infection of control PC	+7.4 %	+17.6 %	+17.6 %
Collect data	+2.5 %	+15.1 %	+16.3 %
Intercept in/out signals	+3.2 %	+12.3 %	+8.0 %
Modify out signals	+0.5 %	+0.7 %	+0.3 %
Cascade centrifuges	+0.8 %	+1.5 %	+0.7 %
other BASs	+0.0 %	+0.0 %	+0.0 %

adapt the case study to our formalism, we left out the probabilistic nodes used in this model.

The goal of Stuxnet in our scenario is to compromise supervisory, control and data acquisition systems (SCADA) of Iranian nuclear enrichment facilities to slow down the production of centrifugal machines. In the considered model, the business corporate network is assumed to be isolated from the SCADA system. Thus, the attack consists of the two phases; first the internal corporate network is compromised and then the SCADA system attacked from there.

As the corporate network is not directly connected to the Internet, an attack can be initiated by infecting an external device which is brought into the facilities and connected to the control system. Once it has installed itself on one PC, the malware tries to infect as many workstations as possible. It then waits until it can reach the Process Control Network, for instance through an infected removable drive. Within the SCADA system it can target modules with two specific CPU types. After gathering data for a longer period of time it sends faked data to the physical infrastructure which slows down and even damages the targeted centrifuges. The attack tree is presented in Fig. 8.

We want to determine the BAS which has the most impact upon the total execution of this attack and conduct a sensitivity analysis as explained above,

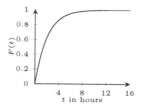

Fig. 9. CDF of the time to attack the IPTV system

i.e., we sequentially change the CDF of one BAS at a time such that its expected execution time doubles. The results are compared to the original model to identify the BASs which are most sensitive with respect to the total execution time. Table 1 highlights the results which suggest that the steps 'Infection of control PC', 'Intercept in/out signals' and 'Collect data' have the greatest impact upon the execution time of the whole attack and should be prioritized when it comes to the application of countermeasures.

IPTV case study. This case study was conducted in the European TREsPASS project [37] to gain insights into the modeling and analysis of socio-technical attacks. It describes a home-payment system designed to support elderly people or people with disabilities, who may have difficulty in leaving their home, in managing their own money. This system is based on the delivery of payments services to individuals via an IPTV set-top box in their own home. It allows the user to order and pay for food and goods of the daily life from home. The system is currently in the development phase and its potential attack vectors are investigated with the help of the following scenario: Since the system is specifically designed for elderly people, we assume that the attacker is a carer who intends to abuse the set-top box to enrich himself. He can for instance try to acquire the payment card and the password of the set-top box, either by stealing it or using his social engineering skills. In total, this case study covers eight major scenarios.

This case study is much more complex than the previous ones, the attack tree contains 148 nodes which are located on up to 14 different levels. More than 90 of its nodes are leaves. Due to confidentiality reasons, we cannot disclose more details about the tree.

The state space of the resulting APH model before compression has a size of about 10^{10}. To evaluate this model in a feasible time we used a shortcut that accelerates the analysis process by orders of magnitudes. Instead of composing the whole APH representation at once, we analyze the model in a compositional manner. At first, we split the attack tree into 9 subtrees which are connected via OR gates. We analyse these subtrees individually by computing the probability of the attacker's success for a set of time-points T. The results are recomposed by using the static computation formula for the OR gate for each $t \in T$. This approach is possible because the subtrees do not share nodes and are thus stochastically independent. This compositional analysis allowed us to evaluate the case

Table 2. Set-up and runtime performance of the case studies

	#Leaves	#Gates	#States before APHzip	#States after APHzip	Runtime in seconds
Steal Exam	12	9	15121	160	9.37
Steal Exam A	12	9	3025	76	1.26
Steal Exam B	12	9	5041	157	5.32
Stuxnet	14	11	94	56	1.13
Stuxnet Sensitivity Analysis	14	11	94	56	16.65
IPTV	92	56	647*	482*	551.62*

* sum over all 9 models of the compositional analysis

study within minutes, whereas the compression and analysis of the entire model at once would take several weeks. The result is presented in Fig.9.

Case Study Evaluation. Each attack tree in the case studies presented has a distinctive structure with leaves on different levels being connected by a mixture of gates. We analyzed each set-up with the APHzip toolchain. The results, as presented in Table 2, were computed with the webservice which implements APHzip, the CDFs were derived with the postprocessing tool on a meachine with a 2.20 GHZ dual-core processor. #States gives the number of states in the graphical representations of the APH of $[\![r]\!]$. The runtime is calculated as the sum of the runtime of both tools.

The smaller models in the first case study can be solved within seconds and even a more involved sensitivity analysis can be performed quickly. Unfortunately, previous work on time-dependent attacks does not offer any figures for comparison. Nonetheless, the results suggest that our analysis technique is extremely efficient in deriving a probability distribution for the execution time of an attack scenario expressed by an attack tree. With the IPTV attack scenario also a more complex case study could be solved in a feasible time.

Another interesting observation is that the complexity of the considered attack tree is not the most important factor when it comes to the computation time. Complex input distributions, such as Erlang distributions with many phases, cause a blow-up of the state space since they are rooted at the lowest level of the composition; and thereby cause longer computation times. Therefore, the computation time of the analysis of a model depends on both its scale as well as the complexity of its input distributions.

7   Conclusion

In this paper we have formalized the semantics of attack trees so as to allow their use for a probabilistic timed evaluation of attack scenarios. The semantics used an effective framework based on acyclic phase-type distributions, and as such enables the derivation of the distribution of the time until the attack is successfully executed. We highlighted that any input distribution at hand for a basic attack step can be cast into the class of APH distributions. Its impact is propagated along the tree, yielding a single monolithic APH distribution for the entire tree. A key component for effective and efficient evaluation is a compression algorithm for APH distributions. This compression can be weaved into the construction process of the monolithic distribution, a feature that is especially interesting in light of the dynamic nature of attack trees: it allows the preprocessing of often appearing attack paths.

We have reported on several distinct case studies demonstrating that this approach can evaluate complex scenarios in a short time. These empirical studies have been carried out with an implementation of the approach as part of a tool chain. As future work we aim at merging and enriching the existing tool with a state-of-the-art APH fitting algorithm [10] as well as a graphical interface. We further aim at support for cost annotations of attack steps, and at support for probabilistic gates, as they appear in the literature on attack trees [21, 22].

Acknowledgements. This research has been partially funded by the NWO project ArRangeer (12238), by the DFG/NWO bilateral project ROCKS (DN 63-257), by the DFG SFB/TR 14 (AVACS), and by the EU FP7 projects no. 295261 (MEALS), 318003 (TREsPASS), and 318490 (SENSATION).

References

1. Basin, D.A., Capkun, S.: The research value of publishing attacks. Commun. ACM 55(11), 22–24 (2012)
2. Köpf, B., Malacaria, P., Palamidessi, C.: Quantitative Security Analysis (Dagstuhl Seminar 12481). Dagstuhl Reports 2(11), 135–154 (2013)
3. Schneier, B.: Attack trees: Modeling security threats. Dr. Dobb's Journal 24(12) (December 1999)
4. Jürgenson, A., Willemson, J.: Computing exact outcomes of multi-parameter attack trees. In: Meersman, R., Tari, Z. (eds.) OTM 2008, Part II. LNCS, vol. 5332, pp. 1036–1051. Springer, Heidelberg (2008)
5. Kordy, B., Pouly, M., Schweitzer, P.: Computational aspects of attack–defense trees. In: Bouvry, P., Kłopotek, M.A., Leprévost, F., Marciniak, M., Mykowiecka, A., Rybiński, H. (eds.) SIIS 2011. LNCS, vol. 7053, pp. 103–116. Springer, Heidelberg (2012)
6. Roy, A., Kim, D., Trivedi, K.: Attack countermeasure trees (act): towards unifying the constructs of attack and defense trees. Sec. and Commun. Netw. 5(8), 929–943 (2012)
7. Zonouz, S., Khurana, H., Sanders, W., Yardley, T.: Rre: A game-theoretic intrusion response and recovery engine. In: IEEE/IFIP International Conference on Dependable Systems Networks, DSN 2009, pp. 439–448 (July 2009)
8. Ray, I., Poolsapassit, N.: Using attack trees to identify malicious attacks from authorized insiders. In: de Capitani di Vimercati, S., Syverson, P.F., Gollmann, D. (eds.) ESORICS 2005. LNCS, vol. 3679, pp. 231–246. Springer, Heidelberg (2005)

9. Horváth, A., Telek, M.: PhFit: A general phase-type fitting tool. In: Field, T., Harrison, P.G., Bradley, J., Harder, U. (eds.) TOOLS 2002. LNCS, vol. 2324, pp. 82–91. Springer, Heidelberg (2002)

10. Thümmler, A., Buchholz, P., Telek, M.: A novel approach for phase-type fitting with the EM algorithm. IEEE Trans. Dependable Sec. Comput. 3(3), 245–258 (2006)

11. Weiss, J.: A system security engineering process. In: Proceedings of the 14th National Computer Security Conference, pp. 572–581 (1991)

12. Amoroso, E.: Fundamentals of computer security technology. Prentice-Hall, Inc., Upper Saddle River (1994)

13. Kordy, B., Pietre-Cambacedes, L., Schweitzer, P.: DAG-based attack and defense modeling: Don't miss the forest for the attack trees. CoRR abs/1303.7397 (2013)

14. Mauw, S., Oostdijk, M.: Foundations of attack trees. In: Won, D.H., Kim, S. (eds.) ICISC 2005. LNCS, vol. 3935, pp. 186–198. Springer, Heidelberg (2006)

15. Bistarelli, S., Peretti, P., Trubitsyna, I.: Analyzing security scenarios using defence trees and answer set programming. Electron. Notes Theor. Comput. Sci. 197(2), 121–129 (2008)

16. Kordy, B., Mauw, S., Radomirović, S., Schweitzer, P.: Foundations of attack–defense trees. In: Degano, P., Etalle, S., Guttman, J. (eds.) FAST 2010. LNCS, vol. 6561, pp. 80–95. Springer, Heidelberg (2011)

17. Sheyner, O., Haines, J., Jha, S., Lippmann, R., Wing, J.: Automated generation and analysis of attack graphs. In: Proceedings of the IEEE Symposium on Security and Privacy, pp. 273–284 (2002)

18. McQueen, M., Boyer, W., Flynn, M., Beitel, G.: Quantitative cyber risk reduction estimation methodology for a small SCADA control system. In: Proceedings of the 39th Annual Hawaii International Conference on System Sciences, HICSS 2006, vol. 9, pp. 226 (2006)

19. LeMay, E., Ford, M.D., Keefe, K., Sanders, W.H., Muehrcke, C.: Model-based security metrics using adversary view security evaluation (advise). In: Proceedings of the 2011 Eighth International Conference on Quantitative Evaluation of SysTems, QEST 2011, pp. 191–200. IEEE Computer Society (2011)

20. McDermott, J.: Attack net penetration testing. In: Proceedings of the 2000 Workshop on New Security Paradigms, NSPW 2000, pp. 15–21. ACM, New York (2000)

21. Piètre-Cambacédès, L., Bouissou, M.: Beyond attack trees: Dynamic security modeling with boolean logic driven Markov processes (BDMP). In: European Dependable Computing Conference (EDCC), pp. 199–208 (April 2010)

22. Piètre-Cambacédès, L., Bouissou, M.: Attack and defense modeling with BDMP. In: Kotenko, I., Skormin, V. (eds.) MMM-ACNS 2010. LNCS, vol. 6258, pp. 86–101. Springer, Heidelberg (2010)

23. Johnson, M.A., Taaffe, M.R.: The denseness of phase distributions. School of Industrial Engineering Research Memoranda 88-20, Purdue University (1988)

24. Asmussen, S., Nerman, O., Olsson, M.: Fitting phase-type distributions via the EM algorithm. Scandinavian Journal of Statistics 23(4), 419–441 (1996)

25. Neuts, M.F.: Matrix-Geometric Solutions in Stochastic Models: An Algorithmic Approach. Dover (1981)

26. He, Q.M., Zhang, H.: Spectral polynomial algorithms for computing bi-diagonal representations for phase type distributions and matrix-exponential distributions. Stochastic Models 2(2), 289–317 (2006)

27. Cox, D.R.: A use of complex probabilities in the theory of stochastic processes. Proceedings of the Cambridge Philosophical Society 51(2), 313–319 (1955)

28. Cumani, A.: Canonical representation of homogeneous Markov processes modelling failure time distributions. Microelectronics and Reliability 2(3), 583–602 (1982)

29. Pulungan, R., Hermanns, H.: Acyclic minimality by construction—almost. In: QEST, pp. 63–72. IEEE Computer Society (2009)

30. Buchholz, P.: Exact and ordinary lumpability in finite Markov chains. Journal of Applied Probability 31, 59–75 (1994)

31. Jonsson, E., Olovsson, T.: A quantitative model of the security intrusion process based on attacker behavior. IEEE Transactions on Software Engineering 23(4), 235–245 (1997)

32. Reibman, A.L., Trivedi, K.S.: Numerical transient analysis of Markov models. Computers & OR 15(1), 19–36 (1988)

33. Fox, B.L., Glynn, P.W.: Computing poisson probabilities. Commun. ACM 31(4), 440–445 (1988)

34. Kwiatkowska, M.Z., Norman, G., Parker, D.: Probabilistic symbolic model checking with prism: a hybrid approach. STTT 6(2), 128–142 (2004)

35. Katoen, J.P., Zapreev, I.S., Hahn, E.M., Hermanns, H., Jansen, D.N.: The ins and outs of the probabilistic model checker mrmc. Perform. Eval. 68(2), 90–104 (2011)

36. Kriaa, S., Bouissou, M., Piètre-Cambacédès, L.: Modeling the stuxnet attack with BDMP: Towards more formal risk assessments. In: 7th International Conference on Risk and Security of Internet and Systems (CRiSIS), pp. 1–8 (October 2012)

37. The TREsPASS project: http://www.trespass-project.eu

Author Index